616.8
W337c

D0854333

THE CLINICAL METHOD IN PSYCHOLOGY

Under the Editorship of
Gardner Murphy

THE CLINICAL METHOD
IN PSYCHOLOGY

Robert I. Watson
Washington University School of Medicine

HARPER & BROTHERS · PUBLISHERS

NEW YORK

Library of Congress catalog card number: 51-11963

To Hazel

Contents

PART III. PSYCHOTHERAPY

Preface

It is customary for the writer to drop his mask and state some of his thoughts concerning his book under the heading of the "Preface." If custom today did not dictate this particular appellation, I would have preferred to use that older and, in this particular case, more expressive phrase, "Apology to the Reader." For here I shall attempt to illuminate some of the objectives of this volume but also call attention to some of its weaknesses.

This book is designed primarily as an advanced undergraduate or graduate text, and accordingly some previous acquaintance with diagnosis and therapy is taken for granted. Generally speaking, diagnosis is treated on a more advanced level and in greater detail than therapy on the assumption that previous acquaintance with diagnostic procedures is greater. This is not the case, however, with the discussion of the nature of diagnostic appraisal with means other than test instruments since these early chapters, concerned with these methods of diagnosis (the interview, observation and rating, and the case study), are pitched at a somewhat lower, more static level. This has been done on the assumption that familiarity may be somewhat less and this volume, if it be used as a text, may be read at a temporal point earlier in the student's acquaintance with clinical materials.

A criticism that may be leveled concerns the omission of an account of the Rorschach and of a considerable number of other currently popular projective measures. (Only two, the P-F study and the Thematic Apperception Test, are given reasonably complete and detailed accounts.) Generally the student of clinical psychology is exposed to a course in projective techniques as such. This volume can be no more than supplementary reading in such a course. Rather, so far as textbook use is concerned, it is designed to be used in other courses in clinical psychology. Moreover, inclusion of the Rorschach at the same level of thoroughness as that given other diagnostic instruments would have lengthened the book beyond the point of practicability. A separate volume is contemplated. Many other excellent tests including those mentioned in page 121 are also omitted primarily on the basis of space considerations.

Some readers may be shocked by the relative paucity of case history material in a book dealing with clinical methodology. Actually it would have required little effort to swell this volume to twice its size by inclusion of case studies, but I am convinced that the best way for the clinician to understand the practice of clinical psychology is to work with his own cases rather than imitate others after perusal of case reports. Because of this conviction case studies as such have been included only when their omission would obscure understanding of basic methods.

The present book has been integrated with a previous one, *Readings in the Clinical Method in Psychology*, so that this text may be supplemented with original contributions by recognized experts. Although the survey of the literature for each diagnostic instrument and for the various aspects of therapy is not exhaustive, only those publications in my opinion representing major contributions being presented, the reviews of the literature in this earlier book supply pertinent material which may have been omitted here.

It will be noted that only about one-third of this volume is devoted to psychotherapy. If used for a semester course this will be sufficient for the most important aspect of the course, the case discussions perforce not included. However, liberal references to cases are supplied. As mentioned previously the chapters devoted to psychotherapy have been pitched at a somewhat lower level of expected previous familiarity than have the chapters dealing with diagnostic material. This was considered desirable because of the anticipated point in training where students would come in contact with the work. It is even possible that their instructors will show this same relative balance between familiarity with diagnostic and with therapeutic materials.

The accounts of psychotherapeutic systems are intended to be primarily descriptive rather than critical. At this level of presentation criticism would be virtually synonymous with offhand dismissal. Since this would be manifestly unfair, a conscientious effort has been made to minimize critical analysis, and in very few instances have I allowed myself the luxury of offering statements of personal predilection. This arises from the conviction that the reader should be allowed first to become somewhat familiar with psychotherapy before he is bewildered with the manifold criticisms that may be leveled at any and all techniques and approaches. Closely related is the deliberate attempt to present basic material at the expense of later innovations. A case in point would be the relatively lengthy discussion of classical psychoanalysis almost to the exclusion of later innovations and ramifications. No attempt is made to "give the last word"; rather, a basis has been laid for understanding the present trends. It may be added in this connection that no textbook writer can be expected to present any point of view with as much enthusiasm as can its protagonists. It is therefore urged that this book be supplemented by prior or simultaneous readings in the references pertaining to systematic point of view as presented in the bibliographies.

The book indicating experimental evidence about psychotherapy is yet to be written, for the very reason that the evidence is in the main yet to be unearthed. To be sure, there are scattered studies representing the launching of an attack on the manifold problems. They are referred to only when relevant to the presentation and not dragged in merely because they are "experimental." The therapeutic contributions of the psychiatrist, which are primarily clinical, not experimental, have not been minimized, as it would be manifestly impossible to write any coherent account depending entirely upon the work of psychologists. Therefore, although Baruch, Blanchard, Blos, Rogers, Thorne, and other psychologists figure prominently in the account given, the indebtedness of psychotherapy to psychiatry is recognized and appreciated.

I have been especially fortunate in spending the last few years in an atmosphere where psychologists, psychiatrists, social workers, and anthropologists enjoy a harmonious relationship. Within the Department of Neuropsychiatry of the Washington University School of Medicine my colleagues have in no small measure contributed much of whatever virtue this volume may possess. To the head of the department, Dr. Edwin F. Gildea, I owe thanks for his forbearance when time was taken in a busy school-hospital setting to work on this book. He did more, however, in offering positive counsel in its preparation. As either past or present members of the department many of my colleagues aided by offering criticisms of one or more chapters. To the following psychologists, Drs. Bettye M. Caldwell, Samuel F. Granick, Ivan N. Mensh, James O. Palmer, Anne M. Ritter, and Saul Rosenzweig; and to the psychiatrists, Drs. Margaret Gildea, Philip H. Starr, and Samuel R. Warson; and to the social workers, Mr. Alfred D. Buchmueller and Mrs. Janet Golden, I am most grateful for various services including critical reading of one or more chapters. A special debt is owned to Dr. Bettye M. Caldwell, who not only offered numerous suggestions as to content but also critically read almost the entire manuscript for suggestions on style and expression. From my students in the Department of Psychology of Washington University who had this volume in manuscript form as a text came some of the sharpest and most penetrating criticisms offered. To them also go my thanks. To my secretary, Mrs. Esther Moloney, goes special thanks for her efficiency and accuracy in helping prepare the manuscript for publication.

In addition I have had the benefit of the reading of one or more specific chapters by the following psychologists and psychiatrists: Drs. Grace Arthur, Dorothy Baruch, Leopold Bellak, Arthur Benton, Phyllis Blanchard, Peter Blos, Psyche Cattell, Edgar Doll, Frederick Gaudet, Roy Hamlin, Arnold Hilden, Max Hutt, Winifred Magsdick, Mina Morris, Henry Peters, Anne Roe, Julian Rotter, Saul Sells, Willam Snyder, Charles Thompson, David Wechsler, Arthur Weider, and Frederick Wyatt. These are in no way, however, to be held responsible for what is said. This is all the more relevant when it is recognized that not in all instances did I accept their comments, perhaps unwittingly committing errors in failing to do so.

Lastly I wish to acknowledge with gratitude the permission to quote the various passages of more than 500 words or of tables given by their copyright holders. Specific acknowledgment is given in the text in these instances. Quotations of less than 500 words end with a reference number to the bibliography for the chapter. Acknowledgment thus given, however, must be supplemented by a general expression of indebtedness to these various sources.

R. I. W.

St. Louis, Missouri
January, 1951

I

Introduction

CHAPTER 1

The Clinical Method

The clinical method has as its one invariant, omnipresent aim the assistance of an individual in distress regardless of the field in which the difficulty occurs. Whether the individual is a patient desperately ill with a raging fever, a child subject to temper tantrums, a college student in danger of being dropped for academic deficiencies, a client beset by vocational perplexities, or a parishioner faced with problems of religious conviction, he seeks help because he or someone about him feels he needs assistance in the solution of his problems. Those from whom he seeks help, if properly trained, have in common both an aim, the alleviation of the distress, and a method, the clinical. The clinician, psychologist or otherwise, steadfastly considers the individual for the sake of that individual.

The Greek term from which the word "clinical" was derived had the meaning of "pertaining to a bed" without, however, the medical connotation it gradually acquired. In the course of linguistic evolution it became limited to medicine and specifically to examinations made in the sickroom. Still later within this field its meaning was extended to include diagnosis and treatment with the patient present, whether at bedside or not. Thus, it encompasses work not only with bedridden patients but also with ambulatory patients whether seen in the physician's office or in so-called clinics.

In the field of medicine educational leaders have given increasing attention to the means whereby relevant training may develop acumen in clinical diagnosis and treatment. This does not mean that the basic sciences of anatomy, biochemistry, physiology, and pathology are neglected. Indeed there is, if anything, an increased respect for the essential scientific substratum of medical activity. Nevertheless, it has been found that clinical skills as well as scientific training may be communicated to the student. The first two years of medical school are devoted primarily to the basic sciences; the last two years of medical school and internship and residency are spent almost exclusively in clinical activities. The skill of the physician in diagnosis and treatment has thus reached levels far in advance of what would have been considered possible just a few short years ago.

Psychology has leaned heavily upon the findings of medicine in the development of its own clinical method. This does not imply that clinical psychology is merely an adjunct to medicine. It has been and continues to be practiced independent of the field of medicine, although the pattern of medicopsychological collaboration is one of the more fruitful signs of present-day growth. It is significant in this connection that the first psychological clinic, founded in 1896 at the University of Pennsylvania by Lightner Witmer, was almost entirely nonmedical in nature.

THE CLINICAL METHOD IN PSYCHOLOGY

It is fortunate that a friend of the first clinical psychologist, Lightner Witmer, has left us an account of the origin of the clinical method in psychology:

In the autumn of 1896, he submitted to the American Psychological Association a new method of research and instruction which he called "the clinical method in psychology and the diagnostic method of teaching." He told his auditors that clinical psychology is derived from the results of an examination of many human beings, one at a time, and that the analytic method of discriminating mental abilities and defects develops an ordered classification of observed behavior, by means of post-analytic generalizations. He put forth the claim that the psychological clinic is an institution for social and public service, for original research, and for the instruction of students in psychological orthogenics which includes vocational, educational, correctional, hygienic, industrial, and social guidance. The only reaction he got from his audience was a slight elevation of the eyebrows on the part of a few of the older members. (Collins, quoted in Brotemarkle, 2, pp. 2–3.)

Although this clinic would be said today to have a somewhat limited point of view, it is nevertheless true that aside from certain differences in expression this is not impossible as a description of the method as it is conceived now. He saw clearly that diagnosis, treatment, and research are major functions of the psychological clinic. A psychological examination of specific functions of the patient is individually conducted; results obtained from many other individuals serve as a reference point or norm and permit analyses of the findings and plans for treatment. This is not an unfair or atypical statement of the method today.

To be sure, many changes have taken place since 1896. Witmer's deliberate exclusion of medical problems does not reflect current thinking. The more dynamic approach which in large measure stems from the influence of Freud has pervaded the field along with the consequent interest in intraindividual comparison. Also many new diagnostic instruments, particularly projective techniques, have appeared. Thus, although the procedures may differ, the essential purpose and spirit of the first psychological clinician has not changed.

The clinical method in psychology as conceived today is the application of psychological principles and techniques to the problems of an individual. The body of knowledge on which it is based stems from the findings of psychology, personality theory, psychiatry, psychoanalysis, and anthropology. Thus, it draws not only from academic psychology but also from all disciplines concerned with the functioning personality. This, of course, is a reciprocally fruitful arrangement, in that research using the findings obtained by means of the clinical method helps to illuminate problems in these fields in turn. However, to discuss the reciprocal relation would be a digression from the main purpose of this presentation. As described here the clinical method is an aspect of applied psychology—applied in the sense that it deals with the problems of an individual in the everyday world, the difficulties of adjustment to both the prosaic and the dramatic issues of living.

If one accepts the *method* as exemplifying the essence of clinical psychology, it follows that certain fairly prevalent views about the nature of clinical psychology may be considered misleading, or even erroneous. Accordingly, it is necessary to examine what clinical psychology is *not*.

1. Clinical psychology is not a subdivision of the subject matter of psychology. Instead it is an area of investigation in which theories and experimental findings drawn from abnormal psychology, child psychology, psychology of personality, and other less closely related fields are integrated and applied in a global approach to an understanding of the individual. In fact, a distinguishing characteristic of the clinical method is the utilization of material from these fields in furtherance of its aims of diagnosis and treatment. There are, of course, research and clinical findings concerned with these aims which cross-fertilize these fields. But there are no clinical psychologists, in the same sense that there are child psychologists; rather, there are psychologists for whom the clinical method is the *sine qua non* of identity.

2. Clinical psychology is not a mere determination of psychometric status. Psychological testing is only one, albeit the most highly publicized, of the techniques at the command of the psychologists. In fact, the clinical psychologist can be distinguished from the psychometrician or psychological technician by the latter's preoccupation with this one technique of testing.

3. Clinical psychology is not an approach to diagnosis alone. Diagnosis and treatment as aspects of the clinical method can be sharply distinguished only for purposes of clarification of discussion. The two merge; diagnosis proceeds throughout all sessions with the patient, and therapeutic effects, whether for good or for ill, start with the first meeting between clinician and patient. To be sure, in some settings and with some psychologists diagnosis is the primary task, but it can never be the only activity. Despite its occurrence with relatively less frequency, specialization in therapeutic efforts is also possible. In this case, the obverse of the shield, diagnosis, must also be understood.

4. Clinical psychology is not an area of employment; nor is it to be identified with a particular sort of person who is the recipient of its services. The fact that common usage gives a much narrower meaning to the word "clinic" than it does to its adjectival form "clinical" is one fertile source of this error. Psychologists do apply the clinical method in clinics and hospitals, but, as will be shown, they also apply it in personnel bureaus, counseling centers, industrial concerns, and many other areas of employment. This means that the gamut of persons who meet the clinical psychologist includes an

extremely diverse population—psychotic and neurotic adults and children, college students, factory workers, the physically handicapped, the mentally defective. That a meaningful distinction cannot be made on the basis of place of employment of the psychologist is borne out by the actual employment situation. A child guidance clinic may have several of its staff primarily concerned with research in the field of electroencephalography, and a university not too far distant may have several persons of faculty rank who devote almost all of their professional efforts to running a psychological clinic. To illustrate this diversity and to make more specific the operation of the clinical method, certain settings for its application will now be examined.

SETTINGS FOR THE APPLICATION OF THE CLINICAL METHOD[1]

THE CLINICAL METHOD IN CHILD GUIDANCE

One of the most encouraging scenes of application of the clinical method is the modern child guidance clinic. With the clinical method as the guiding thread, a pattern of collaboration between the psychologist and his colleagues from other professions has been developed in this kind of setting and has spread to the adult outpatient clinic and to the veterans' hospital among others. In fact, almost all forms of clinical psychological endeavor bear the imprint of the child guidance clinics. It is, therefore, instructive to examine briefly their historical development.

It was recognized at the start that the child's needs cannot be met by one sort of specialist, but rather that the psychologist, the psychiatrist, and what is now called the psychiatric social worker all had legitimate and indispensable functions in the child guidance clinic. A super-clinician, then as now, seemed impracticable and wasteful; so there appeared a pattern of division of labor in both diagnosis and treatment.

This division of labor among psychiatrist, psychologist, and social worker in the early history of the child guidance clinic was relatively simple and specific. During the diagnostic phase the psychologist examined the child, the psychiatric social worker visited the home

---

[1] Descriptions of other settings for the application of the clinical method are given in the bibliography (14) (15) (16) (17) (18) (19) (20) (21) (22).

and saw the parents, and the psychiatrist interviewed him and assumed an overall medicolegal responsibility. At a staff conference the
materials gathered by all were presented, discussed, and evaluated
and a plan of treatment was worked out. Subsequently the psychiatrist treated the child, and the social worker used whatever environmental manipulative procedures seemed pertinent.

This pattern had no sooner found a certain amount of acceptance
than changes were slowly introduced. The clinicians themselves
probably viewed the modifications as minor adjustments in the
division of labor, adjustments aimed at increasing efficiency. The
psychologist, trained in an educational setting and imbued with
the academic tradition, was often found to know quite a bit about
educational, especially remedial, procedures. Particularly in speech
and reading was he considered to be, or easily capable of becoming,
an expert. He thus took on reëducational work. The social worker,
according to the original pattern, was often the person who got
to know the parent best. The not surprising discovery that the
parent, too, had problems led to the application of therapeutic
techniques to the parent by the social worker under the psychiatrist's
direction. The psychiatrist soon saw that, in some instances at least,
parent problems were more deep-seated than those of the child and
that only through working with the parent could the child be
helped. Therefore he began to see parents therapeutically. The
psychologist, who in the meantime had continued to work with diagnostic testing and educational remedial procedures, became increasingly aware that the separation of the child's emotional and educational problems was artificial. Consequently, although continuing
to handle remedial work, in some clinic settings he was given full
therapeutic responsibility.

Today the diagnostic functions continue more or less as in the
earlier clinics. To be sure, there is less emphasis on home visits by
the social worker and an associated diminution in the use of environmental manipulation as a treatment tool. Along with this the
psychologist has considerably extended his diagnostic testing function from the derivation of an IQ and the scores on achievement
tests to a more versatile role, to be discussed shortly. In therapy,
selection criteria as to who will carry the principal role have changed;
no longer is it the particular field of professional specialization as
such, but rather possession of the optimal constellation of training,

experience, and personality attributes which determines who shall work with a specific patient.

Psychologists other than those referred to as clinical psychologists also use the clinical method. Synonyms (or euphemisms) such as counseling or guidance may be used to describe the work that is done. It is clear, however, that fundamentally the task is that of diagnosis and treatment. This may be demonstrated by means of specific uses of the clinical method in student guidance and in industry.

THE CLINICAL METHOD IN STUDENT GUIDANCE

College and high school students are not immune to the development of maladaptive ways of meeting their problems. The three major areas in which the problems arise are the educational, vocational, and emotional spheres. Among psychologists and educators there has emerged a specialization in counseling and guidance in regard to these problems which also involves an application of the clinical method. The work of Williamson and Darley (7) is illustrative of the clinical approach in student guidance. They describe the clinical method explicitly in terms of six steps. The first of these, *analysis*, refers to the application of measuring techniques to bring out the strengths and weaknesses of the individual. This is followed by the second step, *synthesis* of the case material into an integrated coherent picture of the individual. The third step is conceived to be the *diagnosis* of the student's specific problems in one or more of six or seven broad problem areas including the vocational, educational, social, emotional, and financial spheres. From diagnosis comes *prognosis* or *prediction* of the result. Generally speaking, prognoses are given in terms of alternative courses of action presented to the student for his choice, and of estimates of the likely outcome for each of the alternatives. After the student's choice from the variety of alternatives offered, the step of *treatment* is taken. This includes program planning to carry out the objective or solution chosen; referral to a specialist in health, speech, psychiatry, or vocational information; aid in eliminating educational red tape; and the like. The sixth and last step, considered indispensable to any well-rounded clinical program, is that of *follow-up*, i.e., what actually happened after a lapse of time. It is evident that such an approach, adapted to the needs of the individuals concerned, is entirely within the spirit of what has previously been described as the clinical method.

THE CLINICAL METHOD IN INDUSTRY

Although psychologists have been working in industry for many years, their concern has typically been with such activities as personnel selection, turnover, accident prevention, time and motion study, etc. They dealt with individuals, to be sure, but almost always they were interested in making it possible to order the individual to certain continua pertinent to the problem at hand. For example, did a given applicant meet certain standards previously set up by the psychologist as to physique, general intelligence, and special aptitudes? If he did meet the criteria, the psychologist's task was done, and it could be said that the applicant was selected in conformity with the psychological specifications. In the main, the clinical approach is only incidental to their work.[2]

Since about 1935, deliberate attempts to apply the methodology of the clinical approach to problems in industry have become increasingly prominent. This interest in a clinical approach to the adjustment of the whole individual is undoubtedly a concomitant of what Viteles calls the most significant development in industrial psychology in the past decade, ". . . *the growing concern of industrial psychologists with the sentiments, feelings, and the attitudes of workers, supervisors, and managers and with the interplay of people in the social organizations of the industrial enterprise.*" (6, p. 182.)

That this trend is not merely a national phenomenon is demonstrated by a statement from the Institute of Industrial Management, Melbourne, Australia, in which credit for the increase in psychological work by trained personnel in industrial situations is given by Taft to the "tendency to move away from mass psychometrics to a more individual clinical approach, taking into account the individual as an organic whole whose behavior is the result of personality factors and environmental forces as well as abilities." (4, p. 55.) An apt illustration is to be found in the description of the efforts of a consulting firm to offer specialized clinical service directly to individual

---

[2] Viteles, a formally trained psychologist, and those men not formally trained as psychologists who were associated with the studies at the Hawthorne works are distinguished exceptions to this early relative neglect.

business leaders (3). A procedure is outlined for investigating the following factors in key individuals in the concern: intelligence, emotional control, skill in human relations, insight into human behavior, and the ability to organize and direct the activities of others. A detailed personal history is obtained from the executive. This is followed by the administration of those tests considered appropriate to the situation. Therapeutic procedures, both directive and client-centered, are then utilized to bring about optimal job effectiveness.

THE CLINICAL AND SCIENTIFIC METHODS

The person utilizing the clinical method in psychology is first a psychologist and second a clinical specialist. Following the intent both of graduate departments of psychology and of the official organization, the American Psychological Association, he is given training which is very similar in many respects to that given other students of psychology regardless of their later field of specialization. In varying degrees he is allowed to specialize in the later years of graduate study. Psychologists speak a common language and, it is hoped, will continue to do so. Just as a common core of premedical and preclinical training is given the medical student, the student of psychology receives a preclinical training in the basic science of psychology which may be followed by professional specialization. He is thus trained both in the scientific method and in the clinical method.

Since the aim of clinical endeavor is the welfare of the patient rather than the conduct of an experiment, it might appear that the aims of the clinical and scientific methods would conflict. Such is not often the case. Even in the few instances in which there must be a choice, exemplified novelistically in the tribulations of Arrowsmith, the question becomes one of the extent to which the end justifies the means. In their attitude toward this issue clinicians differ in degree, but all adequately trained and experienced practitioners would hold firmly to the conviction that a solid basis of scientific findings is a necessary prerequisite to the advance of clinical practice. Nevertheless, there are differences of emphasis between the clinical and scientific methods which are relevant to the present discussion.

In much, but not all, scientific psychological endeavor the *individual as an individual* is not the object of concern except in so far as he illustrates these uniform phenomena or suggests new fields for this search. Rather, specific instances of behavior in a given individual, once noted, are mingled with similar data concerning other individuals who form the N of that study. A classic design is one in which one variable is isolated and others are controlled. With the advance of statistical methods and increased sophistication in experimental design (particularly analysis of variance), a series of variables capable of later statistical isolation are investigated simultaneously. The individual is not studied; rather he is treated as a contributor to data which will yield a relationship between the independent and dependent variables. It is the phenomena, not the individual, which then are observed or are isolated and measured.

Broadly speaking, in the search for general laws some psychologists-as-scientists are not concerned with individual deviations except for their effect on their overall results. In the course of a study of digit span, although faithfully reporting measures of variability the scientist is not particularly concerned with the reasons for a given individual's low score. The scientific method is more concerned with the discovery of generalizations about natural phenomena, the clinical method with the study and treatment of individual cases. In the latter, the individual, not the general law, is the focus of interest.

But to stop here in the characterization of psychological science would give but a partial and therefore distorted picture. Some psychologists, other than clinicians, are concerned with individuality. Familiarity with the work of Allport and Murphy, to mention but two outstanding contributors, would easily disabuse one of the notion that the account given earlier is entirely accurate if left to stand without qualification. Workers such as these, although still concerned with the derivation of natural laws, are concerned with the laws of *intra-individual* behavior and experience—understanding the individual as an individual.

The picture is further complicated by the fact that in the clinical method the same goals of description, classification, and explanation are sought as in the scientific method. In discussing the scientific methods of child psychology, Anderson offers a description that could apply to the clinical method as well:

It has long been recognized that two characteristics of the scientific method are the *careful observation of phenomena as they occur* and the

accurate recording of these observations in order that they may be tab-
ulated, analyzed, and checked later. The scientist does not depend upon
his memory, but records events as they occur in order to obtain complete
reports and to eliminate bias and retrospective falsification. He devises
situations in which the individual responds directly to stimulation, and
makes permanent records of the performance, as when a test blank is
filled out, a polygraph is used, or a motion picture record made. Where
direct observations or recorded responses cannot be made, he uses ratings
made by other persons and reports from his subjects based on interviews,
questionnaires, and inventories. (1, p. 14.)

Both the clinical method and the scientific method have the
assets of objectivity and quantification, although to different degrees
and in differing respects. Observations are made: in the one case of
blind-alley entries in a maze, in the other of location of the responses
on the Rorschach cards. Objectivity may be achieved through such
devices as the definition of terms—the number of inches of entry
into a cul-de-sac may define a maze error just as the proportionate
number of responses to a given section of a Rorschach blot may
define a "usual detail."

The close relationship and kindred spirit of the two methods are
brought out clearly when the persons concerned and the data with
which they work are considered. If a person is a clinician, he is also
a scientist (although the converse is not true), and his basic data,
the behavior and experience of human beings, are the same.

It would appear that the persons concerned with, and the materials of, the scientific and clinical methods may be, and often are,
identical. For example, a study of the relation of kinds of marital
status to the incidence of various psychoses, or the relation of college
academic failure to size of high school from which these failures
were graduated, would involve individuals in need of psychological
services. Clearly, however, there is a difference in approach. The
psychologist as a clinician is concerned with the individual for the
sake of the individual. In research he is concerned with the establishment of commonly valid generalizations of human behavior whether
these be general laws or laws holding only for a single individual.
Since the basic datum, the behavior of individuals, is always the
same, and the instruments used are often the same, the difference
may be said to lie essentially in the attitude taken toward the problem. *The attitude the psychologist takes toward the subject of his
field, human beings, decides his approach. If the approach is that of*

understanding the individual for the sake of helping him or at least modifying his behavior, the clinical attitude and consequently the clinical method have been adopted. The relationship of the psychologist to the subject of his interest, patients or subjects, may be conceived as a matter of orientation. Either the orientation is clinical or the orientation is scientific, or it may be both simultaneously. The psychologist then will vary his method depending upon whether he deals with subjects, with patients, or with patients as subjects.

Vigorous objection may thus be raised to any distinction based upon the academic psychologist's use of scientific method as contrasted with the clinical psychologist's use of only the clinical method. This is unequivocally not the case. A particular psychologist may, however, use one of these methods to the relative exclusion of the other. Only on this basis are the terms "clinical psychologist" and "experimental psychologist" justified. Pure and applied, academic and clinical, are dichotomies that become blurred on close inspection. This is as it should be. Psychology is both a science and a profession, and a psychologist is both a scientist and a professional man. On the psychological scene today the research man in acoustics may have a governmental contract to investigate improvements in sound transmission; the child guidance clinician may teach a course in psychodynamics at the neighboring university.

THE QUALITATIVE ELEMENT IN THE CLINICAL METHOD

The clinical attitude arises from the conviction that the person is worth helping as a person, and that he can be helped by the efforts of the psychoclinician. Both this attitude and the skills whereby it can be carried through to success are compounded from the psychologist's scientific heritage and from that personal and social heritage of sympathetic understanding, insight into human motives, clinical acumen, clarity of expression, and persuasive ability which also go into the making of a clinician.

A crucial consequence of the clinical attitude is the temporal urgency of his activities. The imperativeness of the situation is quite clear; the clinician, unlike the academician, must *do something*. This necessitates the occasional utilization of imperfectly validated diagnostic procedures and therapeutic techniques of possible but not proved value. He must draw upon every means of psychological understanding. This does not make the clinician any the less a scientist, for to fail to use all possible sources would be to prove himself but a grotesque caricature of the true scientist. A man could withhold possible sources of diagnostic and therapeutic help merely because the techniques involved have not been proved valid; but if he did so when no other approaches seemed feasible, he would be merely a hollow stereotype of the scientist. The worker in the laboratory seeking general laws refuses to draw any conclusions not indisputably compelled by the data. He awaits further evidence on other aspects. In the clinical scene this wait, this pause, for more evidence is sometimes impossible. The clinician must do the best he can, and this best includes drawing upon his personal judgment, his insight, and his "hunches."

Another factor, too, plays a part in the acceptance of qualitative findings by clinicians. In common with their colleagues from other clinical fields they are convinced that their day-to-day experience with patients yields valid findings of diagnostic or therapeutic significance *not yet* objectively proved, and perhaps not yet capable of proof by techniques accepted as "scientific." It is appropriate to point out that all science starts with questions engendered by observations of precisely this nature. A stone may be cast only when the clinician denies the necessity of ultimate proof beyond "clinical experience" or is satisfied with only "empirical evidence." The situation is obviously complicated by the controversy over precisely what constitutes adequate methods of proof, e.g., disputes concerning the demonstration of the validity and reliability of the Rorschach.

Even if tests and the other techniques of the clinical psychologist were purely objective there would still be a necessity for the interpretative synthetic element in clinical practice. Without this, responses to test questions or productions of the patient are well-nigh meaningless. For the sake of argument, it may be postulated that the same answers are given by a particular patient to the examiner whether that examiner is a novice or not. The scores derived, let it be further assumed, would be identical. To this extent objectivity is attained. The novice and the expert might agree to this point and might even make some of the same inferences from the findings. But here they part company. The novice must either stop or elaborate with erroneous or irrelevant statements, whereas the expert could further enrich his "first level" findings with other penetrating and cogent statements on the basis of his clinical experience and knowledge, notwithstanding their lack of objectivity. Although the discussion so far has been concerned with diagnostic procedures, it is even more applicable to the psychotherapeutic aspects of the clinical method. There the clinician depends almost exclusively upon qualitative procedures and findings. Scrutiny of these qualitative elements by use of research methods is one of the major tasks barely begun in present-day clinical psychology.

Advances in clinical acumen, it would appear, must come from scientific advance. Thomas puts the matter appositely:

Synthesis and interpretation, which are among the chief characteristics of the clinical approach, will still be needed. But the data synthesized and interpreted, and the methods employed for doing this, will both be different. Instead of intuitive synthesis and interpretation being compiled upon a mixed basis of equally intuited impressions and "objective" records, the basis will become more and more one of demonstrated quantitative facts covering a field of known mental qualities; and the method of synthesis and interpretation of these facts will become progressively less a matter of merely personal insight and progressively more a matter of reference to empirically established principals and to theories which can be communicated and tested. (5, p. 310.)

THE RELATION OF METHOD AND TECHNIQUES

It should be clear that the term "method" is used here to refer to a general mode of approach to the raw materials or data of a given field. On the other hand, it is not uncommon for "method" sometimes to be used rather loosely in such statements as the "test method," the "interview method," or the "questionnaire method." The term "technique" will be used for these more specific devices and approaches falling within the limits of the clinical method. Later chapters are concerned with diagnostic and therapeutic techniques such as tests, ratings, observation, interview, and the case study.

BIBLIOGRAPHY

1. Anderson, J. E., Methods of child psychology, in Carmichael, L. (ed.), Manual of child psychology, John Wiley & Sons, 1946, pp. 1–42.
2. Brotemarkle, R. A., Clinical psychology. 1896–1946, J. consult. Psychol., 1947, 11:1–4.
3. Flory, C. D., and Janney, J. E., Psychological services to business leaders, J. consult. Psychol., 1946, 10:115–119.

4. Taft, R., The staff psychologist in industry, Amer. Psychologist, 1946, 1:55–61.
5. Thomas, F. C., Intuition or psychometry in the study of personality? Character & Pers., 1939, 7:309–317.
6. Viteles, M. S., Postlude: the past and future of industrial psychology, J. consult. Psychol., 1944, 8:182–186.
7. Williamson, E. G., and Darley, J. G., Student personnel work, McGraw-Hill Book Company, 1937.

Supplementary articles in Watson, R. I. (ed.), Readings in the clinical method in psychology, Harper & Brothers, 1949:

THE CLINICAL METHOD

8. Louttit, C. M., The nature of clinical psychology. Pp. 3–28. (Also in Psychol. Bull., 1939, 36:361–389.)
9. Paterson, D. G., The genesis of modern guidance. Pp. 64–73. (Also in Educ. Rec., 1938, 19:36–46.)
10. Shaffer, L. F., Clinical psychology and psychiatry. Pp. 74–83. (Also in J. consult. Psychol., 1947, 11:5–11.)
11. Shakow, D., Training in clinical psychology—a note on trends. Pp. 84–87. (Also in J. consult. Psychol., 1945, 9:240–242.)
12. Thorne, F. C., The clinical method in science. Pp. 49–63. (Also in Amer. Psychologist, 1947, 2:159–166.)
13. Watson, R. I.., The professional status of the clinical psychologist. Pp. 29–48.

THE FUNCTIONS OF THE CLINICAL PSYCHOLOGIST

14. Campbell, H. M., The role of the clinical psychologist in a Veterans Administration Mental Hygiene Clinic. Pp. 106–114. (Also in J. clin. Psychol., 1947, 3:15–21.)
15. Cornell, E. L., The psychologist in a school system. Pp. 131–146. (Also in J. consult. Psychol., 1942, 6:185–195.)
16. Corsini, R., Functions of the prison psychologist. Pp. 160–165. (Also in J. consult. Psychol., 1945, 9:101–104.)
17. Darley, J. G., and Marquis, D. M., Veterans' guidance centers: a survey of their problems and activities. Pp. 115–124. (Also in J. clin. Psychol., 1946, 2:109–116.)
18. Kinder, E. F., Psychological work at Letchworth Village, Thiells, N.Y. Pp. 154–159. (Also in J. consult. Psychol., 1937, 1:76–80.)
19. Mathews, W. M., Scope of clinical psychology in child guidance. Pp. 125–130. (Also in Amer. J. Orthopsychiat., 1942, 12:388–392.)
20. Watson, R. I., Functions of other clinical psychologists. Pp. 166–175.
21. Wechsler, D., The psychologist in the psychiatric hospital. Pp. 99–105. (Also in J. consult. Psychol., 1944, 8:281–285.)
22. Williamson, E. G., Coordination of student personnel service. Pp. 147–153. (Also in J. consult. Psychol., 1940, 4:229–233.)

II

Diagnostic Appraisal

CHAPTER 2

The Functions of Diagnosis

In its most general terms, diagnosis as an aspect of the clinical method is aimed at acquiring knowledge about the nature and origin of the patient's difficulties. It is the evaluation of the patient's personality characteristics (abilities, achievements, habits, ideals, traits, and temperament) which may help in understanding these difficulties. Diagnosis involves organization and assimilation of all the findings about the patient. The essential elements of diagnosis include (1) securing all relevant information from the available sources, (2) analyzing these data, and (3) planning for the future. Diagnosis encompasses the findings from interviews with the patient and his family, psychological examinations, physical examinations, laboratory findings, school records, and social investigations—the entire gamut of diagnostic techniques to be discussed in subsequent chapters.

DIAGNOSIS AND CLASSIFICATION

Diagnosis as the term is used here must not be conceived too narrowly; its implications go beyond the differentiation and identification of a psychotic or neurotic individual. The appraisal of abilities and aptitudes of school children, the determination of vocational potentialities of college students, and attempts to understand the reactive problems of adults are all diagnostic issues. To force the individual into a pigeonhole does justice neither to the capabilities

of the psychologist nor to the personality resources of the patient. The description of a personality which includes the delineation of any neurotic or psychotic symptoms in evidence is the proper diagnostic task of the psychologist. This is not synonymous with the diagnosis of a neurosis or a psychosis as such.

This restricted concept of diagnosis, of merely labeling or classifying instances of psychological disorders, is rapidly descending from a position of any prominence. With appreciation of the dynamic significance of psychological conditions, a much broader meaning has emerged. The understanding of process is much more important, as expressed in the famous remark of Adolph Meyer's: "We understand this case; we don't need any diagnosis." Diagnosis in the sense of a shorthand label often does not add understanding and may hide or even distort more than it reveals.

It is instructive and sobering to realize that except in a relatively few dramatic instances the psychiatrist does not need the services of a psychologist to help him arrive at a classificatory diagnosis. This does not imply that the psychologist can be oblivious to diagnostic labels, for to some degree he is concerned with them. For example, he may be requested to supply information which will lead to a differential diagnosis either within psychogenic disorders or as between psychogenic and organic involvement, or he may aid in the establishment of the presence of mental deficiency. For the most part, however, his contribution to a diagnostic study is more penetrating and revealing than a mere either-or classification.

The psychologist, so to speak, wears spectacles of a focal length different from those of the psychiatrist. This is not a situation to deplore. On the contrary, his "different" picture is one of the major reasons for his professional existence. The very discrepancy between two observers may be of crucial importance in assaying the total personality resources of the patient.

That some system or systems of classification do aid in diagnostic purposes there can be no doubt. For example, the distinction between psychotic behavior and neurotic behavior is valuable though crude. In some measure, the officially adopted American Psychiatric Association classification of mental disorders is of value. The distinction made between personality problems and behavior problems in work with children frequently helps us to understand and to suggest means of treatment. In addition, diagnostic categories are a con-

venient means of conveying to one's colleagues a short, rough summary of findings in which there will be at least a modicum of agreement and understanding.

DIAGNOSIS AND INTERPRETATION

Diagnosis may be conceived as showing two phases, namely, the descriptive, and the interpretative or inferential. The former consists of the information we have about the patient—his personality make-up, the physical findings, his personal history, his school and work history, family background, and so on. An equally important phase is that of synthetically interpreting these findings. Out of the welter of available material, relevant and irrelevant, the clinician must extract the consistent pattern of meaning that is present.

The task of interpretation in clinical diagnosis is carried out by formulating successive hypotheses, each one being tested and discarded, if necessary, in favor of one more capable of synthesizing the available information.

To enter upon an extended discussion of the nature of interpretation would be to leave the field of methodology and enter the stormy realm of fundamental theory. The systematic point of view, derived from psychoanalysis, Gestalt theory or behaviorism, that somewhat amorphous "dynamic" approach of today, "common-sense" eclecticism—all agitate the "winds of doctrine" that blow upon the current clinical scene. Each clinician is affected by these and sooner or later takes a position which allows him to maintain his equilibrium in the face of the storm and even to agitate it a bit further. Each, in short, has built a set of diagnostic constructs—a way of seeing his patients. Only a rash and short-sighted individual would say that one set of diagnostic constructs is acceptable for all today.

No attempt will be made to urge any one set of diagnostic constructs on the reader. Even to discuss them would take us away from the clinical method and into the realm of the conceptual scheme accepted by the clinician. It is, nevertheless, appropriate to consider the characteristics by which a valid set of diagnostic constructs may be identified. Bordin offers the following account at an operational level:

1. One of the most important characteristics of such a construct is that it enables the clinician to understand more clearly the significance of the individual's behavior. For example, this kind of understanding

would appear to play an important role in the therapist's ability to respond adequately to feelings expressed by the client in a nondirective treatment process. Diagnostic constructs should sensitize the clinician to respond to significant characteristics of the client's behavior that might otherwise have been overlooked. The degree of understanding fostered by the constructs will be reflected by the comprehensiveness of the predictions which can be made about the individual by assigning him to a class. This is the operational significance of understanding. We perceive a distinctive and familiar pattern which is part of a larger pattern the characteristics of which are then predictable from our perception of the smaller pattern. This is the secret of the medical diagnostician's success, namely, that from a few symptoms he is able to predict the other symptoms. In fact, he checks his diagnosis by seeing whether the additional symptoms do conform to expectation.

2. The more a set of diagnostic constructs vary independently, the closer they are assumed to be to the status of "true" causes and the farther from the status of surface symptoms. That is, the more independent a set of constructs, the more sharply focused the prediction yielded. If, for example, fever, coughing and sneezing, blood counts, skin condition, etc., were used as basic constructs in the medical field, it would soon be found that they do not vary independently—that they form patterns—and that the predictions provided by any one construct are very limited. The medical practitioner would explain to us that these characteristics do not predict much because they are symptoms, not causes. To state it another way, a set of constructs based upon the patterns of these limited classifications will provide a basis for a more comprehensive set of predictions. From this point of view the most desirable statistical characteristic of a set of diagnostic classifications is that they vary not only independently but are also mutually exclusive. However, we could no more expect this than we should expect that there will be no individuals who have measles and whooping cough or any other combination of diseases at the same time. By setting a criterion of statistical independence we ask only that various combinations of categories do not occur more frequently than would be expected by chance. We can become most suspicious of the comprehensiveness of a set of categories when we find greater than chance incidence of combinations of three or more of them.

3. From the theoretical as well as from the applied point of view, but particularly from the latter, the most vital characteristic of a set of diagnostic classifications is that they form the basis for the choice of treatment. This means that there should be some understandable and predictable relationship between the characteristics which define the construct and the effects of treatment processes. From the therapist's point of view diagnosis will be of little value unless it points to treatment. Part of the definition of a diagnostic construct should include some statement as to how the condition can be modified, and its validity

will depend in good part on whether this prediction can be verified. (3, pp. 231–232.)[1]

The diagnostic phase of the clinical method culminates in the formulation of a theory or hypothesis of causation. Once causation has been established, emphasis shifts to the questions of what can be done and what corrective steps can be instituted. We then are ready to enter the treatment phase.

DIAGNOSIS AND PROGNOSIS

It is unfortunate that common usage makes a distinction between diagnosis and prognosis. The first term is often thought of as dealing with the present (what it is) and the second with the future (what will happen). The position taken here is that diagnosis always looks to the future. Diagnosis always leads to personal treatment, direct or indirect, or to disposition elsewhere, at which point, presumably, treatment will be given. Diagnosis, then, is concerned with formulating the problem and its most propitious disposition in the light of all circumstances. The sharp distinction between prognosis and diagnosis is considered to be inappropriate and misleading. Only in diagnosis as classification can it hold; diagnostic formulations as conceived here not only easily encompass these factors but also demand that they be included.

Only in one sense, easily embraced in an enlarged concept of diagnosis, can a distinction from prognosis be made. Prognosis, it is sometimes argued, involves consideration of factors which may or may not be changeable and yet which affect the outcome. Factors in the family situation, economic circumstances, or social background may be of such a nature as to make prognosis guarded; these facts do not affect the diagnosis. A child starved for affection may receive it within the home by appropriate modification of the attitude of the parental figures. Another child who exhibits affect hunger, but who is in a large, understaffed orphanage, may diagnostically be said to resemble the first; his prognosis, however, is not so favorable. It is argued that circumstances independent of the individual and immutable may be operative to influence prognosis.

---

[1] Reprinted from "Diagnosis in Counseling and Psychotherapy" by E. S. Bordin, by permission of *Educational and Psychological Measurement*. Copyright 1946 by Science Research Associates.

DIAGNOSIS AND THERAPY

If diagnosis did not imply treatment, the diagnostic study would be of little pragmatic value. The practice prevalent in a particular setting will determine whether the treatment measures will be conducted by the psychologist. The psychologist who is not a staff member but instead is functioning as a consultant to an agency or institution undoubtedly will not handle this phase of the clinical task, but his diagnostic findings will be an integral part of the diagnostic study. Similarly, his diagnostic work may be performed as a member of a team in which other members are charged with the responsibility of carrying out therapeutic measures. Again, he may be in charge of the complete diagnostic-therapeutic process.

Since the diagnostic and therapeutic aspects of the clinical method are sequential in character, there is continuity from diagnosis to treatment. By no means, however, is it rigid, for the two intermingle. During the earlier diagnostic phases certain therapeutic values may result for the patient, e.g., in the form of some relief from tension through the sheer act of talking about his difficulties and a greater understanding of his own personality incidental to his account. The very manner of greeting the patient, of explaining what is to be done and why, of quieting his fears and removing any misconceptions which may interfere with rapport may influence the patient therapeutically.

The psychologist who is acting as diagnostic consultant, i.e., is not in charge of the case, is therapeutically most helpful when his therapeutic activity is restricted to the contributions resulting from the procedures previously mentioned. Although this may seem paradoxical, it must be remembered that at the time of referral to the psychologist the patient has presumably begun the often tenuous task of building the relationship, through which therapy is operative, with the referring therapist. Perhaps he has unburdened himself, which is a painful process, and feels the stirrings of a desire to cooperate. He is trying to be honest and wishes, consciously at least, to be as helpful as possible if only for his own sake. It has been a unique, somewhat terrifying, but certainly dramatic experience. He is referred to the psychologist at a time when he is, so to speak, keyed up. The psychologist often does not know what happened between therapist and patient. If the psychologist in his zeal to understand the problems encourages the patient to talk them over with him, he tries, in effect, to assume full responsibility. The patient may come away badly shaken from the sessions with the psychologist and perhaps resentful of either therapist or psychologist or both. Too many therapeutic cooks, if they do not spoil the broth, at least weaken it.[2]

SYMPTOMS IN RELATION TO DIAGNOSIS

Symptoms, generally speaking, can be identified without the use of any of the distinctively psychological approaches; that is, the presence of symptoms is detected through interview and other means common to all clinicians. Some symptoms are directly observable, such as agitation, euphoria, a rapid pulse, or weeping. In other cases it is the verbal report of the patient, but not the symptom itself, which is observable. Hallucinations, headaches, dizziness, and diplopia are cases in point. The psychologist does not find his greatest usefulness, then, in this area.

It may be observed that the patient is mute, sorrowful, and retarded in movement and thought. These may be recognized as a group of symptoms (syndrome) which have occurred before and may have led to an inclusive identifying name which is now applied when the syndrome is encountered. No matter the name—it is a name for our ignorance unless it somehow leads to a better understanding of the patient. Names based on symptoms rarely do this. Not only do the same symptoms appear in many contexts; they may be brought about by widely varying causes. Not only may the same symptoms have different causes, but different symptoms may have the same causes. Diagnosis which is no more than the name of a group of symptoms is merely an indication of ignorance; only when this is recognized and admitted is there justification for such naming.

This is not to say that symptomatic treatment, to be discussed more fully in later chapters, is not occasionally desirable. As a means of coming to grips with the fundamental difficulties, of focusing attention on more important but less dramatically disturbing conditions, of satisfying the patient's (and the family's) need for action at the onset of treatment, or of making the patient more comfortable —in these circumstances symptomatic treatment is appropriate.

---

[2] This applies with special force to that considerable number of practicing clinical psychologists without training or experience in therapy.

An investigation of the dynamic interrelationships of symptoms which permit several interprctative meanings is the more proper function of diagnostic procedures, including those of the psychologist. Symptoms are transitory and changing; what the patient gains from them is apt to be more constant. Thumb sucking at one time and stealing at another may be symptomatic of affect hunger in a child; these may give way to overeating and the consequent obesity, which may be symptomatic of the same condition in the adult. Symptoms take on real meaning only as they are related to the total personality. One has to know not only that the child is given to temper tantrums and night terrors but also the kind of child he is in general, the influences that shaped him in the past and those affecting him now.

THE PSYCHOLOGIST AND HIS DIAGNOSTIC TASKS

Just how does the psychologist implement these objectives? The theoretical approach varies with the psychological persuasion of the clinician, and so extreme divergences do appear in the *interpretation* of the obtained data. Fortunately, however, there is general agreement concerning the diagnostic task itself. This may be illustrated in the following quotations from psychologists concerning their diagnostic duties. According to the clearly stated account of Shakow, the diagnostic contributions of the psychologist may be classified as: "(1) The description of what the patient in his various conditions is like in certain relevant psychological functions, i.e., *what he is.* (2) The implications which the psychological studies have for therapeutic (educational, vocational, personality, etc.) policy, i.e., *what to do.* (3) The determination of the effects of whatever therapy may have been used on psychological functions, i.e., the evaluation of *what has been done.*" (1, p. 20.)

The account of Campbell is also pertinent. She writes:

The contribution of the psychologist toward the total diagnostic picture consists in offering information relevant to the following main questions: (a) Does the patient show mental or personality deviations? (b) If so, what is their significance for determining the nature and degree of the patient's illness? (c) What psychogenic factors appear to be contributing to the patient's illness? (d) What steps should be taken in treatment? In his effort to answer these questions, the psychologist has available (a) the social, psychiatric and medical history, (b) reports of psychiatric examination and (c) medical, neurological, and laboratory reports. He then examines the patient through informal interview and through the use of whatever diagnostic tests are required to answer, with a fair degree of assurance, the broad diagnostic questions or other special problems pertinent to the case under consideration. (4, pp. 107–108.)

Some psychologists, notably Rapaport and his associates, consider their diagnostic task to involve obtaining knowledge of the patient's personality, ability, and problems without resorting to either the case history or the usual methods of history taking. Nevertheless, their published accounts show considerable methodological and contentual agreement with other accounts in which the psychological report includes case history data.

The collection of psychological findings independent of other data does permit a more clearly separated and distinct evaluation. It is unnecessary, however, to have the psychologist's diagnostic study performed completely independent of other data concerning the patient. As is well known, in general medical practice it is usually considered desirable to have independent diagnoses made by several competent diagnosticians when the case is a difficult one. In such instances, however, certain basic data are not secured by each diagnostician but shared by all.

The previous discussion has been sufficiently general to be applicable in almost any clinical situation. It is desirable, however, to offer more specific accounts in one or another of the settings in which psychologists work. Consequently diagnostic procedures as implemented in psychiatric installations and child guidance clinics will be described.

THE DIAGNOSTIC PROCEDURES OF A PSYCHOLOGIST IN A PSYCHIATRIC INSTITUTION

In a setting in which the psychiatric-psychological collaborative relationship exists, a referral slip is frequently utilized to request a psychological examination. A typical referral slip (used at Washington University Medical School and its affiliated hospitals and clinics) can be found in Figure 1. It is appropriate to disregard the sections concerned with minor details of operating procedure and attend instead to the section concerning the information wanted from the psychological examination.

At one time the determination of the *intellectual level* of the patient was the most important task assigned to the psychological ex-

FIG. 1. Request for Psychological Study Form

Mr.   Clinic or
Mrs. ....   File No. ....
Miss   (Patient's Name)
Address .... Phone ....
            (Street, City, State)
Parent's Name ....
                    (If patient is a minor)
Patient's   Educational
Birthdate .... Level .... Sex ....
                    (Last grade completed)
Limitations on time of
appointment (if any) ....
Treatment Status: Private ..... Out-patient ..... Ward ....
(Check one of each) Staff   ..... In-patient ..... (If hospitalized)
Any record of previous psychological study? ....
If so, where: .... Date(s) ....
Information wanted from present study (Check):
........(a) Intellectual functioning   ....(g) Sources of difficulties of
........(b) Evidence of brain damage   adjustment
........(c) General educational   ....(h) Differential psychiatric
           problem   diagnosis (Specify)
........(d) Particular school subject   ....
           disabilities (Specify)   ....(i) Therapeutic assets
           ....(j) Discrepancy between
........(e) Vocational potentialities   current and previous
........(f) General personality   intellectual levels
           dynamics   ....(k) Change of status
                                       ....(l) Other (Specify)
                                                  ....

Summary of Current Problem:

Present Clinical Impression:

Is more than one *personal* copy of report needed? .... How many? ......
Additional copies sent to ....
Can patient be tested in psychologist's office? Yes .... No ....
Type of current treatment: .... Date started .....
                    (Shock, psychotherapy, etc.)
Type of medication or
sedation (if any) ....
Referring department .... Case referred by:
   (e.g., Med. D, MHC, VA, Children's Hosp.)
Today's date ....
                                       In charge:
                                       ....

aminer. The results centered about the IQ, a measure which placed the individual at some point along a scale in terms of intelligence. The establishment of intellectual level, although important to decisions about commitment to institutions for the mentally defective or the form of therapy most suitable for the individual, is never enough. Even in establishing mental deficiency other factors must be taken into consideration. The degree of social adjustment must be weighed in judging feeble-mindedness as well as, in considering higher intellectual levels. It is more important for diagnosis and treatment to know *how* the individual uses his intelligence than to know merely its level. The ways in which the individual uses his available intelligence and the extent to which he is using it are more meaningful than is a static score called the IQ. Accordingly, the psychologist's report stresses these factors rather than the IQ.

Occasionally the clinician has reason to suspect that the patient may not be functioning at as high an intellectual level at the present time as he had at some time before being seen by the clinician. Referral for measurement of *discrepancy between current and previous intellectual levels* would be indicated. This discrepancy, if established, may be due either to disturbing and limiting central nervous system disorders or to the effect of severe emotional disorders which disturb the individual's ability to handle reality situations. Clues as to the nature of the disturbances and the assets remaining may be obtained from the psychological examinations. Impairment, of course, is apt to affect differentially the various psychological functions, and attention will consequently be paid to differing degrees and kind of impairment demonstrated. In appraising the patient for deficit the ideal approach would be to have a series of measures over a period of years. Since this goal is seldom realized in practice, the clinician must rely on present behavior to infer past performance. A variety of psychological tests, to be considered later, permit this to be done.

The detection of *evidence of brain damage* or "organicity" is closely related to the previous reason for referral because sometimes it is demonstrated through deficit. Deficit may not be primarily a matter of structural change, and, conversely, the problem of brain damage embraces additional factors. Differences in the nature and degree of conceptual thinking, memory change, disturbances in visual-motor and auditory-motor performance, and affective disturbance all contribute to the evidences for and against an "organic" syndrome. In this area the psychologist has the opportunity to supply information of value for diagnosis and treatment. Psychological tests, however, in most instances, are not essential for the establishment of the presence or absence of cerebral alteration. Instead the task of the psychologist centers upon a broader appraisal—the personality changes created in the patient, estimation of present and previous functioning level, the progressive or static nature of the organic involvement, the detection of specific losses in intellectual efficiency, and therapeutic leads for a program of reëducation and therapy.

Differential psychiatric diagnosis as a reason for referral is relatively obvious. Signs and symptoms compatible with more than one diagnostic category, and the presence of somewhat similar but prognostically different syndromes illustrate two situations which might result in a differential diagnosis referral request. Diagnosis is facilitated by the attempts at differentiation of the psychoses from the psychoneuroses, and psychoneuroses from the character disorders, and the various psychotic and psychoneurotic conditions from each other. A word of caution is appropriate here. It is too much to expect fine differentiations to be found by the psychological examinations in all instances. Certainly, however, differentiation between such groups as the "primary behavior problems" and disorders stemming from organic damage is often possible. Implicit in this request for psychological examination is often the idea that the information supplied will touch upon the severity of the disturbance.

General educational problem, particular subject disabilities, and vocational potentialities may conveniently be discussed together. In all of these information is wanted about how the patient behaves or will behave in certain situations removed from direct clinical observation. Is he truant because he is not able to do the work in his present grade in school? Is he deficient in school work because he has never learned to read properly? Is he suited by aptitudes, interests, and past achievements to pursue his present college curriculum? What are his present achievement levels in the basic school subjects? These and related questions form another source of requests for consultation with the psychologist. Psychological reports throw light on these specific issues and also make possible a better understanding of the dynamics of the patient's present difficulties.

Especially valuable to the psychiatrist is the information supplied by the psychologist in regard to *general personality dynamics* and the closely related issues of *sources of difficulties of adjustment* and *therapeutic assets.* Here the issue is not the descriptive but the pathological-dynamic diagnosis. What sort of person is this patient whom we are attempting to help? What are his areas of difficulty, his characteristic methods of handling the vicissitudes of life, the balance of his various personality trends, his conflicts, his ambitions and interest patterns, the relation of his cognitive processes to his emotions, his fantasy life, his overt and latent trends? Is the disturbance of a situational nature? Is it of long standing or of recent origin? The positive and favorable aspects of the patient's resources are brought out, as are the negative, and special attention is given to evaluating the relative strength of each. The likelihood of improvement, the feasibility of therapy, the problems for therapy, and the assets in therapy can thus be indicated.

Another problem which has implications for both the diagnostic and the therapeutic aspects of the clinical method is *change of status.* Individuals showing neuropsychiatric difficulties are relatively unpredictable in terms of changes which occur in particular capacities or general status. Repeated examinations are often given to patients who might show psychological changes following head injuries, infections, functional mental illnesses, and so on. Of particular interest are reëxaminations given after the application of some specific form of therapy, such as shock treatment, lobotomy, or psychotherapy. The benefit or hindrance to mental and emotional status is thus investigated. Children whose environment has been changed by placement in nurseries, foster homes, or institutions are often studied psychologically to determine the degree and areas of improvement, that is, the changes of status which have occurred.

The breakdown into reasons for referral is to some degree artificial but nevertheless necessary. Sometimes referral is for full psychological work-up; i.e., "laboratory studies" are requested. In such instances the psychiatrist is puzzled and hopes more or less vaguely that leads of one sort or another will be gained. However, the adroit use of the psychologist in his diagnostic role requires more precise reasons for referral. The referral slip is only as valuable as the judgment of the person completing it. The particular questions posed by the referring psychiatrist may or may not be the most crucial. If in the judgment of the psychologist a more comprehensive examination is indicated, then other areas are investigated.

The Diagnostic Procedures of a Psychologist in a Child Guidance Clinic

The diagnostic procedures of the majority of child guidance clinics appear to show enough similarity to permit drawing a composite picture of common practice. The first time the child is brought to the attention of the clinic, the presenting problem or problems are indicated in a brief statement by letter, telephone call, or personal visit. The person charged with responsibility for intake selection, generally a social worker, will, on the basis of this material, decide upon the feasibility of an interview. From the adult accompanying the child—parent, teacher, or agency representative—a more complete statement is received. Either a social worker or a psychiatrist spends some time with the child, generally doing little more at this point than allowing the child to get used to the situation in his own way. (Of course, this also supplies information of diagnostic value.) Observations are made of the way the child reacts to the parent and to other adults, of his characteristic mode of dealing with a new situation, of what he spontaneously offers about himself and others. If the decision is reached to accept the referral, future plans and appointments are made. Among these appointments is one with the psychologist.

The prevailing pattern of distribution of services in a child guidance clinic calls for joint diagnostic efforts by psychiatrist, social worker, and psychologist. As a consequence of seeing all (or most) children, the psychologist's contribution takes the form of bringing to bear his clinical acumen on all the psychological problems of the individual.[3] He is charged with the responsibility of using the distinctively psychological approaches to evaluate the difficulties of the child and to offer suggestions for treatment. In short, he is concerned with investigations of all areas of adjustment and maladjustment.

Prior to examination the psychologist has available the statement

---

[3] Symbolizing this shift of emphasis is the absence of a referral slip, common in work with adult psychiatric patients seen only on referral but almost non-existent in child guidance clinic practice where all children are seen.

of complaints, other notes, and, if the clinic procedure involves this step, the notes of the psychiatrist or the person who is to assume full responsibility for the case in later sessions.[4] Either from these notes or from comments made by his colleagues he is aware of the areas of investigation to be especially stressed. Although the arrangement for a psychological examination may be a routine matter, the execution of the examination itself never is. Certain diagnostic areas will be highlighted, according to the nature of the case. For the diagnostic activities of the psychologist in a child guidance clinic the account of Tulchin (2) is representative. He describes the tasks of the clinical psychologist as (1) the determination of the level of intelligence, (2) the determination of educational achievement, (3) the diagnosis of special subject disabilities, (4) the use of tutoring in subject disabilities as a diagnostic function, (5) the determination of special aptitudes, (6) vocational testing and guidance, and (7) the investigation of personality functioning. Thus in a child guidance clinic the tasks of the clinical psychologist seem to be very similar to those obtaining in an adult psychiatric setting. Differences seem to be primarily a matter of emphasis. This should occasion no surprise, since the aim of acquiring knowledge about the nature and origin of the patient's difficulties is similar no matter what the age and circumstances of the patient.

BIBLIOGRAPHY

1. Shakow, D., The functions of the psychologist in the state hospital, *J. consult. Psychol.*, 1939, 3:20–23.
2. Tulchin, S., Present and future diagnostic role of the clinical psychologist, *Amer. J. Orthopsychiat.*, 1942, 12:397–405.

Supplementary articles in Watson, R. I. (ed.), *Readings in the clinical method in psychology*, Harper & Brothers, 1949:

3. Bordin, E. S., Diagnosis in counseling and psychotherapy. Pp. 229–243. (Also in *Educ. Psychol. Measmt.*, 1946, 6:169–184.)
4. Campbell, H. M., The role of the clinical psychologist in a Veterans Administration Mental Hygiene Clinic. Pp. 106–114. (Also in *J. clin. Psychol.*, 1947, 3:15–21.)
5. Carter, J. W., A note on psychodiagnosis. Pp. 183–186. (Also in *J. consult. Psychol.*, 1940, 4:137–139.)
6. Doll, E. A., The social basis of mental diagnosis. Pp. 325–333. (Also in *J. appl. Psychol.*, 1940, 24:160–169.)

---

[4] This may, of course, be the psychologist.

7. Mathews, W. M., Scope of clinical psychology in child guidance. Pp. 125–130. (Also in Amer. J. Orthopsychiat., 1942, 12:388–392.)
8. Thorne, F. C., The clinical method in science. Pp. 49–64. (Also in Amer. Psychologist, 1947, 2:159–166.)
9. Watson, R. I., Diagnosis as an aspect of the clinical method: a review. Pp. 405–427.
10. Wechsler, D., The psychologist in the psychiatric hospital. Pp. 99–105. (Also in J. consult. Psychol., 1944, 8:281–285.)
11. Weiss-Frankl, A., Diagnostic methods in child guidance and psychological counseling. Pp. 366–384. (Also in Ment. Hyg., N.Y., 1937, 21:579–598.)

CHAPTER 3

The Diagnostic Case Study

Diagnostic tasks were the major concern in the previous chapter. Attention now shifts from the diagnostic *tasks* to the *means* utilized to establish diagnosis. The *case study* is the medium through which all the findings about the patient are organized and evaluated. The interview, social history, observation, laboratory examinations, and psychological examinations are among the primary techniques used, and they provide the raw material from which the case study is built.

The individual is the focal point of the case study. In fact, the case study is the technique *par excellence* for dealing with the individual as an individual in all his uniqueness. There is a characteristic pattern or style unique to each patient; yet an implicit assumption made by many psychologists is that individuals differ only in the degree to which particular traits, attitudes, or symptoms are manifested. If for the moment hostility is accepted as a personality trait, an individual may be placed upon a hostile-ahostile continuum. This step is a necessary but not sufficient contribution toward diagnosis. There are differences in the degree to which an individual possesses a given trait or trend; there are also wide variations in the extent to which this trait is manifested, in the manner in which it is exhibited, and, generally, in its pervasiveness, pertinence, or salience.

Hypothetically, two individuals may be equated in terms of amount of hostility possessed. One of these individuals may exhibit

37

hostility in only a few restricted situations and in each instance manifest it with great strength; in the second person the trait may be demonstrated in a large number of contexts with proportionally less strength per manifestation. The latter individual might be said to have a generalized hostility, whereas the former has strong hostile impulses in certain restricted spheres. This is an important trait in the personality structure of both people, but its dynamic significance and the likelihood of initiating changes in the response pattern are probably dissimilar.

In addition there is the closely related issue of the salience of the trait. For one individual, hostility when evinced is very strong and pertinent; for another, who manifests it to an equal degree, it may mean little so far as his personality structure is concerned. In one person it is important in understanding his personality; in another it is not. In one the trait may be expected to show changes after successful therapy; in another no such changes should be expected.

Since individuality coexists with a commonality of characteristics shared with other persons, and since it is not negated even when several individuals are at precisely the same points on any continuum, the portrayal of uniqueness is not enough. It is inevitably judged against a background of similarity. Likeness to others is not ignored, as witness attempts at classification (for classification means placing like with like). An IQ of 103 may in one sense be unique since it is probable that no two response records are identical. Nevertheless, it tells the clinician within certain variable limits of error that in this respect the patient falls within the modal group. How the individual compares with others of his own age and cultural background is an integral aspect of the case study.

When the case study is used clinically there will be differences in the extent to which this uniqueness and similarity will be emphasized The differences are created by the nature of the patient's difficulty, his age, the professional background of the person in charge of the case, the prevailing procedures at a given agency, the time at the disposal of the clinician as well as his skill, and other factors. Thus approaches and findings will differ when the concern is with a behavior problem child as contrasted with a psychotic adult, when a psychiatrist is in charge of the case as distinguished from a psychologist, and when recommendations are made for others to carry out as differentiated from the situation in which the patient receives full diagnostic study and therapeutic care from the same clinician in an inpatient service where the patient may remain for an indefinite length of time. Most important of all, differences will be particularly striking when the case study is a well-intentioned but relatively meaningless chronology of fact and fiction, as contrasted with another case study that is a synthesis of the findings which permits an internally coherent, meaningful, and valid conception of the person, the nature of his problems, and the means whereby they may be worked through.

Objective data about patients are essential for appropriate diagnosis and treatment, but there is always a danger that lack of skill in their collection will result in a confused multitude of unrelated trivia. A simple datum takes on meaning only as it can be related to other data about the patient. In other words, the concern is not with scraps of behavior but with behavior and facts relevant to diagnostic and therapeutic effort. An inordinate fondness for succotash liberally covered with Russian dressing may be considered unique and even help us understand something about a person, but it would be rather difficult to find a situation which demanded an intensive investigation of this particular facet of the patient's gustatory preferences. Similarly, the fact that the patient has read the latest best seller may on occasion be revealing, but its very generality may make it irrelevant. Selection is a necessary prerequisite to organization. In intent this organization, i.e., the case study, bears some similarity to statistical analysis, since both are means of reducing an array of data to a form in which it can be grasped.

TYPES AND SOURCES OF INFORMATION AVAILABLE FOR DIAGNOSTIC STUDY

TYPES OF INFORMATION

It is evident that diagnosis is based upon information about the patient. Generally speaking, three types are available: *observational*, *quantitative*, and *historical*. The clinician observes the patient at first hand in the examining and interview situation and, if possible, indirectly through the contributions of other observers who have known him. Quantitative information is contained in the results of biochemical laboratory examinations and psychological tests. These differ according to the nature of the case. Spinal taps and determination of blood cholesterol illustrate biochemical procedures, and tests of intelligence, memory, and personality functioning exemplify the psychological tests which might be indicated. The third source of information available to the clinician is the historical material about the patient's past life gleaned from records, documents, and interview. The family and past personal history enable the clinician to see the behavior patterns in their longitudinal aspects and thus obtain information on how the maladjustment arose. As pointed out in the previous chapter, concern with the development of a condition, the end result of which faces us as the patient, is necessary for diagnostic formulation. An interest in the patient's past behavior and the various environmental forces—cultural, social, economic, and interpersonal—which molded it is essential.

One of the more fascinating aspects of the development of the case study is the changing perceptions that a patient often shows toward his own history. As the case unfolds with progress in treatment, the patient sees his past experience in a different light and gains in perspective. He therefore becomes a more reliable and valid informant.

In the formulation of the case study both psychometric and anamnestic (biographical) materials are necessary. In the publications of psychologists, e.g., Sarbin (6) and Stouffer (8), some attention has been given to the relative values of these approaches, which they choose to contrast. To the practicing clinician there is a curious air of unreality to a controversy as to the merits of one approach or the other. Both, of course, are necessary and one without the other makes services to the patient incomplete.[1] It is no occasion for surprise that on the basis of a research study Davis (1) concludes that both play significant roles, differing in emphasis according to the types of problem under consideration.

SOURCES OF INFORMATION

The patient himself is among those who contribute the information needed for diagnostic study. He may be able to provide a reliable account of some aspects of his past history. However, his inability to appreciate the significance of other segments of his past

---

[1] This is not to say that because both are necessary both receive equal attention in the training of the clinical psychologist. His training is likely to stress disproportionately psychometric approaches.

history (precisely because he is a patient), as well as memory gaps, limits his usefulness as a source of information. For everyone certain fundamental issues are obscured, if not lost completely, because of the intense emotional overtones coincident upon these experiences. Such deceptions, when they occur, are usually involuntary. In some instances, however, there may be deliberate attempts to mislead. This may happen with some court cases and with other patients who believe it is to their interest to misinform. However, conscious deception is relatively infrequent.

A variety of behavioral manifestations—actions, verbalizations, and products—are secured directly from the patient. The verbal behavior and actions studied include observations not only in the test or laboratory situation but also in informal, extra-test situations. Products may include drawings, modeling in clay, puppet and toy manipulations.

An appreciable number of cases are examined following referral from an agency, professional person, or relatives and friends. It is immediately obvious that good diagnostic practice requires collecting such relevant information as they have. Social work agency records are often a fertile source of information. The central social work information agency, sometimes called the "Social Service Exchange," is a particularly valuable source. School systems also maintain some form of record, often a cumulative one reporting at various temporal points the teacher's observations, test scores, grades, and other material about the student. Courts will be able to supply information at least about delinquencies. Physicians will have the results of their medical examinations. Parents, relatives, and neighbors can rarely supply clinical records, but they offer something else equally important—an intimate acquaintance with the person. Usually they do not understand the psychological significance of their information, especially when the material touches them emotionally. Nevertheless, if the clinician knows what (and how) to ask, they make a valuable contribution to the case study.

Not only do the professional sources supply information about the cases they refer, but also they are in a position to render the same services with other patients. The social worker is frequently charged with the responsibility of seeking such information, although sometimes whatever investigation is made in this sphere is performed by the psychologist or psychiatrist. The social worker, nevertheless, does most of the actual seeking of such information either by letter, telephone, or actual visits, to agency, physician's office, school, neighborhood, or home, in order to acquaint herself directly with the environment and other findings about the patient.

EVALUATION OF SOURCES OF INFORMATION

The source of the data is always indicated in clinical records, and the information should be evaluated in terms of the source. Deliberate attention must be given to the authenticity of the information elicited. A convenient pragmatic classification involving degrees of authenticity is on three levels: unquestioned facts, probabilities, and possibilities. The first, presumably, would include those findings about which there can be little or no doubt; the second, findings for which there appears to be confirmatory independent evidence; and the last, unverified findings against which there is no direct evidence, although the general gestalt of the case makes it unlikely.

Irrespective of the surrounding circumstances, some patients may be so withdrawn or lacking in self-understanding that they are unable to give much meaningful, valid material. Even if in a coma, a patient is capable of giving some information by reflex examination. In all cases it is important to elicit as much information as possible. The difference between one patient who is accessible, trustworthy, and insightful and another who is not, is in one respect merely in the degree to which other sources are needed to supplement and check statements. The reliability of data supplied by the patient can be evaluated in the mental status examination.

In former times it was felt that patients with psychiatric disorders could not be relied upon for a history, and everything told by the patient was categorized as "mental content," implying that it was not factual. In dealing with human behavior it is often very difficult to isolate facts from interpretations. In terms of final purpose (the treatment of the patient) the clinician is often more concerned with the patient's feelings and interpretations than he is with actual events or facts. From other sources varying interpretations of the "facts" should be obtained. Even more important is the task of discovering the attitudes of others toward the patient; how these attitudes may have contributed to the patient's disorder may be an important consideration in the treatment situation. Occasionally patients are so out of contact that one must depend almost completely on others for information. However, even in such situations it is surprising how much the patient can tell to an interested, astute, and persevering observer. Where other informants are used it is advisable to utilize the diagnostic approach described in this and earlier chapters to evaluate their feelings, attitudes, and understanding of the patient's situation.

THE NEED FOR A CASE OUTLINE

There are differences of opinion among clinicians concerning the procedure to be followed in making the case study. Some feel that procedures should have a minimum of similarity from case to case since aspects important in one are of little or no significance in another. Others feel that routine coverage of all aspects is requisite in all cases. The advisability of using printed forms to systematize case study data has been a subject of some discussion. Louttit's arguments for and against the use of such forms (3) are pertinent to the broader issue mentioned.

His arguments against using a definite plan can be expressed as follows: (1) A feeling of being restricted to the items called for may develop. (2) It follows that no provision is made for the special case. (3) On the other hand, when the form calls for much information irrelevant to a particular patient, time and effort are wasted.

Defense of such forms may be stated as follows: (1) If the form is conceived of as a guide and not as a strait jacket, one can omit and add as the immediate situation warrants. Insistence that good procedures necessitate following a rather definite outline does not preclude making allowances for differences in intelligence, age, social background, coöperativeness, and the like. When such allowances are made, the routine form is no longer routine, nor is it a constraining influence. (2) An adequately planned approach will make provision for obtaining additional information in the unusual case. (3) For run-of-the-mill cases on which a considerable amount of information is not desired, good operating procedure still demands a basic minimum of data. There is a certain irreducible minimum of information, then, that must be sought with each case regardless of its seeming irrelevance. Lavish attention need not be given every detail, germane or not. Asking questions of a patient to establish whether or not he is oriented as to place would seem absurdly naïve if he has come alone from his home to the clinic; yet it has been known to occur. (4) The clinic records are more uniform and more conveniently organized for future use. It might be added that a definite case study outline permits both easier and more meaningful learning of the case study technique and more ready grasp of the significance of the findings.

It is known that certain clinicians appear to use little or nothing in the way of a formal guide, much less a printed form. This apparent disregard exists when there is such thorough familiarity with some frame of reference that no necessity exists for a manifest guide in diagnostic sessions. A desirable goal for the clinician is to achieve sufficient familiarity with clinical procedures and appropriate formats so that the diagnostic sessions can proceed in a natural fashion and cover the relevant issues. In any case the student is almost unanimously urged to follow a rather definite procedure.

Some confusion will be avoided if it is remembered that the case study as formulated and recorded may follow any agreed-upon plan, and the actual conduct of the various phases of the study will be much more fluid and dynamic. Diagnostic sessions proceed as events dictate in a particular case.

In connection with neurotic and psychotic conditions there is enough similarity of procedure for it to be possible to prepare an outline of the procedures in a diagnostic case study. Accordingly, in the following section a format appropriate for this setting will be utilized. Although these procedures were primarily designed for use with adults, most of them have direct bearing on work with children.

PROCEDURES IN THE DIAGNOSTIC CASE STUDY[2]

The diagnostic case study when presented in a schematic form, like the one on the pages following, is open to the charge of being static and segmental. It is inevitably also open to the charge of being superficial since the nuances of the dynamic interplay cannot be

---

[2] The description has been adapted from that of Warson and Watson (9). Grateful acknowledgment is extended to the senior author. Another approach to the case study is given in Preu (4), and Wells and Ruesch (10) supply valuable aids to the case study.

captured. Nevertheless, as a preliminary heuristic device it may be defended.[3]

The case study is essentially two-dimensional in character. The first or cross-sectional dimension is derived from the direct findings about the patient (obtained from interview, test, laboratory, or physical examination situations) and the indirect information supplied about the patient's behavior in current situations in which he has not been observed by the clinician (at home, school, work, and elsewhere). The second or longitudinal dimension is concerned with the historical antecedents of the patient's present behavior. Each of these dimensions is essential and complementary; they are synthesized in the process of completing the case study.

THE COMPLAINTS AND THEIR SETTING

Evaluation of the patient's complaints requires considerable skill. In some instances the patient is able to point directly to the problem facing him. More often his description of the difficulties is only remotely or tangentially related to the fundamental issues preventing adequate adaptation. One may err in either of two directions—too literal acceptance of the patient's statement or almost complete disregard of it.

Frequently the clinician does not deal with complaints by the patient but rather with complaints about the patient (many patients will disclaim any difficulties whatsoever). This is especially true when dealing with children's problems, but it is also common among psychotics and psychopaths. In the psychoneurotic disorders the presenting complaints may have a devious relationship to the patient's fundamental difficulties. They serve primarily as a "calling card" to elicit the interest of the clinician. Such a devious approach is understandable in terms of the attitudes of the patient. Even when patients appear to be quite direct and seem to have a great deal of understanding about their problems, an approach like this will require evaluation in terms of previous experiences with psychologists and psychiatrists, reading, etc., because the apparently direct ap-

---

[3] A more advanced and dynamic treatment of the case study is given by implication in the discussion of psychotherapy in Chapters 17 through 23. In these chapters "diagnosis" is presented as a continuing process, not as a separate phase of the clinical method.

proach is somewhat disarming or even challenging in nature. It should be obvious that if the patient really knew the answers he would not be consulting the clinician.

Various sources should be consulted to see how the patient's problems appear to those in his environment. The original complaints should be taken down verbatim as an indication of what the patient or other informant thinks the problems are. Regardless of what the complaint may be it is advisable to encourage the patient to talk about it as much as he wishes. The clinician should neither accept the complaint at face value and start "prescribing" or interpreting nor, on the other hand, question the validity of the complaint. "Quizzing" or "cross-examining" by clinicians can be interpreted by patients as evidence of hostility and rejection and obviously should not be used when the clinician is trying to convey to the patient acceptance of him.

Ignoring the patient's statements of his problems is likely to encourage the development of suspiciousness or feelings of inferiority since it would appear to him that his opinion is not considered important. Even if it is obvious to the clinician that the patient's complaints are not in keeping with the fundamental problem, he should allow and indeed encourage the patient to expand upon them. However tenuous the connection, it has some relation to the real problem or problems. Therefore, it is relevant to therapeutic goals and conducive to establishing rapport. Knowing what the patient *thinks* his problem to be is a starting point for the clinical journey, and even though it may seem to involve a detour it will help lead to the source of the difficulties.

It should be clearly recognized that in formulating his complaints the patient has an opportunity to test out the reactions of the interviewer. If the interviewer reacts to aspersions or demands by "putting the patient in his place," the patient will be alienated and on his guard. It should be taken for granted that very few patients can quickly assume a role in which a new balance of dependence and independence is necessary. The patient may need considerable help in assuming this new role. It is given, not by demanding that the patient conform but by accepting him and permitting him the right to self-determination.

The case study sometimes has the unfortunate result of allowing the patient to assume too passive a role. By furnishing information (no matter how indirectly it was requested) the patient may feel that a tacit bargain is being struck whereby in return for his giving the information the clinician will tell him what to do. Like many other problems arising in the interview situation, this may require working through.

In recording the complaints—their onset, type, and frequency—their relationship with events in the individual's life and the methods employed for relief should be noted. This is the "setting of complaints" and is equivalent to a "history of the present illness" in that it gives the immediate context. It can be relatively brief at this point because emphasis here is primarily on an enlargement of behavioral items into patterns. The setting will be gone into much more thoroughly in the study of dynamics.

This aspect of the case study concerning the complaints is done in conjunction with the mental status examination.

THE MENTAL STATUS EXAMINATION

The mental status examination is based upon the assumption that certain emotional and intellectual patterns of behavior can be elicited which are relevant to our understanding of the patient. Like the physical examination it is essentially a cross-sectional study to ascertain what abnormalities of behavior are present.

For convenience the mental status examination is divided into separate aspects, disturbances in any of which may be a valuable diagnostic indicator. However, the sum total of the observations, plus the history, physical findings, etc., is necessary for proper interpretation and evaluation. In other words, the mental status examination should be merely a description of the behavior of the patient without any attempt to interpret observations until the rest of the case study is completed. (For example, if a patient appears tense and embarrassed during the interview, this fact should be stated as an observation rather than discounted as a "normal" finding because of a feeling on the part of the examiner that he, too, would be embarrassed in such a situation.)

It is appropriate at this point to present an outline of the content of the mental status examination.

APPEARANCE, GENERAL BEHAVIOR, AND ATTITUDES. Observations of the patient's appearance, activity, and attitudes during the interview are recorded. These include a description of the patient's physique,

manner of dressing, motor behavior (underactivity, ovcractivity, incongruous), facial expressions, mannerisms, negativism, etc. The patient's accessibility is described, as are his attitudes toward the examiner (friendly, aggressive, submissive, etc.), toward the interview
situation (tolerant, evasive, enthusiastic, aversive), and toward the
subjects under discussion. Observations of some of the physiological
concomitants of behavior (tenseness, tremors, dilated pupils, flush-
ing, sweating, rapid pulse, etc.) are also noted.

During conversations with the patient the clinician notes the
characteristics of his speech and includes verbatim samples in the
record. Motor disturbances (stuttering, lisping, slurring, scanning)
can be brought to light by using such test phrases as "round the
rugged rock the ragged rascal ran" or "Methodist Episcopal." Tests
for aphasic disturbances may also be pertinent. There may be deviations such as increase or decrease in productivity, acceleration or retardation in rate of verbalization, variations in the richness or poverty
of ideas, or spontaneity, relevance, coherence, and distractibility.
Blocking, flight of ideas with superficial association, disorders of
logical association, autistic reference, stereotypy, perseveration, ech-
olalia, and neologisms indicate how the patient deviates in his use
of symbolic language as a means of expression. An evaluation of the
patient's psychomotor activity can be made on the basis of these
observations.

CONTENT OF THOUGHT. The clinician is interested not in how the
patient verbalizes but rather in what the patient thinks—his ideas,
preoccupations, beliefs, and attitudes.

To properly evaluate mental content one should know something
about the patient's cultural background and the beliefs of his social
group. There are gradations of abnormal thinking from peculiar, unusual, or overevaluated ideas to such misinterpretations of reality as
delusions with varying degrees of systematization, illusions (sensory
misinterpretations), and hallucinations.

The only abnormalities noted on examination of psychoneurotic
patients may be mental trends which reveal relatively fixed ideas and
attitudes (anxious, depressive, hypochondriacal, hostile, obsessive,
rigid, paranoid, etc.). More severe disturbances of thinking processes
are usually indications of more severe states of disorganization or of
disintegration of the personality. The delusional trends most frequently encountered—ideas of reference, persecution, and alien

control—are evidences of paranoid thinking processes. Delusions of sin, guilt, and unworthiness, and somatic, nihilistic, and grandiose delusions are also sometimes found. The presence of delusions may have been elicited incidentally in the course of conversation. If not, the examiner may still have reason to suspect from the patient's behavior that it might be worth while to explore this matter further. Then it will be advisable to ask the patient about his relationships with his friends, family, and colleagues (i.e., how they have treated him), about their interest or desire to help him, whether he believes that they tell stories about him or act suspiciously in his presence, whether other people (the radio, etc.) influence or control his behavior, and the like. Other abnormal manifestations are feelings of unreality and depersonalization, obsessions, compulsions, phobias, and hallucinations in any of the sensory fields.

The areas of hallucinatory experiences are explored with considerable tact whenever there is any reason to suspect their presence. Introducing the idea of "unusual experiences" in connection with a particular sense modality is one means of entering the topic. If evidence of hallucinations is elicited, the clinician should explore the circumstances of their arousal, how long they have been going on, the ideas the patient has as to their purpose, and the person or persons presumed responsible.

EMOTIONAL STATUS (OR STATE OF EMOTIONAL ACTIVITY). The emotional aspect of human functioning is evaluated not only by what the patient says about his inner feelings but also by their overt expression (including physiological concomitants) and by the resonance or feeling aroused in the examiner by the patient. It is sometimes difficult to evaluate these feelings if the patient is very much on the defensive or puts up a front.

The prevailing mood might be described in the following terms:
1. *Prevailing mood.* Certain prevailing moods may be observed such as cheerfulness, gloominess, anxiousness, or indifference. These are noted along with the depth or extent of changes (e.g., patient consistently cheerful to the point of euphoria, indifferent to the point of apathy, etc.).
2. *Consistency or lability of mood.* Mood changes may be extremely labile, the patient shifting rapidly from laughter to tears—the so-called "emotional incontinence." On the other extreme, the mood may be so fixed and unresponsive as to be termed "frozen."

3. *Appropriateness of emotional responses to the expressed mental content.* This section is extremely important because quite frequently somewhat inappropriate and flattened emotional responses are the only evidence of schizophrenic behavior that can be found on mental status examination. In the normal person the affect exhibited varies more or less appropriately with the topic of discussion or the situation in which the individual finds himself. The emotionally disturbed person, on the other hand, is likely to have a persistent trend regardless of circumstances. The appropriateness of the emotional reactions of the patient should be looked for carefully and reported because of its implications.

THE STATE OF THE SENSORIUM AND INTELLECTUAL CAPACITIES. At this point the intent is to evaluate the patient's contact with his environment as demonstrated by his awareness, his memory, and his ability to understand situations and mobilize his intellectual functions so as to deal efficiently with the problems of his environment. Disturbance in this sphere may vary from mild clouding of consciousness to severe delirious or stuporous states.

Evidence of intactness of sensorial-intellectual functioning may be found during the course of the examination and interview. However, for thorough coverage the following items are completed. It should also be borne in mind that fluctuations do occur and repetition therefore is advisable.

1. *Orientation.*
   a. For time: the hour of day, the week, and the month.
   b. For place: particular building, town, state.
   c. For person: recognition of status of people about him.
2. *Memory.*
   a. Immediate: ability to retain and immediately recall a series of digits (seven for average adult) and a name, address, object, and color after a five-minute interval.
   b. Recent: ability to relate events in the recent past (dates of symptoms, names of physicians, recent activities, etc.).
   c. Remote: names of schools attended, occupations, etc.
3. *Grasp.* Slowness in comprehension and difficulty in following simple directions are indications of disturbances in the patient's ability to grasp. Hypothetical problems, such as apparently complicated but essentially simple arithmetic problems, can be used

to test for such a disturbance; e.g.: "If you went to the store with $1.00 and bought 63 cents' worth of articles, how much change would you have left?" A short story or a fable also can be presented to the patient to be read, following which he is to tell or write the story and its meaning in his own words (also tests reading and writing abilities). Knowledge of current events and their meaning is also a good indicator of general grasp, which may be defective on the basis of a lack of intellectual capacity or of a pathological involvement of the sensorium.

4. *Intelligence.* This is most accurately estimated from standard intelligence tests. However, many of the investigative areas previously discussed contribute toward evaluating the degree and scope of the patient's intelligence. Rough estimates may be made on the basis of school achievement, general fund of information and vocabulary, and vocational achievements. In this connection Richards says:

Of particular importance in evaluating capacity from the case history is the evidence regarding school progress and work adjustment. It is a well-known fact that many tests of intelligence are constructed and standardized in terms of the accuracy with which they measure and hence can predict school progress. In a very general sense, assuming schools of average quality, it may be stated that uninterrupted progress through the elementary grades is evidence of at least average mental capacity—IQ, let us say, of 90 to 110; graduation from high school, an IQ of 120 or better, while graduation from college probably indicates 130 or better. But this generalization is very tenuous for there are instances of amazing regular school progress even through high-school of individuals whose maximum test IQ is 75. Unless the clinician can assure himself that the quality of school standards is at least average and that teachers have been impartial in promoting the patient, such assumption is dangerous.

In older individuals much valuable evidence of capacity is shown in the demonstration in school or hobbies of particular skills or abilities. Most educational programs stress a generalized education for all children through the elementary grades so that, until these are completed, individual skills are not obviously apparent in the school history. But by the time the high-school years are reached, some decision usually has been made regarding the individual's adequacy for further academic study or for vocational specialization. Vocational education—i.e., placement in vocational school following the elementary grades—may have been an economic alternative, but more often than not it is an expression of apparent limitation in the academic-type intelligence and because of the fact that other abilities have emerged as more salient. Evidence of skill and abilities is also revealed in the job history. In evaluating the patient's history for evidence of capacity, it is always well to keep in mind the fact that interests and skills go hand in hand in a very real sense. As he develops the child tends to prefer activities in which he is successful—i.e., achieves the greatest ego satisfaction. The consequence of this is that he tends to practice most of these skills and hence to fortify his position, while he tends to discount and therefore neglect those at which he makes a poor exhibition. In later life, vocational choices and successes or rejections and failures are to a great extent conditioned by this early ego drive.

Although earnings are no certain criterion of occupational success and hence skill, they provide a very rough primary index. Of much greater significance is material regarding the individual's advancement in relation to his skills and the reason for changes in employment. Have job changes been in the nature of advancement, or are they signs of impermanence and dissatisfaction and even lack of skill? (5, pp. 45–46.)[4]

Not only may information about intellectual status be elicited without recourse to tests, but it is also possible to arrive at conclusions concerning the relation of present to past status, thus assessing intellectual decline or growth. Indices of decline may be illustrative since their obverse, it is self-evident, would apply to intellectual growth. The interrelation among the factors previously discussed supplies suggestive but not conclusive cues concerning decline, e.g., decrease in occupational status or earning power, loss of jobs, neglect of work, and especially occupational level below that expected on the basis of previous educational accomplishments. In the patient's personal life there may be indications—forgetfulness, carelessness, changes of attitude, loss of sense of responsibility, and other related phenomena—of intellectual deficit.

JUDGMENT AND INSIGHT.   By judgment is meant the ability of the patient to evaluate the relationship of events to one another and to the total situation. This refers to events in the past, present, and future. One questions the patient's ability to reason well (his "common sense"), whether his premises are different from the usually acceptable ones, and whether his behavior supports his stated judgments. Judgment has both general and specific aspects which should

---

⁴ From *Modern Clinical Psychology*, by T. W. Richards. Copyright, 1946. Courtesy of McGraw-Hill Book Co., New York.

be evaluated. Questions leading to an evaluation of the judgment of the patient can be centered around the clarity of mental functioning and relationships of the patient with other individuals (when this is a problem area). However, judgmental difficulties may be investigated in any area of personality functioning where abnormalities are present. A discrepancy between the realities of the objective situation and the patient's reaction to it or way of handling it supplies evidence on the quality of his judgment.

Insight refers to the patient's ability to evaluate his behavior in terms of the total situation (that he is ill and in need of treatment) and also of its more specific relationships (the factors involved in his becoming ill). This is not evaluated merely from what the patient says but on the basis of the total behavioral picture. Varying degrees of insight may be considered to be present, e.g., "none" when the patient does not admit to being sick, "superficial" or "partial" when he recognizes the abnormality of his behavior but does not appreciate its significance, or "formal" (verbal rather than operational) when actions do not support his statements.

Both judgment and insight are complex personality functions involving the use of comprehension, association, memory, reasoning, and planning. These in turn depend on integrative and organizational processes as manifested by the state of the sensorium, the intellectual capacity, emotional attitudes, and personality trends of the individual. Thus disturbances in these processes will be reflected by defects or changes in judgment and insight.

THE HISTORICAL BACKGROUND

Because early experiences are the most deeply impressionistic and important in terms of psychodynamics we try to start with the environment in which the patient was born and those who peopled it. The patterns of conduct and aspiration of the family grow out of their social and cultural standards; all of these form an important part of the environment with which the patient has most intimate contact.

Studies on the effects of heredity in mental disorders have been disappointing to those who would like to simplify the problem to one of eugenics, although familial patterns may be present. However, in addition to familial patterns individuals with mental disorders can create unhealthy emotional environments and, for this reason, evidence of mental disorders in the family should be noted and evaluated. Of greater importance are the personality characteristics of the various members of the family and the evidences of difficulties in interpersonal relationships. For example, personality difficulties of the parents can be reflected in their attitudes toward the patient and in the development of his problems. To obtain this kind of information the techniques of social case work were developed, and their value in both diagnostic and therapeutic situations is clear.

The past personal history is a record of the patient's development and the resultant capacities, achievements, experiences, personality trends, and characteristics. It must, however, be borne in mind that past events which to the observer may appear to have been traumatic may not have been stressful for the patient and vice versa. It is wise to allow the patient to bring out spontaneously the events that were meaningful for him. (For example, the threat of a separation early in life may have been much more traumatizing in terms of disturbing relationships than an actual separation.)

A source of difficulty in the historical section of the case study is that errors of memory are introduced because of the very nature of the task. A considerable period of time generally elapses between the taking of the history and the actual occurrence of the events reported. Often these events were and are emotionally tinged. This makes for omissions and accentuates the distortions that inevitably take place. Parents of feeble-minded children are likely to report a much greater frequency of falls and other possible injuries to the head when the child was an infant. There is little or no real evidence to demonstrate that such incidents occur with significantly greater frequency among feeble-minded than among normal children. In most instances the reason memory plays the parent false is his desire to find a neutral, nonpersonal cause to explain the child's unfortunate condition. Information about the past history of emotionally disturbed patients, especially if these patients are psychotic, is likely to be selectively distorted in the reports of the informants in that strangeness and bizarreness are often stressed.

An outline suggestive of some of the factors of the historical background to be investigated is presented next.

A. *The environment of the patient:* The regional, physical and sociocultural environments including any changes, such as Old World to New, south to north, rural to urban, lower to middle class, poverty to financial sufficiency, working class to business or profession. Family traditions if any.

B. *Family constellation:*
   1. *Father.* Age, occupation, religion, the family and personal background, outstanding personality traits or characteristics, relationship to other members in the home.
   2. *Mother.* Age, family and personal background (differences from the father's should be noted). Characteristics of and relationships to other members of the family.
   3. *Siblings, spouse, and children.* Age, sex, relationships and characteristics, differences in degree of favoritism, etc.
   4. *Other members.* Those who entered or left the family circle and their characteristics and relationships to the patient.

C. *Past personal history:* Any data that patient can recall or remember being told about the circumstances of his birth, his childhood, personality traits, his reactions to birth of siblings, parental attitudes, separations, etc. Possible evidences of emotional disturbances in such behavioral items as feeding or training problems, enuresis, fears, night terrors, speech difficulties, nail biting, temper tantrums, etc.

D. *School history:* An account of the individual's school life, both academic and social, which will give indications of his intellectual capacities, his reactions to discipline and to the need for a broadening of interpersonal relationships.

E. *Occupational history:* The nature of his occupational interests and achievements, reasons for job changes, attitudes toward employers and fellow employees. Military history and type of discharge for patients who have had service experience.

F. *Sexual and marital history:* A good index of the emotional development of the individual. This subject, however, because of cultural and social attitudes may tend to be disturbing if approached directly or abruptly. The patient's interests, activities, and attitudes can be learned indirectly if not given spontaneously or freely. Such inquiries as the attitude of the parents toward sexual interests or activities, the type of companion the patient prefers, and his ideas about marriage may pave the way for a frank discussion of a subject which can otherwise be very distressing to the individual who is already emotionally disturbed.

G. *Medical history:* The patient's attitude toward physical health and well-being as well as the possible relationship between somatic and emotional disturbances. These can be learned by encouraging the patient to discuss his illnesses. Never take a medical diagnosis for granted when given by the patient. (It is surprising how many attacks of "appendicitis," for example, are later revealed as psychoneurotic or psychosomatic in character.)

H. *Interests and habits:* Range and type of interests (vocational and avocational, intellectual, social, religious). Regularity of habits (meticulousness, rigidity, need for perfection). Patient's indulgences of and attitudes toward both his interests and his habits.

THE DEVELOPMENT OF THE DISORDER

From the point of view of causality, personality disorders have both precipitating and predisposing factors. The precipitating factors may be quite obvious and understandable either as overwhelming situations to which the human organism is incapable of adjusting or as changes in integrative structures. In other instances the precipitating factors may be obscure and related to the way in which the individual is handling some life situations. Even when the precipitating factors and their etiological implications are readily discernible, they cannot explain all of the symptomatology. The latter might be divided into "impersonal" and "personal," since each person experiences situations in his own particular way. Such "personal" symptomatology is referred to as "personality-determined" behavior.

The situation in which the individual's difficulties arose should be gone into carefully, not just for its manifest or easily remembered aspects but also for the more latent disturbing elements which may initially be beyond the patient's recall. By an inquiry into reactions to similar situations in the past, the precipitating situation may be utilized as a jumping-off place to clarify general behavior patterns. This will throw some light on any predisposition to the development of such disorders that the patient may have, but since human behavior is more than the product of any one stimulus-response situation this alone is not sufficient. An individual helps make his own environment. Thus to some extent the patient's behavior represents a mode of adjustment to life situations which he helped to create. The development of a disorder, then, will be tied up with those integrative and organizational aspects of the patient's personality which entered into the development of such a situation. In other words, the meaning of the patient's symptoms will be found in the development of his personality.

PSYCHOLOGICAL DIAGNOSTIC TESTING SESSIONS

As a major portion of this volume is devoted to an exhaustive elaboration of procedures and purposes of diagnostic psychological testing sessions, there is little need to forecast future discussions at this point. They are mentioned only to emphasize the proper perspective in which they should be viewed and to illustrate their role in the complete drama of diagnostic appraisal.

In a diagnostic testing session, emphasis is properly placed upon those aspects of the patient's functioning which the psychologist can best evaluate. What can the psychologist with his devices do that is either impossible or difficult for his clinical colleagues to accomplish? Although a referral slip (as described in the previous chapter) is essential, it is also desirable to furnish whatever case material is available. A psychological examination is not to be performed in a vacuum. Valid clinical interpretation of test findings is enriched by knowledge of other sources of information. In research extra-test data may be viewed as a contamination which negates whatever findings emerge; in clinical practice this contamination becomes a source of enrichment of the test findings and makes possible a broader and deeper analysis of the results.

LABORATORY STUDIES

Probably the most commonly indicated laboratory studies are blood counts, urinalyses, blood Kahn's, and basal metabolic rates. Other less common examinations are sometimes specifically indicated. For example, examination of the cerebrospinal fluid, not performed routinely, is made only if some reason for it would appear pertinent. Carbohydrate tolerance tests, electroencephalographic studies, and x-ray examinations also fall in the category of special tests.

Although the psychologist must be familiar with the general nature of these examinations, discussion of them would be inappropriate here. Such matters are, of course, definitely outside the diagnostic and therapeutic purview of the psychologist, falling as they do in a field indisputably the province of the physician. This, however, does not excuse the almost total ignorance of many clinical psychologists in regard to their nature and significance.

DIAGNOSTIC FORMULATIONS

As discussed in the previous chapter, the complexities of the personality and the fact that disorders are the result of the interaction of so many elements of human biology and experience make it difficult to conceive of a diagnostic classification that will be entirely satisfactory from an etiological point of view. The deficiencies of a classificatory system can be minimized by not placing much reliance on the diagnostic label and by adding a formulation of the development of the pathology for the particular patient in relation to his personality dynamics. Such a formulation is in reality a "personality diagnostic appraisal." In spite of this, some attention should be paid to diagnosis in the narrower and more static sense.

The final diagnosis is never made on the basis of the absence of "organic findings" or on the presence of any one abnormal behavioral trend, although either may contribute to a legitimate "impression." The case study provides clues for an understanding of the patient's behavior in terms of his background, development, and life situation at the time of the onset of his difficulties. Although these clues may point in a positive manner toward a personality determination for his symptomatology, it is only when feelings (or their absence), experiences, and behavior are elicited from the patient that a relationship between symptomatology and a primary emotional disturbance can finally be said to exist. This is not always possible in the diagnostic situation, in which case a presumptive diagnosis is usually made on the basis of the clues provided in these areas. A psychiatric diagnosis is in turn never an exclusive one, in that patients may have multiple sources of difficulties not necessarily related. It is yet to be found that the presence of one psychiatric disorder immunizes an individual to any other type of disorder.

The use of the term "disorder" rather than illness is useful in that it indicates that we are dealing primarily with the way the individual is functioning as a person and not with a specific disease entity. However, there may be some factors present which show that the personality disorder is related to disturbances not primarily emotional or psychogenic in origin. In any illness one will find personality-determined symptomatology, since no part of an individual can be disturbed without involvement of the whole person to some degree. The degree of involvement and manner of its expression will depend on the organization of the personality, which should be determined for proper evaluation of the symptomatology.

Similar complications may arise in the diagnosis of a neurotic disorder. The presence of reactions which are characterized as "neurotic" does not necessarily indicate that the individual is "a neurotic"; it may simply be a sign of mild deviations in certain areas. However, if these "neurotic" attitudes and trends are well-ingrained aspects in the organization of the personality, they are termed "character disorders." Although in both character and neurotic disorders we are dealing with personalities that are poorly organized, the former may be well compensated whereas the latter reveal evidences of disorganization and the presence of anxiety that has gotten out of bounds. In both, the neurotic behavior indicates a need for defenses against what might be termed "pathological anxiety." Anxiety, when a normal and constructively useful component of the personality, is described as "objective" in that it can be clearly related to its source in terms of quantity and direction. When it becomes abnormal, anxiety is not thus related but is instead tied up with unconscious meanings. It is when the individual becomes involved in coping with his anxiety to the detriment of his total adjustment that it may become a destructive force. In "character disorders" the pathological anxiety is kept within bounds by the defense mechanisms and compensatory activities. In "neurotic disorders" the pathological anxiety becomes manifest in the symptomatology, and the personality can thus be thought of as "decompensated." In acute reality situations pathological anxiety may take on an objective quality which obscures the neurotic disorder. This occurs frequently when the patient is brought to the clinician for acute and painful disturbance, the convalescence from which becomes complicated by the patient's neurotic problems. It was also seen during the bombing of London, when neurotic disorders seemed to improve spontaneously only to relapse when the danger was over. On the other hand, "catastrophic" reactions can occur in such situations with so rapid a disintegration of the personality that the treatment situation is seriously prejudiced. The only way to understand the symptomatology or predict what might happen is through the use of the clinical approach and a sufficiently thorough case study.

CASE STUDY RECORDS

The Maintenance of Case Study Records

After a diagnostic examination a report is generally necessary. The maintenance of case records is essential, since without them efficient clinical practice would be impossible. The most direct value of a case record is its communicative nature both to the reporting clinician in his subsequent contacts with the patient and to his colleagues and other interested professional personnel. For the individual clinician it is a means of reduction of memory falsification and memory loss. Case notes are needed to refresh memory before an interview, to reopen a case, or to refer the findings to another individual. The sheer act of recording may, as the findings of a case are reviewed, lead to a recognition of different perspectives, of omissions, or of new solutions or interpretations. The idea of the team relationship necessitates the recording of material for the inspection and use by collaborators either through the notes themselves or through a staff conference at which these notes are discussed.

Although facilitation of diagnosis and treatment is the primary purpose, certain other reasons for recording case notes may be identified. The review of case notes is one of the means whereby the senior staff supervises trainees, clinical clerks, residents, and junior staff members, since their activities with and on the behalf of the patient form a part of the record. Individual or group conferences with the case notes as a focus of reference constitute a common in-service training device. Through study of these notes the supervisor can ascertain what was done, what was overlooked, and what possible suggestions might be offered for future steps. Still another value of case notes is the protection they afford the clinician if later misunderstandings arise. The emotionally charged atmosphere of the clinical session may give rise to misinterpretations by the patient or even downright falsehoods. The case notes may give some protection against these unpleasant effects. Finally, the notes become the data of clinical research.

DIFFICULTIES IN MAINTAINING CASE STUDY RECORDS

Although case study records are necessary, a word of caution is in order. Something close to completeness in the maintenance of case study records may be possible, but inevitably this can be accomplished only at the expense of other values. To attempt to maintain literally complete case records would sometimes mean limitation of time for treatment or of case load; in other instances an actual impairment of clinician-patient relationship would occur, e.g., a rigid determination to take notes during the interview despite the patient's evident reluctance to speak because of this practice. It is not completeness *per se* that is of value so much as capturing the essence of that which has transpired.

Of necessity, the identification of the significant and ignoring of the insignificant is not a skill with which the novice is equipped. Only with practice does the sifting process give a valid picture. The implication is obvious. At first, the clinician must err on the side of too many notes, but with practice under guidance he learns to become more succinct. The skilled clinician who holds to a particular interpretative position may be judged by critics of that position as exhibiting the "error" of theoretical bias. There is always danger that the hand of the individual preparing the case study will be heavy upon it. The picture given will reflect the interpreter (or rather his particular professional *Weltanschauung*) more than the patient. At least there will be two pictures—one a clear and vivid portrayal of the clinician's deductions and one, dimmer and smaller in perspective, which gives a distorted image of the patient. The disconcerting aspect of this source of difficulty is the fact that critic and criticized play their roles according merely to whose case is being considered. No solution can be offered by the writer; recognition of this as a problem and a valiant, though probably losing, battle to separate fact and inference are offered as the only guides.

Aside from the clinician's theoretical biases the most prevalent error of case recording appears to be a chracteristically narrow point of view concerning anything but *what was said*. Verbal behavior is important, to be sure, but even the same words may convey vastly different meanings. A quotation from Gill and Brenman (although it places the problem in a therapeutic rather than a diagnostic setting) is so cogent as to be worth repeating:

Emotional intercommunication between people involves much more than literal verbal content. An interview read from the typed or printed page is never the same as the interview heard by electrical transcription; and even the sound-recorded interview is always different from a totally heard and observed session. One need not labor the fact that a single word can be spoken with dozens of intonations, each of which conveys a different meaning; whether the difference lies only in a subtle nuance or in contrasts as clear as that between the angry "no" of a paranoid and the timid "no" of an inhibited patient, both of which would be recorded similarly if verbal content were considered the sole data of the interview.

Translation of content into feeling is done not only by the therapist, but also by the patient, though the latter is usually much less aware of it than the former. The patient reacts to what he hears on the basis of what it conveys to him about the therapist's feeling. Indeed, this is another kind of translation which the therapist must carry out. He must not only tell the patient the "feeling-meaning" of what the patient says, but also what the patient considers the "feeling-meaning" of what the therapist says. It is precisely with regard to this translation that the therapist's judgment comes into play. It is hoped that he will know the meaning of what the patient says, and the meaning of what he says to the patient. Then he must decide which feelings to select from the many expressed by the patient, which of these to translate first, when to translate, and whether to make the translation at all. This will be determined by what he believes will be the "feeling-meaning" the patient will derive from what he says.

In addition to the pitfalls presented by the attempt to translate the verbal content of the psychotherapeutic interview, it must be remembered that much emotional intercommunication takes place through nonverbal means. The most obvious nonverbal emotional communication may be conveyed by a smile, a gesture, a posture. An enormous area of intercommunication is missed if the translation of content into feeling is confined only to a derivative of the patient's words. (2, pp. 102–103.)

If this is the case, what can be done about it in recording? It is self-evident that not all nuances of the interview will be captured and that success in so doing will vary directly with the clinician's skill. What may be done to increase this capacity for appropriately and selectively noting the emotional intercommunication? First must come awareness of it as a challenge facing every clinician. One must ask oneself what the patient is *trying* to say. It is emphatically not just the meaning of the words in their baldest sense that is sought, but the emotional meaning which may run through several apparently disjointed remarks, gestures, and feeling tones. The work of Rogers and his students, particularly Snyder (7), has done much to familiarize psychologists with this issue, particularly their stress on the importance of clarification of feeling. By clarification of feeling they refer to attempts by the clinician to reorganize and synthesize the feelings expressed by the patient regardless of whether the words he used were concerned with this or not.

BIBLIOGRAPHY

1. Davis, F. B., Diagnostic methods in clinical psychology, *Train. Sch. Bull.*, 1945, 42:113–120.

2. Gill, M. M., and Brenman, M., in Brenman, M. (chm.), Research in psychotherapy: round table, 1947, *Amer. J. Orthopsychiat.*, 1948, 18:100–110.
3. Louttit, C. M., A blank for history taking in psychological clinics, *J. appl. Psychol.*, 1934, 18:737–748.
4. Preu, P. W., *Outline of psychiatric case study: a practical handbook*, Paul B. Hoeber, Inc., 2nd ed., 1943.
5. Richards, T. W., *Modern clinical psychology*, McGraw-Hill Book Company, 1946.
6. Sarbin, T. R., Clinical psychology: art or science, *Psychometrika*, 1941, 6:391–399.
7. Snyder, W. U. (ed.), *Casebook of non-directive counseling*, Houghton Mifflin Company, 1947.
8. Stouffer, S. A., Notes on the case study and unique case, *Sociometry*, 1941, 4:349–357.
9. Warson, S. R., and Watson, R. I., Fundamentals of the psychiatric approach: a guide to the psychiatric case study, Washington University Medical School, 1949 (mimeographed).
10. Wells, F. L., and Ruesch, J. (eds.), *Mental examiners handbook*, Psychological Corporation, 2nd ed., 1945.

Supplementary articles in Watson, R. I. (ed.), *Readings in the clinical method in psychology*, Harper & Brothers, 1949:

11. Darley, J. G., The structure of the systematic case study in individual diagnosis and counseling. Pp. 209–216. (Also in *J. consult. Psychol.*, 1940, 4:215–220.)
12. Sarbin, T. R., The case record in psychological counseling. Pp. 217–228. (Also in *J. appl. Psychol.*, 1940, 24:184–197.)
13. Traxler, A. E., Case-study procedures in guidance. Pp. 200–208. (Also in *School Review*, 1938, 46:602–610.)
14. Watson, R. I., Diagnosis as an aspect of the clinical method: a review. Pp. 405–427.

CHAPTER 4

Observation and Rating in Clinical Diagnosis

In one sense the basic technique of all clinical activity is observation—the noting of behavior as it occurs. Without observation there would be no diagnostic interview, no rating scale, no therapeutic session, and no testing. Because of its pervasiveness and indispensability observation is fundamental to all other related techniques. In addition, it is a diagnostic technique in its own right.

Clinical devices utilizing observation in a very direct fashion are not unknown. A test of infant capacity, such as that of Cattell described in Chapter 12, is similar to the popular observational studies of the preschool child; both essentially involve a sampling of behavior. The Vineland Social Maturity Scale depends upon the observation of the clinician to some extent but is far more dependent upon the observations of the parent or other informant with whom the clinician confers. Inclusion of items stressing the age of acquisition of certain behavior characteristics such as crawling, walking, talking, manipulation, and so on clearly demonstrates the observational character of these instruments.

Observations are utilized diagnostically through other than psychometrically standardized devices such as those just mentioned. In general, there appear to be two different motives which lead to their utilization. On the one hand, many aspects of patient behavior of interest to the clinician cannot be directly or objectively measured. Estimating either the degree or the amount of a particular characteristic of. the patient requires the clinician's observations. Thus he reports that the patient "demonstrated an extremely rigid, inflexible approach" to certain areas of daily functioning, "tended to be quite passive and dependent in his dealings with members of the opposite sex," "was pessimistic in regard to his eventual recovery." Rigidity, passivity, and pessimism—though they may be important —are but tentatively and hesitantly measurable by present diagnostic instruments. There is a second reason for the use of observations instead of instruments: either when the pressure of time is too great to permit their utilization or, in other instances, where no more than a rough approximation is needed. The clinician then is satisfied with summarizing his observations. Sometimes these are acquired during sessions primarily devoted to other problems. Thus, reaction time or rate of speech might be measured precisely or observationally evaluated as rapid, average, or slow with some attention paid to any variability which might have been exhibited. Many aspects of the so-called mental status examination described in the previous chapter are of this character.

Observational sources in the psychological diagnostic situation include, of course, scorable test responses. For the sake of clarity of exposition it is possible to separate these psychometric aspects of the test response from the nonscorable ones or from observations. It is also possible, in turn, to distinguish item-bound observations from those which are nonspecific to the test situation but rather reflect various diffuse aspects of his general approach and experiences. Thus, if in response to the question "What is the thing to do if you find an envelope in the street, that is sealed and addressed and has a new stamp?" the patient trembles noticeably, has sweaty palms, is apprehensive, and replies, "Leave it lay, it may be a trap," all three observational aspects—the psychometric, item-bound, and diffuse— are obtained. The score is zero; the nature of the item response suggests a suspicious if not a paranoid trend; the general behavior suggests anxiety of a rather severe nature.

The scorable and item-bound aspects of this behavior will be considered in connection with specific tests, and only general observational material will be treated now. Since psychologists usually make their observations in diagnostic testing sessions, these are the major concern in the discussion to follow.

OBSERVATION IN THE DIAGNOSTIC
TESTING SESSION

The clinician is concerned with observing the behavior samples in the diagnostic sessions as they (1) influence test performance[1] and (2) suggest personality characteristics of the patient. In other words, the psychologist observes the patient in order to appraise his personality for diagnostic purposes and also to evaluate the effect of his present behavior on the test results obtained. To be sure, these two facets of the observational task intermingle and in some instances are simultaneously important in influencing test performance and demonstrating personality characteristics. A report of the general observations made by an experienced psychological clinician concerning a twenty-four-year-old general hospital outpatient veteran referred for evaluation of intellectual and personality functioning will serve to exemplify the procedure.[2] The relevant section of the report follows:

General Observations: The patient is a fairly well developed young man of average height and medium build who came to the Clinic informally but neatly dressed. He was generally oriented as to the nature and purpose of the examination and adjusted readily to the testing situation. His cooperation, effort and attention were good throughout. He seemed interested in and challenged by the various test questions and he worked diligently and methodically on all tasks placed before him. At times he appeared to be exercising excessive caution in his performance which then tended to be fairly slow. This was apparently related to the personal anxiety and lack of confidence which was manifested.

His speech was clear and well-modulated. He answered questions readily, using an average vocabulary and expressing his thoughts adequately. At times he also made some spontaneous comments about himself and the tests. Generally his manner tended to be fairly pleasant and friendly. Although rapport was rather superficial, it seemed adequate for testing purposes.

Anxiety was not severe and interfered relatively little with his performance. He shifted readily from task to task and appeared to have no difficulty in adjusting to the changing situations of the examination. Superficially he presented the picture of a mildly anxious individual who reflects somewhat more than an average amount of personal insecurity and self-consciousness.

---

[1] The concern here is with the general behavior pattern, i.e., behavior not related to specific tests or test items.

[2] Thanks are extended to Dr. Samuel Granick for permission to quote from one of his reports.

Without going into any great detail it is possible to analyze the report into the various elements covered. More or less in order they appear to be the following:

1. Appearance.
2. Orientation to the nature and purpose of the examination.
3. Initial adjustment to the testing situation.
4. Nature of coöperation, effort, and attention.
5. Attitude toward tests and own abilities.
6. Clarity of speech and pitch of voice.
7. Vocabulary level and ability to express self.
8. Spontaneity and initiative during testing.
9. General mood and sociability.
10. Nature of rapport during examination.
11. Evidences of anxiety and tension.
12. Ability to shift.
13. General impression as to the nature of the person that the patient is.

The nature of the report and the topics covered are more or less typical. They by no means exhaust all conceivable general observational findings which might have been reported. In another case different observational data might have been reported if judged noteworthy, e.g., reaction to praise or to recognized failure. The report quoted is relatively less concerned with the influence of the general behavior upon test performance than would be the case with more severely disturbed individuals. The comments in this report suggest behavior conducive to good, if not optimal, adjustment to the testing situation. In spite of differences in test behavior, reports by this clinician in particular (and to a lesser degree clinicians in general) would have some elements in common. Obviously there would be different orders, different highlighting, and the reporting of the inevitable idiosyncratic behavior peculiar to a given patient. In so far as one illustration can be typical, the one quoted may be so considered.

To train interns in psychology to make complete observational reports it is necessary to direct their attention to those aspects of behavior generally worth scrutinizing. The observation guide[3] given

---

[3] This observation guide was developed by the staff of the Division of Medical Psychology, Department of Neuropsychiatry, Washington University School of Medicine. Dr. Bettye M. Caldwell took the major responsibility in its develop-

as Figure 2 serves to bring together in convenient fashion a considerable number of these factors. The major topics, it will be noted, are:

FIG. 2. Test Behavior Observation Guide

Name .... Age ..... Sex ..... Date ....

Description (Appearance, facial expression, attire, posture, motility, voice quality, physical handicaps, presence of glasses, handedness, etc.):

1. *Sensory & Motor Proficiency:*
   Vision: ....
   Hearing: ....
   Manual Control: ....

   | Markedly Deficient | Limited | Average or Better |

2. *Performance Rate:*
   Ext. Rapid .... Rapid .... Average .... Slow ....
   Ext. Slow ....

3. *Orientation to Examination:*
   ....Seems to have complete understanding of nature and purpose of examination.
   ....Shows some insight as to purpose.
   ....Accepts the explanation of purpose of examination.
   ....Occasional evidence of distorted ideas.
   ....Completely misinterprets situation.

4. *Initial Adjustment:* *Final Adjustment:*
   ....Completely at ease, makes good social contact. ....
   ....Better than average social confidence. ....
   ....May show some anxiety, but manages to control it. ....
   ....Rather anxious and poorly poised ....
   ....Extremely ill at ease and apprehensive. ....

5. *Interest:*
   ....Enthusiastic and absorbed.
   ....Definitely interested in the tests.
   ....Shows an adequate amount of interest.
   ....Lack of interest shown.
   ....Completely uninterested.

6. *Coöperation:*
   ....Coöperates enthusiastically—does everything requested.
   ....Coöperates readily, offers no resistance.
   ....Generally good, but may resist certain assignments.
   ....Somewhat negativistic.
   ....Negativistic and uncoöperative, reducing reliability of the test.

ment and her permission, along with that of other members of the division, to publish is gratefully acknowledged.

7. *Amount of Speech:*
........Moderate amount of speech, recognizing limits imposed by test routine.
........Atypical speech pattern, tending toward ......volubility or ....taciturnity.
........Abnormal amount of speech: ....extreme loquacity or ....extreme taciturnity.

8. *Expressive Ability:*
........Excellent
........Good
........Adequate
........Poor
........Very poor

9. *Attention:*
........So attentive to test as to be oblivious to extraneous stimuli.
........Relatively undisturbed by extraneous stimuli.
........Moderately attentive.
........Easily distracted by extraneous stimuli or inner preoccupations.
........Almost impossible to get and hold attention.

10. *Self-Confidence:*
........Extremely self-confident, gives replies with assurance.
........Rather self-confident and assured.
........Somewhat confident, but evinces doubts.
........Definitely inclined to distrust ability.
........Painful uncertainty and vacillation.

11. *Motivation:*
........Intensely motivated, but not to such a degree as to reduce efficiency.
........Strongly motivated to succeed.
........Motivated sufficiently to permit fairly reliable evaluation.
........Rather unconcerned about performance.
........Motivation completely out of proportion to the situation: ....so strong as to render patient over-anxious; .... essentially nil.

12. *Effort:*
........Consistently expends maximum energy to attain success.
........Works diligently on most tasks.
........Strives for success, though possibly not at full pitch.
........Works perfunctorily.
........Lackadaisical, listless, indifferent.

13. *Persistence:*
........Dogged persistence; unable to give up even when failure is obvious.
........Persists even on tasks that are too difficult.
........Persists for a reasonable length of time.

........Admits defeat quickly when difficulty is encountered.

........Anticipates failure—refuses to try.

14. *Ability to Shift:*

........Extreme rigidity, perseveration of ideas.

........Shows difficulty shifting from one idea to another.

........Adequate amount of flexibility.

........Shifts too readily; finds it difficult to carry one task to completion.

........Thought content unstable and fleeting; cannot hold one topic in mind.

15. *Reaction to Praise and Encouragement:*

........Shows renewed or increased self-confidence, but still recognizes limits of ability.

........Stimulated to try harder, even when approaching maximum ability level.

........Stimulated to try a bit harder or persist slightly longer.

........Accepts with considerable reserve; any change in motivation temporary.

........Unmoved and unimpressed.

16. *Reaction to Failure:*

........Adversely affected, manifesting emotional reactions, offering rationalizations and excuses, etc.

........Somewhat upset by failure, tends to magnify it.

........Shows some disappointment, but accepts it realistically as something to be expected.

........Less disturbed than would be expected under the circumstances.

........Unconcerned; no observable reaction.

17. *Self-Criticism:*

........Markedly hypercritical.

........Shows a general tendency to be overcritical.

........Appraises performance accurately.

........Shows a tendency to overrate performance.

........Decidedly uncritical and naive.

18. *Miscellaneous Indicators:*

........Inappropriate laughter and private jokes.

........Irrelevant and bizarre verbalizations.

........Tangential thinking.

........Emotional outbursts.

........Hallucinations.

........Euphoria.

........Flat affect.

........Personal associations.

. ...Speech blocking.

19. *Representativeness of Results:*

........Obtained results definitely not indicative of patient's true capacity.

........Results on most tests contaminated and not optimum.
........Some results satisfactory, others contaminated.
........Some doubt as to complete representativeness of results.
........Obtained findings considered to be a reliable sample of patient's behavior potential.

sensory and motor proficiency, performance rate, orientation to examination, initial and final adjustment, interest, coöperation, amount of speech, expressive ability, attention, self-confidence, motivation, effort, persistence, ability to shift, reaction to praise and encouragement, reaction to failure, self-criticism, miscellaneous indicators, and the representativeness of results. This list of observatinal areas may be compared with those given in the report earlier in this chapter.

One danger of an observational guide such as that just given is that it may encourage some individuals to neglect specific behavioral instances in favor of hasty and careless checking of items. As the patient's particular ways of behaving are the focus of interest, it is imperative that these be noted and utilized to formulate the appropriate specifications. Even when a rating scale is used, there should be no hesitation about including these specific behavior descriptions. Forcing them into the mold set by the items is often undesirable and fallacious.

However, elimination of such sterile use of the guide is one goal of training. On the basis of the ratings made using the guide as a point of reference plus recorded behavioral data, the trainee can prepare a singularly meaningful narrative statement of his observations, as exemplified in the following report:

Appearance, General Behavior, and Attitudes: The patient is a large, obese, 72-year-old woman with very stooped posture whose stiff and hesitant gait suggests long periods of inactivity rather than any structural deformity. Attired in a very untidy dress, she began the session by emitting a stream of vituperative accusations against the hospital personnel for presumably stealing and defacing her clothes. Vision was somewhat limited and manual control hindered by her extreme nervousness, but hearing appeared hyperacute. Her hands, with nails bitten below the quick, were constantly in motion about her body—trembling, drumming on the table, fumbling with combs in her hair, etc. Several times she showed the nails apologetically to the examiner, commenting that it was a shame she "had to be so nervous and do such things." Enjoying to the fullest the attention being given her, she made special attempts to ingratiate herself with the examiner, frequently asking her name but then repeating it incorrectly.

Three sessions were required to complete the examination because of the patient's distractibility and the irresistible urge to talk about her own problems. The nature of the examination was completely misinterpreted, as she thought the results would determine whether or not she was to be transferred to another ward. Because of this fear, her apprehensiveness was intense and did not abate during the entire period of time spent with the examiner. Completely uninterested in the tests themselves, she remained preoccupied with her own thoughts and ideas. This lack of interest made her appear at times more negativistic than was perhaps the case, as it seemed that refusals were caused by inability rather than unwillingness to cooperate.

Throughout the sessions patient was extremely loquacious, exhibiting a veritable push of speech. At times she would suddenly become aware of this and apologize with such remarks as, "You will think I am crazy if I keep talking like that, but it's just that they shouldn't do my clothes that way." Though some blocking was noted, she was for the most part able to express her ideas with no difficulty. As she was equally interested in every extraneous noise occurring outside the office and in the personal thoughts clamoring for expression, it was virtually impossible to get and hold her attention. Definitely inclined to distrust her ability, she repeatedly pleaded for reassurance that she was "intelligent" and "not crazy." Despite this need for and susceptibility to any form of praise and encouragement, she actually showed little motivation to do well on any given test; rather she seemed determined to prove herself in the total situation without applying herself on the individual items. Accordingly she worked perfunctorily and often anticipating failure and refusing to attempt certain tasks. Externally imposed topics could not be kept in mind, but self-initiated ideas were perseverated indefinitely. Because of an uncritical and naive appraisal of her performance, she seldom recognized a failure and thereby evinced little disturbance when such occurred. Though test after test was contaminated by her irrelevant verbalizations, tangential thinking, emotional outbursts, and personal associations, the obtained results are believed to be a representative sample of her present functioning capacity, if not of her potential.

Often the diagnostic testing session stimulates the patient to talk about his experiences and thus to give anamnestic data of some significance.[4] Whenever materials are thus elicited it is customary to present them in the general observations. The psychological report given later on pages 149–151 contains two paragraps under the

_____
[4] In one sense such data are extraneous to the diagnostic testing, and the tendency for the patient to talk is discouraged in some clinics while encouraged in others. This matter of policy was discussed in Chapter 2. Even if clinic procedure calls for its discouragement it will still occasionally occur.

heading "General Observations." The first of these paragraphs is devoted to anamnestic data, and the second is concerned with observational material in the narrower sense.

ACCURACY IN OBSERVATIONS

The clinician directs his attention to an individual's acts, the way in which he behaves, and then infers from them the traits or qualities which he believes are being manifested. To do this accurately he should obviously be a good observer. He may, however, be in the position of observing behavior that cannot lead to relevant inferences or of making inaccurate judgments from relevant behavior.

Without in any way decrying the observational reports given in the preceding section of this chapter, the question can be raised as to the accuracy of these or other similar findings. It is apparent that from observation of what the patient *did* (actual movements, words said, and so on) inferences were drawn as to the meaning of the behavior. This too is typical of psychological observational reports (and those of other clinicians, for that matter).

Separation of observations themselves from inferences about these observations is one of the hardest tasks the clinician faces (2). We so largely "see" things the way we have learned to interpret them that often we may not even realize that we have gone beyond observation to an interpretation of the behavior. For example, a given patient during preliminary instructions for each test looks steadily at the examiner, never showing any awareness of his surroundings or irrelevant stimuli; this is often interpreted as attentiveness—and it might well be attentiveness. On the other hand, the patient might be that not uncommon sort of person who can look at another alertly and yet hardly listen at all (so characteristic of many college students). Or, another patient gazes around the room "instead of paying attention." Perhaps this does represent inattentiveness, but it might be nothing more than a manifestation of his ability to divide attention effectively. Still another patient may ask a series of questions concerning some diagnostic task when customarily the task does not elicit any questioning at all. It might at first appear that he was showing difficulty in concentration. Actually, the possible reasons for his questions may be legion; they may indicate failure to understand, poor hearing, stalling so as not to be compelled to do the task immediately, etc.

Other difficulties appear outstanding, among them is the absolutism of much observational reporting. There is a tendency to lose sight of the fact that the observations reported were obtained in the relatively narrow and, to some degree, artificial situation of an examination. The value of accurate observation and report is attenuated if the write-up assumes or implies that the behavior described holds in *all* situations and at *all* times. Such statements as "This patient is cooperative, submissive and ingratiating" are sometimes more false than true. It may be that although the patient did behave in precisely this way in the examining situation, at home he dominates the entire family (who live in terror of him), cannot get along with his neighbors, and has not a friend in the world. Not only do we sometimes forget that the face the patient shows us is not necessarily his habitual one; we also ignore the fact that it may well suit the purpose of the patient to appear different to us from the way he is on many other occasions. The patient described as "cooperative, submissive, and ingratiating" may have desired to appear so in an attempt to justify some previous conduct. Or he may hold the belief (erroneous or otherwise) that the clinician's aid could be enlisted for some nontherapeutic end, such as an increase in pension. Or he may simply fear the consequences of acting in any other manner. It is imperative, then, for the clinician to evaluate the behavioral evidence secured in the observational situation in the light of the entire case study. Only then can it be seen to be valid for more general aspects of behavior.

Enough has been said to demonstrate that accuracy of observation does not follow automatically from being placed in a situation where one is expected to observe. The surprising thing, in fact, is the accuracy with which many such observations and the ensuing inferences are made. In large measure this acumen must be developed from the self-corrective effect of exposure to patients and the improvements arising from the comments and findings of one's clinical colleagues. Certain steps can be taken both to hasten and to sharpen this accuracy. Appreciation of the significance of systematic as opposed to unsystematic observation, of what makes for reliability of observation, and of the function of ratings in observation all contribute to this end. Accordingly, they will be discussed next.

SYSTEMATIC AND UNSYSTEMATIC OBSERVATION

It is relevant to increasing accuracy in clinical practice to examine the distinction between incidental and systematic observation. Certain of the characteristics which differentiate systematized from unsystematized (incidental) observation as summarized by Goodenough and Anderson apply to clinical study. A major portion of their formulation is as follows (6, pp. 428–429):

	Systematized	Unsystematized
Nature of facts to be recorded	Determined and defined in advance.	Miscellaneous.
Time limits	Either kept uniform for all observations of the records made of time required for a specified unit of behavior.	Frequently unrecorded. No uniform system of time limits.
Place of situation	Always recorded. Sometimes partially controlled by selecting a constant time and place favorable to the free display of the behavior in question and taking all observations under these conditions.	Usually recorded, but in such general descriptive terms as to render classification very difficult.
Manner of making records (a) Terminology	Uniform, all terms defined in advance.	Loosely descriptive, varying from record to record.
(b) Arrangement	Uniform, planned to eliminate all unnecessary writing and to facilitate tabulating.	No formal arrangement. Diary plan most common.
Number of records taken	Number required to yield reliable conclusions determined statistically and observations continued until required amount of data has been secured.	Indefinite.

It would appear that clinical sessions in varying degrees demonstrate the characteristics of the systematized observation periods.

With deliberate attention to these characteristics the tendency toward systematization and consequently accuracy can be increased. Within certain limits clinicians determine in advance the nature of the material to which they will attend (as exemplified in the description both of the case study and of the specific tests); the time limits are roughly uniform, or, if not, recorded; the place is uniform and constant; the terms utilized for description, if not defined in advance, have at least considerable consistency from case to case; there is some degree of uniformity in reporting; the number of records taken, although not so defined as to permit demonstration of reliability in a statistical sense, is such that measurements are repeated many times. This last point, reliability, is of sufficient importance to receive further consideration.

RELIABILITY OF OBSERVATIONS

Reliability of observation (and of rating) involves two approaches (9), one of which is the consistency of observational acumen of a given observer. Does the clinician arrive at the same conclusions when faced with the same behavior constellations? Does he consistently modify his findings when faced with similar modifying factors in those constellations? The application of time sampling techniques to study of the behavior of children, involving observation of specific behavioral indices for repeated periods, is comparable to the situation found in the clinician's office. In both instances there is an attempt to see the same things on repeated occasions. To be sure, the clinician does not necessarily order them to a scale or record them for research purposes, but in essence he does substantially the same thing.[5]

The second approach to reliability is that of agreement by two or more equally competent observers. This conception of reliability is the more important of the two since the consistency of a single observer is included in it. In the clinical field there is considerable effort expended in checking for such consistency of opinion. Separate examinations by collaborating clinicians, the case conference, control analyses, and independent report by the psychologist are directed to this end.

___

[5] Research studies, unfortunately, are lacking so that quantitative support for this position cannot be offered.

THE RATING SCALE IN CLINICAL DIAGNOSIS[6]

After the prior step of delimitation of some common characteristics of human behavior, the essence of rating technique consists
in "placing" the individual at a position along the continuum upon
which this characteristic may be said to lie. Behavior components
are observed and then "fitted" to the rating scale. The individual
is ordered numerically, graphically, or verbally to some position
with respect to the particular characteristic (quality, aptitude,
ability, or trait) in question. The position indicates the clinician's
estimate of the degree or amount of these characteristics.

These characteristics are generally conceived of as present or
absent in varying degrees rather than existing in an all-or-none
fashion. Human characteristics are not dichotomous (social-asocial,
anxious-non-anxious, etc.) but rather possessed in varying intensities,
frequencies, and durations. Rare is the individual who is hostile all
the time and in all situations. Instead his hostility varies in strength,
occurs in some situations but not in others, and endures for some
specifiable length of time. Ratings either deal with these attributes
one by one or, more commonly, summarize them in one continuum.
At any rate, the items are presented in terms of scale steps.

Clinical observations, it was pointed out previously, involve the
making of judgments about the behavior of the patient. While
interviewing and testing patients the psychologist is making judgments about certain qualities, modes of expression, behavior samples, personality traits, or other characteristics that seem to be
detectable. The rating of behavior, then, is an indispensable function
of the clinician, although often no rating *scale* is used. If one stops
for a moment to consider the following typical statement drawn
from a psychological report, "The anxiety that he exhibited during
the examination was minimal, and interfered relatively little with
his performance . . . ," it will be obvious that two rating items
might have been framed somewhat as follows:

---

[6] Certain aspects of the information available about rating scales are considered to be outside the province of this volume. Accordingly, kinds of rating
scales, their construction, statistical procedures, the number of scale steps appropriate under given circumstances, the hazards of rating by untrained individuals, the effect of acquaintance on ratings, and other similar issues are
omitted. Consideration of these problems may be found in Garrett and Schneck
(5), Greene (7), Guilford (8), Symonds (9), and Vernon (10).

1. *Extent of anxiety:* None, Minimal, Moderate, Severe.
2. *Interference of anxiety with test performance:* None, Relatively little, Moderate, Extensive.

Thus rating the patient as "minimal" and "relatively little" would have made the observations fall within the conventional framework of rating scales. A rating scale is nothing more than a format for expressing judgments in which a given patient is assigned to a category, or his position on a scale indicated. The observation schedule given earlier in the chapter contains many rating scale items, although not all sections are cast in the form of continua along a single dimension.

Clinicians are in a particularly strategic position to use ratings. Many of the valid objections that have been raised to their use under ordinary circumstances are nullified by the training and experience of the clinician and the nature of the clinical scene. Ratings have been used apologetically under most conditions not because of intrinsic weakness in the method but because they are often used by individuals who are not experts and because frequently ratings are made even though there has been insufficient observation or inadequate information about the person rated. These objections do not apply to trained clinicians making their usual careful diagnostic studies. In the clinical fields the ultimate criterion applied in diagnosis and treatment is human judgment—the judgment of experts. Since the best judgments possible are wanted, it would appear only reasonable to utilize the systematic sharpening of one's clinical vision by the use of rating scales.

Informal judgment of the kind with which case studies are replete is illuminating and sometimes captures closely the essence of what the clinician is trying to say about the personality of the patient. It does not, however, lend itself to quantitative or exact analysis because of the many different ways in which the same characteristic is expressed and the semantic difficulties this may entail. Then, too literary expressiveness may by its aesthetic appeal hide the actual poverty of the evidence on which the judgments are based. Apt expression is an art the clinician does well to cultivate, but not at the expense of the validity of what he is saying. Rating scales, by their very mundaneness and their inclusion of those many facets of the task which are constant from case to case, help to systematize observation along the lines so aptly described by Goodenough and Anderson (6) in the quotation presented earlier in this chapter.

Clinical opinions are frequently based upon nothing more than a general impression. Too often they are rendered less precise by the tendency to give undue weight to the intrusion of aspects of behavior irrelevant to the matter at hand. Analytical judgment is necessary if valid conclusions are to be reached; i.e., a good evaluation requires that the pertinent characteristics or traits be seen in proper perspective with due weight given to the frequency, duration, and intensity of their component parts. The clinician is practically forced to consider one characteristic at a time when he uses rating scales, and these, if properly constructed, will include the various relevant aspects of the patient's personality.

In spite of such advantages as have been sketched, rating scales are relatively little used in clinical practice. Clinical psychologists rather infrequently use rating scales as such. Presumably they fear that a presentation of their observations in the scale form would fail to capture the nuances of the behavior and thus render static and sterile findings which would be fluid and meaningful if incorporated into the case study in an individual narrative fashion.

Confronted with a rating scale many clinicians would complain that they would feel constrained in its use because it implies that all the units (e.g., personality traits) are equally important in the make-up of the individual. In one patient, they would say, passivity trends are extremely significant and their fluctuation would be indicative of the psychotherapeutic change; in another patient, however, who theoretically has equally strong, numerous, and long-lasting passivity trends, they would merit barely any consideration and would not change with therapy. The concept of saliency in the form given here, which was introduced so far as the writer is aware by Champney (4), can be used to circumvent this difficulty. In a study of child behavior by rating scales he secured ratings in the usual fashion and, in addition, requested the raters to evaluate the potency or significance of the trait in the child's personality. Is it important or unimportant? Is it highly characteristic, or is it negligible in understanding the individual? This concept may be utilized as the basic substratum by the doubting clinician. Thus he may rate characteristics without nullifying the fluidity of judgments as to their importance in a given individual.

SOURCES OF ERROR IN RATING JUDGMENTS

Regardless of whether he uses, abuses or avoids rating scales, any clinician can profit from the experience of those who do use them in regard to sources of error with this technique. The difficulties which face the individual casting his observations in rating scale form also face the clinician who presents his data as a free-running narrative. (Again it can be emphasized that the failure to utilize a rating scale format probably accentuates these errors.) An understanding of the factors which make for unreliable and invalid ratings may help to reduce their effect. The more outstanding of these hazards, therefore, are briefly sketched.

HALO EFFECT. One of the earliest and most faithfully reported findings made by investigators of rating technique was that ratings of one person on different traits showed high intercorrelations even when there was no demonstrable connection between the traits in question. For example, Vernon (10) found a correlation of +.71 between sociability and quickness of movement. Since there is neither logical nor psychological reason for such a high degree of relationship between these obviously disparate facets of behavior, it is plausible to assume that some factor other than a true degree of relationship is affecting the results. In this and many other studies (in which raters and subjects were previously acquainted) there was a definite tendency for a person to be rated characteristically high (favorably), characteristically low (unfavorably), or in between (neutrally). This may be attributed to the favorable, unfavorable, or neutral overall impression which generalized to evaluation of specific traits. That is to say, given characteristics are not judged on the basis of data pertinent to specific behavioral areas but are colored by the general impression. To this Thorndike gave the name "halo effect."

This tendency to create judgments in the image of a general impression should be combated; however, it should also be recognized —though frequently it is not—that there is at least some degree of validity to a positive relationship between specific traits and the general impression of the person. When an invalid halo is eliminated, there still remains a correlation between an over-all evaluation of the individual and at least some specific trait ratings. There appears to be, as Bingham (3) and others show, a valid "halo effect" inherent in the very make-up of the personality.

STEREOTYPING. General impressions affect judgments in ways other than the favorable-unfavorable continuum which gives rise to the halo effect. The general attitude toward a given patient might involve judging him to be "neurotic," "passive," "rigid," or some other of the clichés of psychiatric-psychological judgments. If, for instance, patient A is regarded by the clinician as "an anal-erotic character," A might then have attributed to him all the other traits which the clinician associates with this particular kind of person, and traits which do not fit this preconceived notion might go unnoticed. Paradoxically, the more experienced the clinician the more he needs to guard against generalizations that fit with his previous experience or theoretical bias. If characteristics A, B, and C have in his experience tended to be associated with characteristics X, Y, and Z he is readily tempted to conclude that individuals who possess the former will also demonstrate the latter. Although much and varied experience with patients makes for clinical acumen it can also make for hardening of the arteries of thought, i.e., the ascendance of stereotypes. Clinical psychology and its related disciplines are not immune to the tendency to form stereotypes, which are so aptly described by Allport as an example of the "paralyzing effect of simplification upon the process of judgment." (1, p. 521.)

What may be done to avoid these sources of error in clinical judgment? In general terms and in short compass the answer cannot but be inadequate. At any rate, awareness of these sources of error is the first step in their minimization. Precise definition of the characteristics one is appraising is of methodological help. Realization of at least rough boundaries between one's observations and one's inferences from them is another. Clarity and system of observation, a determination to note exceptions to the general impression, and formulation and research on the problems all contribute to their elimination. In short, in so far as possible the scientific training to which the clinical psychologist is heir should be brought to bear here with as much zest and thoroughness as it is applied to other clinical problems.

BIBLIOGRAPHY

1. Allport, G. W., *Personality: a psychological interpretation*, Henry Holt and Company, 1937.
2. Baumgarten, F., Approach in taking tests: a technique for studying the examinees' behavior, *Occupations*, 1935, 14:115–122.
3. Bingham, W. V., Halo, invalid and valid, *J. appl. Psychol.*, 1939, 23:221–228.
4. Champney, H., The measurement of parent behavior, *Child Developm.*, 1941, 12: 131–166.
5. Garrett, H. E., and Schneck, M. R., *Psychological tests, methods and results*, Harper & Brothers, 1933.
6. Goodenough, F. L., and Anderson, J. E., *Experimental child study*, Appleton-Century-Crofts, Inc., 1931.
7. Greene, E. B., *Measurements of human behavior*, The Odyssey Press, 1941.
8. Guilford, J. P., *Psychometric methods*, McGraw-Hill Book Company, 1936.
9. Symonds, P. M., *Diagnosing personality and conduct,* Appleton-Century-Crofts, Inc., 1931.
10. Vernon, P. E., *The assessment of psychological qualities by verbal methods: a survey of attitude tests, rating scales and personality questionnaires*, His Majesty's Stationery Office, 1938.

Supplementary articles in Watson, R. I. (ed.), *Readings in the clinical method in psychology*, Harper & Brothers, 1949:

11. Watson, R. I., Diagnosis as an aspect of the clinical method: a review. Pp. 405–427.
12. Weiss Frankl, A., Diagnostic methods in child guidance and psychological counseling. Pp. 366–384. (Also in *Ment. Hyg., N.Y.*, 1937, 21:579–598.)
13. Weiss Frankl, A., Play interviews with nursery school children. Pp. 385–394. (Also in *Amer. J. Orthopsychiat.*, 1941, 11:33–39.)

CHAPTER 5

The Diagnostic Interview[1]

In the clinical setting an interview is a face-to-face conversation between clinician and patient, both of whom are attempting to arrive at some resolutions of the latter's difficulties. It is thus a goal-directed conversation—diagnosis and treatment of the patient's psychological difficulties. Not all facets of such interviews will be explored in this presentation. Attention here will be confined to the diagnostic interview, leaving for later discussion the therapeutic interview. The primary aim of this, as well as other diagnostic techniques, is to help the clinician understand the patient. It is a technique used in conjunction with others, possessing points in common with these other approaches as well as features unique unto itself.

The interview, including its standardized variant, the test, is the probing tool of the diagnostic study. It is the only technique available for obtaining certain data. Its distinctive contribution varies from case to case, but probably most often it takes the form of allowing the development of a total picture of the patient. Other aspects of the diagnostic procedure such as observation and rating, though very active processes, do not affect the patient directly. They are essentially receptive processes, their effector component being mediated through the interview. A symptom, a test score, or an inference

[1] The diagnostic interview merges with that which is primarily therapeutic in nature. The presentation of the interview in connection with psychotherapy is pitched at a somewhat higher level of clinical sophistication than is the present chapter. The later chapters are a necessary supplement to the present account.

from observation might be investigated and clarified during the interview and take on new meaning in relation to the personality.

In the task of understanding the patient, the interview provides a method of securing information about the patient's feelings, opinions, attitudes, and personal experiences. This information should consist not of mere "facts" about the patient in the conventional sense; it should also include instances of behavior—inflections, gestures, and facial expressions—which help to portray the attitudes, values, and beliefs of the patient.

During the interview, the clinician is a catalytic agent. The "fact," the "attitude," the "feeling," is something expressed verbally or implied behaviorally by the patient and perceived by the clinician. The dynamic process of the interview is such that it does not stop at this level, for as the information is received there is a process of evaluation embracing not only what has just been expressed but also previously elicited material. In this evaluative transformation the clinician draws upon his background of experience. The interpretation which emerges affects the clinician's subsequent interview behavior, either immediate or remote.

In this chapter a series of comments will be made concerning the conducting of interviews. Even when related as closely as possible to a specific setting, the suggestions will not be applicable to each similar instance. In fact, the experienced clinician may find himself questioning or qualifying any or all the recommendations offered—and rightly so. They are stated positively, somewhat dogmatically, leaving the situations requiring modification to the test of experience. The interview is a flexible technique for which no theorems may be formulated.

THE NATURE OF DIAGNOSTIC INTERVIEWS

The kinds of diagnostic interviews may be clarified if first they are related to other forms of interviews. Berdie (1) makes a distinction between two general forms. His first category is that of interviews in which the aim is to explore situations or environmental factors relatively independent of the personalities of the participants, e.g., sales interviews or public opinion studies. The second category is characterized by its emphasis on the personality of one or both of the participants. These "ego-centric" interviews include the diagnostic interview.

Emphasis on personality is not enough to delimit the diagnostic interview, since many research studies investigating personality use the interview technique and yet cannot be called "diagnostic." Illustrative would be the study of Landis and his associates on psychosexual development. Using as their principal tool a form of interview, they asked the subjects to describe incidents from their early lives. This study, in many ways a model of its kind, recognized more clearly than most that not all personality investigations using the interview approach result in diagnostic interviewing. The distinction was stated as follows:

Some of the questions used in our interview may seem extremely direct and brusque to the clinician. This directness was justified by the nature of the study. There is an important distinction between our investigation and the approaches used by the psychoanalyst, psychiatrist, or general practitioner. We were not directed by an interest in the therapeutic value of discussing current personality problems or from eliciting early memories. The clinician must necessarily proceed in accordance with the psychological needs of the patient. He is more interested in the way an individual handles early memories in relation to present psychological problems than in the nature of the material itself. (3, pp. 12–13.)

Paradoxically, then, such interviews are not diagnostic in a clinical sense because they are not therapeutically oriented. The information is secured as expeditiously and as directly as possible. The person's method of handling the matter is disregarded and the effect of the disclosures upon an individual's own thinking and adjustment is of little or no concern in such research.

The diagnostic interview is not free from other therapeutic implications. If motivating the patient is a goal of therapy it is also a goal of diagnosis if the patient is to reveal appropriate material. The aims of diagnosis do not conflict with those of therapy; rather they merge and become one. Although discussion of therapeutic interviewing would be out of place at this point, it must never be lost sight of that all diagnostic interviews—indeed, all diagnostic procedures—have therapeutic connotations.

FLEXIBILITY IN INTERVIEWS

Diagnostic interviews range in flexibility from the free associative sessions of the psychoanalyst to the rigidly applied psychometric test. Neither of these extremes should be a matter of concern here, since the first is more appropriately dealt with, even in its diagnostic aspects, as an approach to psychotherapy and the second is reserved for later discussion. Instead the concern will be with another variety, ranging from a more or less standardized or directed interview to one which is more or less free or undirected. The nature of the latter is described by Richards as follows:

The clinician finds that many patients, with very little suggestion or stimulus, will elaborate a beautifully organized and fairly complete case history within a short time. It is obvious that it would be not only inefficient but offensive to such a patient to interrupt and restrain him. In such cases, however, it is well to consider that the patient with such a logical account of his own adjustment may well be biased and is using his logic to avoid unpleasant or unacceptable interpretations. Since, as we shall see later, much therapeutic benefit arises from the patient's thinking his own way through his problems, it is well to allow him in most cases a chance at least to tell his story. For many reasons the patient's interpretation of his problem is always an important area of clinical evidence and should always be sought. This relatively free procedure of allowing the patient to interview himself, so to speak, sometimes leads nowhere, as in the case of the patient whose thoughts are disconnected or illogical or irrelevant. In such cases, the clinician can himself gradually assume direction, having already gained a valuable insight into his patient. (5, pp. 34–35.)

The standardized or directed interview, on the other hand, stresses a predetermined list of questions and relatively disregards the directions in which the patient would lead the discussion. Material not related to the question is considered by the clinician as irrelevant or at least extraneous.

Although probably few diagnostic interviews fit these prototypes, it is profitable to make the somewhat artificial distinction in order to state more clearly the advantages and disadvantages of the two contrasting extremes.

Turning to the relative advantages of the standardized interview it may be said that: (1) It often requires relatively less psychological acumen and experience—the person collecting the information must be able merely to gain coöperation and be reasonably persistent. (2) It permits more facile quantification of the data collected. (3) It insures that all the questions considered relevant to the issue at hand are answered in some fashion. (4) It is economical in terms of the time consumed. (5) It facilitates comparison of one individual with another.

There are, however, very weighty disadvantages. A rigid list of questions necessitates a rigid procedure, militating against whole-hearted, friendly coöperation. The interview assumes the character of an oral questionnaire and consequently takes on the defects of such devices.

The free interview, on the other hand, permits expression of the desired information and at the same time allows the conversation to find its own paths with a minimum of direction. Obviously, its great advantage is the naturalness and spontaneity of the procedure. The necessary information is obtained casually and incidentally without, perhaps, awareness by the patient of the nature or importance of the data being elicited. Clues to unsuspected trends and to his unique personal idiom are more likely to appear, thus opening the way to greater understanding of the person. The conduct of such an inter-view—by no means easy—requires considerable training; otherwise it can be extremely wasteful of time or lose the clinician in a maze of irrelevancies.

As said before, the contrast between these two approaches to the interview has been exaggerated. No diagnostic interview is either entirely standardized or entirely free. The form used varies in degree, depending upon circumstances, the training, experience, and person-ality of the clinician, and the purpose of the interview. The more standardized interview seems to be indicated when time is short, when the interviewer is relatively inexperienced, when future quan-tification of the data is anticipated, when the problem is relatively simple, and when the interviewer finds it best suited to his person-ality. The less standardized interview is useful under contrary cir-cumstances. Certainly most clinical situations are such that the freer sort of approach is more desirable. The general outcome is that some compromise between standardization and flexibility is evolved which attempts to preserve the advantages of both and to minimize their disadvantages.

A very common practice is to use a freer approach at certain tem-poral points and a more standardized approach at others. The pa-tient is first encouraged to be spontaneous, to tell his own story and to describe his difficulties. When he has temporarily reached his limits there is recourse to more active probing. This is likely to occur before rapport is well established and before he has had any real experience in the art of self-analysis. With increasing rapport and practice in self-understanding, the character of the interview may become more and more spontaneous.

ROLES IN DIAGNOSTIC INTERVIEWING

Another distinction to be made in regard to kinds of diagnostic interviewing concerns the particular role of the clinician. Whether he is to serve as intake interviewer, as diagnostic tester, or as therapist determines the nature of the diagnostic interviewing he may conduct. Although guided by the common aim of diagnostic understanding, each function creates by virtue of its relatively unique goal differing emphases and procedures.

The intake interviewer, generally but not always a social worker, is usually concerned with clarification of the patient's presenting complaints, the steps he has taken previously to resolve his difficulties, and his expectancies in regard to what may be done for him. This does not mean that the interviewer is oblivious to diagnostic information on other matters, but his role is structured by the necessity of conveying to the patient some understanding of the services available in the particular clinical setting in which the patient finds himself. Since generally he will not be responsible for the later therapeutic sessions he is not so concerned either with allowing the patient free rein or with building up strong rapport with him.

The interview of the test diagnostician, generally a psychologist, is also to a large degree structured by his role. If he is not to have later therapeutic responsibility, he may as a matter of clinic policy attempt to minimize or eliminate interviewing in the narrower sense almost entirely. However, too much limitation on interviewing is generally considered unwise. What might be commonly regarded as an appropriate procedure is described by Kutash:

A psychological interview forms part of the psychological examination and presupposes a knowledge of the case history. It has for its main purposes the elucidation and clarification of the test findings, and the exploration of areas indicated by those findings which had not been covered adequately in the previous case record or the social worker's reports. For example, if the veteran gives an unusually high number of certain sexual responses on the Rorschach, and the previous case record contains no references to sexual problems, it might be fruitful to explore this area by interview to clarify the possible meaning of the pre-occupations with sexual material shown by the patient. (2, p. 325.)

Such a procedure is not obligatory, however. Instead of exploring through interview of the new material revealed in the examination one might call the attention of the referring clinician to the material which needs clarification. For example, the sexual problem mentioned by Kutash might have been explored later by the clinician bearing therapeutic responsibility, merely being reported on by the test diagnostician without further probing on his part.

The role of the diagnostician later to bear the major therapeutic responsibility is the broadest of all. This would be the case whether his professional background is that of psychiatrist, social worker, or psychologist. He is likely to have before him the possibility of a greater number of interviews and will therefore probably be least hampered by his role on any given occasion. Since it is not necessary for him to cover a certain amount of ground in a single session, his interviews may be less structured. Perhaps he is limited only by his theoretical propensities and the necessity of building and maintaining rapport with the patient.

PREPARING FOR AND SUPPLEMENTING THE DIAGNOSTIC INTERVIEW

A diagnostic interview is almost always planned before the appearance of the patient. It may be argued that planning is impracticable because of the inability to predict the direction the interview will take. This contention arises from an erroneous conception of preparing for an interview. Preparation implies that the strategy, not the tactics, may be planned in advance. The tactics (that which is actually said and done) may have unsuspected and unplanned ramifications and therefore must be varied to meet different contingencies.

Questions framed during the information-seeking phase of the interview reflect the general strategy of the clinician. These initiating questions are designed to open up some phase of the patient's personal experience, background, accomplishments, attitudes, or traits. Follow-up questions, which are a matter of tactics, are framed on the basis of answers received to the initiating questions and are used to round out the information given to a point where the interviewer is satisfied. Questions designed to clarify a certain statement, e.g., what the patient meant when he said he quit school because he didn't like it, help to complete the picture and involve tactical maneuvers rather than strategical planning.

The interviewing process may be supplemented by all aspects of the case study. Diagnostic test scores, referral notes, and reports of medical consultations are often indispensable adjuncts to the interview and should be consulted and assimilated as a part of the preparatory process. To make such preparation for the interview as that discussed above implies that appointments of definite duration are made. However, every experienced clinician knows that the secret of good preparation is to have enough skillful flexibility to dispense with careful plans when the occasion demands.

In one sense, the notes taken by the clinician provide a means of supplementing the interview. However, the question of recording any material is a methodological issue on which opinion is divided. To take notes in the presence of the patient is to run the danger of impressing him with the formal character of the interview, thus making him more stilted and self-conscious than he otherwise might be. On the other hand, if notes are not taken, there is a chance that valuable material will be forgotten. Often a compromise solution is indicated. After a casual mention of the necessity and advisability of taking notes, perhaps with a side remark regarding their inviolability, the clinician proceeds unobtrusively to take notes during the session except on matters that may be embarrassing to the patient. Thus essentially it becomes a matter of knowing when to take notes and when to forgo the practice.

ATTITUDES OF THE CLINICIAN IN THE INTERVIEW

It has become almost a truism of clinical practice to say that the clinician's attitude during the interview is one of acceptance of the patient. "Neither to condemn nor to condone, but to understand" might be considered a motto of the clinician. Understanding is actually furthered by this attitude of acceptance, as it implies a certain psychological empathy with the feelings expressed by the patient.

In his present capacity the clinician is neither a judge, a minister, nor a parent; it is not his function to pass judgment, to preach, or to admonish. If the problem the patient is living contains value elements, it is more likely than not that he already knows what he "ought" to do and anything the clinician might add along these lines would be redundant. Even more important, however, are the very evident feelings of rejection that the patient would experience if condemned. Admonishing—no matter how praiseworthy the motives—would be interpreted as rejection. This is precisely what the accepting attitude minimizes, if it does not forestall. A successful clinician is one who succeeds in creating an atmosphere in which there is freedom of expression without fear of judgment or condemnation.

The attitude is by no means easy to maintain, since clinicians are only human. They have learned to curb their own unacceptable behavior within certain limits and in this process have learned to condone similar behavior on the part of others. Violations by others of this pattern of virtues and vices will touch off emotionally toned responses. The situation is further aggravated by the tendencies of the patient himself. Often he will attempt to inveigle the clinician into an argument in order to be able to justify his own hostile trends; or he may be aggressive or disagreeable as a means of testing the clinician and possibly evaluating him. An accepting attitude is necessary if one is to withstand such a bombardment.

This attitude of acceptance may, however, be caricatured if it be forgotten that not to condemn is but one side of a shield, the obverse of which is not to condone. A passive refusal to pass judgment may be interpreted by the patient either as tacit approval, in which case his antisocial behavior may increase, or as a reason for rejecting the clinician as a person unworthy of trust and confidence. Thus if the clinician ignores a child's emotional outbursts, including perhaps violent attacks upon a younger sibling, he will probably find the child either increasing these attacks or protesting about having to see the "bad" clinician at all.

Some clinicians appear to confuse withholding judgment with being impersonal. Mere questioning in a calm dispassionate manner without any indication of real interest defeats the purpose of the interview—the understanding of the patient and his difficulties. A patient does not talk willingly to a clinician who fails to indicate in some fashion interest in him. Warmth arising from a genuine interest in the patient is essential.

As yet nothing has been said about the clinician's personal insecurities and their influence upon the course of the interview. Nothing is more prominent in the work of young clinicians than the anxiety, sometimes bordering on panic, with which they first approach a patient to discuss his psychological problems. Untutored in being comfortable in a clinician-patient relationship, they find a refuge in the concise statements of the case outline that they are to follow. Hence they use this outline mechanically and, in their intentness upon securing answers to their questions, quite forget that the feelings of the patient are being ignored. Consequently the therapeutic relationship is upset before it has an opportunity to develop. Some anxiety on first entering a psychodiagnostic and psychotherapeutic situation is perhaps inevitable; however, its persistence suggests an inability to handle properly the psychological interview.

ATTITUDES OF THE PATIENT IN THE INTERVIEW

When a patient first faces the clinician, the stage is set for ambivalent feelings and attitudes. His presence, regardless of reason, puts him temporarily in a dependent position, a status almost always resented and feared. His sense of individuality is threatened because he does not know what will be done to him; he is doubtful of his reception and not at all certain that he will be understood. On the other hand, he is no doubt curious about what is to happen, even hopeful that something may be done. Thus there is a spark of receptivity—a desire to find a solution. The clinician must be alert to capitalize on both the positive and the negative swings of feeling lest they cancel each other and cause the patient to retreat from the situation.

Sometimes the patient who most urgently needs the clinician's service is unable to use it once it is sought. He may be unable to talk about his problems in general or simply not want to talk about certain aspects of his problems and conflicts, especially those that touch him most deeply (and therefore are etiologically important). Through action of his various mechanisms of adjustment, he unconsciously seeks to hide the very feelings and experiences most essential to an understanding of his problems. He cannot reveal his basic conflicts merely by being asked to do so; therefore a frontal attack using cross-examination methods is doomed to failure. It is because of this inability to speak readily on fundamental problems that elaboration upon trivial or even irrelevant items is apt to occur during the course of diagnostic interviews. The patient thus avoids the real issues and thereby allays his anxieties.

Inability to speak of one's difficulties or the avoidance of some aspects of these difficulties may conveniently be referred to as resistance. It is also expressed in other ways—hostility, belligerence, forgetfulness of or lateness to appointments, and the like—all of which have in common an impedance, a slowing of the diagnostic-therapeutic process.

Another attitude which the clinician will occasionally face in the patient is that of quasi sophistication. The patient may strive desperately to demonstrate that he knows what is wrong, and may even postulate a solution. In this connection it is well to point out that no matter how psychiatrically and psychologically sophisticated the patient may be, he still does not know the solution to his problem— his very presence proves this. Occasionally the clinician is so impressed with the depth of the patient's insight, the astuteness of his conclusions, or the beautifully formulated account of his difficulties and their origin that he may be dazzled into believing the contrary. Nevertheless, if what he says could solve the problem it would already have done so.

Out of the feelings aroused by the act of seeking help from the clinician, the patient sometimes develops an overdependence to a greater or lesser degree. This the clinician neither avoids (which would be interpreted as rejection) nor stimulates (which could only serve his own, not the patient's, needs). Instead, as in the case of resistance, the feelings are utilized for diagnostic and therapeutic ends by being brought to the attention of the patient.   ·

Whatever the attitudes evinced by the patient, his behavior must be considered the expression of his personality. His actions—affectionate, docile, dependent, admiring, hostile, critical, domineering, or antagonistic—are diagnostic materials to be noted, studied, and interpreted in the same way as his responses to the Rorschach blots.

RAPPORT AND THE INITIAL CONTACT

It follows from the preceding discussion that it is the atypical patient who does not find the initial session with the clinician an ordeal. His feelings are apt to be near the surface ready to operate. More often than not he is ill at ease, self-conscious, and defensive as he speculates about what is going to happen. Even if there by his own choice, he feels himself in a position of inferiority before the "expert." This awkwardness may be intensified if he has been persuaded or coerced into coming. He is faimiliar neither with the situation in which he finds himself nor with the personality of the clinician. Some sort of tentative adjustment to both must be made, and it is clearly the responsibility of the clinician to carry the burden of the initial contact. The first goal of the clinician may be expressed as the establishment of rapport with the patient.

Rapport exists when the patient's tendency to be on the defensive is overcome; when his confidence, trust, good will, and friendship are gained; when his resistance to discussing his problems is dissipated or minimized; and when he is motivated to discuss his problems. Without rapport both diagnostic and therapeutic effort will be relatively unsuccessful, for neither truthful nor complete data can be obtained from the patient who does not have confidence and trust in the clinician.

It is primarily the responsibility of the clinician to establish and maintain this warm, positive, coöperative relationship. The earlier discussion of the attitude of the clinician is directly pertinent since the characteristics discussed are precisely those that make for adequate rapport—acceptance, friendliness, interest, and personal understanding through which he inspires the patient. Since people differ, the relationship differs, and there are no rules which fit all situations. All procedures of the interview should contribute to rapport, but at the onset certain techniques of rather wide applicability may be useful in its creation.

As much as circumstances will permit, an atmosphere of leisure and absorption in the problem of the particular patient should be mustered. A clear desk, privacy, and arrangements for telephone calls to be diverted are aspects of the physical situation that contribute to rapport. The interviewer must make a genuine attempt to put the patient at ease and must avoid giving the impression that he is such a busy man that he must hurry on to the next "case." The ordinary rules of good manners prevail—a cordial greeting by name, informal conversation, and a few pleasantries are not so time-consuming as to be prohibitive. Rather than direct questions, remarks of a neutral character are appropriate. These should make no particular demands upon the conversational capacity of the patient.

If the conversation does not provide the necessary transposition into the nature of the problem, an appropriate starting point is the patient's presenting complaint. Only when the patient appears to have exhausted his first statement are more specific questions introduced. In this period the interview is guided by the clinician to unembarrassing aspects of the patient's life relevant to the problem as stated by him. Special interests, hobbies, matters of common knowledge, or other topics about which the patient may speak with knowledge and assurance are particularly suitable for this period, in which the patient seems to be at a loss as to how to proceed. No question should be asked which the clinician suspects the patient is not ready to answer. By observing him for clues of rapport in comments, inflections, gestures, and general attitude, the clinician gains help in determining the time when the patient is psychologically receptive to deeper and more pertinent discussion.

Though these suggestions may be helpful, they suffer from superficiality and obvious limitations as to the breadth of their applicability. Genuine feeling with and for the patient, for example, is more conducive to rapport than all such external trappings. It takes no great acumen to see that some patients would hardly take kindly to these procedures despite their general usefulness. A woman obsessed with thoughts of suicide is in no mood to discuss the vagaries of the weather, and an extremely verbal patient may show manifest impatience, if not agitation, to get on with a description of some problem. In such instances all rules may go by the boards, and what the patient thrusts upon the clinician comes first. Silence punctuated only by expressions of understanding may be all that is necessary from the clinician until the flood subsides and greater calmness ensues.

Rapport is a relationship which must be maintained; its establishment does not guarantee its continuance. Sensitive spots should not be trampled roughshod, and a circuitous approach to the emotional area may be utilized in response to such cues as speech blocking, blushing, or nervousness. Humor, sincere praise, generous approval of accomplishment, and a stressing of the favorable aspects of the person are not out of place in maintaining rapport. Even though rapport is most often thought of as positive or friendly, it may continue to exist even in conjunction with expressions of hostility, resentment, and anger by the patient. Such behavior need not be disturbing to the interviewer if an undercurrent of understanding remains, pragmatically demonstrated by the productivity of the interview.

HAZARDS IN THE INTERVIEW PROCESS

Certain procedural hazards appear in the course of diagnostic interviewing that are of sufficient general importance to be described. These processes if not understood and averted are traps for the unwary. In large measure they appear in the interview because they are common phenomena in ordinary conversation, and they ensnare the interviewer because the clinically appropriate response is the antithesis of that which happens in conversation. In everyday conversation we disregard a fair amount of what is said as irrelevant to our interests; dismiss shifts of the topic of conversation as unimportant; find periods of silence a challenge to say something; override our conversational partner blithely by talking before he is finished; use vaguely defined terms and suggest by our very method of statements the replies we would like to hear. Only an obtuse person would plead not guilty to these practices at one time or another. The diagnostician, then, must guard against these all too human tendencies because of their ability to reduce the diagnostic value of the interview. Accordingly, these conversational errors of omission and commission will be examined one by one.

Although allowing the patient to tell his story in his own way has been urged as an appropriate procedure, it sometimes stimulates what some individuals mistakenly interpret as irrelevant talk. "He goes on talking but says nothing," complain some novices in interviewing. As Whitehorn says: "If one is studying the personality of a patient, there is no such thing as 'irrelevant talk.' The irrelevance is merely a condition of the interviewer's mind—he doesn't know what to make of it. The observer may listen, out of politeness, or because he has been told there is psychotherapeutic value in letting the patient talk, but he may not know what to listen for; in that case, the psychotherapeutic value may not be very great, for the patient may sense that no progress is being made." (6, p. 200.)

What, then, is the solution? In a further quotation Whitehorn states:

Without getting into deeper meanings at this stage, I may say that the patient's "irrelevant talk" usually means that he feels the need of self justification, for some reason or other. To discover the "some reason or other" may be sometimes of much greater medical importance than anything else the physician can do. He should not, therefore, merely wait for the talk to subside or impatiently brush it aside. . . . The interviewer does well, in general, to keep his mouth shut and his mind alert to all evidences from which he can infer the nature of the implied accusation or guilt against which the "irrelevant talk" or behavior constitutes a defense. He has the opportunity to learn in this way what "it is all about," by a process somewhat analogous to the surveyor's triangulation, thus: He may take two statements of the patient and imaginatively construct a statement to which they could be the logical replies. If a considerable number of these construction lines converge toward the same point, the interviewer thus acquires a tentative idea as to what the talk is all "about." He may even throw out tentative questions or remarks to check his inferences. It is not recommended to seize the patient, so to speak, and make him face this central issue. In whatever the interviewer says he should keep to the same tangential lines which the patient has already laid down and use so far as possible words which the patient has used. (6, p. 201.)

The significance of shifts in the topic of conversation initiated by the patient is often difficult to understand. Some changes in conversational direction are fairly obvious and quickly understood. Other shifts—those dismissed as meaningless in casual conversation —are generally of much greater significance. These shifts that occur without immediately obvious connection are likely to be the very ones most important for diagnostic understanding: the connection is there and must be sought in order that it may be understood and, if necessary, followed up. A patient may be telling of his inability to get along with his wife and then switch to a discussion of his sister's separation from her husband, demonstrating that in his own mind his problem is connected with his sister's similar difficulties. By the process of triangulation previously described the question arises as to whether these in turn are related to something in the parental home of both the patient and his sister. Shifts also may indicate that the patient feels he is telling too much about the topic he abandons and that it would be too painful or too personal to proceed further.

The clinician, especially the less experienced one, is apt to find periods of silence uncomfortable if not unendurable. The temptation is to rush in and fill this seemingly endless void with some remark, almost any remark. This is in most instances a definite mistake, as pauses do not represent a real absence of activity. They may mean periods in which the patient is collecting his thoughts, nerv-

ing himself to bring up a previously avoided point, digesting some
new point of view, or engaging in other clinically useful activity.

A closely related mistake is to override the patient—to break into
a sentence or to supply what is apparently the missing word for
which he is fumbling. This putting of words into his mouth may
well be accepted by the patient for a variety of reasons other than
the appositeness of the remark or word. "Who am I to argue?" he
might decide, or else find in the interjected remark a more plausible
or convenient way to express the matter. Questions requiring for an
answer simple affirmation or negation should be avoided. Not only
do they shift the burden of the discussion to the interviewer, but
also their answers are more readily misunderstood since they are
interpreted only in the interviewer's frame of reference. The clinician may never be aware that the patient meant something quite
different by his monosyllabic reply from the interpretation he put
upon it.

Word meanings often impede the free conversational interchange
of the interview. There may be mutual misunderstandings arising
from the use of words by one which the other does not understand,
or from failure to grasp the intended implication of a shade or nuance of meaning. In order to circumvent this difficulty definitions of
the terms the patient uses should often be sought. To "love," to
"hate," to be "dumb," "to be sick," to be "afraid of everything" are
not academic matters, and the definitions sought are not academic
ones. These words are concerned with emotional matters and cannot be accepted at their face value but instead must be explored for
the *feelings* associated with them.

Misdirected and unintentional suggestion may jeopardize the success of diagnostic interviewing. The clinician should not directly
suggest responses, but by his inflection, his choice of words, and
other signs he may unwittingly lead the patient to a reply which he
would like to hear, or a reply which is the socially acceptable response, or one which the very form of the question compels as an
answer. Some patients are prone to be obliging, and if the clinician
conveys the impression that he wants a certain answer he may get
it regardless of its accuracy. To the question "Your home life was
happy, wasn't it?" the odds are strongly in favor of getting an affirmative reply.

When it is necessary to interject a question or comment owing to

the obscurity of the material, the lack of relevant detail, the fact that
the patient has run down, or the necessity for a tactful reminder that
the conversation has wandered too far afield, this question or statement may often be in an unequivocal, nonsuggestive, nonleading
form. This is not to imply that only very general questions stated
neutrally are productive, for the use of a variety of simultaneously
presented alternatives is equally useful. As Macfarlane puts it:

. . . Fruitful results are more apt to be obtained if he is presented
with an array of alternative answers, which inform him indirectly that
the interviewer realizes people behave differently and that the interviewer is not passing moral judgment on any particular way that people
behave. Let us take a specific example. If one wishes to obtain from
a ten-year-old boy his description and evaluation of his habits of expressing anger, an approach such as the following has been found to
bring a rich array of material: "All of us get 'mad,' at times, but 'kids'
differ in the way they show it. Grown-ups do too, for that matter. Some
people fly off the handle at the least thing, other people hold it in for
a long time and brood, others hold it and then explode all over the
place, others flare up in a hurry and get over it just as quickly, some
people sit tight lipped and don't say a word. What about you? Do you
hold it in or flare up easily or what? Or do you hold in around some
people, and flare up at others?" If he says he explodes, again he may
be given alternatives, including even extravagant ones so that his own
less extravagant behavior will be easier to divulge: "Do you kick, bite,
scream, use your fists, swear, get sarcastic, or what, when you are really
boiling?" And to continue, "Do you feel better or worse after an explosion? Does it sort of clear the atmosphere for you, or are you apt to
feel like a fool afterwards, or what?" When that is settled, "Who really
inspires you to your biggest 'mads,' your brother, father, teacher, mother,
playmates, or whom? Over what do you get most excited, when you
lose a game, or can't do what you want, or when the 'kids' tease you or
your sister gets into your things? Do you get 'maddest' at people or at
things that you can't get to come out right, or what? How often do you
really get 'boiling mad'—several times a day, every day, once a week,
once a month, once a year, or what? How often do you flare up—not
really explode—daily, etc.?" On the whole, those who explode easily
rather enjoy expanding upon this topic. For those who inhibit irritation,
and, therefore, do not get the same satisfaction, the approach obviously
has to be altered. (4, pp. 65–66.)

TERMINATING THE INTERVIEW

An interview may come to an end at no definite point, its closing
being determined only by the end of the period of time allowed.
Or it may come to a definitely fitting closing period, fruitfully occu-

pied by several acts: a brief summary of the discussion in order to insure that the clinician and the patient are in accord in understanding the significance of the conversation, an outline of plans to be carried out before the next session, or a statement about what may be taken up at the next meeting.

The last few minutes of an interview period, with the patient aware of the termination, are often very productive. Sometimes this is because the patient unconsciously wishes to hold the clinician a trifle longer and therefore inserts an interesting point as a means of extending the session. On other occasions, he may have been nerving himself to go into some matter and, finding it still undiscussed with the session drawing to a close, thrusts it in abruptly to accomplish his objective. Again, there is perhaps a distinction in his thinking between the interview hour proper and these closing minutes or seconds in which the interview is "over" and he can be himself and not a patient. Whatever the reason, these few minutes are likely to be diagnostically important.

BIBLIOGRAPHY

1. Berdie, R. F., Psychological processes in the interview, *J. soc. Psychol.*, 1943, 18:3–31.
2. Kutash, S. B., The psychologist's role in clinical practice, *J. clin. Psychol.*, 1947, 3:321–329.
3. Landis, C., et al., *Sex in development*, Paul B. Hoeber, Inc., 1940.
4. Macfarlane, J. W., Interview techniques, *Nat. Assoc. Deans Wom. J.*, 1943, 6:61–66.
5. Richards, T. W., *Modern clinical psychology*, McGraw-Hill Book Company, 1946.
6. Whitehorn, J. C., Guide to interviewing and clinical personality study, *Arch. Neurol. & Psychiat.*, 1944, 52:197–216.

SUPPLEMENTARY READINGS

7. Bingham, W. V., and Moore, B. V., *How to interview*, Harper & Brothers, 3rd ed., 1941.
8. Garrett, A., *Counseling methods for personnel workers*, Family Welfare Association of America, 1945.
9. Oldfield, R. C., *The psychology of the interview*, Methuen & Co., 1941.
10. Watson, R. I., Interviewing, in Kaplan, O. (ed.), *Encyclopedia of vocational guidance*, Philosophical Library, 1948, pp. 627–639.
11. Woodward, L. E., and Rennie, T. A. C., *Jobs and the man*, Charles C. Thomas, 1946.

CHAPTER 6

Tests as Diagnostic Instruments[1]

Psychological tests provide one approach to the task of diagnosis. However, it is well to emphasize at the outset that they cannot properly be used as *the* tools of diagnosis. Regardless of the nature of the clinical problem, it is unlikely that any one battery of tests will permit the derivation of a complete diagnostic appraisal. The valid interpretation of their results demands complementation from other techniques described in the previous chapters. The developmental and school history, the mental status examination, and, in fact, the entire case study bear upon the test findings and are needed for adequate interpretation.

Occasionally the value of tests in general is questioned. This distrust, expressed in sweeping statements of disbelief in their value, would perhaps be more justifiable if directed at a particular instrument or a specific clinician. There is no doubt that many tests have serious shortcomings; similar conditions exist in all fields where instruments and tools are used. Refinement, development, and elimination of tests is indeed necessary, but this does not nullify their use at the present time. Improvements in telescopes have been going on for centuries, but the fact that in certain respects there is still room for improvement does not prevent utilization of them in their present state of development. Similarly, tests, crude though some of

---

[1] The therapeutic use of testing materials will be discussed in a later chapter.

them may be, are useful in diagnostic functions, despite this need for further refinement.

The same individual who condemns tests is likely to be proud of his own observational and inferential prowess and the resulting ability to "size up" an individual. Though he may be highly skillful, his techniques are often esoteric and uncommunicable, whereas tests are open to inspection and criticism and their reliability and validity are matters of investigation. The intuitionist who scoffs at tests makes himself the measure of all things, and since standard errors of measurement are not calculated about his capabilities along these lines, he blithely ignores errors in his own judgments—indeed, often treating them as nonexistent. It should be emphasized that the fact that such observations are not open to scrutiny by others does not make judgments based upon them any more free of these errors. Making the conclusions reached difficult or impossible to verify may hide sources of error but will not remove them.

BASIC PRINCIPLES IN THE USE OF DIAGNOSTIC TESTS

Basic to the diagnostic usage of tests, if not for all uses of tests, are certain principles which give them meaning in this task. Although not original, they profitably can be formulated here because sometimes they are accepted implicitly rather than being explicitly stated. Briefly, these principles are as follows: (1) Tests are samples of behavior. (2) Tests do not reveal traits or capacities directly. (3) Psychological maladjustments selectively and differentially affect the test scores. (4) The psychometric and projective approaches, although distinguishable, are mutually complementary.

TESTS AS SAMPLES OF BEHAVIOR

A clinician's interest centers upon the experience and behavior of the individual patient—upon what he thinks, feels, and does, the nature of his symptoms, characteristic ways of dealing with his problems, and the assets he may possess which are not being utilized in his fight for emotional-mental health. In short, the clinician learns about the patient as a person and something about the environment from which he comes. But he learns much of this second-hand by hearing the patient or someone else talk about his experiences and behavior. Though his behavior in the interview may be studied and observed, much of this is structured by the particular nature of the sessions themselves, and the usual interview-observation-rating techniques are not subject to as precise measurement as might be wished. Psychological tests meet this need for supplementing other behavior samples.

It would be of little or no moment to know how an individual performs on the short array of tasks placed before him in the psychological test if this behavior had no wider import. It is only insofar as this behavior gives a basis for estimating behavior in his day-to-day living that it assumes significance. A test is a sample of the patient's behavior on the assumption that his behavior in the test situation is indicative of his behavior in other non-test situations. Confusion in approach to the test material suggests a confused inner state; a patient showing a rigid approach may also be suspected of being rigid in other things.

It might be argued that the most valid method of obtaining diagnostic material would be to obtain an actual sample of the behavior in question in the situations in which it was exhibited. In theory the best way to gather information about parental rejection would be to observe the mother and child in their day-to-day interpersonal relationships. However, this not only would be impracticable in terms of time and trouble for its collection but also would have restricted validity as the sheer presence of the observer would exert an influence which would to some degree change the situation. If an individual attempted to find out his flair for medicine by attending medical school, a sure "test" of his ability to enter the field would thus be given. But as such a procedure is neither administratively feasible nor practical, a need has arisen for predictions rather than demonstrations.

Tests, whatever their faults, are relatively economical of time. They permit a sampling of behavior requiring hours, not months or years. Although one could conceivably observe a student in the classroom over a considerable period of time for the purpose of gaining information about his educational prowess, a diagnostic achievement test of an hour's duration might yield just as much or more information. Furthermore, such an appraisal would allow application of a wealth of normative material denied even the most skilled observer who does not use such an instrument.

A psychological test is more than a random sample of the patient's behavior taken during a given period of time; it is a sample taken under standardized and relatively objective conditions. The tasks presented are similar for all patients (the test materials); the method of presentation is similar for all examiners (the instructions and administration); and the results are judged according to the same standards (scoring criteria). Thus actual behavior under circumscribed, previously defined, and relatively objective conditions forms the datum of the psychological test. As Hunt (30) points out, the manipulation of the data implied in scoring should not blind us to that with which we have started—behavior in a situation.

Some of this behavior is not weighed in the scale of numerical scoring. In order to derive a score (a number) many intrinsically different sorts of behavior must be reduced to their common elements, thus providing a yardstick for interindividual comparison. This yardstick (scoring criteria) is ordered to one dimension of the behavior segment, and those aspects of the behavior which cannot be matched against the yardstick must be considered irrelevant to the scoring, though they are not to be disregarded. As Cornell and Coxe aptly express it, a test instead of being compared to a yardstick may be likened to a telescope—an instrument for refinement of observations. They go on to say that the psychologist ". . . uses tests to enable him to describe better what he sees, to reveal some things not evident to the naked eye, in order to give him a better basis for predicting probable outcomes. He can be successful in this just to the extent that he is able to interpret the measured results in the light of a great variety of observable but unmeasured, and as yet unmeasurable, qualitative factors that are of equal importance in the total picture." (2, p. 1.)

TESTS AS MEASURES OF FUNCTIONS, TRAITS, OR CAPACITIES

If the sampling of behavior is accepted as the most valid way of describing the nature of psychological tests, it follows that a function, trait, or capacity is never measured directly, but rather that some behavior is considered indicative of the trait. Direct determination of "intelligence" is impossible; instead presumed products of this capacity are measured. For example, the relative size of an individual's vocabulary is considered a good measure of verbal intelligence, and differences in the magnitude and precision of vocabulary are taken to be results of differences in ability. However, vocabulary size is not always the direct result of intelligence; differences in educational opportunity, cultural background, and physical and emotional factors may distort the results. The test may be fair to one person and not to another because of these distorting features.

It becomes apparent, then, that hypothecating behavior which will represent certain traits or capacities may be hazardous, and the factors which distort inferences from behavior on the test to functions or capacities apply with equal force in all areas of testing—aptitudes, achievement, personality, etc. This evinces the fact that there are "good" tests and "bad" tests, and the common clinical practice is to select the test demonstrated to give the fairest appraisal of the function in question. Such an instrument must attenuate errors which would reduce the representativeness of the behavior sample obtained, thereby decreasing its reliability and validity. To this issue further attention will be given in the discussion of selection of tests.

It is relevant to offer a reminder at this point: the diagnostic appraisal that is made through the material is not a "label" diagnosis but a means of identifying personality characteristics (22). The clinician is interested not in calling the patient a schizophrenic, but rather in the presence, or absence, and interrelation of certain personality characteristics which aid in understanding the patient. As Schafer (22) reminds us, not all hysterics are equally labile, nor are depressives equally guilt ridden. There are no infallible diagnostic indicators or "signs"; there is instead a constellation of characteristics in a particular patient. Tests measure behavior indicative of traits, functions, or capacities from the interrelationship of which a diagnostic appraisal is made.

SELECTIVE IMPAIRMENT ON TEST RESULTS

Since the time of Kraepelin and Bleuler there has been an interest in the selective impairment of psychological functions in the various mental disorders (15). Today, because of improvements in instruments and advances in theoretical and experimental psychology and psychiatry, there has been a resurgence of such interest. Most baldly stated, psychological maladjustments encroach upon one or more of the functions tapped by a test whereas other functions may be relatively or absolutely unimpaired. Thus psychological maladjustments selectively and differentially affect functions reflected in the test scores. The process has been described by Menninger, Rapaport, and Schafer as follows:

It appears that the following interlocking sequence is fundamentally important for the test assessment of patients in adjustment and mal-adjustment: certain patterns of defense mechanisms are adopted and these determine specific strengths and weaknesses and (sic) in psychological functioning which then become characteristic of the adjustment of the personality; with the onset of maladjustment, an exaggeration or breakdown in these strengths and weaknesses characteristic for that maladjustment occurs which can be measured; this leads to a diagnostic differentiation.

For the psychological examiner the interlocking sequence should be, first, knowledge of the dynamic etiology of the mental disorder as productive of specific defenses or their breakdown; second, the theoretical knowledge of the psychological functions which are related to specific defenses or their breakdown; and finally the knowledge of tests of the psychological functions. (15, pp. 475–476.)

THE PSYCHOMETRIC AND PROJECTIVE APPROACHES[2]

Two approaches to diagnostic testing may be distinguished—the psychometric and the projective. The first approach stresses the measurement of some characteristic of the individual by a previously established scale. Psychometric instruments involve stimulus-response situations in which the responses have definite predetermined values. In short, both the stimulus and the response are structured. A relatively fixed stimulus with a relatively narrow range of meanings creates a situation in which the response range is correspondingly narrow. Thus the question "What is the capital of Italy?" may produce the correct response, statements expressing inability to answer, various incorrect cities or countries, or perhaps a few tangential responses—such as "the Pope." In scoring, the correct response gets full credit, the others nothing. Scores are summed and appropriate statistical transformations made. The psychometric approach in the scientific tradition stresses *measurement* of part functioning.

The projective instrument attempts to reveal the quality of the subject's personality. Stimuli are chosen which allow the subject to impose upon them his own meaning and organization, private and idiosyncratic though it may be. Only with considerable difficulty (and often not at all) are such interpretations ordered to a scale.

---

[2] A more complete discussion of the projective approach is reserved for later chapters.

The projective approach in the artistic tradition stresses *understanding* of the total personality.

It may be noted that the psychometric and projective distinction involves primarily different *approaches* rather than different *tests.* Fundamentally it is not the instrument but the way one approaches the diagnostic task which is important. The Wechsler-Bellevue Scale is more readily conceived in the psychometric and the Rorschach in the projective tradition, yet the Wechsler-Bellevue Scale may be approached projectively, as Rapaport (18) approaches it, and the Rorschach Ink Blots approached psychometrically, as Zubin (27) approaches them.

On the present clinical scene the projective approach is dominant. In describing his application of a battery of tests to a group of neurotic and psychotic patients Rapaport has this to say:

> In order to develop a psychological rationale for these tests and the types of responses on them, we adopted the "projective hypothesis"— namely, that every reaction of a subject is a reflection, or projection, of his private world. This approach to testing contrasts sharply with that usually characterized as "psychometric." The main aim was not to attribute to a person a percentile rank in the population or any other numerical measure allegedly representative of him. The aim was rather to understand the individual: to give him a chance to express himself in a sufficient number and variety of controlled situations, the nature of which has been well enough explored to enable the psychologist to infer, out of the subject's reactions, the gross outlines of his personality makeup. This expectancy, however, implies the "projective hypothesis"; it implies that every action or reaction of a human individual bears the characteristic features of his individual makeup. The choice of tests on the basis of this hypothesis would favor tests whose material is unconventional and not limited to eliciting habitual reactions. This hypothesis would find the Rorschach Ink-Blot Test most satisfactory; the Thematic Apperception Test less satisfactory; and the standard intelligence tests least satisfactory, because the intelligence test questions themselves would appear, at first glance, aimed at eliciting highly conventional responses. We included in this battery not only clearly projective tests; but we attempted to demonstrate that the projective hypothesis, though in generalized form, can be applied even to intelligence tests. In fact, we approached all of these tests with this hypothesis. (18, pp. 10–11.)

In essence, then, all tests may be conceived of as projective techniques in that the patient projects his inner life into his reactions, and his organization of these reactions (test results) may be used for interpreting his personality. Learning, comprehension, attention are as truly aspects of the functioning personality as are drives and emotions. Thus any test can be used as a projective device especially when qualitative and idiosyncratic behavior is interpreted in conjunction with the quantitative findings. However, it must be reiterated that this does not mean abandonment of the psychometric approach.

It is the conviction of most clinicians that the "psychometric" and the "projective" approaches to testing are compatible and mutually strengthen each other. Both are legitimate; they reinforce rather than exclude each other. Even Rapaport and his associates, who stress the projective hypothesis, report the IQ of the patients they test. One approach may be stressed over another according to the needs of the case, but both are needed in most instances. The IQ of the child for whom institutionalization for mental deficiency is being considered may be more important than how he reveals himself projectively on these materials. But even here attention has been given for some time to this aspect of test behavior.

THE SELECTION OF DIAGNOSTIC TESTS[3]

The selection of specific tests for work in clinical diagnosis is adequate only if certain criteria are met. The test or tests selected must be relevant to the problem, appropriate for the patient, familiar to the clinician, adaptable to the time available, and must meet certain established standards of reliability, validity, and normative breadth. In addition, there is a question of whether a routine battery meeting these criteria should be used or a new battery selected for each case. These criteria and this last issue will be discussed in turn.

RELEVANCE TO THE PROBLEM

The selection of the specific tests will be determined in considerable measure by the diagnostic impression that one has of the patient, based partially upon the reasons for referral. Dominating all criteria of selection is the criterion of relevance—the chosen instruments should be those most likely to result in a resolution of the

---

[3] The criteria of selection of tests for individual diagnostic work differ from those which would be applicable under other circumstances. For example, certain of the criteria of selection of tests for group usage are ignored as irrelevant. In such testing situations price, simplicity of administration and scoring, and similar characteristics loom large (cf. Freeman, 8).

diagnostic problem presented by the patient. Final selection of instruments is decided by what the clinician expects them to reveal about the particular patient under consideration.

Tests, then, are selected to explore the hypotheses suggested by the reasons for the examination as described in Chapter 2. Selection may be made on the basis of function—intelligence, personality, achievement, etc.—as well as on the basis of the diagnostic problem. To give an illustration, differential diagnosis in a forty-five-year-old rural farm hand between mental deterioration and mental deficiency would certainly warrant selection of an appropriate intelligence test such as the Wechsler-Bellevue. In addition a measure of memory such as the Graham-Kendall Memory for Designs Test and a measure of conceptual thinking such as the Object Sorting Test may be indicated. Since the Rorschach frequently reveals evidence concerning differences between past and present functioning this too might be included in the battery.

It is not necessary to select the entire battery in advance. Previously disregarded aspects of the patient's condition may be appreciated as testing progresses, necessitating a change of plans. Again, unexpected slowness may prevent completion of all instruments tentatively planned in the time allotted.

APPROPRIATENESS FOR THE PATIENT

A decision must be made about each test as to its appropriateness for a particular patient. In making it, certain characteristics of the group or groups on which the test was standardized must be known and the same characteristics of the patient considered. Tests are selected as appropriate to the following characteristics of the patient: age (or grade), sex, intellectual level, experience level, physical handicaps and general physical condition, and socioeconomic status. If the patient does not resemble the standardization group in these characteristics, there should be some way of inferring the effect of his atypicality upon the results and an adjustment should be made accordingly.

FAMILIARITY TO THE CLINICIAN

It almost goes without saying that in deciding any crucial diagnostic point, tests with which the examiner is unfamiliar should not be used. Other things being equal, thorough familiarity with a few instruments is of greater clinical value than superficial acquaintance with many, despite the glowing (and often unverified) claims with which many new instruments are thrown upon the market. This does not mean that unfamiliar tests should not be tried; rather, they should not be depended upon clinically until familiarity is achieved. In familiarizing oneself with a new test a good working rule is to select for inclusion in the battery not only the new test but also a familiar one heretofore used for the same purposes as the new instrument.

ADAPTABILITY TO THE TIME AVAILABLE

Another consideration pertinent to the choice of testing devices is the time available for administration, scoring, interpretation and write-up. Frequently time allowances are liberal, sometimes not. This, of course, is a relative matter, varying according to the problem, the setting, the age of the patient, the policy of the institution, and so on.

Time considerations achieve prominence in many clinic situations where there are drastic restrictions of the time available for any one patient. Under such conditions some of the group tests, the functions of which are discussed in a later section, are applicable. Group testing is not the only solution, however, as not all the individual tests are tremendously time-consuming. Short forms of the Wechsler-Bellevue, a short-form TAT, individual subtests included in the Arthur Performance Scale for which there are individual norms, and other tests are appropriately used under time pressure. The *Mental Examiners Handbook* of Wells and Ruesch (25) contains many valuable short testing devices.

Under circumstances in which time is at the absolute minimum it is well for the clinician to ask himself if testing is appropriate at all. The psychological diagnostic sessions which the clinician encounters vary from those in which many tests are imperative to the occasional situation in which no formal tests are indicated or in which they may even be contraindicated. If one can ascertain from a few minutes' inquiry about school history and from other indices such as vocabulary level that a child is of better than average intellectual capacity, it is sometimes a waste of precious time to administer a short intelligence test. Rather, some of the procedures concerning intellectual status described in Chapter 3 may be applied and the time saved used to greater advantage elsewhere. However, assuming a good working relationship and experienced colleagues, referrals in which time is of the utmost importance generally are not so easily solved. Frequently the referring clinicians have applied these mental status techniques and are still at a loss concerning at least some aspect of intellectual functioning of the referred patient.

In this connection there is a deplorable tendency among a few psychologists to be rather unyielding about the time necessary for a psychological examination. The psychologist when a member of the clinical team is not immune to an overrigid demand for completeness; one too common form is the occasional insistence on doing a *complete* psychological work-up on all cases. He is distressed or resentful (according to his nature) if asked to utilize a single technique on short notice when scheduling does not permit more extended study. Psychological examinations at a precise moment are hardly life-and-death matters and are not emergencies in that sense. Nevertheless occasions do arise when some level of evaluation is urgent. For example, suppose a child from a remote area, in the hospital for a general pediatric examination (arranged to last only a day or so), revealed on this examination an unsuspected problem making psychological consultation desirable. Should the psychologist deny this service because customarily a complete study would take a day in itself? The interests of the patient demand bowing to time limitations and doing as much as possible in the available hour, perhaps emphasizing in the report the need for a more complete and definite examination.

If a greater amount of time is available, perhaps approaching the optimal, then this criterion may not be so important. However, time is always a dimension of psychological practice, and it is the sign of professional maturity to use enough, but not more than enough, time to do an adequate job according to the demands of the diagnostic services required.

RELIABILITY

Although tests give a retrospective view of the past and a measurement of the present, their greatest value is the insight they provide into the future behavior of the individual. An essential criterion of selection of a testing instrument is information about its dependability (or undependability) in doing this. Reliability is concerned with the dependability of measurement either on repeated administration, from one portion to another portion of the test, or from one form to another form of the test, and it has become a truism to say that a diagnostic instrument should be reliable. There are separable meanings of this concept of dependability so that it is more appropriate to speak of *reliabilities* than *reliability*. Other than the hypothetical self-correlation for which no adequate estimates exist, "reliability" according to Cronbach (3) may be said to take three forms, for which he proposes the names "coefficient of stability," "coefficient of stability and equivalence," and "coefficient of equivalence." His definitions follow:

Definition (1): *Reliability is the degree to which the test score indicates unchanging . . . individual differences in any traits. (Coefficient of stability.)*
Definition (2): *Reliability is the degree to which the test score indicates unchanging individual differences in the general and group factors defined by the test. (Coefficient of stability and equivalence.)*
Definition (3): *Reliability is the degree to which the test score indicates the status of the individual at the present instant in the general and group factors defined by the test. (Coefficient of equivalence.)* Internal consistency tests are generally measures of equivalence. These coefficients predict the correlation of the test with a hypothetical equivalent test, as like the first test as the parts of the first test are like each other. (3, pp. 5–6.)

The coefficient of stability is estimated by the test-retest correlation, the coefficient of stability and equivalence by the correlation of parallel tests, and the coefficient of equivalence by the parallel-split (split-half) and other methods. Cronbach goes on to point out that in describing a test separate estimates of coefficients of equivalence and stability should be provided since they have different meanings and different implications for attenuation, standard errors of measurement, etc.[4]

Techniques for measurement of these various reliabilities, although important, tell nothing about maintaining or increasing consistency and stability. Statistics measure but do not produce reliability. The clinician must exercise care that the conditions under which he tests produce the reliability for which he strives. Factors

---

[4] Discussion of statistical methodology is beyond the scope of this volume (though emphatically not outside the province of the clinical psychologist).

such as clarity of instructions and maintenance of optimal motivation not only are of general importance but also increase reliability. Reliability is partly a function of the clinician as his experience determines whether the instrument is a reliable one for *him*. As he works with the instrument he learns many facts about its reliability. This is not to imply that he should neglect published studies of reliability but serves to emphasize the importance of experience in understanding reliability. The clinician is responsible for knowing the reliability of his instruments. As Magaret says:

The clinician who is not aware of the need for interpreting and critically evaluating the reliability of the instruments he uses opens himself to serious error in understanding his client's general intelligence. Let us suppose that he uses the 1937 Stanford-Binet scale and makes a series of measures of intelligence on the same client over a period of years. He notes an unsystematic variation from year to year of five or six IQ points. This is the expected variation for his measure, within the limits of reliability for the Stanford-Binet IQ. Unless he realizes this, however, the clinical psychologist may attempt unjustifiably to explain, in terms of his client's possible instability or deterioration, a change which is only an expected characteristic of a fallible instrument. . . . Or suppose he attempts, unsuccessfully, to diagnose psychiatric disorder on the basis of a pattern of subtest scores obtained on the Wechsler-Bellevue adult intelligence scale. Unless he takes into consideration the reliability of these scores, he may again attribute to his client's responses a capriciousness which is rather the result of the characteristics of the instrument he is using. (13, pp. 359–360.)

VALIDITY[5]

Tests selected for diagnostic use should measure what they are said to measure. If a test of so-called vocational interest does not actually measure vocational interest or some aspect of it, then it is not useful for diagnostic purposes in instances in which this is a problem. Thus it would appear that the validity of a test has direct bearing on its selection according to the criterion of relevance.

In appraising validity it is not enough to know what the author has christened his instrument. A test labeled as a measure of conceptual thinking does not forthwith become such a measure. It may

---

[5] It is well to point out at this juncture that the entire discussion of each specific test given later is concerned with validity since content, standardization, the groups to which applied and on which standardized, information about diagnostic usage, qualitative cues, and many more aspects of test information have direct bearing on a test's validity.

not differentiate at all the abilities of individuals to think conceptually. In some instances different labels are attached to identical procedures. Digit span is sometimes identified as a measure of memory span and sometimes as a measure of attention. It may be, of course, that both of the interpretations are correct (or it may be that both are incorrect). Many tests are not at all clear cut in the delimitations of the functions they tap. Often tests measure a composite of emotional and intellectual functions and it is even plausible to believe that sometimes they test different functions in different individuals.

As mentioned before, interest in diagnostic testing centers on predicting the future behavior of an individual on the basis of what is known about him at a particular moment. This means it is necessary to ascertain the relationship between certain test findings and subsequent behavior. Knowing the nature and magnitude of this relationship it is possible to predict the patient's behavior from performance on the test.

As with reliability, information about validity can in some measure be gained from reading the literature but the best criteria of validity develop from the clinician's day-to-day experience with the instrument. He matches his test findings with the findings of others who have used different techniques and submits them to the test of time. Validity is conceived of in operational terms: what the test measures becomes clear only through use. Each administration of a test is a venture in exploring its validity. This position is forced upon the clinician by the fact that what it measures varies with the patient, his mood, his coöperativeness, and, in some measures at least, his age and mental level. All diagnostic material gives us information about validity and can be compared with other material obtained by other techniques. The question is not "What is this test's validity?" but "What is its validity for this patient?"

In a sense, correlation with other measures is indirect evidence of validity. To the extent that one instrument correlates with another, they may be measuring the same thing. If the magnitude of this relationship is very great, the possibility arises that the second or new measure is to some degree superfluous. There are certain dangers of misinterpretation which must be appreciated to understand the nature of this relationship. Cronbach puts it as follows:

A high correlation is often erroneously interpreted as showing that one factor causes the other. There are at least three possible explanations for a high correlation between two variables, A and B. A may cause or influence the size of B, B may cause A, or both A and B may be influenced by some common factor or factors. The correlation between score on a vocabulary test and score on a reading test may be taken as an example. Does good vocabulary cause one to be a good reader? Possibly. Or does ability to read well cause one to acquire a good vocabulary? An equally likely explanation. But the results could also be explained as resulting from high intelligence, a home in which books and serious conversation abounded, or superior teaching in the elementary schools. Only a theoretical understanding of the processes involved, or controlled experiments, permit us to state what causes underlie a particular correlation. Otherwise, the only safe conclusion is that correlated measures are influenced by a common factor. (4, pp. 36–38.)

The correlation of one variable with another, then, is an estimate of validity since the magnitude of the correlation yields information about the extent to which they overlap or measure the same thing.

The correlational approach is only one among many approaches to validity. Indeed, there is at present considerable dissatisfaction with some instances of its application to problems of validity in clinical materials. The wealth of relatively new developments in statistical techniques available for use with clinical data is reviewed by Mensh (16). He describes the shift as being from "group-centered" to "individual-centered" statistics. The individual case, not the group, is the focus of interest. To explore these methods is, however, beyond the scope of the present discussion.

Methods of measuring validity should in no wise be confused with arranging conditions so that a valid test behavior sample is secured. In effect, all procedures which make for accurate diagnosis contribute to validity. Validity is a function of the use to which the results are put; test results in themselves are not valid or invalid. They possess validity only when they are used for some purpose, and their degree of validity must be evaluated in terms of their use. If, as is often the case, more than one purpose is served by the same test it has several validities. Hence it is impossible to speak of a test's "validity"; rather its "validities" must be known. Peatman puts it as follows:

The single-function implication of the phrase, "the validity of a test," is apt to be an understatement of a test's functional possibilities. A test, such as the Terman Group Test of Mental Ability, may be found to have a fair degree of validity in differentiating the scholastic achievement and aptitude of 14-year-olds of our culture, some validity in differentiat-

ing their aptitude for a broad range of occupations as well as a degree of
validity in differentiating their aptitude for the subdivisions of a given
occupation. A test may have *validities*, and to varying degrees. In other
words, test scores may have empirically discovered relations with behavioral criteria of different types of populations as well as with differen-
tiable types of situation-demands. (17, p. 39.)

Realization of the greater or lesser degree of invalidity to which
all diagnostic tests are heir should temper any tendency toward dog-
matism which the psychologist might otherwise be prone to exhibit.
Presumably all commonly used and generally accepted clinical instruments supply valid information on occasion, but with just as
much certainty it may be said that at least occasionally they are just
as invalid.

THE CLINICAL USEFULNESS OF TEST NORMS

Diagnostic tests are also selected on the basis of the clinical usefulness of the norms available. It is necessary, therefore, to sketch
the meaning of norms, their derivation from statistical transformation of scores and from clinical experience, and other issues which
enter when considering their application to diagnostic testing.

An individual is diagnosed in the broad sense simply by differentiating him from other individuals. It was pointed out earlier that
to understand a patient's behavior it is first necessary to understand
his deviations from and similarities to both normal and atypical
individuals of his age and cultural group. Information about these
similarities and differences can be supplied with considerable accuracy by comparative data in the form of test norms. Qualitative
and historical materials obtained in other aspects of the diagnostic
case study are not as cogent precisely because they have not been
quantitatively determined. Norms provide points of reference which
permit differentiation as well as the drawing of inferences about
commonalities. Interpretation of a patient's score is possible only
when anchored by some point of reference, i.e., norms.

Since statistical norms are dependent upon scores it is necessary
to examine for a moment the nature of a score. The cumulative raw
score results directly from a computation based on the answers themselves. It may be calculated as one or more points per item correct
with or without some correction for incorrect answers. Total raw
score may be based upon successful completion within certain time

limits, upon accuracy alone, or upon an intermingling of time and accuracy credits. Raw scores such as these are much less meaningful than scores which can be related either to a table of norms or to subjective norms acquired through clinical experience. For the former, a derived scoring system which permits comparison with scores of others on some meaningful continuum appears to be necessary. Derived scores pertain to a system of scoring values such as centiles or standard scores (or age-grade equivalents deduced from them), which results in a common meaning for a given numerical value assigned two or more tests or subtests. Suppose a patient achieved raw scores on the Vocabulary and Similarities subtests of the Wechsler-Bellevue Scale of 25 and 13 respectively. Without a system of weighted scores the clinician would be at a loss to evaluate these scores properly. When it is discovered that on both subtests the weighted score is 11 he knows that the patient did relatively as well on one as on the other.

It is sometimes overlooked that for derived scores on two or more tests to have comparable positional meaning it is necessary that the normative population be the same or highly similar. Suppose, for example, the standardization population for a given intelligence test was drawn from a culturally enriched college town and the raw scores were converted into standard scores with a mean of 50 and standard deviation of 10. Another test, on the other hand, took its sample from a mill town population. Though the standard scores were similarly derived, a given individual's standard score of 50 on the first test might really be more comparable to 65 on the second test than to 50 *if he did equally well on both*. Thus the positional value of a test score depends most fundamentally upon the sample used for the computation of the derived scores.

Even more essential to the proper understanding of a derived test score is knowledge of the appropriateness of the normative group for the individual patient. Note that the question is not the comparison of two derived scores on the same individual but the valid interpretation of a single score of an individual when that score is evaluated by means of a table of norms. The score can be properly interpreted only if the normative group is an appropriate one, i.e., a population with which the patient may justifiably be compared. A test of reading achievement standardized on New York school children and with norms stated in grade equivalents is not so catholic that one

can administer it to a rural Mississippi Negro school child and report
he reads at the fourth-grade level (with the further comment that
he actually is in the sixth grade) if this grade level is thought of as
applying in his own school system. Actually in his own school this
might be tantamount to seventh-grade reading.

Scores have little meaning until expressed in terms of their relationship to an actual distribution of scores, as it is necessary to know
how a particular score deviates from the normative group average.
This distribution of scores is properly either that obtained by a group
of individuals similar to the one whose score is to be interpreted or
that obtained by a group of individuals with whom the individual
in question is in some way to be brought into contact. The first type
of comparison is the more common, as it involves the relationship
of an individual to his peers; i.e., the patient is a member of the
population of which the normative group is a sample. The second
kind of distribution is somewhat more unusual in that it involves
normative comparison of individuals who, strictly speaking, do not
fall in the general population of which the normative group is a
sample. For example, it would be appropriate to evaluate a Negro
against white norms if the reason for comparison involved participation in some direct way in a situation in which the white members
of the group set the standards. Illustrative would be the selection of
Negro naval recruits for specialist training who would be required
to meet the same standards as white recruits. Similarly, selection for
psychotherapy, a highly verbal process, would require about the same
minimum verbal intellectual level irrespective of other considerations such as race.

Selection of appropriate norms, then, is not an automatic or
routine practice. Consideration should always be given to the appropriateness of the norms available in the *particular* case. If more
than one set of norms is available, the compositions of which are
defined, selection of the normative material most appropriate for the
individual is possible.

In a large measure the lack of adequately described normative
groups has popularized subjective standards among clinicians. As
experience with roughly delimited groups of patients accrues and
correlation of their behavior with subsequent clinical course can be
observed, the psychologist begins to develop a set of norms that are
qualitative and without benefit of formal tabulation. This does not
mean that they are necessarily fuzzy or lack precision; in fact, among

some such clinicians they appear to be astonishingly accurate. Despite their accuracy, however, there is the indisputable necessity of objectifying these qualitative norms whenever possible. If this can be done, the value of local norms specifically designed for the situation at hand is significantly enhanced.

Despite the values of established norms, their limitations must be recognized. Similarity-dissimilarity to position on a normative scale supplies valuable information, but for many aspects of an individual's behavior repertory no norms exist. Foremost among the examples which might be given is that of the patient's style of life, the integrated pattern of uniqueness which he presents to the clinician. This as a unit cannot be ordered to a set of norms although norms may supply information that goes into this portrayal. Norms may allow us to place the scores on a psychograph; they cannot give entire expression to the individuality that marks off this particular person from others. For a further discussion of this issue in a setting in projective techniques see Chapter 14.

THE ADVISABILITY OF A ROUTINE TESTING BATTERY

The problem of whether or not to use a routine battery of tests is intimately related to the preceding discussion. It is with the intent of applying these or similar criteria of test selection that both proponents and opponents of a routine battery take their stand. Therefore it is appropriate to consider the advisability of applying a routine battery in individual diagnostic work.

Some clinicians argue that clinical aims are best served by the routine use of an identical battery of tests for all, or almost all, patients. Rapaport, who argues for the established battery approach, states that "The advantages of . . . a battery of tests are that indicators, which for some reason are absent in one or several of the tests, are likely to be present in others; that indicators in the different tests are likely to support and supplement each other; and that the presence of indicators in some of the tests may call attention to more subtle indicators in others which might otherwise have been overlooked." (18, p. 6.) It would appear that these are essentially arguments for the use of several tests rather than arguments in favor of a fixed battery of tests. Very few clinicians would plead for "single test" diagnosis. Indeed, most psychologists use several instruments with a single patient for precisely the reasons given, but vary the battery from patient to patient.

Hutt summarizes some other arguments in favor of the routine battery, namely, ". . . (1) comparable data on a number of tests become available for research; (2) a routine battery of tests offers a systematic check on the most important phases of the patient's personality; and (3) the psychologist gains familiarity with the battery and is more readily able to integrate the findings successfully." (9, p. 9.)

Although, as he points out, these advantages do exist, he goes on to suggest that such a procedure is very wasteful of both the clinician's and the patient's time, tends to invite a mechanical approach, and does not provide for a particularly intensive probing of a given area when such would appear to be indicated. Sensitivity to the problems of the patient favors the utilization of instruments according to need and not according to the demands of clinic routine. Nevertheless, competent clinicians follow both practices. As a matter of fact, many who would insist that they select a new battery for each patient will be found using the same instruments time after time nearly as often as those who hold the opposed position.

KINDS OF DIAGNOSTIC TESTS

A semblance of order in discussing diagnostic tests may be achieved if they are classified according to certain criteria. Each of the tests to be discussed in later chapters will be classified by the major psychological function which it appears to tap, the ages for which it is most appropriate, and the diagnostic problems for which it is particularly suited. The classification of the kinds of problems for which diagnostic testing is pertinent, described in Chapter 2, will then be utilized for a further classification of tests in terms of these problems. Next, brief mention will be made of the distinctions between group and individual testing. Finally, the question of the use of personality questionnaires in clinical practice will be considered.

CLASSIFICATION OF DIAGNOSTIC TESTS BY PSYCHOLOGICAL FUNCTION, AGE, AND PROBLEM

Table 1 presents a summary of the instruments discussed in detail in later chapters.[6] Each one is classified according to the scheme

---

[6] One diagnostic instrument which is included in this table is not later discussed in detail. The Rorschach Ink Blots, although essential in diagnostic appraisal, is omitted for the reasons stated in the Preface.

described above. The tests reported in the table are those remaining after a rigorous elimination. The aim was to select the minimum number and variety of instruments to cover the majority of diagnostic problems the psychologist might encounter. Inclusion of these seventeen instruments in the clinician's repertory should prepare him for many of the clinical tasks he will encounter. Obviously not all eventualities of clinical practice could be covered. It was decided that since intellectual and emotional problems (mental deficiency, personality deviations, neurotic and psychotic conditions of the child and the adult) would be the focus of interest, the more narrowly educational and vocational problems would have to be minimized. Accordingly, vocational interest, aptitude, and educational achievement tests will not be included because of this emphasis and space considerations.

To further the aim of selection, the criteria for selecting a diagnostic test discussed in the preceding section of the chapter were applied. No test was selected which would be open to the charge that it failed to meet in large measure these criteria. Other considerations also tempered selection. It was decided that the tests must be in common use in clinical settings; the materials must be available at present; and they must make a contribution which, under at least certain circumstances, no other selected instrument could make.

That someone else would have made a different selection is evident from examination of the table. Conspicuous absences are the Minnesota Multiphasic, the Hanfmann-Kasanin, the Shipley Institute of Living, the Worcester-Wells, the Szondi, the Bender-Gestalt, the Goodenough Draw A Man, the Draw A Person, the Merrill-Palmer, the Gesell Developmental Schedule, the Minnesota Preschool, and the Cornell-Coxe. The explanation is that selection, where possible, was made on the basis of all of the above criteria, resulting in the omission of some otherwise excellent instruments.[7]

Tests may be classified in terms of the kinds of psychological processes they purport to reveal. Unfortunately not a single scientifically rooted system of classification is generally accepted. This is attributable in turn to the failure of psychologists to agree upon a well-defined classification of psychological processes. Nevertheless,

---

[7] The omission of personality questionnaires is discussed later in the chapter.

TABLE 1. A Summary of Certain Diagnostic Test Instruments

Instrument	Major Area Tapped	Ages for Which Most Appropriate	Diagnostic Problems for Which Particularly Appropriate
Arthur Point Scale of Performance Tests	Intellectual functioning	5 to 12 years	Intellectual functioning of a nonverbal or performance sort. Useful when there is a foreign language handicap, cultural deprivation, speech or hearing defect, or when major concern is with suspected mental deficiency or differences between verbal and performance factors (the last in conjunction with a verbal test)
Cattell Infant Intelligence Tests	Intellectual functioning	1 year to 3 years	Intellectual and motor functioning (general developmental rate) in infants whether retarded, normal, or advanced
Goldstein-Scheerer Cube Test	Conceptual thinking	Adolescents and adults	Logicalness and flexibility of thinking, differences in abstract and concrete thinking, brain damage, mental deficiency, and dementia praecox
Graham-Kendall Memory-for-Designs Test	Memory	6 years through adult	Visual-motor memory, brain damage
Digit Span Test	Memory	5 years through adult	Used as a measure either of memory or of attention, useful when organicity is suspected
Healy Pictorial Completion Test II	Conceptual thinking	5 years through adult	Issues in which conceptual thinking aspect of intellectual functioning is important, schizophrenic thinking
Kohs Block Design Test	Conceptual thinking	5 years through adult	Issues in which conceptual thinking aspect of intellectual functioning is important, deficit in analytic-synthetic ability

Test	Function	Age range	Description
Object Sorting Test	Conceptual thinking	5 years through adult	Personality functioning under disorganization, relation adequacy of sorting to verbalization, level of sorting, "everyday" concept formation, looseness or narrowness of sorting, schizophrenic thinking
Porteus Maze Tests	Intellectual functioning	5 years through adult of normal intelligence	Issues in which planning ability, common sense, impulsiveness are important, mental deficiency, delinquency, consideration of lobotomy
Rorschach Ink Blots	Personality functioning	8 years through adult	Personality dynamics and organization, severity of psychological illness, evaluation of personality "checks and balances," intellectual level, thinking and imagination, temperament, therapeutic assets, brain damage, differential psychiatric diagnosis
Rosenzweig Picture-Frustration Study	Personality functioning	4 years through adult	Relative strength and interrelationship of methods by which frustrations are handled
Revised Stanford-Binet Tests of Intelligence	Intellectual functioning	2 to 14 years	Intellectual level particularly in relation to verbal functioning and to school adjustment. Mental deficiency
Thematic Apperception Test	Personality functioning	8 years through adult	Fantasies, themes, motives, drives, ambitions, preoccupations, attitudes, interpersonal relationships, level of functioning, sources of difficulties
Vineland Social Maturity Scale	Intellectual functioning	1 year through 10 years	Social developmental level as related to intellectual and motor functioning, smoothness of development, areas of retardation
Wechsler-Bellevue Intelligence Scale	Intellectual functioning	12 years through adult	Patterning of intellectual functioning, verbal and performance levels, mental deficiency, relation of emotional states to intellectual functioning, brain damage, presence of pathological thinking
Wechsler Memory Scale	Memory	Adolescents and adults	Visual and oral memory functioning, memory deficit, organic pathology
Weigl Color-Form Sorting Test	Conceptual thinking	5 years through adult	Ability to shift in thinking, evidence of deterioration, rigidity of approach

there is a pragmatic classification in fairly common use which offers a convenient frame of reference. The following major functions tapped by specific instruments will be used: intellectual functioning, conceptual thinking, memory, and personality functioning.

It is immediately apparent that certain contradictions exist in this classification, conventional though it may be. Intellectual functioning, for example, includes in its scope memory and conceptual thinking. The omnibus term, personality functioning, is generally understood to include the part-functions of memory, intelligence, and the like. Here it is construed to include also a general, more dynamic configuration in which a part is played not only by these part-functions but also by the interrelations arising from them plus unique factors attributable to the personality as a unit.

It follows that because a test is classified in terms of its major function its diagnostically useful contributions are not limited to this area only. The area tapped, used for classificatory purposes, is almost without exception but one in which the test is most useful. Enthusiastic protagonists of the Rorschach, for example, might urge that it supplies information about practically all the functions of the personality.

Another system of classification used in this table is that of the ages for which each diagnostic test is particularly appropriate. This system was adopted because it is considered more useful functionally than the more conventional statement of the range of ages for which the test may be used. Thus, in most instances the range of ages for which a given test is considered most appropriate is narrower than the potential or possible range. On the other hand, a more subjective personal note is introduced than would be the case if the author's ranges were objectively reported. Nevertheless, clinical opinion would have it that there is an optimal range as well as a potential range despite the disagreement with the authors of the tests concerned. Arthur and Doll would consider the instruments they developed, respectively the Point Scale of Performance Tests and the Vineland Social Maturity Scale, as suitable for adult ages, instead of having the older limit set at twelve years for the former and ten for the latter. General clinical practice, however, appears to be to use them much less often for individuals older than the upper limits set in the table. The "most appropriate" range is, therefore, more useful for present purposes, although the subsequent detailed discussion of each instrument will include findings with adults. The ages given in the table refer to mental as well as chronological age.

The last column of the table gives the diagnostic problems for which each instrument is particularly appropriate. Some tests, regardless of the major area of functioning, are more relevant for a particular problem than are others. For example, it is commonplace in clinical practice to consider the Thematic Apperception Test as throwing more light on the content of a patient's difficulties than does the Rorschach, although both are tests of personality functioning. An attempt has been made to give not only some of the nuances of the test's appropriateness in the major area tapped but also the classes of patients for which it is particularly suitable in terms both of psychiatric diagnostic classifications and of social or physical limitations. To exemplify, the Arthur Point Scale of Performance Tests would be particularly appropriate in testing the nonverbal intellectual functioning of a deaf child suspected of being mentally defective.

CLASSIFICATION OF DIAGNOSTIC TESTS BY REASONS FOR REFERRAL

Reasons for referral for diagnostic testing were presented in Chapter 2. Tests especially indicated for certain categories of referral are given in Table 2, further subdivided into the age level for which they are most appropriate. Since the table does not repeat all of the previously described reasons for referral or include all age levels, some explanatory comments are necessary. Certain diagnostic problems either never occur or occur with such infrequency at particular age levels that they have been omitted in the table, e.g., a general educational problem in a preschool child. For the present purpose it was not necessary to treat separately the problems of "sources of difficulties of adjustment," "differential psychiatric diagnosis," "personality dynamics," and "therapeutic assets," since the battery selected from among these tests would be substantially the same for all these categories of referral. Nevertheless, a given instrument may contribute somewhat more to one and somewhat less to another of these problems. For example, the Rorschach is likely to be most crucial in investigating general personality dynamics, whereas the TAT is more sensitive to sources of difficulties of adjustment. Differential handling of this group of problems depends less on choice of instruments than on analysis and organization of findings.

TABLE 2. Tests Indicated for Particular Reasons for Referral

Intellectual Level			Evidence of Brain Damage		
Infant and Preschool	Child	Adoles. Adult	Infant and Preschool	Child	Adoles. Adult
Cattell	Arthur	Wechsler-Bellevue	Cattell	Arthur	Object Sorting
Stanford-Binet	Stanford-Binet		Stanford-Binet	Goldstein-Scheerer Cube	Goldstein-Scheerer Cube
Vineland	Vineland		Vineland	Graham-Kendall	Graham-Kendall
				Object Sorting	Rorschach
				Rorschach	Wechsler-Bellevue
				Stanford-Binet	Wechsler Memory
				Vineland	Weigl
				Weigl	

Discrepancy Current and Previous Intelligence			General Personality Problems		
Infant and Preschool	Child	Adoles. Adult	Infant and Preschool	Child	Adoles. Adult
Cattell	Arthur	Graham-Kendall		Rorschach	Rorschach
Stanford-Binet	Rorschach	Rorschach		Rosenzweig P-F	Rosenzweig P-F
Vineland	Object Sorting	Object Sorting		TAT	TAT
	Stanford-Binet	Vineland		Stanford-Binet	Wechsler-Bellevue
	Vineland	Wechsler-Bellevue		Object Sorting	Object Sorting
		Wechsler Memory			

Omitted from the table is any indication of tests suitable for appraising the personality problems of infants and preschool children. Although occasionally the devices mentioned for older children may be applied this is not often the case. Play materials or an interview with a reliable informant are probably to be more indicated. Referrals for investigation of vocational potentialities, general educational problems, or school subject disabilities, considered collectively as a group, as well as referrals for investigating change of status do not appear in the table because tests bearing most directly upon the first group are not included in this volume (interest, aptitude, and achievement measures) and the battery used in the second is related not to the kind of diagnostic problem but to any or all the other reasons for referral.

In one sense the classification under discussion is the reverse of that in Table 1. There the individual test as related to particular diagnostic functions was the focus of interest. Now the referral problem receives emphasis and a test is evaluated in terms of its relevance to the problem. Mention of several tests in connection with one problem is not meant to imply either that all of them are necessary with each patient or that tests other than those listed are not useful. Sometimes a shorter minimal battery is indicated.

INDIVIDUAL AND GROUP TESTING

It is possible to classify psychological tests by the number of individuals to whom they are administered at a given time. Accordingly the distinction between individual and group tests has arisen. Although in a few instances either group or individual administration is permissible, the tests described in this presentation are almost exclusively individually administered. To be sure, *screening* which may precede diagnosis is possible with group tests, but the diagnostic functions herein described can be carried out only in a rather crude fashion by measurements given to more than one person at a time. More often than not group measures are compromises in the face of large numbers to be dealt with in a short time and are used only to identify those in need of more intensive individual examination. As emphasis here is upon the individual and his adjustment, discussion of these more superficial measures would not be apropos.

Although objectivity perhaps may be achieved in group testing, clinicians are almost unanimous in their preference for individual administration. The advantages of individual tests are not difficult to isolate. As Hunt (30) points out, the principal advantage of the individual test over the group test is the opportunity it provides for observing the subject as he works. Not only is there a probability of understanding the patient better through such observations, but also they give the examiner a chance to adjust the testing situation to fit the patient. Group testing ignores inevitable variation in the motivation with which each individual being tested approaches the tasks and tacitly equates this factor for all subjects in the final analysis that is carried out. In individual testing, however, the clinician can take into account differences in motivation in interpreting the results or perhaps alter the drive level when it is recognized as being below the optimum. Certain conditions which are commonplace in individual sessions—procedure oriented toward establishing and maintaining rapport, variation of conditions to meet the needs of the patient, selection of tests designed to stimulate interest and offer encouragement—are almost unattainable in group testing.

THE USE OF PERSONALITY QUESTIONNAIRES IN CLINICAL PRACTICE

The various objections to structured personality questionnaires are quite well known (e.g., Ellis, 6; Ellis and Conrad, 7) and need not be reviewed here. Quite apart from such limitations, certain more specific issues must be considered when the clinical scene is the focus of interest. The uses of personality questionnaires that touch most directly upon the work of the clinician are their utilization as screening devices and as substitutes for the interview. As a screening device the questionnaire is a prolegomenon for clinical activity; it aids in locating some disturbed individuals with relative economy of time and effort of skilled personnel. Once the person in need of diagnostic and therapeutic services is located the questionnaire loses much of its value. Dealing with the single patient the clinician is interested not in identification, because this has already taken place, but in understanding and appraising him in a broader diagnostic sense. Screening, which is more in keeping with the tradition of group testing, is thus outside the major stream of diagnostic testing as here conceptualized, and the attendant problems of construction and validation of screening devices are somewhat alien to other diagnostic activities considered here.[8]

---

[8] For a recent discussion of personality tests used as screening devices see Zubin (26).

More pertinent to the present concern with tests used as diagnostic devices is the value of the questionnaire type of personality test in revealing something of what the patient thinks about himself, or more strictly what the patient consciously thinks he thinks about himself and what he is willing to reveal under the circumstances. In this way a personality questionnaire is a standardized interview in which the patient's self-report is secured. His opinions may or may not be valid in any real sense. It is erroneous to assume that the individual knows himself and is willing to tell the facts about himself. With the clinician's recognition of the dynamic nature of personality, with his acceptance of the importance of factors about which the patient is characteristically unaware, and with his appreciation of the semantic difficulties involved in answers to questionnaire items, there exists a denial of such a naïve misconception.

Most advocates of structured personality tests reject the ingenuous belief that a questionnaire response bears a one-to-one relation with either feeling or behavior. Meehl (14), for example, argues very persuasively that it is not necessary to accept answers to questionnaire items as surrogates for actual behavior. (Illustrative would be the acceptance of an affirmative answer to the question "Do you avoid crowds?" as one bit of information pointing to an introvertive tendency on the part of the respondent.) Instead, he contends, self-ratings on various items constitute "verbal behavior, the non-test correlates of which must be discovered by empirical means." (14, p. 297.)

This use of the questionnaire to find out the individual's beliefs is not unimportant because it offers a means whereby appreciation of the problems facing him and the means whereby they are being met may be analyzed. Since appraisal of the patient's insight is a necessary step in any complete study, the questionnaire affords a means of making it.

Despite the fact that this approach may be used for this purpose there is some question as to whether or not it is the most effective method therefor. One of the objections to the clinical use of personality questionnaires was the inescapable requirement of forcing answers into only two or three categories. Just as the requirements in courts of law for an answer of yes or no force the witness into stating what is a half-truth, so do the items of a questionnaire very often place a similar restriction upon the unhappy patient. This is a serious limitation in that the flexibility so prized in the interview is lost. Closely related to this limiting factor in the use of personality questionnaires in clinical practice is the customary treatment of a response to an item as if it had the same emotional import for each person tested. This cannot be accepted as sensible practice in the clinical setting. "Failing to make new friends easily" may be reported by an anxiety-ridden neurotic or by a mature person aware of his limitations. In rebuttal to both these arguments it might be argued that the patient may be questioned further once he has expressed himself concerning the items. This is, of course, possible but instigates the question of why a rigid compartmentalization should be forced when what is wanted is an "open end" answer.

Even if some limited usefulness in this area is admitted it would still be unnecessary to explore the various questionnaires in the same fashion as other diagnostic instruments are examined because their use does not depend upon a particular instrument. Indeed, to further this aim a judicious selection of items from a variety of different questionnaires to suit the convenience of the clinician and the unique characteristics of the patient might be the most profitable approach. If the items are thus treated, then scores or clusters of supposedly related items become pointless.

Lest this necessarily brief discussion be misinterpreted, a reiteration is in order: it is not contended that personality questionnaires are useless in all situations, but merely that in the clinical scene as described herein they have less value.

Bibliography follows Chapter 7.

Procedures in Diagnostic Testing

In the previous chapter emphasis was placed upon selection and description of diagnostic tests. In completing this discussion it is necessary to consider certain procedures involved in diagnostic testing apart from the instruments themselves. To be sure, the selection of tests for diagnostic use is intimately associated with that which goes on in a testing session. However, a variety of issues remain which are more directly procedural in nature. Among these are the manner of opening the testing session, administering tests, utilizing qualitative cues in diagnostic testing, recording test data, and preparing diagnostic testing reports.

OPENING THE TESTING SESSION

It is assumed that the clinician does not proceed with actual test administration until initial rapport has been established with the patient. The development of rapport as an aspect of diagnostic interviewing, discussed in Chapter 5, applies in all essentials to the sessions devoted primarily to psychological testing.[1] Sears makes the point that the maladjusted person to an even greater degree than the normal will react to the examiner or examination in such a fashion as to make it "symbolize (often on an unconscious level) parental dominance, schoolroom atmosphere, authority or 'the law'

---

[1] Chapter 12, concerned with diagnostic testing of infants and preschool children, considers development of rapport in a manner specific to these ages.

in ways tending to arouse hostile or fearful attitudes." (23, p. 480.) If for no other reason than to avert such attitudes, special care must be taken in opening the testing session.

This period of initial adjustment occupied with getting acquainted and placing the patient as much at ease as circumstances permit may be profitably used to ascertain pertinent background material such as educational level, a rough idea of his intelligence, presence or absence of physical handicaps, and so on. It is a period that may also be used to explore with the patient his understanding of the reasons for seeing the psychologist. This naturally leads to an explanation by the clinician of the purpose of the examination and attempts at eliciting coöperation, generally stated in terms of how the test results will help the patient with his difficulties.

The order of presentation of test instruments is of some significance in producing optimal motivation. Test order may be influenced by the patient's foreknowledge of the reasons for the examination. If he has been referred for exploration of vocational potentialities, tests obviously bearing on this might be given first in order to set the scene and to produce acceptance and coöperation. Measures considered worth while though not so obviously bearing on the reason for referral could be given later.

Other factors influencing test order may conflict with this consideration, though likewise they encourage optimal motivation. A test allowing some success (or at least not emphasizing that the patient is failing) is desirable as a first instrument; on the other hand, it should not be of insulting ease. Sometimes performance tests such as form boards are utilized as introductory tests because they serve as intermediate objects of neutral character which render the situation less personal. This sort of focus rather than a face-to-face question-and-answer period ameliorates the tension for the patient. Kent (11) stresses the inherent interest value of some test materials and suggests opening the examination not with standardized materials but with some task not subject to fixed rules and permitting interruption if interest fails to develop. She urges having available several highly varied instruments which may be used flexibly as the opening tasks.

There are, of course, situations which make for exceptions to these fairly common practices. With the very young, the psychotic, the negativistic, and the apprehensive different procedures might be followed. For example, with apprehensive patients who view the testing session as an ordeal it is well to cut short the preliminaries and proceed directly to the testing. Sometimes with juvenile delinquents or adult criminals one cannot enlist their coöperation in the time available, so that it is necessary to keep a firm hand on the situation.

Other considerations such as the necessity of economizing on time might influence test order. In such instances an initial test taking little time and allowing a quick rough grasp of some characteristic of the patient might be indicated. The results obtained might be sufficient to obviate more elaborate testing. For example, the Stanford-Binet Vocabulary is used by many clinicians, both as an icebreaker and as a means of helping to decide about further intelligence testing. Using this particular instrument does not have the earlier mentioned advantage of creating an initial situation softened by some material object and therefore beginning with this test is sometimes contraindicated.

ADMINISTERING DIAGNOSTIC TESTS

Every diagnostic testing device has something in the way of directions for administration that are to be adhered to in a more or less faithful fashion. Despite the fact that tests are made for man, and not man for tests, it is imperative that the clinician know the directions so well that he can follow them exactly (even if occasionally he knowingly violates them). Identical habits of administration make possible comparability from one patient to the next for the individual diagnostician, from one diagnostician to another within a given clinic, and from these to clinicians in other settings. Without adherence to directions for administration the testing scene would be utterly chaotic.

The greatest source of danger from differences in administration occurs not in deliberate recognized changes but in the unwitting changes that repeated administration may bring in its wake. Little "tricks" of handling the material are likely to appear and become so subtly ingrained that the clinician is not even aware that there has been a change of procedure. Mutual checking of techniques by fellow clinicians at intervals of about six months, although not common practice, is a reasonable precaution offering the additional advantage of making it possible to share those innovations judged desirable.

A controversial but crucial problem is the question of varying the administration to fit the characteristics of the particular patient. To vary or not to vary the test procedure is the dilemma of the Hamlet in psychological dress. Both alternatives can plausibly be defended in the sacred name of validity. The normative population has been given the test under standard directions and the validity of these norms hinges upon adherence to a similar procedure by the clinician. And yet the patient owing to his illness is not as motivated as the normative subjects, or is from a different age or cultural group, or has some handicap such as deafness which renders the typical procedure impracticable. Should the test be adapted to him, or should these differences be ignored in administration and appear only in discussion of results?

The individual most adequately compared to the norms is the one to whom the situation meant the same as it did to those comprising the standardization group. The question of whether or not to change the directions to suit circumstances arises because of a desire to examine the patient under the same conditions as those prevailing when the standardization group was examined. If the conditions are not the same a comparison to this group is difficult. In the opinion of the writer modifying the directions for testing in a fashion that would make the test *mean* the same to the patient as it did to this composite person is more important than rigid adherence to the directions. Preservation of literal directions in the face of personal variations makes it impossible to maintain equivalence of conditions and thus defeats the purpose of the instructions. Wells has expressed this point of view so cogently that a quotation is in order. He says:

An intelligent South Sea Islander, observing a psychometric examination, would be likely to regard it as a magic rite designed to propitiate friendly spirits in the patient's behalf. Should he observe a conscientious examiner in the apprentice stage, tightly clinging to forms prescribed, his idea would be confirmed, for none knows better than himself how slight a departure from the required formulae will not only destroy their beneficence but may well deliver the hapless sufferer into the hands of the malignant ghosts. Over against such esoteric views of psychometric methods is the customary and pragmatic one. The function of psychometrics is not the accomplishment of a ritual, but the understanding of the patient. The ceremony of mental tests is valuable so far as it serves to reach this end. When it fails, or stands in the way of doing this, proper technique demands that it be modified. Ability to do this intelligently is what distinguishes the psychologist, properly so called, from the "mental tester." (24, p. 27.)

There are still other occasions when exact administration may be sacrificed. These occur when the patient is stimulated by the situation to reveal important diagnostic material not relevant to the test material as such but nevertheless superseding it in importance. For example, the individual may expound at length on an important issue about which he has heretofore been very reticent, or he may reveal unsuspected deeper pathological trends such as delusions or hallucinations. It is the clinician's manifest duty in such instances to sacrifice exactitude of testing to exploration of this area with him. It is equally his responsibility to stress in his report the fact that scores obtained during this period of testing are suspect and should not have the significance which otherwise might be attached to them.[2]

If variation in administration when circumstances dictate is accepted as an integral part of clinical procedure, it follows that learning clinical adroitness in this area is an essential aspect of the training of the clinician. By the very nature of the problem there can be no blanket prescription, telling when and where to vary, as the cues for doing so are learned in the course of clinical experience. It should be obvious that such deviations from directions are not matters to be taken lightly and are to be avoided whenever possible; until experience is achieved the beginning clinician does well to follow rather exactly the directions for administration.

UTILIZING QUALITATIVE CUES IN DIAGNOSTIC TESTING

Cues significant both to personality dynamics and to diagnostic classification may be obtained by considering qualitative aspects of the responses given by the patient irrespective of their scoring. Questioning, in the form permissible under the directions for administration, aims not only at clarification of scoring but also at

---

[2] Common clinical practice calls for any alteration in techniques to be marked conspicuously on the test blank.

understanding why a particular response was chosen from the wealth of possibilities potentially open to the patient. Peculiar verbalizations or associations make mandatory inquiry into their meaning and significance.

The discussion of observation in the diagnostic testing session in Chapter 4 alluded to the fact that the clinician is interested in the patient's behavior because it influences test performance in addition to suggesting personality characteristics of diagnostic significance. If the performance is interfered with to the extent that a transitory personality picture is all that emerges, then the results cannot be said to be representative of the patient. Accordingly, it is necessary for the clinician to reach some decision as to whether or not his findings are representative, i.e., whether similar ones would be reported if the patient were retested after a brief period. The qualitative aspects of behavior provide valuable clues for making this judgment.

It would be manifestly impossible to describe all cues which point in the direction of nonrepresentativeness of the obtained results. Some suggestions have already been given in the rating report form in an earlier chapter—difficulty of establishing rapport, anxiety to such a degree as to lower functioning level, negativism, easy distractibility, etc. Jewett and Blanchard have supplied a useful list:

Slowness of response, necessity for repetition of instructions in order to elicit any reaction, irrelevant responses which indicate disordered associative processes rather than failure to comprehend the given situation, tendency to continued elaboration of the response to a preceding situation which interferes with the transference of the attention to the next problem presented, reaction to a situation in harmony with instructions given in connection with previous situations (perseveration)— these and other peculiarities of behavior should lead one to suspect the accuracy of results, because they are symptomatic of effective disturbances which interfere with intellectual accomplishment, even though the patient appears to put forth much effort on the examination. Indeed, this very intensity of effort is necessitated by the affective blocking, since the patient must make an exertion in order to overcome it and answer at all coherently. (10, p. 46.)

Attention now shifts to the use of these qualitative cues in identifying personality characteristics. Cofer regards the problem as an analysis of the concept of clinical intuition and reports upon the various kinds of subjective features which he believes enter into his diagnostic testing approach. No claim to novelty is made; on the contrary, both his experience in learning from other clinicians and the presumed commonality of his findings are stressed. His statement of the specific forms which these features take is of sufficient importance and clarity to quote extensively:

(1) The manner of verbal expression of the answer. This particular indication is of especial value in schizophrenic or schizoid conditions . . . although it may have significance in other conditions and for personality evaluation. For example, one patient, diagnosed schizoid personality, replied to the question, "Why should we stay away from bad company?", much as follows: "If one green apple is put with rotten apples, it will become rotten too." Asked to explain this further, he stated, "Birds of a feather flock together." When further explanation was requested, he said, "A person is known by the company he keeps." This manner of expression, obviously unusual, seems to reflect the inability to come to the point, the use of stilted, formal modes of expression often seen in the schizoid process. The patient apparently has the right idea; but he is unable to formulate it in any precise, straightforward way. . . .

(2) The quality of the reasoning. In his verbal expressions, as well as in his concrete performances, a patient may reveal the quality of his reasoning. It may be orderly, loose or bizarre. The goal may be lost. Or some structural deviation in the thinking may be revealed. For example, another schizoid patient, giving the similarity of a dog to a lion, responded in this way, 'They are not the same. They are different strains of animals. The dog comes from the wolf family, the lion from the cat family." Pressed further for a similarity, he stated that "both are meat eating animals." In this sequence, it is easily seen that the components of the correct answer are present. Yet the patient is unable to synthesize them, and in his final formulation stresses that they eat meat; the more abstract concept, animals, is underemphasized. In this instance we have clear indication of faulty reasoning and peculiar reasoning at that. The intellectual structure seems disorganized, even fractionated. Still other patients may show even more disorganization. . . .

(3) Rigidity or flexibility of method. It is noteworthy that on many tests, in addition to Goldstein's, patients are unable to adjust themselves to situations requiring different patterns of thought than those to which they are perhaps pathologically devoted. For example, I can recall one patient who did very poorly on the abstraction test of the Shipley-Hartford Scale. Among others, he was unable to solve the item which requires that the alphabet be continued backward. Asked what was his trouble on this test, he pointed out that you couldn't have the alphabet backwards. It doesn't go that way. Or we may have instances of series continuation such as 4, 5, 6, 7, 8, . . . instead of the correct 4, 5, 6, 5, 4, or phrase completions, such as "plank *steak* meals" rather than "plank

board meals." Such errors are almost always strongly suggestive diagnostically, always dependent of course upon the context in which they occur.

(4) Special aids to performance, such as tracing or covering parts of the material. In giving tests, one will occasionally encounter behavior such as this from a patient. In a Rorschach examination the other day, a patient who apparently was having considerable difficulty in deciding what he saw resorted to tracing the blot areas on which he was concentrating, or using his hands or a match book cover to cover the area in which he was not momentarily interested. It was as though he needed to reinforce his visual impressions through another sense that led to his tracing and as though conflicting or distracting stimulation had to be excluded by some very effective means (covering). In his case, such behavior seemed to stem from an organic disturbance, although I have seen such behavior in patients in whom there were no other organic indicators. One occasionally sees what is perhaps the same sort of thing in the digit memory test, in which a patient will in haste repeat the digits as though he could not "hold on" to them if he delayed a moment. This has occurred in cases with clear cut brain disease.

(5) Manipulation of the test material: "edging," rotation etc. Again in the Rorschach test one will sometimes encounter a patient who holds the cards at peculiar angles, and who thus gets peculiar views of the cards. This behavior seems to occur most often in schizophrenics. . . . We all have seen similar rotations in the block design tests or in the design memory tests from the Binet. Such behavior seems to come sometimes from organics, sometimes from schizophrenics. But it is always noteworthy and capable of providing clinical hunches.

(6) Lastly, I should like to consider the significance of specific responses. It is perhaps dubious that any given response can be pathognomic of a certain disorder. . . . Such features of performance may sometimes occur in the absence of other positive signs, and then the so-called intuitive process comes into being. (1, pp. 222–224.)[3]

Cofer concludes that these and other bases for qualitative or intuitive judgments really are unanalyzed, unrecorded, or even unverbalized observations, and that it is the task of the clinician to bring them into the open with the implication that they too may be objectified. However, a word of caution is imperative. Qualitative observations should not be neglected, but they should not be dignified by the belief that *inferences* about them are statements of certainty. All too often clinical inferences are not put to the crucial test of verification from other sources. Psychological super-

---

[3] Reprinted from "An analysis of the Concept of 'Clinical Intuition'" by C. N. Cofer in G. A. Kelly (ed.), "New Methods in Applied Psychology," (MS.), by permission of G. A. Kelly and the University of Maryland Student's Supply Store.

stition is decried, and yet if not careful a clinician can create flights of fancy only slightly more sophisticated but just as erroneous.

Clinical judgment of certain kinds of qualitative material, such as the manner of verbal expression, has been put to the test of controlled conditions. In a recent study by Klehr (12) test material consisting of the responses of the Comprehension and Similarities subtests of the Wechsler-Bellevue Scale and a short vocabulary test was available on three populations. The subjects consisted of twelve schizophrenics, twelve mental defectives, and twelve normals. Care was taken that clinicial opinion was unanimous in regard to the correctness of the diagnostic classification of each of these individuals. Fifteen experienced clinical psychologists and an equal number of relatively inexperienced graduate students served as judges. The responses of each of the thirty-six subjects were mimeographed on separate sheets, and the judges were asked to read the test responses and make a purely qualitative decision, unaided by objective scoring, of the group (schizophrenic, mentally defective, normal) into which each subject fell. These decisions were reached with the knowledge that among the thirty-six there were representatives of each of the three groups but without knowing how many of each type. Chance expectancy would lead to correct identification of four out of each group of twelve cases. The experienced clinicians as a group operated considerably above chance; the graduate students did not. For example, the experienced clinicians, on the average, correctly identified about seven out of the twelve schizophrenics, only five being incorrectly identified as defective or normal. When it is remembered that the situation was artificial—the only material available being a mimeographed statement of some thirty-six test item responses—it is reasonable to state, as does Klehr, that clinical judgment in the actual testing situation would be even more effective. Clinical experience, it would appear, does improve diagnostic accuracy.

The need is imperative to objectify, or at least to specify, the various clinical signs which are interpreted by the clinical psychologist as demonstrating the presence of some conditions of diagnostic significance. A beginning has been made in such studies as that of Rashkis and Welsh (19). They were concerned with the detection of anxiety when the Wechsler-Bellevue Scale was being administered. Some anxiety, of course, is natural on facing a psychological examination. The problem is to identify cases in which anxiety is a prominent feature and to be able to differentiate these from cases in which anxiety plays little or no part. The four of the twelve signs they isolated which appear to be most effective will serve as illustrations:

T (emporary) I (nefficiency) on Block Design. (a) Simple errors in the placing of one or two blocks in the more difficult designs. The error is usually in the lower right hand corner of the pattern. (b) Loss of time due to failure to begin immediately, stopping temporarily during the course of the solution, or fumbling in turning up the proper face of the block and fitting it into the design. (See also *Compensatory Psychomotor Activity.*)

Apprehension. (a) Continual questioning of the examiner as to the purpose of the test. (b) Expressions of inadequacy. (c) Excessive concern as to the correctness of the response. (d) Insistence on knowing the correct response after an admitted failure.

Compensatory Psychomotor Activity. Fidgeting, squirming and shifting the position in the chair, gum chewing, laughing, whistling, making vague exclamatory noises, toying with the test materials, drumming on the table, tapping the foot, etc. (to be distinguished by the examiner from hebephrenic or hypomanic behavior).

Distractibility. (a) Undue attention to stimuli external to the test situation, or to irrelevant stimuli within the test situation. (b) Fluctuation of interest and attentivity. (19, p. 355.)

Somatic complaints and physical signs and other forms of temporary inefficiency, including inefficiency of Digit Span, were generally less discriminating. Their data contained too few cases to establish any statistical significance for the differences found but their results are extremely suggestive and point to an approach worthy of further investigation. It is of some significance that three of the four most useful "signs" are of more general applicability than merely in the Wechsler-Bellevue testing situation. Apprehension, compensatory psychomotor activity, and distractibility as indicators of anxiety may have similar significance irrespective of the testing instrument. Nevertheless, anchoring the findings to a specific test and the simultaneous use of signs drawn directly from the materials (such as temporary inefficiency on Block Design) will help in the objectification of such diagnostic aids.

The results of these studies might be said to lend some encouragement to the conviction held by most clinicians that judgments they make on test materials exclusive of the psychometric findings.

approach a fairly high level of accuracy and also that these signs may be objectified. As there is a paucity of experimental evidence these must be considered more as optimistic hopes than verified convictions. Nevertheless, clinical psychologists will continue to utilize such judgments. By accepting this privilege it becomes their obligation as research men to submit the judgments to scientific scrutiny.

RECORDING TEST DATA

Essential both to clinical practice and to research is the complete recording of the patient's responses. The actual phrases and sentences used and the movements made often are highly illuminating. Experience has shown that it is not enough to record only those responses which strike the clinician as significant at the time they occur; retrospective examination by the psychologist or by other clinicians may bring out overlooked inferences which would have been lost if the full response had not been recorded. Since the relatively inexperienced examiner is less likely to sense the significance of the response at the time it is given he finds it necessary to record responses verbatim to an even greater extent than the more experienced clinician. To err on the side of copiousness is generally considered better than to do so in the direction of skimpy recording. To use the former emphasis means at most a few minutes' more work whereas if the latter is adopted the material may be irretrievably lost.

Stereotyped abbreviations or symbols for right and wrong are not encouraged unless it is manifestly impossible to find any meaning in the response except its psychometric value. "DK" for the answer "I don't know" and "+" for the correct single-word answers may be suitable, but even in such apparently simple matters one can err in failing to use verbatim recording. For example, nuances of meaning of interpretative significance may be lost as a result of too cursory recording of the various ways of disclaiming knowledge. Entries of "DK" for "don't know" may conceivably mean any one of the following: "I don't know"; "How should I know?"; "I don't know, it's my fault I don't know, I'm not good at this sort of thing or anything else"; "I once knew but the Masons have robbed me of my thought"; "It is something that was once within my powers of awareness"; "This is really using my imagination, but

—no I really can't say." No pathognomic significance can be attached to any one of these responses in itself, but in conjunction with the rest of the record it may be diagnostically meaningful. The recording of test responses is but a means to an end—the diagnostic interpretation of the findings. This matter of interpretation either for the clinician's own application in the therapeutic tasks that lie ahead or for the guidance of his colleagues can best be stated through the framework of a discussion of reports on psychological testing.

REPORTS OF DIAGNOSTIC TESTING SESSIONS

Judging by the dearth of publications on the *format* of psychological reports, clinical psychologists have not been particularly concerned with the format as a problem. Many excellent reports have appeared. It is evident, however, that the skill they demonstrate in reporting is not so much a matter of explicit deliberation and common agreement as it is a matter of individual flair, often unverbalized, that has led to the development of a particular appropriate style. In any case, hardly anything specifically concerned with this aspect of the work of the clinical psychologist has appeared in the professional journals. This is in marked contrast to the situation prevailing among the members of both the social work and the psychiatric professions, particularly the former. For some time now they have given both explicit and extensive consideration to the nature of their reports in terms of generally accepted principles adapted to the purposes at hand. This lack of explicit discussion among psychologists is all the more surprising when one considers the self-evident fact that the qualifications of a psychologist are often judged by his professional colleagues on the basis of the quality of the reports he renders concerning the patients seen by him.

AIMS OF THE REPORT OF DIAGNOSTIC TESTING

A report of diagnostic testing differs according to the setting in which it is made and, more important, according to the patient. The focus of the report is the patient: In what way can the results be used to understand and help the patient? In what ways can the results be given so that they may be used in dealing with the patient therapeutically?

The most useful report is concise and attempts to answer the questions directed at the psychologist when the case is referred to him. (This would include self-referral when the psychologist is acting as the sole clinician.) In effect, the reasons for referral are hypotheses advanced by the referring clinician as worthy of investigation because he feels they account at least in part for the patient's difficulties. Accordingly, the psychologist explores these areas, reports his findings, and evaluates their validity. The intent of the report thus never becomes routinized since the material that emerges reveals a new pattern with each case.

This emphasis on answering the questions put to the psychologist does not mean that other material should be excluded, especially if there is reason to believe that what has been found might not be known to the referring clinician or agency. Discrepancies between psychological findings and information from other sources also should be recognized and explicitly but tactfully mentioned. If reasons for these discrepancies are recognized, they too should be given in the report.

INTERPRETATION IN THE DIAGNOSTIC TESTING REPORT

The primacy of the interpretative phase over the merely descriptive discussed in Chapter 2 is fundamental in psychological reporting not only when the psychologist has full case responsibility but also when he functions as a consultant. In the situation in which he carries on beyond diagnosis, he will generally be on the alert for clues which give him understanding about what has happened, and thus will have some leads as to what to do. Unfortunately this is not always the case when he is acting as a consultant and disposition, so far as he personally is concerned, culminates in his written report. We psychologists are sometimes too enamored of our test scores. They are reported as if they automatically sum up the particular case. It is too much to expect that the sheer reporting of scores will confer upon the referring clinician the ability to utilize them. Psychiatrists are likely to find a certain nightmarish quality to the psychologist's examination when the principal facts triumphantly reported are that the IQ is 92, the child reads at the fifth-grade level although he is actually in the sixth grade, and he coöperated readily. Meanwhile the child is driving the mother (and the psychiatrist) to distraction, is headed for the reform school or mental hospital, and is making his younger sister's life a miniature hell. The findings of the psychologist

are undoubtedly correct and the description is accurate, but in a
report they are almost as meaningless as a count of the freckles on
the child's face. Test scores are not enough; the interpretation of
what they mean in the setting of the difficulties exhibited must be
included.

Rosenzweig presents the matter so well that a quotation is highly
appropriate.

Such interpretation requires not only a knowledge of the several test
instruments but an understanding of personality dynamics—the principles in terms of which the person expresses his capacities, needs and
traits at various levels of organization—and the ability to comprehend in
terms of such principles the syntax and semantics of the individual as
these emerge from the subject's every psychologic expression. In such a
framework every act or statement of the person can be construed to yield
an understanding of him; and the incidental examination behavior as
well as the more formal test findings fall into place according to the
psychodynamics of personality through which all individual expression is
mediated.

Under the circumstances described, it is obviously impossible to expound any set of rules or even principles which will assure the accomplishment of an integrated understanding of the individual subject. It
may, however, be briefly indicated how the psychologist, operating with
the assumed special aptitudes, knowledge and experience, ordinarily attempts, explicitly or implicitly, to fit together his observations in a psychologic report. Taking it for granted that all expressions of the personality are, if properly understood, meaningfully related to each other, the
interpreter attempts to single out the cardinal strengths and weaknesses,
drives and interests, attitudes and symptoms in terms of which the various manifestations of the person seem to be most significantly oriented.
To arrive at such basic axes of the personality considerable cogitative experimentation is required in every case analysis. One hypothesis as to
these cardinal forces or facets may be adopted, tried, found wanting or
corroborated up to a certain point; then dropped, perhaps, in favor of
some other hypothesis which must in turn be subjected to similar experimental manipulation. The process demands time and persistence as
well as skill. Without the weighing and balancing of one finding against
another and of both against some third or fourth aspect of the behavior,
repeatedly and patiently, the process of insightful comprehension demanded of the clinician cannot be achieved. In this context it may be
decided to employ some previously unconsidered test or other mode of
observation as a basis for checking an hypothesis that has emerged. Thus
every individual subject becomes a research project in his own right.

The method of interpretation outlined may with certain advantages
be designated that of the *minimum hypothesis*. The picture of the sub-

ject that will in the end be embodied in the psychologic report must account for the largest number of possible observations and facts in terms of the smallest number of underlying or explanatory variables. When two alternative interpretations are in competition, the foregoing statement provides the only currently accepted basis for deciding between them. Such an approach, while not explicit in the text books, is implicit in the actual work of every psychodynamic clinician. (20, pp. 187–188.)[4]

Schafer (21) indicates that the process whereby test findings assume interpretative significance is that of insight on the part of the examiner—the field becomes structured in such a fashion that there is an internally consistent and coherent picture of the individual patient. Such subjective integration is essential because many aspects of the patient's behavior elude quantification, just as does an overall conception of his personality.

This does not mean, however, that the synthesis is not objective, but quite the contrary, as Schafer says:

That the diagnostic process will occur "within" the clinician is of course obvious; in this sense it will be subjective; it will not be worked out on a comptometer. However, that the diagnostic process is neither verifiable nor communicable—and in this sense not objective—is an entirely different proposition and one which we must reject. Objectivity is not established by popular agreement or by purely quantitative thinking but only by agreement among *competent* observers. In this word *competent* lies the necessary condition for establishing the validity of test findings. Verifiability of diagnostic conclusions or predictions is possible where competent analysis of case history and current status has been carried out separately from diagnostic analysis and where the results of these two processes of insight are checked against each other. *Communicability* is a more difficult criterion of objectivity to meet. Recognizing as we do that every case represents an essentially unique dynamic picture, we cannot justifiably attempt to teach mechanical rules of interpretation. But we should attempt to introduce into the thinking of the apt student a number of figural considerations—in other words, a frame of reference—which will limit and specify the directions available to the process of diagnostic insight. This frame of reference will include *basic psychodynamic theory, test rationale, familiarity with previous findings and self-knowledge.* This is the basis on which agreement among competent diagnosticians or in other words objectivity can be established. (21, pp. 6–7.)

[4] Reprinted from *Psychodiagnosis* by S. Rosenzweig with K. L. Kogan, by permission of Grune & Stratton. Copyright 1949 by Grune & Stratton.

ORGANIZATION OF THE REPORT

Since clinicians are busy people some thought must be given to the organization of the findings of the psychologist in a fashion to permit selection. Solid pages of material—relevant and irrelevant, important and unimportant—will probably result in a quick skimming with a good chance that the referring clinician will miss what the psychologist especially wants him to know. Some organization is indispensable. Two customary procedures lend themselves readily to this need for organization: either the use of subheads (these may name the specific tests used or the phases of personality investigated), a summary, or both. Sometimes the summary is given as the first, not the last, section of the report! The essential quantitative findings are set off from the rest of the report by some means of emphasis such as centering on the page.

Generally it is customary for the psychologist to report to his nonpsychologically trained colleagues his interpretation of his findings—not the original test protocols or details of the scoring. (These are kept in a psychological test file along with a copy of the report open to those who have the necessary background to evaluate the findings at this level of organization.)

The findings presented in the formal reports to the referring party are, for the most part, kept free of the esoteric but convenient shorthand that has developed around test instruments, e.g., M:ΣC, vocabulary scatter and K score. This technical jargon is useful in discussion with psychologist and other initiates. However, in *psychological reports* in the clinical setting it must be avoided. Its appearance in such reports will be interpreted by the colleagues of the psychologist as a sign of either inability to make or insecurity about making the translation to the language shared with other clinicians.

In almost all instances more than one psychological instrument is used along with the findings from other aspects of the case study which are relevant and available. Accordingly, the task of the psychologist includes integration of all findings in his report rather than mere reporting of isolated material. Thus test data of diagnostic value arise from the reinforcement of conclusions drawn from findings on one instrument by those obtained with another. For example, the findings in regard to intellectual functioning obtained with the Wechsler-Bellevue Intelligence Scales are frequently better understood when considered in conjunction with information on intellectual functioning obtained from the Rorschach Ink Blots. Failure to function at full capacity, suspected by the clinician on the basis of the results of the former instrument, may or may not be verified by analysis of the responses to the Rorschach Blots. The cumulative consistency (or inconsistency) emerging from the analysis of the findings of several instruments does much to establish the plausibility, if not the validity, of the final formulation.

The approaches utilized by several clinicians will be examined. In this connection the formats used by Sarason and Sarason (32) and Rosenzweig and Clark (31) are pertinent. The account of Sarason and Sarason, concerned with a diagnostic problem in feeble-mindedness, illustrates effectively the approach through organization around tests. After a report of an interview with the parents (not necessarily conducted by the psychologist) a psychological report in the narrower sense is given. First general observations are presented. These include the child's appearance, degree of contact with the testing sessions, mood changes, the nature and extent of the emotion exhibited, and so on.[5] Test results are presented in a tabular summary and then discussed one by one, e.g., Terman-Merrill, Metropolitan Achievement, Rorschach, etc.

Rosenzweig and Clark (31) in their account of the integration of psychiatric and psychological findings present a case report concerning a psychotic ex-soldier which illustrates the approach through division of the psychological report into aspects of personality. A very short summary of test results stated in terms of test instruments is presented, e.g., "Wells Memory Test—Memory Quotient 76— Interpretation: Memory loss. Not optimal." Then the patient's attitude during the testing sessions is analyzed in terms of cooperation, attention, muscular activity, speech, posture, and general representativeness of the results elicited. The bulk of the report is organized around the headings of (1) intellectual functions, (2) personality structure and dynamics, (3) reactions to frustration, (4) indications of insight. The findings are presented in this sequence, each beginning with a short summary followed by test-by-test description.

---

[5] More detailed examination of observation as a technique of the clinical method was made in Chapter 4.

Whenever pertinent, a test discussed in another section is again mentioned, and any relevant related information is integrated with that previously presented.

Both the approach through tests as the focal point and that through aspects of personality have much to recommend them, and they merge imperceptibly since diverse tests are generally more revealing of one aspect of personality than another. In the "test centering approach" there is the implication that intellectual functioning is identified more with a specific test, e.g., "Stanford-Binet Findings," than with some other instruments used with the same patient. Thus in essence both approaches use aspects of the patient's personality as the method of organization. It is generally agreed even by those who organize their reports under test headings that emphasis should be on the patient, not the test.

Regardless of the individuality which may characterize the body of reports a summary and recommendation section is often included. The recommendations consist of suggestions as to how the psychological findings may be utilized for therapeutic ends either by further referral to other sources or through the psychotherapeutic efforts of the therapist who requested the diagnostic study. Special emphasis is placed upon the problems posed by the referring source. It is in the summary that clinical acumen of the highest order is necessary. Here, more than in any other section of the report, ability to integrate the findings from tests, observations, and history is necessary.

An Illustrative Psychological Report

As a means of summarizing the previous discussion, a psychological report is given.[6] The psychiatrist attending this patient while she was on the ward of an inpatient service in a general hospital referred her to the psychologist with the request that there be an evaluation of intellectual level and personality functioning.

This report might be read with the following points of the previous general presentation in mind. It should be noted that more than one testing device was used and that the findings from the various instruments were integrated into a coherent whole. For example, there was reinforcement of the material elicited about intellectual

---

[6] Permission to quote this report was extended by Dr. Ivan N. Mensh. This courtesy is gratefully acknowledged.

functioning as demonstrated by the intelligence test findings and other findings arising from use of the projective measures. The focus, it will be noted, is the patient, not the test.[7] Test scores, as such, are not stressed.

The report is written with the more general reasons for referral (evaluation of intellectual level and personality functioning) in mind. On the other hand, aspects of the patient's functioning perhaps not known to the referring clinician and not directly in line with these reasons for referral are discussed. The report is atypical only in its brevity and relative simplicity. For the present purposes these are not disadvantages.

PSYCHOLOGICAL REPORT ON MRS. W.

Age: 25
Date of Examination: 3–25/49
Referred for evaluation of intellectual level and personality functioning.

General Observations: Mrs. W. is a 25-year-old brunette who married at 15 and was divorced at 21. She has two children, ages 8 and 6. One of 11 children herself, she said that the children married as soon as they were old enough to get out of the home. She reports as her principal complaints crying spells, itchy feelings, feelings of tension, and a dread in expecting something "terrible to happen." People "get on her nerves" and "bother" her a lot. She says that she has no appetite, can't lie down for a rest, gets the jitters if she stays in bed, believes she is more nervous in the hospital than at home where she could "get up and do something." She was told that she had a "nervous breakdown," and she emphasizes her weight loss (nearly 80 pounds in less than one year). Although a gain in weight from 134 to 194 pounds which she experienced during her first pregnancy, two years after her marriage, seems as significant, to her the weight loss is much more important.

The general picture of test behavior was one of euphoria and hyperactivity. In structured test situations this euphoria and hyperactivity was especially noticeable. However, in the unstructured situations in which projective materials were used she was more controlled, quieter, and frequently rejected stimulation. For example, in response to one set of materials she could "think of nothing to write"; she was extremely defensive; her euphoria dropped away almost completely; she smiled anx-

---

[7] In fact, in this report the tests are not even mentioned by name. It might be added that they include the Wechsler-Bellevue, the Rorschach Ink Blots, and the Thematic Apperception Test.

iously; and her responses were highly superficial. She rejected nearly 50 per cent of the material, and despite these rejections took more than three times the average response time.

This change from euphoria and hyperactivity was even more noticeable with the TAT cards. She very suddenly developed a "splitting headache," could make nothing out of the material, asked if it could be done at some other time, looked out of the window and at the examiner. Nervous movements ceased, and she repeatedly stalled for time. In 36 minutes of testing she was able to report only one line for each of 6 stimulus cards. The picture was that of a person who had had the wind taken out of her sails.

Intellectual Functioning: Mrs. W. earned a full scale I.Q. of 80, which is at the lower limit of the dull normal intellect. The Verbal I.Q. of 74 is in the borderline defective range; performance quality I.Q. of 89 approaches the level of the average adult of her age. The vocabulary level and facility is dull normal. The peak performance on any item was at the average intellectual level, and her poorest performance was within the range of the mentally defective. She did most poorly on items sampling fund of information, attention and concentration, and mental alertness. There was a typically dull quality to items testing new learning, social intelligence and those requiring analysis and abstraction. Although the intellectual performance must be evaluated against the background of her education (fifth-grade), home environment and work situation—none of which suggest intellectual stimulation—the test results obtained appear to be representative of the intellectual functioning of this patient.

Personality Evaluation: This is an uncritical, impractical individual who feels inferior and frequently verbalizes self-depreciating statements. The record suggests mental deficiency with an inability to see human percepts, few popular responses, many uncritical whole responses. The record is generally unproductive. There is an absence of fantasy life, but a high level of emotionality which is poorly controlled and immature. She lacks the ability to handle adequately emotional stimulation and her own responses to such stimulation. She is quickly reactive to affective stimuli, but only in one instance did she show evidence of any adult control. The principal area of concern seems to be in heterosexual relationships, with three-fourths of her responses concerning anatomy or sex; one-third of these, an unusually high proportion, refer specifically to the sex organs. Furthermore, she rejected the cards which usually elicit frank sexual responses. The content of her thinking reveals principally anxiety, concern about illness and consequent depression and hostility as well as difficulty in relationships with men.

Problems for therapy seem to be numerous and include low intellectual level, a guarding of material, absence of fantasy, poor emotional control and lack of aggressive energy. Assets in therapy presently are seen only in the measure of intellectual control maintained, and the potentiality for more mature affective relationships.

Summary: This 25-year-old divorcee has dull normal intelligence. Vocabulary level (dull normal) is higher than her general verbal intelligence which is in the borderline defective range. The handling of manual and other performance items is significantly better than of verbal tasks. Fifth grade education plus little stimulation in the home and work situations are reflected in the intellectual performance.

The personality picture is that of an unanalytical, impractical individual, without aggressive energy, who is much concerned with sexual material. Although she is quickly reactive to emotional stimulation, her control is poor, and she lacks the ability to handle adequately her emotional responses.

There are problems for therapy in the low intellectual level, absence of fantasy activity, poor emotional control, lack of aggressive energy, anxiety, and self-depreciating attitude. Affective contact and the maintenance of intellectual control are presently the only assets which appear to be available.

Euphoria and hyperactivity characterized her behavior at one stage of the examination, but later in unstructured situations completely disappeared, leaving her quiet, defensive, guarded, and hypoactive.

BIBLIOGRAPHY

1. Cofer, C. N., An analysis of the concept of "clinical intuition," in Kelly, G. A. (ed.), New methods in applied psychology (MS.), University of Maryland, 1947, pp. 219–227.
2. Cornell, E. L., and Coxe, W. W., A *performance ability scale: examination manual*, World Book Co., 1934.
3. Cronbach, L. J., Test "reliability": its meaning and determination, *Psychometrika*, 1947, 12:1–16.
4. Cronbach, L. J., *Essentials of psychological testing*, Harper & Brothers, 1949.
5. DiMichael, S. G., Characteristics of a desirable psychological report to the vocational counselor, *J. consult. Psychol.*, 1948, 12:432–437.
6. Ellis, A., The validity of personality questionnaires, *Psychol. Bull.*, 1946, 43:385–440.
7. Ellis, A., and Conrad, H. S., The validity of personality inventories in military practice, *Psychol. Bull.*, 1948, 45:385–426.
8. Freeman, F. N., *Mental tests: their history, principles and applications*, Houghton Mifflin Company, rev. ed., 1939.
9. Hutt, M. L., What did the clinical psychologist learn from the war? *Ann. N.Y. Acad. Sci.*, 1948, 49:907–912.
10. Jewett, S., and Blanchard, P., The influence of affective disturbance on responses to the Stanford-Binet test, *Ment. Hyg., N.Y.*, 1922, 6:39–56.
11. Kent, G. H., Use and abuse of mental tests in clinical diagnosis, *Psychol. Rec.*, 1938, 2:391–400.

12. Klehr, H., Clinical intuition and test scores as a basis for diagnosis, *J. consult. Psychol.*, 1949, 13:34–38.
13. Magaret, A., Intelligence testing and clinical practice, in Pennington, L. A., and Berg, I. A. (eds.), *An introduction to clinical psychology*, The Ronald Press Company, 1948, pp. 353–379.
14. Meehl, P. E., The dynamics of "structured" personality tests, *J. clin. Psychol.*, 1945, 1:296–303.
15. Menninger, K., Rapaport, D., and Schafer, R., The new role of psychological testing in psychiatry, *Amer. J. Psychiat.*, 1947, 103:473–476.
16. Mensh, I. N., Statistical techniques in present-day psychodiagnostics. *Psychol. Bull.*, 1950, 47:475–492.
17. Peatman, J. G., On the meaning of a test score in psychological measurement, *Amer. J. Orthopsychiat.*, 1939, 9:23–47.
18. Rapaport, D., et al., *Diagnostic psychological testing*, Vol. I, Year Book Publishers, 1945.
19. Rashkis, H. A., and Welsh, G. S., Detection of anxiety by use of the Wechsler Scale, *J. clin. Psychol.*, 1946, 2:354–357.
20. Rosenzweig, S., with Kogan, K. L., *Psychodiagnosis: an introduction to tests in the clinical practice of psychodynamics*, Grune & Stratton, 1949.
21. Schafer, R., On the objective and subjective aspects of diagnostic testing, *J. consult. Psychol.*, 1948, 12:4–7.
22. Schafer, R., Psychological tests in clinical research, *J. consult. Psychol.*, 1949, 13:328–334.
23. Sears, R., Motivation factors in aptitude testing, *Amer. J. Orthopsychiat.*, 1943, 13:468–492.
24. Wells, F. L., *Mental tests in clinical practice*, World Book Co., 1927.
25. Wells, F. L., and Ruesch, J. (eds.), *Mental examiners handbook*, Psychological Corporation, 2nd ed., 1945.
26. Zubin, J., Recent advances in screening the emotionally maladjusted, *J. clin. Psychol.*, 1948, 4:56–63.
27. Zubin, J., with Young, K. M., Manual of projective and cognate techniques, College Typing Co., 1948 (mimeographed).

Supplementary articles in Watson, R. I. (ed.), *Readings in the clinical method in psychology*, Harper & Brothers, 1949:

28. Doll, E. A., Psychometric pitfalls in clinical practice. Pp. 187–199. (Also in *J. consult. Psychol.*, 1947, 11:12–20.)
29. Hubbard, R. M., What constitutes a psychological examination? Pp. 334–348. (Also in *Amer. J. Orthopsychiat.*, 1940, 10:152–162.)
30. Hunt, W. A., The future of diagnostic testing in clinical psychology. Pp. 395–404. (Also in *J. clin. Psychol.*, 1946, 2:311–317.)

DIAGNOSTIC TESTING REPORTS

31. Rosenzweig, S., and Clark, R. A., The personality of a psychotic ex-soldier. Pp. 299–313. (Also in *J. abnorm. Soc. Psychol.*, 1945, 40:195–204.)
32. Sarason, E. K., and Sarason, S. B., A problem in diagnosing feeble-mindedness. Pp. 314–324. (Also in *J. abnorm. Soc. Psychol.*, 1945, 40:323–329.)
33. Taylor, J. L., and Teicher, A., A clinical approach to reporting psychological test data. Pp. 244–258. (Also in *J. clin. Psychol.*, 1946, 2:323–332.)

GENERAL SOURCES OF TEST INFORMATION

34. Buros, O. K., (ed.), Educational, psychological and personality tests of 1933, 1934, and 1935. Studies in Education No. 9., *Rutgers University Bulletin*, 1936, No. 13.
35. Buros, O. K., (ed.), *The 1938 mental measurements yearbook*, Rutgers University Press, 1938.
36. Buros, O. K., (ed.), *The 1940 mental measurements yearbook*, Mental Measurements Yearbook, 1941.
37. Buros, O. K., (ed.), *The third mental measurements yearbook*, Rutgers University Press, 1949.
38. Garrett, H. E., and Schneck, M. R., *Psychological tests, methods, and results*, Harper & Brothers, 1933.
39. Hildreth, G. H., A *bibliography of mental tests and rating scales*, Psychological Corporation, 2nd. rev. ed., 1939.
40. Hildreth, G., A *bibliography of mental tests and rating scales: 1945* supplement, Psychological Corporation, 1946.

CHAPTER 8

The Wechsler-Bellevue Intelligence Scale[1]

The difficulties which until recently faced the clinician when he was called upon to evaluate the intellectual functioning of adults are well known. Such individually administered devices as the Stanford-Binet were standardized upon children, and their use with adults went beyond the age groups upon which they were standardized. In addition the assumption of a constant mental age which neither increased nor decreased after a given point of chronological age created certain theoretical and practical difficulties to be discussed later. Tests standardized on younger subjects purposely contained items which would appeal to their level of interests. By the same token, many of the items would appear childish to older individuals. Another limitation not confined particularly to any age group was the frequently encountered necessity of supplementing an intelligence test predominantly or entirely verbal in nature with a test less dependent upon verbal abilities. Thus "performance" testing requiring the use of a different set of norms would be introduced, with the consequent uncertainty about the relation of the two sets of scores. The Wechsler-Bellevue Intelligence Scale was explicitly designed to

---

[1] This chapter is intended to supplement Wechsler (59), *The Measurement of Adult Intelligence*. Familiarity with this volume is essential to the use of the test. Consequently much pertinent material is not covered here. Reviews of the literature concerning this test have been published by Rabin (48) and Watson (58).

overcome these inadequacies and accordingly its appearance in 1939 was hailed with enthusiasm.

Subjects for standardization were adults selected from a wide age range and with a correction introduced for differences in age (to be described later). Quite apart from this immediately obvious value of its standardization on adults, it possessed certain other features which recommended it to practicing clinicians. The standardization was careful and included tryout and normative groups of a sufficiently large size; speed was to some degree minimized and power quite properly stressed; the subtests were selected with an eye to their clinical meaningfulness as well as for their contribution to the total score; both performance and verbal materials were included in defining an individual patient's general intelligence level; administration time is comparatively brief; satisfactory validity and reliability have been demonstrated, and the application of the statistical technique of the standard score made it possible for comparison of subtest scores to be carried out readily and meaningfully. A description and evaluation of this measure is the purpose of this chapter.

Wechsler explicitly states his conception of the nature of intelligence: "Intelligence is the aggregate or global capacity of the individual to act purposefully, to think rationally and to deal effectively with his environment." (59, p. 3.) He goes on to point out it is global in the sense of embracing the person's behavior as a unit and yet it is an aggregate because the functions of which it is composed may be differentiated. Behavior is determined also by other factors such as drives and incentives which influence this inclusive capacity.

DESCRIPTION OF THE SCALE

The Wechsler-Bellevue Intelligence Scale, an individually administered point scale, consists of eleven subtests applicable for ages ten to sixty and older.[2] The six subtests which Wechsler calls collectively

---

[2] There are two forms of the scale available but since at present most of our information is couched in terms of Form I it will suffice to say that Form II is constructed on the same general pattern and is composed of material similar to that of the more commonly used Form I. At present the literature on the standardization of the second form is quite scanty. Essentially the only data supplied by Wechsler in the manual (60) are to the effect that norms are based on 1000 male adults, eighteen to forty, that preliminary comparison shows a "high correlation" between the scales, that there is a mean difference of less than two points between the Full Scale scores of Forms I and II, and that there is only a "small difference" in retest scores in the subtests. Although

the Verbal Scale are entitled General Information, General Comprehension, Digit Span, Arithmetic, Similarities, and Vocabulary. The
so-called Performance Scale includes Picture Arrangement, Picture
Completion, Block Design, Object Assembly, and Digit Symbol. In
the Verbal subtests the responses to verbal stimuli are given orally
by the patient. The Performance subtests include some in which
manipulation by the patient is important and others in which this
element is at a minimum.

The items within a given subtest are arranged in order of difficulty
as found by Wechsler on standardization. Nevertheless, evidence
has been advanced by Jastak (33) on the basis of an item analysis of
1600 cases that many items are misplaced. On only one subtest, Digit
Span, did he find perfect agreement with Wechsler's order of presentation. Familiarity with his findings would aid the clinician in understanding otherwise puzzling discrepancies in the sequence of successes and failures.

A brief description of each of these subjects seems indicated.

GENERAL INFORMATION

There are twenty-five items in the General Information subtest
which become progressively more difficult to answer. A representative easy item is "How many pints make a quart?" "What is ethnol-
ogy?" is an example of one of the more difficult ones. Each response
is scored either 1 (correct) or 0 (incorrect). The total score is the
sum of the raw scores of all correct responses.

---

the directions are deceptively similar, close scrutiny will show a considerable
number of minor changes in wording which make for greater surface clarity
than do the directions for Form I.

The only study at time of writing that has appeared concerning the relationship between the Wechsler-Bellevue Form I and Form II is that of Gibby (19).
Only thirty-two psychoneurotic males were involved, necessitating cautious
interpretation of the results, but his findings, nevertheless, are disconcerting.
He found that although the correlations between verbal, performance, and
total IQ's on the two forms were substantial, ranging from .76 to .87, subtest
differences were very prominent. These differences took the form of both substantial score differences on the same subtest and low correlations between the
same subtests. Comprehension and Arithmetic were substantially more difficult
on Form II. The correlation between subtests of Form I and Form II ranged
from .20 in Comprehension to .93 in Vocabulary.

In the absence of other information it is well to withhold judgment on the
apparently serious discrepancies that exist. Certainly any other application of
Form II as the equivalent of Form I except in the derivation of IQ's is hazardous at the present time.

GENERAL COMPREHENSION

The ten items in General Comprehension tap a minimum of educationally acquired information and stress instead qualities of practical judgment. Responses are scored either o, 1, or 2. Among the easier items is "Why should we keep away from bad company?" A somewhat more difficult one is "Why does the state require people to get a license in order to be married?"

ARITHMETIC

The Arithmetic subtest comprises ten problems to be solved without benefit of pencil or paper. It has, unlike the previous two subtests, time limits for each item as well as bonus time credits for the last two problems. For the person of average intellectual ability the time limits are rather generous. A representative easier item asks, "How many oranges can you buy for thirty-six cents if one orange costs four cents?" One of the two more difficult items (presented in writing rather than orally) asks, "If a train goes 150 yards in ten seconds, how many *feet* can it go in one fifth of a second?"

DIGITS

The Digits subtest involves verbal repetition by the subject of series of digits presented orally by the clinician. They increase in length a digit a time every two trials. The largest number of digits correctly reproduced forward and backward are added, and the total score for the subtest is this sum of the two.

SIMILARITIES

In Similarities two apparently disparate objects or categories are presented verbally and the subject is expected to deduce their similarity. Responses are scored either o, 1, or 2 depending upon the quality and the degree of abstraction involved. The introductory item is "In what way are an orange and a banana the same?" More difficult items leave the realm of concrete objects and include such items as "praise or punishment," obviously requiring a more complex degree of conceptualization.

VOCABULARY

The subject is required to the best of his ability to define the meaning of various words. A typical easier word is "donkey," and a more difficult one appearing in the list of forty-two is "aseptic." Examples of scoring criteria are supplied in the manual (59), and with their aid the examiner scores the responses for either full or half credit.

PICTURE COMPLETION

Picture Completion is scored for the number of pictures for which the missing essential parts can be correctly identified within the time limit of fifteen or twenty seconds (which is really long enough to remove it from the category of a timed test for most patients). A typical easier item shows the line drawing of a man in which only one-half the mustache is given, whereas in a more difficult item the threads of an electric light bulb are missing.

PICTURE ARRANGEMENT

Sets of pictures are presented to the subject in a prescribed irregular order, and it is his task to arrange them in the correct temporal order which tells a story. Both accuracy and time credits are scored. A typical series shows (when arranged in proper order) first, a man carrying a dressmaker's dummy, then calling a cab, sitting in the cab with only the dummy's head visible on his shoulder, turning around to look out the rear window, blushing, and finally with the dummy shoved far over in the other corner of the cab.

OBJECT ASSEMBLY

There are three different items on Object Assembly—a manikin, a head of a woman in profile, and a hand. These become progressively more difficult. The task that the patient faces is to arrange the parts as if in a jigsaw puzzle. In the manikin the various parts are reasonably unitary sections of the human body, recognizable as such, and the lines upon the pieces make it a relatively easy item. In the profile the drawing of the features upon the various portions aids in its assembly although the cut portions do not follow discrete parts of the profile. The hand, however, has no lines upon the surface of the parts, and thus does not offer this form of clue to its proper solution. Both time and accuracy credits are given.

BLOCK DESIGN

The task facing the subject is to reproduce with colored blocks a design which he has on a card in front of him. The blocks are painted on different sides in blue, red, white, and yellow, red and white, and blue and yellow although only various combinations of red, white, and red and white appear in the designs. Two demonstrations and four test designs require four blocks each; later more complex designs require nine and sixteen blocks. Time and accuracy scores are given.

DIGIT SYMBOL

The subject is asked to transcribe beneath a series of single digits the symbols which correspond to these particular digits as indicated in a key which he has before him. The score is the total number of symbols correctly reproduced in ninety seconds.

STANDARDIZATION AND NORMATIVE GROUPS

Norms for the Wechsler-Bellevue are based upon 1750 subjects ranging in age from seven to seventy who were selected from 3500 on the basis of the occupational distribution of the adult white population of the country as indicated by the 1930 census. Number of cases at each five-year interval ranged from 50 cases in the group used for the later fifties to 195 cases in the later twenties. Most of them were from New York City and many of the remainder were from New York State and all were white. Although correction for occupational distribution may have removed a certain amount of the provincial element thus introduced, it is not clear that it has entirely done so.

Both the means and the standard deviations for all three IQ's (Full, Verbal, and Performance) show considerable constancy from ages ten to sixty (Wechsler, 59) in the standardization groups. An IQ of 100 was the modal figure, and none were either below 98.0 or above 102.5. The modal standard deviation was 14, with a range from 12.60 to 16.85. Of the forty-eight standard deviations reported, only five fell outside the range of 13 to 15. No age trends were to be found, which fact demonstrates that this method of standardization successfully took into account both changes in score and differences in variability with age.

ADMINISTRATION AND SCORING

The directions and scoring are prescribed by Wechsler and are designed to be followed explicitly. Detailed directions are given in the manual (59).[3] Following administration of each subtest in the prescribed fashion it is permissible and virtually obligatory to probe for understanding of the responses, provided the additional material does not enter into the scoring and the questioning is not of such a nature as to affect other subtests.

The order of presentation of the subtests fortunately may be varied. Wechsler recommends the Information subtest, if there are not contraindications, as the initial one to be used. Occasionally a Performance subtest is preferable, especially if the patient seems reluctant to talk or appears ill at ease when talking to the examiner in the pretest period. Once started upon either Verbal or Performance subtests, the subject need not continue them without variation. Interspersing verbal and manipulative subtests is a common clinical practice. If a patient has obviously overreacted to a failure on a particular subtest, one on which some success or appearance of success is probable, such as the Digit Symbol subtest, might then be introduced.

THE DERIVATION OF THE INTELLIGENCE QUOTIENT

The item scores within each subtest are summed to yield total raw scores, the magnitude of which may vary from possible maximums of 14 to 67. Because of the obvious lack of equivalence of magnitude of raw scores from one subtest to another, a table of weighted scores is used in the derivation of the intelligence quotients. The weighted scores were derived from the raw scores by use of Hull's method of standard scores. A mean of ten and a standard deviation of three was arbitrarily assigned, thus equating each subtest with all the others.

These weighted scores are used in three summations to derive intelligence quotients. The weighted scores of the Verbal subtests are separately summed, as are the weighted scores of the Performance subtests. From these summed scores a Verbal IQ and a Performance IQ are derived. Addition of the two weighted score totals gives a

---

[3] The arrangement of the section of the manual concerned with administration is such that considerable turning of pages from one section of the book to another is necessary. Consequently, for those not entirely proficient in the test's administration, the copying of the essential directions on 6- by 9-inch cards is suggested. The directions for a given subtest will, with one or two exceptions, fit upon a single card.

grand total which is the score used for the derivation of the Full Scale IQ.[4]

These three quotients show a considerable degree of relationship one to another. In the standardization sample, necessarily a heterogeneous one, the correlation among the three IQ's were .90 ± .01 between Full Scale and Verbal IQ, .88 ± .01 between Full Scale and Performance IQ, and .71 ± .02 between Verbal and Performance IQ. The first two, it must be noted, are spuriously high because either the Verbal or the Performance Scale, as the case may be, was included in the Full Scale with which it was correlated. Lewinski (40) found substantially similar, although slightly higher, correlations in a sample of 1000 naval personnel. Thus closely interrelated, if not identical, functions are being measured.

IQ's are not obtained from the relationship of mental to chronological age, as is the case in the Stanford-Binet. Wechsler supplies tables from which IQ's may be read directly. Entry is made into these tables by the appropriate total score in relation to the subject's age group. A patient who earns a total weighted score of 100 would have an IQ of 101 at age 22, an IQ of 108 at age 37, an IQ of 112 at age 47, and an IQ of 115 at age 57. It is evident that the meaning of the intelligence quotient when using this particular scale is different from that customarily associated with this term. Wechsler (59) points out that, after all, the IQ is the ratio between the obtained or actual score and the expected mean score for the age of the particular subject. He notes that when a child receives a mental age of 122 months on the Stanford-Binet it means essentially that he has a score such that he passed or received automatic credit for sixty-one test items. A point scale suffices for the derivation of a mental age measure and, in a sense, always precedes it. The tables of intelligence quotients that Wechsler supplies contain norms extending over a considerable age range, namely, ten to sixty. The tables are so adjusted as to make the IQ's for all ages comparable. Following cus-

---

[4] Wechsler (59) originally assumed during the standardization of the test that the Vocabulary subtest was unfair for illiterates and persons with a language handicap. His investigation revealed that this assumption was incorrect. However, the normative table for the derivation of a Verbal and Full IQ was designed on the assumption that respectively five and ten tests would be used. Prorating is therefore necessary if one follows the current recommendation to administer the Vocabulary subtest and to use it in the derivation of the intelligence quotients.

tomary procedure Wechsler presents a classification of total IQ's which in a modified form is shown in Table 3. The actual method of construction of Table 3 and also of the IQ tables in the manual is of

TABLE 3.   Intelligence Classifications for IQ's Derived from the Wechsler-Bellevue Intelligence Scales[5]

IQ	Classification	Limits in Terms of PE	Percent Included
65 and below	Mental defective	−3 PE and over	2.2
66–79	Borderline	−2 PE to −3 PE	6.7
80–90	Dull normal	−1 PE to −2 PE	16.1
91–110	Average	−1 PE to +1 PE	50.0
111–119	Bright normal	+1 PE to +2 PE	16.1
120–127	Superior	+2 PE to +3 PE	6.7
128 and over	Very superior	+3 PE and over	2.2

considerable importance, since the method of derivation of IQ's is somewhat different from that often used. It will be noted from the table that IQ's 91–110, or the classification of average, include 50 percent of the population. This was not fortuitous. Accepting, as he did, the convention of the mean IQ as being 100 and the further convention of 90 as being the lowest limit of average intelligence, Wechsler selected the appropriate statistical measure of variability to apply to the scores of the standardization samples for each age group. Since it is reasonable to suppose that the middle 50 percent of the general population could be called average in intelligence, the probable error (or Q) for this purpose was the appropriate statistic. This measure was selected since 25 percent of the cases lie between the mean and an ordinate point one probable error from the mean. If both positive and negative deviations are included, ±1 PE includes 50 percent of the cases. Thus ±1 PE were given values of 90 and 110. Once "anchored" by the decision to use −1 PE from the mean of the weighted scores for a given age group as IQ 90 (also assumed to be the lower limit of average), the other values in the IQ scale fell into place, and it then became merely a matter of naming the other steps. This method of anchoring IQ 90 and 110 at 1 PE from the mean was used for each age group. A consequence of some signifi-

⁵ Adapted from *The Measurement of Adult Intelligence* by D. Wechsler (59), by permission of The Williams & Wilkins Company. Copyright 1944 by The Williams & Wilkins Company.

cance is that this made variability from the mean of 100 constant from age to age.

The use of the probable error has the further advantage that the lowest category, traditionally labeled mentally defective, would require on the basis of the properties of the normal curve that 2.15 percent fall three or more PE below the mean. Since most research investigations show 2 or 3 percent of the population to be mentally defective (in the psychometric sense), the use of this statistical method of derivation of the IQ had the effect of agreeing with the commonly accepted finding.

It will be noted that an IQ of 65 is the upper limit for the classification of mentally defective instead of the more commonly used figure of 70. Arrival at IQ 65 was not arbitrary but was an outcome of the statistical method used, which in this case defines a mental defective as an individual whose score is such that it falls −3 PE or more from the mean of the weighted scores for his age group. Wechsler has some doubts whether the percentage of 2.2 included in this category is not too small and suggests that a "truer" figure might be 3 percent, in which case a mental defective would have an IQ of 68 or below. Lest this latter figure tempt one to use the Terman-Merrill classification, in which IQ 70 is set as the upper limit of mental deficiency, it is well to mention that Wechsler emphatically warns against the use of any scheme of verbal interpretation of IQ's with Wechsler-Bellevue results except the one given above.

This method of derivation of the intelligence quotient abandons the concept of mental age. Beyond a certain point, MA equivalents are only hypothetically related to the actual data from which they are derived, since they are extrapolated values. Mental age as a method of defining intelligence is suspect according to Wechsler. Each test constructor who bases his measure of intelligence upon a MA score must of necessity select as a divisor the highest CA beyond which the MA scores cease to increase. The figure used as the highest CA turns out to be a function of the test, as it would vary from test to test. Designating the year where MA scores cease to increase as maximum divisor ignores the decline that sets in with increasing age. The experimental literature seems to be uniform in finding that the curve of mental growth declines more or less regularly with increasing age. The loss seems to be relatively slight up to age twenty-five and not too great up to approximately thirty-five. Beyond this the curve of decline becomes more and more rapid. These and other considerations led Wechsler to forgo using the mental age approach. In this connection he says:

The classification offered above, like all others making use of IQ's is based essentially on a statistical concept of intelligence. It differs from other classifications of this kind in that our statistics have been more rigorously developed, and above all by the fact that our assumptions have been more explicitly stated. But the important thing about all such classifications (whether one admits it or not) is that they abandon all attempts at an absolute definition of intelligence. An IQ merely tells you how much better or worse, or how much above or below the average any individual is, when compared with persons of his own age. What that average represents we really do not know. In a point scale it is some numerical score; in a mental age scale, an M.A. equivalent. Most people can readily see that a point score has no absolute significance, because among other things its numerical value is so obviously dependent upon the number of items that happen to comprise the scale. In the case of the mental age scores, even psychologists are often under the impression that we are dealing with some absolute quantity, and the impression is even more common among psychiatrists. There is a rather widespread view that in defining intelligence in terms of mental age, we are doing so in terms of some basic unit of amount. That, as we have seen, is a mistake. A mental age is just a test score and differs from other arithmetical summaries, only by the fact that it happens to be in a year-month notation. The mental age notation has a number of advantages, but among these is not the magical one of being able to transmute a relative into an absolute quantity. In brief, mental age is no more an absolute measure of intelligence than any other test score. (59, pp. 41–42.)

It is apparent, then, that the Wechsler-Bellevue IQ implies a different meaning from that which the Stanford-Binet IQ, for example, would connote. The method of derivation is different, as are the groups with whom the individual subject is being compared. In the Stanford-Binet a comparison is made with the general population within the limits of the standardization sample as a whole; in the Wechsler-Bellevue there is a comparison of the individual only with other individuals falling in the same age group. There has been some objection to Wechsler's use of the term "IQ" when applied in the manner just described. However, in actual clinical practice it does not appear to be particularly misleading.

Wechsler also supplies what he calls an "Efficiency Quotient," which is an individual's mental ability score on the Full Scale when compared with the score of average individuals aged twenty to twenty-four. This particular age group was chosen as the one in which intellectual ability is at its maximum. Thus an individual of fifty who had an IQ of 100 when this index was derived in the customary fashion for the scale would when his score was compared with the scores of the twenty to twenty-four age group be found to have an efficiency quotient of 84.

VALIDITY

The validity of the scale, Wechsler (59, pp. 127 ff.) argues, ultimately rests upon clinical judgment of its value. That it has passed this test of empirical expert judgment hardly anyone who has used it would doubt. Nevertheless, there are other procedures which may be used to throw very direct light upon its validity.

Approaches to examination of its validity to be presented include correlation with judgment of experts, effectiveness in discriminating among groups, and prognostic efficiency. Although the question of its relationship to other tests and the results of factor analysis might be taken up at this point since they also supply information about validity, other considerations made it advisable to defer such discussion until later.

Wechsler (59, pp. 129 ff.) reports correlational studies made between test scores and judges' ratings. One group of trade school students and another of students in a commercial high school as rated by their teachers on intelligence yielded contingency coefficients respectively of .43 and .52.

A general method used to investigate the effectiveness of the subtests involved calculation of the significance of the difference between the means of each subtest for groups differentiated on the basis of the sum of the subtest scores. The question to be answered is whether or not each subtest contributes to the discrimination of the groups, since differences in total score among the groups do not necessarily mean that each subtest differentiates the groups. Wechsler, Israel, and Balinsky (61) investigated the effectiveness of each of the subtests of the Bellevue Scale in discriminating between a borderline group with IQ's between 66 and 79 and a mentally defective group with IQ's between 50 and 65. They found the magnitude of the mean scores for the two groups in the expected direction and concluded that each test did discriminate, with Digit Span the least discriminatory of all the subtests. Object Assembly was also relatively weak, since more individuals made a standard score of 9 or more on this than on any of the other subtests. The weighted score of 9 is of significance because it is close to the lower limit for the average younger adult (age twenty to twenty-four). Ten subtests each with a weighted score of 9 yield an IQ of about 95 at these ages. Thus, many of these psychometrically borderline and mentally defective individuals reached or exceeded a score on Object Assembly expected of individuals normal in intelligence. The opinion might be hazarded that their relatively good showing on this particular subtest is related to the fact that sheer persistence in trial-and-error attack will permit an occasional high score, perhaps more than is the case with any other subtest.

Another study (39), using the Verbal subtests with naval recruits as subjects, corroborated and extended these findings. The investigator found that each subtest distinguished not only between mentally defective and borderline cases but also between borderline dull normal and normal individuals. Unlike the previous study, Digit Span was found to be as discriminatory as any other subtest.

MacPhee, Wright, and Cummings (41) present evidence that the subtests of the Verbal Scale are useful and dependable for military screening purposes in appraising the general intellectual ability of rural southern Negro naval recruits. They found subtest differences between each level of intelligence investigated. This is of some importance when it is remembered that the scale was standardized on whites, and Wechsler (59, p. 107) warned against using the present norms for a Negro population.

One criterion of validity of a psychometric test is its relative prognostic efficiency. This efficiency may be judged by comparing test forecast with ultimate psychiatric diagnosis. Although this criterion would be considered weak for many diagnostic categories it perhaps is strongest in the realm of mental deficiency. A relevant study was performed by Balinsky, Israel, and Wechsler (6), who compared the relative effectiveness of the 1916 revision of the Stanford-Binet Scale and the Wechsler-Bellevue Scale. The subjects in question had been referred to Bellevue Hospital because of suspected mental retardation. The question posited was whether or not commitment to a state institution for mental defectives should be recommended after diagnostic study. The ultimate decision was made by the psychiatrist, who had at his command the facts from the case history, the psychiatric interviews, and the psychological examination and observations. For the groups in which the psychiatrist had both the results of the Binet and the Bellevue before him the Bellevue was clearly superior in prognostic efficiency. Representative biserial correlations with recommendation for commitment or non-commitment were .27 for the Binet and .78 for the Bellevue. It must be noted that this study was performed at Bellevue Hospital, which fact introduces an uncontrolled factor of the possibility on the part of the psychologists to urge and the psychiatrists to accept as more valid the findings of a scale developed at their own hospital. It is doubtful, however, if the differing efficiencies can be attributed entirely to this factor in view of the consistency of their results among several groups, including some in which results of either the Binet alone or the Bellevue alone constituted the psychometric instrument available for consideration by the psychiatrist. There was one group in which this factor definitely could not operate since the Wechsler-Bellevue was given to the subjects two or three years *after* the recommendation for commitment or non-commitment was made. For the thirty-six cases the biserial correlation for the Wechsler-Bellevue was .72 ± .09 whereas that for the Stanford-Binet was .61 ± .10. Although still showing the superiority of the Wechsler-Bellevue, the difference found is presumably statistically nonsignificant.

The relative efficacy of these two tests in this investigation was not studied in relation to age. Since a considerable number of the subjects studied, apparently over 50 percent for all groups, were within the age range of fourteen to seventeen, it is quite possible that the Wechsler-Bellevue was considerably more efficient with these relatively older subjects but not at all superior to the Stanford-Binet with the younger subjects. In any case, the Wechsler-Bellevue in general seems to be somewhat more efficacious than the 1916 Stanford-Binet in terms of its agreement with diagnosis of mental deficiency.

In this study the evidence thus seems to favor the Wechsler-Bellevue as a diagnostic tool for distinguishing between borderline and mentally defective levels, but failure to isolate different age levels makes it impossible to judge whether or not this holds for children aged ten to fourteen as well as for older adolescents and adults.

RELIABILITY

The consistency with which the Wechsler-Bellevue Scale measures whatever it does measure has been investigated in a variety of ways. The results that Wechsler (59) himself presents as a measure of reliability may be summarized first. He states that the standard error of measurement for the Full Scale IQ with a median of 100 and a standard deviation of 14.7 was found to be 5.7. Correlation on retest with twenty adults aged twenty to thirty-four was found to be .94 ± .02. Likewise correlation among various portions of the scale (four subtests vs. four other subtests) for 355 adults aged twenty to thirty-four was .90 when estimated by the Spearman-Brown formula. In a way, calling this last coefficient a reliability measure is somewhat misleading. What is really demonstrated, as Derner, Aborn, and Canter (12) point out, is the consistency with which the two groups of four subtests measure some common factor. For the same groups the correlation between Verbal and Performance IQ's was .83.

A study by Rabin (47) using institutionalized mentally ill patients is of interest since it demonstrates that, despite the particular group of subjects used, the Wechsler-Bellevue is remarkably constant from test to retest. Rabin's sixty subjects included thirty schizophrenics and thirty of other diagnostic classifications including manic depressives and psychoneurotics. The group had a mean age of thirty-three and a range of sixteen to sixty-three. With retest intervals ranging from one to thirty-five months, mean thirteen months, the correlation between test and retest for Total Scale weighted scores was .84. This coefficient of stability compares favorably with ones obtained on normal adults on other tests. The Verbal Scale changed very little, and the Performance Scale showed a slight increase. The findings of both Wechsler (59) with normals and Rabin (47) with psychiatric patients suggest that the scale as a unit may be employed in individual (as contrasted with group) differentiation and classification.

There remains the problem of the reliability of the individual subtests. In Rabin's study the test-retest correlations for the various subtests (excluding Vocabulary, which was not administered) ranged from .99 for Information to .44 for Comprehension. Digit Span and Block Design were in the seventies; all the remaining subtests were in the sixties, except Digit Symbol, which was in the fifties.

Other published studies include those of Hamister (26), Gilhooly (21), Cronbach (11), and Derner, Aborn, and Canter (12). In the study of Hamister the sample used was fifty-three neuropsychiatric patients of whom thirty-four were schizophrenic and the remainder scattered through a variety of other diagnostic categories. They were retested after either one week or one month. The two temporal groups were combined in reporting results, since the differences in scores obtained at the two delay periods were statistically nonsignificant. In both groups there was considerable learning effect reflected in a mean increase in weighted score on retest of nearly eleven points. For the group the highest test-retest correlation was .94 for Information, and the lowest was .59 for Digit Span. Two of the six Verbal subtests were in the nineties, two in the eighties, one was in the seventies, and one in the fifties. The Performance subtests included one in the eighties, three in the seventies and one in the sixties.

The split-half technique was used with certain subtests in the study of Gilhooly (21). Information, Comprehension, Similarities, and Vocabulary were selected, partly because they have no time limits and make a split-half coefficient more meaningful. The subjects were 122 white male veterans with diagnosis of psychoneurosis. Corrected by the Spearman-Brown formula, the correlations were .94 for Vocaublary, .79 for Information, .77 for Similarities, and .56 for Comprehension. The limits of accuracy vary from .91 to .96 for Vocabulary to .37 to .70 for Comprehension. In other words, the Comprehension coefficient might vary from as low as .37 to as high as .70 owing to chance factors of sampling. Of the four subtests, Vocabulary alone could be expected on this basis to yield consistent results from sample to sample. Standard errors denoting the amount of fluctuation that can be expected in the test scores if the same subject is retested were also calculated with equally sobering results. Using weighted scores for the Information subtest one would expect on the basis of this sample that a variation of six points might be due to the imperfections of the measuring instrument. In other words, a person tested once and obtaining a score of 8 might once in a hundred times get a score of 14 on retesting, owing to the imperfections of the subtest itself. The minimum difference that would be necessary for statistical significance at the one percent level was also calculated and was found to vary from four to six among the four subtests. Specifically, a difference of 5.10 weighted score points between Information and Similarities would be necessary for statistical significance at that level. And yet, it is sometimes recommended that a difference of two or three weighted score points is enough to draw conclusions concerning the differential balance of traits presumed to be measured by two subtests.

Cronbach (11) reports, without going into detail, some findings of Wechsler concerning the correlation between Forms I and II and then estimates what the presumed reliability of the individual subtests would be in an unrestricted population. One of these presumed reliability coefficients is in the nineties (Digit Symbol); two are in the eighties (Information and Block Design); five in the seventies (Comprehension, Similarities, Digit Span, Arithmetic, and Picture Arrangement); and two in the fifties (Picture Completion and Object Assembly). The study of reliability of Derner, Aborn, and Canter (12) is the latest to appear and contains an exhaustive review and comparison of the previous reliability studies. Using a population of 156 normal subjects with 60 subjects retested after one week, 60 subjects retested at the end of four weeks, and 38 subjects retested after a period of six months, they found that there was no significant difference between the stability coefficients at any one of the retest intervals. Accordingly, the coefficients were averaged with correlations found to range from .62 (Arithmetic) to .88 (Vocabulary). Five of the coefficients were in the eighties, two in the seventies, and the remainder in the sixties.

That much credence can be placed on the stability of the individual subtest scores, standing alone, is to be doubted. A further discussion will be reserved for consideration of the significance of scatter among the subtests.

CORRELATION WITH OTHER INSTRUMENTS

The clinical usefulness of a test is increased when we have some knowledge of the degree of relationship that it may bear to other measures. Viewed in general terms this information is valuable for two reasons. First, by knowing the degree of relationship it has to another instrument we are in a better position to understand the nature of what the test is and is not measuring. Second, by the same token, such knowledge aids in interpretation when results of both are available for a particular patient.

CORRELATION WITH STANFORD-BINET

A considerable number of studies have been directed to the exploration of the relationship of the Wechsler-Bellevue Scale and the Stanford-Binet, Form L. This is hardly surprising when one considers the popularity that they both enjoy as diagnostic instruments.

There have been a variety of investigations following the identical pattern of applying both Stanford-Binet Form L and Wechsler-Bellevue to the same populations, then calculating correlations and measures of central tendency and variability. Table 4 summarizes the findings of these studies. It will be noted that the nature, age, and mean IQ of the samples vary widely. In each, however, substantial correlations were obtained between IQ scores on the Stanford-Binet Form L and the Wechsler-Bellevue scales. Seven of the eight studies report correlations with Stanford-Binet involving Total, Verbal, and Performance scales. A pattern is readily apparent: either Total or Verbal Scale shows the highest correlation with Stanford-Binet, but within the confines of a given study there is an insignificant difference between them. The correlation of the Stanford-Binet with the Performance Scale is typically about twenty correlational units lower. Moreover, the substantial correlation between the two measures does not seem to change with age, as reported by Halpern (25) and others.

The magnitude of the correlations is naturally larger when there is greater variability in the population under consideration. Certain of the Total and Verbal Scale correlations with Stanford-Binet are .90 or more, thus approaching the level of the correlation found on retest with an identical instrument. When variability is restricted, as in the study of mental defectives or college students, the correlations are lower, although never dropping below .65 between Stanford-Binet and Total or Verbal Wechsler scales. Quite obviously a high degree of relationship exists. These correlations are somewhat higher than that briefly mentioned by Wechsler (59) using the 1916 version of the Stanford-Binet with seventy-five male and female adolescents aged fourteen to sixteen. He reports a correlation of .82 ± .03 of Stanford-Binet IQ with the Total Scale IQ. If one makes the assumption that the unreported standard deviation of Wechsler's group was about that which he reports for his fourteen-sixteen-year standardization groups, namely, 15, it will be seen that his findings

Table 4. Correlational Studies of Wechsler-Bellevue and Stanford-Binet, Form L

Investigator	Sample	Age	N	r with SB	Mean IQ	σ	Range
Benton, Weider, and Blauvelt (7)	60 mental hospital patients diagnosed, for the most part, manic depressive, dementia praecox, and involutional melancholia	Range 16–59 Mean 35		Total .93 ± .01	SB 105	27.7	41–149
				Verb. .92 ± .01	WB Total 100	18.5	59–132
				Perf. .73 ± .04	WB Verb. 105	20.2	55–136
					WB Perf. 99	18.4	47–122
Goldfarb (22)	60 foster-home children	Range 11–17 Mean 14		Total .86	SB 95	16.3	58–146
				Verb. .80	WB Total 90	15.5	47–126
				Perf. .67	WB Verb. 94	15.0	53–122
					WB Perf. 89	15.6	55–123
Halpern (25)	133 mental hygiene clinic outpatients				SB Total WB	Verb. WB	Perf. WB
		A 10–14	37	Total .92 ± .02	84 79	75	87
		B 15–24	55	Total .91 ± .01	87 86	84	88
		C 25–34	23	Total .90 ± .03	81 82	83	86
		D 35+	18	Total .90 ± .04	82 91	89	95

				Mean IQ Differences		
			Age	N	Total WB minus SB	Verb. WB minus SB	Perf. WB minus SB
---	---	---	---	---	---	---	---
Kutash (36)	50 adult institutionalized male mental defectives	Range 16–59 Mean 35	Total .76 ± .04 Verb. .73 ± .04 Perf. .51 ± .07	15–30 / 31–45 / 46–60 / Total	15 / 27 / 8 / 50	4.67 / 11.59 / 20.38 / 10.92	7.54 / 14.96 / 22.33 / 12.50	7.21 / 11.86 / 22.45 / 13.78
Mitchell (45)	227 Iowa state mental hospital psychotics and alcoholics	Range approx. 15–65 Mean by interpolation approx. 37	Total .89 Verb. .91 Perf. .80	SB / WB Total / WB Verb. / WB Perf.		87 / 89 / 91 / 89	26.5 / 19.6 / 19.0 / 19.2	28–150 / 39–134 / 52–132 / 39–134
Weider, Levi, and Risch (63)	61 white children referred for behavior and personality disorders	Range 8–16 Mean 12	Total .81 ± .03 Verb. .87 ± .02 Perf. .56 ± .06	SB / WB Total / WB Verb. / WB Perf.		86 / 87 / 82 / 94	15.6 / 16.6 / 16.1 / 17.5	58–122 / 57–126 / 58–120 / 52–138
Sartain (54)	51 college freshmen	Unspecified	Total .77 Verb. .80 Perf. .51	SB / WB Total / WB Verb. / WB Perf.		129.5 / 117.5 / 115.4 / 115.1	10.9 / 10.5 / 10.6 / 10.4	Unspecified
Anderson et al. (4)	112 college freshmen	Unspecified	Total .62 ± .04 Verb. .65 ± .04 Perf. .39 ± .05	SB / WB Total / WB Verb. / WB Perf.		128 / 118 / 116 / 116	9.9 / 7.2 / 7.0 / 8.8	Unspecified

resemble those of Weider, Levi, and Risch (63) and Goldfarb (22). The studies of Benton, Weider, and Blauvelt (7), and Mitchell (45), using adult mental hospital patients, not only showed greater variability of test scores but also higher correlation coefficients— approximately .90.

In diagnosis clinicians are concerned not only with relative positions on a scale, which appear to be substantially similar on the Wechsler-Bellevue and Stanford-Binet scales, but also with the magnitude of the score. In other words, despite perfect linear relationship between two sets of scores, one set could classify all individuals as normal while the other might label them as mentally defective.

Benton, Weider, and Blauvelt (7) and Mitchell (45) found greater variability, as shown by the standard deviations, for the Stanford-Binet than for the Wechsler-Bellevue. This suggests that the Stanford-Binet would have more high scores and more low scores than the Bellevue, which has been found by investigation to be the case. Although he does not report measures of variability, Kutash (36) in his study with mental defectives cites the differences between percentages of cases falling in various IQ groups. The lowest of these reported, IQ 30–49, shows that 20 percent of the total group tested were included in this IQ range on the basis of Stanford-Binet IQ, whereas but 2 percent would be so placed by the Wechsler-Bellevue Full Scale. Other similar findings reported by Kutash corroborate this tendency for the Stanford-Binet to yield lower scores. Despite the similarity of the standard deviations of the scores on the two tests, Weider, Levi, and Risch (63) also obtained lesser variability on the Wechsler-Bellevue than on the Stanford-Binet. On the basis of data too detailed to present here, there seems to be general agreement among these investigators that individuals falling in the lower IQ brackets are likely to test higher on the Wechsler-Bellevue and lower on the Stanford-Binet, and the reverse is true in the superior range, where higher Stanford-Binet IQ's are found as compared with Wechsler-Bellevue IQ's on the same person. IQ's in the middle ranges seem to agree more closely, but the trend is apparent as one goes away from IQ 100 in either direction. Table 5, adapted from Benton, Weider, and Blauvelt (7), brings this out clearly.

Rather consistent differences at different age levels within the same sample have been reported in the studies of Halpern (25),

The Wechsler-Bellevue Intelligence Scale   175

TABLE 5. Equivalent Binet and Bellevue Full Scale IQ Scores for a Group
of Psychiatric Patients[6]

Binet	Bellevue	Binet	Bellevue	Binet	Bellevue
IQ	IQ	IQ	IQ	IQ	IQ
40	59	78	83	116	107
42	60	80	84	118	108
44	62	82	86	120	110
46	63	84	87	122	111
48	64	86	88	124	112
50	66	88	89	126	113
52	67	90	91	128	115
54	68	92	92	130	116
56	69	94	93	132	117
58	71	96	94	134	118
60	72	98	95	136	120
62	73	100	97	138	121
64	74	102	98	140	122
66	76	104	100	142	123
68	77	106	101	144	125
70	78	108	102	146	126
72	79	110	103	148	127
74	81	112	105	150	129
76	82	114	106	...	...

Kutash (36), and Mitchell (45). At ages ten to fourteen (Halpern) and ten to nineteen (Mitchell) the Stanford-Binet IQ is higher, whereas in their studies of those above thirty-five or forty the Wechsler-Bellevue seems to be greater. Between the ages of fifteen and thirty-four the two tests will yield approximately the same quotient. Thus it would appear that at the younger ages the Stanford-Binet is consistently higher, with the reverse being found at thirty-five and above. However, Kutash, working with mental defectives, found a mean difference always in favor of higher IQ on the Wechsler-Bellevue. As age increased the difference increased until at ages forty-six to sixty the difference was over twenty IQ points. As he was dealing only with institutionalized mental defectives between the ages of fifteen and thirty, his group was much

[6] Adapted from "Performance of Adult Patients on the Bellevue Intelligence Scales and the Revised Stanford-Binet" by A. L. Benton, A. Weider, and J. Blauvelt (7), by permission of the *Psychiatric Quarterly*. Copyright 1941 by the New York State Department of Mental Hygiene.

more restricted in variability than that of Halpern or Mitchell, which perhaps accounts for this different finding.

The relatively higher IQ's on the Wechsler-Bellevue with increasing age are in large measure a function of the method of construction of the scale. Wechsler, it will be recalled, made allowance for decline with age by using adults from older age groups in the standardization population. He summarizes his opinion on these issues as follows:

> In general, *adult* I.Q.'s obtained on the Binet will differ from those obtained on the Bellevue Scale, in proportion to the degree to which the Binet fails to make allowance for the age factor. Accordingly, I.Q.'s obtained on the Bellevue Scale will show close agreement with those obtained on the various revisions of the Binet up to about age 15, because up to this age they both take into consideration the age factor. But from this age on the Bellevue I.Q. will begin to be systematically higher than the Binet I.Q. Between ages 15 to 30 the differences will be small. Beyond age 30 Bellevue I.Q.'s will grow larger and increase with the increasing age of the subject, so that when age 50 is reached they may be as much as 20 points higher than the Binet I.Q. (59, p. 142.)

In summary, two general trends appear to influence differences in the IQ's obtained with the Stanford-Binet and Wechsler-Bellevue —age and IQ level. At earlier ages, approximately ten to nineteen, Stanford-Binet IQ is likely to be higher, in later adolescence and to about age thirty-five they are roughly the same, and above this age the Wechsler-Bellevue yields definitely higher IQ's. On the other hand, the IQ level seems also to create differences in that at the lower levels the Wechsler-Bellevue is prone to yield a higher quotient than the Binet, whereas at the upper levels the converse is to be expected. In a given patient, age and IQ level may be so related as to accentuate or diminish the difference or similarity of the IQ's obtained.

CORRELATION WITH OTHER TESTS AND COLLEGE GRADES

That the IQ score of Wechsler-Bellevue is rather highly related both to scores on other intelligence tests and to academic standing is brought out clearly by correlations reported in the studies of Anderson et al. (4) and Sartain (54). The correlations for Total and Verbal Wechsler-Bellevue scores with freshman-year college grades were respectively .41 and .50 in the study of Anderson, and .53 and .58 in the study of Sartain. In the study of Sartain correlation of Wechsler-Bellevue Total and Verbal IQ with Alpha Form 5, Otis Self Administering Tests (Higher Examination, Form A), and the American Council on Education Psychological Examination ranged from .68 to .77; in the study of Anderson two forms of the latter test gave correlations of from .48 to .56. With all of these tests, Full Scale scores yielded lower correlations than did the Verbal Scale alone. Correlations with the Performance Scale of the Wechsler-Bellevue and these tests were about twenty or thirty correlation points lower. It would appear that a substantial degree of relationship exists between the Wechsler-Bellevue and college grades, Alpha, Otis, and ACE, and that a higher relationship is present with the Verbal Scale than with the Total Scale. The Performance Scale is substantially less correlated to such a degree that it is not measuring an ability markedly involved either in college scholastic success or in certain other intelligence tests.

On the other hand, the Performance Scale shows a high degree of relationship with the Revised Minnesota Paper Form Board. In a study by Janke and Havighurst (30) of practically all sixteen-year-old boys and girls in a midwestern community the correlation is reported to be .73 ± .02. Evidently, then, scores on the form board presumably measuring ability to perceive spatial configurations are related to whatever the Performance Scale may be measuring.

Another relationship investigated by Rudolf (53) is that between the Verbal Scale IQ and the Social Age of the Vineland Social Maturity Scale. This latter measures some aspects of social adjustment, particularly responsibility for self-help, self-responsibility, and, to some degree, responsibility for other individuals. With over 500 mental defectives Rudolf found the correlation between Verbal Scale IQ and Vineland Social Age to be .93 ± .04, thus indicating a very substantial relationship. Inspection of the table presenting the correlation data shows wide variation in IQ, ranging from about 40 to over 120, and in Social Age, ranging from about 2 to 24, despite the nature of the sample. This variability is sufficient to offer a caution against any hasty decision that the Vineland Social Maturity Scale, or conversely the Wechsler-Bellevue Scale, may be dispensed with in clinical practice. Wide variation in individual cases may well be present and may be crucial in clinical appraisal. For a further discussion of the Vineland Social Maturity Scale the reader is referred to Chapter 11.

ABBREVIATED SCALES

Attempts to develop abbreviated scales drawing upon some, but not all, of the subtests were made inevitable by the comparability of their weighted scores. Pro-rata weighting of the subtests selected to form a shorter scale makes possible the application of the normative tables supplied for the full scale while saving time in administration. This economy, of course, presumably entails some sacrifice of reliability and validity, but the intent of the various workers who have published accounts of shorter scales has been to show that the sacrifice is not so great as to preclude the use of shorter scales. Consequently, a short scale has been sought which would estimate with considerable accuracy the results that would have been obtained had the full scale been given instead of only selected subtests.

The shorter scale arrived at by Kriegman and Hansen (35) is representative of the dozen or so that have been published. It is described here both because of the careful and complete study made and because of the method of original selection of the subtests that was used. The scale was made up of Vocabulary, Information, Block Design, and Similarities and called VIBS from the initial letters of the subtests selected. These four subtests were reported by Wechsler (59) to be among the best of the subtests on the basis of correlation with the entire scale. In this selection Kriegman and Hansen include both Verbal and Performance subtests and furthermore subtests found to be sensitive to psychopathies, thereby increasing the value of the shortened scale as a diagnostic instrument. The correlations of VIBS with the total score and with the IQ on the Full Scale were found to be .91 and .94 respectively. These correlations are typical of some of the other relatively valid abbreviated scales found in other studies using different arrays of subtests. The particular combination of Kriegman and Hansen is confirmed as among the more valid, at least for some groups, by the study of McNemar (42). He correlated various subtest combinations with the total score based on all of them. Using the data of Wechsler's norm group, aged twenty to thirty-four, for all subtests except Vocabulary, he found one of the best triads to be Information, Block Design, and Similarities.

Although defensible as a screening device on the grounds of rapid administration and the ease of teaching inexperienced personnel, these short forms cannot be recommended for other purposes.[7] A considerable amount of the experience gained in regard to pattern analysis, qualitative cues, and understanding of the individual through the rationale of the subtests is no longer applicable if an abridgment is used.

DIAGNOSTIC USAGE OF THE WECHSLER-BELLEVUE INTELLIGENCE SCALE

Performance on the Wechsler-Bellevue Intelligence Scale, like other measures in this area of functioning, is not only a means of appraising the intellectual level of an individual but also a method of studying many other facets of his behavior. The performance sampled by the Wechsler-Bellevue is an expression not of intelligence alone but of the personality as a whole.

It is customarily held that the great advantage of the Wechsler-Bellevue Scale as a diagnostic instrument used with the individual patient arises from the equating of weighted scores of the subtests. Each weighted subtest score is considered to be a discrete measure capable of direct comparison with the scores from other subtests. It will be remembered that in the standardization population the weighted subtest scores on each test were such that many individuals would show approximately equal weighted scores on all. As a consequence, a subject's score deviation has to some degree been considered characteristic of him as an individual. Thus the pattern of scores reveals something about both the nature of the personality of the individual under consideration and, in the event of psychopathy, the impingement of the disease upon the processes of the individual measured by the test. Directly attributable to the method of standardization are the close interrelations of attempts (1) to identify the psychological functions measured by each subtest (rationale) and the related qualitative findings, (2) to derive analyses of different diagnostic groups (diagnostic scatter patterns), and (3) to utilize certain combinations of subtests to predict mental deterioration

---

[7] Wechsler (59, p. 71) considers no less than eight tests necessary for the derivation of a Full Scale IQ, if for some reason omissions must occur, and would not as a general rule omit tests at all.

(mental deterioration index). Each of these developments will be considered in turn.

RATIONALE AND QUALITATIVE ASPECTS

If a test is to be considered as providing a broad sample of behavior, some concept must be derived as to the meaning of the type of behavior sampled. This the concept of rationale supplies. It is by no means a new departure, as witness an "intelligence" test or a "mechanical aptitude" test. In this instance the method of attack is to examine critically the content of the subtests themselves rather than accepting such terms as "digit span" or "picture arrangement," satisfied that the meaning is implicit in the label. What is the individual called upon to do when he repeats a series of digits or arranges pictures in sequence? Wechsler has offered no systematic explicit presentation of rationale except to say that the subtests were selected with the thought of their clinical meaningfulness in mind, but *The Measurement of Adult Intelligence* (59) contains many scattered comments on this issue. Rapaport (49) (50), another authority on the Wechsler-Bellevue Scale, has discussed this matter in detail and has adeptly isolated a veritable flood of clinical cues concerning each of the subtests. The opinions of these two authors about the rationale of each subtest are worthy of review.

That the rationale to be described may be incorrect at least in part and reflect merely our state of ignorance is quite possible, or even probable. However, Rapaport (49) maintains that pointing out the necessity of a rationale cannot be incorrect. Scatter does exist, and enough evidence has accumulated to suggest strongly that it is a function not only of the test but also of the individual. To explore the scatter pattern one must advance certain hypotheses about the meaning and significance of this scatter. To do so, some attempt should be made to develop a rationale for each subtest.

VOCABULARY

There is relatively little discussion of the rationale of the Vocabulary subtest given by either Wechsler or Rapaport. It would appear to be simultaneously a measure of the patient's fund of information, range of ideas, and learning ability. There is no reason to anticipate much disagreement with the statement that it reflects previously learned materials; and similarly undisputed is the belief that scores made upon it are relatively impervious to the influences of disease processes. Rapaport (49) states that performance is to a considerable degree dependent upon the wealth or poverty of early educational influences and is comparatively unmodified by later schooling and life experiences. He bases this upon the observation that many individuals from culturally poor childhoods do not enlarge their vocabulary despite later richer life experiences. Still another speculation ot some interest is his attitude toward the role played by vocabulary acquisition in the patient's individual functioning. It is his contention that undisturbed functioning allows the individual to organize and assimilate the wealth of material to which he is exposed. If this functioning is disturbed, in some instances either repression may extend its influence to include vocabulary, or knowledge (including vocabulary) may be sought as a defense, resulting in overintellectualization. Thus he finds that the hysterical group, characterized by the presence of repression, tends to have relatively low vocabulary scores, whereas the obsessive-compulsive group, characterized by overintellectualization, achieves relatively high vocabulary scores.

Wechsler and Rapaport agree that vocabulary is quite refractory to impairment. This results in part from acceptance in the scoring system with equal credit of different and conceptually lower levels of definitions. Thus, it does not necessarily mean that there is no change in verbal functioning following impairment or deterioration. Actually the individual may function verbally at a somewhat lower level than would have been the case when his vocabulary was at its peak of scope and efficiency and yet manage to give barely satisfactory definitions. Despite the fact, then, that many individuals consider this subtest the most plausible one for obtaining an estimate of pre-trauma functioning level, it is apparent that the estimate so acquired is not necessarily precise. In this respect the Wechsler Vocabulary suffers from the difficulties discussed in the next chapter in connection with the Stanford-Binet Vocabulary test.

Wechsler (59) stresses the qualitative material that is obtained with this subtest. He points out that in defining a word the patient gives much more than its mere meaning; the quality and the nature of his thought processes are also to some extent laid bare. The social setting from which the patient comes may often be inferred from his responses, as in getting "vesper" and "pewter" correct but failing "gamble" or "brim." Schizophrenic thinking, not merely in its more obvious forms such as neologisms or "word salads" but in its more subtle manifestations, is also indicated on the Vocabulary subtest. For example, pedantry, rigidity, perseveration, redundancy, and incoherence may appear. Rapaport et al. (49) and Schafer (67) also give illustrations of these patterns of thinking.

An interesting beginning toward analyzing Vocabulary responses which will throw light on this problem has been made by Gerstein (18). She has systematically analyzed and categorized Vocabulary subtest responses as descriptive, functional, and categorical, corresponding roughly to the three methods of forming concepts developed by Reichard, Schneider, and Rapaport (52) for the Weigl Color-Form and Object Sorting Test as described in Chapter 13. When fully developed this method may prove fruitful clinically in analyzing Wechsler-Bellevue Vocabulary subtest responses.

INFORMATION

The Information subtest, according to Wechsler, measures "range of a man's knowledge." (59, p. 78.) This seems to be in agreement with the position taken by Rapaport (49), who points out that it is a test of remote memory in which the availability of the appropriate memories depends on one's own particular pattern of striving and interest. He indicates that these motivations affect delivery of that particular memory into consciousness.

Since both the Information and the Vocabulary subtests require from the patient statement of facts learned, the previous discussion of the rationale of Vocabulary is relevant. Scores on the Information subtest may be similarly affected, though perhaps they are slightly less stable.

COMPREHENSION

Wechsler considers the Comprehension subtest to be essentially a test of common sense. He offers as a definition: ". . . the possession of a certain amount of practical information and a general ability to evaluate past experience." (59, p. 81.) The judgmental character of this subtest is very evident from the phrasing in the six of the ten items which ask, "What should you do. . . ." (59, p. 81.) Rapaport regards the subtest as involving something akin to judgment, viz., appropriate and relevant responses to a situation.

Correct answers depend upon selection from an existing fund of knowledge and use in a fashion both emotionally and intellectually appropriate. There is thus a close relation to the current conception of reality testing. The issue hinges less on knowledge of the "right" answer than on selection of the most appropriate one from the wide array of potential responses.

Rapaport (49) offers certain cautions in the interpretation of results obtained from this subtest. For example, one may get only a stereotyped response from patients who manage to maintain a front to conceal their essentially inadequate judgment. "To keep out of trouble," given in response to the question "Why should we keep away from bad company?" may be a mere verbal cliché. On a slightly higher level, the response "to support the government" to the question "Why should people pay taxes?" is sometimes given for a similar reason. The psychologist must be on the alert for such "fronts" and search for incongruities, rigidity, and lack of understanding, which may become manifest if the patient is pressed further.

Other observations on this subtest are worthy of attention. The impulsive, for example, may be noted to make mistakes which they subsequently correct. Conditional responses of the doubt-ridden are easy to obtain. Psychotics, especially those showing evidences of deterioration, may respond to the individual items in a fashion indicative of their difficulties. For example, one might reply that the proper thing to do upon finding a sealed, addressed, and stamped envelope is to avoid it as it is really a trap. Another might remark that nothing should be done about the situation of a fire in a theater because "I like to watch fires."

SIMILARITIES

The logical character of the individual's thinking is the most basic ability measured by the Similarities subtest. Thus, Wechsler (59, p. 86) seems to agree with the position taken by Rapaport (49, p. 146), who speaks of it as a measure of verbal concept formation. It is a means of gauging an individual's ability to select appropriately and then to verbalize relationships between two ostensibly disparate qualities. Poor performance seems to be related to loss in conceptual thinking or to rigidity or distortion in the thought processes. Individuals who fail to give similarities but instead give differences when by their level of intelligence (not mentally defective) they can be expected to do the former are most often psychotic.

Deduction of similarities involves comprehension of the nature of a given conceptual realm. Three levels of response may be distinguished—the concrete, the functional, and the conceptual. A patient whose thinking is entirely concrete would deny any similarity whereas another on a slightly different concrete plane would perhaps point out a superficial likeness, e.g., dogs and lions are similar in that they both have legs. A response at the functional level might indicate that they both eat, and a conceptual response would involve a really essential similarity, pointing out that they are both animals. To those familiar with the scoring categories of Wechsler it is immediately apparent that scores of o, 1, or 2 are not strictly equated to these levels. Indeed, some conceptual responses gain one credit as do some at the concrete level. The scoring, however, does roughly follow this sequence, with conceptual, functional, and concrete responses obtaining scores of 2, 1, and o respectively.

DIGIT SPAN

Rapaport (49) considers the Digit Span and Arithmetic subtests to be radically different from those previously discussed, referring to the latter as the "essentially verbal subtests." His arguments are based both upon statistical considerations and upon rationale. He has found, as have other investigators, that Digit Span and Arithmetic are more vulnerable to maladjustment, indicated by low averages and large standard deviations as compared with other subtests in his various patient groups. As he puts it, these two subtests depend not so much on *verbalization* as on *vocalization*. In Digit Span, instead of the inseparable content and the verbalization which communicates it, visual or auditory imagery may replace verbal imagery. In addition there is no content specific to the subject or to the communication of the response. A similar condition exists in the Arithmetic subtest, where abstract spatial images may comprise the content.

The full title for this subtest as given by Wechsler is Memory Span for Digits, which presumably may be regarded as the rationale he attributes to this particular subtest. However, he does also point out that "low scores . . . are frequently associated with attention defects." (59, p. 84.) He goes on to point out that the backward span is especially prone to show this particular difficulty. Rapaport regards this subtest as primarily a test of attention, by which he means "effortless, passive, non-selective intake of stimulation." (50, p. 45.) Free receptivity unclouded by side issues makes an individual especially adept on this subtest, and digit span achievement is presumably highest if intake is effortless. When the digits are transformed by voluntary effort into meaningful or grouped numbers, there is a corresponding transformation of the functions that these materials serve. They then measure, in part at least, concentration rather than merely this effortless intake labeled "attention."

In this connection Rapaport presents some clinical evidence that certain patients who show high scores on memory material such as recalled stories exhibit a low digit span, and vice versa. He also protests the assumption that memory is being measured on the grounds that memory refers to "logically meaningful and emotionally relevant material" (49, p. 176) which has been both assimilated and organized in the individual. On the basis of analysis of scatter he concludes that impairment is not necessarily indicative of maladjustment, but rather of the extent to which anxiety disturbs the ability to carry out this effortless passive process. However, anxiety is not the sole cause of poor performance in Digit Span, as is borne out by the attention disturbance of paretics, who are apparently not disturbed by anxiety. Shakow (in a personal communication to Rapaport, 49, p. 178) makes the very plausible point that possibly both immediate learning and attention are involved, with the latter more prominent in digits forward and the former more so in digits backward.

Anastasi (3), in the course of a study involving intercorrelation among memory tests, found that digit span, one of the tests used in her preliminary work, had such a low correlation (average +.11) with the others that she dropped it from her battery concluding that it was not a test of memory but a measure "depending on incidental factors, such as attention, an active attitude, desire to do well on the test, etc." (2, p. 40.) This lack of correlation with other memory measures has not been the experience of all investigators. Eysenck and Halstead (13) found it to correlate quite highly with other tests of immediate memory—as highly, in fact, as practically any of fifteen used. It is necessary to add, however, that factor analysis led them to conclude that all of the tests were measuring a general factor which could be equated with "g." Thus digit span is to them a measure of intelligence and nothing else.

ARITHMETICAL REASONING

It is evident from the name that Wechsler regarded this particular subtest as somehow or other tapping the ability to reason with arithmetical formulations. In the opinion of the writer, Rapaport (49, pp. 195 ff.) is more correct, at least for adult patients of normal intellectual level, when he points out that it seems to be a measure of concentration and involves voluntary, effortful, selective intake. This implies an active relationship—a deliberate effort to keep out of the flow of consciousness all irrelevant material. The four basic calculations ingrained in the subject are utilized more or less automatically, and the problem is to be solved by precise, correct thinking about it. In solving the problem the subject reflects and selects the appropriate numbers. Although he does not state so specifically, Rapaport apparently feels that reasoning cannot be performed without first concentrating.

That Arithmetic measures something other than concentration is obvious when mentally defective individuals are being considered. The illiterate southern Negro is not showing a relative weakness in concentration when he has a characteristically low score on this subtest; rather, many of the factors that are part of his environmental background—poor schooling, less need for learning arithmetical calculations, and so on—are presumably operating. He just doesn't know how to do the arithmetical problems. In such instances arithmetical reasoning is, as the name of the test implies, being measured.

PICTURE ARRANGEMENT

In Picture Arrangement the "subject's ability to comprehend and size up a total situation" (59, p. 88) is measured, according to Wechsler. The subject must "understand the whole, must get the 'idea' of the story before he is able to set himself effectively to the task." (59, p. 88.) In another connection Wechsler (59, p. 156) refers to it as a measure of social alertness. Rapaport would place this subtest in the visual organization group, in which "anticipatory and planning ability are tapped." (49, p. 215.) The patient must anticipate the consequences that might arise in such a series of pictures to be arranged in a sequence.

If unusual arrangements occur, it occasionally proves profitable to have the patient relate the story that the pictures represent. Paranoid trends are sometimes revealed in the introduction of elements which have no concrete representation in the pictures themselves.

PICTURE COMPLETION

Wechsler regards Picture Completion as a measure of the "ability of the individual to differentiate essential from unessential details." (59, p. 91.) This is dependent upon the perceptual and conceptual abilities of the patient. Rapaport would again classify this subtest in the visual organization group, for, like Picture Arrangement, no manual activity of any consequence is needed. He considers it a measure of visual concentration, i.e., the ability to detect visually some inconsistency created by an omission. The use of a time limit creates a pressure which removes it from the category of tests requiring effortless attention. To this, Wechsler would object on the grounds that the time is sufficient to remove this pressure. This test provides another instance in which the individual at the lower intellectual level might be facing a considerably different task from what the aforementioned rationale would imply.

BLOCK DESIGN

Wechsler stresses that Block Design is a measure of synthetic and analytic ability (59, p. 92). Both Wechsler and Rapaport agree that it is a measure of visual motor organization or coördination. Rapaport considers that the common psychological denominator for three subtests—Block Design, Object Assembly, and Digit Symbol—is the presence of motor activity guided by visual organization. He therefore refers to all three as tests of visual-motor coördination. It would appear that these are more strictly "performance" tests than either Picture Arrangement or Picture Completion since manual activity assumes a crucial place in the execution of the tasks demanded. The task depends upon differentiation of the designs into parts equivalent to the block faces and subsequent restructuralization of the unified design out of the discrete parts.

Much can be learned, as Wechsler (59) stresses, from watching how the patient performs the tasks set for him. A great variety of qualitative areas may be observed—haste, persistence, trial-and-error behavior, ability to assume an abstract approach, and so on. All in all, this is one of the most clinically valuable subtests in the scale. Further consideration, however, will be reserved for discussions in later chapters of the Arthur Performance Scales, the Kohs Block Design Test (to which the Wechsler Block Design is basically similar), and the Goldstein-Scheerer Cube Test.

OBJECT ASSEMBLY

Wechsler does not define precisely what he regards Object Assembly as measuring, although he speaks of it as a measure "which requires putting things together into a familiar configuration." (59, p. 97.) He refers to "a secondary value" which seems to be "capacity to persist at a task." (59, p. 98.)

Rapaport regards this as another measure of visual-motor coordination guided by visual organization, which in this case consists in "the forming of anticipations from the parts to the unknown whole pattern." (50, p. 49.) Different pieces are fitted together into a pattern which these parts form. Production, as compared to reproduction in Block Design, is being measured in this subtest. Visual organization may be sharp and fully anticipatory, with recognition and even labeling of the object prior to moving the pieces into place. Again, total significance of the object may not be apprehended, and the procedure may be guided only by trial and error and pattern coherence; i.e., lines and edges are used in a concrete and piecemeal fashion without appreciation of the total design.

Object Assembly is a behavior sample in which the method of attack often reveals pertinent data about the individual's techniques of problem-solving. Some immediately react to the whole and then seek to understand the relationship of the individual parts. Contrariwise, others react with trial-and-error procedures, relating one segment to another and regarding the emerging totality as a more or less immaterial corollary. Sometimes there is no concern at all with what is being assembled. As Wechsler (59) points out, this test is especially valuable because of the information it gives about mode of perception, reliance on trial and error, and manner of reacting to mistakes.

DIGIT SYMBOL

According to Wechsler (59), Digit Symbol measures associative flexibility when one is faced with a new learning task. On the other hand, Rapaport (49) regards it as primarily a matter of visual-motor coördination, in which the learning process, he insists, is of an abortive nature because of the nonsense and fleeting character of the material to be learned. In this instance the coördinated activity consists essentially of imitating certain symbols not heretofore learned. It is the element of *imitation* which differentiates this test from Block Design (involving *reproduction*) and Object Assembly (involving *production*).

By the nature of the task this subtest is especially sensitive to psychomotor retardation. Goldfarb (22) found it consistently negatively related to various reaction time measures. Also as a measure of new learning, it is useful in instances in which organicity is suspected. It is limited, however, because of the precise muscular movements required. If there is motor area involvement this may affect performance. Thus an additional variable of unknown importance complicates interpretation of the scores.

DIAGNOSTIC SCATTER PATTERNS

For many years clinical psychologists have realized that uneven attainment on different kinds of items on intelligence tests reflects differences among individual patients that help in discriminating among various diagnostic categories and, more important, in understanding of the patients. These cues developed through personal experience and relevant observations of consistent behavior exhibited on a given test by patients fitting various psychiatric syndromes. Naturally the psychologist was not satisfied with this anecdotal state of affairs and proceeded to develop methods of objective investigation of the relation between items or subtest scores and other aspects of the patient's behavior. In other words, he investigated scatter. Although intratest scatter among items within a given subtest has proved qualitatively valuable diagnostically, according to the findings of Rapaport and his associates (49) (50), and a beginning has been made looking toward quantification of intratest scatter by Holzberg and Deane (27), the present concern is with intertest scatter. Intertest scatter refers to unevenness of attainment among score units from some fixed reference point, such as a measure of central tendency. The analysis of scatter when treated alone (as it must be in reporting summary data on groups) is an oversimplification of the problem. Nevertheless, some information of diagnostic value has emerged.

The investigators of scatter on the Wechsler-Bellevue with various clinical groups have used a bewildering array of methods of presenting their results. Many of the approaches used unfortunately obscured the value of their findings for individual application. For example, rank order of magnitude of subtest scores in differing diagnostic groups is of little or no help to the clinician. Others attempted to study scatter after first averaging all the scores for each subtest. Some clue concerning the variability of the scores from these subtest means could be gathered from the standard deviations; nevertheless, it is extremely difficult to infer very much from them. For example, suppose a certain group has a total mean score for the ten subtests of 85 and a given subtest mean score of 8.5. With the consequent deviation of zero for this subtest, it is impossible to know whether or not a number of extremely high and an equal number of extremely low scores have not canceled one another and thus could not be distinguished from subtest scores showing little or no deviation. The standard deviation of the mean of a subtest score is of some value but is open to suspicion because of the failure to take into account skewness, which, as far as the writer is aware, has never been reported in any study of mean scatter on the Wechsler-Bellevue. Another limitation is the false impression given by the manner of presentation of certain studies. Some writers appear to make the assumption that failure of the average to bear out a suggested criterion proves it of no value. What is ignored is that the clinician is interested in the conclusions he can draw about each individual patient from the subtest pattern, and it is not necessary that all criteria be met in each case to be useful diagnostically. Some cases might meet the criterion on a given subtest despite failure of the mean to do so. In the analysis to follow the investigation utilizing rank order or mean subtest score will be referred to as studies of group trends.

A more clinically meaningful approach would be to apply the specified criteria to each individual case and then report the number in each diagnostic group meeting all of the criteria, all minus one, and so on. In studies involving such conditions as schizophrenia and mental deficiency the criteria specific to each group should be applied to both groups. One would then have measures of positives, false positives, negatives, and false negatives. Another approach is to calculate the actual percentage of the cases deviating by various amounts from the mean scores. Investigations presenting their results in these and similar fashion will be referred to in the subsequent discussion as studies of individual patient patterns.

An interesting new approach to pattern analysis through factor analysis has been described by Jastak (32). Although he did not use the Wechsler-Bellevue Scale, his procedure and results have implications for it. Using a group of twelve tests Jastak isolated one general and four group factors. To illustrate the results, there was one cluster of subtests comprising a group factor to which the name "reality perception" was given. By reality perception (orthotude) is meant relevance and appropriateness of thought and action, high reality perception being exhibited by a person demonstrating awareness of reality relatively free from distortion. The tests in this cluster were judged to correspond to Comprehension, Picture Arrangement, Picture Completion, Block Design, and Object Assembly in the Wechsler-Bellevue Scale. Summing the weighted scores of this cluster of subtests yielded a total score which at a statistically significant level distinguished between schizophrenics and normal control groups, with the schizophrenics having distinctly lower scores on the tests presumed to measure reality perception. Since the factor analysis was not done using the Wechsler-Bellevue itself, this finding and other results are merely suggestive. Nevertheless, enough has been done to establish what might be referred to as a "cluster" approach promising leads for subsequent studies. If more conclusive evidence appears, a valuable new approach may then be made available.

Before presentation of the results of certain studies of scatter pattern in various clinical groups it is desirable to consider the situation facing the psychologist in clinical practice. What he has before him for each patient as the result of the administration of the Wechsler-Bellevue is a list of ten or eleven subtest scores, the individual responses to each item, and some information about the patient's general behavior. For the moment, primary concern is with the first—the subtest scores.

The clinician wishes to relate these data to the findings concerning others in the clearest, most convenient, and most unequivocal fashion possible. If this method is one in common use, so much the better. Wechsler's own method would appear to meet these requirements. He points out (59) that since the subtests have been equated in terms of weighted scores the average expected score for a subtest could be ascertained by dividing the total score by 10. He also points out that the mean of the Performance and Verbal subtest scales may be calculated separately by dividing the subtotals by 5. Deviations, plus and minus, from this expected score could then be calculated. The question arises next as to what is a significant difference from expectancy. He proceeds to define this on rational grounds and offers as a working arrangement the following categories (59, p. 153):

+ a deviation of from 1.5 to 2.5 units above the mean subtest score

+ + a deviation of 3 or more units above the mean subtest score

− a deviation of from 1.5 to 2.5 units below the mean subtest score

− − a deviation of 3 or more units below the mean subtest score

o a deviation of + 1.5 to − 1.5 units from the mean subtest score

The amount by which a given subtest must deviate from the mean in order to be significant is roughly proportional to the magnitude of the total score. An individual earning a smaller score shows a significant deviation in terms of a smaller absolute score than does ·a person having a larger score. Accordingly Wechsler suggests that these categories be applied only with individuals whose weighted scores fall within the limits 80–110. Larger and smaller scores call respectively for larger and smaller deviation values calculated by a method which Wechsler describes in his manual (59).

GROUP TRENDS

On the basis of his extensive clinical experience Wechsler supplies a table of signs, a portion of which appears in Table 7. The five clinical groups for whom he presents deviation patterns are organic brain disease, schizophrenia, neuroses, adolescent psychopathy, and mental deficiency. Since Wechsler and his co-workers have had more clinical experience with this scale than anyone else, it would seem important to compare the findings of other workers with these empirical formulations. Accordingly it would be highly desirable to present results of other investigations in a similar fashion.

Unfortunately, many investigations are not presented in this fashion directly but instead follow the approaches previously described (rank order and mean).

Despite this it is possible to calculate and report the magnitude of the deviations from the means of all subtests for various patient groups. The results for schizophrenic patient groups reported by various investigators will illustrate the findings. The results of the studies of Magaret and Wright, Rabin, Weider, and Rapaport[8] accordingly will be summarized. Table 6 gives a summary of their results in terms of a short description of the sample including mean age, the mean deviation for each subtest from the total mean, and certain other values considered of differential diagnostic value.

At first glance, perhaps, it might appear that there was little agreement from one patient group to the next. There are, nevertheless, several very suggestive group trends. Whenever Vocabulary was utilized its mean score was quite definitely and unequivocally plus. The mean of the Information subtest is characteristically above the mean of all subtest scores, although on several occasions it is quite close to the mean. The mean on Comprehension is also plus in general, but in the study of Magaret and Wright and in one of Rapaport's groups (group 2) its mean falls below the mean of all subtest scores. Another subtest found to be plus, although sometimes very close to the mean, was Similarities. It is hard to characterize the results found with Block Design. Rabin and Weider found little deviation from the mean, whereas Magaret and Wright, and to an even greater degree Rapaport, found a positive deviation. It would appear, then, that like Similarities there is a trend toward plus scores. Digit Span and Arithmetic tend to show no strong deviations in any of the groups in either the minus or the plus direction. Accordingly they can be said to fall close to the mean. Object Assembly shows substantially the same pattern. On the other hand, Picture Arrangement and Picture Completion tend to be below the mean of the subtest scores. Digit Symbol seems to be the subtest most unequivocally minus.

---

[8] Rapaport reports mean subtest scores for all his groups. Attention in this analysis is directed to his acute and chronic unclassified schizophrenics and his acute and chronic paranoid schizophrenics, because they are considered as the most comparable to the groups used in other studies. They are also the ones which he frequently combines in discussing his results.

Table 6. Wechsler-Bellevue Subtest Mean Deviations from Total Means among Schizophrenic Groups

Investigator:	Magaret and Wright (44)	Rabin (46)	Weider (62)	Weider (62)	Rapaport (49)	Rapaport (49)	Rapaport (49)	Rapaport (49)
Sample:	80 Hospitalized Patients	30 Recently Hospitalized Patients	20 Younger Hospitalized Female Patients	30 Older Hospitalized Female Patients	17 Acute Unclassified	13 Chronic Unclassified	11 Acute Paranoid	10 Chronic Paranoid
Mean age	35	28	23	42	28	25	37	34
Information	+1.5	+1.9	+0.8	+0.5	+1.7	+1.7	+1.8	+0.9
Comprehension	−0.6	+1.0	+1.3	+0.8	+0.6	−0.7	+0.6	+0.7
Digit Span	+1.0	−0.7	+0.1	0.0	+1.0	−1.3	−1.4	+0.6
Arithmetic	−1.1	−0.5	−0.2	−0.3	−0.8	−0.8	+0.6	−0.1
Similarities	+0.2	+0.4	+1.0	+0.8	+1.0	+1.3	+2.2	+0.6
Vocabulary	+2.0				+1.8	+1.6	+2.0	+2.0
Picture Arrange.	−1.2	−0.9	0.0	−0.7	−1.0	+0.2	−1.2	−0.8
Picture Complet.	−0.8	−0.7	−0.5	0.0	−1.1	−0.5	−1.1	−1.1
Block Design	+0.6	+0.2	−0.1	+0.3	+0.3	+1.0	+0.8	+0.6
Object Assembly	+0.9	+0.2	−0.6	−0.1	−1.3	−0.4	−1.1	−0.1
Digit Symbol	−1.3	−0.7	−1.6	−1.3	−4.0	−0.3	−1.2	−0.4
Σ Verb.	32.9	42.9	49.0	44.3	54.0	54.2	53.3	51.8
Σ Perf.	31.0	38.7	43.2	40.7	47.0	54.0	45.7	47.7
PA + PC	11.2	14.5	17.9	16.3	18.1	21.3	17.5	17.9
Inf + BD	15.3	18.5	19.1	17.8	22.2	24.3	22.4	21.3
OA	7.4	8.5	8.6	8.4	8.8	10.4	8.8	9.8
BD	7.2	8.5	9.1	8.8	10.4	11.8	10.7	10.5

A comparison of these findings with the empirical contentions of Wechsler would appear to be pertinent. (See Table 7.) Apparently in the Verbal subtests, including Vocabulary, there is close correspondence of the summarized findings and Wechsler's modal sign (the first mentioned for any given subtest). Among the Performance subtests there is agreement only that Picture Arrangement and Digit Symbol are minus. In the other three subtests there is disagreement. Block Design apparently was found to be plus more often than Wechsler would contend (although he does suggest a trend to plus), and Object Assembly is closer to zero in contrast to his belief that this subtest is characteristically minus. Finally, Picture Completion was found in this analysis to be minus although variable, whereas he would consider it more characteristically neutral with a trend in the direction of minus. Indeed, a few extreme minus deviations in a group medially showing zero deviation might produce a mean minus deviation such as is found here.

TABLE 7. Comparison of Summarized Findings of Studies of Scatter and Wechsler's Contentions Concerning Schizophrenics

	Summary Impression	Wechsler
Inf.	+	+ to ++
Comp.	+ but var.	+ to −
Dig. Span	o but var.	o to +
Arith.	o but var.	o to −
Sim.	+	+ to − −
Vocab.	++	++
PA	− but var.	− to o
PC	− but var.	o to − −
BD	+ but var.	o to +
OA	o but var.	−
DS	−	−

Certain other findings reported in Table 6 by these investigators may now be summarized. In all except one instance the sum of the Verbal subtests is greater than the sum of the Performance subtests. In the one exception the means are practically identical. Inspection of the individual subtest means shows this superiority of Verbal subtests is due primarily to the Information, Comprehension, Similarities, and, when used, Vocabulary subtests. It would appear that the processes affected in schizophrenic disturbances show their greatest influence in the Performance subtests and the least in what Rapaport calls the essentially verbal subtests.

Wechsler suggests that the sum of the Picture Arrangement and Picture Completion subtests are characteristically less than the sum of the Information and Block Design subtests. In each group the formula when applied yields means which favor this prediction. This might well prove to be a valuable diagnostic sign.

The last sign—Object Assembly much below Block Design— can hardly be said to be substantiated for the groups qua groups. In four groups the differences are nonexistent or slight, and it is only in Rapaport's groups that significantly smaller means occur for the Object Assembly subtest.

So much for trends in groups. What of individual cases, examined individually? How often do they meet the criteria and to what degree?

INDIVIDUAL PATIENT PATTERNS

The patterns found can be reduced to something dangerously close to an absurdity. Let us imagine that Tables 6 and 7 and the table of patterns presented by Wechsler (59) are used by an earnest but uncritical clinician when faced with the subtest scores of an individual. There would doubtless be a bewildering array of partial agreements and disagreements—six points for schizophrenia according to one investigator, only three according to another, and possibly organicity and psychopathy indicated as well. If only the more or less self-consistent table reported in Wechsler is used, the contradictions will not, of course, be so apparent, but even here there is evidence of considerable overlap.

A design which would allow scores of the individual patient to be compared with the diagnostic pattern was utilized by Brecher (9). The individual subtest scores of forty state hospital patients clinically diagnosed as schizophrenic were compared with the signs for each of the clinical groups for which Wechsler presented scatter patterns. A patient showing an excess of positive schizophrenic signs was called schizophrenic, another showing an excess of neurotic signs was called neurotic, and so on. If there was a considerable number of positive signs for more than one group the patient was placed in the one for which he had the largest number. If diagnosed by signs alone only 32.5 percent would have been properly classed as schizophrenic whereas 25 percent would have been called psychopathic, 10 percent mentally defective, and the rest variously classified, including 17.5 percent borderline (equal number of signs for more than one group) and unclassified. Thus an incorrect diagnosis would have been reached in 67.5 percent of the cases. Since there are five clinical groups in which an individual might fall, chance alone would have called for 20 percent correct diagnoses. No one, of course, in actual clinical work would have proceeded so mechanically, but this study does bring out the danger of too much dependence upon signs in diagnosis.

Another approach to subtest patterns was utilized by Levine (38), viz., the accuracy of diagnosis from scatter patterns. A Veterans' Administration hospital supplied a population of 110 consecutive admissions. Nearly half were diagnosed as schizophrenic, the remainder predominantly psychoneurotic with a sprinkling of other diagnoses. The task given five clinical psychologists was to utilize the diagnostic signs and methodology of Wechsler with transcriptions of the Wechsler-Bellevue record form. The tests had been scored and the deviation symbols indicated. With a blank for each case they were to arrive at one or another of the diagnoses or place it in a category of unclassified. With final hospital diagnosis as the criterion, all the cases were divided into two categories, schizophrenia and non-schizophrenia, and a comparison was made for each individual psychologist of the success he had in duplicating this classification. The percentage of agreement with criteria diagnoses ranged from 60 to 67 percent for the individual psychologist. Chance agreement would be about 50 percent so they were functioning above chance, but this greater agreement was of borderline statistical significance. The agreement from one psychologist to the next ran from 68 through 83 percent. Although the results may be due to the relative inexperience of the psychologists participating, there is no reason to believe that another group would do particularly better. If this is the case, the large percentage of error and the large percentage of disagreement among the psychologists tend to raise doubts about the practical clinical validity of the pattern approach.

A study of Garfield (15) is especially informative, since he reports not merely means and standard deviations but the actual percentages of subtest deviations in terms of those showing deviations of − 2.50 and over, − 1.50 to − 2.49, − 1.49 to + 1.49, 1.50 to 2.49, and 2.50 and over. When compared with a control group of non-schizophrenic, non-psychotic hospitalized patients on several subtests, the performance of the two groups was essentially similar, whereas for others either the schizophrenic or the control group was slightly higher. The overlapping was marked, and extensive intragroup variability was exhibited. Garfield did to some degree substantiate Wechsler's formula that in the schizophrenic the sum of Picture Arrangement and Picture Completion is less than that of Information and Block Design, since 63 percent of the schizophrenics exhibited this relation as contrasted with but 39 percent of the controls.

Rapaport and his associates (49) have had considerable success in the use of diagnostic signs only when certain conditions were fulfilled, i.e., when the Wechsler-Bellevue was used as part of a battery, when each patient was considered as an individual, and when qualitative cues were utilized as well as test scatter. Since they did achieve this success in diagnostic formulation it is of some interest to analyze the subtest scores of their patients to see if Wechsler's signs would be applicable. The procedure applied was as follows: Each subtest of each patient of four groups of schizophrenics[9] was assigned the appropriate plus, minus, or zero symbol, the Verbal and Performance subtests being treated separately. Then the percentage for each subtest meeting the criteria for − −, −, 0, +, and + + was calculated. Table 8 reports these findings. The table is to be read as follows: On the Vocabulary subtest none scored − −, 2 percent −, 63 percent zero, 12 percent +, and 24 percent + +. Results for other subtests are to be read similarly. Certain findings are immediately evident. In almost all subtests half or nearly half the patients showed zero deviation from their means. The Performance subtests, with the exception of Block Design, had about an equal percentage of those − and − − as they had + and + +. Block Design was positive (+ or + +) in 65 percent of the cases.

---

[9] The groups included were acute unclassified, chronic unclassified, acute paranoid, and chronic paranoid schizophrenics. The practice of Rapaport in combining these groups has been followed.

TABLE 8. Percentage Summary of Rapaport's Group of 51 Schizophrenics

	− −	−	o	+	++	Trend
Vocab.		2	63	12	24	o+
Comp.	18	16	47	14	6	oo
Inf.		6	63	12	20	o+
Sim.	6	10	49	22	14	oo
Dig. Span	31	18	31	6	14	− − −
Arith.	28	12	47	14		o−
PA	12	16	49	20	4	oo
PC	14	10	63	4	10	oo
BD			35	43	22	+++
OA	20	6	55	6	14	oo
DS	20	12	41	8	20	oo

In the Verbal subtests, Arithmetic and Digit Span showed a trend toward minus, but in each instance over 50 percent of the patients were zero or plus. Vocabulary, to be sure, had 36 percent + or ++, but 63 percent fell in the zero category as well. Information showed substantially the same relationship, with 32 percent + or ++ and 63 percent zero. Similarities and Comprehension can hardly be said to show any trend with nearly half at zero.

How do these results compare with those found by Wechsler? Block Design, reported by Wechsler as o to + in schizophrenics, is found in this sample to agree. With the other performance subtests his contentions can hardly be said to have been supported since no trend really was found. Arithmetic, reported by Wechsler as a subtest characteristically o to − in the schizophrenic patients, as well as Vocabulary and Information, characteristically plus, receive some confirmation in these data. Digit Span, which according to Wechsler should be o to +, is actually more o to −.

The results, then, support previous contentions that making any judgment based upon signs is extremely hazardous if not impossible.[10] And yet, Rapaport was singularly persuasive in offering evidence of clinical usefulness of sign interpretation. Herein lies a paradox: application of signs individually seems to work, but when

---

[10] Even a cursory inspection in Rapaport's table (49, pp. 516 ff.) of the scores of these four schizophrenic groups will show that many cases meet few (two to four) of the signs posited by Wechsler.

the findings for a group are summarized only certain vague trends can be detected.

One might argue that Wechsler and Rapaport do not agree entirely in what is expected on the Wechsler-Bellevue scatter pattern of a schizophrenic. In some measure this is quite true, but careful reading of Rapaport's *Diagnostic Psychological Testing* (49) will show that if he had offered a summary, which by the nature of his findings he was not then prepared to do, more agreement than disagreement with Wechsler regarding what to expect would probably be found.

For the sake of argument let us ignore Wechsler's pattern entirely and consider only the findings of Rapaport's cases summarized in Table 8, so far as it offers evidence concerning a scatter pattern. For each subtest the high percentage of zeros, the roughly equal percentage division of plus and minus scores of the remaining cases, and other findings reported earlier would make it almost impossible to use any really useful clear-cut findings that could be applied to individual cases.

One of the reasons that pattern analysis has not been as successful as might be expected is the tacit assumption by some investigators that a diagnostic group should show one major pattern of subtest scores, with other combinations of scores merely variations of this pattern. Although the data of Rapaport and his collaborators (49) might be used to illustrate the fallacy of this point of view (to which fallacy they do not, of course, subscribe), an especially pertinent study is that of Goldman, Greenblatt, and Coon (24). In the course of psychological examination at Boston Psychopathic Hospital, the psychologist encountered a considerable number of cases whose performance on subtests of the Wechsler-Bellevue led her to suspect that brain damage existed. On the great majority of patients this had not been suspected before. Clinical examination including EEG, cerebral spinal fluid, and x-ray examinations was then carried out. Of ninety-two cases, sixty-six (72 percent) were found to show clinical abnormalities suggesting brain damage; in the remaining cases either there were no supporting clinical findings or the evidence was equivocal. On a control group of forty hospitalized cases with nothing on the subtests to suggest brain damage a similar clinical study revealed but 17 percent with any findings even suggestive of brain damage.

What of the subtest scores? It was found impossible to give more than a very rough summarization of all the cases at once. The authors consider such tabulations, including their own, as gross oversimplifications. To convey adequately the results they found it necessary to present *seven* patterns, not one (although none was specific to a disease entity). Illustrative would be type A, including those of moderately high original endowment who showed preservation on Comprehension and Information with loss on all other subtests (Vocabulary was not used). Clinically they demonstrated marked aggressiveness and irritability of an explosive sort. On the other hand, pattern type G, of average endowment, had a loss of function on all subtests. Clinically there was impaired memory and clouding of consciousness. In another pattern among other characteristics is a high Block Design score, better in fact than that in Comprehension or Information. Block Design is generally agreed to be one of the best tests for detecting brain damage by the presence of low scores.

In spite of this diversity these cases were diagnosed from the psychological examination. This paradox of successful appraisal and diversity of pattern is explicable only if it is understood both that there is more than one pattern and that qualitative cues of a considerable variety and scope were not only observed but correctly interpreted. In summary:

> Both quantitative and qualitative signs are found in patients with "brain damage." The quantitative signs consist essentially in marked discrepancy in the weighted scores between various sub-test items. As a rule, performance on non-verbal items (Picture Arrangement, Picture Completion and Block Designs) is most markedly affected but there is always at least *one* verbal sub-test on which there is also loss in ability to function. The qualitative signs are best displayed on the non-verbal test items where the patients show rigidity, inability to shift attention or change the mode of responding, inability to ignore superficial or extraneous stimuli and difficulty in organizing material into either a required pattern (Block Designs) or into a meaningful logical sequence (Picture Arrangement). The same signs do appear in the verbal material but are more difficult to recognize and may often be missed. Where both quantitative and qualitative irregularity of performance are found, clinical analysis reveals a very high incidence of brain damage. (24, p. 178.)

An additional factor deserves consideration at this point. Only clinical experience will allow the psychologist correctly to disregard many test "signs" in one case whereas in another the presence of even a single "sign" may be considered pathognomonic. For example, in looking over a record in which a patient had a Vocabulary score of 12 and a Similarities score of 3, most experienced clinicians would not hesitate to say that this is the performance of a schizophrenic because they have never seen it in a record of any other than a schizophrenic. The difficulty, of course, is that a performance of this kind is met so infrequently as to be almost a useless guide for the novice clinician.

CRITICISMS OF PATTERN ANALYSIS

The proponents of a diagnostic pattern analysis with the Wechsler-Bellevue face a number of obstacles. Some of these have been mentioned explicitly; others were implicit in the previous discussion. It is worth while to summarize systematically:

1. The degree of intelligence may influence the test pattern. Marked differences in subtest pattern may be expected because of shifts in subtest scores occurring with differences in the level of general intellectual ability. For example, MacPhee, Wright, and Cummings (41) found considerable irregularity in mean verbal subtest score among several hundred subnormal southern Negro naval recruits. The patterning of scores was quite different at different levels of ability. At the lowest level (mean IQ 52), Similarities is well above and Arithmetic considerably below the other three clustered subtests. At a higher level (mean IQ 64), although Similarities is still highest, both Comprehension and Digit Span approximate it. Information, on the other hand, has dropped markedly, and Arithmetic is still the lowest. One need look no further than Wechsler's data concerning mental defectives to illustrate the same point. If a pattern exists for mental defectives, certainly there must be differences attributable to intelligence quite apart from other diagnostic categories. At different levels of intelligence different patterns of scores may be expected. Sheer differences in intelligence run through all records. One must, then, take into consideration the magnitude of the scores when interpreting patterns. As yet, however, there is insufficient evidence to warrant description of a so-called neurotic pattern obtained by a genius and one obtained by a moron, so that reliance on the same pattern remains obligatory if a pattern is to be used at all.

2. A factor which is likely to be neglected in interpretation of pattern analysis is the influence of age. The weighted subtest score, unlike the intelligence quotient, is not adjusted to age differences. If it were, many ostensible discrepancies might be attenuated. This is illustrated by Jastak's analysis (31) of the data on Rapaport's schizophrenics and depressives. When age is kept constant, the differences between schizophrenics and depressives in the form of greater degree of impairment on the Performance subtests on the part of the latter group tend to disappear. Foster (14) earlier had ilustrated the effect of age differences with a sixty-year-old deteriorated schizophrenic whose subtest scores when adjusted for age differences using Wechsler's data on various age groups tended to vary little one to the other. As another example, in the mentally defective group the superiority on the Performance Scale as compared to the Verbal Scale is quite well established in the age range where the psychological examination is of actual diagnostic value (that is, the younger ages). However, erroneous conclusions could be reached about the older mental defective if the differential age deficit in these two scales were not taken into consideration. The greater loss in Performance subtests with increase in age would result in there being either no particular difference or perhaps a higher Verbal score. This is borne out by the data from Wechsler, Israel, and Balinsky (61), which permit calculation of the mean Performance and Verbal Scale scores for forty-five mental defectives aged twenty to forty-nine. The means are respectively 19.63 and 16.63, implying that probably there are quite a few with higher Verbal than Performance Scale scores. This trend is also evident from inspection of the data reported by Magaret and Wright on adult morons with an average age of thirty-five. Likewise, factor analysis does not encourage extensive dependence upon the subtests as independent nonvariable measures of psychological functions. The results of Balinsky's (5) factor analysis of the subtest scores based upon cases aged nine to sixty used in the original standardization are such as to suggest caution about treating the subtests as functional entities. Not only did different factors emerge at different age levels, but in addition the same subtests did not necessarily contribute to a given factor when it appeared with another age group. The general conclusion is offered that mental traits change and undergo reorganization over the

years though verbal and performance factors appeared the most consistent. If a given subtest measures different psychological functions at different age levels, then matters of rationale and pattern analysis become extremely complicated. Thus the clinician must exercise extreme caution in interpreting the significance of subtest scores of an individual patient.

3. Sex differences may distort interpretation of scatter. Jastak (31), without giving his source, says that males are superior on Picture Completion, Object Assembly, Arithmetic, Information, and Digit Span. Females are said to be superior on Block Design, Digit Symbol, Picture Arrangement, Vocabulary, and Comprehension. This, he claims, would distort the description of the personality and the diagnostic indications inferred from the pattern. The present writer considers this criticism less serious than are most of the others because so far as is known data bearing it out conclusively have not been published.

4. Diagnostic nomenclature for neurotic and psychotic conditions is in a state approaching confusion. Without the thread of etiological information which saves other clinical disciplines from this disorganization to some degree, psychiatry and psychology depend upon any one of several classifications which combine etiological, dynamic, and symptomatic guides. The combining of various subgroups (as in the schizophrenic subtypes), although perhaps necessary in certain research investigations, certainly does not help to secure clear-cut findings. The confusion may be more the fault of present nosological formulations than of the test. In fact, a hypothesis to keep in mind is that eventually lack of agreement in regard to scatter may force revision in our thinking about nosological entities. The search for patterns of selective impairment reflecting a type of maladjustment may extend our understanding beyond the present clinical patterns. This is still only a possibility; if such a state does ever come into being the Wechsler-Bellevue Scale presumably will be considered one of the more important pioneer devices.

5. Even if characteristic patterns can be established, there is no guarantee that a diagnostic aid is thus established, since other diagnostic groups may show many or even all of the same trends of characteristically low and high scores. Unless all important clinical groups are investigated systematically, it may well be that the pattern accepted as characteristic of the known and investigated group is

also characteristic of another group not investigated. That the explored and unexplored groups will be a source of differential-diagnostic confusion is almost inevitable.

6. Degree of illness will affect the pattern. It is reasonable to expect that the temporal relationship between testing and onset of illness will affect the degree of impairment.

7. Latent or covert personality forces not reflected in the diagnosis and not attributable to the present neurotic or psychotic pattern now being manifested will also influence scatter. As Schafer (55) points out, a person relying upon obsessive defenses before developing a schizophrenic process will show test patterns referable to obsessiveness, and another patient who previously showed premorbid hysteric reactions will evince these in the test findings. Hence one obsessive-like schizophrenic and one hysteric-like schizophrenic will in their tests show different patterns. The assumption that all variations in test results are attributable to the psychotic processes is again untenable.

8. Differences may reflect characteristics of the instrument rather than the individual. Specific reference must be made to the reliability of the subtests, their placement within the total scale, and the resistance of the scale to the effects of impairment. We have relatively little evidence that the subtests are sufficiently long to give a reliability satisfactory for individual diagnostic usage. The subtests contain from ten to forty-two items; there is limited sampling of situations in which the presumed function is expressed. Scores based upon such short measures are generally rather unreliable. The reliability of the total test is not now in question; but if subtests are to be treated as independent entities it is necessary to have information about the consistency of measurement of each. The results of the study on test-retest reliability of Hamister (26) previously referred to are such as to discourage placing much credence in subtest reliability, as but two coefficients in the nineties were found. He computed standard errors of measurement and found that for seven of the subtests plus and minus 2 SE M is equal to or greater than six weighted score points. Thus, in these subtests deviations of three weighted scores above or below the mean might be functions of the error of measurement. In effect, Wechsler's plus and minus deviations referred to earlier might even in the case of − − and + + deviations show nothing more than error brought about by the lack

of reliability of the individual subtests. The study of Gilhooly (21) using split-half coefficients, also previously described, supports his findings and reinforces the contention that the utmost caution is needed in interpreting scatter.

Still another characteristic of the test which might produce differences in subtest performance is the position of the subtest within the total scale during administration. Klugman (34) administered the Digit Span subtest either as first, middle, or last of the eleven subtests to 300 psychoneurotic veterans and found significant differences among the three means. It would appear that similar investigations of other subtests might well reveal similar differences created by the order of administration, despite Wechsler's contention that there is no appreciable effect.

It must also be remembered that the Wechsler-Bellevue Scale is primarily a structured test even when used projectively. Many seriously maladjusted individuals preserve enough of a façade and sufficient intellectual control to prevent the seriousness of their difficulties from being apparent. Verbal shells and clichés are present often enough to affect the scores on the various subtests and thus make the findings equivocal.

9. The most important obstacle of all to unequivocal and unvarying interpretation of diagnostic Wechsler-Bellevue patterns is the unique traits of the personality of the individual arising from his individual expression of his needs, wishes, and drives. Each individual has developed out of the matrix of environmental and hereditary factors characteristic ways of handling life's problems. Some traits are strengthened, others aborted or modified by his experiences. If the measuring instrument is sensitive to expressions of personality through its items, then to some degree personality differences will appear. The restraining or accelerating factors making for these differences may or may not be pathological. For example, wide variation in intra-individual patterns may occur as the result of normal development and may reflect cultural background, race, or schooling. A pattern involving a low Performance and a high Verbal score may at times be diagnostically significant for schizophrenia, but at times such discrepancies mean nothing more than that the individual in question has poorer manipulative than verbal ability for reasons quite apart from pathological processes.

In summary one can do no better than to quote Hunt and Older:

"If tests are devised in which scatter is a sole function of some specific factor in pathology, then this scatter will be *diagnostic* rather than *indicative*. In the meantime, since scatter is a function of numerous factors, it is impossible to set hard and fast rules for its interpretation and to provide infallible statistical norms for its recognition. Scatter remains indicative, and any subsequent diagnosis must come only after a careful clinical evaluation of the subject, his history, and his background." (28, p. 123.) The results, then, of scatter analysis are equivocal and to some degree disappointing. This disappointment, however, should be tempered by a realization that, after all, such procedures devoted to the assignment of diagnostic labels are a rather insignificant portion of the labors of the professional clinical psychologist.

A resolution of many of these difficulties might be accomplished by a return on the part of the clinician to an emphasis on the individual and his unique characteristics. Fundamentally much research concerning diagnostic scatter patterns has been misdirected. As Schafer (55) says in a masterly paper concerning clinical research, the assumption that a diagnostic indicator is directly related to a diagnostic label is essentially incomplete because it ignores the fact that the indicators must necessarily be expressions of personality characteristics. If it is held firmly in mind that personality characteristics are thus reflected, and that patients of a given diagnostic category need not more than other individuals all possess the same characteristics to the same degree and manifest them in the same way, much confusion may be avoided. It is apparent that there is no infallible indicator since even the most "characteristic" personality trait need not invariably be present in a given patient group. The task of the psychologist is not to attach a label but to describe a personality.

MENTAL DETERIORATION INDEX

A diagnostic problem frequently facing the clinical psychologist is that of stating in meaningful quantitative terms a comparison between the patient's actual or present functioning ability and his previous functioning level. The ideal but manifestly impossible situation in which patients would have had earlier psychological examinations identical to the one to be applied when they are now seen as patients, with deficit suspected, may be disregarded. Lacking this, dependence is placed upon the fact that there appears to be a differential loss among various abilities. For example, it is often said that the vocabulary of an individual seems to be more resistant to pathological processes both of disease and of aging than is his ability to learn new tasks or to solve problems at a conceptual level.

Processes which cause these losses are varied, including such conditions as cerebral arteriosclerosis, general paresis, traumatic brain injuries, and many others of a similar nature.

The differential-test-score method of measuring psychological deficit has been described by Wechsler and his associates (37) (59). Knowing from his own and other work that there is differential loss among abilities measured by the Wechsler-Bellevue and other scales, he attempted to develop a method of determining loss in intellectual abilities by the comparison of the sums of weighted scores for two groups of subtests. Certain subtests were found to be relatively unaffected by the age of the individual; other subtests declined considerably with age. These are referred to respectively as "Hold" and "Don't Hold" subtests. The sum of the Hold subtests—Vocabulary (or, if not available, Comprehension), Information, Picture Completion, and Object Assembly—is compared with the sum of the Don't Hold subtests—Digit Span, Arithmetic, Block Design, and Digit Symbol—by application of the formula, $\dfrac{\text{Hold–Don't Hold}}{\text{Hold}}$.

This is referred to as the Mental Deterioration Index and gives the percentage of intellectual loss. Deficit is presumed to have taken place if the loss is greater than a critical amount for each age level. Wechsler himself adopted the convention of considering a loss of 20 percent as evidence of definite deterioration.

It has been indicated previously that basic to the construction of the Wechsler-Bellevue Scale is an allowance for intellectual decline with increase in age beyond full intellectual maturity. Some consideration must be given to this natural progressive impairment because clinical interest centers in deficit greater than that expected on these grounds. By using the means for the standardization groups of each subtest at each successive age period it is possible to sum the two groups of Hold and Don't Hold subtests and thus know the average amount of loss to be expected. This Wechsler presents in tabular form (59, p. 66) for correction by subtraction from the obtained percentage loss. For example, in the case of W. F. presented below the Hold subtests give a score of 34 while the Don't Hold subtests total 15. Dividing the difference between the two sums (19) by the sum of the Hold subtests (34) gives 56 percent. Since the patient was forty-five years of age a correction of 11 percent for normal age loss is necessary. On subtraction the deterioration index is 45 percent. By this method information is available which bears not only upon the patient's present functioning ability but also upon the level at which he (hypothetically) previously functioned.

It has been suggested that the deterioration index is useful in differential diagnosis in distinguishing between organic memory impairment and hysterical amnesia, between mental deficiency and intellectual deterioration, between a psychosis with and without organic deterioration, and in finding corroborative evidence where neurological data are equivocal. Two short cases reported by Levi, Oppenheim, and Wechsler (37) are illustrative of its clinical usefulness:

A. B., female, 18, admitted in an unconscious alcoholic state. The subsequent psychiatric interview revealed complaints of amnesia, dizziness, uncertainty, confusion. She was considered to be mentally defective and of unstable, delinquent make-up. A psychometric examination was requested for possible placement. The Bellevue-Wechsler composite IQ of 95 indicated average intellectual functioning, but with a deterioration index of 20 per cent.

Hold Subtests		Don't Hold	
Comp.	8	Digits	7
Int.	10	Arith.	7
P. Comp.	9	Blocks	10
Obj. A.	12	D. Sym.	7
	39		31

$\frac{8}{39}$ = 20 per cent

The verbal and performance IQ's were almost identical (94 and 96, respectively). The psychometric findings, so much at variance with psychiatric evaluation, stimulated closer neurological examination, which disclosed anomalies leading to a diagnosis of psychosis with organic brain damage due to heredito-degenerative disease, with aphasia.

W. F., male, 45, was admitted when his parents died, because a sister who tried to take care of him was unable to tolerate his temper outbursts and was afraid to trust him with her children. He had been considered defective almost all of his life and had been taken care of by his parents. He was admitted for possible commitment, and considered mentally defective by the psychiatrist. The psychometric examination revealed dull normal functioning (IQ of 83), but with a deterioration index of 45 per cent.

Hold Subtests		Don't Hold	
Voc.	11	Digits	4
Info.	10	Arith.	4
P. Comp.	8	Blocks	3
Obj. A.	5	D. Sym.	4
	34		15

$15/34 = 56$ per cent $- 11$ per cent $= 45$ per cent
The performance IQ of 88 was slightly higher than the verbal IQ of 83. Final diagnosis was "psychosis with mental deterioration." (37, pp. 405–406.)[11]

The authors make no claim, of course, that results of the application of this index are always so unequivocal. That this formula is more open to question when applied to some patients and patient groups than they appear to suggest is brought out clearly in certain studies of brain-injured and mentally defective patients.

In applying Wechsler's index to fifty brain-injured veterans Allen (1) found the formula to screen only 54 percent of the total group. Its use did not disclose any appreciable loss in 20 percent. Nearly half of presumably unequivocal clinically diagnosed cases were not detected. The Object Assembly subtest included in Wechsler's formula as relatively invulnerable was found, on the contrary, to be apparently especially vulnerable to post-traumatic organicity. Its mean subtest score with the brain-injured patients was third lowest of the eleven, suggesting its placement in the "Don't Hold" rather than its present acceptance in the "Hold" category.

For at least one other diagnostic group there appears to be rather stringent evidence that the deterioration index is invalid. This is the mentally defective group. Certain research studies and empirical considerations indicate that application of the ratio will lead to erroneous conclusions. In a study by Boehm and Sarason (8) it was found that a group of twenty-two familial defectives in whom the possibility of a previously significantly higher level of functioning was practically ruled out showed considerable deterioration loss. Corroboration of these results is to be found in a study by Sloan (57) of eighty male high-grade "familial" or "undifferentiated" mental

---

[11] Reprinted from "Clinical Use of the Mental Deterioration Index of the Bellevue-Wechsler Scale" by J. Levi, S. Oppenheim, and D. Wechsler, by permission of the *Journal of Abnormal and Social Psychology*. Copyright 1945 by the American Psychological Association.

defectives with a mean IQ of 58 on the Wechsler-Bellevue Full Scale. In addition to a failure to find clinically any evidence of the presence of a traumatic causative condition, on fifty-six of the eighty subjects a testing with the Stanford-Binet on the average of ten years previously yielded an average drop of less than one IQ point when compared with the present retest. And yet, the mean DQ of the group was 71, thus indicating deterioration. The fact that such a high incidence of deterioration was found in groups not likely ever to have functioned at higher levels strongly suggests that the results concerning the deterioration index are an artifact of the statistical construction of the formula and not an actual representation of their present status. This, of course, does not mean, if other corroborative evidence of deterioration is available, that a score falling in the mental defective range cannot indicate deficit. But it does mean, as Boehm and Sarason point out, that a logical error seems to have occurred in violating the initial assumption that when deterioration is present certain scores are comparatively low. To infer that the converse is invariably true would be a *non sequitur*.

Confirmation of the possibility that such findings with mentally defective individuals is fortuitous can be further illustrated. Let us assume the hypothetical case of an individual aged twenty with an IQ of 59 and a weighted total score of 40. If the most common pattern of subtest scores for mental defectives according to Wechsler (59) is accepted for the moment as valid, the following distribution of weighted scores would seem plausible:

Information (o)	5
Comprehension (+)	6
Arithmetic (− −)	1
Digit Span (−)	2
Similarities (o)	4
Picture Completion (−)	2
Picture Arrangement (o)	5
Object Assembly (+)	7
Block Design (o)	5
Digit Symbol (−)	3

Applying the formula, a net loss of 45 percent would be obtained. Since the "typical" mentally defective individual is not known to show such deterioration, the application of the deterioration ratio in the "most characteristic" mental defective would appear to be inappropriate. It is immediately apparent that other such patterns arising from similar circumstances may exist, suggesting again extreme caution in the use of this ratio with mental defectives.

The research evidence in the field of psychotic deterioration is not so clear-cut. One available study, although interpreted by its author as evidence against the validity of the index, may be differently interpreted. Rabin (47), using groups of aged patients including senile psychotics and cerebral arteriosclerotics, claimed that the ratio was not substantiated. His evidence was based not upon any calculation of an index but upon the fact that when the subtests were ranked on magnitude of mean score, the Hold and Don't Hold tests were not necessarily among the four subtests with the highest and the four subtests with the lowest scores respectively. What he failed to take into consideration (which was also the case with Hunt, 29) was the fact that it was explicitly stated by Wechsler that an equal number of both Performance and Verbal subtests should appear in the divisor and the dividend of the index to rule out a possible unfairness to individuals whose scores happened to stress one over the other.

Inspection of the mean scores on the subtests in Rabin's four groups of aged patients shows that in all instances the means of the Verbal Hold subtests are the two highest of the five Verbal subtests, and the means for the Verbal Don't Hold subtests are the two lowest. The same situation exists in the Performance section, except that the substitution of Picture Arrangement for Block Design would have enlarged the difference between Hold and Don't Hold.[12] Inspection of the data makes plausible the inference that calculation of deterioration ratios (which Rabin did not make) would have shown some deterioration beyond that expected on the basis of age alone. Consequently, then, it would appear the deterioration index is substantiated in this particular study of aged hospital patients.

Schlosser and Kantor (56), in a study on 163 inpatient admissions to a Veterans Administration NP hospital, found a statistically nonsignificant difference between the deterioration indices of schizo-

---

[12] Two other sources corroborate this finding that Picture Arrangement might be substituted for Block Design as a Don't Hold subtest. Goldfarb (22) found in both males and females eighteen to sixty-five years of age that the negative correlation with age is greater for the former than the latter subtest, and inspection of Wechsler's table of means for Performance subtests according to age (59, p. 222) shows a slightly sharper decline with age for Picture Arrangement than for Block Design.

phrenic and psychoneurotic patients. Although they were newly admitted patients, some evidences of deficit should have been present if the ratio is to have diagnostic significance. It is rather difficult to reconcile the authors' negative findings with expectancy, if the deterioration index is valid. Moreover, in a study of ten schizophrenic cases on which they had pre-psychotic test results, Rappaport and Webb (51) found that using Information, Comprehension, and Vocabulary (three of the Hold tests) either singly or in combination was not a reliable measure of premorbid IQ. The results of these studies, then, would appear to call for extreme caution in applying the deterioration index.

In some measure the possible unreliability of the subtests, previously discussed, influences the derivation of the deterioration index. There is no evidence that the subtests of numerator and of denominator are reliable enough to carry the burden, even when used collectively.

It must be emphasized that the approach to deficit through the deterioration index is but one among many possible means of operationally defining the issue. Wechsler states the position that the impairment or loss of function reflected in differential subtest performance is both related to decrease with chronological age in normal persons and characteristic of patients showing psychiatric deterioration. This is an assumption as yet unproved. In fact, there is some evidence, presented by Cameron (10), that senile deterioration and schizophrenic disorganization are somewhat different. There is evidence from the studies of Garfield and Fey (17) and Magaret and Simpson (43) that the Shipley Institute of Living Scale for Measuring Intellectual Impairment and the Mental Deterioration Index are correlated with each other to a degree only slightly greater than zero. The Shipley Institute Scale is constructed on the assumption that deterioration may be demonstrated by the differences between scores on a test of conceptual thinking and scores on a measure of vocabulary knowledge, with significantly lower scores on the former being indicative of impairment and with the ratio between vocabulary and abstraction scores stated in terms of a quotient (conceptual quotient). Calculation of the quotient to isolate cases with problem pathology yielded a group whose composition did not overlap to any degree with those whose Wechsler-Bellevue Mental Deterioration indices would also be considered indicative of deterioration. In the

Magaret and Simpson study (43) psychiatrists' ratings of deterioration correlated nonsignificantly with the findings for either measure. Since this lack of agreement with another measure of deficit exists, there is all the more need for caution in application of the Mental Deterioration Index.

In contrast to Wechsler's more cautious approach, others have applied this measure of mental deterioration widely and somewhat promiscuously.[13] This indiscriminate usage has caused some confusion among psychiatrists, especially in view of the rather unfortunate choice of the term "deterioration." Psychiatrists tend to regard "deterioration" as an irreversible process arising from organic lesions or prolonged mental disease, and when such involvements are clearly absent they are likely to see little meaning in such a ratio. An operational definition rather than a bald unqualified statement of "deterioration" might ameliorate the situation somewhat. In a diagnostic testing report, the statement, "In analyzing the subtest scores of this patient there is found to be an impairment or loss of function when comparing previous and present functioning ability greater than that expected as a result of normal decline with age to the extent that the deterioration ratio is 36 per cent," is more meaningful than mere reporting of the ratio. One may then present relevant evidence and speculate upon the probable causes of this finding.

As yet, there has been little positive evidence to substantiate the contentions of Wechsler and his associates regarding the deterioration index. It would appear that, awaiting such evidence, only guarded claims should be made by the clinician on the basis of his findings with this index.

SUMMARY

The Wechsler-Bellevue Intelligence Scale has proved its value in the clinical market place. As a consequence of its value as a clinical instrument many valuable studies have appeared. Nevertheless, because of its popularity, uncritical usage and poorly planned research are also rather widespread.

Though the test as a whole has been found to show validities and reliabilities in a variety of clinical settings, the situation when sub-

---

[13] The fact that the Record Form supplied by Wechsler contains space for calculating deterioration has invited the derivation and application of this ratio in cases that Wechsler perhaps never intended.

tests are treated separately is not so clearly favorable. In particular, the reliabilities of each subtest are not as high as some of the uses to which they have been put would demand. The problem of the validities of each subtest and the diagnostic usage of the Wechsler-Bellevue are inextricably bound together. Since the equating of weighting scores for the subtests has proved to be such a valuable clinical tool the questions of rationale, diagnostic scatter patterns, and the mental deterioration index received rather detailed consideration in this chapter. For the most part, evidence concerning the rationale of a particular subtest has not been developed from a direct research attack upon the problem. Instead, research implications plus a wealth of clinical findings have been drawn upon to formulate that which it appears to measure. It is evident that much research aimed at experimentally demonstrating these hypotheses remains to be done.

Perhaps in no other area in present clinical research has there been so much busy work as in the exploration of the diagnostic scatter patterns of the Wechsler-Bellevue. This is not to say that some studies are not valuable, and the ones judged to be most commendable have been presented. When it is realized that perhaps forty or fifty other studies have necessarily been omitted, the full flood of research in this area with this instrument may be realized. Whence comes the popularity of this form of research investigation? It may be suggested that in part there is the desire to find a psychological counterpart to the philosophers' stone; in his desire to extend clinical services and to make them more objective the psychologist searches for the open-sesame to diagnostic appraisal that does not rely heavily upon clinical experience and opinions of the psychologist. Although such a goal may be laudable, in the foreseeable future it will not be reached.

As in all tests the value of the Wechsler-Bellevue is dependent in a fundamental sense upon the direct experience of the clinician. In reviewing the findings which investigators have furnished there is an attempt to share this experience. Still, without personal acquaintance, many of the findings will be misinterpreted no matter how carefully and correctly stated. To illustrate from the findings concerning pattern analysis, Wechsler supplied tables designed to aid in diagnosis but emphasized their dependence upon the accumulated experience of the clinician. This experience may justify in one case disregard of many test signs and in others judging the presence of even a single one as pathognomonic.

BIBLIOGRAPHY

1. Allen, R. M., A note on the use of the Bellevue-Wechsler Scale Mental Deterioration Index with brain injured patients, *J. clin. Psychol.*, 1948, 4:88–89.
2. Altus, W. D., and Clark, J. H., Subtest variation of the Wechsler-Bellevue for two institutionalized behavior problem groups, *J. consult. Psychol.*, 1949, 13:444–447.
3. Anastasi, A., A group factor in immediate memory, *Arch. Psychol.*, 1930, No. 120.
4. Anderson, E. E., Anderson, S. F., Ferguson, C., Gray, J., Hittinger, J., McKinstry, E., Motter, M. E., and Vick, G., Wilson College studies in psychology: I. A comparison of the Wechsler-Bellevue, Revised Stanford-Binet, and the American Council on Education tests at the college level, *J. Psychol.*, 1942, 14:317–326.
5. Balinsky, B., Analysis of the mental factors of various age groups from nine to sixty, *Genet. Psychol. Monogr.*, 1941, 23:191–234.
6. Balinsky, B., Israel, H., and Wechsler, D., The relative effectiveness of the Stanford-Binet and the Bellevue Intelligence Scale in diagnosing mental deficiency, *Amer. J. Orthopsychiat.*, 1939, 9:798–801.
7. Benton, A. L., Weider, A., and Blauvelt, J., Performance of adult patients on the Bellevue Intelligence Scales and the Revised Stanford-Binet, *Psychiat. Quart.*, 1941, 15:802–806.
8. Boehm, A. E., and Sarason, S. B., Does Wechsler's formula distinguish intellectual deterioration from mental deficiency? *J. abnorm. soc. Psychol.*, 1947, 42:356–358.
9. Brecher, S., The value of diagnostic signs for schizophrenia on the Wechsler-Bellevue Adult Intelligence Test, *Psychiat. Quart. Suppl.*, 1946, 20:58–64.
10. Cameron, N., A study of thinking in senile deterioration and schizophrenic disorganization, *Amer. J. Psychol.*, 1938, 51:650–665.
11. Cronbach, L. J., *Essentials of psychological testing*, Harper & Brothers, 1949.
12. Derner, G. F., Aborn, M., and Canter, A. H., The reliability of the Wechsler-Bellevue subtests and scales, *J. consult. Psychol.*, 1950, 14:172–179.
13. Eysenck, H. J., and Halstead, H., The memory function. I. A. factorial study of fifteen clinical tests, *Amer. J. Psychiat.*, 1945, 102:174–179.
14. Foster, A., Age and the Wechsler-Bellevue scattergraph, *J. clin. Psychol.*, 1947, 3:396–397.
15. Garfield, S. L., A preliminary appraisal of Wechsler-Bellevue scatter patterns in schizophrenia, *J. consult. Psychol.*, 1948, 12:32–36.

16. Garfield, S. L., An evaluation of Wechsler-Bellevue patterns in schizophrenia, *J. consult. Psychol.*, 1949, 13:279–287.
17. Garfield, S. L., and Fey, W. F., A comparison of the Wechsler-Bellevue and Shipley-Hartford Scales as measures of mental impairment, *J. consult, Psychol.*, 1948, 12:259–264.
18. Gerstein, R. A., A suggested method for analyzing and extending the use of the Bellevue-Wechsler vocabulary responses, *J. consult. Psychol.*, 1949, 13:366–370.
19. Gibby, R. G., A preliminary survey of certain aspects of Form II of the Wechsler-Bellevue Scale as compared to Form I, *J. clin. Psychol.*, 1949, 5:165–169.
20. Gilhooly, F. M., The relationship between variability and ability on the Wechsler-Bellevue, *J. consult. Psychol.*, 1950, 14:46–48.
21. Gilhooly, F. M., Wechsler-Bellevue reliability and the validity of certain diagnostic signs of the neuroses, *J. consult. Psychol.*, 1950, 14:82–87.
22. Goldfarb, W., An investigation of reaction time in older adults and its relationship to certain observed mental test patterns, *Columbia University T.C. Cont. Educ.*, 1941, No. 831.
23. Goldfarb, W., Adolescent performance in the Wechsler-Bellevue Intelligence Scales and the Revised Stanford-Binet Examination, Form L, *J. educ. Psychol.*, 1944, 35:503–507.
24. Goldman, R., Greenblatt, M., and Coon, G. P., Use of the Bellevue-Wechsler Scale in clinical psychiatry with particular reference to cases with brain damage, *J. nerv. ment. Dis.*, 1946, 104:144–179.
25. Halpern, F., A comparison of the Revised Stanford L and the Bellevue Adult Intelligence Test as clinical instruments, *Psychiat. Quart. Suppl.*, 1942, 16:206–211.
26. Hamister, R. C., The test-retest reliability of the Wechsler-Bellevue Intelligence Test (Form I) for a neuropsychiatric population, *J. consult. Psychol.*, 1949, 13:39–43.
27. Holzberg, J. D., and Deane, M. A., The diagnostic significance of an objective measure of intratest scatter on the Wechsler-Bellevue Intelligence Scale, *J. consult. Psychol.*, 1950, 14:180–188.
28. Hunt, W. A., and Older, H. J., Psychometric scatter pattern as a diagnostic aid, *J. abnorm. soc. Psychol.*, 1944, 39:118–123.
29. Hunt, W. L., The relative rates of decline of Wechsler-Bellevue "Hold" and "Don't-Hold" tests, *J. consult. Psychol.*, 1949, 13:440–443.
30. Janke, L. L., and Havighurst, R. J., Relations between ability and social status in a midwestern community. II. Sixteen-year-old boys and girls, *J. educ. Psychol.*, 1945, 36:499–509.
31. Jastak, J., Problems of psychometric scatter analysis, *Psychol. Bull.*, 1949, 46:177–197.
32. Jastak, J., Psychometric personality traits, *Del. St. med. J.*, 1949, 21:165–169.

33. Jastak, J., An item analysis of the Wechsler-Bellevue Tests, *J. consult. Psychol.*, 1950, 14:88–94.
34. Klugman, S. F., The effect of placement of the digit test in the Wechsler-Bellevue Intelligence Scale, *J. consult. Psychol.*, 1948, 12:345–348.
35. Kriegman, G., and Hansen, F. W., VIBS: a short form of the Wechsler-Bellevue Intelligence Scale, *J. clin. Psychol.*, 1947, 3:209–216.
36. Kutash, S. B., A comparison of the Wechsler-Bellevue and the Revised Stanford-Binet Scales for adult defective delinquents, *Psychiat. Quart.*, 1945, 19:677–685.
37. Levi, J., Oppenheim, S., and Wechsler, D., Clinical use of the Mental Deterioration Index of the Bellevue-Wechsler Scale, *J. abnorm. soc. Psychol.*, 1945, 40: 405–407.
38. Levine, L. S., The utility of Wechsler's patterns in the diagnosis of schizophrenia, *J. consult. Psychol.*, 1949, 13:28–31.
39. Lewinski, R. J., Discriminative value of the sub-tests of the Bellevue Verbal Scale in the examination of naval recruits, *J. gen. Psychol.*, 1944, 31:95–99.
40. Lewinski, R. J., Vocabulary and mental measurements: a quantitative investigation and review of research, *J. genet. Psychol.*, 1948, 72:247–281.
41. MacPhee, H. M., Wright, H. F., and Cummings, S. B., Jr., The performance of mentally subnormal rural southern Negroes on the Verbal Scale of the Bellevue Intelligence Examination, *J. soc. Psychol.*, 1947, 25:217–229.
42. McNemar, Q., On abbreviated Wechsler-Bellevue Scales, *J. consult. Psychol.*, 1950, 14:79–81.
43. Magaret, A., and Simpson, M. M., A comparison of two measures of deterioration in psychotic patients, *J. consult. Psychol.*, 1948, 12: 265–269.
44. Magaret, A., and Wright, C., Limitations in the use of test performance to detect mental disturbance, *J. appl. Psychol.*, 1943, 27:387–398.
45. Mitchell, M. B., Performance of mental hospital patients on the Wechsler-Bellevue and the Revised Stanford-Binet, Form L, *J. educ. Psychol.*, 1942, 33:538–544.
46. Rabin, A. I., Fluctuations in the mental level of schizophrenic patients, *Psychiat. Quart.*, 1944, 18:78–91.
47. Rabin, A. I., Test constancy and variation in the mentally ill, *J. gen. Psychol.*, 1944, 31:231–239.
48. Rabin, A. I., The use of the Wechsler-Bellevue Scales with normal and abnormal persons, *Psychol. Bull.*, 1945, 42:410–422.
49. Rapaport, D., and Gill, M., and Schafer, R., *Diagnostic psychological testing; the theory, statistical evaluation, and diagnostic application of a battery of tests*, Vol. I, Year Book Publishers, 1945.

50. Rapaport, D., with collaboration of Schafer, R., and Gill, M., *Manual of diagnostic psychological testing*. I. Diagnostic testing of intelligence and concept formation, Josiah Macy Jr. Foundation Review Series, 1944, 2, No. 2.
51. Rappaport, S. R., and Webb, W. B., An attempt to study intellectual deterioration by premorbid and psychotic testing, *J. consult. Psychol.*, 1950, 14:95–98.
52. Reichard, S., Schneider, M., and Rapaport, D., The development of concept formation in children, *Amer. J. Orthopsychiat.*, 1944, 14:156–161.
53. Rudolf, G. de M., Comparison of the intelligence quotient with behaviour, *J. ment. Sci.*, 1949, 95:703–705.
54. Sartain, A. Q., A comparison of the New Revised Stanford-Binet, the Bellevue Scale, and certain group tests of intelligence, *J. soc. Psychol.*, 1946, 23:237–239.
55. Schafer, R., Psychological tests in clinical research, *J. consult. Psychol.*, 1949, 13:328–334.
56. Schlosser, J. R., and Kantor, R. E., A comparison of Wechsler's deterioration ratio in psychoneurosis and schizophrenia, *J. consult. Psychol.*, 1949, 13:108–110.
57. Sloan, W., Validity of Wechsler's deterioration quotient in high grade mental defectives, *J. clin. Psychol.*, 1947, 3:287–288.
58. Watson, R. I., The use of the Wechsler-Bellevue Scales: a supplement, *Psychol. Bull.*, 1946, 43:61–68.
59. Wechsler, D., *The measurement of adult intelligence*, The Williams & Wilkins Company, 3rd ed., 1944.
60. Wechsler, D., *The Wechsler-Bellevue Intelligence Scale: Form II manual for administering and scoring the test*, Psychological Corporation, 1946.
61. Wechsler, D., Israel, H., and Balinsky, B., A study of the sub tests of the Bellevue Intelligence Scale in borderline and mental defective cases, *Amer. J. ment. Def.*, 1941, 45:555–558.
62. Weider, A., Effects of age on the Bellevue Intelligence Scales in schizophrenic patients, *Psychiat. Quart.*, 1943, 17:337–346.
63. Weider, A., Levi, J., and Risch, F., Performances of problem children on the Wechsler-Bellevue Intelligence Scales and the Revised Stanford-Binet, *Psychiat. Quart.*, 1943, 17:695–701.
64. Wittenborn, J. R., An evaluation of the use of Bellevue-Wechsler subtest scores as an aid in psychiatric diagnosis, *J. consult. Psychol.*, 1949, 13:433–439.

DIAGNOSTIC TESTING REPORTS INVOLVING THE WECHSLER-BELLEVUE SCALE

65. Rosenzweig, S., and Clark, R. A., The personality of a psychotic ex-soldier, in Watson, R. I. (ed.), *Readings in the clinical method in*

psychology, Harper & Brothers, 1949, pp. 299–313. (Also in *J. abnorm. soc. Psychol.*, 1945, 40:195–204.)

66. Rosenzweig, S., with Kogan, K. L., *Psychodiagnosis: an introduction to tests in the clinical practice of psychodynamics*, Grune & Stratton, 1949, pp. 237–268, 271–286.

67. Schafer, R., *The clinical application of psychological tests: diagnostic summaries and case studies*, International Universities Press, 1948.

CHAPTER 9

Revised Stanford-Binet Tests of Intelligence[1]

The 1937 revision of the Stanford-Binet Intelligence Scale developed by Terman and Merrill is a modification of the 1916 Stanford-Binet, which in turn was an extension and adaptation of the scales developed previously in France by Binet. The earlier Stanford-Binet, certain aspects of which will be discussed later, was for many years the standard psychometric instrument, and all other instruments were relegated to positions of lesser importance. It is no exaggeration to say that at one time the major task of the psychometrician was to administer the Stanford-Binet. In all probability no other individually administered test was given so often, as it was used extensively both in clinical practice and in research here and abroad. In fact, it was paid the compliment of being the standard against which newly developed scales were validated.[2] It is not surprising, then, that the 1937 revision was met with enthusiasm and immediately became widely used. The high correlation, repeatedly found, between scores on this new scale, as well as the older revision, and ability in school-work has particularly recommended it in working with children of

[1] This chapter is considered as merely supplementary to the standard volume describing the Revised Stanford-Binet Scales, *Measuring Intelligence* by Terman and Merrill (53), and consequently certain points of importance are not discussed.

[2] Since many writers adopted this position on the relationship of the Stanford-Binet to other measures, the literature on its correlation with other tests is discussed in connection with them and not in the present chapter.

school age and younger. It is also very successfully used with mentally defective individuals of all ages. Accordingly its application with these groups, children and mental defectives, will be stressed in the account to follow.

DESCRIPTION OF THE SCALES

The Revised Stanford-Binet provides two complete scales designated as Form L and Form M. When either of these is referred to as a unitary test series it is called a scale. The various kinds of units found at the age levels into which the scale is divided are referred to as tests, and divisions of tests, if any, are called items. Both scales were designated for children aged two and upward and for adults. These two scales, intended to be essentially different in item content, are specified to be equivalent in "difficulty, range, reliability, and validity." (53, p. 3.)[3] In further describing the scales, Terman and Merrill contrast them with the original form: "In content Form L bears greater resemblance to the original Stanford-Binet, but neither form can be recommended above the other. Both, we believe, are relatively free from the grosser faults of the old scale. They cover a far wider range, they are more accurately standardized throughout, the tests provide a richer sampling of abilities, and the procedures have been more rigidly defined. On the whole they are somewhat less verbal than the old scale, especially in the lower years." (53, pp. 3–4.)

Each scale contains 129 tests, distributed over twenty age levels. Below age five the levels cover half-year intervals; from age five through fourteen the intervals are yearly; and beyond age fourteen there are four adult levels, designated as "Average Adult" and "Superior Adult I, II, and III." All levels have six tests, except "Average Adult," which has eight. In addition, there is an alternate test for each of the seven youngest levels.

Vividly demonstrated only through use of the scales is the fact that the test materials are sufficiently interesting to the child to stimulate considerable effort. The content is not so interesting and stimulating to an adult, as it is often necessary in testing him to

---

[3] In this they are successful to the point that little attention will be paid to one scale as contrasted with the other. Unless otherwise indicated comments apply to both scales; however, Form L is used where there is direct reference either to levels or to tests.

include material appealing to and standardized upon younger individuals.

The bewildering variety of tests involved in the scales is apparent even on casual inspection of the material. Attempts at classification in order to reduce them to an intelligible form have been manifold. The tentative classification arrived at by Porteus has much to recommend it. He classifies the tests as follows:

(1) Memory. These include memory span for digits, sentences, commissions, items read in a story or news paragraph, pictures, and designs—21½ tests.
(2) School Attainments. There are 4½ tests involving school attainments—4 of arithmetic and the "Reading and Report" test.
(3) Verbal Ability. These are tests of vocabulary, verbal comprehension and expression, description, definitions, verbal reasoning, rhymes, word associations, and verbal classifications—32 tests.
(4) Common Knowledge and Comprehension of Practical Situations. These include similarities, picture interpretation, picture absurdities, problems of fact, and aesthetic comparison—19 tests.
(5) Practical Judgment and Abilities. These are tests of manipulative skill, drawing, form board, planning, induction, and ingenuity—20 tests. (39, pp. 120–121.)

In considering the tests of the Terman-Merrill Scales it is important to keep in mind that no person takes all tests at all levels. In the classification of Porteus just given, levels III through Average Adult were included. A given patient would hardly extend his successes and failures over this entire range, and no one individual takes precisely the tests thus classified. There is wide variety in the items measuring a given function at the different levels of the scales whenever such functions (e.g., rote memory and language ability) extend throughout most of the scale. The majority of particular kinds of tests, however, appear only at certain levels and not at others, e.g., arithmetic problems. This procedure may be contrasted with that followed, for example, in the Wechsler-Bellevue, in which all of the tests extend throughout the entire chronological age range for which the scale is suitable.

The activities required of the younger child (levels II through III-6) on both scales are very often nonverbal, and for this the constructors of the tests are to be commended. However, part of this presumed advantage is lost because of the considerable verbal comprehension needed to respond to the questions; e.g., "Show me the

one that we can buy candy with" requires more than merely pointing, as the child can execute the proper movement only if he understood the directions.

Inspection of the upper levels reveals that they are heavily
weighted with verbal material often of an abstract nature. This is in
keeping with Terman and Merrill's contention that "At these levels
the major intellectual differences between subjects reduce largely to
differences in the ability to do conceptual thinking, and facility in
dealing with concepts is most readily sampled by the use of verbal
tests. Language, essentially, is the shorthand of the higher thought
processes, and the level at which this shorthand functions is one of
the most important determinants of the level of the processes themselves." (53, p. 5.)

This opinion appears to be plausible concerning the upper levels
but some authorities, e.g., Krugman (27) and Porteus (39), believe
there has been an undue emphasis on verbal material at the middle
levels. Krugman, for example, finds levels VIII and XI of Form L
especially open to this criticism. Porteus would go further and extend the criticism to levels VIII through XIV, as he found but four
nonverbal tests between these levels. Over the entire range covered
in his classification (levels III to Average Adult), only about 17
percent of the tests were nonverbal. These opinions seem reinforced
by the findings of McNemar (29), who attempted to develop a nonverbal scale covering all age levels. He could include no tests from
level VIII and but one each from Forms L and M at level XI. Levels
XIV and upward are almost entirely verbal in character.

Since Terman and Merrill (53) do not offer either a definition of
intelligence[4] or a discussion of the theoretical basis of test selection,
it is necessary to use item content to understand their conception of
the nature of intelligence. No particular definition of intelligence
advocated by the authors is discernible from a survey of test content
as such. It is evident that the materials provide "for the sinking of
shafts at critical points" (53, p. 4) and are of considerable variety.
It is apparent, moreover, that in following Binet they eschewed
discrete segmental response categories, e.g., reaction time and memory, and thought of intelligence as a sum total of many varied activities. They also state that intelligence is "of necessity modified and

---

[4] It is of some significance that in the index of their volume (53) the only
entry under "intelligence" refers to the importance of experience and training.

moulded" (53, p. 65) by experience and training, and the results of both formal instruction and incidental learning will obviously be reflected in test performance.

STANDARDIZATION AND NORMATIVE GROUPS

The Revised Stanford-Binet Scale is an age scale; in other words, the tests are grouped at various age levels. Test performance is evaluated in terms of the chronological age of those who made up the standardization group. The objective of the standardization of the Revised Stanford-Binet was to construct scales "so standardized for difficulty as to yield mean I.Q.'s of approximately 100 at all age levels." (29, p. 3.) Accordingly a representative sample of American-born white children was sought. Subjects for standardization were chosen from seventeen communities in eleven states in such a fashion as to represent the East, South, Middle West, and West. Rural and urban populations, the various occupational levels, and school and out-of-school individuals were sampled so as to be roughly proportionate to the percentages found in the population of the country as a whole. There were about 3000 subjects in the standardization group, with all subjects taking both Forms L and M in an alternate order and in close temporal proximity. About 80 children were tested at each half-year to age five, 110 at five and one-half, 200 at each age from six through fourteen, and 100 at each age thereafter through eighteen. Apparently no individuals over eighteen were tested; if so they did not appear in the standardization.

A preliminary tryout on a population for whom mental ages on the original Stanford-Binet were available but who would not be used for final standardization aided in the selection of items, e.g., elimination of those showing a slow rise of percents passing at successive age levels. To quote from Terman and Merrill on the procedure thereafter:

This preliminary tryout provided the necessary data for the selection of tests for the provisional scales. . . . The retention[1] or rejection of items was based upon several criteria. In order of importance these were: (1) validity, (2) ease and objectivity of scoring, and (3) various practical considerations such as time economy, interest to the subject, the need for variety, etc.

Validity in turn was judged by two criteria: (1) increase in percents passing from one age (or mental age) to the next, and (2) a weight based on the ratio of the difference to the standard error of the difference between the mean age (or mental age) of subjects passing the test and of subjects failing it. The use of such a weighting scheme was prompted by the obvious advantage of being able to utilize the data for all of the subjects who were tested with a given item. Since this weight is based upon the total number of successes and failures for the item in question, and because it is a unitary index, it affords a better basis for judging the relative validity of items than a series of percents passing. (53, pp. 9–10.)

Unfortunately there is no account available of how much relative weight these criteria had in the final selection and placement of the items retained. In any event, the less satisfactory tests were eliminated.

One of the criteria of validity, increase in percent passing, deserves further consideration. There is a prevalent but erroneous belief that the correct location level of a given test is at the point where 50 percent of the subjects pass it. On this point Terman has this to say:

The plan which some have advocated whereby all tests would be located at the age where 50 per cent of unselected subjects pass them simply does not work, as it yields mental ages that are much too high in the lower range and much too low in the upper range. For a scale of the Binet type there is no one "correct" per cent for locating all the tests. The fact that adjacent mental ages become progressively closer together from the lower to the upper ranges, with the scatter of an individual's performance increasing correspondingly, means that tests located correctly at a lower age will show a higher per cent of at-age passes than will a test correctly placed at a higher age. Moreover, the correct placement of tests for a particular age depends in part on the tests in the preceding and succeeding ages. For example, the correct per cent of at-age passes for tests in year XII depends partly on whether there are tests at years XI and XIII, as in the New Revision, or none, as in the original Stanford-Binet. (29, p. 9.)

In spite of the care in selection of the standardization cases it was recognized by Terman and Merrill that the sample was biased in the direction of more from superior occupational groups and a proportionately smaller representation from the rural population. They believe that these inadequacies are successfully overcome by virtue of the fact that their reported average IQ's for each chronological age group run slightly over 100. This slightly higher than 100 average IQ represents an attempt to adjust for the inadequacies of sampling; a truly random sampling at a given age would theoretically yield an average IQ of 100. To arrive at a group of tests (not an individual test) in which the median mental age would correspond with median chronological age meant much adjustment and juggling of tests until the desired result was obtained. In this, data in Terman and Merrill (53) and McNemar (29) show that they are reasonably successful. Certain criticisms, however, of the representativeness of their sample may be made. It is not representative of the *total* population of the United States. Because it excludes roughly one-tenth of the population by not including Negroes and sampling "average schools" (53, p. 12), and since the tests admittedly correlate highly with school achievement, the bias in sampling produces lower IQ's in general for the total population, and overemphasizes scholastic competence from about age VI and upward. Moreover, it places all children not represented in the original sample at a distinct disadvantage—i.e., those of Negro, poor rural, and/or poor school background.

The process of "cutting and filling" which went into this attempt to arrange the tests so as to yield a median IQ for each age level at about 100 has sometimes led to the erroneous charge that the IQ of any child was thus made to remain constant. The purpose behind this process was to yield tests in which an IQ of 100 would have the same meaning at different age levels. Median IQ constancy in the standardization population such as this does not mean a given individual's IQ will remain constant. To this question attention will be given later.

ADMINISTRATION AND SCORING

The manual *Measuring Intelligence* (53) contains both general and specific instructions for the administration of both forms along with scoring standards. A separate volume, *Directions for Administering* (52), is often used during actual administration because of its relatively smaller size, thinness, and compactness. Responses are entered on a record form (short) or a record booklet (long).

Two scoring guides for Form L have appeared which are supplementary to that contained in the manual. The earlier and shorter guide prepared by the staff of the test division of the New York City Board of Education (1) contained unique or questionable responses which they submitted both to a group of other experienced psychologists and to Terman and Merrill. Plus and minus scorings, both of the group and of Terman and Merrill separately, are reported. In only one of 311 instances was there complete unanimity of opinion about scoring and only rarely as much as 85 percent agreement by the fifty-seven psychologists participating. Occasionally a majority would disagree with Terman and Merrill. Although it must be remembered that these were responses deliberately selected as questionable it would appear that objectivity of scoring is not so easy to achieve as is sometimes thought. A subsequent scoring guide, prepared by Pintner, Dragositz, and Kushner (38) with a forward by Terman and Merrill, contains rather detailed examples of scoring plus some general statements about testing procedure and administration. It was prepared primarily to be of service to beginning students.

Terman and Merrill insist that the clinician using the scales make no deviation from the standard order assigned the test items.[5] However, some degree of serial testing of similar items consecutively (e.g., the vocabulary test) is worked into the regular order, but many other tests (e.g., digit span) are scattered throughout several age levels with the consequent necessity of repeating directions and making other wasteful moves. Terman and Merrill state that to test serially is to change the difficulty of the tests to an unknown extent. To this topic attention will be directed later.

The general scheme of scoring is to accumulate mental age credits for each success. Passing a given test earns one, two, four, five, or six months' credit according to the level at which it occurs. Differential scoring of the items of some tests permits credit at more than one level; e.g., Verbal Absurdities II, which occurs both at levels IX and XII, is credited at the lower level if there are three items correct and at the upper if there are four.

Administration places very little emphasis on speed, and time limits are infrequently imposed. The scales were planned so that roughly fifty minutes are needed for younger children and not more than seventy-five minutes for older children.

Terman and Merrill (53) offer as a general rule that the examination should begin at a level not only requiring some effort from the subject but also likely to permit success. If the age level has been overestimated, demonstrated by failure to pass one or more tests, it

---

[5] An exception to this is made when children, especially of preschool age, show resistance to a particular type of test and necessitate deviation for the sake of easing the situation.

is necessary to go to a lower age level until a point is reached at which all tests of a given level are passed. This is the "basal" year. The tests are then administered at successively higher levels until the subject fails all tests for a given age level. This is frequently referred to as the "maximal" year. Terman and Merrill (53) mention that occasionally failures below basal and successes above maximal years occur but that the error is small if one discontinues testing after finding the original basal and maximal years. They do point out nevertheless that any successes above maximal or failures below basal years should be taken into account in computing mental age.

DIFFICULTIES IN THE LOCATION OF BASAL AND MAXIMAL YEARS

Though failures below basal and successes beyond maximal ages may not be too common their occasional appearance decreases the certainty with which a clinician can feel he has established the range of a subject's abilities. Krugman (27) made a survey of 1200 reports of Form L examinations and found 15 percent with double basal, double maximal or both. However, the differences of score thus obtained from that which would have occurred if testing had gone only to single basal and maximal years are not always of consequence. A random sampling of twenty cases from the group with double basal or maximal ages revealed twelve with differences of five or fewer IQ points and three with differences of more than ten points. In seven of the twenty the new IQ changed the classification of the child with regard to degree of intelligence. This would suggest that further inquiry into the issue should be made.

Studies made by Berger and Speevack (3) (4) are pertinent. They examined with Forms L and M 200 school children between the ages of seven and fifteen referred for suspected mental retardation. By extending the criteria of maximal year to require failure on all tests at two successive levels they found that 42 and 32 percent respectively for Forms L and M showed an increase in mental age over that which would have been obtained if testing had stopped at a single maximal year. In the individuals who did show an increase in MA the average increases were slightly over three months for both forms, though maximum increase was as great as fourteen months. In many instances a child (although the group was a typically mentally retarded one) succeeded on tests several years above his chronological age. The authors drew the apparently reasonable conclusion that with retarded children the testing should be extended to at least a point where two levels have been failed.

In a study by Carlton (9) 215 children resident in a state institution for the mentally defective (mean IQ = 62, mean CA = 14-2, mean MA = 8-5) were given Form L with the examination extended until they failed three successive levels. Of this number, forty passed tests in later levels after failing all tests in one or more levels. Gain of from one to four IQ points resulted. Although Carlton concludes that to obtain the greatest accuracy the child should be examined through three maximal years, this appears to be somewhat excessive in view of the relatively small maximum IQ gain.

No dogmatic formula for determining when testing should continue beyond the first basal and maximal years may be given. Economy of time, the nature and severity of the problem, the importance of the results of testing, the level of testing at which failure occurred, and other factors must be weighed. Certainly if time does permit and other factors make it desirable, extending testing to two basal and maximal years is appropriate, though as always the individual patient is the crux of the matter. There may be indications from marginal successes or failures that it is desirable to go beyond one basal or maximal. On the other hand, it may be suspected that further basal testing would be emotionally upsetting to the patient, who sometimes regards being asked the easy items as something close to insulting; conversely, the additional tension engendered by introducing further frustrating material at the maximal end might be too high a price to pay for the slight gain in precision of measurement.

Levels XII and XIII

The previously mentioned study by Carlton (9) noted that of the forty subjects passing tests beyond the maximal year twenty-seven had complete failure at level XII followed by some success at levels XIII and higher. This would imply that level XIII might be easier than level XII, and actually it was for 65 percent of the cases. Krugman (27) and colleagues also felt that three tests at level XIII were too easy and that no other age level had this many tests misplaced. These three were the Plan of Search, Word Memory, and Paper Cutting. In addition Harriman (19) found that 200 Pennsylvania school children in the fifth and sixth grades with a mean age of

11–7 and a mean IQ of 112 showed the distribution of successes given in Table 9.

TABLE 9. Percentages of Successes on One or More Test Items at a Given Age Level on the Stanford-Binet Scale, Form L[6]

Age Level	Percent
X	91
XI	77
XII	63
XIII	78
XIV	52
Average Adult	27
Superior Adult I	12
Superior Adult II	8
Superior Adult III	3

That something is amiss at level XIII is apparent. Actually there was about the same percentage of success in passing one or more tests at level XI (77 percent) in this group as at level XIII (78 percent). One or more tests at age XII were passed by 63 percent. The progressions of figures suggest, or at least are not incompatible with, the interpretation that level XIII is too easy rather than level XII too hard.

There is some contrary evidence which refutes this contention. Mitchell (34) found that with groups of college freshman and senior medical students level XIII is more difficult than XII and Plan of Search (XIII–1) a particularly difficult test. Since testing college students with the Stanford-Binet is hardly a common procedure her findings are of but academic interest. Highly pertinent, however, is the analysis by McNemar (29) of the percentage within each age group of the standardization population used by Terman and Merrill who passed each test. His results do not appear to confirm either the general findings about the relative ease of level XIII or with one exception findings on specific tests. This exception is Plan of Search, which was passed by as much as 22 percent of the standardization group aged eight years whereas only 60 percent of

[6] Adapted from "Irregularity of Successes on the 1937 Stanford Revision" by P. L. Harriman (19), by permission of the Journal of Consulting Psychology. Copyright 1939 by the American Psychological Association.

the thirteen-year-olds passed. Inspection of his data shows very few tests with as slow a rise in percents passing below the level finally established for the test. Aside from the findings on this one test nothing unusual can be observed.

Two possibilities remain: either for some reason the standardization group for level XIII was atypical, or the findings of the several studies represent an artifact. It would appear that the course of conservative clinical practice would be to test beyond level XII if complete failure occurred there. Nothing is lost, and something may be gained.

THE DERIVATION AND SIGNIFICANCE OF MENTAL AGE AND INTELLIGENCE QUOTIENT

THE MENTAL AGE

The mental age (MA) is derived by crediting the individual with all years and months at and below the basal mental age (e.g., passing all six tests at level III–6 gives a child credit for forty-two months) and adding to this the amount of credit allotted to every test passed beyond that point. The mental age found with this instrument is the basic indicator of intelligence, though what this intelligence is, is not precisely defined. In the words of Terman and Merrill mental age on the test "tells us merely that the ability of a given subject corresponds to the average ability of children of such and such an age." (53, p. 25.)

Often a given mental age is interpreted rigidly in terms of the expectancies of the clinician. Many workers appear to underestimate the range of non-test behavior possible for individuals of a single mental age level. Wile and Davis (57) studied 250 boys and girls of MA ten years on the 1916 Stanford-Binet who had been referred to the Children's Health Class of a New York City hospital. Reading disability cases and mental defectives were excluded. Among other findings it was observed that grade placement ranged from 2A to 9B with less than 50 percent appropriately placed according to city standards. Reading and arithmetic comprehension ranged just as much or more, with the nature of the problems running the entire gamut of conceivable issues. As the authors conclude, "The concept of Mental Age may suggest abstract homogeneity but factually it represents a wide degree of heterogeneity." (57, p. 708.) Age-grade groupings in relation to MA in the standardization group as reported by McNemar (29) show variability which might to some appear astonishing. For example, below grade 7 MA's in each grade ranged over about five to eight years becoming progressively greater the higher the grade. From grades 8 through 12, six standard deviations embraced twelve years. Therefore it might be deduced that mental age is but a single phase, although an important one, of the complex process which is investigated when a child is studied diagnostically.

It is important to note that the Stanford-Binet is standardized as a mental age scale rather than as a point scale. The clinical significance of the method of derivation (and standardization) warrants examination. As some critics have pointed out, e.g., Kent (26), the mental age method of standardization results in a very rigid instrument. It is incapable of having tests added or subtracted or norms revised without arduous labor. Even more important, there results a very cumbersome test. Moreover, as Kent says, it is wasteful of valuable material in that it does not take into account correct items, insufficient to gain credit at one level but greater than the number required for credit at an earlier level. For example, eight correctly defined words earn credit at level VIII and eleven words credit at level X, but no credit is given at level IX for nine or ten words. Another criticism which arises because it is a mental age scale is that as a composite rather than a functional unit (battery) measure its primary yield is a score—the mental age. Arrived at by summing a variety of tests passed, the Stanford-Binet is incapable of yielding anything approaching the richness of diagnostic information of the battery or functional-unit approach (such as in the Wechsler-Bellevue), which permits the development of a rationale for each component part. That this is not impossible to do will be illustrated later; nevertheless, the task is complicated by the method of derivation.

THE INTELLIGENCE QUOTIENT

In order to appraise the intelligence of a given individual it is necessary to know not only his mental age but also his brightness or dullness in comparison with his fellows of similar choronological age. The index of relative brightness used by Terman and Merrill is the intelligence quotient (IQ), a measure based upon mental age as related to choronological age (CA).[7] The conventional formula for calculating this index, $\dfrac{MA}{CA} \times 100 = IQ$, need not be applied each time the test is administered, as a table in the manual obviates this step and thereby eliminates a frequent source of error in the use of the older revision. IQ's are given in this table for MA-CA relationships as low as 30 and as high as 170. Calculation of other IQ's not included in the limits is, of course, possible, except that the maximum IQ for an adult, i.e., CA 16–0 or older, is 152.

A device to prevent a too rapid decline in IQ with increasing CA is introduced for ages above thirteen. In computation of the IQ, ages from thirteen to sixteen are adjusted downward by one-third of the months over thirteen years. In order to compute the IQ of a fourteen-year-old child, one divides his mental age score by 156 + 8 or 164 (thirteen years plus two-thirds the number of months beyond thirteen). For an adult, sixteen and over, the mental age score is divided by fifteen years (thirteen plus two-thirds of the three years between thirteen and sixteen). The base line or denominator used for those sixteen or older then is the same no matter what the chronological age may be. This abrupt termination of increase in the denominator is by no means a basic phenomenon of mental growth but is apparently due to the materials used in the Stanford-Binet and thus a function of the scale.

Terman and Merrill deal straightforwardly with this issue. They say, "In this connection it should be noted that mental ages above thirteen years cease to have the same significance as at lower levels, since they are no longer equivalent to the median performances of unselected populations of the corresponding chronological ages. A mental age of fifteen years represents the norm for all subjects who are sixteen years of age or older. Beyond fifteen the mental ages are entirely artificial and are to be thought of as simply numerical scores. As such they are useful in marking off the higher intellectual altitudes measured by the scale and in providing a basis for computing a subject's I.Q. score." (53, pp. 30–31.)

VARIABILITY IN INTELLIGENCE QUOTIENT AT DIFFERENT AGES

As mentioned before, the authors were successful in arranging the tests so that a mean IQ 100 meant the same thing at the various

[7] The use of the IQ makes age norms as such unnecessary.

age levels (barring the difficulties arising as a consequence of the manipulations for ages above thirteen). However, this does not demonstrate that other IQ's, 80 or 120 for example, would have the same meaning at different age levels. For them to serve as indices of relative brightness with the same meaning at any age level requires that the variations in IQ from the mean IQ assume roughly the same distribution. In other words, if the distribution curve is different, IQ's of the same numerical value might stand at different distances from the mean and thus not denote the same things when considered as indices of brightness. Therefore, attention must be given to the variation exhibited from this measure of central tendency. The standard deviations of the IQ's on the scale at the different age levels have a mean of 16.4.[8] However, inspection of Table 10, reporting IQ variability in relation to age in the standardization group for Form L and Form M, shows two age levels (CA 2½ and 12) having standard deviations of about 20, two age levels (CA 3 and CA 15) having standard deviations of about 19, and one age level (CA 6) with a standard deviation of about 13. This creates a situation in which to some extent IQ's do not have consistent meaning and some variability in IQ from age to age might reflect this source of error.

As Goodenough (18) points out, a child who on Form L received an IQ of 162 at 2½ years would, if he maintained his constant position of +3σ from the mean, at age six receive an IQ of 138. Similarly another child −2σ from the mean at six and twelve would receive respectively IQ's of 75 and 60. Accordingly, a child may obtain widely different IQ's at different ages though his relative brightness (as measured in standard deviation units from the mean) might have remained unchanged. Differences of fifteen or twenty IQ points to an individual two or three sigmas from the mean are serious, especially in view of the fact that the clinician's concern is so often with patients at one or another of the extremes.

Are these differences due to perhaps an atypical sample in the standardization population, so that it is possible to disregard these

---

[8] This figure of 16.4 points may be contrasted with that of about 12 points found with the old scale. The increase in variability calls for a readjustment in the thinking of an individual familiar with the old scale. Terman and Merrill cite certain evidence which tends to support the validity of the larger standard deviations found with the present scales.

TABLE 10.   IQ Variability in Relation to Age[9]

CA	N	σ L IQ	σ M IQ
2	102	16.7	15.5
2½	102	20.6	20.7
3	99	19.0	18.7
3½	103	17.3	16.3
4	105	16.9	15.6
4½	101	16.2	15.3
5	109	14.2	14.1
5½	110	14.3	14.0
6	203	12.5	13.2
7	202	16.2	15.6
8	203	15.8	15.5
9	204	16.4	16.7
10	201	16.5	15.9
11	204	18.0	17.3
12	202	20.0	19.5
13	204	17.9	17.8
14	202	16.1	16.7
15	107	19.0	19.3
16	102	16.5	17.4
17	109	14.5	14.3
18	101	17.2	16.6

findings in practice? Studies on other samples offer the only answer; the crucial test of repeated examination of the same population over the years is as yet unavailable. Goodenough (18) reporting on three independent samples for 2½, 6, and 12 years of age and Brown (7) for age 6 on still another sample seem to rule out inadequacy of sampling in the standardization population as an explanation of these variations. McNemar does not attribute them to the sampling but considers them an artifact of the scale, offering the following explanation:

. . . A closer scrutiny of the curves for per cent passing has convinced us that the difference in variability is an artifact of the scale. It results from strange, and undetected, accidents. It is well known that the extent of variability is partly a function of item difficulty. It so happens that no items yield curves for per cents passing which cross the ordinate for age 6 between the 35 and 65 per cent levels of difficulty.

[9] Reprinted from Measuring Intelligence by L. M. Terman and M. A. Merrill (53), by permission of Houghton Mifflin Company. Copyright 1937 by Houghton Mifflin Company.

This fact will definitely result in a narrower spread of M.A.'s and I.Q.'s for 6-year-olds than would have resulted had this imperfection been absent. The same situation as regards lack of items of medium difficulty exists for ages 5 and 5½, though not so markedly as for age 6. The greater variability at ages 11 and 12 may be due to a concentration of items of medium difficulty for these ages, a concentration which is greater than that at other ages, except at 2½, 3, and 3½. There is, however, nothing about the item difficulties for age 15 which would enable one to predict the rather large S.D.'s for I.Q.'s at that age. (29, pp. 85–86.)

In view of the existing evidence the use of a conversion table in deriving the IQ at these ages seems indicated. Table 11, reproduced from McNemar, seems suitable. It presents IQ adjustments for

TABLE 11.   IQ Adjustments for Variability Differences[10]

Obtained IQ's	2–4 to 3–3	4–10 to 6–6	11–6 to 12–5	14–6 to 15–5
148	140	159	142	143
146	139	157	140	141
144	137	154	138	139
142	135	152	137	137
140	134	149	135	136
138	132	147	133	134
136	130	144	131	132
134	129	142	130	130
132	127	139	128	128
130	125	137	126	127
128	124	134	124	125
126	122	132	123	123
124	120	130	121	121
122	119	127	119	120
120	117	125	117	118
118	115	122	116	116
116	113	120	114	114
114	112	117	112	112
112	110	115	110	111
110	108	112	109	109

[10] Reprinted from *The Revision of the Stanford-Binet Scale* by Q. McNemar (29), by permission of Houghton Mifflin Company. Copyright 1942 by Houghton Mifflin Company.

Obtained IQ's	2–4 to 3–3	4–10 to 6–6	11–6 to 12–5	14–6 to 15–5
108	107	110	107	107
106	105	107	105	105
104	103	105	103	104
102	102	102	102	102
100	100	100	100	100
98	98	98	98	98
96	97	95	97	96
94	95	93	95	95
92	93	90	93	93
90	92	88	91	91
88	90	85	90	89
86	88	83	88	88
84	87	80	86	86
82	85	78	84	84
80	83	75	83	82
78	81	73	81	80
76	80	70	79	79
74	78	68	77	77
72	76	66	76	75
70	75	63	74	73
68	73	61	72	72
66	71	58	70	70
64	70	56	69	68
62	68	53	67	66
60	66	51	65	64
58	65	48	63	63
56	63	46	62	61
54	61	43	60	59
52	60	41	58	57
50	58	39	56	56

variability differences at and near those ages just discussed. It is not suitable except at the indicated ages.

In using the table, entry is made with the obtained IQ in the column containing the chronological age of the patient. For example, if the obtained IQ was 130 and the chronological age was 12–1 the adjusted IQ value would be 126.

On the basis of the same findings it would appear that the table of IQ equivalents of standard scores given by Terman and Merrill (53) is not suitable for application at the ages under consideration because it ignores change of variability with age. One standard score equivalent for a given IQ at all ages is impossible with unequal variability at different ages. However, if tables of standard scores are desired, it is quite feasible to construct them for different age levels thereby taking their unequal·variabilities into account.

A descriptive classification of IQ's has been offered with the 1937 revision, which is reproduced in Table 12. In reference to this table

TABLE 12. Distributions of Composite L—M IQ's of the Standardization Group[11]

IQ	N	Percent	Classifications
160–169	1	0.03 ⎫	
150–159	6	0.2 ⎬	Very superior
140–149	32	1.1 ⎭	
130–139	89	3.1 ⎫	Superior
120–129	239	8.2 ⎭	
110–119	524	18.1	High average
100–109	685	23.5 ⎫	Normal or average
90–99	667	23.0 ⎭	
80–89	422	14.5	Low average
70–79	164	5.6	Borderline defective
60–69	57	2.0 ⎫	
50–59	12	0.4 ⎬	Mentally defective
40–49	6	0.2 ⎪	
30–39	1	0.03 ⎭	

it cannot be overstressed that an IQ below the borderline limit (70–79) does not necessarily imply feeble-mindedness or an IQ in this borderline exclude it. IQ's may rise and fall, necessitating consideration of other factors as well. Indeed, this is explicitly stated by Merrill (32) in her presentation of the table. Her choice of the term "mentally defective" for the lowest classification was made on the basis of a distinction between low intelligence and "feeble-mindedness," a term reserved for those who legally and socially cannot function in society for lack of intellectual prowess. The diagnosis

[11] Reprinted from "The Significance of IQ's on the Revised Stanford-Binet Scales" by M. A. Merrill (32), by permission of the *Journal of Educational Psychology.* Copyright 1938 by Warwick and York.

of mental deficiency from psychometric data, if we can go this far and speak of diagnosis on this basis at all, must be supported by evidences of vocational inadequacy, social incompetence, and educational failure. The entire configuration must be taken into account to arrive at a valid appraisal. An intelligence quotient of 65 may imply mental deficiency, but it also may indicate a cultural handicap, a psychotic reaction, lack of rapport, or illiteracy. The test cannot decide; the clinician must.

VALIDITY

Validity is not a topic which permits easy compartmentalization, as evidence for and against validity permeates all test findings. The career of the Stanford-Binet, possibly by virtue of its wide popularity, has been particularly stormy in this respect. Although *Measuring Intelligence* contains no reference to validity as such, Terman has stated elsewhere, ". . . The ultimate criterion of validity was correlation with mental age. . . . In no case was percent passing by chronological age the final criterion of validity. It is necessary to emphasize this fact because of mis-statements that have been made by some of the critics of the age-scale method." (29, p. 4.) This rebuttal refers to the oft-repeated charge that anything that showed increase with CA might have been included in the scale without violating the selection principle. The critics charged further that the principles, whether verbalized or not, which led to the decision to try a given item in preliminary standardization must have been something other than the increase in percent passing with increasing CA since such items as height or speed of reaction or number of teeth were not included. The criterion is a necessary, but not a sufficient, index of intelligence. The difficulty would appear to be that a tautological argument is involved. MA is based upon mean CA results, so mental age is based upon chronological age. The fact that the tests do show a correlation with mental age, to say nothing of other direct indices of validity such as correlation with other tests and clinical usefulness, makes it plausible to conclude that whether this charge of an irrelevant criterion of validity is correct or incorrect, the test does show considerable evidence of validity. A correlation with mental age, as Terman would contend, does not solve the problem because the question then becomes one of determining what is measured by mental age and the resultant IQ.

FACTOR ANALYSIS

Factor analysis of test results is of practical importance to the clinician because of the information yielded about the nature of what the test is measuring. McNemar says the presence of a large general factor and the relative exclusion of group factors is ". . . necessary if the scores of individuals are to be comparable—the presence of a large group factor, or factors, permits two equal scores to be qualitatively different and two different scores to be quantitatively (with respect to the central function being measured) the same." (29, p. 99.) A satisfactory attack upon this problem involves two issues: (1) Is there a common factor of sufficient saturation to satisfy the need expressed above? (2) Does this common factor at one level correspond to the common factor at other levels?

To these problems McNemar addressed himself. Using Thurstone's centroid method with the standardization sample of Terman and Merrill he performed fourteen separate factor analyses. The test items included in each were so arranged as to overlap, e.g., tests from level III appeared not only with the group of CA 3 but also with the group of CA 3½. The results show conclusively that a strong first factor is to be found in all fourteen factor analyses with about 35–50 percent of the variance thus being accounted for. Since about 35 percent of test variance is due to unreliability, little is left to be attributed to group factors. The overlap device is utilized to present evidence that this first factor is measuring an ability which is consistent throughout all levels of the scale. The second and third factors isolated are of such dubious nature that it is reasonably safe to disregard them. Thus, McNemar has offered evidence that the need for comparability is satisfied as there is a common factor found throughout the scale. As Terman (29) points out, this needs checking by the retest method over a period of years.

McNemar refers to the major factor found in his results as the "first," "common," or "general" factor, leaving for others any further identification of its nature. It is generally considered that tests having high loadings in this factor require ability to solve problems involving words and numbers. Tests with low factor loadings are those which depend more upon manipulative skill and less upon language skill.

In England, Burt and John (8), who used the bipolar factor

method on the results of testing 483 boys and girls between 10 and 14½ years of age, also found that the first or general factor had a strong verbal bias. The contribution of the first factor to general intelligence was very similar to that found by McNemar, namely, about 40 percent of the total variance. There were three bipolar factors isolated in addition to the general factor. The bipolar factors are described as indicating the effect on test performance of age; of verbal, spatial, and numerical abilities; and, somewhat less conclusively, of immediate memory, understanding words, and understanding situations.

SCHOLASTIC SUCCESS

The test originally developed by Binet and Simon was validated against scholastic progress and, in fact, was commissioned in order to weed out intellectual misfits from the Paris schools. The Terman-Merrill revision is closely related to factors which make for success in highly verbal activities or school subjects. McNemar (29) presents detailed findings about the standardization group on this point. As Mursell (36) points out, to assume, as is sometimes done, that something so closely related to scholastic success is not in turn related to intelligence borders on the absurd. Therefore, evidence of validity is found in the uniformly high correlations reported.

It is both a weakness and a strength that its results are so closely related to school progress. A quotation from Wells is appropriate. He reminds us that "The original function of the Binet scale was as a gauge of proper school progress. For this function it is still reasonably suited; if clinical psychologists object that it is ververbalistic, the answer is that so is the curriculum." (56, p. 113.) The Stanford-Binet cannot be dismissed or minimized because, as some of its critics disparagingly claim, it is "merely a scholastic aptitude test." The scholastic milieu, aside from the home, exerts the most important environmental influence upon the make-up of the child. That the Stanford-Binet is not as useful where the patient's problems touch less upon school influences may be a cause for regret but not for dismissal of it as an instrument.

RELIABILITY

Terman and Merrill (53) point out that no single reliability coefficient may be cited as representative, as the coefficients vary according to IQ. For the standardization group they report reliability coefficients of about .98 for those subjects below 70 IQ, about .92 at IQ 100, and about .90 at 130 IQ and above. Reliability increases, then, as IQ level decreases. It is gratifying to note that the reliability is greatest in the region of 70 IQ, where IQ findings are often of crucial importance.

Reliability coefficients (of stability and equivalence) found by correlating Form L and Form M at each of the twenty-one age levels ranged from .85 to .95 with a median of .91. Since the subjects were all within four weeks of a birthday (or half-birthday) there is a greater restriction of range than that existing when the customary twelve months' spread at a given age is used in calculating reliability. Consequently these coefficients may be said to compare favorably with the somewhat higher coefficients of .92 or .95 sometimes reported in the literature for other tests.

A statistical measure relevant in the present discussion is the standard error of measurement. Perhaps the simplest method of determining standard errors of measurement for Stanford-Binet results is through mental age findings. There is a choice to be made between calculating the standard error of measurement either for mental age or for the intelligence quotient. The table of the standard error of the IQ given in *Measuring Intelligence* (53, p. 46) provides only a rough approximation and is not precise enough because it reports σe (IQ) without considering the fact that the *mental age level* at which this IQ falls influences its magnitude in a very real sense. Flanagan (16) deals with this point clearly. After pointing out that by consulting Terman and Merrill's table of standard errors of measurement just referred to one would learn that for an IQ of 100 there is a standard error of measurement of 4.51, he goes on to say:

This might appear to be satisfactory, but let us further examine the situation for individuals having an IQ of 100 but who are placed at differing age levels. If the chronological age of such an individual is 100 months, we may deduce that the standard error of measurement in terms of mental age would be 4.51 months, for an error of 4.51 months in the mental age would produce an error of 4.51 points in the IQ at this chronological age. If however, the individual was 150 months old, the error of measurement in terms of mental age which would produce an error of 4.51 points in the IQ would be 6.76 months. It is seen that . . . [their table] could only be a correct description of the situation if the error of measurement in terms of mental-age scores of any point on the scale were directly proportional to the mental age at that point. That this situation exists seems unlikely since there are the same number of tests, six, at each age level from VI to XIV and it is unreasonable to suppose that the tests at successive age levels are progressively less discriminatory. We are thus forced to the conclusion that it is impossible to determine the standard error of measurement of any particular IQ with the type of information represented in . . . [their table]. (16, pp. 132–133.)

In the light of this, it seems reasonable to recommend that the table given by McNemar (29) of the standard errors of measurement of mental age reproduced as Table 13 be used for securing the appropriate values. The values given in the table are for specific MA's and not for a range of values. Thus, the standard error of measurement for MA 100 months is 4.6, and to find the value for

TABLE 13. Standard Error of Measurement in Months for Mental Age Scores (Approximate)[12]

MA	σe (MA)	MA	σe (MA)
180	7.0	100	4.6
170	6.5	90	4.2
160	6.2	80	3.9
150	6.0	70	3.5
140	5.8	60	2.9
130	5.5	50	2.5
120	5.2	40	2.2
110	4.9	30	1.9

MA 95 months it is necessary to interpolate between the standard error of measurement of 4.6 for MA 100 and 4.2 for MA 90 and thus obtain the desired value of 4.4. For MA's greater than 180 months, 7.5 is a fair estimate, according to McNemar. If the standard error of an IQ is desired, entry of the IQ tables of Terman and Merrill (53), beginning on page 415, knowing MA, CA, and σe (MA), will readily yield an approximate value. Thus with MA 70 months, CA 120 months, and σe (MA) 3.5, the σe (IQ) is about two IQ points, while with MA 120 months, CA 70 months, and σe (MA) 5.2, the σe (IQ) is about six IQ points. These standard

[12] Reprinted from *The Revision of the Stanford-Binet Scale* by Q. McNemar (29), by permission of Houghton Mifflin Company. Copyright 1942 by Houghton Mifflin Company.

errors of measurement are not large when one compares them with the findings on other tests. Nevertheless, it is sobering and perhaps conducive to caution to realize that the exactitude of the Stanford-Binet is such that an individual with an MA of 170 months might vary as much as twenty-one months owing entirely to errors of measurement inherent in the instrument.

Test-retest results on this instrument like any other used in clinical practice must be considered both from the standpoint of reliability (stability), which assumes no particular change in those tested except normal growth, and also from the point of view of constancy, in which there is at least a possibility of change in the person to be reflected in the test results. Retests in varying degrees involve administration of new material to the subject. The test is the same in name, but the content differs even with the same form. For example, a retest taking place three years after the original test, assuming normal intellectual growth, might have as its basal year level X and run through Average Adult. The original test might have started initially at level VII and run through level XII; thus the overlap might not be too great. To be sure, the results of factor analysis indicate a common factor throughout the scale, but the fact remains that different material possessing different first-factor loadings will be used. Variation on retest is thus to some degree introduced by this fact.

In the course of her investigation of intellectual growth, Bayley (2) reports certain retest findings with the Stanford-Binet Form L that may be used as indicators of stability. Using forty-five non-clinic children who had been tested at regular intervals from the time they were one month of age, she reports for CA 8 and 9 (the two ages at which Form L was used) both the correlation between the results of the two testings and the change in IQ points from one year to the next. The means and standard deviations for the IQ's were respectively 120 ± 19 and 139 ± 22. The correlation between results of CA 8 and 9 was .91.[13] Thus, despite the upward movement of the IQ's there was close correspondence between relative positions.

The most exhaustive study of IQ stability is that of Honzik,

---

[13] Testing was conducted very close to the birthday of the child (within one month), introducing a restriction of range which undoubtedly acted to lower the coefficient.

Macfarlane, and Allen (23), who followed a fairly representative (but rather superior) sample of Berkeley, California, children from age twenty-one months to eighteen years. From age eight years through fifteen years the Stanford-Binet, Form L or M, was used and consequently the results are pertinent for this period. Without regard to the distinction between Form L and Form M (the differences being nonsignificant), there were differences of not more than five IQ points in the mean IQ for the total group at the successive testing periods. Test-retest correlations disregarding the length of interval between testings were mostly in the high eighties or low nineties. However, individual changes in variability were quite wide. Since different tests were used before and after the Stanford-Binet, the summary of the variability presented which covers ages six through eighteen does not deal only with Stanford-Binet changes, so a pertinent summary statement is impossible.

Hilden (22) found variability to be quite extensive on repeated annual testings of from nine to seventeen years of thirty normal children. For example, three cases had differences in IQ as great as forty-five points over the years. The least extreme variation was seven points. Nevertheless, the group trends were stable, e.g., the mean of the highest IQ's at twelve years of age or before did not differ significantly from the final IQ which was secured some four or five years later. It should be noted that Hilden found the highest IQ twelve years CA or before to predict most adequately the IQ obtained at the oldest age tested. This might be taken as an exemplification of the dictum that many nonintellectual factors may act to depress the obtained IQ, but not the reverse, and that the highest IQ is more nearly representative.

A retest study with mental defectives is also pertinent. Spaulding (50) utilized the results of nearly all Stanford-Binet Form L retests given in an institution between certain dates yielding a group of seventy-one of mean CA on initial test of 14–2. The mean time elapsing before retest was slightly under four years. On both test and retest most of the subjects were imbeciles, morons, or borderline defectives. Retesting was not done routinely, but generally on the request of the previous examiner because he felt there was some indication of possible deterioration or improvement. As a group, there was no particular change since the mean IQ's for test and retest were respectively 56.0 and 57.6. The correlation was again .91. Case study information was sought upon the eight cases showing increases in IQ of ten or more points and the seven cases showing decreases to a corresponding extent. Behavior problems either complicating the original (test) period or the later (retest) period accounted for many of these changes. Expected deterioration, psychoses, or lues accounted for some of the decreases. For only two could no satisfactory explanation be found. Thus the differences in almost all instances were accounted for by examination of the circumstances of the particular case. Although this may appear dangerously close to *post hoc, ergo propter hoc* reasoning, the clinical scene too often demonstrates this sort of situation for it to be dismissed in this fashion. Individuals seen by clinicians show such changes; they are suspected and then confirmed by retesting. In such instances the problem is not reliability (because reliability assumes consistency of the person as well as the instrument) but constancy—or better, inconstancy—as changes occur or are presumed to occur in the individual.

IQ CONSTANCY AND THE CLINICAL SCENE[14]

The studies on the constancy of the IQ, particularly those emanating from the University of Iowa, have renewed interest in the relationship and relative influence of nature and nurture. To deal with any of the ramifications of this issue would be too far afield from the present methodological aim. However, they are of interest to the clinician since he is concerned with prediction of the future intellectual level of the child. Whether or not one accepts as exemplary the rationale and technique of such studies, the rather common observation of improvement in intellectual functioning upon removal to a more stimulating and healthful environment stands undisputed. It is the sensitive instrument, not the unreliable one, which reflects these changes.

Changes in IQ on retest may be due not to relatively permanent modifications but to transitory changes in the patient or in the situation. Undoubtedly, the total interpersonal situation and the degree and kind of relationship with the clinician affect the patient's scores, just as they do in a situation more narrowly thera-

---

[14] The question of constancy of IQ obtained on the Stanford-Binet of the preschool child when retested in later childhood or adolescence will be considered in connection with the chapter on preschool testing.

peutic in nature. On the basis of clinical experience psychologists exhibit little surprise when an emotionally disturbed child earns a substantially higher IQ upon retest. Though he found the test situation originally traumatic, on retest he may be in a more favorable state for testing and find the situation no longer so difficult to take. Under the circumstances an increased IQ should not be hard to understand. A discussion of this point is given by Blanchard (59). Likewise, circumstances might act to depress the retest IQ.

A study by Tulchin (55), although conducted some years ago with the 1916 Stanford-Binet, illustrates what may be done in recognizing the inadequacy of original test results and their relation to results found on retesting. He divided his subjects into a group who coöperated well and whose results were consequently considered reliable, and several groups in which to varying degrees the results were not considered reliable. Emotional blocking, speech, reading, and language handicaps were some of the factors which were considered as making for unreliability. On retest the clinician's estimates were confirmed in that the IQ's did not vary more than five IQ points for over 80 percent of the reliable group; but only about 30 percent of those in a typical one of the groups considered unreliable stayed within the limit of five IQ points' variation.

Implicit in the findings reported and the recommendations made by the clinical psychologist based upon the application of the Stanford-Binet (or other intelligence tests) is that the IQ as an index of the rate of mental growth or brightness tends to remain constant. When no qualifications are reported the assumption is made that if the patient were retested any change would be relatively slight (or to put it on a more statistically sophisticated level, the changes would be those expected from the magnitude of the standard error of measurement).

THE RELATION OF THE 1916 AND 1937 STANFORD-BINET SCALES

For some years subsequent to its appearance in 1937, comparison of the present revision and the 1916 Stanford-Binet was popular. Many of the detailed findings of such studies are now irrelevant because of the virtual disappearance of the 1916 Stanford-Binet from the clinical scene. Nevertheless, some attention must be paid to it because occasionally records of psychometric examinations given with the earlier revision are appealed to in present clinical contacts.[15]

Under no circumstances is the original or 1916 classification of IQ's by Terman appropriate with the Revised Stanford-Binet. The article by Davis (13) brings this out clearly. He shows, for example, that an IQ of 70 on the 1937 Binet would be equivalent at age seven to a 1916 Binet IQ of 81. His table of IQ equivalents is based on the use of the standard deviation for the entire 1937 standardization group (16.4) and therefore introduces the errors discussed in connection with IQ interpretation at the ages having smaller and larger standard deviations. Merrill (32) gives a tabulation reproduced as Table 14 which will serve as a rough indication of the nature of the changes in IQ from one revision to the other. This table shows the shifting that has occurred in the direction of a wider IQ spread for the present revision. High IQ's are higher in the new scales and low IQ's are slightly reduced.

The greater variability of the Revised Stanford-Binet Scales has been attributed to the wider geographical and socioeconomic sampling. As Rheingold and Perce (42) point out, the greater number and diversity of items as well as the possibly greater discriminatory value of the items of the new scale may also contribute.

THE SIGNIFICANCE OF SCATTER ON THE REVISED STANFORD-BINET

If an individual passed all tests at a certain age level and thereafter failed all tests there would be no irregularity or scatter—the basal year would also be the maximal year. Such consistency is not expected and is rarely found. As McNemar points out, scatter may be attributed to a variety of factors: ". . . item unreliability, low intercorrelations among items, lack of high correlation of items with age (those are highest for items at the lower end of the scale), the presence of a series of items which call for some special ability, and

---

[15] It is the conviction of the writer that, despite the considerable amount of research on the 1916 Binet, the 1937 version is sufficiently different to make it almost impossible to transfer detailed clinical findings about tests and test items from the old to the new form. As a consequence the 1916 literature is not exhaustively reviewed.

TABLE 14. Percentage Distribution of Stanford-Binet and
Revised Stanford-Binet IQ's[16]

Percentile	IQ Stanford-Binet	IQ Revised Stanford-Binet L—M
99	130	143
98	128	138
97	125	134
95	122	131
90	116	124
85	113	121
80	110	117
75	108	114
66.6	106	111
33.3	95	96
25	92	93
20	91	90
15	88	87
10	85	83
5	78	77
3	76	73
2	73	70
1	70	65
N	905	2,904

lastly faulty age placement of items." (29, p. 167.) All of these are functions of the scale itself; the question at issue is whether or not there is also scatter attributable to the characteristics of the individual. This takes more generalized form in the question of whether or not diagnostic groups show characteristic scatter, i.e., whether the flow of successes and failures is revelatory of certain significant attributes.

The tendency for some subjects to show irregular performance (scatter) has been quantitatively investigated through various formulas. For example, the so-called Pressy scatter (20) is based upon giving weights to tests passed above and failed below the test level nearest the MA. These weights are proportional to the distance from it. Thus a child with MA 8–0 would have a greater weight attached

[16] Adapted from "The Significance of IQ's on the Revised Stanford-Binet Scales" by M. A. Merrill (32), by permission of the *Journal of Educational Psychology*. Copyright 1938 by Warwick and York.

to a failure on a test at level V than on a success at level IX. The sum of these weights is the measure of scatter.

Although studies of scatter with psychotic adults were not infrequent with the 1916 Stanford-Binet (20) (21) (24), their results were inconclusive, if not contradictory. With the advent of more suitable instruments, particularly the Wechsler-Bellevue Scale, this area of investigation with the Binet scales has been largely abandoned. It is perhaps significant that only two major studies (5) (37) using the Revised Stanford-Binet Scales in the investigation of patterns of psychotic adults have appeared. Although the studies were carefully conducted, the results again are disappointing in their yield for actual clinical practice. Apparently this dearth of studies mirrors the clinical practice of today, with hardly any use of the Revised Stanford-Binet in diagnostic work with neurotic or psychotic adults. With Harris and Shakow (21), it is agreed that the point-scale technique is superior for the evaluation of scatter in that each variety of performance is measured continuously rather than changing in almost all instances at successive age levels.

A curious state of affairs is found on considering the extent of scatter shown by problem children as compared to that exhibited by normal children. On one hand we have the rather widely held, but by no means unanimous, clinical opinion that children demonstrating emotional difficulties are prone to have wider scatter on the Stanford-Binet than do normal children, although it is recognized that for individuals in the latter group other factors may be operating to make for unevenness of development and consequent wider scatter. On the other hand, there are apparently no published definitive studies of scatter involving matched groups of normal and problem children in which the 1937 revision was used! It may be that the impressions of some clinicians are correct but no research evidence can be cited. Certainly under this state of affairs the novice clinician is in the uncomfortable position of not knowing just how wide "wide" scatter is. Caution in the interpretation of scatter as diagnostically significant is indicated.

Probably at this time a scatter of, say, more than six years (including both maximal and basal) should make the results of the examination "suspect." Such a scatter may not necessarily be indicative of emotional maladjustment, but it leaves open to suspicion the adequacy of its numerical result (i.e., the IQ) in characterizing the subject's intelligence. Such wide scatter may be due to many factors (atypical culture or educational background for the test, maladministration or inaccurate scoring of the test, poor rapport, poor effort or motivation, as well as emotional difficulty), but at least the examiner may tentatively conclude that "something is amiss."

TEST PATTERNS IN NORMALS AND MENTAL DEFECTIVES

The failing or passing of a given test on the Stanford-Binet is viewed by many clinicians as throwing light on broader aspects of personality as well as on relative intellectual strengths and weaknesses. McNemar (29) warns that the individual tests have relatively low reliabilities, and consequently such a procedure must be used with caution.

An even more fundamental difficulty barring ready interpretation of such relative strengths and weaknesses is the method of placement of items at a given age level during standardization. It must never be overlooked that the tests were not primarily arranged according to a certain fixed percentage of cases of a certain CA passing each of them, but rather in such a fashion that for any age group the mean IQ would be as close to 100 as possible. For example, McNemar (29) reports that at CA 7, for items at level VII of Form L, the percents passing tests 1 through 6 respectively were 59, 51, 69, 59, 55, and 70. Comparable variation in percent passing found with the standardization group at each age level results from selection of those tests for a given age level which in combination made it possible to derive an IQ of 100 for the group.

Tests, then, are not equal in difficulty at a given age level; differences are inherent in the scale itself. Therefore, any attempt at a pattern of test scores must take into account what might for convenience be called the normative pattern. To illustrate, an analysis of successes and failures with mentally defective individuals may yield a certain pattern. This does not mean per se that it is characteristic of the mentally defective alone. It may be that normal individuals of the same MA would yield the same pattern. Therefore, studies using select groups without comparing them with a normal group are difficult to interpret.

The results of two studies concerned with the relative difficulty of test items for the mentally defective might serve to illustrate the

difficulties of identifying a characteristic pattern. In one study Rautman (41) used the Revised Stanford-Binet Form L with 1000 institutionalized mental defectives with a mean IQ of 50, a standard
deviation of 15 and a range from 13 through 79. The average CA
was about twenty years with a standard deviation of about 10. He
calculated for each age group the percents passing each test and then
calculated the significance of the difference from other tests. Thus
he was able to show which tests were reliably different from other
tests at the same level. Sloan and Cutts (45) utilized substantially
the same procedure using the same form with 406 mental defectives
who had almost identical mean CA and IQ to those found by Rautman. Between mental age levels IV and XIII they compared each
test with the five others of that level. They considered a test to fall in
the category of "easy" if it was passed by a significantly higher percent than at least three other tests. The same rule was applied to
hard tests, i.e., passed by a lower percent than three other tests.

Fortunately the data of Rautman permit these same rules to be
applied, making it possible to compare the two studies in terms of
hard and easy tests. Between the mental age levels of IV and XI
(those in which the two studies overlap) there are fifty-four
tests.

Rautman found many more tests easy and hard, in the sense that
these terms are used here, than did Sloan and Cutts. In fact, forty-
eight of the fifty-four tests equally subdivided between the two categories are so designated. Sloan and Cutts, on the other hand, found
but eleven tests to meet these criteria. This greater discriminatory
prowess of the former study is to be attributed in part at least to the
large sample on which it is based.

Despite the disparity in number of tests classified, the two agree
except in one instance in finding certain tests characteristically hard
or easy for mental defectives. It is still important to know whether
these same tests are also characteristically hard or easy for normal
individuals.[17]

A partial answer is supplied from the findings on the standardization group as reported by McNemar (29, pp. 89 ff.). As the data do

---

[17] In fairness to these investigators it must be pointed out that they did not
state that these patterns were different from those obtained from normal individuals. They merely presented the results as characteristic of mental defectives,
saying nothing about normals.

not include calculations similar to those made in the previous studies, the following plan was used: The two easiest tests and the two hardest tests as demonstrated by percent passing for the sample at that age level were selected as easy or hard. In the nine instances in which Rautman and Sloan and Cutts agreed, five were substantiated by McNemar's findings, one was neutral, but three were contradicted by the figures on normals. These three which reversed the trend in the mental defectives as compared to the standardization group were Vocabulary and Mutilated Pictures at level VI, easy for the mental defectives and hard for the normals, and Verbal Absurdities at level XI, in which the reverse occurred. Another possible comparison is between the hard and easy tests of McNemar and the findings of Rautman alone. It was found that in ten instances both groups found a test hard, in ten both found it easy, and in only thirteen was there disagreement. Chance expectancy would, of course, point to less agreement.

There is evidence from these sources that many of the differences supposedly characteristic of the mentally defective are actually characteristic of a normal group as well. Thus caution is advised in making inferences about individual cases.

A study which takes into account the relative difficulty of the test with normal individuals is that of Thompson and Magaret (54). Their subjects were all the mental defectives referred to a clinic during a specified period and the members of the standardization group for the Revised Stanford-Binet Scale whose mental ages were the same as those found in the defective group. This type of matching held constant the mental age factor in the two groups. The defective group was chronologically older but naturally had a lower average IQ. The authors found that out of seventy-three tests only thirty differentiated between the two groups with statistical significance.

Their data provided a golden opportunity for investigating certain hypotheses regarding the difference between the normal and the subnormal intellect. Accordingly, they explored the belief that tests easier for the defective include those which depend more upon his broader experience as compared to that of his peer of normal mental age. Without awareness of the findings on specific tests just given, two skilled psychologists rated each of the tests for their dependence upon past experience. The mean experience ratings of tests easier and harder for the mentally defective were practically identical. What difference there was occurred in the direction opposite to expectancy under the hypothesis.

Another hypothesis investigated was that of the presumed compensatory memory ability of the mentally defective. Contrary to common clinical impression, rote memory items are not a forte of the mentally defective, for none of these tests proved easier for the mentally defective whereas several were among those in which the normals surpassed the defectives of the same mental age.

The hypothesis defended as most plausibly accounting for the results is that the tests in which the defectives do poorly as compared to normals are those more heavily saturated with the general first factor found by factorial analysis, finding evidence in the previously described factor analysis of McNemar. The mean factor loading for the tests easier for the defectives was .49 and the mean for the tests that proved more difficult was .60, the difference being statistically significant. Confirmation of the thesis of Thompson and Magaret is to be found in the data of Sloan and Cutts in the study previously referred to. For each "hard" and each "easy" item the writer found the first factor loading as reported by McNemar. The median factor loadings for these two groups were respectively .718 and .427. Thompson and Magaret say that the differences may be interpreted in terms of chronological age or intelligence quotient—the two features on which the groups differed. After discussion they decided tentatively that the variable accounting for the differential successes and failures in the two groups was whatever it is that is measured by the IQ. In other words, mental defectives failed items heavily saturated with the first factor, not because they are older but because they have lower IQ's. They reach this decision because they consider it unreasonable to assume that the young subjects they studied would show a decrease in factor loadings with increase in chronological age. Magaret and Thompson (30) have recently extended their investigation by studying a third group in addition to the normal and mentally defective, namely, a superior group (120 IQ or above). They found their previously reported results to hold throughout the intelligence distribution, since the results with this third group supported their hypothesis concerning the first factor.

QUALITATIVE ASPECTS

The variety of tests of the Revised Stanford-Binet provides the clinician with numerous opportunities for behavioral observations, although the previous account should serve to sober the person too prone to interpret the pattern of success and failure as diagnostically revealing. Nevertheless, there are certain systematic approaches to the qualitative aspects of diagnostic testing. Two valuable sources of incidental comments about specific tests of the Revised Stanford-Binet are Terman and Merrill (53) and Carter and Bowles (11).

The classificatory terms for various kinds of responses developed by Strauss and Werner (51) for certain items of the 1916 Stanford-Binet still have value and are given below, and a sampling page from the scoring guide using these terms (adapted to the 1937 revision) is presented as Table 15.

1. "Correct." A correct answer. The principal import of the problem is recognized and it is solved in a sufficiently specific, comprehensive and general way.
2. "Correct-incomplete." A less correct but still satisfactory answer. The principal import of the problem may not be fully recognized; the answer may lack either specificity or comprehensiveness.
3. "Superficial." The answer is either irrelevant or it is based on purely verbal association.
4. "Wrong." The answer contradicts general facts or specific facts involved in the problem.
5. "Egocentric." The answer indicates a retreat into a personal emotional sphere.
6. "Nonsensical." A logically absurd or meaningless answer.
7. "Misunderstanding." An answer based on a misunderstanding of the question.
8. "Inadequate." An answer reached by adding factors not inherent in the question, or through comprehension of the question from an aberrant point of view.
9. "Don't know." The answer: I don't know.
10. "Ambiguous." Some of the main points of the solution, not explicitly stated, may be inferred. This descriptive term is used only in connection with terms 1 and 2.

The plan was modified somewhat and applied by Martinson and Strauss (31) to normal and mentally defective children of mental ages 8 through 11. Through MA 10, the mentally defective gave a considerably greater percentage of answers based on term 7 (misunderstanding). "Don't know" answers were much more often given

Revised Stanford-Binet Tests of Intelligence   257

TABLE 15.   Qualitative Scoring of Revised Stanford-Binet, Form L, VII, Test 4, Item A[18]

Question: What's the thing for you to do when you have broken something which belongs to someone else?

Terms	Answers	Comment
1. "Correct."	Give them something instead of it.	Precise statement.
2. "Correct-incomplete."	Paste it.	Not precise, but still correct.
3. "Superficial."	Tell them.	Superficial statement.
4. "Wrong."	Just leave it broken.	Contradictory to reasonable behavior.
5. "Egocentric."	Be ashamed.	Egocentric emotional statement.
6. "Nonsensical."	Sit down.	Meaningless, absurd.
7. "Misunderstanding."	I tell my mother she should buy me a new one.	Misunderstood—the thing belonged to someone else.
8. "Inadequate."	a	
9. "Don't know."		
10. "Ambiguous."	Feel sorry.	May imply: I feel sorry, excuse me. The answer is then "correct incomplete."

a Examples do not occur in this test.

by normals than by the mentally defective children. Other categories either showed negligible differences or too few instances falling within the category to be of significance. Following their lead from item studies with the 1916 Binet, it would appear that almost all levels of the Revised Stanford-Binet from III-6 through Superior Adult III supply items capable of similar analysis, viz., comprehension, responses to pictures, verbal and picture absurdities, similarities, finding reasons, abstract words, proverbs, and vocabulary.

Cruickshank (12) in a study involving normal and mentally retarded children of a mean MA of 10 found in the ingenuity test, level XIV, 4, of the Revised Stanford-Binet Form L very useful in

[18] Adapted from "Qualitative Analysis of the Binet Test" by A. A. Strauss and H. Werner (51), by permission of the American Journal of Mental Deficiency. Copyright 1940 by the American Association of Mental Deficiency.

this regard. It was deliberately selected to see the quality of the responses to what for the most part would be a problem beyond their powers. The normals either solved it or said, "Don't know," whereas the mentally defective boys gave most often nonsensical, superficial, or inadequate answers. This particular method of analysis, although apparently not in wide use, can be recommended. It is especially noteworthy in that it is an attempt to systematize qualitative features and therefore is more readily transmitted both to colleagues and to students.

In a very succinct fashion Murphy (35) discusses the qualitative use of the Stanford-Binet. After dividing the approaches to this task into three—content analysis, form analysis of drawing, and analysis of the distribution of successes and failures—she writes:

Much of the verbal material can be useful for content analysis. The words-in-one-minute test is of course one kind of free-association test. With practice the words, pauses, groupings, etc. can be recorded. Doubtless any experienced tester could give illustrations like the following: a girl who had poor relations with children gave a list of objective words from her immediate surroundings much as other children do, but interpolated the group crazy-blame-fear. Discussion with her teacher revealed that the children had been calling her crazy because of her excessively shy detached behavior. A tense boy who alternated between very controlled behavior and explosions of aggressiveness toward other boys gave sequences in which ambitious adult abstract words alternated with words of violence, destruction, and hostility. In such instances, the verbal material serves to highlight the behavior of the child and reveal the depth of emotional patterns which might otherwise be taken less seriously than they deserve. Definitions, abstract words, etc. are important to watch: one child of average I.Q. gave definitions in highly sensory and colorful terms suggesting artistic possibilities which were later confirmed but had not previously been suspected.

The areas of clarity in definition may be indicative; the child who can define "obedience" but not "defend" is giving us hints about his relations to adults and to children which should be followed up.   .

Reading memory distortions may be revealing, as also inadequate picture interpretations. For example the child who comments on Colonial Days that the man shouldn't have a gun to shoot because it is wrong to shoot, is giving a moralistic interpretation which ignores the life and death reality problem of the picture; such unrealistic moralizing would make the child's social relations difficult if it were generally characteristic of him.

In studying the content of the full Binet record it is of course important to watch for repetitions and congruent deviations. One swallow doesn't make a summer, but a flock of birds flying in the same direction usually means something.

Form analysis of an elementary sort may be done with all drawings produced by the child before, during or after the test; the paper cutting drawings, drawings made for the memory-for-designs test, the purse lost in the field, together with a spontaneous drawing or two collected at the beginning and end of the test, all offer records of the child's graphic patterns. Oversensitiveness to limits, overimpulsiveness, etc. may give clues related to what is found in the content analysis.

The distribution of successes and failures is inspected for consistent and inconsistent patterns. Occasionally a child will pass high tests where he has failed lower ones; while this may sometimes be due to learning that has taken place during the test, it also appears in children who are bored by easy material and stimulated by harder material. When a child succeeds consistently with digits and other precisely defined tasks, and fails in tests requiring insight, it is worth asking whether he is dependent on authority and precise tangible accomplishments. Where the opposite pattern appears, anxiety may have stimulated a concentrated effort to understand and deal with social relations at the expense of routine learning. More study of the meaning of such patterns in the total picture of a child's personality is needed.

As in any personality appraisal, the total picture is more important than separate items taken alone. The child who overcautiously stays within limits on the drawing tests, leans on digits, shows poor insight, defines "obedience" but not aggressive words, may be giving important clues to a personality structure; he may be anxious about authority to the extent of inhibition of normal childish spontaneity, and this would affect work as well as social relations in a modern school. (35, pp. 16–17.)[19]

ADAPTATIONS OF THE REVISED
STANFORD-BINET SCALES

ABBREVIATED SCALES

A considerable number of studies have been concerned with the use of abbreviated scales as substitutes for the complete Revised Stanford-Binet. With economy of time the goal, they are devoted to a comparison of the MA's and IQ's obtained from a shorter scale with those found from use of the full scale. The design of these studies involves administration of the full scale and then derivation of the shorter scales by means of separate scoring. Implicit in this practice of applying different scoring methods to the tests of the full

---

[19] Reprinted from "The appraisal of child personality" by L. B. Murphy, by permission of the *Journal of Consulting Psychology*. Copyright 1948 by the American Psychological Association.

scale is the assumption that the application of a different scoring method yields the same results as administration of the test according to the shortened procedure. Shotwell and McCulloch have pointed out that this is not necessarily justified, as ". . . a different juxtaposition of test items and the compression of the whole test into a much shorter time interval might produce unpredictable transfer effects which would significantly influence total scores." (44, p. 164.) No study investigating this possibility is known so all that can be said is that this is a possibility which must be kept in mind in weighing the evidence.

The two shortened scales[20] used in the investigations to be considered were the tests designated by Terman and Merrill (53) to be administered when time does not permit complete testing (the starred items) and the modification by Wright (58) of this abbreviated scale. The short scale of Terman and Merrill includes four tests at each level selected on the basis of their representativeness and validity. Wright's modification extends the testing at the basal and the maximal years to include the two remaining tests for each of these levels. In other words, if failure occurs at a point presumed to be the basal year, or if success occurs at the level thought on the basis of four failures to be the maximal year, testing proceeds on the short scale until another basal or maximal is reached. At this point, all six tests of the new basal or maximal are also administered. Testing ceases when six tests at a given level are passed and six tests at another level are failed. The Terman-Merrill abbreviation saves about 33 percent of the time required to administer the full scale, whereas Wright's modification eliminates only about 20 percent of the total time.

Particularly relevant to this evaluation of the results of studies of the shorter scales are their findings on correlation of the short and full scale, the mean differences obtained, the tendency to overestimate or underestimate the full scale results, and the likelihood of deviation on the short scale beyond a certain number of IQ points or MA units. This last factor is especially important because of

---

[20] The so-called nonverbal and memory scales described by McNemar (29) are not especially recommended by him and apparently little, if at all, used in clinical practice; they can consequently be disregarded. What in effect is the reverse of the nonverbal, i.e., the "verbal" tests not appearing in it, might sometime be tried as an independent scale since it would contain the tests highly saturated with the first factor.

clinical interest in the scores of individuals. Means on both the scales may be quite similar, yet there may be individuals whose scores deviate considerably from those on the full scale. There is no generally accepted amount of deviation that is considered serious, but some criterion is desirable in this presentation. Therefore, somewhat arbitrarily, a deviation of more than five IQ points will be considered as seriously in error. It may be argued that this is an excessively rigorous standard. For "group" studies and purposes it might well be, but in clinical activities it can be defended.

The findings of the several studies concerned with the relationship of abbreviated scale to full scale are summarized in Table 16. Despite the high correlations found rather consistently, the Terman and Merrill Short Form and Wright's modification have slightly lower mean IQ's than those found for the full scale. However, in no case is the mean difference obtained between a short and the full scale statistically significant. The three studies involving both forms show a slightly greater correspondence between the means of the full scale and that of Wright's modification. Moreover, the amount of deviation, expressed here in the percentage of cases exhibiting more than five IQ points difference between the full scale and one or another of the short scales, clearly favors Wright's modification. Another point which favors the Wright modification over the Terman-Merrill Short Form is the presence of inversion, or the passing of tests at a level above that where all are failed. As mentioned earlier, this is a serious matter when using the Stanford-Binet, since wide-range testing seems to change the IQ. Spache (48) in the study referred to in Table 16 found such inversions in the Terman-Merrill short scale in 19 percent and in Wright's modification in 6 percent of the cases.

The results are unequivocal in pointing to an underestimation of full scale IQ by the short scales in more than half the cases. The mean scores would suggest this, but the direction of deviations reported in percentage form bring it out much more clearly. In each case where it was investigated, more than 50 percent of the subjects received lower IQ's on the abbreviated form and about 30 percent received higher.

A difference related to mean intellectual level that may be observed in the table is that Brown's "normal" and Spache's "superior" group show a tendency for a progressively greater number of individ-

TABLE 16. Findings on Abbreviated Stanford-Binet Scales

Investigator	Sample	CA	Scale	IQ	r	Percent of Cases Showing Deviations of More Than 5 IQ Points	Direction of All Deviations
Wright (58)	275 outpatient and institutionalized morons and borderline individuals	Mean σ 13.3 5.4	Full Scale IQ Short Scale IQ Wright's Mod. IQ	Mean 66.4 65.1[a] 65.7[a]		T-M Short 10.5 Wright's Mod. 1.8	Short, no trend. Wright's Mod., slight tendency to underestimate
Shotwell and McCulloch (44)	100 institutionalized grand mal epileptics	Range 16-4 to 49-1	Full Scale IQ Short Scale IQ Wright's Mod. IQ	Mean 49.2 49.0 48.8		T-M Short 6.0 Wright's Mod. 2.0	Short
Spaulding (49)	500 institutionalized mental defectives	Mean 17.8	Full Scale MA Short Scale MA	Mean 6-11 6-9	.99	T-M Short 3.8[b]	Higher 31% Same 16% Lower 53% Short
Kvaraceus (28)	214 school children referred because of some maladjustment	Median Q 10.4 2.5	Full Scale IQ Short Scale IQ	Median 90.7 89.4			Higher 31% Same 15% Lower 54%
Brown (6)	300 randomly selected kindergarten children drawn from a year's entering class of a large city	Mean σ 5-10 2.2	Full Scale IQ Short Scale IQ	Mean σ 109 11 108 11	.94	T-M Short 13.2	Short Higher 24% Same 19% Lower 57%
Spache (48)	100 nursery and private school students in New York City	Mean Approx. 6-0	Full Scale IQ Short Scale IQ Wright's Mod. IQ	Mean 123.35 121.75 124.05		T-M Short 33 Wright's Mod. 26	

[a] Calculated from Wright's data.
[b] Deviation of more than 8 MA months. This figure was chosen because in the region of the mean MA, 8 MA units correspond to 5 IQ points.

uals to exhibit deviations greater than five IQ points than is the case with the subjects of the studies whose mean IQ is 70 or lower. This suggests that the two abbreviated scales are less accurate in predicting full scale IQ's at these levels than at the mentally defective level although, according to Spache (48), Wright's modification is still slightly superior to the regular short scale.

The question of whether the short scales should be used can be answered only in terms of the precision needed, the importance of saving time, and the use to which the results are to be put. For example, if the IQ is used with mental defectives after institutionalization, then perhaps a shorter form might be used, whereas to judge desirability of commitment the full scale would seem obligatory. With individuals falling at or above the normal level the evidence tends to suggest that even more caution should be exercised about the use of either shorter scale because of the increase in the percentage of deviations of more than five IQ points. Of the two, Wright's modification seems the instrument of choice, but the time element enters, for with slightly less accuracy the Terman-Merrill abbreviation may be utilized with an appreciably greater saving of time.

THE VOCABULARY TEST

The vocabulary test used as an independent instrument is, in a sense, an adaptation of the Revised Stanford-Binet Scales. In clinical practice it is not uncommon to use it as a single test standing by itself, as it has been found to have a high correlation with the entire scale. Using the word list of the 1916 scale Terman and Merrill (53) found that the correlation between mental age and vocabulary score was .91 for a group ranging in age from seven to adult. Within a given age level and with the 1937 revision the correlation is generally lower, with coefficients of .71, .83, .86, and .83 reported for ages eight, eleven, fourteen, and eighteen (McNemar, 29). Elwood (14), using a heterogeneous sample of 1100 city school children of mean CA of 11 and mean MA of 9–1, found a correlation between vocabulary score and mental age of .978. A study by Spache (46) gave correlations between full scale MA and both vocabulary score and vocabulary MA. They were respectively .85 and .91. His group of sixty-five nursery and private school children had a mean of 8–8, a vocabulary score of 9.4, and a mean vocabulary MA of 9–1. Since the average IQ was "well over 100" it was a superior group intellectually.

In 14 percent of the cases there was an underestimation of the full scale MA by approximately one year, and overestimation by a similar amount occurred in 49 percent. This same investigator (47) in summarizing his several investigations of short forms reports the vocabulary test the least accurate in predicting full scale MA's when compared with the Terman-Merrill Short Form and Wright's modification. The standard error of estimate is about one year of mental age. If the vocabulary test is used as an individual instrument, predictions in error by this amount or more must be anticipated. The magnitude of the correlation suggests a high degree of relationship between the vocabulary test and the full scale within the various groups. Nevertheless, the findings about individual overestimation and underestimation of MA and the magnitude of the standard error of estimate lead to the inference that the vocabulary test should be substituted for the entire scale only with considerable caution and with full awareness of the tentative results thus obtained.

The findings reported up to this point used normal children as subjects. Because certain additional factors must be evaluated when the vocabulary test is used as an individual instrument with neurotic or psychotic children or adults, the findings concerning these individuals are considered separately. Since the test measures an individual's ability to define orally a selected list of words it does not tap as many functions as does the entire battery, and consequently diagnostic clues are limited though still possible. Another difficulty arises from the nature of the task which the vocabulary test structures for the patient. As Kent (26) has indicated, the test measures the patient's willingness to offer a definition and not necessarily his ability to offer a *correct* definition. The standard of accuracy varies considerably among patients; consequently a patient less autocritical than another may offer and receive credit for a definition which the second patient considered and rejected as not adequate.

In addition, the hypothesis has been advanced that the Stanford-Binet vocabulary test is such as to give credit on many levels and kinds of definitions, thus permitting success at easier levels even when more difficult conceptual organization which receives the same credit is no longer possible. This is true for patients as compared to normals as found in a carefully controlled investigation of Feifel (15). He found that patients offered (and received credit for) "easier" definitions than did normals. This helps to account for the apparent maintenance of former level with patients whereas other tests show deficit.

Of even more consequence are the findings in regard to age. Using the 1916 Stanford-Binet word list from which the 1937 vocabulary test was derived,. Shakow and Goldman (43) studied score differences in relation to age. They found with a representative population a mean level of fifty-seven words relatively constant to the seventh decade. A different approach was followed by Rabin (40), who was interested in the relationship between Form L vocabulary and the Wechsler-Bellevue scale. Using a group of 268 psychotic and non-psychotic mental hospital patients of wide age range he found a correlation of .78. The vocabulary IQ was on the average thirteen points higher than the Wechsler-Bellevue Full Scale IQ. Overestimation by vocabulary IQ increased as age increased until at ages sixty to sixty-nine it was twenty-five IQ points. The psychotic groups showed a greater discrepancy between vocabulary and Wechsler-Bellevue IQ than did the non-psychotic group. Shakow and Goldman (43) argue that the explanation of vocabulary differences between either children and adults or younger and older feeble-minded is attributable not to increase of vocabulary with increase in chronological age but to a decrease in achievement on the other tests of the scale with the advance of age. Thus a proportionately greater vocabulary score results. This seems to be the general consensus of clinical opinion on the matter. However, the phenomena described by Feifel mentioned above may also be operative, although his results are not as clear-cut concerning younger as compared with older adults as they were with normal as compared with abnormal subjects.

Both clinical experience and research findings warrant the conclusion that an older individual of low IQ would have a higher vocabulary score than would a child of the same MA on the full scale. For example, Carlton (10), using Form L, investigated this problem with institutionalized imbecile and moron groups aged 10–6 to 17–5 and found by analysis of covariance that chronological age with mental age constant made a difference in vocabulary score with mean vocabulary score increasing as CA increased.

In keeping with the evidence presented and with a wealth of other material on other tests and other populations which might be cited (cf., for example, Chapter 8 on the Wechsler-Bellevue Scale), it would appear that a distinction must be made between the Stanford-Binet vocabulary test as a measure of present level of functioning and the test as a measure of past level of functioning. With psychiatric patients, especially adults, the vocabulary test must be considered as reflecting fairly adequately perhaps the previous level of functioning but as an overestimation of the present level of functioning. As age or severity of psychotic involvement increases, so does this disparity, and thus the vocabulary test becomes an even poorer indicator of present functioning.

If the vocabulary test of the Stanford-Binet is used individually as a measure of intellectual level, it erroneously may be construed to be a substitute for the entire scale. Distortions will inevitably ensue with an overestimation of the functioning intelligence of older individuals as compared to younger individuals of the same mental level. It may be that use of the vocabulary test with older persons gives a truer picture than does the entire scale; nevertheless, vocabulary mental age cannot be substituted for full scale mental age with confidence that one is comparable to the other in the upper age range.

ADAPTIVE TESTING

From time to time suggestions have been put forth that the Stanford-Binet should not be administered in the order directed in the manual but should be adapted to the particular needs of the patient. The adaptation suggested by Hutt (25) was instigated by a desire not to save time but to motivate the patient maximally so as to obtain the most valid measure possible. He believes that strict adherence to directions does not necessarily mean a standardized testing situation (cf. Chapter 7). In regard to the Revised Stanford-Binet, he pointed out that the consecutive ordering of tests of constantly increasing difficulty with the concomitant increase in frustration engendered thereby resulted in decreasing motivation. This decrease in motivation was predicted to be more or less proportionate to the patient's degree of maladjustment.

Thus the Stanford-Binet was visualized as systematically penalizing the very individuals with whom the clinician is most often concerned. The adaptive procedure that Hutt suggested and tried has as its guiding principle: "Any adaptation of the procedure of testing which offers more favorable motivation for subjects who would be unduly affected by the standard procedure of being given all of the more difficult items toward the end of the testing situation, and which does not affect the medium age-placement of the items, does not disturb the norms of the test." (25, p. 95.) Hutt believed that maximum motivation could be achieved by abandoning consecutive testing and using alternating hard and easy tests instead. Accordingly he framed the following procedure:

I. Begin the New Revised Stanford-Binet with an item from a year level sufficiently below the anticipated mental level to insure the subject's success with this item. . . .

II. Begin the test with an item which does not require considerable concentration, rapid response, or prolonged and involved verbal directions. . . .

III. Alternate "easy" and "hard" items. (In other words, after the subject fails an item give him an easier one; after he passes an item he may be given a more difficult one.)

IV. Administer "serial" tests serially and as early as possible, after the subject has "warmed up." (This is done, not so much as a time-saver but as a means of helping to establish both the basal and maximal early in the test. . . .)

V. Establish both the basal and maximal as early in the test as feasible. (This means, in practice, alternating items from the presumed basal and maximal as soon as there is some evidence that these will, in fact, become the two extremes of the test range.)

VI. Ordinarily, do not administer tests below the presumptive basal or above the presumptive maximal. (25, p. 97.)

There was full agreement on his part that in order to use Terman and Merrill's norms the standardized directions for administering and scoring each specific test must be followed, but he questioned the assumption that the order of presentation made a difference in the difficulty of the items and the motivation for attempting these items. He cited as difficulties with the assumption the following:

For one thing, two subjects who "take" the same items of the test, both scoring the same basal and both completing the test at the same upper level (hereafter called "maximal" in this study) do not necessarily face the same situation. The succession of items may remain the same but the succession of passes and failures may not. This may be true even though both subjects actually obtain the same mental age. This variation in the pattern of successes and failures may, and likely will, affect the motivation of the subjects. In addition, the nature of each subject's reaction to the necessary succession of failures at the maximal may be quite different; we have no right to assume equal capacities for frustration tolerance on the part of different subjects.

For another thing, two subjects who obtain the same mental age may be given different batteries of test items to secure this rating. One may establish a lower basal or a lower maximal or some other variation in the pattern may obtain. Hence, the degree of practice with items of the scale may vary. For example, one subject may have had 5 digits forward at year level VII before getting to 6 digits forward at year level X, while another may not. The same may be true for other types of items such as verbal absurdities, digits backward, abstract words, picture absurdities, etc. (25, pp. 95–96.)

This procedure was put to empirical test through utilization of Stanford-Binet examinations administered by the staff psychologists of an educational clinic in New York City. They used the standard and adaptive procedures alternately with successive cases. Drawing from a sample of over 1100 test records, they selected 640 which met certain criteria and made it possible to have two groups matched closely in CA, school grade, and Binet vocabulary scores. (This last was administered in the same manner to both groups.) In three subgroups based on division by school grade, consecutive and adaptive testing did not make for any appreciable difference in median IQ, the largest difference being 0.7 IQ points.

This does not mean that there may not have been effects of adaptive testing upon specific items on specific individuals. Indeed, if there were not, there would be no point to the modification. Despite the similarity of *median* IQ, the *mean* IQ was consistently larger in the adaptive as compared with the standard groups to the point of significance at the 5 percent level. This led to further inquiry in an effort to account for this difference. On the basis of careful matching of case history data, two extreme groups of very well adjusted and very poorly adjusted subjects were selected for both the usual and the adaptive method. The method of testing, standard or adaptive, made no difference in the mean IQ score for the very well adjusted groups. In the two poorly adjusted groups both means were lower than those from the well adjusted groups. For the adaptive method, however, it was only about seven IQ points lower, whereas for the standard method it was about 18 IQ points lower. Since there was careful matching of the groups, these results suggest that the systematically varied factor of difference of method of testing accounts for the differences in mean IQ. The argument is further reinforced by the fact that the mean vocabulary scores of the two poorly adjusted groups were nearly identical (12.0 and 12.2), and the group adaptively tested had a total IQ fairly commensurate with such a vocabulary, whereas the IQ for the group given the test in the usual fashion had a mean IQ considerably lower than would be expected from the vocabulary score. Hutt points out that these data do not unequivocally demonstrate the validity of this method of testing, as much more evidence drawn from external criteria would be necessary; nevertheless, they are highly suggestive.

The adaptive approach to Stanford-Binet administration by use of serial testing is shown by Frandsen, McCullough, and Stone (17) not to have any significant effect on IQ with forty-seven normal subjects aged five to eighteen. Sixty-eight of the 122 items of Form L were arranged for serial testing with a similar arrangement in Form M. A balanced schedule for all subjects of test and retest, and consecutive and serial administration were arranged, e.g., Form L consecutive with retest by Form M serial and so on. It was found that the mean IQ's for serial and consecutive testing were 109 and 108 respectively with a correlation of .93 between the results of the two testings. The mean IQ difference between serial and consecutive was 5.48, only slightly higher than the mean test-retest difference of 5.09 reported by Terman and Merrill (53). So the hypothesis that serial and consecutive testing would not lead to significant differences was upheld, making possible confident use of Terman and Merrill's norms despite differences in testing procedures.

It may well be that the method of varying the approach with different patients leads to more valid results than does the rigid lockstep of the usual method. This is the opinion of Carter and Bowles (11), who stress selection of tasks from the scale for first presentation which will not only stimulate interest but also aid the examiner in gaining an impression of the probable age range through which the individual will perform. They also speak of using easy tasks to reassure and interesting ones to capture attention. An incidental advantage that Hutt (25) advances is that adaptive testing circumvents the difficulty in obtaining the "final" basal and maximal years which, as pointed out earlier in the chapter, was a source of error in the IQ.

BIBLIOGRAPHY

1. Anon., *A supplementary guide for scoring the Revised Stanford-Binet Intelligence Scale, Form L*, Division of Tests and Measurements, New York City Board of Education, 1941.

2. Bayley, N., Mental growth in young children, in *Intelligence: its nature and nurture*, 39th Yrbk. Nat. Soc. Stud. Educ., Public School Publishing Company, 1940, pp. 11–47.

3. Berger, A., and Speevack, M., An analysis of the range of testing and scattering among retarded children on Form L of the Revised Stanford-Binet, *J. educ. Psychol.*, 1940, 31:39–44.

4. Berger, A., and Speevack, M., An analysis of the range of testing and scattering among retarded children on Form M of the Revised Stanford-Binet Scale, *J. educ. Psychol.*, 1942, 33:72–75.

5. Brody, M. B., The measurement of dementia, *J. ment. Sci.*, 1942, 88:317–327.

6. Brown, F., A comparison of the abbreviated and the complete Stanford-Binet Scales, *J. consult. Psychol.*, 1942, 6:240–242.

7. Brown, F., The significance of the IQ variability in relation to age on the Revised Stanford-Binet Scale, *J. genet. Psychol.*, 1943, 63:177–181.

8. Burt, C.. and John, E., A factorial analysis of Terman Binet tests. Part II, *Brit. J. educ. Psychol.*, 1942, 12:156–161.

9. Carlton, T., Performances of mental defectives on the Revised Stanford-Binet, Form L, *J. consult. Psychol.*, 1940, 4:61–65.

10. Carlton, T., The effect of chronological age on Revised Stanford-Binet vocabulary score at the moron and imbecile levels, *J. genet. Psychol.*, 1942, 61:321–326.

11. Carter, J. W., and Bowles, J. W., A manual on qualitative aspects of psychological examining, *J. clin. Psychol.*, 1948, 4:109–150. (Also as *Clin. Psychol. Monogr.*, 1948, No. 2.)

12. Cruickshank, W. M., Qualitative analysis of intelligence test responses, *J. clin. Psychol.*, 1947, 3:381–386.

13. Davis, F. B., The interpretation of IQ's derived from the 1937 Revision of the Stanford-Binet Scales, *J. appl. Psychol.*, 1940, 24:595–604.

14. Elwood, M. I., A preliminary note on the vocabulary test in the Revised Stanford-Binet Scale, Form L, *J. educ. Psychol.*, 1939, 30:632–634.

15. Feifel, H., Qualitative differences in the vocabulary responses of normals and abnormals, *Genet. Psychol. Monogr.*, 1949, 39:151–204.

16. Flanagan, J. C., review of *Measuring intelligence*, by Terman and Merrill, *Harvard educ. Rev.*, 1938, 8:130–133.

17. Frandsen, A. N., McCullough, B. R., and Stone, D. R., Serial versus consecutive order administration of the Stanford-Binet Intelligence Scales, *J. consult. Psychol.*, 1950, 14:316–320.

18. Goodenough, F. L., Studies of the 1937 Revision of the Stanford-Binet Scale. I. Variability of the IQ at successive age levels, *J. educ. Psychol.*, 1941, 32:241–251.

19. Harriman, P. L., Irregularity of successes on the 1937 Stanford Revision, *J. consult. Psychol.*, 1939, 3:83–85.
20. Harris, A. J., and Shakow, D., The clinical significance of numerical measures of scatter on the Stanford-Binet, *Psychol. Bull.*, 1937, 34:134–150.
21. Harris, A. J., and Shakow, D., Scatter on the Stanford-Binet in schizophrenic, normal, and delinquent adults. *J. abnorm. soc. Psychol.*, 1938, 33:100–111.
22. Hilden, A. H., A longitudinal study of intellectual development, *J. Psychol.*, 1949, 28:187–214.
23. Honzik, M. P., Macfarlane, J. W., and Allen, L., The stability of mental test performance between two and eighteen years, *J. exper. Educ.*, 1948, 17:309–324.
24. Hunt, J. McV., and Cofer, C. N., Psychological deficit, in Hunt, J. McV. (ed.), *Personality and the behavior disorders*, The Ronald Press Company, 1944, pp. 971–1032.
25. Hutt, M. L., A clinical study of "consecutive" and "adaptive" testing with the Revised Stanford-Binet, *J. consult. Psychol.*, 1947, 11:93–103.
26. Kent, G. H., Suggestions for the next revision of the Stanford-Binet, *Psychol. Rec.*, 1937, 1:409–433.
27. Krugman, M., Some impressions of the Revised Stanford-Binet Scale, *J. educ. Psychol.*, 1939, 30:594–603.
28. Kvaraceus, W. C., Pupil performances on the abbreviated and complete New Stanford-Binet Scales, Form L, *J. educ. Psychol.*, 1940, 31:627–630.
29. McNemar, Q., *The revision of the Stanford-Binet Scale: an analysis of the standardization data*, Houghton Mifflin Company, 1942.
30. Magaret, A., and Thompson, C. W., Differential test responses of normal, superior and mentally defective subjects, *J. abnorm. soc. Psychol.*, 1950, 45:163–167.
31. Martinson, B., and Strauss, A. A., A method of clinical evaluation of the responses to the Stanford-Binet Intelligence Test, *Amer. J. ment. Def.*, 1941, 46:48–59.
32. Merrill, M. A., The significance of IQ's on the Revised Stanford-Binet Scales, *J. educ. Psychol.*, 1938, 29:641–651.
33. Merrill, M. A., personal communication, 1948.
34. Mitchell, M. B., Irregularities of university students on the Revised Stanford-Binet, *J. educ. Psychol.*, 1941, 32:513–522.
35. Murphy, L. B., The appraisal of child personality, *J. consult. Psychol.*, 1948, 12:16–19.
36. Mursell, J. L., *Psychological testing*, Longmans Green and Company, 1947.
37. Myers, C. R., and Gifford, E. V., Measuring abnormal pattern on the Revised Stanford-Binet Scale (Form L), *J. ment. Sci.*, 1943, 89:92–101.

38. Pintner, R., Dragositz, A., and Kushner, R., Supplementary guide for the Revised Stanford-Binet Scale (Form L), Appl. Psychol. Monogr., 1944, No. 3.
39. Porteus, S. D., The practice of clinical psychology, American Book Company, 1941.
40. Rabin, A. I., The relationship between vocabulary levels and levels of general intelligence in psychotic and non-psychotic individuals of a wide age range, J. educ. Psychol., 1944, 35:411–422.
41. Rautman, A. L., Relative difficulty of test items of the Revised Stanford-Binet: an analysis of records from a low intelligence group, J. exper. Educ., 1942, 10:183–194.
42. Rheingold, H. L., and Perce, F. C., Comparison of ratings on the Original and Revised Stanford-Binet Intelligence Scales at the borderline and mental defective levels, Proc. Amer. Ass. ment. Def., 1939, 44:110–119.
43. Shakow, D., and Goldman, R., The effect of age on the Stanford-Binet vocabulary score of adults, J. educ. Psychol., 1938, 29:241–256.
44. Shotwell, A. M., and McCulloch, T. L., Accuracy of abbreviated forms of the Revised Stanford-Binet Scale with institutionalized epileptics, Amer. J. ment. Def., 1944, 49:162–164.
45. Sloan, W., and Cutts, R. A., Test patterns of mental defectives on the Revised Stanford-Binet Scale, Amer. J. ment. Def., 1947, 51:394–396.
46. Spache, G., The vocabulary tests of the Revised Stanford-Binet as independent measures of intelligence, J. educ. Res., 1943, 36:512–516.
47. Spache, G., Methods of predicting results of full scale Stanford-Binet, Amer. J. Orthopsychiat., 1944, 14:480–482.
48. Spache, G., The abbreviated Stanford-Binet Scale in a superior population, J. educ. Psychol., 1944, 35:314–318.
49. Spaulding, P. J., Comparison of 500 complete and abbreviated Revised Stanford Scales administered to mental defectives, Amer. J. ment. Def., 1945, 50:81–88.
50. Spaulding, P. J., Retest results on the Stanford L with mental defectives, Amer. J. ment. Def., 1946, 51:35–42.
51. Strauss, A. A., and Werner, H., Qualitative analysis of the Binet test, Amer. J. ment. Def., 1940, 45:50–55.
52. Terman, L. M., and Merrill, M. A., Directions for administering Forms L and M: Revision of the Stanford-Binet Tests of Intelligence, Houghton Mifflin Company, 1937.
53. Terman, L. M., and Merrill, M. A., Measuring intelligence, Houghton Mifflin Company, 1937.
54. Thompson, C. W., and Magaret, A., Differential test responses of normals and mental defectives, J. abnorm. soc. Psychol., 1947, 42:285–293.

55. Tulchin, S. H., Clinical studies of mental tests, Amer. J. Psychiat., 1934, 90:1237–1248.
56. Wells, F. L., Revised Stanford-Binet Scale, in Buros, O. K. (ed.), The 1938 Mental Measurements Yearbook, Rutgers University Press, 1938, pp. 113–114.
57. Wile, I. S., and Davis, R. M., A study of the behavior of 250 children with mental age ten years, Amer. J. Orthopsychiat., 1938, 8:689–709.
58. Wright, C., A modified procedure for the abbreviated Revised Stanford-Binet Scale in determining the intelligence of mental defectives, Amer. J. ment. Def., 1942, 47:178–184.

Supplementary Articles in Watson, R. I. (ed.), Readings in the clinical method in psychology, Harper & Brothers, 1949:

DIAGNOSTIC TESTING REPORTS INVOLVING THE REVISED STANFORD-BINET

59. Blanchard, P., The interpretation of psychological tests in clinical work with children. Pp. 349–365. (Also in Ment. Hyg., N.Y., 1941, 25:58–75.)
60. Sarason, E. K., and Sarason, S. B., A problem in diagnosing feeble-mindedness. Pp. 314–324. (Also in J. abnorm. soc. Psychol., 1945, 40:323–329.)

ADDITIONAL DIAGNOSTIC TESTING REPORTS INVOLVING THE REVISED STANFORD-BINET

61. Escalona, S. K., The use of a battery of psychological tests for diagnosis of maladjustment in young children—a case report, Trans. Kans. Acad. Sci., 1945, 48:218–223.
62. Rosenzweig, S., with Kogan, K. L., Psychodiagnosis: an introduction to tests in the clinical practice of psychodynamics, Grune & Stratton, 1949, pp. 16–24.

CHAPTER 10

Performance Tests of Intelligence

THE NATURE OF PERFORMANCE TESTS

The major function of performance tests is to afford standardized settings for observation of the behavior of an individual in situations other than the type provided by verbal tests. This is not to say that verbal sampling is unimportant—the attention given it in earlier chapters attests the contrary.

In a sense the term "performance tests" is a misnomer. Every test reaction, verbal or otherwise, is a performance. But since such tests originated in manipulative material, particularly form boards, it is easy to see how the term came to be applied. In the most narrow sense, performance tests are those which can be administered without any speech or the use of written words on the part of either the examiner or the subject. There are several well-standardized scales that conform to this requirement and are consequently useful in testing cases of speech defect, deafness, foreign language handicap, specific reading disability, lack of schooling, and extreme shyness.

Most so-called performance tests, however, involve verbal instructions, but as Carter and Bowles say: ". . . Performance tasks differ from certain Binet-type items in that the former involve 'concrete' language situations in which the individual is in direct contact with the object to which reference is made. Such tasks tend to be less dependent upon language (oral or gestural) than the 'remote' language situation, which characterizes many Binet items in which the

274

individual is not in visual contact with the object." (14, p. 135.) The "Performance Scale" of the Wechsler-Bellevue Scale not only requires verbal instructions but includes test items that demand verbal response.

The development of the performance scale for the measurement of nonverbal intelligence has followed closely the history of the development of the verbal scales, including the Binet. As it was utilized first in clinics to obtain a more accurate estimate of the ability of the patient who was not able to earn a rating on the Binet or other verbal scales appropriate to his capacity to adjust to life situations, an impression developed that dull individuals tend to do better on nonverbal scales than on those requiring verbal response. This impression has not been uniformly supported by research data. In 1927, Arthur (6) reported that, for a group of 435 clinic cases made up of individuals with Binet IQ of less than 95, the median difference (with differences arranged according to algebraic magnitude) between the Binet IQ and that obtained with Form I of the Point Scale of Performance Tests was ±0. There was no tendency on the part of the dull individuals in this group to do better in the nonverbal than in the verbal field. These findings have been supported by a later study made by Arthur (6). Sixty cases of general mental retardation with chronological ages between fifteen and twenty years were selected on the basis of lack of special disabilities. They were simple aments without physical handicaps. Each individual had an IQ of less than 75 on both the Binet Scale and on Form I of the Point Scale of Performance Tests. The differences between the Binet and the performance scale IQ for these individuals were arranged according to algebraic magnitude. The median difference for the girls was ±0. For the boys, it was +1.0. For the whole group, the median difference was +0.5, of a point of IQ. That is, the group of sixty cases showed an average of one-half point higher on the performance scale than on the Binet. It is possible, then, that the discrepancy between results such as Arthur's and the fairly common clinical impression in regard to relative success in verbal and nonverbal situations is due to the fact that she gave the performance scale routinely. This would yield a very different conclusion from that arrived at in situations where the performance scale was given only when it was suspected that the patient might be more successful on that than he had been on the Binet or other verbal scale.

Performance tests are of considerable general significance in the appraisal of an individual. Although Porteus was speaking of but one kind of performance test—that stressing manipulation—the following quotation is cogent:

One of the important gaps that are not filled by the verbal tests is the testing of manipulative ability. There are, especially in early childhood, quite a number of situations in which this capacity is valuable. Every child must learn to dress himself, and the management of buttons and laces requires considerable manipulation. Playing with mechanical toys and games of skill, together with the operation of household devices, calls for a certain degree of manual dexterity of a rather simple nature. The capacity seems to have only a moderate amount of exercise in later childhood and that mainly in such mechanical operations as learning to draw and write in school. Perhaps for this reason scales such as the Binet make little provision for testing manipulative skill. . . . [Nevertheless] it is well to remember that, though so little attention is paid to testing manipulative ability in the Binet scale, a large number of children will ultimately earn their living as skilled or semiskilled manual workers, a condition which should be taken into account in our intelligence testing program. (33, pp. 139–140.)

The exigencies of the clinical setting—referrals of persons not speaking English, illiterates, deaf individuals, and those with severe speech defects—emphasize the need for performance scales in psychological and psychiatric clinics. Of equal importance is the fact that performance tests tap intellectual functions of importance in evaluating the ability of the individual. Sometimes there is unequal development in an individual of verbal and nonverbal abilities. There may be considerable learning ability revealed by the Binet Scale, but it may be accompanied by a deficiency in the ability to do independent thinking. The high Binet rating may indicate that the pupil is bright enough to do good work in high school, but a low rating on the performance scale indicates the reason for his failure in high school mathematics and laboratory science.

In 50 percent of clinic cases in one study by Arthur (6) the performance scale tended to yield a higher estimate of the general ability of the patient than the reaction level reported by the Binet IQ. This higher rating is considered by Arthur as likely to be the more accurate estimate since it has been found that after therapy (corrective speech, remedial reading, glandular therapy, lip reading, hearing aids, etc.) the Binet rating tends to approach the Arthur

Scale of Performance Tests PQ. It is seldom, if ever, that the non-verbal rating changes with the modification of handicaps other than vision and hypothyroidism. This should be taken into account whenever a diagnosis of "normal" or "feeble-minded" ("mentally deficient") is to be made. To ascertain whether there is a discrepancy between verbal learning ability and capacity for nonverbal thinking in cases free from obvious handicaps, complementation of "verbal" tests such as the Revised Stanford-Binet by a performance scale is indisputably indicated.

Carl (13) comments that in decisions about mental deficiency, performance tests should receive equal weight with verbal tests (with, of course, attention to other factors revealed by these and other measures—particularly those of social competence and personality adjustment). Why, then, have they not received the attention that other, more verbal, instruments have been given? Speaking of mental defectives, Hamlin has this to say:

. . . The so-called performance batteries have never come into their own as tests of intelligence with dull and defective subjects. They are widely used but are generally considered to be less valuable than verbal tests like the Binet. Several reasons may account for this. First, verbal symbolism *does* play an important part in many aspects of intelligence. Second, the Binet has the support of long tradition. Third, mental deficiency is usually recognized early, in the school situation where verbal intelligence is at a premium. And fourth, the performance scales have never been as successfully developed as the verbal type of tests; success depends too much on factors other than intelligence. (18, p. 162.)

It is possible to disagree with the fourth conclusion offered by Hamlin, although many clinicians would agree with him, in view of close accord found between Binet and performance scale results in homogeneous groups. "Factors other than intelligence," such as speech defects and hearing defects, also affect verbal scales as well.

Another restriction on the usefulness of performance tests occurs when the entire scope of intellectual prowess is considered. Many, but not all, performance tests have their optimal usefulness with children of preschool and school age or with adults of these mental ages. In effect this is saying that beyond a certain mental age (in the neighborhood of ten or twelve) they become of less relevance in considering diagnostic problems. That there are exceptions to this age restriction in certain of the component tests will be amply illustrated later in the discussion of some of the tests of the Arthur Performance Scale used as independent instruments, such as the Kohs Block Design Tests. Nevertheless, some of the elements, as in most performance scales, have very definitely this limitation. As Carl (13) points out, differences in performance test scores among normal adults often have another meaning than is the case with scores on the same tests of younger or mentally defective persons. Among older normal individuals, variations in scores may indicate merely variation in motor reaction speed, or differences in confidence, initiative, and aggressiveness and have little or nothing to do with varying degrees of comprehension of the problem presented as a performance task. Illustrative of this point are the comments of R. B. Cattell (15) about the Seguin Form Board. He considers it a fairly valid test of "g" below mental ages of about ten; thereafter it becomes a test of manual dexterity. This exemplification of Spearman's "Law of Diminishing Returns" is fairly common with performance tests although not unknown with verbal material, e.g., the change of functions of the arithmetical problems of the Wechsler-Bellevue Scale with increase in intellectual level.

Although the foregoing is but an introduction to the nature of performance tests it will suffice to set the stage for the examination of a typical performance scale.

THE ARTHUR POINT SCALE OF PERFORMANCE TESTS[1]

This battery of performance tests, each component part of which was standardized simultaneously on the same sample of children aged 5.0 to 15.99 years, inclusive, is a very useful instrument, serving to complement any verbal scale. The total test score and the component test scores throw light on intellectual functioning under conditions differing from those prevailing in a verbal test situation. The child's method of approach to concrete tasks, his motor coördination, his confidence, and his persistence may be noted and evaluated. It is most useful with individuals of the chronological ages for which it was standardized, or their mental age equivalents. In effect, this means it is unsuitable, for example, for a five-year-old Mongolian

---

[1] The manual (3) for Form I of this scale contains information essential to administering, scoring, and interpreting results. Instructions should be followed precisely when using this scale.

imbecile, but valuable in determining the ability of a mentally defective eighteen-year-old. Since the component tests were for the most part already known to the clinician, it received immediate acceptance on its publication in 1930 and has maintained a position of prominence ever since. It is probably the most valuable and the most popular performance scale in use with school-age children today, especially since the publication of a satisfactory alternate form for retest purposes, the Revised Form II.

A Description of Form I

Each of the tests composing the battery will be examined in turn. A brief description of the instrument will be followed by an account of the task before the child and some idea of the scoring.

KNOX CUBE. Four black one-inch cubes two inches apart are placed in front of the child (or adult) to be tested. After telling the child to do as he does, the psychologist, with a fifth cube, taps the cubes in prescribed order at the rate of one per second. The child then attempts to repeat the order of tapping. The series are simple at first and progressively become more difficult. This test is given as both the first and the last test of the battery. The score is the average number correct on the first and second trial.

SEGUIN FORM BOARD. The form board consists of ten geometric figures (star, rectangle, etc.) to be placed by the child in their appropriate recesses as quickly as possible. Three trials are given and the shortest time is used as the score.

TWO-FIGURE FORM BOARD. A square and a cross can be constructed from nine pieces. In the instructions the child is directed to put the pieces back as quickly as he can. A five-minute time limit is set. This test is not used in the scoring but serves as an introduction into "puzzle-test" procedure in which a variety of pieces are combined to make one form on the board, as contrasted with the solid one-piece entries of the Seguin Form Board.

CASUIST FORM BOARD. Into four recesses—three circles of varying sizes and a "rectangle" with curved ends—twelve pieces are to be fitted to make the figures. Time is recorded; five minutes are allowed. If all figures are not completed within the time limit, partial credit is given for the number finished.

MANIKIN. The Manikin consists of six pieces—two arms, two legs, head, and trunk—which when fitted together make a conventionalized figure of a man. Directions are "Now put these together." Scoring is on the basis of time and errors.

FEATURE-PROFILE. The Feature-Profile has parts to be correctly placed. If the seven parts are fitted together properly with the large piece they form the profile and the ear of the head. Partial successes of "ear correct" or "profile correct" are recorded within the limits of five minutes; scoring is on the basis of time required to complete, or the part correct, if not completed. The ultimate point score is for a combination of Feature-Profile and Manikin.

MARE AND FOAL. The Mare and Foal is a picture puzzle of several animals in a field. Seven cut-out pieces are to be returned to their appropriate places by the child. The directions are simple: "Put these back as fast as you can." The score is based on the time in seconds required for completion. As Healy (12) points out, this is a bright, puzzle-like picture which does much to evoke interest.

HEALY PICTURE COMPLETION I. A colored picture board depicts an outdoor scene in the country in which several children and one adult carry out a variety of activities. On the board there are nine empty squares to which the activities of these people and the kinds of objects in the picture are related. Each empty square should be filled by a picture of a significant object necessary for the understanding of the activity. There are fifty squares which would fit any of the nine empty spaces. On these squares are representations of a great variety of objects—a stool, a mouse, a hatchet, a wheel, a broken window, a closed window, a flying bird, a standing bird, and so on. The directions center upon having the child find the block which completes the pictured activity. Recording is made of the numbers of the blocks placed in each square with scoring based on weights developed prior to Arthur's use of the test.

PORTEUS MAZE. The materials are a series of "paper mazes" graded in difficulty, developed by Porteus in 1924. The instructions speak of driving an automobile along the road with cul-de-sacs referred to as closed roads and guide lines as fences. Retracing is not allowed. Two trials are permitted at all levels if necessary except for ages twelve and fourteen, in which four trials each are allowed. Testing continues through two successive failures, with scoring based on full and partial credit for accuracy and completion on first or subsequent trials, with higher credit the fewer trials necessary. There is no time limit.

KOHS BLOCK DESIGN. The blocks are identical one-inch cubes. On the six sides they are red, blue, yellow, white, yellow and blue, red and white. There are seventeen test cards to be preceded by two trial cards. The task is to reproduce with blocks the design. The. design card is kept in front of the child. The first nine designs require four blocks; thereafter the number of blocks necessary increases to nine and then to sixteen. Each design has a time limit after which no credit is given. Bonuses for rapid work are given. Testing continues through three successive failures.

STANDARDIZATION AND NORMATIVE GROUPS

The Arthur Point Scale of Performance Tests is a point scale. In other words, the yield is not a mental age directly but a point score, which may then be transformed into an equivalent MA. In the case of the Arthur Scale each of the different tests takes its score values from its ability to discriminate between successive age levels. These values were found by the formula,

$$DV = \frac{Av_2 - Av_1}{\dfrac{PE_2 + PE_1}{2}}$$

in which for each of two successive ages Av_1 is the mean for the lower age group and AV_2 is the mean for the higher age group. The difference between the two averages is divided by the denominator of the formula above, which contains measures of variability. The resultant figure is regarded as a point score. The greater its discriminative value the larger this figure, and thus the greater the value attached and the greater the contribution to the combined score. For each test, point values were found for every possible raw score; and the raw scores of a person given each of the tests were converted into point scores from the table that resulted. The point norms for each level were added to obtain a series of combined point norms for the battery as a whole. In arriving at this standardization, about 1100 public school children aged five to fifteen years inclusive from a middle-class "American" district were tested, with about 100 cases at each age level. This kind of standardization may be contrasted with that used in the Wechsler-Bellevue.

In the Arthur Performance Scale the various tests are differentially weighted at the same age level. Thus one given test may count more in the final sum than does another. In the Wechsler-Bellevue each subtest is weighted equally in the final sum at the same MA level. In both instruments the weighting varies at different age levels. At one point a test in the Arthur Scale may contribute a great deal, at another proportionately less. For example, combined Manikin and Feature-Profile could hardly yield more than 5.0 for the person getting the highest score. The Kohs Block Design maximum is 8.44. And yet at 6.5 years the former yields a point score of 0.80 and the latter gives 0.86, or practically the same amount. It is probable that at the lower age levels comprehension of the task is an important factor determining success or failure. If both tests are measuring the same ability at this level, they should earn approximately equal weighting, as they appear to do.

ADMINISTRATION AND SCORING

The Clinical Manual (3) supplies specific, clear instructions for the administration of the scale and for scoring the tests. Details were given previously in connection with the description of the tests. It is urged by Arthur that the tests be administered in a definite order since any other order "appears to have a noticeable effect upon the norms." (3, p. 26.) This order is as follows:

1. Knox Cube
2. Seguin Form Board
3. Two-Figure Form Board
4. Casuist Form Board
5. Manikin and Feature-Profile
6. Mare and Foal
7. Healy Picture Completion I
8. Porteus Mazes
9. Kohs Block Design
10. Knox Cube

The time required for administration is generally from about forty-five to sixty minutes (more often the latter in the writer's experience).

The tests can be given by gestural directions with one or two exceptions. Although verbal directions were used in the standardization, the test results when secured by pantomime would probably not be too unusable. Probably the same norms can be applied with some safety. Fortunately Form II, to be discussed later, obviates to a considerable extent the necessity of this plainly risky procedure. Scoring to arrive at the raw score values was briefly described in connection with the account of the nature of the tests. Once the raw scores for any of the tests are obtained, entry is made into the appropriate point-value tables. The measures derived will be described in the next section, concerned with mental age and intelligence quotient.

If, as is usually the case, some verbal test such as the Stanford-Binet is also administered to the patient, it is good clinical practice to administer the Arthur Scale first. This places the test less demanding of an interpersonal relationship before the more demanding verbal scale.

ABRIDGMENTS OF THE SCALE

The tests were originally selected for inclusion in the battery only on the basis of their discriminative value. A recognition of the resultant overweighting with form boards prompted Arthur to develop an abridgment of the scale. She found that omitting the Casuist Form Board and the Manikin-Feature-Profile Test, the tests showing poorer discriminative value, appeared to allow the scale to work as well as when they were included. Her evidence is stated in terms of comparison of performance on the Binet (Stanford-Binet and Kuhlmann-Binet), the full Arthur Scale Form I, and the scale abridged as just described. Intelligence quotients did not differ appreciably one from the other. For example, the differences between the median and quartile of Form I as compared to the abridgment of Form I ranged from zero to minus two and a half for medians, and quartile deviations were hardly more. If these tests are omitted, a table for converting total point scores into mental ages with this abridged form is supplied by Arthur (3). In the opinion of the writer, omission of the Casuist Form Board and Manikin-Feature-Profile strengthens the scale for individuals not accustomed to working under time pressure. Form boards to some degree at least require rapid trial and error rather than circumspectness and deliberation. As Arthur (3) noted, the child who stops to think out procedures on these tests is handicapped as compared to the impulsive hyperactive one who uses rapid trial and error. It might be objected that the same criticisms apply to the Seguin Form Board, which is a speed test. Its inclusion, however, can be defended on the basis of the need for inclusion of (but not overweighting with) a task measuring speed of reaction to a simple task.

If other tests are omitted owing to mischance or deliberate elimination (for example, the Healy because the person is unfamiliar with the situation depicted), it is possible to adjust the results obtained so as to use the full norms by finding first the actual earned point score MA level, followed by entry into the omitted test tables at that level and subsequent adjustment by the point values found there.

THE DERIVATION AND SIGNIFICANCE OF MENTAL AGE AND INTELLIGENCE QUOTIENT

Mental age norms were obtained from a group of 574 subjects out of the larger standardization group. The smaller sample had been given either the 1916 Stanford-Binet or the Kuhlmann-Binet. The results of these tests decided placement of the mental age levels thereafter used. In the volume concerned with standardization Arthur (2) shows that this was successfully done. At the higher levels the agreement became less than is the case at the lower levels.

From her findings, tables were prepared giving the equivalent MA for each point-score value for each test. The tables supply not only the points which when summed give the total point score but also MA levels for each of the tests. It is these MA levels which supply information about the individual's relative strengths and weaknesses. The point values, it must be remembered, are weighted according to the discriminative value of the particular test—the greater the discrimination the higher the point value. Thus a child might achieve a point value of 4.44 on the Feature-Profile and a point value of 4.22 on the Casuist Form Board, but his MA level in the first instance would be 15.5 and, despite an almost as large point value, only 10.5 in the second instance.

The total point value is converted into years and months of mental age by entry into still another table. Intelligence quotients are calculated by the usual formula, $\frac{MA}{CA} \times 100 = IQ$. Although Arthur uses the term "intelligence quotient," a rather common practice is to refer to it by the term "performance quotient." This serves to distinguish it from the Stanford-Binet or other verbal test quotients. This practice will be followed in the ensuing discussion although it is one to which Arthur objects. She writes (6): "If learning capacity (memorizing) is a more significant index of intelligence than reasoning ability and capacity to adjust to concrete situations, then the verbal scale would yield an I.Q. and the nonverbal scale would not. As I feel that reasoning ability is a more valid symptom of intelligence than memory for verbal material, I would like to see *Binet I.Q.* and *Performance I.Q.* used. Scales other than these, I believe, cannot yield I.Q.'s, as the Binet concept of mental age is essential to the derivation of the I.Q."

Although extrapolated norms below MA 6 and above 15 are supplied, Arthur indicates that use of them involves a relatively inaccurate procedure, particularly with respect to the lower extension (to age four). Clinical opinion would have it that at this level one of the preschool tests, such as the Cattell, might be more suitable. Arthur (6) herself recommends the use of the Revised Form II for those whose anticipated mental age will fall below the six-year level. This alternate form will be described in the next section of the chapter before considering other matters.

REVISED FORM II

Arthur (5) has stated that the primary purpose of the Revised Form II is to serve as an alternate for Form I. Thus, Form I is generally given first to patients of school age and older. Agreement is closer between the two forms when only the tests that parallel those in Form II are included in Form I. This means, in effect, elimination of the Casuist Form Board, the Manikin and Feature-Profile, and the Mare and Foal. For children below six years of age the Revised Form II should be given first, and supplemented, Arthur recommends, with the Arthur Adaptation of the Leiter International Performance Scale. The Revised Form II has derived norms that extend down to 4.5 years, one age group lower than Form I. The Arthur Adaptation of the Leiter Scale provides norms extending down to 3.5 years. Where Form I is given first, the Revised Form II is used for retest purposes. When the Revised Form II and Arthur Adaptation of the Leiter Scale are given first, Form I is used for retesting. For most clinical purposes use of the abridged scale, Form I, and then Form II if necessary, is indicated.

The Revised Form II is designed to measure ability from five

years of age to adulthood, but its greatest value and derived norms
(for converting point score into MA) are from five to fifteen. Extrapolated norms below 4.5 years and above 15.5 years are provided.
Norms from 4.5 to 15.5 years were derived from the scores of 968
pupils from the same middle-class district used in standardizing
Form I, and the method of standardization was substantially the
same. Since considerable attention was paid to making the directions
suitable for deaf children, it can also be recommended highly for
use with this group. A description of each of the tests follows:

REVISED KNOX CUBE.   The revision is very similar to the Knox
Cube Test of Form I. The four cubes are fastened on a base, and
a different tapping order is used. It is, however, administered non-
verbally to all taking it, whether they are deaf or not. If a hearing
child is puzzled by this, he is told that if he were deaf, words could
not be used, and that he should be as bright as a deaf boy or girl
in understanding what is to be done. A second trial is given after
the Porteus Maze Test.

REVISED SEGUIN FORM BOARD.   The standard Seguin Form Board is
reduced to five-sixths its customary size. The board's position is the
reverse of that in Form I—the star is toward instead of away from
the psychologist. The inserts are stacked with the child watching,
and then, according to whether or not the child is deaf, directions
are given in words or by gesture.

ARTHUR STENCIL DESIGN I.   Twenty increasingly complex designs
are presented one at a time to the child. He is to reproduce them
from a supply of six square colored cards and twelve colored stencils.
The designs are made by placing stencils and square cards one on top
of the other in such a sequence as to reproduce the design both in
shape and in color. A sample design requires merely that the child
select the solid white card and lay over it a red octagonal stencil.
Testing continues until three successive designs are failed. There is
a time limit of four minutes per design, with the score being the
number correctly reproduced, each within the time limit. This test
is presumed to measure logical thinking (Arthur, 5).

The test was introduced on the revision of Form II because the
Kohs Block Design Test, formerly included in both Form I and
Form II, had exhibited too high a degree of practice effect. In addition to the color and form elements of the Kohs a three-dimensional
problem is introduced by the necessity of arranging the parts one
on top of another.

PORTEUS MAZE (ARTHUR REVISION). The specially designed mazes rotate those of Form I by 180 degrees except for the first, which is a new design. This new design, introduced to make the task easier for deaf or non-English-speaking subjects, is an octagon with one side omitted. The problem of finding the way out is thus introduced at the start. Additional designs for the five- and six-year mazes have been introduced from another later revision of mazes by Porteus.

HEALY PICTORIAL COMPLETION II. The picture shows a series of events in the daily routine of a schoolboy—getting dressed, eating breakfast, walking to school, etc. In each of the ten test panels and one trial panel there is a blank space for a one-inch-square insert. A set of sixty inserts is supplied the child, and his task is to select the appropriate insert for each panel. Various selections are plausible but for each panel there is clearly one best response. Scoring values for a variety of pieces are supplied. Some of the objects which may be selected will partially but not entirely comply with the demands of the situation and consequently receive partial credit. (This credit was in part statistically and in part empirically derived.) The test is non-timed and instructions are nonverbal. Otherwise the procedure and scoring are the same as originally used by Healy.

A COMPARISON OF FORMS I AND II. Comparison of Form I, Form II, and the Stanford-Binet was carried out with ninety-four clinic patients (5). An extremely diverse clinic population was deliberately selected as being the most realistic to work with, although this diversity presumably acted to reduce agreement between verbal and nonverbal tests. More or less equally divided between boys and girls, the CA's ranged from 8–5 to 21 years. The interval between test on Form I and retest on Form II ranged from one week to three years. In spite of these features of the situation acting to reduce agreement, Form I and Revised Form II showed a difference of but five PQ points algebraic median difference (lower on Form II), and but six PQ points arithmetic median difference (higher on Form II). This shows a rather high degree of resemblance between the results of the two forms.

VALIDITY

The discriminative value of the tests at successive age levels on the basis of which the tests were first selected and then weighted was used as the major criterion of validity. It will be remembered that the revisions of the Stanford-Binet also used this criterion. The reader is referred to the earlier discussion since it is applicable in the present instance.

Since mental ages were derived from the 1916 Stanford-Binet and Kuhlmann-Binet, correlation with them is also a criterion. In connection with IQ differences between the Performance Scale and the Kuhlmann-Stanford-Binets, Arthur has this to say: "For fifty per cent of the cases tested on Form I, the IQ falls within five points of the IQ obtained on either the Kuhlmann-Binet or the Stanford-Binet scale. This means that results obtained with this form of the performance scale agree almost as closely with those obtained with either of these Binet scales as Stanford-Binet IQ's agree with retests on the Stanford-Binet scale." (3, p. 3.) Utilizing her data for investigating the abridged scale previously discussed, Arthur (4) found that a comparison of the 974 Form I PQ's and Binet IQ's (Kuhlmann and Stanford 1916) for a group of clinic cases in which there were no deaf, blind, spastic, dyslexic, or acutely upset individuals gave a probable error of less than five points at all levels except twelve, fifteen, and sixteen years and adult. This greater difference at the older levels she attributes to the low ceiling on the 1916 Stanford-Binet. The Kuhlmann-Binet had been used for the examination of the younger patients.

Goodenough and Maurer (17), in a study of the standardization data, found that the correlations between Arthur Form I PQ's and Binet (1916 Stanford-Binet and Kuhlmann-Binet) IQ's ranged in magnitude from .54 to .81 for year-age groups six through ten. Wallin (42) also investigated this relationship. His samples were mentally defective, retarded, or behavior problem children referred to a psychoeducational clinic. There were 290 cases given the 1916 Stanford-Binet and 172 given the 1937 Stanford-Binet. The correlations with Form I were respectively .72 and .53. Concerning differences between Arthur PQ's and Revised Stanford-Binet IQ's, Wallin found 57 percent showed differences of zero to ten PQ-IQ points, 27 percent eleven to twenty points, 13 percent twenty-one to thirty points, and the rest even greater differences. In 74 percent of the cases the Arthur PQ was the higher of the two. The mean IQ was 74 and the mean PQ was 82.

Another study of Form I, more or less representative of the several that have been made, is that of Hilden and Skeels (21). With 384 residents of orphanages and a training school they investigated the relationship of the Arthur Performance Scale Form I and the 1916 Stanford-Binet. The group ranged in age from six to twenty. For all ages combined the correlation was .74 ± .02. In correlations year by year, no age trends were apparent. The probable error of estimate for the Stanford-Binet Scale on the Arthur Point Scale is ten points. The Arthur Scale tended to yield higher IQ's than the Binet Scale with an average difference in favor of the Arthur of 5.4 PQ points. The closest correspondence between IQ's on the two tests is exhibited at IQ levels of 60 and 70, the lowest for which they have data.

In the investigation that Arthur (5) performed of the relationship between Form I and Revised Form II with ninety-four diversified clinical patients, information was also available concerning the relationship between Revised Form II and the Stanford-Binet (probably the 1937 revision). The algebraic median difference was 0, and the arithmetic median difference was 6 (Revised Form II higher). Comparison of these results with the differences between Form I and Form II shows less difference between these different tests than between the two forms of the same test when the form boards are included in Form I. Arthur (4) also reports that Revised Form II shows a correlation of .78 with Binet (presumably the 1937 revision) for 171 subjects. The characteristics of the group are not specified.

The magnitude of the correlations and the differences in PQ-IQ found demonstrate that the two forms of the Arthur Performance Scale are related to the Stanford-Binet Scale, yet not so extensively as to render one of them superfluous.

RELIABILITY

Arthur does not report reliability coefficients either of equivalence or of stability. Her attitude toward this problem is best expressed in her own words (6): "If validity and predictive value are high, it seems to me that reliability, that has significance beyond a numerical value, is inevitable. With tests selected on the basis of difference in the kind of ability measured, there is not expected or desired too great an agreement between the separate tests; and with a scale in which the puzzle element and problem solving plays so large a part, comparison of test and retest ratings is significant as a measure of rate of learning, but does not serve as a measure of reliability." There is no doubt that repetition reflects considerable effects of practice.

Patterson (28) reports a correlation coefficient of .85 between the first and third annual administration of the performance scale. The group consisted of sixty-one institutionalized high-grade mentally deficient boys (mean Stanford-Binet IQ of 67). For the same two-year interval, correlations of Porteus, Kohs, Seguin, Healy I, and Knox were respectively .80, .78, .75, .72, and 69. In view of the restricted range these may be considered as showing considerable stability on retest. Over this period there was a mean gain of about ten PQ points as contrasted with a mean loss of one IQ point. This and other evidence points to the differences as being due to practice.

It has been recommended (6) that retests on the same form of the Point Scale of Performance Tests should not be given within a minimum of three years of the first examination with that form. The brighter the patient, the longer should be the interval before attempting a reëxamination with the same material.

THE ARTHUR SCALE AND PSYCHOMETRIC PATTERNS

Something akin to the scatter approach described in connection with the Wechsler-Bellevue has been used with the Arthur Performance Scale. Generally it took the form of finding the relation between an individual's standing on another test and his standing on the Arthur Scale. This other test has frequently been the Revised Stanford-Binet Scale. Following custom this will be referred to as the psychometric pattern approach. Its nature is stated very clearly by Bijou: "A psychometric pattern may be defined as a statement, numerical or verbal, of the relationship existing between two or more test ratings. If there are only two scores in the pattern, the relationship may be expressed by a ratio, or by the difference between them. If there are more than two test values, the pattern may be stated in absolute terms, such as, Terman Vocabulary Quotient 100, Stanford-Binet Quotient 80, and Grace Arthur Performance Quotient 60, or the same three scores may be noted in relational terms by merely indicating that the Terman Vocabulary score is high, the Binet is intermediate, and the Arthur is low." (10, p. 354.)

Many of the studies point to the general conclusion that for groups a higher performance score (variously defined) than verbal score is indicative of better educational and personal adjustment in the mentally defective and delinquent. The reverse pattern, higher verbal than performance, is considered to point to their being aggressive, maladjusted, educationally inferior, and poor parole risks. Typical is a study of Bijou based on results found at Wayne County Training School for boys that he reviews briefly:

The patterns, composed of the revised Stanford-Binet and the Grace Arthur Performance Scale, of all the boys residing in three of the ten cottages were selected for study. One cottage was composed of well-behaved self-governing boys, one of typical training school boys, and the third of aggressive boys. The low performance pattern was found in 8 per cent of the well-behaved boys, in 25 per cent of the typical boys, and in 48 per cent of the aggressive boys. Or reversing the analysis, the greater the number of recognized well-adjusted boys in these cottages the greater the proportion of high performance patterns in the group. (*10*, p. 359.)

Other studies which support this have been performed by Abel (1) and Bijou (*11*).

Not all studies are so clearly in favor of such an hypothesis. For example, Wallin and Hultsch (43), using a school psychoeducational clinic population, found no more than chance relationship between psychometric patterns and type of adjustment. The reason for such discrepancies as these is quite clear. As Carter and Bowles state:

Although various test score patterns may be obtained in an individual case, they have little or no significance unless the child's history and his behavior in the examining situation are taken into account. For example, many children present pictures of personality disturbance but do not show markedly low performance scores in contrast with their Binet test quotients. On the other hand, a low performance score can result from a variety of conditions other than serious personality difficulties: poor coordination, unusually slow tempo of response because of health conditions or other circumstances, inadequate opportunities to build up skills in manipulating objects, or anxiety in the examination situation not necessarily typical of the child in every day life circumstances. A wide discrepancy between the Binet and performance test scores of an individual is not in itself "diagnostic" of anything in particular.

Similarly, the significance of low Binet results with contrastingly higher performance scores may reflect the not uncommon finding that children from families of low socio-economic status tend to do less well on tests essentially linguistic in nature; on the other hand, such results may occur because of an inadequate child-examiner relationship. The association of such a pattern with delinquency may indicate simply the children charged with delinquency tend to come from families of lower socio-economic status. (*14*, p. 140.)

Proponents of the pattern hypothesis base their case on what they believe to be ample evidence that such patterns occur with sufficient frequency to be of diagnostic value. Actually the evidence is not complete enough to show whether this is so or not. Varying standards regarding the magnitude of the difference necessary to place an individual in one or another of the groups, relatively small samples, and diversely selected populations all militate against unequivocal findings. Also the fact that the Arthur Performance Scale is made up of many tests measuring different functions is somehow lost sight of in these attempts to arrive at patterns. Performance level on the Kohs, the Seguin, and the Porteus Maze, for example, is apt to differ in the same individual. These differences are obscured in the final quotient.

Perhaps, then, an omnibus battery of functionally somewhat different tests is not as good discriminatory test patterning as is a single unit from the battery. Certain studies to be discussed in connection with the individual tests of the Arthur battery tend to support this view. Even in such instances, however, exceptions inevitably appear. No high or low score on a test invariably has the same absolute meaning.

THE RATIONALE AND INDEPENDENT USEFULNESS OF SOME OF THE TESTS INCLUDED IN ARTHUR'S BATTERIES

One of the reasons that the Arthur Scale was so well received by clinicians was that the tests included were, for the most part, already well known to them. The progenitor of the Arthur Scale—the Pintner-Paterson Performance Scale—was in wide use before Arthur selected and adapted some of its tests. Other performance scales also included some of them. Both before and subsequent to its appearance, some of the tests included in the Arthur Scale have been used independently in diagnostic situations.

There have also been inevitable variations from the Arthur administrative procedures in subsequent investigations. Time limits have been different; errors were scored in addition to time; the sequence of items has been changed; introductory instructions have been differently given. Separate norms for some of these have been adequately developed (12), though, of course, they are not applicable to the tests when used as a portion of the Arthur batteries.

On the other hand, if what the test is measuring does not seem to be changed by these variations, then the material is still pertinent and aids in understanding the Arthur Scale. Some of the tests will receive only brief mention, but the Kohs Block Design, the Healy Pictorial Completion II, and the Porteus Mazes are diagnostic instruments often used as independent measures, which will accordingly receive more detailed attention.

KNOX CUBE

Often considered a test of memory span, the Knox Cube Test can also be plausibly defended as a test of attention. Pintner (29) considered that success depended largely, although not exclusively, upon ability to imitate. This may be so, but such ability as is manifested depends more basically upon attention and/or memory. Although formerly used quite often as a separate instrument, there is some evidence that the test is not reliable enough for independent use. Certainly its discriminative value in the Arthur Performance Scale is not great after CA 9.5 years. In spite of the fact that whatever ability is tested by the Knox Cube Test appears to reach its maximal development early in the life of the individual, this test is of major importance in the diagnosis of feeble-mindedness. Though normal individuals develop this ability early, the mentally defective develop it very little. This tends to confirm Spearman's conclusions that attention is of the very essence of intelligence. According to Arthur (6), of sixty cases of simple aments of chronological ages between fifteen and twenty years, without special disabilities of any kind, only three were able to earn scores on the Knox Cube Test that, when translated into mental age, approached normal limits. For the group of sixty the median mental age earned on the Knox Cube Test was 6.5 years. On Form I as a whole, the median mental age for this group was nine years and four months.

When used as part of the Arthur Scale, administration both at the beginning and at the end of the examination occasionally produces interesting qualitative results. About this feature Arthur has the following to say:

> On the average, individuals do slightly better on the second presentation of the Knox Cube series, given at the end of the examination, than on the first series, given at the beginning. Any wide deviation from this pattern may be significant. A frightened child, or one who is slow in

adjusting to new situations, may do very poorly on the first trial, but on the second giving of the series may earn a score commensurate with his mental age on the scale as a whole. A child of a contrasting type exerts himself to make a good first impression and does well the first time the series is presented, but after an hour of work with the examiner may feel so at ease that he lapses into his usual careless attention habits. (3, p. 10.)

SEGUIN FORM BOARD

The Seguin Form Board has a long and distinguished history, as summarized by Bronner et al. (12). Originated as a device for training defective children, it was not until many years later, in 1906, that it was used as a diagnostic test by Norsworthy. There have been many minor modifications of design and many methods of scoring—shortest of three trials, average of three trials, and first trial, to name several—and many rationales offered for each adaptation. Also, a tremendous number of theories have been advanced as to the nature of the psychological functions involved. In one article Young lists as many as forty-nine functions, capacities, or traits to account for some of the more elementary factors involved (12). As Bronner and her associates (12) point out, what the test measures depends in large part on the manner in which it is given and the point of view from which the results are interpreted. As a test in the Arthur Performance Scale it probably measures, as Arthur says, speed of psychomotor reaction.

MANIKIN AND FEATURE-PROFILE

It appears, according to various authorities, that Manikin and Feature-Profile demand a kind of synthetic ability to see the parts of a whole and to put them together. The least discriminatory of all tests in the Arthur battery over all age ranges, their principal value is at the younger ages. The discussion of these two tests (with addition of the Hand) as the Object Assembly subtest of the Wechsler-Bellevue in Chapter 8 is pertinent.

THE KOHS BLOCK DESIGN TEST

The Kohs Block Design Test appears to have a high intrinsic appeal at all ages for which it is suitable. Kohs (25) mentioned that no subject tested fails to manifest a tendency to combine the cubes in some fashion, correct or incorrect. The test also supplies an opportunity for qualitative observation, especially of habits of work or method of attack upon a problem. It requires very simple material and very little in the way of language. On these various grounds it would appear to be of considerable value in a clinical situation. It is as difficult as the Knox Cube for the feeble-minded (6).

STANDARDIZATION, ADMINISTRATION, AND SCORING. In standardizing the test Kohs' major sample consisted of 291 subjects drawn from public school children ranging in age from four to sixteen from three widely separated geographical areas, and of seventy-five feeble-minded inmates ranging in age from nine to thirty-seven drawn from two homes for the feeble-minded.

His method of administration and scoring are described in the book which serves as a manual (25). Certain differences from the approach that Arthur used are found. Kohs administered through five instead of three failures and subtracted scores for excess moves; e.g., if on design 7 the subject took more than ten moves, a point was subtracted from the score he would otherwise have received. The test as a whole took on the average thirty to forty minutes. Although his work forms the basis for later developments, certain changes in procedure and scoring are generally followed today, and those introduced by Hutt and Benton will be described briefly.

Arthur (2) found during the course of the standardization of Form I of the Performance Scale that scoring on the basis of time only yielded as high discrimination as scoring of both time and errors. Hutt (23), following the lead of Arthur's use of the Kohs, investigated the simplified scoring system based on time and success of the completed design but eliminating counting and scoring of moves because of errors by examiners in the scoring of moves. This change was instituted for economy of time and also to allow the clinician opportunity to observe qualitative aspects of behavior impossible when he was occupied with scoring number of moves. The change is essentially very simple—elimination of subtraction of credits for performance taking more than a certain number of moves. A subject earns as much credit as before for completing a design successfully and has credits subtracted for overtime but not for excess moves.

Hutt (22) (23) presents evidence justifying use of this revised scoring method. The subjects were 100 children, CA 6 to 15, examined in a New York City pediatric clinic because of maladjustment. On the 1916 Stanford-Binet the median IQ was 94.7, with a range from 59 to 155. The new derived scores as well as the original Kohs scoring were converted into Kohs MA's. It was found that the two scorings correlated .99, whereas with the 1916 Stanford-Binet original and revised scorings were respectively .70 and .71. Amount of change in months from the original to the revised scoring was on the average 1.9 months, and the most probable changes (middle 50 percent) 0 to + 2 months (0 to + 2 IQ points). In no case was the discrepancy greater than six months. Applying the Kohs to a small group of adults, Benton (7) found the same correlation (.99) between the two scoring systems. The differences, however, tended to run in the reverse direction, with the middle 50 percent of the changes ranging from − 2 to + 0.5 points.

Benton (8) has also prepared and reported norms for various groups of adults in the age range of twenty to twenty-nine, none of whom were hospitalized or under psychiatric care. Nevertheless, several made extremely poor scores; e.g., had the norms for children been consulted, a college instructor would have made an age score of eight years. The inference is obvious: a poor score cannot be interpreted routinely. The influence of age was striking enough (older individuals tending to do less well) for him to adopt the procedure of presenting norms only for the age group for which he had a considerable number of cases. At the present time there are no adequate norms for older ages on the Kohs Block Designs.

The same investigator (9) suggests the use of a shorter form of the Kohs, based on the first twelve designs, which will save about twenty minutes in administration time. He found with a group of 180 adults with a mean total point score of 105 that these twelve designs correlated .90 with the entire test of seventeen designs. This correlation was considered of sufficient magnitude to warrant substitution of the shortened form in clinical situations, especially those in which time is at a premium. He also developed equivalent scores for the shortened and full test, making possible use of the original norms and findings despite administration of only a portion of the complete test. In applying this test it is suggested that Hutt's scoring, and when appropriate Benton's norms, and Benton's shorter form may often be used. There will, however, certainly be occasions in which there is a distinct need for the complete test.

RATIONALE. Kohs' conception of the rationale of the Block Design Test is certainly related to that of Arthur, who regards it as a test of logical thinking. More specifically, however, Kohs (25) considers it a measure of analytic-synthetic activity which may for clarity be separated into the two aspects. Analysis connotes a capacity to discover parts or differences in objects or qualities which otherwise seem unitary in nature. By synthesis is meant a capacity to construct a higher order concept from more fragmentary experiences. Successful completion of the items of the Kohs Block Design Test appears to require the patient to analyze the design into its constituent parts and then synthesize these impressions in the correct reproduction of the design with the blocks. It will be remembered that this is substantially the opinion of Wechsler and Rapaport concerning the Block Design subtest of the Wechsler-Bellevue.

Kohs extended the scope of this analytic-synthetic process to encompass intelligence in general. The direct evidence for this extension he obtained from his study of the correlation of the Block Design Test and the 1916 Stanford-Binet in the standardization sample. In what emerged as the standardized designs, the correlations between Binet MA and Block Design MA for the public school children and the feeble-minded were respectively .81 and .67. With the two groups combined, the correlation of Block Design score points and Stanford-Binet vocabulary score was .77. These relatively high correlations have been verified by Hutt (22) and Wile and Davis (45).

Because of the magnitude of such correlations Kohs in 1923 decided that no matter how the Block Design Test and the Stanford-Binet appear "to differ radically in character, the mental manipulations making for successful achievement are fundamentally the same." (25, p. 199.) He goes on to suggest that because of these high correlations the Block Design Test could be substituted for the Stanford-Binet, since relatively little understanding of language is necessary for the former. Clinical opinion then as today was solidly against such a procedure. For example, Wile and Davis (45) found discrepancies between results on the Block Design and those obtained with the Stanford-Binet despite a high correlation between the two. They present evidence that in the crucial borderline area (Binet 70–80 IQ), out of fifty-four children at this level the Kohs classified 50 percent below 70 while 11 percent got normal ratings, concluding that the Block Design Test should not be substituted for the Stanford-Binet. This is not to say that the results of the Binet were considered the ultimate criterion, as the authors felt that neither Binet nor Kohs taken separately or together is an infallibly decisive measure.

Although Kohs' ideas about the rationale have received some acceptance and at least by this author are considered acceptable, his extension of what is essentially one aspect to cover a considerably wider area of intellectual functioning is not warranted. Rather, the Block Design Test is a valuable measure comprising one aspect of a more global functioning intelligence. In the opinion of the writer the emphasis on *thinking* that Arthur and others place upon it is the crucial point. Accordingly, when discussing instruments useful in the measurement of the thought processes of the individual, the test and its derivative, the Goldstein-Scheerer Cube Test, will be taken up again.

HEALY PICTORIAL COMPLETION II

The Healy Pictorial Completion Test I is relatively little used today except as a test in the Arthur Scale, Form I. Its cartoon-like atmosphere invites facetiousness, precipitating inferior performance by adults as compared to children. In addition, the norms presented by Healy are too low, and the test is not designed in such a fashion that there is one and only one absolutely logical choice. Healy Test II, the instrument now under consideration, was designed in part to overcome these difficulties. As Bronner and her associates state, "Pictorial Completion II has none of the crude features of the earlier completion test. A very well-drawn and attractively colored series of pictures is represented, each of which depends essentially on the one that has gone before. Only one absolutely logical choice is possible for each of the eleven pictures. Graded scores for answers partially correct have been statistically determined." (12, p. 185.)

STANDARDIZATION, ADMINISTRATION, AND SCORING. The test was originally standardized by Healy (20) on over 1500 individuals. No further information is given about the sample except the statement that no subjects were feeble-minded or psychotic. From details of normative material presented (in terms of percentiles) by age it is fair to assume that they ranged in age from seven to fifty.

Directions according to the Arthur method of administration, it will be remembered, are nonverbal. The procedure used by Healy as described in the article which serves as a manual (20)[2] verbally acquaints the subject with the sequential nature of the pictures, pointing out that each has an element missing and that he is to find the very best one from the pieces supplied.

The score assigned a correct solution of a given picture was based on a weighting inversely proportionate to the frequency with which it was correctly solved, i.e., the picture least often chosen was given highest weight. In scoring solutions other than the "correct" one the weights were related to the frequency of choice but in part were empirical. Responses other than the correct or partially correct are penalized by being scored − 5. The maximum possible score is 100. This scoring was used in all particulars by Arthur. Though generally not needed, twenty minutes is allowed. Arthur allows unlimited time, which is essentially the same.

CORRELATION WITH 1916 STANFORD-BINET AND OTHER TESTS. The correlations with the 1916 Stanford-Binet show it to be rather low. Some of the more important studies yield the following correlations: (1) .40 MA and PC score for 136 adult criminals (41); (2) .51 and .50 for MA's of 200 boys and 192 girls referred to a child guidance clinic (44); (This last investigator [44] found about the same correlation between the Ferguson Form Boards and the Stanford-Binet in the same sample. With this test the partial correlation, Binet MA held constant, with Healy II was .35 for both boys and girls. This was the highest partial correlation that he found in the study of several tests.) (3) .32 for twenty-five six-year-old first-grade children (46). And yet, these same investigators found correlations of .52 and .53 between Gates Primary Type 2 and Type 3 Reading Tests and Healy Pictorial Completion II. It would appear that there is some correlation between the two tests though not of sufficient magnitude to render plausible substitution of one for the other. The Healy Pictorial Completion Test II measures something independent of that measured by the Stanford-Binet.

---

[2] The directions, scoring criteria, and norms are also reported in Bronner et al. (12).

QUALITATIVE ASPECTS. The mistakes made with this test are qualitatively more interesting than the correct responses. Deviations from the correct solution may be minor or they may be bizarre and idiosyncratic. In any case they often give clues as to the thinking of the patient. Although setting limits on correct responses, the test offers the possibility of a wide selection of attempted solutions. This, as Hanfmann (19) says, makes it especially suitable for a qualitative analysis of the patient's performance. She distinguished three major factors operative in each of the scenes—action, general situation, and clue. By action is meant that in each scene there is an activity being carried out indicated by position, gesture, and sometimes facial expression, such as getting a shoe or hanging up a coat. This action takes place in a general situation—a classroom, a dining room, a street—in which the material environment and spatial determinants play a part, so that grasping the situation is also involved. Lastly, there are clues within a situation such as the reflection of the missing window in IV, or clues carried over from earlier frames—as the color and number of books missing in II may be deduced by observation of I. For correct solution, in the sense of selecting the only square which fits all of the aspects of the situation depicted, the individual must appreciate the relation of previous pictures in the series to the one in question. If the clue is once appreciated, as Healy himself points out, it acts to determine the correct response in a clear and unequivocal fashion. Once the shadow with the crosspieces is seen, there can be no doubt that the answer is a window and a window of a specific kind. Only by appreciation of clues can there be optimal score. Some are harder to grasp because they are carried over from a previous scene or are relatively extraneous, i.e., not "built" into the scene by its general nature. They are not related to the central theme and unless sought would be missed.

The degree of connectiveness of clue and situation was investigated by Hanfmann. She found that psychologists independently judging the degree of connectedness of the situation and the clue on a three-point scale gave results which correlated almost perfectly with the scores given for optimal completions. She writes:

The pictures in which the optimal solution is most easily obtained, and consequently given the least credit in scoring, are those in which the completion follows more or less directly from the action or general situation (IX, VII, I); next highest scores are given to pictures in which the clue is of a more additive character, yet still related to the situation (V, VI). The carried-over clues present a still more difficult problem, and the extraneous clues, totally isolated from the action-situation, although sufficiently conspicuous in themselves, prove the most difficult ones to grasp. Thus our assumption that the difficulty of finding the optimal completion is the function of the degree of isolation of the clue from the general situation, is confirmed by the analysis of the numerical results obtained during the standardization of the test. . . .

One may expect a picture to be the better completed, the less ambiguous the represented action, the more fully it is integrated with a clear-cut background to a well defined general situation, and the more naturally the special clue follows from this central action-situation of the picture. While the general term "apperception" used by Healy designates the totality of processes leading to completion, a closer analysis shows that qualitatively different psychological processes seem to be involved in the grasping of the three aspects of the picture. The results of a preliminary analysis of placements made by normal and abnormal subjects seem to indicate that these qualitative differences correspond to three degrees of difficulty in the solution of the task. Action, in the given picture series, is grasped most readily even by abnormal subjects; the general situation is clear to all normal adults, but seems to make no impression on many psychotic patients; the clue is often missed even by normal adults and thus gives the differentiation on the highest level. (19, p. 329.)

RATIONALE. That this test is measuring a special ability is either explicitly stated by the various investigators or implied in their treatment of the data. It is related to whatever the Stanford-Binet measures but independent enough of it to be conceived as measuring a separate function or functions. According to Bronner, Healy et al., the test requires "ability to see the relationship between the objects and activities depicted and the missing pieces, and to interpret the meaning of one element in the light of others." (12, p. 186.) Arthur (3) apparently agrees but specifically states that the Healy is related to language ability. At any rate, there appears to be considerable agreement that ability to "size up" a situation is involved.

Since the Stanford-Binet is so obviously a verbal test, the suggestion of Arthur that the Healy Picture Completion II is related to language ability (and yet is not substantially correlated with Stanford-Binet) must be viewed with reserve. It is true that a relatively high correlation with the Gates Reading Tests has been reported (46), but this is based on very few cases. Even if the correlation could be substantiated by other investigators, it is more likely that whatever both the tests measure is more fundamental, perhaps the ability to see or educe relationships.

DIAGNOSTIC USAGE. This test is a valuable clinical instrument which appears to be measuring a function or functions of diagnostic significance. Yet despite the fact that its application offers the opportunity for qualitative observations of considerable significance, it has many weaknesses. It suffers from a lack of a definitive analysis; the groups used are in some way always nonrepresentative or equivocal; the normative group received hardly more than two or three lines' description; reliability is not well established. Some of the difficulties are illustrated in the work with delinquents and criminals. The groups with whom the results are compared seem always to require rescoring of the results to meet local procedures (41), and elaborate statistical stratagems are necessary before any sort of more or less definitive comparison can be made. This is not meant as a criticism of the workers with this instrument. They have shown considerable adroitness and resourcefulness in working with the inadequate data available, but the need for more basic and carefully planned studies must be emphasized.

PORTEUS MAZE TEST

The Porteus Mazes have had a long and somewhat stormy history. Originally developed in 1914, the test has passed through several revisions including the one utilized by Arthur (the 1924 revision) and a later revision commonly used when the test is applied independent of the Arthur battery (the 1933 Vineland Revision). It has been applied to many populations, clinical and nonclinical, primitive and nonprimitive, literate and illiterate, young and old. Some clinicians have found it very valuable; others reject it with vehemence.

The test is regarded by Porteus as a measure of "commonsense," with the principal advantage being "that it provides a problem which because of the capacities required for success, approaches most nearly a real life situation." (30, p. 29.) The element of planning ability is stressed.

ADMINISTRATION AND SCORING. Directions for administration are given in the manual of the test (31). They are substantially the same as those that Arthur uses but involve a different later standardized set of mazes (Vineland Revision-New Series) running from the third year to adult. Scoring is on the basis of the years of the mazes passed. In calculating the test quotient (TQ), an adjustment for the age of the child is made in the divisor for ages thirteen to fifteen akin to the arrangement made in the 1937 Revision of the Stanford-Binet.

The implication of general procedure and the scoring of time and errors is stated as follows:

> The conditions of application of the maze tests are such that the subject in every case is given an opportunity to realize his own errors and by a system of repeated trials to profit by his experience and to readapt his methods. This latter characteristic is the most important feature in the Porteus Maze tests and one that is lacking in most performance tests, especially those of the puzzle solving variety where trial and error methods are allowed without penalty in the scoring. . . .
>
> It is not sufficiently recognized that a maze test in which no account of errors is taken or one which is scored with a time limit is not, properly speaking, a test of temperamental qualities at all. When errors are not taken as the basis of the scoring it ceases to be a test of prudence in behavior but merely of a special kind of mental alertness. This is true not only of the maze test but of any test in which false moves are allowed. It is obvious that the impulsive person who rushes into error but has sufficient mental alertness to retrieve himself quickly suffers hardly any handicap in time of performance at all. He sees no necessity therefore to modify his method of attacking the task. In a maze test of the "slot" variety where the task set the child is to pass an object through a slotted maze in the quickest possible time, it is evident that little, if any, distinction is made between a child who makes a number of impulsive errors but corrects them quickly and one who by prudent reconsideration avoids all errors. The one child is mentally alert but imprudent, the other puts caution above speed. In the Porteus maze test immediately an error is made the subject is stopped and the test must be begun over again. The need for more prudent action is thus made apparent. It is impossible to evaluate, at the same time, speed for decision and prudent preconsideration. The one precludes the other. For tests of this nature the attempt to combine speed and errors in the one scoring combination seems to be wasted ingenuity. (30, pp. 6–7.)

Porteus (37) has never placed much stress on the adult mazes. There is some evidence that there is a ceiling effect which makes the test unsuitable for use with adults of more than average intelligence (16). It has not been used by any means as much with adults as with children, except that its usefulness with mental defectives and criminals has been explored.

QUALITATIVE SCORING. Porteus (34) has recently developed and applied another scoring of the mazes consisting of qualitative errors which when summed give the Q score. With the Q score the task is still the same—to draw a line between the guide lines to a terminal point, with attention in the main directed to avoiding blind alleys. The subject does not realize that the quality of his responses can also be judged. As Porteus says, ". . . Since nothing has been said about the quality of his drawing, habits of slovenliness, impulsiveness, haphazard work are given an opportunity to show themselves." (34, pp. 11–12.) In a way, although Porteus might object to such designation, it is a projective device of restricted scope and narrow meaning.

Directions for scoring, including setting up a critical score, are given in a specially prepared manual (34), but later normative material (36) has also appeared. So far as the administration is concerned the changes are minor—principally less repetition of instructions about not lifting the pencil after an emphatic warning about this. Qualitative scoring does not apply to the adult tests.

The qualitative errors include crossing or touching lines, cutting corners, lifting pencil, wavy lines (scores arrived at by comparison with samples), wrong direction although self-corrected before failure, failures in the first and/or last third of the test, and qualitative errors at the fifth- and sixth-year levels. Failure in the first third of the maze is scored as a qualitative error in that it indicates greater impulsiveness than later failure whereas failure in the last third with the "goal in sight" is indicative of carelessness or overconfidence. Qualitative errors at the fifth- and sixth-year levels are penalized additionally in this scoring because the mazes are so relatively simple at these levels.

Wherein lies the difference in significance of this measure as compared to quantitative scoring? No extended or explicit discussion of this precise point has appeared, but in discussing the origin of the need for qualitative scoring (in studying the behavior of delinquents) Porteus (35) contrasts planning capacity with careless, impulsive, haphazard reactions. These he regards as temperamental factors.

Three areas of intensive application of the Porteus Maze Test of special interest to the clinician are its use with mental defectives, both children and adults; with juvenile delinquents and criminals; and with patients who have received lobotomies. The results are presented both as instances of application and as evidence for and against the validities of the Porteus Maze Test.

MENTAL DEFICIENCY. The first of these—use with mental defectives—was thoroughly investigated by Porteus (31) and his collaborators in a considerable number of related studies. In his early work with the mental defectives he was struck by their lack of planning capacity (as well as by their failure to think abstractly). After preliminary work, the first edition of the Porteus Maze Test emerged as an attempt to measure this. Early work, in keeping with the times, stressed its relationship with the Binet. Accumulated evidence demonstrated that the original standardization was too easy at some ages and too difficult at others, so a revision was prepared, and at Vineland a series of studies of its validity were carried out. Many of these utilized the ratings of the director of educational activities, who knew the children intimately over long periods of time. These studies pointed to the superiority of prediction of educational capacity by the Binet, but a superiority of the Porteus in predicting industrial and social capacity. Binet and Porteus combined were better than either one alone. It was concluded after an intensive series of investigations that the Porteus Mazes had "a closer relation to social sufficiency than the Binet." (31, p. 99.)

Much of this work was prompted by the finding, according to Porteus, that interpretation of feeble-mindedness through the Stanford-Binet IQ alone would have resulted in the classification as feeble-minded of an absurdly large number of individuals, running into the millions in the United States alone. The Maze Test was offered as a corrective, since it purports to measure a form of social adjustment which the Stanford-Binet or Binet-type test did not measure.

DELINQUENTS. It is unnecessary to explore in any detail the relationship between regular quantitative scoring of the Porteus Mazes in delinquents and criminals; it is fairly well established that many of them do quite well on this measure and consequently such method of scoring is relatively nondiscriminating. As Porteus himself points out, "The scores of individual delinquents were not by any means, consistently below those of normals of equal social status."

306   The Clinical Method in Psychology

(34, pp. 13–14.) To be sure, there are studies of juvenile delinquents
which found that on the average they scored lower on the Porteus
than they did on the 1916 Stanford-Binet (Porteus, 34), and that
delinquents divided into socially adjusted and maladjusted showed,
for the latter groups, significantly lower scores on the Porteus than
they did on the Binet (24, 39). On the other hand, Shakow and
Millard (41) found adult criminals did better on the average on the
Porteus than on the Stanford-Binet. Whatever the direction and
statistical significance of differences between Porteus and Stanford-
Binet, there is still considerable overlapping in respect to the capacities being measured.

The most promising development in the use of the Porteus Mazes
with delinquents would appear to be in the use of the Q score.
Porteus describes the reasoning behind them as follows:

. . . The typical delinquent response is marked by careless, haphazard
work, persistent disregard of instructions, and satisfaction with an inferior grade of execution or poor workmanship in the task. He does not,
of course, know that his effort is being scored in these particulars, and
concentrates all his attention on finding his way through the maze; thus,
in many cases he gains a good quantitative score. It is when the delinquent is off guard that his habitual reactions are exhibited without
check. It should be emphasized, however, that this is not true of all
delinquents, some of whom are as meticulous in performance as any
non-delinquent. (35, p. 269.)

The results obtained by Porteus regarding qualitative errors in
various groups are summarized in Table 17. The designation of the

TABLE 17. Weighted Q Scores of Delinquent and Non-Delinquent Groups[3]

Group	Average Q Score	σ	Critical Ratio
Delinquent girls	52.9	24.4	
Normal girls	24.7	14.5	9.9
Delinquent boys	49.3	25.2	
Normal boys	21.8	12.9	9.7
Criminal adults	56.7	26.2	
Bus drivers	17.8	12.8	13.3

[3] Adapted from Qualitative Performance in the Maze Test by S. D. Porteus
(34), by permission of S. D. Porteus. Copyright 1942 by S. D. Porteus.

group is sufficient description for present purposes, and on each group 100 subjects were involved. It will be noted that there were fewer errors for the normal boys and girls and for the bus drivers. In each instance their paired group has a significantly greater number of errors with a mean score at least double in magnitude. The degree to which the Q score is affected by mental age scoring in the usual fashion was investigated by correlational technique. For the delinquent girls and adult criminals the correlations were respectively −.40 and −.37. This was justifiably considered by Porteus not to be a high degree of relationship. It is plausible to infer that the two systems of scoring are measuring, to some degree at least, different functions. A later paper by Porteus (35) reviews the findings just given and supplies additional confirmatory evidence concerning Q scores in delinquent and non-delinquent groups.

These findings of Porteus were based upon residents of Hawaii. In view of the possibility that crime and delinquency were due more to general easygoing habits in Hawaii than would be the case elsewhere, Porteus urged that they be checked within the continental limits. This Wright (47) did on delinquent boys in a California training school. Her results using the same statistical measures were almost identical with those obtained by Porteus. It is interesting to note that on quanitative scoring the mean test quotient was 94.6 as compared to a 1937 Revised Stanford-Binet mean IQ of 97.2. The difference is not statistically significant. The subjects thus were working up to capacity on the Porteus Maze Test if the Stanford-Binet be used for comparison.

Porteus' norms on Q scores were based on scores of subjects fourteen years old or older. Sanderson (40) investigated this matter with 150 younger as well as older children drawn from the fifth, sixth, and eleventh grades of an Illinois public school. A relationship to age was found, and statistically significant differences between the fifth- and eighth-grade groups. The mean score of the fifth-graders was such that it was greater than the critical score set by Porteus (34). Since these subjects were regular public school children, and not delinquents, this suggests extreme caution in applying the same interpretation to a Q score of a younger child as one would to that of an older child. On the other hand, this in no way contravenes the rationale that has been applied. Carelessness, haphazardness, and impulsiveness in younger children is probably characteristic of developmental level and not necessarily suggestive of delinquent trends. Such a finding offers evidence of the validity of this method of scoring, not the contrary.

LOBOTOMIES. Another area in which the Porteus Maze Test appears to have considerable promise is in the investigation of the psychological functioning of patients after brain surgery, especially lobotomies and related operative procedures. Psychologists have been singularly unsuccessful in demonstrating psychometric change after such operations, despite a wealth of clinical evidence that changes of some sort or another have taken place. Loss of initiative, if some of these clinically observed changes may be crudely summarized, is generally accepted as one of the effects. This suggests that the Porteus would be appropriate to apply since loss of initiative must somehow be related to planfulness. One of the studies on this problem is that of Porteus and Peters (38). They utilized the results of repeated examinations of fifty-five lobotomized mental hospital patients, principally schizophrenics and manic-depressives. They found a marked decline in score on the first postoperative examination with subsequent improvement. A control group showed the expected practice effect of a considerable gain on retest. When the patients are divided into three groups on the basis of improved social adjustment, the two improved groups, although showing a greater decline in first retest score than did the unimproved groups, on repeated tests made larger subsequent gains. The authors conclude that there is loss in planfulness reflected in the scores, and that recovery of planfulness, when it occurs, is also reflected in the scores. Again the test is demonstrated to be valid in that it discriminates in the direction expected from its rationale.

RELATIONSHIP WITH HEALY PICTORIAL COMPLETION II AND STANFORD-BINET. It has not been overlooked that the claims for the Porteus Maze Test and for the Healy Pictorial Completion Test to some degree overlap. Planfulness and ability to size up a situation must be related in some fashion. Several studies, as a matter of fact, touched upon the relationship of scores on the two tests and the relation of both to the Stanford-Binet. Two of the most adequately controlled studies were those of Morgenthau (27) and Shakow and Millard (41). With over 100 children, excluding mental defectives and drawn from various sources, Morgenthau found identical correlations (.54) between the 1916 Stanford-Binet and Healy Pictorial Completion II and Porteus. The correlation between Pictorial Completion II and Porteus was .70. In the study of Shakow and Millard (41), dealing with criminals with a mean age of twenty-six, among other tests the Healy Pictorial Completion II was administered to 136 of the group, the Porteus Mazes through XIV to 116 of the group, and the 1916 Stanford-Binet to all of them. The correlations among MA's were as follows: Healy and Porteus .38, Porteus and Stanford-Binet .41, and Healy and Stanford-Binet .40. In both studies the substantial correlations of both instruments were equally high with the Stanford-Binet and just as high or higher between themselves. They both appear to measure something related to the Binet but in a sufficiently independent fashion so that both might be useful. On the other hand, the correlation between Porteus and Healy is not so low as to raise the suspicion that one or the other is not measuring what it is purported to be measuring.

Another relevant study was concerned with the relationship of Porteus to Stanford-Binet. In a careful study of the correlation between Porteus and Stanford-Binet for 100 boys and 100 girls, CA 5 to 14, referred to a psychological clinic Louttit and Stackman (26) found the correlations, with CA constant, to be respectively .54 and .68. Their analysis of the literature reported shows the trend to be such that the first of these more nearly approximates the average. If the coefficient of .54 is accepted as approximately the relation between the Binet and the Porteus tests, only 30 percent of the factors making for successful performance are common to both.

DIAGNOSTIC USAGE. There does seem to be some confusion about the claims made for the Porteus Maze Test. In over thirty years that Porteus has worked with this instrument he has with consummate patience and considerable ingenuity investigated its usefulness in many settings, clinical and nonclinical, with many sorts of people. This intensive exploration of its usefulness to the relative exclusion of other research endeavors has contributed to the erroneous impression that he considers it the be-all and end-all of test development. To be sure, he has defended it with considerable vehemence (cf. 31, 32, 37), but he has always insisted that it is a test to be used in conjunction with others (and with other data). In situations where the Stanford-Binet is appropriate he contends that it is a valuable supplementary tool because it seems to evaluate planning capacity and prudence more effectively than does the Binet. With this the writer is prepared to agree. In addition it might be well to add that probably the greatest future value of the Porteus Maze Test will come from its qualitative scoring. Certainly studies exploring its validity are urgently needed in view of the extremely promising results thus far attained.

It is particularly suited for use with the mentally defective, the delinquent, and the patient being considered for lobotomy, as the previous discussion has demonstrated. Certain of its values point to its particularly appropriate usage with these groups. It does not require superior language training; it seldom arouses the set, "I didn't have much schooling"; and all the elements of the problem are perceptually (visually) present in concrete form. These values are what make it especially useful for the groups mentioned earlier; by the same token it is valuable with other groups, such as psychotics, where the same features are likely to be prominent.

BIBLIOGRAPHY

1. Abel, T. M., The relationship between academic success and personality organization among subnormal girls, Amer. J. ment. Def., 1945, 50:251–256.
2. Arthur, G., A point scale of performance tests, Vol. II, The process of standardization, Commonwealth Fund, 1933.
3. Arthur, G., A point scale of performance tests, Vol. I, Clinical manual, Commonwealth Fund, 2nd ed., 1943.
4. Arthur, G., Performance tests, in Harriman, P. L. (ed.), Encyclopedia of psychology, Philosophical Library, 1946, pp. 447–451.
5. Arthur, G., A point scale of performance tests. Revised Form II. Manual for administering and scoring the tests, Psychological Corporation, 1947.
6. Arthur, G., personal communication, 1949.
7. Benton, A. L., Application of Hutt's revised scoring of the Kohs Block Design Test to the performance of adult subjects, Amer. J. Psychol., 1941, 54:131–132.
8. Benton, A. L., A study of the performances of young adults on the Kohs Block Designs Test, J. appl. Psychol., 1941, 25:420–427.
9. Benton, A. L., and Perry, J. D., Short method of administering the Kohs Block Designs Test, Amer. J. Orthopsychiat., 1942, 12:231–233.
10. Bijou, S. W., The psychometric pattern approach as aid to clinical analysis—a review, Amer. J. ment. Def., 1942, 44:354–362.
11. Bijou, S. W., An experimental analysis of Arthur Performance Quotients, J. consult. Psychol., 1942, 6:247–252.
12. Bronner, A. F., Healy, W., Lowe, G. M., and Shimberg, M. E., A manual of individual mental tests and testing, Little, Brown and Company, 1927.
13. Carl, G. P., The role of psychometrics in appraisal of mental deficiency, Nerv. Child, 1942, 2:29–36.

14. Carter, J. W., and Bowles, J. W., A manual on qualitative aspects of psychological examining, *J. clin. Psychol.*, 1948, 4:109–150. (Also as *Clin. Psychol. Monogr.*, 1948, No. 2.)
15. Cattell, R. B., *A guide to mental testing*, University of London Press, 1936.
16. Cornell, E. L., and Lowden, G. L., A comparison of the Stanford and Porteus tests in several types of social inadequacy, *J. abnorm. soc. Psychol.*, 1923, 18:33–42.
17. Goodenough, F. L., and Maurer, K. M., *The mental growth of children from two to fourteen years*, University of Minnesota Press, 1942.
18. Hamlin, R., The role of intelligence in manipulative tests, *Amer. J. ment. Def.*, 1943, 48:162–168.
19. Hanfmann, E., A qualitative analysis of the Healy Pictorial Completion Test II, *Amer. J. Orthopsychiat.*, 1939, 9:325–329.
20. Healy, W., Pictorial Completion Test II, *J. appl. Psychol.*, 1921, 5:225–239.
21. Hilden, A. H., and Skeels, H. M., A comparison of the Stanford-Binet Scale, the Kuhlmann-Anderson Group Test, the Arthur Point Scale of Performance Tests and the Unit Scales of Attainment, *J. exper. Educ.*, 1935, 4:214–230.
22. Hutt, M. L., A simplified scoring method for the Kohs Block-Designs Tests, *Amer. J. Psychol.*, 1930, 42:450–452.
23. Hutt, M. L., The Kohs Block-Designs Tests: a revision for clinical practice, *J. appl. Psychol.*, 1932, 16:298–307.
24. Karpeles, L. M., A further investigation of the Porteus Maze as a discriminative measure in delinquency, *J. appl. Psychol.*, 1932, 16:426–437.
25. Kohs, S. C., *Intelligence measurement: a psychological and statistical study based upon the Block-Design Tests*, The Macmillan Company, 1923.
26. Louttit, C. M., and Stackman, H., The relationship between Porteus maze and Binet test performance, *J. educ. Psychol.*, 1936, 27:18–25.
27. Morgenthau, D. R., Some well-known mental tests evaluated and compared, *Arch. Psychol.*, 1922, No. 52.
28. Patterson, R. M., The significance of practice effect upon readministration of the Grace Arthur Performance Scale to high grade mentally deficient children, *Amer. J. ment. Def.*, 1946, 50:393–401.
29. Pintner, R., The standardization of Knox's Cube Test, *Psychol. Rev.*, 1915, 22:377–401.
30. Porteus, S. D., *Guide to Porteus Maze Test*, The Training School (Vineland, N.J.), 1924.
31. Porteus, S. D., *The maze test and mental differences*, Smith Publishing Company, 1933.
32. Porteus, S. D., The validity of the Porteus maze test, *J. educ. Psychol.*, 1939, 30:172–178.

33. Porteus, S. D., *The practice of clinical psychology*, American Book Company, 1941.
34. Porteus, S. D., *Qualitative performance in the Maze Test*, Psychological Corporation, 1942.
35. Porteus, S. D., Porteus maze tests: applications in medical and allied fields, *Brit. J. med. Psychol.*, 1945, 20:267–270.
36. Porteus, S. D., Q scores, temperament, and delinquency, *J. soc. Psychol.*, 1945, 21:81–103.
37. Porteus, S. D., Porteus maze tests, in Harriman, P. L. (ed.), *Encyclopedia of psychology*, Philosophical Library, 1946, pp. 537–544.
38. Porteus, S. D., and Peters, H. N., Maze test validation and psychosurgery, *Genet. Psychol. Monogr.*, 1947, 36:3–86.
39. Poull, L. E., and Montgomery, R. P., The Porteus Maze Test as a discriminative measure in delinquency, *J. appl. Psychol.*, 1929, 13:145–151.
40. Sanderson, M. H., Performance of fifth, eighth and eleventh grade children in the Porteus Qualitative Maze Tests, *J. genet. Psychol.*, 1945, 67:57–65.
41. Shakow, D., and Millard, M. S., A psychometric study of 150 adult delinquents, *J. soc. Psychol.*, 1935, 6:437–457.
42. Wallin, J. E. W., A comparison of the Stanford 1916 and 1937 (Form L) test results with those from the Arthur Performance Scale (Form I) based on the same subjects, *J. genet. Psychol.*, 1946, 69:45–55.
43. Wallin, J. E. W., and Hultsch, C. L., The pathognomonic significance of psychometric patterns, *Amer. J. ment. Def.*, 1944, 48:269–277.
44. Werner, H., A comparative study of a small group of clinical tests, *J. appl. Psychol.*, 1940, 24:231–236.
45. Wile, I. S., and Davis, R., A comparative study of the Kohs Block Design Test, *Amer. J. Orthopsychiat.*, 1930, 1:89–103.
46. Wilson, F. T., and Flemming, C. W., Correlations of performance tests with other abilities and traits in grade I, *Child Developm.*, 1937, 8:80–88.
47. Wright, C., The qualitative performance of delinquent boys on the Porteus Maze Test, *J. consult. Psychol.*, 1944, 8:24–26.

DIAGNOSTIC TESTING REPORTS INVOLVING THE ARTHUR PERFORMANCE SCALE

48. Rosenzweig, S., with Kogan, K. L., *Psychodiagnosis: an introduction to tests in the clinical practice of psychodynamics*, Grune & Stratton, 1949, pp. 34–39.
49. Sarason, E. K., and Sarason, S. B., A problem in diagnosing feeblemindedness, in Watson, R. I. (ed.), *Readings in the clinical method in psychology*, Harper & Brothers, 1949, pp. 314–324. (Also in *J. abnorm. soc. Psychol.*, 1945, 40:323–329.)

CHAPTER 11

The Vineland Social Maturity Scale

The Vineland Social Maturity Scale is a measure of social development widely used with children and adults. In the words of Doll, its author, it "provides a definite outline of detailed performances in respect to which children show a progressive capacity for looking after themselves and for participating in those activities which lead toward ultimate independence as adults." (7, p. 1.) It thus taps an area of development important in many diagnostic problems—actual functioning level rather than estimated potential. Habitual performance is evaluated, not predicted capacity. Bradway, one of Doll's early co-workers, describes the scale as emphasizing different qualities at different age levels. She states: "The Vineland Social Maturity Scale measures social development in terms of personal independence and responsibility. In infancy and early childhood social maturity is reflected in self-help, at adolescence in self-direction and in adult life as assumption of responsibility for others." (3, p. 326.)

The usefulness of such a scale, which objectifies impressions of growth and development generally observed by the clinician who works with the problems of children, is self-evident. Instead of depending alone upon clinical impression and past experience for judging the significance of certain types of behavior, the clinician has at his command a standardized diagnostic tool. Because it is standardized, because norms have been developed, and because he can share in the experiences of others who have used it, the clinician is in a position to make more accurate diagnostic appraisals than would be the case if he had to depend upon personal experience alone. It is especially useful in cases where the diagnosis of mental deficiency is involved. As two of the criteria of mental deficiency are social incompetence and arrested development, the Vineland Social Maturity Scale is directly suitable for diagnostic appraisal within this area.

Strictly speaking, the Vineland is not a test but a standardized developmental schedule in the sense that the operation performed by the clinician is a consideration of a diversity of information and a decision about the presence or absence of the behavior relevant to the item in question. This information is gathered through what, in effect, is a guided interview. Instead of eliciting behavior samples by administering test materials, the clinician gathers data from an informant who may or may not be the child or adult in question. Thus the scale samples behavior outside the somewhat artificial confines of a clinical setting. The informant does not make the necessary judgments; instead he or she supplies information from which the clinician makes certain inferences.

Despite points of similarity, the scale is not to be confused with rating scales in that scores on the Vineland are not based on general opinion but are standardized. Because of this Doll (7) objects to calling it a rating scale. Nevertheless, it certainly is not a test in the sense the word is used here—a sampling of behavior in the presence of an examiner. The term "developmental schedule" serves to distinguish it both from a rating scale and from a test. In many ways its dissimilarity to the orthodox test merits approbation rather than criticism. One advantage over a test in evaluating development, quite apart from its special aim of measuring social maturity, is the breadth of behavior that can be judged in a relatively short period. If a test in sampling behavior is to be at all economical of time, the individual cannot be placed in more than a rather limited variety of situations. The Vineland Social Maturity Scale permits wide sampling from an informant who knows the subject, without, however, requiring this untrained person to make critical evaluations.

DESCRIPTION OF THE SCALE

The scale as entered on the report blank consists of 117 items divided into age groups from 0–1 to 25 years. Typical items at the lowest level concern balancing the head, pulling self upright, and grasping with thumb and finger. Items included at level IV–V include dressing self (except tying), washing face unassisted, and using a pencil for drawing. At level XII–XV (the first in larger than single-year units) buying clothing accessories, engaging in adolescent group activities, and performing responsible routine chores are included. At the highest level, XXV, such items as promoting civic progress, directing or managing affairs of others, and sharing community responsibility are involved.

Other than listing the items sequentially it is also possible to catalogue them under one or another aspect of social maturity. This Doll does in terms of eight categories: self-help general (e.g., balancing head, standing alone, and avoiding simple hazards); self-help eating (e.g., masticating food, and eating with spoon); self-help dressing (pulling off socks, washing hands unaided, and exercising complete care of dress); locomotion (e.g., walking upstairs unassisted and going to distant places alone); occupation (e.g., cutting with scissors, doing routine household tasks, and performing skilled work); communication (e.g., following simple instructions, relating experiences, and making telephone calls); self-direction (e.g., being trusted with money, buying own clothing, and providing for future); and socialization (e.g., demanding personal attention, playing simple table games, and promoting civic progress). These may be regarded as the areas which make up social maturity as Doll conceives it. Although the items in one category have functional similarity, Doll does not insist that such a classification is more than a matter of convenience. Some of the items are those that form the basis for test items in intelligence scales, especially at the preschool level. Thus sitting unsupported, grasping with thumb and finger, following simple instructions, using names of familiar objects, cutting with scissors, and using a pencil appear in other measures as skills to be demonstrated. At older age levels characterized by greater individuation of behavior this is not so much the case, as there is greater diversity of items which reflect social and intellectual maturity.

In speaking of the item content Doll has this to say:

In the present formulation there is an ample number of items in the pre-school range where our knowledge of social behavior is most definite, and where individual differences are least extensive. The number of items decreases in the later periods of early childhood and especially during the period of adolescence. This is partly due to the rather rapid decline in the rate of social growth coupled with the increasing scope and variety of social behavior. The number of items is seriously limited in the superior adult level and this affects the measurement of average adult level as well. (4, pp. 767–768.)

The paucity of items at the adult level provides one explanation for the relative concentration of diagnostic and research usage of the scale at the younger ages or with mental defectives at a similar level. Although there is a limited number of adult and adolescent items, this is partly a matter of formulation since the number of items could be increased by fractionating the present items.

STANDARDIZATION AND NORMATIVE GROUPS

The standardization as described by Doll (5) rests upon the examination of ten normal persons of each sex at each CA level through thirty years, or 620 subjects in all. They were drawn so as to be representative of social status based on paternal occupation.

The method of construction yielded a year scale based on a method suggested by Thomson (16) for using Hardy's summation technique. Thomson's method is akin to a 50 percent passing technique but yields the average of the ages at which the item is passed. This involves all the data and is hardly more laborious than finding the point at which 50 percent pass the item by interpolation from the percentages immediately on both sides of this point. The result is a complete standardization curve for each scale item. An average standardization value for each item is provided as well as standard deviations from these values. However, the values and standard deviations have not yet been reported by Doll. He states that the items are arranged in order of difficulty based on the average values for the total distribution of scores for the item. The distribution of scores for each item extended over several years. They are separated into year groups according to standard age scores obtained for the scale as a unit. As sex differences on the items used were not found either with the standardization group or with subsequent feeble-minded groups, separate norms are unnecessary (5). Only those items which showed no significant sex differences were used.

There is some confusion about whether this is an age scale or a point scale. Doll states:

This scale is both a point scale and an age scale. As a point scale the individual items have been standardized in progressive order of difficulty.

As a year scale the average point scores at successive life ages have been used as test-age scores. In such a year scale the average normal annual increments in score are always equal to corresponding increments in life age up to the maturational limit or "ceiling" of the scale. This ceiling represents the total range of normal adult scores. For the 1916 Stanford Binet, for example, this normal range is from a lower limit of about 9 years to an upper limit of 19 years, with the average at 14 years, and the mid-range between 12 and 16 years. For the Social Maturity Scale the corresponding adult range is from about 20 to 30 years, with the average at 25 years and the mid-range between 23 and 27 years. Since test scores cannot be standardized in terms of age beyond the average adult level, the upper test ages are obtained by statistical . . . [extrapolation]. (6, p. 90.)

ADMINISTRATION AND SCORING

The manual of directions (7) supplies information about the general precautions to be observed in administering the scale and detailed instructions for each item. A record form facilitates both administration and scoring. In using the scale the clinician starts well below the anticipated final level and goes through the items of each functional category one by one until failures occur. This is not a requirement for administration; the clinician may use another approach if he so desires, such as presenting the items in the sequence in which they appear in the record booklet. Doll advises that the basal score below which items are assumed to be passed requires two consecutive successes within each category. Likewise two 'consecutive failures in each category are necessary for the determination of the ceiling.

Rather explicit criteria of scoring are given for each item. A quotation from self-help items will serve as an illustration:

25. Drinks from cup or glass unassisted.
    Uses cup or glass, unassisted, for drinking, by grasping handle or by using either or both hands on sides of glass and without serious spilling.
28. Eats with spoon.
    Uses spoon at table or high chair for eating from bowl, cup or plate and does so without help and without appreciable spilling.
30. Discriminates edible substances.
    Avoids eating trash, and readily discriminates between ordinary substances suitable or unsuitable for eating without necessity of sampling them. May bite hard objects but does not require watching in this respect.

33. Unwraps candy.
  Given candy or food enclosed in wrapping, removes wrapping without suggestion or help before eating. (7, p. 20.)

These item definitions do not provide for all contingencies; nor do they tell the clinician how to direct the interview so that a full and unequivocal answer may be obtained. Questions are asked about the behavior of the child by the clinician more or less as he sees fit until he is satisfied that he can accurately judge the habitual presence or absence of the behavior to which the item refers. Doll offers only a general orientation, making it very clear that the crux of the matter is to determine the extent to which the person in question is capable of performing the activities in question.

The person being examined does not necessarily (or even usually) supply the information which determines the score. An informant who knows the person well supplies the material necessary for the examiner to make the judgment. Provided certain precautions are observed the use of self-report is sanctioned by Doll (7) with individuals whose Stanford-Binet mental age is as low as five years. In this connection rapport is especially important. If the subject is uncoöperative, only invalid results can be obtained. Furthermore, in spite of good rapport certain characteristics of the patient may serve to render dubious the obtained results. Modesty, an uncritical attitude, or a tendency toward self-deprecation must be detected if the patient is used as an informant. Under many circumstances a desirable precaution is to check a few items with another informant.

An item is scored "plus" (+) if it is apparent that the criteria for it have been satisfied, and that it is habitually performed without unusual or artificial incentive. Those items measuring behavior which the patient formerly performed but does not currently because of special restraint are scored "+F" and receive full credit. Those an individual has not performed because of lack of opportunity are scored "+N.O." and receive full credit when they occur in an otherwise continuous series of plus scores, no credit in an otherwise continuous minus series, and half-credit within the intermediate or mixed range. Items are scored "±" if the behavior is in an emergent state wherein it is occasionally but not habitually performed and receive half-credit. Items are scored "−" if the person has not yet or only rarely performs the act in question.

The sum of the scores (plus those below basal) gives the total score, which is converted to an age score by interpolation on the record sheet. For example, on finding that the total score is 48, inspection will show it falls at level III–IV. The precise value is calculated by expressing as a fraction of the total array of the scores for that age level the difference between the obtained score and the highest score of the preceding year group. In this instance, 48 is four-sixths of the distance between 3.0 and 4.0, or 3.7. This is the social age (SA). A table for converting scores into SA is provided in the manual (7). SA may be converted into SQ by the formula similar to that used for determining the IQ. The highest divisor used is 25 since there is a steady rise in score to this CA in contrast with the usual intelligence test where 14 or 16 usually marks the CA at which there is a leveling off. Concerning the SQ Doll says, "The scale provides a measure of social level as an absolute index of present status. This index of level may be converted into a relative index of brightness; that is, the social age score may be converted into a social quotient. This quotient gives an index of relative social development which may have some value for prognosis." (4, p. 768.) Although the SQ is calculated and used it is not as interpretatively unequivocal as is SA. Doll (10) himself states this method of expression is not entirely satisfactory and should be considered tentative because preciseness of interpretation has not been established.

VALIDITY

The validity of the Vineland Social Maturity Scale has been repeatedly investigated. Item validity was indicated by the standard deviations of the normative item curves, by relation to chronological age, and more particularly by similar curves for feeble-minded subjects classified by SA. Using as subjects 436 patients of the Training School at Vineland (an institution for mental defectives), Doll found that the item standardization curves were "steep, smooth and parallel." (5, p. 289.) These findings are evidence of validity since they were independent of the standardization group. The results he obtained also showed a consistent progression of item difficulty when the successive social age groups were studied; i.e., the items at a specific social age were equally difficult for a given social age group. When normal CA (and SA) groups were compared with feeble-minded of the same SA, although naturally of higher CA, they were again very similar in spite of the greater experience and training open to the feeble-minded group. On these issues Doll unfortunately does not cite detailed evidence so that these statements must for the moment be accepted on faith.[1]

Estimations of social age from informants independent of the scale were compared with SA's obtained from the scale. In a group of resident patients (5) at Vineland the correlation was .85. When the total group was broken into subgroups it was found that lower SA's were estimated more accurately than the higher; up to SA 12 the estimated SA's averaged within one year of the obtained SA, accuracy of estimates decreasing markedly thereafter.

Doll also investigated validity by study of the differentiating capacity of the scale to discriminate feeble-mindedness. In this connection he writes:

From practical considerations the minimum normal adult social age may be tentatively placed at 18 to 20 years. All scores of our institutionally committed feeble-minded subjects fall below these limits. Also 5 patients discharged to employee status all have scores slightly above 18 years.

Summarizing the data on social quotients, we have a total of 446 subjects, 10 of whom (not included in our feeble-minded data) are diagnosed as "not feeble-minded," and 7 as "doubtful." Of these 446 subjects, 65 have I.Q.'s above 70, but only 25 have S.Q.'s above 70. Of these 25 with S.Q.'s above 70, 13 are diagnosed as feeble-minded and 4 as doubtful, and 8 as not feeble-minded; all the 13 feeble-minded are under 15 years L.A. (with prospect of S.Q. falling with increased age).

From this we infer that S.Q. is a better diagnostic aid than I.Q., and that S.Q. below 80, and certainly below 70, marks the upper limit of feeble-minded social competence. (5, p. 290.)

In the same study Doll (5) reported that feeble-minded subjects have lower social ages as compared with normal subjects and further that idiots, imbeciles, and morons can be satisfactorily differentiated. In addition, Doll and Fitch (8) (9), using as subjects ninety-one juvenile delinquents in a state home, had informants who knew the boys well make an estimate of their social age. This was found to correlate .80 with obtained SA.

Some evidence from comparison of institutionalized and extra-

---

[1] For some years Doll has promised that a forthcoming book will give more complete evidence, which presumably would include data on this or comparable groups. This book is now in the process of publication by the Educational Test Bureau.

instutionalized feeble-minded has been advanced by Doll and Long-well (10). The patients receiving extra-institutional care such as those boarding or paroled had social ages significantly higher than their mental ages although placed in such status before being examined with the Vineland Scale. Indirect evidence of validity is discernible in the study of Ordahl, Keyt, and Wright (14). Selecting as subjects those institutionalized high-grade defectives who contribute to the institution as workers, they investigated their SA and SQ. The mean 1916 Stanford-Binet IQ was 62 and the mean MA was 9–8 years. The mean SQ was 57 and the mean SA was 11–6 years (corrected by elimination of +F credits because of evidence that these reflected repeated unsuccessful attempts rather than habitual performance). Thus the mean SA was higher than the MA, but the SQ smaller than the IQ. As the authors indicate, this is the expected pattern for the mentally deficient. The mental defective who performs the day-to-day routine activities of the institution has a social age considerably higher than his mental age. Although this study does not given comparative figures of the nonworking mental defectives of comparable MA there is enough indirect evidence (cf. 5, 11) that the difference of almost two years between average MA and SA is greater than that found with unselected institutionalized mental defective populations.

It is well known that many of the pupils in special classes in the public school system have IQ's as low as many institutionalized mental defectives. In the selection of a given child for special classwork rather than institutionalization it is anticipated that the child will be able eventually to manage his own affairs. This is in contrast with placement in a home for the mentally deficient, where such eventual independence would be expected to be the exception. It was the hypothesis of Doll and McKay (11) that the factor of social competence would be revealed by differences in the social maturity age and quotient of children drawn from these two groups. Accordingly, they matched a small group of children for sex, CA, and MA. One member of the pair was in a training school for the mentally deficient; the other member was in a special class in the regular school system. Since they were matched for CA and MA they were also matched for IQ. The mean SA's were respectively 7.0 and 9.4 and mean SQ's were 57 and 78. These differences are statistically significant, showing the superior social competence of the special-class children. In terms of SQ about 50 percent of the special-class children had SQ's above 80 whereas none of the institutional children had SQ's above 80. There is the possibility that these differences are due to the greater environmental opportunity of the special-class students living more or less freely in their own homes. Analysis of the superiority on specific items in the special-class group (on which in all except one instance the special-class students were equal or superior) does not show this to be the case. Doll and McKay (11) conclude that facilitating as well as inhibiting effects are at work in the institutional environment. This discrepancy between verbal intelligence as measured by the Binet and social competence as measured by the Vineland probably accounts partly for the children's presence in the respective groups. In other words, the intellectually deficient and socially incompetent is institutionalized; the intellectually deficient but relatively socially competent is not. In this connection, "It seems reasonable, therefore, to suggest the hypothesis that when both S.Q. and Binet I.Q. are below 70, the individual may be feebleminded; that when both S.Q. and Binet I.Q. are above 80 the individual may be normal, even if dull-normal; and that when either S.Q. or I.Q. is below 80 the individual may be borderline. In the last group we may also hypothecate a suspicion of normality when the S.Q. is above the I.Q." (11, p. 101.) As Doll and McKay point out, this is to be considered in the nature of a hypothesis to be applied anew in each individual case with due regard to the complete diagnostic study. Within these limits it appears a reasonable approach.

RELIABILITY

Reliability (stability) was studied and reported by Doll (5) for 123 repeated examinations given after lapses of one day to nine months to feeble-minded residents at the Training School. The correlation obtained was .92 with the probable error amounting to about one-half year. Some of the original and repeat examinations had the same examiner and informant, some the same examiner and different informants, some different examiners and the same informant, and some different examiners and different informants. Analysis of the data for each of these variables revealed that the order of variation was not particularly different from one variable to another.

After a median time interval of 1.85 years, 250 of the 620 normative subjects were retested (6). This group was quite comparable to the original sample. The average increase in SA was 1.95 years (as compared to the time interval of 1.85). The median SQ increase was two points. A second retesting for 196 of these 250 was performed after an additional 1.35 years, with results in keeping with those just reported. Nevertheless there were considerable individual differences, with the rate of increase above twenty years CA being considerably below expectation whereas below twenty years it was somewhat higher than expectation (59 and 119 respectively instead of 100). The probable error of social age increment was ±.7 years for the 250 examined after almost two years. On the basis of this and testings after still longer intervals, Doll concluded that there are marked individual differences in rates of growth over short-time intervals but that over longer periods approximately the expected rate is obtained.

Patterson (15), using as subjects Fels Research Institute children aged 6 to 120 months, calculated several measures of reliability. The coefficients of stability were respectively .66, .63, and .42 after six, nine, and twelve months for thirty-one to fifty-one cases. Thirty-two cases tested by one examiner with the child as the informant gave a correlation of .50 with the results of a different examiner who retested within six months with the mother as the informant. With twenty cases and different examiners but the same informant a coefficient of .85 was found.

The summary that Patterson offers seems to express adequately his own and the previously reported findings. He states that "These correlations indicate a satisfactory reliability for the scale when used by a skilled examiner with informants with whom he is acquainted and who in turn are acquainted with the subjects. In such circumstances the main source of unreliability, other than the scale itself, is probably the source of information." (15, p. 278.)

CORRELATION WITH STANFORD-BINET

Despite the intent of Doll to develop an instrument going beyond the accepted concept of mental age as most adequately reflecting competence to adjust in society, the Vineland Social Maturity Scale has frequently been compared to various intelligence measures, particularly the Stanford-Binet. The intent has been primarily to demonstrate differences, but similarities have inevitably appeared. In a sense, the studies now to be discussed are related to the previous reports of validity. There is a difference, however, in that the intent of these workers, through examining the relationship, was to bring out the uniqueness of the scale. Almost needless to say, correlation does not mean identification. In other words, the rather high positive correlation between MA and SA, to be found in the data to be discussed, does not mean that both scales are measuring precisely the same functions.

The approaches to this problem include not only correlational technique but also comparison of the standing of the subjects with respect to the relative magnitude of SA and MA (or SQ and IQ). In considering the relationship it is important to note that there is a choice to be made between using SQ-IQ correlations and SA-MA. The latter is considered the more appropriate both because SQ is not so fully established and so stable a measure as SA for reasons given earlier, and, if the influence of CA (which is involved in a quotient measure such as IQ or SQ) be partialled out, because the lower degree of relationship might be misinterpreted. The SQ and the IQ are not obtained with the same divisors, in one case reaching a maximum of 25 and in the other of 16 (with the 1916 Stanford-Binet). This is likely to create confusion unless kept in mind, e.g., in the study of Ordahl, Keyt, and Wright (14), their finding of SQ smaller than IQ is partly, at least, a direct result of their difference in maximum divisor. The standard deviations of the two scales are likewise unequal. Since interest focuses on *tests*, MA-SA relationship is primary. Accordingly, whenever possible, the results will be given in age terms.

Table 18 gives a representative sample of the studies concerned with the relationship. It is no great surprise to find that there is a considerable degree of relationship. It would appear that the correlation is greatest with mental defectives on the one hand (5), (11), (17) and superior children on the other (15), (17). With the borderline, dull-normal, and normal (1), (3), (11), (12), (13) the correlation tends to be somewhat lower. Lack of knowledge of variability within the various samples makes this conclusion very tentative, since restriction of range in one study as compared to another would lower the obtained coefficient. However, in the study of Doll and McKay (11) the variability is very similar for mental defectives

TABLE 18.   Correlation Between the Vineland Social Maturity Scale and the
1916 and 1937 Stanford-Binet

Investigator	Sample	S-B	Correlation SA and MA	Relative Standing
Doll (5)	436 institution-alized mental defectives. Median CA 19–0	1916	.80	Median MA 7.2 Median SA 8.0 Median IQ 56 Median SQ 45
Doll and McKay (11)	38 special-class children. Mean CA 12.6	1916	.61	Mean MA 7.2 Mean SA 9.4
	38 paired institu-tionalized feeble-minded. Mean CA 12.2		.70	Mean MA 7.3 Mean SA 7.0
Bradway (3)	310 school chil-dren fourth through eighth grade	1916	.73	Class N SA MA Grade 4 slow to ret. 13 9.0 8.3 Regular 41 10.3 9.9 Grade 5 slow to ret. 9 9.0 8.4 Regular 42 11.1 10.8 Gifted 18 12.2 13.2 Grade 6 slow to ret. 15 9.2 8.7 Regular 43 11.6 11.7 Gifted 13 12.5 15.3 Grade 7 Retarded 9 9.7 9.7 Gifted 17 14.0 16.6 Grade 8 Retarded 12 10.5 10.1 Gifted 19 15.6 16.8
Wile and Davis (17)	100 children, IQ's 120 and above. Median CA 8–8	1916	.88	Mean SA 2 years, 3 months below MA and one month above CA
	100 children, IQ'S 79 and below. Median CA 10–4		.91	Mean SA 2 months above MA and 2 years, 8 months below CA
Louttit and Watson (13)	62 first-grade children. Mean IQ in normal range	1916	.38 (IQ and SQ cor-rected for age)	
Anderson (1)	60 special-class children younger than 12.	1916	.40[a]	Median SQ 92 Median IQ 65
	250 special-class children. CA 14–16			Median SQ 86 Median IQ 66
Patterson (15)	91 Fels Research Institute chil-dren. Mean CA 6 years	?	.96	Mean MA 7.1 Mean SA 6.8
Gamboro (12)	Special-class children.	1937		
	171 boys, CA 14–16		.19	Mean MA 10.2 Mean SA 12.2
	115 boys, CA 12–14		.29	Mean MA 8.8 Mean SA 12.9
	61 girls, CA 14–16		.09	Mean MA 9.5 Mean SA 12.6

[a] As calculated by Louttit and Watson (13).

and special-class children, and the differences in magnitude of correlation in favor of the defectives tend to corroborate this conclusion that there is a lesser degree of relationship in borderline groups. The authors suggest that the MA's of the special-class children may be less representative of their true intelligence than is the case with the institutionalized mental defectives.

The study of Louttit and Watson (13) does not report results in SA-MA terms, and, therefore, the correlation found between IQ and SQ has been corrected for CA, lowering the correlation to some degree. The study of Gamboro (12), the only one reporting statistically nonsignificant correlations, is found to have an extraordinarily restricted MA dispersion with sigmas of .9, .8, and .9 for mean MA's of 10.2, 8.8, and 9.5 respectively. The study of Anderson (1) does not report standard deviations, and, further, the correlation found was based upon SQ and IQ. It would appear, then, that these studies do not contradict the major trend of a substantial correlation between SA and MA. However, this general degree of relationship is not so great as to suggest that the Vineland Social Maturity Scale is superfluous.

The situation concerning relative standing of SA and MA is less equivocal. In mental defectives SA tends to exceed MA; in special-class children the trend is accentuated; with normal children they tend to be about the same; and for superior children the MA tends to exceed the SA. Those instances in which SQ-IQ results must perforce be used verify the trends found with MA and SA.

DIAGNOSTIC USAGE

The preceding discussion supplied information relevant to diagnostic usage, but there are other matters concerning use of the scale which deserve brief mention. It would be erroneous to assume that the Vineland Social Maturity Scale is useful only in connection with diagnostic problems in which mental deficiency or borderline intelligence is suspected; it has other very pertinent uses. Poor adjustment may arise in instances in which the individual is intellectually superior but relatively lacking in social competence. This discrepancy between intellectual and social maturity is at the root of some behavior problems in children. The scale also may be used to advantage with deaf children. Bradway (2) made a careful study at a residential school for the deaf and concluded that it may be applied without modification.

A distinction is to be made between conduct and competence (10). The scale is not a direct measure of conduct (socially accepted behavior). Doll urges that this be judged on other bases. Thus a person may be socially mature enough to adjust to society in terms of his SA but still unable to adjust because of other facets of his behavior. This must be kept in mind, else confusion will result when dealing with certain problem children, delinquents, or criminals.

The argument that the scale is too subjective has sometimes been advanced. Proponents of this view say that the examiner is left too much to his own devices when faced with an informant. He has to know what to ask the informant and to decide when he has secured both enough relevant and sufficiently valid information to make a decision about the scoring of the relevant items. It requires a high level of professional competence to secure reliable and valid results and to judge when sufficient information to reach a decision has been secured. This is true enough so far as it goes, but it can be ignored as beside the point when skilled clinicians are concerned. True, it takes training and the appropriate experience to apply the Vineland Social Maturity Scale, but so does every other test. If the person conducting the interview is competent enough to be entrusted with making such interviews at all, the scale is a guide which aids immensely as contrasted, let us say, with a free interview conducted without it.

It should be emphasized that the person evaluated is not necessarily present. This instrument has the advantage that occasionally it may be applied as a means of making an evaluation of the child's social maturity without subjecting him to a disturbing test situation. The informant, however, must be in a position to know the habitual activities of the patient if the application of the scale is to be valid.

The collection of information in order to decide if the patient meets the criteria for passing the items frequently yields a dividend of other diagnostically useful material. This is in the form of information about the attitude of the informant, often the mother. The way in which the questions are answered helps to show the attitudes the mother takes toward the child and to reveal his status in the total family constellation. The scale may also serve occasionally as a standard or normative guide for the parent who is pushing the child beyond capacity because of disproportionately high standards. Although this procedure does not get at the more fundamental problem of why the parent is pushing the child, it does serve to demonstrate convincingly the discrepancy between aspirations and expectancy and what may justifiably be expected.

After establishment of the level of social competence as measured by the Vineland Scale, an individual training program may be set up with greater assurance than would be the case if it had not been used. Specific items failed below the general level may be the first point of attack, and then those falling immediately above his present functioning level. The "category" approach is of special usefulness here, since the groups of self-help, self-direction, socialization, etc., show specific areas of weakness and strength.

The measurement of SA is specifically influenced by limiting variables to self-expression such as physical handicaps, social handicaps, and other circumstances. However, one of the virtues of the scale is that it permits the measurement of the influence of such variables.

SUMMARY

Everything considered, the Vineland Social Maturity Scale is a useful clinical instrument, filling a gap which other measures do not fit. With the mentally defective, the delinquent, and the problem child it is especially pertinent because it tells the clinician something about a very relevant facet of their behavior, viz., social competence. Nevertheless, like all other diagnostic measuring devices it is not a panacea for the problems of the clinician. It provides one approach to the assessment of social adjustment, but does not measure all aspects of such adjustment.

BIBLIOGRAPHY

1. Anderson, M. L., Education for social maturity, *Train. Sch. Bull.*, 1937, 33:185–192.
2. Bradway, K. P., The social competence of deaf children, *Amer. Ann. Deaf*, 1937, 82:122–140.
3. Bradway, K. P., Social competence of grade school children, *J. exper. Educ.*, 1938, 6:326–331.
4. Doll, E. A., The clinical significance of social maturity, *J. ment. Sci.*, 1935, 81:766–782.
5. Doll, E. A., Preliminary standardization of the Vineland Social Maturity Scale, *Amer. J. Orthopsychiat.*, 1936, 6:283–293.

6. Doll, E. A., Growth studies in social competence, *Proc. Amer. Ass. ment. Def.*, 1939, 44:90–96.
7. Doll, E. A., *Vineland Social Maturity Scale: manual of directions*, Educational Test Bureau, 1947.
8. Doll, E. A., and Fitch, K. A., Social competence of delinquent boys, *Proc. Amer. Ass. ment. Def.*, 1938, 43:137–141.
9. Doll, E. A., and Fitch, K. A., Social competence of juvenile delinquents, *J. crim. Law Criminol.*, 1939, 30:52–67.
10. Doll, E. A., and Longwell, S. G., Social competence of the feeble minded under extra institutional care, *Psychiat. Quart.*, 1937, 11:450–464.
11. Doll, E. A., and McKay, B. E., The social competence of special class children, *J. educ. Res.*, 1937, 31:90–106.
12. Gamboro, P. K., Analysis of Vineland Social Maturity Scale, *Amer. J. ment. Def.*, 1944, 48:359–363.
13. Louttit, C. M., and Watson, R., Vineland social maturity scores for entering first grade children, *Train. Sch. Bull.*, 1941, 38:133–137.
14. Ordahl, G., Keyt, N. L., and Wright, C., The social competence of high-grade mental defectives determined by self-report, *Amer. J. ment. Def.*, 1944, 48:367–373.
15. Patterson, C. H., The Vineland Social Maturity Scale and some of its correlates, *J. genet. Psychol.*, 1943, 62:275–287.
16. Thomson, G. H., A note on scaling tests, *J. educ. Psychol.*, 1926, 17:550–552.
17. Wile, I. S., and Davis, R. M.., Behavior differentials of children with IQ's 120 and above and IQ's 79 and below with some reference to socio-economic status, *Amer. J. Orthopsychiat.*, 1939, 9:529–539.

DIAGNOSTIC TESTING REPORTS INVOLVING THE VINELAND SOCIAL MATURITY SCALE

18. Bice, H. V., Mental deficiency, moron level, in Burton, A., and Harris, R. E., *Case histories in clinical and abnormal psychology*, Harper & Brothers, 1947, pp. 383–397.

Supplementary article in Watson, R. I. (ed.), *Readings in the clinical method in psychology*, Harper & Brothers, 1949.

19. Doll, E. A., The social basis of mental diagnosis. Pp. 325–333. (Also in *J. appl. Psychol.*, 1940, 24:160–169.)

CHAPTER 12

Diagnostic Testing of Infants
and Preschool Children

The years from birth to the end of the fifth year are frequently divided into two periods—the infancy and the preschool periods. Infancy is considered to extend from birth to somewhere toward the end of the second year, and, in terms of characteristics relevant to diagnostic testing, it is the period in which the infant is tested either prone or supported on the mother's lap. Walking has barely begun; precise or exact movements of the hands are hardly possible; and verbal communication through language is just emerging. In the preschool period, extending from the end of infancy through the age of five, both gross and fine muscular coördinations are developed to a point where the child may be seated at a table, use his hands skillfully, move about with ease, and, furthermore, communicate through speech.

The effective ranges of the relevant tests do not necessarily coincide with one or another of these periods. For example, the Cattell Infant Intelligence Scale and the Vineland Social Maturity Scale may be applied in infancy and in the preschool period as well. Diagnostic instruments used during the preschool period include the Revised Stanford-Binet Scale and in the later stages of the period the Rorschach, the Weigl Color-Form, and the Arthur Performance Scale. Only two of these instruments are discussed at this juncture —the Cattell Scale and the Revised Stanford-Binet. First, however, certain general comments concerning the diagnostic testing of infants will be made, following which the Cattell Scale will be described and evaluated. Thereafter, preschool testing will be described, and then a short account offered of the Stanford-Binet Scale as a preschool instrument.

THE DIAGNOSTIC TESTING OF INFANTS

Attempts at the development of tests for infants have not met with the success that those for older children have achieved. Opposing the acquisition of valid and reliable results in infant testing are certain inherent characteristics of infants—inability to understand oral directions, short attention span, and easy fatigability. At this stage physical development plays a much larger part in deciding the functioning status than it does in an older child and therefore distorts the interpretation of psychological functioning. Variations in IQ at this age level and the correspondingly lower reliability and validity coefficients are considered by Cattell (4) and others to result not from the inadequacy of the tests but rather from irregularities of the tempo of development. Cattell's evidence in individual cases is in keeping with a host of evidence which points to an uneven rate of intellectual development in infancy. Whether the unstable state of affairs in infant testing be due to psychological characteristics, physical development, irregularities in the tempo of mental development, or all three, diagnostic testing of infants is only approximate.

What, then, is the clinical value of the psychological testing of infants? Carter and Bowles put the matter very well:

In the more formal aspects of the psychological examination of infants, the task is, essentially, a rough screening job endeavoring to classify individuals into one of three groups: (1) Those found to have made unusual developmental progress; (2) those making satisfactory or average development progress; and (3) those whose developmental progress is subnormal or questionable. Consistent evidence of unusual developmental progress found in several successive examinations of an infant may indicate promise of being able to take advantage of unusual opportunities. However, the authors know of no more reliable basis for this assumption than that it seems clinically justified in terms of the mores governing the placement of children for adoption. Satisfactory developmental progress in an infant means little more than that there is no discernible reason for questioning the infant's potentialities for taking advantage of normal opportunities for development. Subnormal or questionable developmental progress in an infant, however, may well indicate biological or emotional traumas or deprivational conditions that may impose serious limitations upon future developmental progress. Cases so identified are referred for medical examination and observed over a period of time to check on progress. In terms of the predictive value of infant examinations, little more than this is possible since what behavior equipment the infant will build up is so highly dependent upon the physiological and psychological events in his future, i.e., upon health factors and the nature of his future contacts with persons, objects, and events. (3, p. 114.)

Only if the essentially modest scope of infant testing is realized can a worth-while diagnostic contribution be made in this area. Inferences are justified only if tentative and cautious, and, in general, recommendations for retesting are in order to provide an additional safety value.

Certain procedural precautions in the testing of infants are worth stating. Generally speaking, to prevent undue fatigue the session should not last more than half an hour. Fortunately, the Cattell Infant Intelligence Scale, the instrument of choice, can usually be given in this time.[1] With this and other infant tests the mother or an attendant is customarily present during the testing, and, except when the child is in a supine or prone position, he is held upon her lap. The mother should be warned that the child is not expected to do all the tasks placed before him and that she should not interfere with the testing to encourage or help the baby unless specifically requested.

The examination needs to be conducted in a smooth, unhurried, quiet manner. Loud noises and sudden movements may serve to divert attention or cause undue emotional arousal and therefore should be avoided. As an infant becomes aware of strangers after the first six months or so a period of time to adjust to the testing situation is desirable.

Carter and Bowles offer the following very able summary of the diagnostic attitude necessary for the clinician to assume:

In addition to obtaining information relevant to scoring test items, other observations are an important part of the infant examination. Even though the infant fails to pass a given test item, it may be determined whether or not he is approaching that level of performance. For exam-

---

[1] In the opinion of Cattell (5) often a half-hour is too long for a sitting. She usually requires a second sitting about one week later. She believes that this procedure appreciably increases the reliability of the results.

ple, he may fail to turn his head to a voice or a ringing bell, yet postural adjustments may reveal that he hears the sounding object. He may be unable to grasp an object placed before him, but increased tension and straining may show that he is making an approach to the object. It is important to notice such things as the alertness of the infant, interest in surrounding objects, the quality of his responses to persons and objects, the general tempo of his responses, his stability, and his adjustment to the situation. Such information, combined with the mother's reports, will add to the picture of the baby's developmental progress. (3, p. 116.)

THE CATTELL INFANT INTELLIGENCE TESTS[2]

The Cattell Infant Intelligence Tests were developed as a downward extension of the Revised Stanford-Binet Intelligence Tests, Form L, which fact in itself gives the scale an advantage over other tests for infants. The tests are organized into a scale; the directions for administration are clear and definite; the scoring has been made reasonably objective and well defined; and the material has proved to have an appeal for infants and young children. Prolonged effort is not generally necessary on the part of the child, which is a definite advantage at this age level. The testing materials are relatively inexpensive and easily available, and the results possess clinical validity, at least in the opinion of some experienced psychologists. For these and other reasons the Cattell Scale was selected for exposition.

Description of the Scale

Many of the tests used in the scale were adopted from items developed by Gesell and his co-workers. Others were collected from various sources including the Revised Stanford-Binet, and still others were original. Items deliberately not selected from these sources included those Cattell judged to be unduly influenced by home training or too dependent upon large muscular control. The first criterion of elimination was not fully adhered to since home training influences many tests that were included. Of course, in any strict sense this criterion would be impossible to apply. Elimination of items of the latter type is entirely in keeping with the usual negative findings concerning the relationship between muscular control and intelligence. Some motor tests (lifting head, holding head erect, etc.) were included nevertheless.

---

[2] The manual, *The Measurement of Intelligence of Infants and Young Children*, by Cattell (4) contains much detailed information not covered here.

The scale, following the format of the Stanford-Binet, is divided into age levels. There are twenty-two levels, at one-month, two-month, three-month, and half-year intervals. During the first year each level covers only one month, and during the second year two months. In the first half of the third year there are three-month intervals, and from thirty months to the end of the fourth year each interval covers six months. Strictly speaking, the test extends only from the second through the thirtieth month, as beyond this point the items are taken directly from the Stanford-Binet, Form L. Each level has five tests with either one or, more often, two alternates. The number of tests at each level as well as the small intervals offer the possibility that this is a more accurate instrument than certain scales developed earlier.

A SUMMARY OF TEST CONTENT

The tests at the earlier levels are naturally nonverbal and involve response to sensory stimulation by turning head, regarding objects, grasping, manipulating, and so on. At the sixth-month level, for example, the infant, while in a sitting position on the lap of an adult, is required to pick up a cube from the table, lift a cup, reach out and finger his reflection in a mirror, reach for a key or similar object held perpendicularly in the hand of the examiner, and reach for several seconds for a cube just out of his grasp. These early tests have as their principal materials a large ring, cubes, and small pellets.

At the youngest levels the tasks are mostly perceptive in nature— for example, attending to a voice or following a ring in vertical motion. There is a gradual change in the nature of the tests in the direction of more manipulatory tasks beginning at about five months. The first verbal responses are those of adjustment to words (performing an act in response to a spoken request), appearing at nine months. A speaking vocabulary test appears at eleven months. From this point on more and more verbal tests are utilized although manipulatory tasks still predominate. At the level of nineteen to twenty months the child is expected to build a tower of three cubes, to place a square in a large form board, to use a stick to obtain a toy out of reach, to place a doll in a chair and give it a drink, and to point to parts of a doll. At these age levels the principal materials are pegboards, pencils, blocks, form boards, and dolls. The upper levels of Cattell's own tests (through the thirtieth month) include these same materials and also make use of identification of objects from pictures and replicas. Certain of the tests used for age levels twenty to thirty months are drawn from the Revised Stanford-Binet Scale. They are interspersed among Cattell's own tests and restandardized along with the others.

STANDARDIZATION AND NORMATIVE GROUPS

The standardization population consisted of 274 children, who received a varying number of retests, averaging five examinations. The tests were given at the ages of three, six, nine, twelve, eighteen, twenty-four, thirty, and thirty-six months. In all, 1346 examinations were made. For a variety of reasons the number of children who were tested and retested at each of these points varied.

The individual children used for standardization were subjects in a comprehensive pediatric-psychological study planned to run over a period of years. Therefore criteria for inclusion in the project limited those in the sample. The children were selected before birth from parents willing to have their child included; only those families offering evidence of sufficient stability of work and residence to be available over a period of years were selected. Therefore, socially or mentally inadequate parents were not selected. Prospective parents with an income above a certain figure were not eligible for clinic services, from which the sample originated. As a consequence, the family groups selected were mostly lower middle class. Northern European stock was another requirement. Cattell quite properly did not claim this was a random sample. The method of selection and the exigencies of the project limited somewhat the systematic composition of the sample. For example, some tests were tried out on smaller groups than others, time per child was limited by the number to be tested for the project in a given period, and so on.

Items were eliminated as unsatisfactory which showed insufficient, irregular, or too great increase in the percentage of passes from one age group to another. Failure to hold attention, cumbersome equipment, and difficulties in administration were among the other reasons for elimination.

It will be remembered that children were tested at three, six, nine, twelve, eighteen, twenty-four, and thirty months of age. For levels between these ages, tests were placed by estimation from percents passed. Items at fourteen and sixteen months were those too difficult for twelve months and too easy for eighteen months. These between-age-group placements were checked by a very small sample tested every month with close agreement to the between-age placement after twelve months. Deviation was greater below twelve months, which is in keeping with Cattell's contention that the test norms themselves are less satisfactory at these early months.

Percent passing was the only method of item analysis applied. Even here the spread of months at which children were tested was not very large. Inspection of the table in Cattell (4) presenting results shows that typically a given test was applied only at three of the intervals, e.g., eighteen, twenty-four, and thirty months. However, there was often a fairly sharp rise. This implies that a wider age range would not have helped matters appreciably since at the youngest age a test was tried almost all children failed whereas at the oldest age almost all passed. Nevertheless, if supplementary methods and testing at shorter age intervals had been applied, a more adequately standardized instrument might have resulted.

The test items were so placed as to bring the median IQ of the groups aged thirty months and under (the Cattell test items proper) to coincide as closely as possible with that which each group obtained on the Stanford-Binet Form L at thirty-six months. In this Cattell was successful in that the median IQ for each younger group does not differ by more than two points from that obtained on the Stanford-Binet at thirty-six months. It was on this basis that the Cattell Infant Intelligence Tests became a downward extension of the Revised Stanford-Binet.

What of individual variation in IQ? The median variation in IQ between one age and another in the standardization group is given in Table 19. Before twelve months, variation, disregarding signs, is somewhat larger, centering around ten IQ points. Thereafter it tends to be about six or seven IQ points (except for the very small group tested and retested at ages thirty-six and forty-two months with the Stanford-Binet, Form L).

ADMINISTRATION AND SCORING

Directions for administration and scoring are given in the manual (4), and a convenient record form is available. Each test, one by one, is described in terms of the material, procedure, and criteria to be met for credit to be achieved. All tests are scored plus or minus

TABLE 19. Median IQ Changes Between Successive Age Groups. Cattell IQ's from 3 to 30 Months and S-B IQ's at 36 and 42 Months[3]

Age in Months	N	Signs Disregarded	Signs Considered
3–6	60	10.5	+2.4
6–9	61	11.0	−1.6
9–12	58	9.3	−0.2
12–18	67	6.8	+2.1
18–24	66	7.0	−3.0
24–30	51	6.5	+2.8
30–36	42	5.0	−1.5
36–42	20	10.5	−4.5

with no partial credits allowed. Photographs of responses to the test situations aid in scoring.

Testing proceeds very much as it does in the Revised Stanford-Binet Scale. However, the tests do not have to be administered in a definite order, and serial testing is consequently quite feasible and is even recommended. A basal and maximal year decide the limits of testing. The child may be held in the mother's lap if this is considered desirable. Cattell recommends that items which are given in prone position be given first. (These occur up to and including the five-month level.) The tests having the greatest appeal may be given first. With an older child, for example, if he wants the pencil the test involving its use may be given; if he expresses interest in a certain box its contents should be used for testing.

Cattell (5) states that if an item is refused an alternate should be used. If only four items are scorable, each item may be given proportionately greater weight. If less than four items are scorable the test should be declared invalid and repeated a week or two later.

A criticism (3) that has been directed against the Cattell Scale is that in the upper ranges the increasing number of tests necessitating execution of verbal requests or requiring verbal responses sometimes meets the resistance characteristic of the two-year-old. These tests are best introduced only after a satisfactory adjustment to the

---

[3] Adapted from *The Measurement of Intelligence of Infants and Young Children* by P. Cattell (4), by permission of P. Cattell. Copyright 1940 by P. Cattell.

testing situation has been achieved and any resistance handled by the methods subsequently presented. Although time limits and timed tests are avoided, the total scale is such that it takes about twenty to thirty minutes to administer.

Since the tests are standardized as a mental age scale, derivation of IQ follows the procedure outlined in regard to the Revised Stanford-Binet. The calculations are on the basis of fractions of a month per test successfully completed, with the smallest unit being o.2 month credit. The tests at each level, as in the Stanford-Binet, cover the preceding period.

VALIDITY

The validity of the test was reported by Cattell (4) in terms of its ability to predict Revised Stanford-Binet IQ. This is in keeping with the avowed purpose of constructing a downward extension of this scale. As mentioned previously, the tests were placed in such a manner as to produce a median IQ as close as possible to that obtained with the Revised Stanford-Binet, Form L, at three years. In spite of this, the IQ's of this same group at the earlier age-testings did not correlate appreciably with the Stanford-Binet. The correlations of Cattell IQ for three, six, and nine months and the Stanford-Binet IQ for thirty-six months were respectively .10, .34, and .18. Thereafter the correlations became larger, with those for twelve, eighteen, twenty-four, and thirty months being .56, .67, .71, and .83 respectively. To throw some light on the meaningfulness of these correlations it might be mentioned that the correlation between Form L administered at thirty-six and again at forty-two months was .75. In the light of these measures, the scale may be regarded as of doubtful validity below twelve months (although useful in detecting extreme variations) and quite adequate after twelve months.

RELIABILITY

The corrected odd-even reliability (equivalence) coefficients are presented in Table 20. Before considering them it is well to indicate, as does Cattell, that the method for selection stressed the widest diversification of tests at a level as possible. Heterogeneity then made it impossible to divide the tests into anything resembling comparable halves, which would presumably act to reduce the obtained coefficients. There are no test-retest (stability) coefficients reported—

TABLE 20.   Reliability Coefficients on Cattell Infant Intelligence Tests[4]

N	Age in Months	r
87	3	.56
100	6	.88
83	9	.86
101	12	.89
100	18	.90
80	24	.85
56	30	.71
62	36 (S-B)	.87

in this case a more crucial measure. In any case the reliability coefficient of .56 at age level three months suggests that extreme caution be applied when interpreting results at this low level. Thereafter, with one exception, the coefficients are .85 or higher. All in all, reliability, except at the youngest age, compares favorably with tests used with school-age children.

DIAGNOSTIC USAGE

No published study other than that of Cattell concerning this scale is known. Nevertheless, it is in fairly widespread use because of the desirable features discussed in introducing it. It would appear to have its greatest value between twelve and thirty months. At younger ages, as is true of other infant measures, it is too erratic to be given much credence as predictive of later IQ. But even here it is of some value. Cattell claims (on the basis of a very few cases) that an infant who achieves a high rating at three months has an appreciably better than average chance of rating above average at three years. On the other hand, a low IQ at three months does not seem to indicate whether the child will be low, average, or high at the end of three years except in extreme cases. As has been said many times before, the entire case study must be taken into consideration and clinical judgment applied in interpreting the results. Nevertheless, application of the Cattell Scale gives an opportunity for quanti-

[4] Adapted from The Measurement of Intelligence of Infants and Young Children by P. Cattell (4), by permission of P. Cattell. Copyright 1940 by P. Cattell.

fication of impressions, and in the clinical setting it is of considerable assistance in diagnostic appraisal.

THE DIAGNOSTIC TESTING OF
PRESCHOOL CHILDREN

The same difficulties inherent in infant testing also exist at the preschool level though perhaps to a lesser degree. From the point of view of prognostic efficiency tests at these ages are somewhat more successful, showing a higher degree of relationship with intellectual status at later years than do infant tests. This was apparent in the discussion of the Cattell Scale, in which it is clear that the older the child the more closely do his findings on the Cattell resemble those on the Binet.   .

New problems make their appearance. These may be stated in terms of characteristics particularly noticeable at these ages which make for below optimum performance on the part of the child. Goodenough's (7) classification of such characteristics admirably clarifies the issue. The three traits finally selected by her as showing only a small amount of overlapping were shyness, negativism, and distractibility. She presents the following rating scale, which will serve to amplify the discussion:

Shyness: . . .
1. Child comes to examining room readily, talks freely, seems entirely at ease throughout test.
2. Child shows some hesitation at first, but does not cry or seem frightened. After a few minutes acquaintance, is entirely willing to remain with examiner and appears to be completely at ease thereafter.
3. Child requires much persuasion before he can be induced to remain in room without mother. Eventually yields, but continues to show some anxiety as to mother's whereabouts; has to be frequently reassured. May cry a little at the outset.
4. Child cannot be persuaded to remain in examining room without mother. With mother present, goes through the tests in a fairly satisfactory manner.
5. Child continues to cry or to cling to mother, and cannot be persuaded to take the tests, even with mother present, takes too few to justify a test rating.
Negativism: This may be an accompaniment of the behavior described under shyness, but it frequently occurs independently.
1. Child is entirely obedient and docile throughout tests, is willing at least to attempt whatever he is asked to do.

2. Child offers minor objection to some of the tests, but when urged and encouraged goes ahead with apparently undiminished effort.
3. Child requires much urging on any test which does not immediately appeal to his interest. May refuse flatly to try them at first, but objections can be overcome by subterfuge. Tests which arouse his interest are responded to readily.
4. Child shows a tendency to negativistic behavior on practically all of the tests. Even tests which attract his interest are likely to be performéd in the uppusite way from that which he has been told, Subterfuge, bribery and special firmness has to be used throughout in order to secure results.
5. Child refuses to take any of the tests, or takes too few to warrant a test rating.

Distractibility:
1. Child sits quietly during tests, gives good attention to directions throughout. Is not unduly distracted by outside stimuli, and does not interrupt test with irrelevant remarks.
2. Child sits quietly during tests, but is inclined to chatter on irrelevant subjects, and is rather easily distracted by outside stimuli.
3. Child is somewhat restless, frequently climbing on table and attempting to handle material not then in use. Attention wanders easily but is also easily recalled.
4. Child is distinctly hyperactive, runs about room, snatches material, inquires into everything he sees or hears. Attention can be held only for brief intervals, but by catching him "on the fly" he can be made to go through the tests.
5. Child shows extreme hyperactivity. Attention span so brief that he often loses track of what he is to do before completing a test. Results are too incomplete to warrant a test rating. (7, p. 205.)[5]

In large measure these new problems stem from the fact that diagnostic testing becomes during this age a highly interpersonal affair. No longer does the clinician function merely, as Carter and Bowles put it, "to bring the infant into contact with various objects." (3, p. 116.) Instead, tasks are introduced which require more direct interpersonal relations between the child and the examiner. Verbal items, for example, require a high degree of interaction and rob the examiner of anonymity that he or she may have maintained before.

In testing preschool children resistant behavior must be anticipated and handled appropriately. It may assume protean forms—refusal to comply with directions, shyness, distractibility, complete

---

[5] Reprinted from "The Emotional Behavior of Young Children During Mental Tests" by F. L. Goodenough, by permission of the *Journal of Juvenile Research*. Copyright 1929 by the California Bureau of Juvenile Research.

silence, loud continuous shrieks. Although there is perhaps an inevitable amount of resistive behavior occurring as a normal phenomenon of development, there is likely to be an increase of this in the testing session arising from a fear of the unfamiliar due to sheer inexperience outside the home. Furthermore, previous experience with hospitals and clinics for vaccination, dental work, operation, or hospitalization may have conditioned the child to expect that in some way or another the present situation is going to be painful. Parents not uncommonly use subterfuge to get their children to accompany them on such visits, and a natural suspicion may well arise that they again are being tricked. Whatever form the resistance assumes, it is important for the clinician to overcome it if rapport is to be developed and the test results are to reflect optimum performance on the part of the child.

Although no substitute for having "a way with children" can be offered, there are certain techniques for smoothing the sometimes rough road of preschool testing. Resistant behavior is not interminable, and a few simple precautions which help to reduce it to a minimum are frequently utilized. Meeting the child before he becomes too interested in the waiting room and its toys, or, if this is not possible, letting him have a few minutes' play in the reception room; a visit to the toilet; having furniture adjusted to his physical proportions; having the door partly ajar; beginning the testing session with material judged to be of intrinsic interest to the child; having the testing material readily available, facilitating transition— all these strategic moves operate to reduce the intensity and scope of behavior which prevents proper rapport. In her discussion of this problem Symmes suggests certain valuable approaches:

(1) *The Challenge Method:* The specified directions are prefaced by words, "I'll bet you can't do this" or "I'll bet you can't say this." Frequently an immediate and triumphant reply bursts forth, and the entire examination can be finished by interjecting this method throughout the test when the routine procedure fails. Immediate praise for success upon such a performance should be given. The writer's experience has been that boys some times respond more readily than girls to this method. The drawing test items can often be elicited when crayon or pencil fail, by appealing to the child's ego in speculating outloud whether he is big enough to write on a blackboard, or challenging his ability to do so. This privilege, as it seems to be regarded, is a boon in securing visible response, although it unfortunately has the disadvantage

of being only a temporary record of skill, but the efforts can, of course, be copied on to paper for permanent incorporation with the psychological findings.

(2) *Projection Method:* The withdrawing, shy child who remains quiet and firm in refusals to do the tests can sometimes be drawn out by the *projection method* by projecting the function of the test performance on something other than the child. "Let's see if the doll can do this," holding a crayon in the doll's hand and illustrating, asking the child if he can make her do it, or show the doll how to do it. Repetition of digits and words belong to that group of tests most difficult to obtain responses to, with pre-school children. Items requiring an immediate verbal response, a kind of interchange of question and answer between examiner and child, various investigators have been found to meet with the greatest per cent of refusals. . . . If the challenge method fails, the projection method sometimes works, and using a toy telephone may bring forth prompt repetition of digits or words.

(3) *Disguise Method:* This method has proved itself in cases where negativism seems to take the form of a refusal where the child has enough insight into the goal of the test to do the opposite or to exploit the test in some other fashion. If a child has pushed the formboard away, after it has been presented several times, perhaps at different intervals, with no cooperation, the immediate absorbing interest of the child can be used to good advantage in securing the desired response, as is shown in the following case. One young lady, who was completely wrapped up in building towers of blocks to the exclusion of the formboard, was persuaded to build one of her towers on top of the circle belonging to the formboard, and then place both in the circular hole. This, of course, changed the test directions slightly, and actually made the test somewhat more difficult, but the young lady in question seemed able to cope with this additional difficulty.

(4) *The Choice Method:* This is particularly useful in the period from approximately 18 months on, where investigation and exploration of the room and its contents forms a characteristic picture of activity, the absence of which may be significant. Test materials can be placed strategically in various parts of the room and as the child approaches them and begins to manipulate them, the routine test procedure can be carried through with satisfactory results. (9, pp. 188–189.)[6]

Other techniques for handling resistance are discussed by Dwyer (6). These may conveniently be identified as "withdrawal" and "distraction" and will be illustrated in turn. A child aged forty-two months was still weeping copiously after one or two tests had been presented especially to arouse interest. The psychologist then left

---

[6] Reprinted from "Some Techniques in Securing Rapport with Pre-School Children" by E. F. Symmes, by permission of the *American Journal of Orthopsychiatry.* Copyright 1933 by the American Orthopsychiatric Association.

him alone, busied himself with other work or left the room to answer the phone. Upon the examiner's return the child was playing with the materials, and testing could be begun without incident. Another child heretofore untestable was attracted by the sound of an auto starting. A trip to the window to watch the car facilitated rapport and testing proceeded. Deliberate introduction of a distraction—showing blocks on the floor, a short walk, a drink of water, etc.—may be used instead of depending on fortuitous circumstances.

Postponement either of a specific test or item or of the whole session is another method of handling the situation. Dropping a given item only to return to it later may seem mundane but is surprisingly effective. Postponement of the entire testing session is generally not necessary, and certainly the other techniques should be tried first.

According to Symmes (9) the various studies show that at about age two to three years a peak stage of resistance occurs. Mayer (8), among others, would place it at a somewhat older age. At any rate, by the time the child has reached school age of about six he has usually some degree of adaptability to people and will treat the psychological examination either as part of school routine or as some new game.

Although because of the acuteness of this problem at the preschool ages discussion of obstacles to rapport has been given what may appear to be a disportionate amount of space, the earlier, more general discussion of diagnostic testing in Chapter 7 is still applicable and relevant.

THE REVISED STANFORD-BINET SCALE IN PRESCHOOL TESTING

The earlier presentation of the Revised Stanford-Binet Scale stressed its use with school children, not those of preschool age. Since the 1937 revision of the Stanford-Binet covers an age range down to two years it is possible to use it during the preschool period. Certain attributes, particularly its predictive value for IQ at later years, are of importance in evaluating the use of this instrument in preschool years. The problem of constancy figures at the preschool level because of the well-established finding that there is greater inconstancy on retest during the school ages when the original testing was performed at preschool ages.

A study of IQ constancy with this instrument was performed by Bradway (2). It was a ten-year follow-up study of children originally tested during the standardization of the scale when they were from two to six years of age. The retesting was performed when the children were twelve to sixteen, using Form L of the scale. There were 138 subjects divided into two groups: fifty-two children initially examined at two to three and a half years of age, and eighty-six children initially examined at four to five and a half years. It was found that these groups were similar in distribution of parental occupations to the entire age level standardization groups from which they came.

Table 21 gives some pertinent data about the findings. Elimina-

TABLE 21. Results on Initial and Retest IQ's[7]

	Ages 2 and 3			Ages 4 and 5		
	Mean	σ	r with Retest IQ	Mean	σ	r with Retest IQ
Initial Form L IQ	115.7	17.0	.58 ± .06	105.9	14.9	.67 ± .04
Initial Form M IQ	116.3	18.1	.67 ± .05	105.4	13.3	.63 ± .04
Retest Form L IQ	114.5	18.4		108.4	16.5	

tion in the retest group of those who initially failed more than one item of the lowest age level (to avoid the possibility of including subjects whose IQ would be artificially raised) probably contributed heavily to the findings that the mean IQ's were 114–116 for the group aged two and three, and 105–108 for the group aged four and five both on test and retest, instead of closer to 100. The correlation between test and retest after a lapse of ten years is substantial. The different magnitudes of the correlations using different forms (superiority of Form M at ages two and three and superiority of Form L at ages four and five) are of little moment. Correlations based on MA instead of IQ reversed the differences.

It should be noted that the correlations of the younger group are not appreciably lower than the correlations for the older group. This is encouraging considering the strictures laid down about the varia-

---

[7] Adapted from "IQ Constancy on the Revised Stanford-Binet from the Preschool to the Junior High School Level" by K. P. Bradway (2), by permission of the *Journal of Genetic Psychology*. Copyright 1944 by the Journal Press.

bility of retest IQ's for very young children. However, there is greater homogeneity (as seen from the magnitude of the standard deviations) in the groups aged four and five, which suggests the superiority of the predictive correlations at these ages. This is borne out by the calculation of the IQ differences between test and retest. In her summary Bradway says, ". . . The IQ's of about one-fourth of the 2- and 3-year group and one-third of the 4- and 5-year group changed less than five points after 10 years. The IQ's of one-half of the 2- and 3-year group and three-fifths of the 4- and 5-year group changed less than 10 points. The IQ's of two-thirds of the 2- and 3-year group and three-fourths of the 4- and 5-year group changed less than 15 points." (2, p. 214.) It is to be noted that in each instance the older group showed less change. Despite this slight inferiority of the Revised Stanford-Binet at ages two and three as compared with four and five, it is even more important to note the rather small amount of IQ changes over the years.

When both these correlations and IQ differences are compared with those found in studies using other instruments the relatively superior predictive value of the Revised Stanford-Binet becomes apparent. With Bradway it is agreed that it "is as good as or better than any other objective index in predicting the future intellectual functioning of a pre-school child." (2, p. 214.)

In the study just discussed the interval between test and retest was ten years. Naturally with shorter intervals the correlation is even higher. For example, Black (1) found that a superior nursery school group with an age range of two and a half to six and a half, retested with Form L one year later, showed a correlation between IQ's of .94.

A comment or two concerning administration of the scale to preschool children is necessary. A weakness of the Revised Stanford-Binet Scale is the lack of any specific technique for handling refusals without scoring them as failures. Since problem children are especially prone to exhibit opposition it becomes a serious issue in a clinical setting. Sometimes an alternate test is introduced to replace one that has been refused. It is by no means clear in the directions that this is the examiner's prerogative, as Terman and Merrill (10) state only that alternate tests may be given at this level when the original test was "spoiled" in administration. At any rate, the use of alternate tests under such circumstances of refusal appears to be a sensible procedure. A particularly persuasive discussion of the advisability of using adaptive testing at this level is offered by Carter and Bowles (3).

These are, however, minor matters as compared to the predictive capacity of the scale. It would appear that as a preschool test the Revised Stanford-Binet is an excellent instrument for prediction of success along the same lines as those for which the scale is appropriate in later years. It has the tremendous advantage of being a portion of an instrument used with such success in connection with problems related to the school situation. When used in conjunction with the Cattell Scale at the appropriate age levels, and when supplemented by the Vineland Social Maturity Scale (and occasionally joined by the Rorschach, the Weigl Color-Form, and the Arthur Performance) it may provide the nucleus of a battery suitable for many of the diagnostic problems in this age range with which the clinician is confronted.

BIBLIOGRAPHY

1. Black, I. S., The use of the Stanford-Binet (1937 revision) in a group of nursery school children, *Child Developm.*, 1939, 10:157–171.
2. Bradway, K. P., IQ constancy on the Revised Stanford-Binet from the preschool to the junior high school level, *J. genet. Psychol.*, 1944, 65:197–217.
3. Carter, J. W., and Bowles, J. W., A manual on qualitative aspects of psychological examining, *J. clin. Psychol.*, 1948, 4:109–150. (Also in *Clin. Psychol. Monogr.*, 1948, No. 2.)
4. Cattell, P., *The measurement of intelligence of infants and young children*, Psychological Corporation, 1940.
5. Cattell, P., personal communication, 1950.
6. Dwyer, F. M., A note on resistance and rapport in psychological tests of young children, *J. genet. Psychol.*, 1937, 51:451–454.
7. Goodenough, F. L., The emotional behavior of young children during mental tests, *J. juv. Res.*, 1929, 13:204–219.
8. Mayer, B. A., Negativistic reactions of pre-school children on the New Revision of the Stanford-Binet, *J. genet. Psychol.*, 1935, 46:311–334.
9. Symmes, E. F., Some techniques in securing rapport with pre-school children, *Amer. J. Orthopsychiat.*, 1933, 3:181–190.
10. Terman, L. M., and Merrill, M. A., *Measuring intelligence*, Houghton Mifflin Company, 1937.

CHAPTER 13

Tests of Memory and Conceptual Thinking

Concept formation and memory are basic components of intellectual functioning which play a unique role in meeting the exigencies of daily existence. Under the influence of stress, psychogenic or histogenic, there are generally retrogressive changes or inadequate development of these intellectual functions varying to a greater or lesser degree according to the individual and the nature of the stress.

In general, the problem facing a clinician interested in the memory and conceptual thinking of his patient is the extent to which there has been a loss or deficit. Customarily he is not concerned with unusual prowess or ability in such functions, perhaps too readily dismissing them as "negative" findings, but rather with the extent and nature of any demonstrated disability or deficiency. This interest in specific functions, however, need not blind him to the inescapable fact that they are but part functions of a more or less integrated functioning entity—the patient as an individual. Memory and conceptual thinking are but constituents of a more global functioning toward which affective as well as intellectual components contribute significantly.

In the discussion to follow, the tests described as measures of memory are the Wechsler Memory Scales, the Graham-Kendall Memory-for-Designs Test, and the auditory-vocal Digit Span Test. Tests of conceptual thinking include the Kohs Block Design, the Goldstein-Scheerer Cube Test, the Healy Pictorial Completion Test

II, the Wechsler-Bellevue Similarities subtest, the Weigl Color-Form Sorting Test, and the Rapaport adaptation of the Object Sorting Test.

TESTS OF MEMORY FUNCTIONS

In the measurement of retention no one test will serve all purposes. Benton puts the matter forcefully:

Experimental psychologic investigation has indicated that when a number of retention tests are given to a group of subjects, the intercorrelations of the scores are not high enough to warrant the substitution of one test for another. Statistical analysis of test results . . . have yielded evidence for the existence of an "immediate memory factor," but as yet an adequate single test for the valid assessment of this "immediate memory factor" has not been devised. The practical implications of the experimental work on the problem are clear. In the present state of knowledge of memory functions and of mastery of the technic of their measurement, one cannot depend on one test alone to give a valid index of a patient's retentive capacity. (1, pp. 212–213.)

In accordance with this admonition the tests to be described in this chapter sample memory in such a fashion as to cover a variety of functions. Retention does not appear to be a unitary attribute, with distinctions being observed between immediate and remote memory, between rote and substance memory, and between auditory-vocal and visual-graphic performance. All these differentiations will be exemplified and related to specific instruments in the succeeding discussion.

THE WECHSLER MEMORY SCALES

The Wechlser Memory Scales are two equated alternate forms possessing as advantages clear and explicit directions, relative ease and brevity of administration, varied and interesting subject matter, and objective and explicit scoring criteria. Their value is enhanced by the availability of two forms in the event a retest is desired. Even more important, they have been more adequately standardized than other memory measures and make allowance for memory variations with age. The memory quotient obtained is directly comparable to the intelligence quotient as derived from the Wechsler-Bellevue Scales, permitting intertest comparison, a valuable diagnostic aid. It must be mentioned, however, that this comparison of memory quotient and intelligence quotient implies that memory is a unitary factor, the evidence of which is, to say the least, equivocal.

DESCRIPTION, ADMINISTRATION, AND SCORING. Form I (32), consisting of seven subtests, will be described.[1] The first of these, Personal and Current Information, includes six items such as age of the subject, the name of the governor, etc., scored on the basis of correctness. The second subtest, Orientation, requires the patient to supply the year, month, and day, and the name of the place he is in, and the city. Mental Control, the third subtest, involves counting backward from twenty to one, saying the alphabet as rapidly as possible, and counting by threes, with credit given for speed as well as accuracy. The fourth subtest consists of two prose selections read aloud to the patient about which he is to tell everything that has been read. Each of the passages has been divided into units or "ideas"—e.g., "The American/ liner/ New York/ struck a mine/. . . ." Scoring is on the basis of the number of items correctly reproduced, with the final score the average on both passages. The fifth subtest is the well-known digits-forward-and-backward, scored by maximum number of digits repeated correctly for both. If the Wechsler-Bellevue Intelligence Scale has already been administered to the patient, this subtest is not readministered since the same series of digits are used, although in the Memory Scale subtest the maximum number of digits used is limited to eight forward and seven backward. The sixth subtest requires the only special equipment other than the record sheet necessary in the entire test. This consists of three cards upon each of which there is a rather elaborate geometric design of increasing difficulty. After ten seconds' exposure of a single design the patient is asked to reproduce it. Scoring is on the basis of accuracy of reproduction with explicit instructions for point-by-point scoring. The seventh and last subtest, called Associate Learning, involves the learning of paired associates in orthodox

---

[1] Form II, standardized by Stone et al. (30), follows substantially the same format and differs primarily in content. In fact, subtests in two instances are identical. The nature of the items, some selected from the same sources used by Wechsler, and the information available from other researches before tryout pointed to equal difficulty of the first and second forms. Administration of the two forms to three small intellectually superior groups within a two-weeks interval, no matter which form was administered first, resulted in mean differences of only one or two raw score points, the differences being statistically nonsignificant.

fashion. Some pairs are relatively easy—e.g., baby-cries, up-down—whereas others are hard—e.g., obey-inch. The list of ten pairs is presented three times, each in a different order, and three recall tests are given with the patient informed of the correctness or incorrectness of each response. Scoring is on the basis of number of items correct for all three recalls with the hard associates given double the weight (one raw score point) of the easy associates.

The scores of the seven subtests are summed for 'the total raw score. The method of transformation of raw scores into a more meaningful summary figure will be discussed after the method of standardization has been described.

STANDARDIZATION AND NORMATIVE GROUPS. The group used for standardization consisted of about 200 non-hospital "normal" adults of ages twenty-five to fifty. Mean raw scores for this population sample were obtained and divided into groups for each five- or ten-year interval. Available on about 100 of these subjects were Wechsler-Bellevue Intelligence Scale results. The mean raw scores for different ages were plotted against the total weighted scores on the Wechsler-Bellevue (age group twenty to twenty-four), and constants were found which kept the mean memory quotient (MQ) for each group equivalent to the mean IQ of that group. Thus in deriving the MQ the clinician adds to the obtained raw score a correction for age (smaller amounts at younger ages and larger amounts at older). This gives a weighted or corrected memory score. Then entry is made into a table of MQ equivalents to find the memory quotient. A concrete illustration might clarify both the method of standardization and the derivation of the MQ for a particular person. Suppose a forty-two-year-old man made a total raw score of 58. The correction for his age group is 40. The sum of these two, a corrected memory score of 98, is found to be equivalent to MQ 100. In this particular instance his raw score of 58 evidently was exactly at the mean for his age group in the standardization population.

VALIDITY AND RELIABILITY. Evidence for validity and reliability in the psychometric sense is distressingly meager. No studies reporting coefficients either of equivalence or of stability are known; nor are there either intratest or intertest coefficients which demonstrate validity. There is no doubt that these are necessary, and until more information is available results from this instrument must be interpreted with considerable caution. It may be seriously questioned whether or not "memory" is a unitary factor, and, therefore, it is not established that there is need to throw all these subtests together. For those who prefer to continue to regard memory as unitary the total score and its relation to IQ presumably has more meaning than for those who reject this interpretation.

In view of these inadequacies the question may be raised as to why the Wechsler Memory Scales were considered worthy of inclusion. Despite the lack of concrete validity and reliability studies, the method of standardization, the normative group, and so on make them a commendable instrument. Just as important are the indirect and inferential evidences of validity implied in the discussion of diagnostic usage to follow.

DIAGNOSTIC USAGE. The various subtests which make up the test are composed of material used many times before, about which there is considerable information available. Digit span, for example, has been used clinically for years. What it measures precisely has been a matter of controversy, as the discussion of its use in the Wechsler-Bellevue Scale attests. Whether it be a measure of attention (reception) or of immediate memory or of both according to circumstances and the patient is a moot point, but certainly its inclusion can be defended on either grounds. Memory for connected prose, a learning task such as paired associates, personal and current information, and orientation are essentially somewhat objectified portions of the mental status examination (see Chapter 3), and reproduction of visual designs has high "face" validity as a sample of memory functioning.

Although part scores for the subtests have not been separately standardized, the scale nevertheless provides an opportunity to evaluate remote memory of extremely well-learned material, such as that involved in the items concerned with personal and current information and mental control, as compared to immediate recall, characteristic of the material included in the prose passages, the digit span, visual reproduction, and associate materials (poor performance in these last often being indicative of attention and concentration difficulties as well). In addition, performance on rote and meaningful material may be compared, and disturbances in specific areas investigated such as auditory-vocal (digit span), visual-motor (visual reproduction), and so on. Notwithstanding these attributes, the lack of separate (and comparable) standardization of the tests makes comparison a rather difficult task possible only after considerable clinical experience with the tests comprising the instrument. The correction for age, possible with the total score, is not applicable with part scores, which factor adds to the hazards of test-to-test comparison.

Against the test of clinical usage the Wechsler Memory Scales have demonstrated their sensitivity. For example, Stone found that the test "is remarkably sensitive, considering its ease and brevity, to the temporary intellectual impairment associated with electro-convulsive shock." (30, p. 206.) The study, described in another paper (29), involved two groups, to one of which Form I was administered one day before the application of the first electro-convulsive shock and Form II one day after the last shock. There was a loss in mean MQ of seventeen points, equivalent to 15 percent of the initial score. The other group was given Form I one day after the last shock and Form II two to three weeks thereafter. There was a mean gain of twenty-three MQ points, equivalent to 28 percent. In the first group there were statistically significant losses in all subtests except memory for designs, in which there was a nonsignificant gain. Stone's contention about the sensitivity of the instruments would therefore appear to be borne out.

THE GRAHAM-KENDALL MEMORY-FOR-DESIGNS TEST[2]

The Graham-Kendall Memory-for-Designs Test is a short, easily administered test suitable in cases in which brain damage is suspected (11). Its relatively low correlation with measures of intelligence, its fair ability to discriminate brain-damaged cases from normals, its tapping of a function (visual-motor ability) not otherwise measured by the usual tests, and its relative independence of the influence of age all serve to recommend its use. By the same token it should be conceived as part of a battery—not as *the* test of memory loss in general.

[2] This test may be obtained from the Department of Neuropsychiatry, Washington University School of Medicine, St. Louis, Missouri. To a greater degree than probably was the case with the choice of any other instrument the selection of this one for presentation was dictated by provincial considerations. Certainly it cannot be said to be clearly superior to the Benton Visual Retention Test (1). On the other hand, the author is not aware that the Benton Visual Retention Test is either more widely used or essentially a "better" test. Therefore, the choice between two presumably more or less equally useful tests went to the one used locally.

DESCRIPTION, ADMINISTRATION, AND SCORING. The Memory-for-Designs Test consists of fifteen straight-line designs on white cards, one design to a card. To reduce the influence of intelligence, designs with meaningful associations were avoided. Administration involves informing the patient of the following procedure—exposure of the card for five seconds, withdrawal, and immediate reproduction. The total time for the fifteen designs averages less than ten minutes.

Scoring for errors (described and illustrated in a manual that accompanies the test) is on a range of four points for each design with the total score the sum of the scores for all the designs. A score of zero is given for a reproduced design with not more than two errors. (In a subsequent article Graham and Kendall (12) indicate that omitted or incomplete drawings are scored zero, the same as a satisfactorily reproduced design—contrary to the statement in the original article which serves as the manual. This somewhat unusual procedure arises from the fact that scoring an omission as an error did not aid in differentiating between control and brain-damaged cases. They plausibly defend this procedure with·the remark that awareness of forgetting so as to leave unfinished or to refrain from starting a design at all, is a higher level of performance than typical brain-damaged cases demonstrate. A positive score given for omissions would imply a contribution toward a brain-damaged score, which is not the case according to their data.) A score of one is given when more than two errors are made but the general configuration is retained. A score of two is given when the configuration is lost, and a score of three when the designs have been turned either 90 or 180 degrees. Thus, unfavorable scores are larger than favorable ones. Interpretation of these scores will be considered after standardization has been discussed.

STANDARDIZATION AND NORMATIVE GROUPS. The normative populations consisted of two groups, 194 children aged 8.5[3] to 15 and 239 adults aged 16 to 69, with a mean of 33 (18). Part of the adult normative group was treated separately in an earlier normative study (11). The treatment of the data obtained necessitated the fitting of linear equations, which proved to be difficult unless this separation into two age groups was made. The bulk of both groups were patients in various affiliated psychiatric and medical installations.

---

[3] Children younger than 8.5 were tested, but the test proved to be too difficult below this age.

Individuals with IQ below 70 were excluded from both groups, as were cases even remotely suspected of brain damage. From the adult group were excluded all individuals whose formal schooling did not include the third grade. On all subjects there were also available intelligence test data. In the case of the children either Revised Stanford-Binet or Wechsler-Bellevue results were secured; in the case of the adults there were either Stanford-Binet or Wechsler-Bellevue vocabulary scores. The correlations between Memory-for-Designs Test scores and age and intelligence were −.34 and −.39 respectively for the children and .27 and −.31 for the adults. The correlation of intelligence and age was .54 and .14 for children and for adults. Regression equations were prepared involving the correlation of raw scores with intelligence and age so that a score adjusted for these factors might be derived. This adjustment is subtracted from the obtained raw score, yielding the so-called difference score. It is not necessary for the user of the test to make such calculations each time since tables are supplied to be entered according to age and intelligence test or vocabulary results.

VALIDITY.   So far no mention has been made of the capacity of the test for discriminating non-brain-damaged individuals from those known to have suffered organic brain insult. A group of 103 adults from the same clinic and hospital sources all with a diagnosis of cerebral brain damage were also given the test and difference scores calculated. Instances of congenital conditions, childhood trauma, and birth injury were excluded so that arrested development would not complicate the picture. The brain-damaged cases included central nervous system syphilis, multiple sclerosis, postencephalitic syndrome, brain tumor, and so on.

It was decided to use a reference point, the difference score above which only 4 percent of the normative population falls, in comparing these groups. The question, then, was to determine how many of the brain-damaged cases scored above this critical point. Table 22 reports a summary of the data. Inspection shows that 50 percent of the brain-damaged cases received difference scores of 7 or above whereas but 4 percent of both normative groups made such scores. The next category, "borderline," included roughly the same percentage in all groups (which was the intent of the authors), while the so-called "normal" group included 79 percent of the adults, 74 percent of the children, and but 28 percent of the brain-damaged

TABLE 22.   Percentage Distribution of Difference Scores for Normative and Brain-Damaged Groups[4]

Score	Normative Adults	Normative Children	Brain-Damaged Adults	Interpretation
7 to 24	4	4	50	"critical"
2 to 6	17	22	22	"borderline"
−6 to 1	79	74	28	"normal"

cases. Obviously, this last group is not "normal" in the sense of not exhibiting brain damage—they were selected because they did. It would appear, then, that the test discriminates a large proportion of the brain-damaged cases but by no means all. The recommendation of the authors seems to hold that "high scores are suggestive of brain damage while low scores would not indicate absence of brain damage." (11, p. 310.)

RELIABILITY.   Using fifty-five cases from one or the other of the normative groups an immediate retest was made, yielding a coefficient of stability of .80. This group, however, was not unselected, in that they were retested because of clinical interest; consequently an unduly large proportion were picked who had initially high scores. Presumably this lowers the coefficient somewhat. Contrary to expectation, retest scores show little improvement with practice. For score categories 1–9 and 10–16 lower scores of only one and two points respectively were found on the average. The coefficient of equivalence found by split-half technique and corrected for length was .92 in a sample of seventy normative controls and seventy experimental (brain-damaged) cases.

DIAGNOSTIC USAGE.   Graham and Kendall did not, of course, intend this test to be used alone in the investigation of brain-damaged cases. They believe (11), and rightly so in the writer's opinion, that this instrument contributes diagnostic information of a different sort from that supplied by other instruments.[5] Originally showing very

---

[4] Adapted from "Further Standardization of the Memory-for-Designs Test on Children and Adults" by B. S. Kendall and F. K. Graham (18), by permission of the *Journal of Consulting Psychology.* Copyright 1948 by the American Psychological Association.

[5] The Benton Visual Retention Test, an instrument in many ways similar, is an exception.

little correlation with either age or intelligence, the small remaining relation has been statistically eliminated. In an attempt to isolate a function related to brain damage and yet independent of age or intelligence, they seem to have been reasonably successful. To the extent that they have been, the test becomes a valuable instrument to be used in conjunction with others.

It might be noted that this independence from the influence of age and intelligence presumably acted to make the discriminatory ability of the instrument less impressive than would otherwise have been the case. Other instruments more vulnerable to the influence of deficit in the "higher functions" and therefore more global in nature might show a higher relationship and yet not be as useful diagnostically. This instrument may well be more independent of other tests in the complete battery than is often the case.

The investigation of the various diagnostic subgroups within the brain-damaged category has not been completed, and as yet there are no conclusive findings. It might appear that this instrument would be useful in indicating difficulties on the part of reading disability cases. Such is not the case, however. In a study of the relationship between retardation in reading as measured by various reading tests and scores on the Memory-for-Designs Test, little or no relationship was found (17). Brain-damaged cases were excluded, and the question of whether or not this lack of relationship holds with such patients is a matter for future research. At any rate, in the absence of clear-cut brain pathology poor readers do not perform this visual-motor activity more poorly than good readers.

A beginning has been made in isolating qualitative indicators of diagnostic value which do not enter into the scoring system (11). For example, drawings turned 90 degrees (as distinguished from those turned 180 degrees) are nine times as frequent in brain-injured cases as in the normative controls. This is not reflected in the scoring but can carry weight in qualitative interpretation. Cases of severe psychiatric illness were found to produce scores above the critical value, but often they could be differentiated from brain-damaged cases by qualitative indicators not included in the scoring system. For example, schizophrenics sometimes began with an inner detail rather than the main outline. On the whole, however, qualitative interpretation with this instrument is as yet not thoroughly formulated.

THE DIGIT SPAN TEST

Any discussion of clinical tests of memory would be incomplete if digit span were omitted. Originally described in 1887 by Jacobs (16), it has been a popular device used by psychiatrists and psychologists alike in their diagnostic investigations. Simplicity of administration and ease of scoring are among its obvious advantages. Perhaps because of these attributes clinicians have sometimes been lured into considering it the sufficient measure of immediate memory functioning. It is, however, no definitive and all-embracing test of memory.

In fact, it has many quite serious limitations, not the least of which is the possibility that it is not a test of memory at all. The discussion in Chapter 8 concerning the Digit Span subtest of the Wechsler-Bellevue is pertinent in this connection. It will be remembered that Rapaport believed it more properly to be considered as a measure of attention. There is no doubt clinically that tension in an emotionally disturbed patient can produce impairment in performance. Whether this tension produces anxiety which in turn affects attention, as Rapaport claims, or whether the tension operates in some other fashion to produce poor performance is not absolutely clear. Even if one speculates that it is a test of retention and rejects the proposal that it is a measure of attention, there are still difficulties that make for equivocal interpretation. One must still distinguish between poor performance due to emotional tension and impairment indicative of poor retentive capacity. Is there poor immediate memory, emotional tension, or both? Such are the questions that face the clinician.

The situation is further complicated by the possible differential significance of repetition of digits forward as opposed to digits backward, as discussed in the earlier chapter on the Wechsler-Bellevue Scale. The opinion has been ventured that these do not really represent two aspects of the same task but are actually measures of different capacities. Shakow (24) has claimed that digits forward are more impaired by defects of attention and digits backward by impaired immediate learning. Wells and Ruesch (34) found that performance on digits backward is particularly impaired in hebephrenic and unclassified dementia praecox and in general paresis and other conditions. They go on to say that there appears to be a closer relationship between mental disease and backward span.

Another difficulty inherent in this test is the relatively low reliability (stability) it seems to demonstrate. In the study of Hamister (14), referred to in the chapter concerned with the Wechsler-Bellevue Test, it was indicated that the Digit Span subtest yielded a reliability coefficient of but .59 and that this was the lowest coefficient found of all the subtests of the Wechsler Scale. This low correlation coefficient, of course, is not necessarily found under conditions of administration other than those obtaining when Hamister administered the test. This is a matter for further experimental investigation.

A thorough study of forward digit span was performed by Peatman and Locke (22) using college students as subjects. The span measured ranged from four to thirteen digits for a single series. The score was the total number of reproductions correct irrespective of misses on earlier or later series. Although they investigated a variety of problems of mode and regularity of presentation, present interest focuses on auditory presentation at the rate of one per second. Vocal recall was not used; instead the responses were written. Four series were given and the coefficient of equivalence was found by correlating the two odd and two even series. This coefficient of reliability was found to be .87. With another group of subjects one series repeated after the lapse of two months (coefficient of stability) correlated .56. These results, coupled with rather low intercorrelations among this and various other methods of presentation, will give pause to the careful clinician when called upon to interpret the results of the Digit Span Test.

The seriousness of this matter is reflected in the attention given it by two committees of the Clinical Division of the American Psychological Association (7). They are investigating the reliability of the various methods of administration and scoring, and offer a comment that lacking this information the test should not be used for diagnostic purposes. This is probably too severe a restriction.

The Digit Span Test is a part both of the Stanford-Binet and of the Wechsler-Bellevue scales. If the various age level tests in the former are administered serially it is possible to use this as a measure. The Wechsler-Bellevue subtest may be used directly. If neither scale has been administered it may be given separately.

The manual of Wells and Ruesch (34) contains pertinent material if the latter course is to be followed. They find the norm for adults to be six to seven forward and one or two fewer backward, giving a total of eleven to twelve. Bronner et al. (5) present norms for children.

TESTS OF CONCEPTUAL THINKING

Tests in the category of conceptual thinking are used to investigate the ability of the subject to form concepts and the level at which this may be done. The ability to abstract, to synthesize, to educe relations is demonstrated by these measures. Deficit in conceptual thinking is particularly prominent in the brain-injured and the schizophrenic. Such patients find great difficulty in dealing with problems of deduction and eduction; they cannot shift easily from one concept to another. Nevertheless, tests of conceptual thinking have wider import than merely as instruments to be used with these particular patient groups. Conceptual thinking, as admirably demonstrated by Rapaport and his associates (24), is not a thing apart, but of the very warp and woof of the functioning personality.

Characteristically, clinical interest in conceptual thinking centers not so much on the end result or product of the thinking as it does upon the process by which this result was achieved. Consequently the tests focus the attention of the clinician upon the *procedures* followed by the patient. The clinician goes behind the curtain of the test response to observe the mechanics of the production.

It is not surprising, then, that tests of conceptual thinking used in clinical practice today depend almost entirely upon qualitative indicators. Standardization of directions has been achieved, but not the development of norms or studies of validity and reliability in the conventional sense. Since the results are stated in terms of *process* rather than achievement, norms have been slow in appearing. They are still needed, even if stated to some degree in terms other than numerical progressions. The problem is rendered particularly acute because in the absence of normative data one is likely to have considerable difficulty in interpreting results outside a particular sphere of reference. Within such a sphere of experience, e.g., adult brain-injured, a clinician may build a considerable background of knowledge and be in a good position to interpret adequately his findings on such patients. Once he steps out of the familiar framework, however, he may be lost because of the lack of easily communicated findings of others (in the form of norms and other objectified results). Witness the difficulty many clinicians have in working with brain-injured children. In children the processes of abstraction are still in formation. That they are still nascent means that the clinician cannot by any means always be certain the results obtained are due to brain-injury *per se*, as they might well reflect the current developmental level.

Performance tests such as those to be described are in many cases more suitable than verbal tests for assessing level of conceptualization because a patient may be able to preserve an appearance of normality at the level of speech whereas essentially his thinking has changed radically (10). However, this does not mean that verbal tests are useless, e.g., the Wechsler Similarities subtest is presented in this chapter. Other measures to be described include the Goldstein-Scheerer adaptations of the Weigl Color-Form Test and the Kohs Block Design Test (Cube Test), the Rapaport adaptation of the Object Sorting Test, the Kohs Block Design in original form, and the Healy Pictorial Completion Test II. Certain of these instruments—the Similarities subtest of the Wechsler-Bellevue Scale, the Kohs Block Design, and the Healy Pictorial Completion Test II of the Arthur Scale—were described previously in chapters dealing with intellectual functioning, at which time only incidental mention was made of the fact that they also sampled conceptual thinking. With the latter objective they may be used as parts of their respective scales or independently. Before discussing instruments not heretofore mentioned in any detail, each of these familiar tests shall be presented in a setting which emphasizes their conceptual character.

WECHSLER-BELLEVUE SIMILARITIES SUBTEST

In chapter 8, concerning the Wechsler-Bellevue Scale, it was pointed out that there seems to be some agreement that the Similarities subtest measures verbal concept formation. This ability to apprehend verbal relationships is certainly an aspect of thinking relevant to the present discussion. It was also indicated that three levels of abstraction might be given—the concrete, the functional, and the conceptual. As Rapaport (24) emphasizes, the similarities can be responded to on these levels of coherence. The task requires substitution of a verbal symbol for a conceptual category, and he feels that failure of development rather than impairment of abstract thinking produces the functional or concrete response. In his estimation, once the abstract level has been achieved, it may persevere in spite of present deficit. The items may then be responded to on the basis of habitual verbal associations or clichés which are but a shell empty of meaning. If this is suspected, the clinician may verify his suspicion by further questioning to see if the subject understands the reply he has given. Frequently his attempt at explanation will be at a concrete or functional level.

Other investigators feel, however, that the Similarities subtest can reflect deficit as failure of abstract thinking. For example, Trist et al. (31) used it in investigating nosological groups. For twenty-five paretics they found consistently persistent giving of differences despite the attempts to stop this by prompting, as well as elaborate verbosity generally leading away from rather than toward giving a similarity, and failure to increase their score under prompting. All three findings were present in seventeen of the twenty-five cases whereas not one of the control neurotic cases simultaneously demonstrated all three criteria. In any case, the inability to give similarities appears to be a special, although not pathognomonic, feature of deficit.

HEALY PICTORIAL COMPLETION TEST II

The Healy Pictorial Completion Test II, consisting of a series of sequential pictures each with some important part missing and a multitude of available choices, was described earlier as tapping abilities associated with apperception of a situation. Also indicated was the fact that mistakes are more revealing than correct selections. Illustrative of what may be learned about the thinking of the patient, especially the seriously disturbed patient, from its application is brought out in a study by Hanfmann (15) of thought disturbances in schizophrenics.

She investigated schizophrenic thinking with the Healy Pictorial Completion Test II, modifying the usual instructions by omission of the explicit statement that only one solution is correct and merely telling the patient to find the blocks which would best complete the pictures. After completion the patient was asked to give reasons for his choices. Eliminating placements based on a complete lack of understanding, i.e., blocks chosen for irrelevant reasons such as matching color of some prominent adjacent object or just liking it there, she found solutions capable of rough subdivision into seven categories:

1. *Isolated action.* If person in picture is shown in action—looking at, pointing to, or reaching for something—patient fills in without regard to the rest of the situation, e.g., a cat or flag in the sky.

2. *Assumed psychological act.* This response is one more step removed from physical reality in that patients do not mention at all the outward action, but instead refer to the thoughts or needs of the person—tie placed on the horizon because the boy needs a tie; a horse in the room because the boy wants to travel.

3. *Belongingness to the situation or parts of it.* Although not thought of by the boy, the object belongs to the situation—a tie (on the wall) goes with his hat (which the boy does have); milk bottle (on the wall) is relevant since the boy is having breakfast.

4. *Summary of represented situation—its keynote.* A book because it is the spirit of school lessons; clock on sidewalk because it is time to go to school.

5. *Verbal connections—relation between words.* A plant in the cloakroom because brush = plant and you brush coats; mail truck in air because of air mail.

6. *Transportation into the reality plane—picture is given status of reality and therefore needs of patient become operative.* The refusal to place spilt ink in picture because patient didn't want to spill the ink.

7. *Incomprehensible, far-fetched, or irrelevant explanations.* A book in with a group of boys because one of them has a T on his sweater.

These categories do tend to overlap somewhat, and results are therefore not treated statistically for each category. They all have in common the disregard of the representation of space; i.e., the spatial system is not appreciated, permitting physically impossible juxtapositions. This is in spite of the fact that the patients' descriptions of the pictures one by one showed that the nature of the environment was correctly perceived; e.g., it might be known that the boys were playing in a field and a clock be placed in the sky nevertheless. Responses justifying their placements fell in four categories—admission of incongruity, defense by some rationalization, indifference to the criticism, or claim that the question of spatial position is irrelevant.

The arrangements reminded Hanfmann of nonrealistic art, but with the difference that the schizophrenics do not voluntarily adopt that attitude. There may be absurd responses in some, realistic ones in others, but unawareness of the difference. This conclusion finds confirmation in other studies of concept formation—i.e., the patients failed to reconcile the conceptual system with their solution in sorting tasks just as they failed to recognize spatial incompatibilities in their choices in the Picture Completion Test. This is a concrete way of thinking.

In applying the Picture Completion Test to schizophrenics, organics (general paretics and arteriosclerotics), and normals it was found that two-thirds of the schizophrenics and three-fourths of the organics made incongruous responses, which were practically absent from the normal group.

Kohs Block Design Test

The Kohs Block Design Test, as has been said before, permits not only the derivation of a score reflecting analytic-synthetic ability but observations concerning the thinking processes whereby the solution is achieved. It is, therefore, a measure of conceptual thinking and as such is relevant to the present discussion, as is the earlier presentation in Chapter 10.

This test apparently is especially sensitive to the absence of deterioration of the ability to generalize, although subject to the cautions given in the earlier chapter. The patient "sees" the design card, is aware of the color differences in the blocks, understands he is to reproduce the design using these blocks, but cannot perform the thought processes necessary to make the generalization from the design to the blocks. Patients showing organic deficit are especially prone to have difficulty with the Kohs Block Design Test.

A study by Lidz, Gay, and Tietze (19) illustrates both its usefulness and its limitations. The authors were interested in studying patients who suffered from definite cerebral lesions with deterioration as compared to schizophrenics. They made the usual assumption concerning vocabulary age, i.e., that it is relatively resistant to intellectual impairment and may be used as a measure of previous intellectual functioning level. For this purpose the 1916 Stanford-Binet Vocabulary test was used. The cases with active cerebral damage performed at a level about four years below their vocabulary age whereas for the schizophrenic cases there was only a negligible difference between average performances on the two measures. In discussing this study Richards brought out very well the diagnostic limitations of this sort of approach. After reviewing the findings he says, "This certainly does not mean that a score on the Block Designs test that is poor relative to the verbal tests indicates that the patient is not psychotic, for the psychotic patient may be relatively poor on any test—the Block Designs test is no exception. Hence, in cases where the explanation of deficit is in doubt (as to whether it is or is not organic), good relative performance on the Block Designs suggests only that cerebral damage is a less likely possibility." (27, p. 73.)

One other point that Lidz, Gay, and Tietze (19) make concerning their study is worth mentioning. They point out that the relatively good performance of the schizophrenic on the Kohs Block Design Test as contrasted with the poor performance of the cerebrally deficient should induce caution in uncritically equating the thinking disorders of the schizophrenic with those demonstrated by cases with disability following brain damage. On this problem there will be further comment when the Goldstein-Scheerer modification of the Kohs Block Design Test is evaluated.

Although not stressing the conceptual character of the Kohs Test, a study which serves to illustrate its clinical usefulness in the sphere of feeble-mindedness may be mentioned. This was performed by Sarason and Sarason (28). Although they had available scores for all tests of Form I of the Arthur they were particularly interested in the Kohs Block Design Test because of the work of Goldstein and others, to be described shortly, showing a relation between a modification of this test and indications of cerebral pathology. Their subjects were feeble-minded inmates of a training school and they wished to find a test pattern discriminating the relatively well-adjusted high-grade familial mental defectives from those whose adjustment is relatively poor. The two groups used, insignificantly different in average Binet MA, were (1) those whose Kohs mental age was at least eighteen months beyond Binet MA and (2) those whose Kohs mental age was eighteen months below

Binet MA. These two groups were compared as to their adjustment. It was found that the well adjusted (as shown by Rorschach and observations of institutional behavior) fell in the Kohs-above-Binet group. It was also found that the group whose adjustment was poor (Kohs-below-Binet) had a test pattern characteristic of organic pathology and had many abnormal EEG records.

THE GOLDSTEIN-SCHEERER CUBE TEST

The Goldstein-Scheerer Cube Test is a modification of the Kohs Block Design Test and consequently is logically introduced at this point. The modifications introduced had one basic aim—permitting greater opportunity to observe the thought processes of the patient. Particular interest was not in getting a score but in knowing, instead, how the patient approached the task and what steps were used in attempting to bring about a solution. In keeping with this aim it was made progressively simpler for the patient to break down the design perceptually. In effect, if failure at harder levels occurred, the modification was akin to "testing the limits" in the Rorschach technique.

DESCRIPTION OF THE TEST AND OF THE PROCEDURE. The cubes used in this test are identical with the blocks of the Kohs, the Wechsler-Bellevue, and the Arthur. The designs are, with one exception, those used by Kohs, though presented in a different order. The sequence used is related to increasing difficulty as found by Goldstein and Scheerer (10) in an analysis of the data on patients used by Nadel (21). Full directions are given by Goldstein and Scheerer in their monograph (10) and in a supplementary manual.

There are six possible presentation steps which may be followed with each of the twelve designs: (1) small unlined design; (2) actual block size unlined design; (3) small design with lines superimposed to show division into blocks; (4) actual block size design with superimposed lines; (5) block model (exact replica); and (6) three block models one of which is a replica, patient's task being to indicate which is correct. Not all patients need all these progressions to reproduce the design. Success not only consists of correct performance at a given level, but involves also return thereafter to the original small unlined design of Step 1, reproduction with this as a guide, and acknowledgment of the correctness of the construction. To illustrate, suppose the patient fails steps 1, 2, and 3. On step 4 with the actual block size design he copies it. At this point step 1 is reintroduced. If he succeeds on step 1 and states it is correct, the next new design is introduced; if not, step 5 of the old design is presented. Testing always continues until the step 1 design is completed and is acknowledged to be correct by the patient. It ceases when a design is failed at step 6. The designs made, correct or incorrect, are copied by the examiner on specially prepared record forms and the patient is questioned about the accuracy of his productions.

It can be seen that the procedure is a time-consuming one and testing is sometimes curtailed by elimination of some of the later designs.

A variation in procedure sometimes occurs in clinical practice when the Wechsler-Bellevue Scales have been administered. On the Block Design subtest, behavior of the patient is sometimes sufficiently aberrant to suggest that the Goldstein-Scheerer procedure might be of diagnostic value. Since qualitative findings and not a score are the principle yield at the present time, the practice is followed of now administrating the Cube Test with Goldstein's designs and procedure. In spite of the previous practice with the Block Design subtest, no particular differences have been observed as compared to the patients given the Cube Test alone. This contention, however, is based on limited and personal clinical observation and should be checked by a research investigation.

BEHAVIORAL ANALYSIS. A clear description of what seems to occur in attempts to duplicate the designs has been offered by Nadel. He identifies two methods of response to the task: "(1) By breaking down the design into its component block elements, constructing the required design by the single blocks; (2) By following the 'figures' created by the design, thus building the 'figure' of the design. The latter method may lead to success on some occasions, but the blocks are so arranged that response to the 'figure' usually leads to an unsuccessful result. Usually two or three blocks together are needed to complete a 'figure.' Thus the method of using the single blocks is essential for success." (21, p. 23.) In his study normal subjects seem to prefer the first method, although capable of using the second, and brain-damaged subjects appear to favor the second. The normals were capable of shifting from one to the other; the brain-damaged were not.

According to Goldstein and Scheerer there are two types of approach to this task—the concrete and the abstract. In their manual they both describe these approaches and indicate how they may be identified. The former approach is realistic, bound to the immediate experience and more passive in nature. The abstract attitude, on the other hand, requires the ability:

1. To detach our ego from the outerworld or from inner experiences.
2. To assume a mental set.
3. To account for acts to oneself; to verbalize the account.
4. To shift reflectively from one aspect of the situation to another.
5. To hold in mind simultaneously various aspects.
6. To grasp the essential of a given whole; to break up a given whole into parts, to isolate and to synthesize them.
7. To abstract common properties reflectively; to form hierarchic concepts.
8. To plan ahead ideationally; to assume an attitude towards the "mere possible" and to think or perform symbolically. (10, p. 4.)

The authors indicate that the normal person utilizes both attitudes and is capable of shifting from one to the other according to the exigencies of the situation; the patient with a brain lesion and the schizophrenic have impaired capacity for abstract behavior and are reduced to a mere concrete level of behavior. But neither they nor other workers mean to imply that the organic and schizophrenic processes are identical (9).

Goldstein and Scheerer then proceed to illustrate these attitudes by typical mistakes made by patient groups because of concreteness or rigidity. Examples include: (1) dependence upon size (a reproduction by a single block, instead of four blocks, since it reproduces the actual size of the model); (2) dependence upon total configuration including white surrounding field (reproduction with white surrounding or on some sides of the figure block or blocks); (3) dependence upon a global impression but not specific parts ("stripedness" of figure resulting in a reproduction which has diagonals but not the entire pattern); (4) dependence upon impression of certain color aspects (perhaps only one of two colors used, or with correct colors but not in the shape of the figure).

In discussing cases of brain concussion Goldstein (8) presents a very succinct summary which may be taken as indicative of the results obtained. He states that deviations from the normal are indicated by:

A) Exceptionally prolonged solution time, and increase in number of trials before success on each design. However, if the patient is finally successful without assistance, length of solution time or increase in number of trials does not necessarily indicate pathological change, but the latter should be suspected. If the patient is better able to reproduce another design, the protracted solution time on the first test may mean little. Normal persons may start to duplicate total figures or the upper or lower parts of the design, or they may begin by building two figure parts of the corners, thereby losing time. Normal individuals soon see that they cannot reach a correct solution in this way; or if they do arrive accidentally at a correct solution, they will recognize that it is more expedient to proceed by the simpler division method. If the subject persists in proceeding in this total or subwhole manner, even after the other procedure has been demonstrated to him, impairment of abstraction is indicated, even if he should eventually succeed.

B) If the subject was successful in constructing a larger design or one with lines, and thereafter is unable to do the small unlined standard design, impairment of abstraction is definitely indicated. The same is the case if he is unable to duplicate the next standard design after he had been previously successful on a large design or a design with lines. The test may be repeated after certain intervals to bring out changes in behavior indicating progress in capacity.

C) A person with good capacity for visualization may reach a correct solution simply on the basis of imagery, in spite of a persistent defect in abstraction. His handicap will come to the fore if he is confronted with a design he has never seen before. The most important point is whether the subject is able to *learn the piecemeal* procedure. If not it indicates *impairment of abstraction.* (8, p. 333.)

DIAGNOSTIC USAGE. A valiant preliminary attempt to develop quantitative scoring and norms for the Cube Test has appeared recently. Boyd (4) utilized the Goldstein-Scheerer administrative procedure by assigning weights to each step; the earlier the step at which success occurs the greater the weight. Unfortunately, the groups were small and the weights rather arbitrary.

Normal adults in most instances are expected by Goldstein and Scheerer (10) to score perfectly on the first step and thus not to need a simplified presentation. If they do, they are generally able to profit quickly from the aids offered. This may be more or less valid but lacks experimental verification. Certainly with IQ's even as high as 90 it is not invariably so, as found, for example, in the evidence of Boyd (4).

The Weigl Color-Form Sorting Test

The Weigl Color-Form Sorting Test sets the task for the patient of sorting various colored geometric shapes. Two possible solutions are successively sought—sorting by color and sorting by form, although not necessarily in this order. The test is both brief, five minutes generally being sufficient for administration, and relatively simple. Success or failure is much less equivocal than in the other conceptual tests. It is suitable, as later discussion will demonstrate, for children as young as four or five years of age. By virtue of its simplicity, however, it is less discriminatory in mild or early cases of suspected brain pathology. If failure in the adult is found it is likely to be of diagnostic significance, though the converse is not necessarily true. Normally adults have no difficulty in sorting both by form and by color and shifting with ease from the one which they first adopted to the other.

DESCRIPTION OF THE TEST AND OF THE PROCEDURE. Today the adaptation of the Weigl Color-Form Sorting Test prepared by Goldstein and Scheerer (10) is probably the most popular, and attention will be concentrated on this particular method of administration and scoring. Variations from the original procedure of Weigl (33) are relatively insignificant.

The material used consists of twelve cardboard or composition figures of different forms and colors—four circles, four squares, and four triangles in red, green, yellow, and blue. On their reverse sides they are all neutral (white) in color. The figures in random order are placed before the patient with instructions to place together those that belong together. Questions about procedure are met with noncommittal statements, so that any decision is left up to the subject. All conversations and spontaneous remarks are recorded. A graphic record is made of whatever sorting emerges, and the subject is asked to explain his grouping. He is then requested to put the pieces together in another way and afterwards again queried as to his reasons for the second grouping. If form and color sortings unequivocally emerge at this point the examination may be concluded; but if mixed form and color or disregard of form and color appear, it is necessary to proceed further. If the patient grouped in part 1 according to form and was unable to shift to color in part 2, the examiner then arranges the proper color groupings and asks why they were thus sorted. If the patient accepts a color grouping the figures are again shuffled and parts 1 and 2 repeated to see if he can now shift from form to color. If he originally grouped according to color and in part 2 was unable to shift to form, the figures are turned over to their neutral side and a sorting is requested. If now grouped by form, parts 1 and 2 are repeated to see if the shift can be made. If patterns are made or verbalizations are ambiguous, a variety of control steps described in the manual should be taken. As Weigl (33) himself stressed, it is important not only to note whether a shift in sorting behavior has occurred but also to recognize the factors, personal and situational, which give rise to this alteration in sorting on the part of the patient. What situation had to be created in order for the patient to make the shift? This question the examiner must attempt to answer.

BEHAVIORAL ANALYSIS. According to Goldstein and Scheerer (10) it is imperative to understand that there are concrete and abstract approaches to the task. In the setting of the Color-Form Test these approaches are manifested as follows:

I. *Abstract.* The subject assumes a conceptual attitude from the very start. He carries out the instruction by volitionally abstracting from the various individual sense impressions and orients himself toward a conceptual frame of reference, the category of form or of color. To elaborate: the subject transcends the immediate experience of each figure as *one given thing*; he disregards this thing-like character which comprises shape and coloration in *one* and segregates the two properties, shape and coloration, from each other. He consciously generalizes the so-segregated sensory properties of each figure according to form and color hue and systematizes them into a principle of classification. He subsumes the various figures under a particular class concept, taking the single figure as a representative of a category; that of form or that of color hue. Among others this procedure is frequently manifested by the subject's questions during such behavior: "Shall I sort according to form or according to color?"—and by the subject's ability to give account of his sorting procedure, of its conceptual basis, to himself and to others.

In arranging the material spatially, the subject will casually "throw" the forms he chooses in different heaps or piles, not being particular about the spatial position of the individual figure within each heap.

He will either form four piles of equally *colored* figures, corresponding to the number of color hues present; or he will form three piles of equally *shaped* figures according to the number of shapes present. He does so because he can treat the single figures *collectively* as falling under the category of color with the subclassification of green, yellow, blue, red—or under the category of shape with the subclassification of triangular, square, circular.

II. *Concrete.* . . . The subject unreflectively surrenders to the experience of the various figures as individual "things." Yet these "things" are no objects of real palpable usage. The only tangible properties they have consist of "*colored*" shape or "*shaped*" color. Therefore the subject is delivered to the sense impressions as they arise from the properties of the given material. These properties of shape and color *belong* to the given figure as an undivided whole, and do not particularly gravitate in themselves towards favoring the color aspect or the shape aspect. Therefore the subject's immediate apprehension will be guided by either one of the two following impressions: (1) That of a motley variety. In glancing over this color variety, one particular color is easily thrust phenomenally into the foreground (be it the red, the blue, the green, the yellow). Thereby the like colored objects tend to join together in uniform "color spots." (2) Or the subject's impression is that of a variety of shapes. In glancing over this shape variety, easily one particular shape element is thrust experientially into the foreground (be it the circle, the triangle, the square). Thereby the congruently shaped objects tend to stand out as belonging together. Which one of the two impressions, the *color* congruency or the *form* congruency obtrudes phenomenally depends upon the present personality make-up and background of the subject. (10, pp. 110–112.)[6]

Goldstein and Scheerer go on to point out that the patient adopting the concrete attitude may follow the dominating sense impression of color, place, or shape. But in so doing he does not put the figures casually in a heap. Instead he is likely to follow a definite spatial and temporal order. For example, he may arrange the red, blue, green, and yellow circles consecutively in a line and then turn to the squares and finally the triangles, arranging them in a second and third line in the same color sequence. In this arrangement the shape aspect prevailed. Or, he may sort the red triangle, circle, and square in a line in that sequence and go on to arrange the green, blue, and yellow shapes in the same sequences. Here the color aspect predominates. In explaining why this happens, Goldstein and Scheerer say:

. . . In the concrete attitude the subject cannot break asunder the unity of the given thing and hold apart systematically its properties— in this instance shape and color.
Hence, the subject never actually separates in his grouping the prevalent color—or shape aspect—from the given figures, in an abstract sense. He does not deliberately single out that prevalent aspect as a common denominator so that he can deposit the figures heapwise from a collective

─────────
    [6] Reprinted from "Abstract and Concrete Behavior" by K. Goldstein and M. Scheerer, by permission of *Psychological Monographs.* Copyright 1941 by the American Psychological Association.

point of view. His spatial arrangement of the figures cannot be arbitrary. Even though the subject follows one prevalent impression, e.g., that of shape, his placement of the figures still remains under the influence of his taking them as individual "things"! Thus he fits the differently colored, congruent shapes so that the colors, too, fit a definite pattern and, in the case of prevalent color aspect, he fits the differently shaped colors so that the shapes, too, fit a definite pattern. (10, pp. 112–113.)

The normal person is capable of assuming both attitudes but can shift from color to form and vice versa. "Individuals with disturbance of cortical funtion are unable to assume the abstract approach and therefore discharge the task on an exclusively concrete level of responding." (10, p. 113.) The tendency to build patterns of an ornamental spatial kind, the inability to grasp what sorting means, failure to shift, and inability to generalize are specific behavioral manifestations of abnormal concreteness which these authors illustrate in some detail.

DIAGNOSTIC USAGE. Bolles (2) tested normal children, dements (hebephrenics), and mental defectives with a variety of tests. These included a forerunner to the present Goldstein-Sheerer Cube Test procedure (although involving fewer steps), two object sorting tests, and the Weigl Color-Form Test. The subject groups were matched for mean Stanford-Binet MA, and differences in procedures and results in these and other tests were explored. In the sorting tests they were also required to state the basis by which the groupings were made, or, as Bolles referred to it, the basis of pertinence. In this study normal children (mean MA 9–3) showed no preferences for first sorting on the basis of form or of color, but all were capable of voluntary shift and verbalized the basis of their classification. Dements and aments of the same mental age were unable to shift voluntarily, and whereas the former group had a tendency to sort for form, aments tended to sort on the basis of color.

By CA 8, all the subjects of Reichard, Schneider, and Rapaport (26) were able to sort by either color or form, only a negligible percentage of six-year-olds being unable to make at least one successful sorting. From age seven onward there was a strong tendency on the part of the children to make form sortings (whether first or not) to the extent that two thirds were form and one third was color. Although these data are not directly comparable to Bolles' results on preference, or rather lack of preference, it would appear that form tends to be a first or a preferred sorting. The larger size of the groups in this latter study makes its results the more acceptable.

Both studies agree in finding that by ages eight or nine normal children are capable of sorting both by color and by form. Since in both groups they were capable of doing so voluntarily, without prompting, this would appear to be significant for clinical usage. The usefulness arises because the results offer a base line, crude to be sure, for appraising the behavior of patients on this test. If voluntary shift from color to form or vice versa cannot be made by children older than eight or nine, the results may be viewed as showing some interference in conceptual thinking.

In discussing both the Cube Test and the Color-Form Test the present account has leaned heavily upon the work of Goldstein and his fellow workers. It is appropriate at this point to consider certain implications of their efforts. Many of the tests of conceptual thinking described in this chapter have achieved particular prominence in appraising organic brain disorders. Goldstein, both in his own work and in work inspired by his findings and guidance, has been inclined unintentionally to further two intimately related misconceptions. On the one hand, there is a fairly prevalent mistaken belief that tests of conceptual thinking are suitable only when organicity is suspected. The work of Rapaport and his associates on other kinds of patients has intended to dispel this notion, but it has by no means eradicated it. On the other hand, sometimes the tacit assumption is made that the type of impairment found by Goldstein, best described in short compass as "impairment of the abstract attitude," is such that all individuals with cortical defect manifest it in greater or lesser degree. Such is by no means the case. Individuals with known cerebral pathology do not always demonstrate this particular kind of impairment.

It must be emphasized that the work of Goldstein and Scheerer, admirably acute in capturing the nuances of the behavior of a group of selected patients as it was, did not in any sense pretend to be an experimental study. Nowhere is the number or type of patients studied mentioned; nowhere are there control data on normal subjects; and exceptions which must have occurred are not mentioned. Essentially the data are anecdotal. Clinically skilled though these authors are, other reputable investigators are not as convinced of the prevalence and significance of their findings (cf., e.g., reviews of the Goldstein-Scheerer monograph in Buros, 6).

THE OBJECT SORTING TEST[7]

The Object Sorting Test is still another instrument used for the exploration of concept formation. "Putting together that which belongs together" by the process of sorting (selection) demands conceptualization. The patient must make choices and, as this test is administered, present his reasons for the choices. In large measure the process of choice is guided by conventional concepts, which factor actually limits choice. However, under the disorganization created by psychological problems, the patient adheres less to conventional patterns, giving the clinician the opportunity to study the personality of the patient.

Both sorting behavior and verbal explanation of the sorting are essential conditions to the understanding of the concept formation of the patient. One aspect may be disturbed and not the other, although the usual finding is a disturbance of the relationship of the two. The exploration of this relationship is permitted by the Object Sorting Test.

MATERIALS AND PROCEDURES. The test material consists of thirty-three common objects[8] which are, to quote Rapaport and his associates, "A real knife, fork, and spoon; a miniature knife, fork and spoon; a real screwdriver and pair of pliers; a miniature screwdriver, pair of pliers, hammer and hatchet; two nails; a block of wood with a nail in the center of it; two corks; two sugar cubes; a pipe; a real cigar and cigarette; an imitation cigar and cigarette; a matchbook; a rubber ball; a rubber eraser; a rubber sink stopper; a white filing card; a green cardboard square; a red paper circle; a lock; and a bicycle bell." (24, p. 397.)

---

[7] As in the Cube Test, there is some question as to just whose name should be used to identify this test. Apparently it is agreed that Gelb introduced it, and that Weigl first described it fully, but modifications by Goldstein and Scheerer (10), Bolles, Rosen, and Landis (3), Zubin and Thompson (35), and Rapaport (24) make for a somewhat confused picture. The problem is here "solved" by avoidance.

[8] The material is not sold commercially. It may, however, be purchased in local stores. If it is desired to reproduce Rapaport's group of objects, a picture of them has appeared in Reichard and Rapaport (25) which is an aid if the verbal descriptions are found to be unclear. The illustration is especially valuable for ascertaining relative sizes and proportions.

With the objects spread before him, the patient has the task of sorting them in various ways. The objects are such that groupings may be made on the basis of *use* (eating, utensils, smoking, equipment, toys and tools), *material* (metal, paper, rubber), *shape* (round, rectangle), *color* (red, white), and *size* (regular and miniature). There are two parts to the test presenting different kinds of conceptual problems. In Part I the task is actively to form conceptual groups and then define them. A sample object is before the patient and he is asked to select all of the other objects which belong with it. All but one of the seven introductory items (given in Table 23) are presented by the clinician; the first sample object is selected by the patient. If by chance he picks an object that is later presented by the clinician, the item should be given a second time at its place in the regular order to see if any changes have occurred. After each sorting the subject is asked why the group of objects selected belong together. Grouping and verbalizations are recorded along with behavior notes and side comments. In Part II the task of the patient is to state the principle of sorting involved in a group of objects placed before him. Thus a more passive form of conceptualization is involved here than in Part I. There are twelve such item groups with frequent overlap of objects from one group to another. However, a different attribute of the object is relevant in each instance. For example, the sink stopper in one group is a "round" object and in another a "red" object.

The approach to Object Sorting used by Rapaport (24) has certain advantages of greater clarity and more objectivity in scoring which makes it the procedure of choice for exposition.[9] Many of the earlier investigations using this test were stimulated by the work of Goldstein. Consequently, the schema they utilized stressed the "abstract" and "concrete" attitudes discussed earlier in connection with the Color-Form Test and the Cube Test. It is, of course, quite possible to use this approach to analysis of the data yielded by the Object Sorting Test. In fact, the manual by Goldstein and Scheerer (10) for the Cube Test and the Object Sorting Test also includes details of administration and the behavioral analysis of a closely

---

[9] A greater amount of detail, including specific instructions for administration and inquiry, is given in Rapaport (24). As many findings are not reviewed here, this reference should be consulted when administering the test.

related Object Sorting Test.[10] The approach of Rapaport et al. (24) was selected for exposition for three reasons: (1) It was considered advisable to present another point of view; (2) Rapaport's approach appears to possess greater objectivity, communicability, and richness than does the Goldstein-Scheerer approach; and (3) the dichotomy set up by Goldstein and Scheerer (10), pertinent with deteriorated schizophrenics and those with organic pathology, is not applicable with many other patient groups who show little or no impairment of the "abstract attitude" but nevertheless have some psychological deficit.

SCORING. Before examining the actual scoring procedure for the sortings and the verbalizations it is necessary to consider in some detail the rationale of the scoring as conceived by Rapaport and his associates. They state:

Our scoring system takes account of: (a) uniform scoring of active and compliant concept formation; (b) both sorting and verbalization; (c) the adequacy of sorting and verbalization, which is the degree to which sorting or verbalization approximates the conceptual norms of the population; (d) conceptual levels of definition; (e) the *concept span*, or whether objects belonging to the group were left out or irrelevant ones included.

We shall divide our discussion into: (a) that of active and compliant concept formation; (b) that of adequacy; (c) that of conceptual level; (d) that of the concept span.

(a) The Scoring of Active (Part I.) and Compliant (Part II.) Concept Formation. On Part I., the sorting is scored for its adequacy and span, and the verbalization for its adequacy and conceptual level. On Part II., the definition of the presented sorting is scored for adequacy of verbalization, and for conceptual level.

(b) Adequacy. A sorting is adequate . . . [if] all the objects put with the sample object are relevant to it, and homogeneous among themselves. The verbalization is adequate if it is congruent with the group of objects to which it refers.

Adequate Sorting. With the rubber ball as sample, the rubber cigar, rubber cigarette, rubber sink pad, and rubber eraser make an adequate sorting. It is meaningful, and statistically most frequent of the sortings made around the ball. Adequate, but quite rare, is the sorting of the round objects with the ball. It is adequate because it segregates from the other objects a well-circumscribed group and a sufficient number of

---

[10] Other groups of objects, methods of evaluation, and procedures have been used by Bolles (2), Bolles, Rosen, and Landis (3), Halstead (13), Lynn, Levine, and Hewson (20), and Zubin and Thompson (35).

objects according to a clear conceptual content. Thus adequate grouping is: (1) relevant to the sample object; (2) so common as to be acceptable; (3) or rare, but based on a well-defined concept which segregates a sufficient number of objects. Adequate sorting is scored "plus."

Inadequate Sorting. The sorting of toy silverware with the real fork, omitting the other real silverware, is an inadequate sorting; it disregards the difference between the sample and the sorted objects. Sorting the small hatchet with a green handle with the green cardboard square is inadequate; it disregards a sizable group of paper objects which would make a more relevant sorting. Inadequate sorting is not relevant to the sample object, and is inappropriate in view of the other objects at disposal for sorting. Inadequate sortings are scored "minus."

If from a correct sorting an essential object is omitted, or one that does not belong is added, though hereby the conceptual content of the sorting—as established from the verbalization—is not affected, the score is "plus/minus." If a reasonably good sorting is seriously affected by additions or omissions of this kind, or if a generally inadequate sorting has some lucid features to it, the score is "minus/plus."

Adequate Verbalization. If the adequate sorting of all rubber objects with the rubber ball is defined as "all rubber," the verbalization is adequate. If the inadequate sorting of the green square with the green handled hatchet is defined as "both green," the verbalization is also adequate. A verbalization is adequate if it covers correctly the group sorted; its score is "plus."

Inadequate Verbalization. Definition of all the rubber objects as "all have some red on them" is an inadequate verbalization; many red test objects are not part of this group. The verbalization of inadequate sorting is usually inadequate; but it is the inadequate verbalization of *adequate* sorting which is indicative of malign disorganization. A mild form of this type is seen when the toys are defined as "all limitations" or "all small"; and a malign form is seen when the same group is defined as "all used to break something."

Inadequate verbalizations do not cover the sorting, and do not differentiate the objects within the realm from those outside it. They are most malign if they diverge from good active sortings or, in compliant concept formation, from the sorting to be defined. The score given is "minus." Small peculiarities, or deviations in otherwise adequate verbalizations, obtain the score "plus/minus." Inadequate verbalizations with some glimmer of the correct idea are scored "minus/plus."

(c) *The Conceptual Level of Sorting.* On the concrete level of concept formation, "things" are considered to belong together because of a common unessential property or because of a contiguity in everyday experience; on the functional level, "things" are considered to belong together because of a common function. These levels refer to partial characteristics; the third and highest level refers to abstract-conceptual common content, as expressed by an abstract generic term.

In the Sorting Test, the conceptual level is determined mainly from the verbalization. To define the adequate sorting of the tablespoon and table knife with the big fork as "eating utensils" shows an *abstract-conceptual level;* "we eat with them" shows a *functional level;* "all are on the table" shows a *concrete level.* At times the sorting can be more revealing than the verbalization: though sorting the table utensils with the sugar may be defined in abstract-conceptual terms as "tableware," the sorting itself shows that the level of concept formation is concrete.

Definitions on the concrete level are scored C (concrete), on the functional level F.D. (functional definition), and on the abstract-conceptual level C.D. (conceptual definition). The following four types of definitions are more or less related to the functional and concrete levels, and have pathological implications:

Syncretistic Definition. Syncretistic definitions of a functional type are "We use them all," or "They all give us pleasure." Syncretistic definitions of a concrete type may refer to location, as "all found in a house"; to origin, as "all come from plants"; or to belonging, as "all belong to men." Here the concept basis has become tremendously enlarged, and the definition does not differentiate "realm" from "not-realm"; in fact, almost everything might be subsumed with realms so defined.

Fabulation. This type of definition is seen when a subject starts out with the big screwdriver as "belonging to a workman," and puts the rest of the tools with it, meanwhile relating the workman's daily chores; then includes the sugar and eating utensils, as the workman has lunch; and the lock, with which he has locked his tool-kit on going to lunch; and finally, at the end of lunch, all the smoking utensils. Fabulations resemble definitions on a functional level; however, they refer not to *common* functions of objects, but to *different* functions woven into a story. Fabulation is the extreme of a concrete type of concept formation; in it the objects are isolated from the conceptual contents of each other, and can be chained together only by extraneous stories. Fabulations may be innocuous looking, but they should always arouse suspicion of serious pathology.

Symbolic Definition. Interpreting a round piece of paper as an ashtray, and a square piece of paper as a table, and sorting with them the silverware, is a mild form of this type. Defining the large and small silverware as "mother and child" is a full-fledged one. The symbolic type of conceptualization re-interprets radically the meaning of the objects, and makes the new symbolic meaning the basis of sorting. This type is a sign of the encroachment of "affective-evaluative" concept formation upon consciousness.

Chain Definitions. Here, with a red sample a red object which is rectangular may be sorted; with this is sorted a rectangular wooden block; with this, in turn, is sorted a wood-handled tool, and so on. The concepts here are narrow and on a concrete level; but due to a generalized disturbance the concept becomes fluid, so that the conceptual frame of reference changes from one object to another.

(d) The Concept Span: Loose and Narrow Sortings. A sorting of appropriate concept span segregates a well-defined group of objects, and includes *all* the objects that belong with the sample and excludes *all* the objects that do not. A sorting which includes objects not belonging with the content of the concept, or one whose concept is too inclusive in reference to the test objects, is called here "loose." One not including objects that belong with the concept, or one whose concept is too limited in reference to the test objects, is called here "narrow."

Loose sorting results from the subject's having little perseverance with his concepts, and being led by each object to a further generalization. Thus, with small pliers, other small tools, then the big tools, then the nails, the block of wood, the lock, the cigars, the cork, the sugar, may all be sorted to make a workman's kit.

Loose sortings come about usually as an expression of the type of thinking in which "everything belongs with everything"; but they may also result from anxious and haphazard performance.

Narrow sortings result from determining the conceptual content of the sample without reference to the test objects available, and rigidly not modifying it. Thus, to decide that the content of the sample object *ball* is "red, round, and rubber" will result in sorting only the red rubber sink stopper with it.

Such rigid preconceived decisions are frequent in compulsive, over-meticulous persons who, in surveying the test objects, find that most objects do not "fit" the sample because of small—but to them significant—differences. Narrow sortings may be due also to depressive retardation, wariness, lack of interest and/or understanding. Careful observation reveals the type.

Neither rigid deductions from the sample, nor endless induction with every new object sorted, will make for appropriate concept span; this results only when equal weight is given to the available objects and to the conceptual content of the sample. This is a *tacit* implication of the instructions, well understood by most "normal" subjects.

Scoring of Loose Sorting. Mild looseness—as, sugar put with the silverware—is scored "l," if it does not impair the concept underlying the sorting.

Loose sorting—as, lock put with tools "to lock the tool kit"—in which the underlying concept is impaired, but not yet disrupted, is scored "(L)."

Essential looseness—as, putting the knife with the ball because its end is round, the nail because its head is round—which includes nearly all the test-objects in a sorting, is scored "L." Yet an essentially loose sorting may consist of only few objects, as sorting the pliers with the fork because "you pick things up with both." Not the extensiveness of the sorting, but rather the degree of "not-belonging together" of the objects sorted, determines the degree of looseness. Only active sorting is scored "l," "(L)" and "L."

Scoring of Narrow Sorting. Narrow sorting—as, omission of one rubber object from the well-defined rubber sorting—is scored "(N)."

Here the concept is on a conceptual level not affected by the narrowness itself.

Essentially narrow sorting finds "nothing belongs" with the ball, or groups only big pliers with small pliers as "both pliers." Such sorting which includes no or few objects with the sample, where it is possible to sort many more with it, is scored "N."

The scores "N" and "(N)" pertain to active sorting only. On Part II., narrowing of the concept span splits the groups into parts and defines each separately. Such definitions are labeled "split-narrow," and scored "S/N." (23, pp. 166–176.)[11]

There seems to be agreement on the part of other investigators about the phenomena isolated and described by Rapaport et al. (24). Although they do not use the same schema or nomenclature, the phenomena are substantially similar. Bolles (2), for example, speaks of classification by use, of concrete and abstract classifications, and gives illustrations of what Rapaport (24) would call syncretistic, symbolic, and fabulated classifications. This is encouraging in that it lends support to the commonality of their rationale.

No total score is derived, not only because there are but nineteen items but also because the scoring system is designed merely to permit a more facile survey of the results. For convenience, scoring illustrations are given in Tables 23 and 24. In both tables heavy reliance is placed upon the findings of Rapaport and his associates. Table 23, concerned with Part I, gives item by item the commonest adequate sorting of the objects, typical narrowings or loosenings of the concept span, and illustrations of abstract-conceptual, functional, and conrete definitions. In some instances there are omissions in the tables; e.g., a typical loosening on item 4 (bicycle bell) is not reported. These omissions are to be understood as implying either that there is no typical response or that for the item this particular kind of response is impossible or so nearly so that it may be disregarded.

Not all possible scoring categories are given in the table. Inability to sort or no response at all occurs in some instances. For scoring purposes it would be entered as "failure." In Part I no response is most common with item 4 (bell), and is not diagnostically significant. It does occur with other items—e.g., item 7 (rubber ball), responded to with the statement that nothing goes with it. Generally

---

[11] Reprinted from *Manual of Diagnostic Psychological Testing*, I, by D. Rapaport, R. Schafer, and M. Gill, by permission of the Josiah Macy Jr. Foundation. Copyright 1944 by the Josiah Macy Jr. Foundation.

TABLE 23. Scoring Part I of the Sorting Test

Item	Sample	Adequate Sorting	Typical Narrowing	Typical Loosening	Abstract-Conceptual	Functional	Concrete
1	Chosen by patient						
2	1.ᵃ Fork	l. knife l. spoon m.ᵇ fork m. knife m. spoon	Excludes m. silverware = (N)	Adds to others sugar cubes = 1 (if all metal objects grouped as "metal"—mild loosening although adequate)	"Silverware" "Eating utensils"	"You eat with them" "Used for eating"	"Find them on the table" "In the kitchen"
3	Pipe	r.ᶜ cigar r. cigarette i.ᵈ cigar i. cigarette	Excludes i. cigar, i. cigarette = (N) or inclusion of matches only	None typical; if occurs, sign of pathology	"Smoking equipment" "Smoking utensils" "Smoking set" (this may be concrete—inquire)	"You smoke them" "Used in smoking"	"Smoking set" (this may be abstract—inquire); if matches added only, "you use to light pipe"
4	Bicycle bell	Round objects Metal objects Toys (rare to get correct)	Omits some of whatever is sorted		Round Metal Toys	If lock and/or tools sorted, "used on bicycle"	If screwdriver selected, "use to take off"; if tools (except hatchet) selected, "tools for repairs" = 1
5	Red paper circle	Red objects Round objects Paper objects	Omits some of whatever is sorted		Red Round Paper		With eraser included, "if you write on paper might need eraser"

6	Toy pliers	(no signif. omiss. of cigarette) 4 m. tools 2 l. tools or 4 m. tools and other toys	Excludes 4 l. tools or less = (N); adds only l. pliers	Adds to others 4 m. tools, 2 l. tools, 2 nails · With block "nail it" = l; "all toys" = l	"Tools" "Toys"	"Use them to make something" "Fix something" "Use in carpentry"	"Found in a tool chest"; l. pliers only added = "pliers"; block with nail only added = "use pliers to pull out nail"
7	Red Round *Rubber* Ball	Eraser Sink stopper Rubber cigar Rubber cigarette	Omission of cigar and/or cigarette	Indecision concerning corks for "spongy"	"Rubber"		
	Red *Round* Rubber Ball	Two corks Bell Paper circle			"Round"		
	Red Round Rubber Ball	Red objects			"Red"		
	Red Round Rubber *Ball*	Toys			"Toys"	"To play with"	"You find them in a play-room"

a l. = large
b m. = miniature
c r. = real
d i. = imitation

such failures occur because the individual, responding on a concrete level, cannot identify the object with any of the others as associated in a concrete situation—"It doesn't need anything." Syncretistic and fabulated responses, not reported in the table, are given by some patients. Item 5 (red paper circle) is especially sensitive to tendencies in these directions. A typical syncretistic response is to sort various objects with the circle and offer the definition of "geometric shapes." A fabulated response might be a circle as a table mat with which the silverware and sugar are grouped as a "place setting."

One or two points of importance concerning conceptual level and concept span, not brought out in the table, should be mentioned. The conceptual level may be mixed; for example, to item 6 (toy pliers), several tools may be added and the explanation given that they are "all tools—something to build with." Thus, a mixed conceptual and functional conceptual level appeared in this response. Narrowing of the span of sorting may occur by failing to include one or more than one of the usually included objects. For example, with the ball of item 7 the sink stopper, eraser, and rubber cigarette might be selected, but not the rubber cigar, so that a mildly narrow sorting is given.

According to Rapaport, on the general significance of items on Part I, inadequate sorting on item 4 (the hardest item) may almost always be disregarded, whereas failure on items 3 and 6 (the easiest items) are indicative of maladjustment. Items 2, 5, and 7 are considered to be intermediate, and only if several inadequacies appear are they said to indicate maladjustment.

Table 24, concerned with Part II, presents for each item the objects sorted for the patient, and, where applicable, the typical abstract-conceptual, functional, and concrete responses. Illustrations of split-narrow concept spans, syncretistic and fabulated responses are also given when they are pertinent. The omission of functional or concrete level responses for a given item implies that they are either impossible or almost impossible. Consequently, the great majority of such responses will be false and therefore inadequate.

False responses may, of course, appear. In item 1 (red), the response "for a child to play with" is false in that objects are included which are hardly considered playthings, e.g., the match book. Or in item 5 (paper), the answer "used to write on," although it fits some of the objects included, hardly applies to the cigarette. Again, in item 6 (pairs) several of the pairs are of real and imitation objects, but several are composed of identical objects, so it is false to give this basis for scoring. These, then, are failures.

Failures are considered to have occurred when neither an adequate abstract-conceptual nor a functional definition has been given. On this basis Rapaport et al. (24) found that items 2, 4, 5, 8, 9, and 10 are very easy in that not more than 9 percent of their control group failed any one of them. On the other hand, in items, 1, 3, 6, 7, 11, and 12 the controls failed from 20 to 50 percent. The authors draw the conclusion that failures on the easy items, especially if massed, should be considered indicative of impairment. Fabulated or other bizarre responses are indicative of pathology whether in hard or easy items.

DIAGNOSTIC USAGE.   In dealing with the various patient groups they studied, Rapaport et al. (24) report in detail their findings. It is impossible in short compass to summarize them adequately for each of the patient groups or for even one such group. Instead, a description will be given of the diagnostic indicators they used when considering general differentiation of the groups instead of the influence of single indicators. They believe, on the basis of their experience with the test, that scores falling above or below these limits, as the case may be, indicate at least a tendency toward impairment of conceptual thinking. These indicators are:

(1) Fewer than five adequate or nearly adequate (plus or plus/minus) sortings on Part I.
(2) Two or more loose sortings on Part I.
(3) Fewer than three abstract-conceptual definitions on Part I.
(4) One or more syncretistic definitions on Part I.
(5) More than one fabulated or symbolic definition on Part I.
(6) Fewer than eight adequate or nearly adequate definitions on Part II.
(7) Fewer than six conceptual definitions on Part II.
(8) More than two syncretistic definitions on Part II.
(9) More than two fabulated or symbolic definitions on Part II. (24, p. 450.)

In about 50 percent of the unclassified and paranoid schizophrenics three or more signs of impairment appeared. For other patient groups the findings were as follows: depressives, 45 percent; mixed neurotics, anxious and depressed, and neurasthenic (collectively), 42 percent; preschizophrenic, 35 percent; and hysteric and obsessive-compulsive, 15 percent. In the control group of Kansas highway

TABLE 24. Scoring Part II of the Sorting Test

Item	Sorting Presented	Abstract-Conceptual	Functional	Concrete	Split-Narrow	Syncretistic	Fabulated
1	Ball Paper circle Match book Sink stopper Eraser	"Red"			"Rubber and paper"	"All manufactured" "All come from plants" "We use them"	
2	3 l.[a] silverware 3 m.[b] silverware Bell Lock 2 Nails 2 Pliers	"Metal" "All steel" "All iron" (latter two have concrete tinge)			"Silverware and toys" "Silverware, bicycle and tool-kit"	"All used by man" "All used in every-day life"	"With these you eat your breakfast and then you go to work with these and this is a lock for your tool chest and this is a warning bell"
3	Ball Sink stopper 2 Corks Bicycle bell Paper circle	"Round"			"Rubber" vs. "non-rubber" "Red" vs. "non-red"	"All found in the house" "All used by man" "All manufactured"	Relates to specific everyday activities
4	l. screwdriver l. pliers m. screwdriver m. pliers m. hammer m. hatchet	"Tools" "For carpentry" "Builder's equipment"	"Use to make things"	"In the tool-kit"	"Real tools" vs. "imitation" "For children and for adults"		"For father in his work and these are for child who is imitating"
5	Red paper circle Green cardboard square White filing card Match book r.[c] cigarette	"Paper"			"Cigarette" considered an exception	"All come from plants" "They burn"	"A man working at a desk (filing card) smoking, etc."
6	2 Forks 2 Knives 2 Spoons 2 Corks 2 Nails 2 Sugar cubes 2 Screwdrivers	"Pairs"				"Use them all" "Find them all in the house" "All objects of pleasure"	In re "father and son," or "family"

No.	Objects						
7	2 Pliers 2 Cigars 2 Cigarettes r. cigarette 2 Sugar cubes Filing card Green rectangle turned to white side	"White" "Colorless"		"Cigarette" considered an exception	"All afford pleasure"		"Sugar could go in coffee, these could be doilies (card and rectangle), and smoke cigarettes"
8	Sink stopper i.[d] cigar i. cigarette Ball Eraser	"Rubber"		Exception to "metal ring"			
9	Pipe r. cigar r. cigarette i. cigar i. cigarette Match book	"Smoking material"	"Use them to smoke with" "Smoke them"	"Find them on a smoking stand"	"Imitations" differentiated	"All come from plants"	
10	3 l. silverware 3 m. silverware	"Silverware" "Eating utensils" "Table service"	"Eat with them" "Used in eating"	"Found on a table"	"Imitations" differentiated		"Father-child"
11	4 m. tools 3 m. eating utensils i. cigar i. cigarette Ball	"Toys" "Playthings"	"You play with them all"	"For a child" "Find them in a child's room"	"Metal and rubber"	"Things we use every day"	
12	Filing card green cardboard Block of wood with nails Match book 2 Sugar cubes	"Rectangles" "Squares" "Right angles"				"Materials" "Things we use every day" "All come from the earth"	

[a] l. = large
[b] m. = miniature
[c] r. = real
[d] i. = imitation

patrolmen only 9 percent showed three or more of these indicators. Certain signs were found to be characteristic of the schizophrenic, namely, in Part I, two or more loose sortings, one or more syncretistic definitions, and more than one fabulated or symbolic definition, and on Part II, more than two syncretistic and two or more fabulated or symbolic definitions. Only 9 percent of the control group had more than one of these signs whereas 32 percent of the schizophrenic groups did so.

A study of the development of concept formation in children by Reichard, Schneider, and Rapaport (26) is of interest in that it reports the percentage of adequate sortings on Part I and adequate verbalizations on Part II (+ and ± scorings) for children aged four to fourteen. At age four the percentage of adequate sortings and verbalizations for Parts I and II respectively were 29 and 12 percent. By age nine they were respectively 81 and 56 percent. Thereafter, there was no appreciable increase in percentage on Part I, but in Part II there was an increase to 86 percent at age fourteen. The authors conclude that with the development of intellectual maturation "a compliance with socially-accepted norms of thinking becomes progressively greater and more adequate; while active concept formation, though it develops earlier, remains more autonomous, uncompliant, and less adequate." (24, p. 417.) This conclusion, based upon the differences in percentage of adequacy between Part II (compliant) and Part I (active) concept formation, also holds for the control and clinical groups in the study of patient groups previously referred to (24).

In conjunction with the Object Sorting Test, the findings of the Wechsler Similarities subtest assume prominence, and Rapaport et al. (24) considered the tests complementary.[12] The Similarities, a purely verbal test, gives information concerning verbally stereotyped concept formation, and the Object Sorting Test yields information as to how the patient deals with the objects of the everyday world. Further, it requires performance as well as verbalization. From the

---

[12] The Hanfmann-Kasanin Test, which has the advantages of confronting the patient with a new conceptual problem, was along with the Wechsler Similarities subtest ("purely verbal" concept formation) and the Object Sorting Test ("everyday" concept formation) used in a three-pronged attack on the problem. The Hanfmann-Kasanin Test, cumbersome and time-consuming for the yield it gives, is no longer used as part of the routine battery at the Menninger Clinic (39).

relation of the findings on the two tests it is possible to secure additional material of diagnostic significance. Rapaport and his associates (24) found a substantial degree of relationship between impairment on Similarities (defined as a Similarities subtest score three or more units below Vocabulary subtest score) and impaired sorting behavior (defined in terms of the signs of impairment previously discussed). This was especially noticeable among schizophrenics in which a biserial r of .69 was found. Nevertheless, on these two tests, there are schizophrenics (and others) who preserve a good verbal front and demonstrate their impairment only on the Object Sorting Test. Preschizophrenics are especially likely to give themselves away on Part I. Schizophrenics, however, are likely to be impaired on both Part I and Part II.

BIBLIOGRAPHY

1. Benton, A. L., A visual retention test for clinical use, *Arch. Neurol. & Psychiat.*, 1945, 54:212–216.
2. Bolles, M., The basis of pertinence, *Arch. Psychol.*, 1937, No. 212.
3. Bolles, M. M., Rosen, G. P., and Landis, C., Psychological performance tests as prognostic agents for the efficacy of insulin therapy in schizophrenia, *Psychiat. Quart.*, 1938, 12:733–737.
4. Boyd, F.., A provisional quantitative scoring with preliminary norms for the Goldstein-Scheerer Cube Test, *J. clin. Psychol.*, 1949, 5:148–153.
5. Bronner, A. F., Healy, W., Lowe, G. M., and Shimberg, M. E., A manual of individual mental tests and testing, Little, Brown and Company, 1927.
6. Buros, O. K. (ed.), *The third mental measurements yearbook*, Rutgers University Press, 1949.
7. Cofer, C. N. (chm.), Report of the committee on the teaching of clinical psychology, *Newsletter, Div. clin. abnorm. Psychol.*, 1949, 2:9–10.
8. Goldstein, K., Brain concussion: evaluation of the after effects by special tests, *Dis. nerv. Syst.*, 1943, 4:325–334.
9. Goldstein, K., Methodological approach to the study of schizophrenic language and thought, in Kasanin, J. S. (ed.), *Language and thought in schizophrenia*, University of California Press, 1944, pp. 17–39.
10. Goldstein, K., and Scheerer, M., Abstract and concrete behavior; an experimental study with special tests, *Psychol. Monogr.*, 1941, 53, No. 239.
11. Graham, F. K., and Kendall, B. S., Performance of brain-damaged cases on a memory-for-designs test, *J. abnorm. soc. Psychol.*, 1946, 41:303–314.

12. Graham, F. K., and Kendall, B. S., Note on the scoring of the Memory-for-Designs Test, *J. abnorm. soc. Psychol.*, 1947, 42:253.

13. Halstead, W. C., Preliminary analysis of grouping behavior in patients with cerebral injury by the method of equivalent and nonequivalent stimuli, *Amer. J. Psychiat.*, 1940, 96:1263–1294.

14. Hamister, R. C., The test re-test reliability of the Wechsler-Bellevue Intelligence Test (Form 1) for a neuropsychiatric population, *J. consult. Psychol.*, 1949, 13:39–43.

15. Hanfmann, E., Thought disturbances in schizophrenia as revealed by performance in a picture completion test, *J. abnorm. soc. Psychol.*, 1939, 34:249–264.

16. Jacobs, J., Experiments on "prehension," *Mind*, 1887, 12:75–79.

17. Kendall, B. S., A note on the relation of retardation in reading to performance on a Memory-for-Designs Test, *J. educ. Psychol.*, 1948, 39:370–373.

18. Kendall, B. S., and Graham, F. K., Further standardization of the Memory-for-Designs Test on children and adults, *J. consult. Psychol.*, 1948, 12:349–354.

19. Lidz, T., Gay, J. R., and Tietze, C., Intelligence in cerebral deficit states and schizophrenia measured by Kohs Block Test, *Arch. Neurol. & Psychiat.*, 1942, 48:568–582.

20. Lynn, J. G., Levine, K. N., and Hewson, L. R., Psychologic tests for the clinical evaluation of late "diffuse organic," "neurotic," and "normal" reactions after closed head injury, *Res. Publ. Ass. nerv. ment. Dis.*, 1945, 24:296–378.

21. Nadel, A. B., A qualitative analysis of behavior following cerebral lesions diagnosed as primarily affecting the frontal lobes, *Arch. Psychol.*, 1938, No. 224.

22. Peatman, J. G., and Locke, N. M., Studies in the methodology of the digit-span test, *Arch. Psychol.*, 1934, No. 167.

23. Rapaport, D., with collaboration of Schafer, R., and Gill, M., *Manual of diagnostic psychological testing*. I. Diagnostic testing of intelligence and concept formation, Josiah Macy Jr. Foundation Review Series, 1944, 2, No. 2.

24. Rapaport, D., Gill, M., and Schafer, R., *Diagnostic psychological testing*, Vol. I, Year Book Publishers, 1945.

25. Reichard, S., and Rapaport, D., The role of testing concept formation in clinical psychological work, *Bull. Menninger Clin.*, 1943, 7:99–105.

26. Reichard, S., Schneider, M., and Rapaport, D., The development of concept formation in children, *Amer. J. Orthopsychiat.*, 1944, 14:156–161.

27. Richards, T. W., *Modern clinical psychology*, McGraw-Hill Book Company, 1946.

28. Sarason, S. B., and Sarason, E. K., The discriminatory value of a test pattern in the high grade familial defective, *J. clin. Psychol.*, 1946, 2:38–49.

29. Stone, C. P., Losses and gains in cognitive functions as related to electro-convulsive shocks, *J. abnorm. soc. Psychol.*, 1947, 42:206–214.
30. Stone, C. P., Girdner, J., and Albrecht, R., An alternate form of the Wechsler Memory Scale, *J. Psychol.*, 1946, 22:199–206.
31. Trist, E. L., Trist, V., and Brody, M. B., Discussion on the quality of mental test performance in intellectual deterioration, *Proc. R. Soc. Med.*, 1943, 36:243–252.
32. Wechsler, D., A standardized memory scale for clinical use, *J. Psychol.*, 1945, 19:87–95.
33. Weigl, E., On the psychology of the so-called process of abstraction, *J. abnorm. soc. Psychol.*, 1941, 36:3–33.
34. Wells, F. L., and Ruesch, J. (eds.), *Mental examiners handbook*, Psychological Corporation, 2nd ed., 1945.
35. Zubin, J., and Thompson, J., *Sorting tests in relation to drug therapy in schizophrenia*, New York State Psychiatric Institute, 1941.

DIAGNOSTIC TESTING REPORTS INVOLVING THE TESTS DISCUSSED

36. Benton, A. L., and Howell, I. L., The use of psychological tests in the evaluation of intellectual function following head injury: report of a case of post-traumatic personality disorder, *Psychosom. Med.*, 1941, 3:138–151.
37. Bolles, M., and Goldstein, K., A study of the impairment of "abstract behavior" in schizophrenic patients, *Psychiat. Quart.*, 1938, 12:42–65.
38. Roscnzweig, S., with Kogan, K. L., *Psychodiagnosis: an introduction to tests in the clinical practice of psychodynamics*, Grune & Stratton, 1949, pp. 55–66, 70–73, 304–310.
39. Schafer, R., *The clinical application of psychological tests: diagnostic summaries and case studies*, International Universities Press, 1948.

CHAPTER 14

The Projective Approach to
Personality Evaluation[1]

Mirroring many of the turmoils of the present clinical scene is the projective approach to personality evaluation. Arising from contributions in the psychological and psychiatric fields, projective materials and theories bear the imprint of both. Brilliant and unquantified clinical insights go hand in hand with the more pedestrian but equally important attempts to bring the results of such approaches within the confines of scientific exactitude. In a very real sense clinical insights, both of psychiatrists and of psychologists, have taken the place formerly occupied by the contributions of philosophers in revealing the unexplored territories of the human psyche. It is manifestly the task of psychologists as scientists to attempt to submit such insights to scrutiny by the scientific method.

The principal theoretical influences upon projective approaches appear to be psychoanalytically oriented thinking, traditional psychological theories and findings, global (Gestalt) theory, and certain general trends in modern scientific thinking with particular emphasis upon theoretical physics. It may be hazarded that these influences

---

[1] It is unnecessary here to sketch the history of projective techniques. For a brilliant and thorough statement the review by Sargent (18) is unexcelled. For marshaling support by analogy from other scientific fields the paper of Frank (22) is especially persuasive.

have been presented in the order of their importance in directing thinking about the projective approach. Psychoanalytic thinking, with its emphasis upon psychic determinism and the influence of unconscious motivation, has contributed a dynamic orientation which dominates projective methodology and theory. Although traditional psychological theory occasionally comes to grips with projective techniques, with some (but not all) adherents to such views finding in projective material an irritating as well as stimulating source of knowledge about human motivation and personality, it has made a major contribution by emphasizing observation of scientific caution and the need for integration of findings with the main stream of psychological thought. The influence of the global approach is most evident in the position clinical workers take concerning interpretation of projective materials. They contend that interpretation must take place in a setting in which part functions (scores and the like) take on their meaning in relation to the pattern which they form. The part measures, if considered in isolation, lose most if not all of their meaning. An atomistic position, on the basis of the assumption that personality is conceived to be composed of functionally autonomous discrete and independent variables, is found to be untenable. Rather, there is a continual interaction among components of the personality, and this interaction is, in itself, an aspect of the study of personality. Although the weight of more general scientific theorizing is perhaps less direct, the projective approach reflects the climate of the times and finds many plausible analogies in discoveries from other fields. The presentation of clinical projective techniques to follow will bear in varying degrees these imprints.

In Chapter 6 the psychometric and projective approaches were compared and the conviction was expressed that both are necessary because they mutually strengthen each other. It is now necessary to examine the projective approach in more detail. Accordingly, the nature of projection first will be formulated. The projective approach as such will then be restated and further examined. Following this, the similarities and differences between projective and nonprojective devices will be considered. Next, the advantages of the projective approach will be analyzed and some of its difficulties will be presented. Lastly, the necessity of multiple projective approaches will be urged.

THE NATURE OF PROJECTION

The term "projection" was used by Freud to identify a mechanism by which the ego defends itself against anxiety (Bellak, 2). According to his point of view the ego protects itself against anxiety by attributing unacceptable thoughts or impulses, not to the unconscious where they originate, but to persons or objects in the environment. The mechanism is accepted generally by clinical workers whether or not they subscribe to psychoanalytic doctrine. In other words, the phenomenon of projection, whether psychoanalytically interpreted or not, has been found to exist and to have heuristic value.

In applying the adjectival form of the term "projection" to the techniques under discussion, Frank (22) did not theoretically justify his selection. Although the term is in many ways a happy choice, its rapid and well-nigh universal acceptance is not without dangers. On the one hand, there is the chance that it will be taken by some to have a meaning identical with the narrower psychoanalytic concept of projection as a defense characteristic of the paranoid patient. This point of view is entirely too narrow and psychopathologically oriented. On the other hand, there is that somewhat loose and amorphous meaning given to the term in which it is supposed to encompass all instances in which the thoughts, desires, and feelings of one person are attributed to another. This, too, is wide of the mark. A meaning more in keeping with actual practice has been suggested by Rapaport. He compares it to a projector and screen and goes on to state that "In this sense, a projection has occurred when the psychological structure of the subject becomes palpable in his actions, choices, products, and creations. Therefore, when a procedure is so designed as to enable the subject to demonstrate his psychological structure unstilted by conventional modes, it is projective. The subject matter used in the procedure serves as a lens of projection, and the recorded material of elicited behavior is the screen with the picture projected on it." (14, p. 7.) This is very close to the meaning which Bell (1) suggests. He points out that the term stems from a Latin root meaning "to cast forward" and calls attention to the fact that the subject thrusts out his personality where it may be inspected.

THE PROJECTIVE APPROACH

If projection is conceived in the fashion just stated it carries certain implications, of which the most important may be referred to as the projective hypothesis. In Chapter 6 this hypothesis was briefly examined, and it was argued that all tests may be conceived projectively. It is now necessary to reëxamine this point of view. Another formulation by Rapaport may serve as a reminder. He writes, "All behavior manifestations of the human being, including the least and the most significant, are revealing and expressive of his personality, by which we mean that individual principle of which he is the carrier." (12, pp. 213–214.)

The projective approach embraces techniques which permit the individual to reveal aspects of his personality by the organization of stimulus material, into which he projects the meaning that it has for him. Since idiosyncratic and spontaneous responses are sought, no external criterion of what is right and wrong is imposed. In applying the projective hypothesis it is not the correctness or incorrectness of the performance but the style of expression which is diagnostically revealing. Since the stimuli are such that the subject does not know what is expected of him, by his spontaneous way of handling them he reveals his method of organizing experiences. The manner in which he interprets, constructs, or distorts the stimulus to which he is exposed makes it possible for the astute clinician to trace significant aspects of personality functioning. In other words, in the course of structuring the material the patient reveals his structuring principles, which are, it is hypothesized, the principles of his personality. In topological psychology the concepts of psychological fields and ego boundaries and the reactions between the two may be considered the theoretical soil from which springs the clinical concept of structuring.

THE MATERIALS UTILIZED IN
PROJECTIVE TECHNIQUES

The materials generally most suitable for application of the projective hypothesis are those which impart relatively unclear or equivocal meaning, thus permitting the patient to interpret or structure them himself. Structured tests of the sort discussed earlier emphasize material that is relatively clear, fixed, and unequivocal in meaning.

Because the situation is structured by the individual and his own meaning is imposed thereon, the material itself becomes secondary. Nevertheless, the materials cannot be ignored, as they do to some degree set the stage and establish boundaries within which he is free to move but beyond which he is not to go. For example, sentence completion forms may vary widely in the freedom of response permitted. Less structured statements, reaching the epitome in "I . . . ," or statements designed to touch upon some particular area may be chosen. For example, in some research (3) with aged persons the following representative items are included which purport to mirror if possible the rigidity which is so characteristic of the aged:

When I face a new situation . . .

A person has a right to be stubborn when . . .

Before making a decision I . . .

Changing my routine often . . .

Once I have started something . . .

The same principle applies to the instructions given the patient, as they also impart a certain degree of structuralization and thereby impose certain limitations. Relatively more or less structured directions may be used with the same materials. "Draw something" permits more freedom of expression than "draw a man." Allowing a child to choose from among toys and to play with them or not at will is less structured than setting up a family of dolls with one labeled father, another mother, another little sister, and still another the child himself.

Unstructured materials are a ready soil for the emergence of projective phenomena, but other materials may be and are utilized. To the extent that the patient gives other than traditional or conventional responses in any setting he demonstrates the individuality which is the necessary prerequisite for personality appraisal under the projective hypothesis. In the unstilted, nonconventional reactions which any psychological testing material (or any other sort of situation even to the level of casual conversation) may elicit is to be found the sort of information which makes possible the application of the projective hypothesis. The case history, the conventional intelligence test, and many other tools of diagnosis may be said to exemplify the projective hypothesis in the sense that they are taken on the assumption that from them the patient's personality functioning may be inferred. As Frank (6) points out, almost any thing or any experience may be used provided the examiner searches for the idiomatic mode of responding. Thus by unstandardized procedures projective reflections of the personality may be elicited, but by no means has a projective technique been established. Certain specific procedures offer a more abundant yield because of their relatively more unstructured character; these rather few procedures are commonly called projective techniques. In clinical practice, then, certain materials and approaches have proved more revealing of personality functioning than others, and it is to these that the term "projective techniques" has been applied.

Even among the projective techniques proper a classification may be made as to the degree of structuralization. Such a conception is preferred to one which would make the distinction more of a dichotomy and seem to connote terminal points. For example, Hutt (8) speaks of "partially structured" and "unstructured" personality techniques. In the subsequent discussion the Thematic Apperception Test and the Rosenzweig Picture-Frustration Study would be classified as less unstructured. In these measures the stimulus material to some degree limits the situation by being somewhat conventionalized, but still the patient may respond in a relatively free or idiosyncratic way. For example, in the Thematic Apperception Test there are pictures of events and persons only slightly blurred as to outline or detail. The subject works within a frame of reference which limits the potentially possible responses. Classified as more unstructured is the Rorschach technique. In this the responses are not so easily channeled by the demands of convention. The stimulus, vague and diffuse, lacks intrinsic meaning and acquires it only after the subject breathes meaning into it. Projective techniques, then, are means of investigating personality characterized by more or less free responses to more or less unstructured stimuli.

The range of projective techniques (in the sense of "especially appropriate" devices) is very wide. Borrowing from Sargent (18) her ways of classifying them, we see that they vary as to the nature of the *materials* (ink blots, pictures, words, stories, art media, dramatic play); *the functional uses to which put* (imposition of structure, catharsis, interpretation of meaning, etc.); *the degrees of control* (for example, from unstructured clay to specific toys); *the degrees of interpretative fixity* (from empiricism to elaborate conceptualizations); and the purposes (diagnosis, therapy, and research).

THE SIMILARITIES AND DIFFERENCES BETWEEN PROJECTIVE AND NONPROJECTIVE TECHNIQUES

It has been previously stated that with projective techniques inferences about the patient's personality functioning are drawn most readily from relatively unstructured material, while with nonprojective techniques such inferences are made from structured material. This distinction on closer examination tends to become blurred; nevertheless it is still one of the bases for the clearest differentiation of the two approaches. The distinction, moreover, ignores the fact that the approach of the patient to the material is more important than what is presumed to be the nature of the material itself.

For many years the clinician has been struggling with the problem of the appropriate level at which to interpret the projective responses of his patients. In a TAT story to card 1 (boy with violin), for example, a patient responds with an account stressing ascent of the boy to fame and fortune. The clinician is faced with a problem: Does this story merely represent what the patient thinks is expected of him, the conventional and socially approved solution? In actuality, he may not believe this would be the outcome at all. Again, this solution may express his own consciously experienced and observable way of meeting obstacles. Lastly, it may represent unconscious trends in which this solution is contradicted by his own conscious way of formulating it. Obviously the significance attached to the story clinically would vary considerably according to which of these levels (or combination of levels) is being demonstrated at the moment. It remained for Rosenzweig (17) to think through systematically and put in sharper focus this common clinical dilemma, although he offers no ready-made solution for the practicing clinician.

The three levels of personality appraisal he posits are the subjective (I), the objective (II), and the projective (III), which are described in Table 25. Although the levels are stated in terms of all varieties of personality appraisal, not merely so-called projective techniques, emphasis is properly placed upon the present subject of discussion. Projective techniques were developed as a means of

TABLE 25. Levels of Response in Typical Methods of Personality Appraisal[2]

Level	Psychodiagnostic Methods	Behavior Elicited in Test Situation	Mode of Prediction
I	*Subjective:* the subject takes himself as the object of observation and communicates the results to the observer. (E.g., inventory or questionnaire, opinion or attitude poll, autobiography.)	*Opinion:* the subject gives self-critical or censored responses in keeping with his perception of himself or with his ideas of what is proper and socially acceptable. The data obtained are *adaptive* responses to questions.	*Extrapolation:* from present performance to past or future behavior in other situations where the subject is asked his opinion of himself.
II	*Objective:* the examiner takes the subject as the object of observation, either in an everyday situation or as he performs an assigned task, the results of which are communicated to the examiner. (E.g., time-sampling observations, miniature life situations, some rating scales, intelligence or aptitude tests.)	*Overt:* the subject functions as he observably would in everyday life. The data are *adaptive* reactions of the subject to actual life situations or to tests that represent a standardized reproduction of such situations.	*Extrapolation:* to overt behavior in similar externally defined situations.
III	*Projective:* both subject and examiner "look the other way" at some ego-neutral object. The subject performs an assigned task which does not involve self-observation and shares the results with the examiner. (E.g., Rorschach, TAT, word association, play technique, etc.)	*Implicit:* the subject responds impersonally in terms of unconscious or unexpressed attitudes, feelings, or thoughts. The data are the *autistic* reactions of the subject rather than his reality-oriented behavior.	*Interpretation:* from manifest content to underlying factors in the personality.

[2] The present chart is a revision by Rosenzweig of the one originally published by him (17) and is quoted in its present form with his permission.

investigating at level III, but this in practice is by no means exclusively the case. "Projective" material may lead to responses properly categorized as objective and subjective. Detailed examination will be forgone until specific projective techniques are examined in later chapters.

Although thus far differences between projective and nonprojective techniques have been stressed, Levinson (9), for one, insists that the similarities between "ability" tests (intelligence, aptitudes, etc.) and projective techniques are at least as important as their differences. He holds that they are methodologically similar in that there is a standardized testing situation identical for all subjects. In the behavior sample that is a test situation individual differences characterize the subject. If these differences in behavior are to be intelligible they must be attributed to differences in the individual's make-up. This aspect of the situation is identical whether the stimulus consists of an ability or a projective test. A problem to be worked out by the subjects is presented which was selected so as to produce a maximum of individual differences among the subjects in the behavioral functions under investigation. Tests of both kinds are standardized under physical conditions which make the examining situation as comfortable and as free from distraction as possible. There is likewise a uniformity in the relation between clinician and subject. Although friendly and encouraging the clinician is neutral in all ways that would directly affect the behavior function or functions under consideration. Individual differences in such dimensions must not be attributable to the differential behavior of the clinician. In addition, the patient's relation to the task is standardized on an optimal level of interest and effort. Finally, the patient in both types of tests is not restricted in expression of test-relevant behavior but instead is allowed free expression in these variables.

Levinson (9) also discusses the two kinds of tests in terms of selectivity of cues. All kinds of tests are such that only certain dimensions of behavior are selected for measurement and inference. To be sure, more often than not, ability tests are ordered to a dimension or dichotomy of correctness—incorrectness, whereas projective instruments tend to be concerned with other types of behavior crudely subsumed for present purposes under the rubric of personality factors.

If, instead of considering ability tests as distinguished from projective techniques, as did Levinson, one broadens the discussion to contrast projective and all kinds of nonprojective tests, whether of ability or not, it is immediately apparent that many nonprojective tests measuring *not* ability but other psychological factors do not measure correctness. Rapaport discusses this matter, indicating that ". . . Nonprojective tests do not *all* ask for statements concerning which verifiability, social agreement, and logical necessity are all present." (13, p. 644.) He illustrates this with an item from a personality questionnaire that inquires as to feelings of tiredness, and points out that the verifiability of an answer to such a question is of quite a different order from that on questions of common knowledge. It would appear that this distinction when applied to many nonprojective tests would not hold and that no fundamental difference between the two approaches can hinge upon "correctness" of response as the hallmark of the nonprojective test.

A distinction sometimes made between structured and unstructured tests which appears to have little point refers to interpretation. It is sometimes said that structured tests are objective, and the interpretation of the clinician or other test administrator plays a very small part or, according to some, has no role at all. They would contrast this with projective tests, which in their estimation require the clinician to make interpretations to such an extent as to demand almost entirely an artistic or intuitive process. Here, it is seemingly lost sight of that interpretation of some sort and at some level is necessary with any test. Results must be interpreted—no test performs this service of itself. What appears to be different in projective devices is the relatively greater breadth within which interpretations are made and the temporal point at which these occur. Munroe puts the matter cogently:

It is worthwhile to point out that interpretation of the results of standardized tests in the individual case also depends upon the judgment of the psychologist—except in so far as they are delivered over to the lay administrator for judgment. Everyone knows that all of the standardized tests, even intelligence tests, may be simply erroneous in some cases and that the significance of an accurate score on a particular trait must be seen in relation to scores on other traits and background data. It seems proper to emphasize that the projective method attempts to apply *within the confines of the, test situation* a process of judgment fully accepted in clinical psychology generally. The novelty seems really to lie more in the point at which judgment is introduced rather than in the introduction of judgment. (11, p. 11.)

Frank (6) (22) would contrast the psychometric with the projective approach on the basis of conformity to group norms. He feels that the standardized test employs group norms to gauge an individual's adherence to or deviation from the standard or conventional performance. On the other hand, the projective method is concerned with the idiomatic, unique expression of the individual as manifested in relation to his other thoughts, feelings, and actions and thus does not need norms.

His approach stresses the fact that "standardized," i.e., structured, tests do not tell us as much about the individual personality as do the projective techniques, but it is nonetheless possible to object to such a distinction on two grounds. First, there is available some normative material on projective instruments that is used in clinical practice, e.g., popular trends and the number of responses of various populations on the Rorschach, or cataloguing of themes on the TAT. Second, and more important, intra-individual comparisons may be made from the results of structured tests, as materials presented about each of the tests in earlier chapters would appear to testify.

These two points require additional elaboration, but the latter will not be discussed further until the next section of the chapter. Concerning the former issue, Rosenzweig (16) has offered in the context of a discussion of the TAT an account of the problem of norms in projective methodology. One crucial point that he makes concerns the need for norms; he points out that recognizing unique responses requires prior knowledge of what is common.

Neglect of this need to know similarity in order to appreciate differences sometimes leads to difficulties. Consider, for example, the clinician's preoccupation with patient populations. Sometimes he is startled to discover how "pathologically" laden are the projective responses of normal individuals. In part, at least, this may be due to his lack of norms. The availability of norms in this and other situations aids the clinician. The fact that norms currently available for use with projective techniques are limited and partial is not a source of virtue unique to the projective approach, as Frank would have it, but rather a challenge to the psychologist to fill these gaps as thoroughly and as thoughtfully as possible. To be sure, it is evident that the nature of these norms will be somewhat different from that of norms for other kinds of tests, but a norm's a norm for all that.

It might appear that the intent of this discussion has been to demonstrate that there is no essential difference between projective and nonprojective testing. Such is not the case, since the original distinction that projective tests deal with relatively unstructured material and nonprojective tests deal with relatively structured material still holds. More important than this, the projective hypothesis, as previously described, makes for essential differences. Or, to combine both material and process, it might be said that in the projective test the patient organizes the unstructured material and in the process casts light upon his personality structure, whereas in the nonprojective test the material is already organized to a great extent and a comparison of his responses with those of others is essential in order to cast light upon his personality.

THE ADVANTAGES OF THE PROJECTIVE APPROACH

In now turning to the advantages of the projective approach there is, in one sense, a continuation of the previous discussion of differences between projective and nonprojective techniques, since the advantages also serve to distinguish between the two approaches. The advantages of the projective approach involve functions which the nonprojective cannot serve as readily or completely.

The variety and richness of the material which the projective approach provides, while fascinating to the clinician, irritate the experimentalist. What precisely are the presumed advantages of the projective approach? White (21) would find in the interpretation of such imaginative productions (as he called them) at least a partial answer to problems not open, or at least not as readily open, to investigation by other personality test methods such as the questionnaire. In sketching the territory not thus open he writes:

In the first place there are the things that a person knows about himself but will not tell. Here belong the secret wishes and daydreams, the weaknesses and humiliations, very likely also the triumphs and deepest joys, the disclosure of which would embarrass the subject beyond bearing. Even a patient who understands that his cure depends on telling everything may take several months to overcome his repugnance at mentioning certain topics of which he is fully aware. In the second place there are the things that a person cannot tell about himself because they are repressed: the imaginings and strivings which are inaccessible because their recognition would give rise to unbearable anxiety. Finally there are the things that a person cannot tell about himself because they work so silently and diffusely as to escape his notice and afford him no ground for comparison with others. In this zone belong his unrealized emotional dependencies, his habitual expectations as to how his fellows will treat him, his fundamental courage or despair, his deeply ingrained patterns of defense, and beyond these the perceptual preferences, intellectual peculiarities, and mood climates which lie at the boundary where personality shades off into temperament. (21, p. 214.)

How do projective techniques meet these problems? Even a cursory inspection of projective findings reveals that often the subject is unaware or but dimly cognizant of the significance of what he is telling and thus opens the way to revelation of material such as that characterized by White. The fact that the patient is not aware (or only dimly aware) of the significance of his responses allows the clinician to deal with something other than conscious, guarded, or superficial responses. Of course, projective devices differ in the degree to which patients are consciously aware of the source of the material they are using. For example, in the Thematic Apperception Test the subject may use material that will be freely acknowledged to come from his own personal experience. In any case, it is impossible for him to guess the intricacies of the scoring even if some level of sophistication about the nature of the scoring has been reached.

Projective devices are relatively immune to attempts to conceal or modify personality facets under scrutiny. In effect, this is saying that the tests are behavioral rather than a means of securing the opinions of the patient. In addition, since the patient is not aware of the purposes of the techniques, he consequently does not know how to dissimulate. Deliberate attempts to mislead or misconceptions on the part of the patient are thus held to a minimum.

Not only does he not understand the significance of the material, but the very nature of the material and task—judging a picture, making up a story, or modeling clay, to name but a few—diverts attention from the self. Questions of a personal nature are not asked; instead material of an apparently innocuous character not requiring ego-defensive responses is placed before him. The last consideration which lends credence to the advantages of the projective devices as revelatory of more than a superficial view of personality is their ability to tap unconscious motivational factors. As Sargent puts it:

In any direct question situation, even the cooperative subject who has no intent to falsify results can tell only what he knows about himself. He can provide a self-portrait only as it appears to him. Whether or not one subscribes to the Freudian theory of the unconscious, it is a generally accepted fact that we are inclined to deny many of our true motives and to rationalize impulses in order to make our behavior more socially and personally acceptable. The material brought forth by means of projective methods goes beyond these superficial defenses. For example, a child who has been taught to reply dutifully that he loves his mother, may give that answer to a direct question, yet in drawing, story telling, or manipulation of play materials he will consistently attack, mutilate, or destroy mother figures. The revealing nature of such observations has been too frequently confirmed by subsequent clinical study to leave, in the mind of the practical clinician, much doubt of its significance, in spite of the fact that crucial experiments have not yet been devised to demonstrate the facts in a manner entirely satisfactory from the standpoint of exact science. (19, p. 420.)

Even more important, however, than the advantages so far attributed to the projective approach is the fruitfulness in regard to intra-individual comparison. These devices purport to allow interpretation of a total personality picture—not simply isolated traits and attitudes but an interrelated structured personality in which an intra-individual rather than an inter-individual study is made. On the clinical scene the individual is the focus of attention, and such techniques as these allow an appraisal of the individual as an individual. As Frank (6) points out, clinical medicine has long known it is the magnitude of one function or organ in relation to other functions or organs which is important for understanding a total organism.

Projective techniques are a means of appraising the individual personality as a unitary configuration; specific responses are interpreted in the light of this configuration. It is axiomatic in the clinical interpretation of the behavior sample secured by use of a projective technique that the specimen so secured must be interpreted in all of its uniqueness and complexity. Isolated sub-observations must be related to the total picture. One response must be compared with others, perhaps taking on a new and different meaning because of this comparison. Within the behavior constellation derived from a projective technique a specific item may have a variety of meanings according to the way it is related to the total pattern. This may be contrasted with a more atomistic approach emphasizing specific units (traits, etc.) which may be considered independent of the pattern in which they arise. This is not to say that the behavior trends isolated by means of projective techniques are not related to one another additively, multiplicatively, or otherwise. In fact, it is characteristic of much of the research being performed with projective devices that subscores, ratios, and the like are utilized in order to discriminate among various groups. But in the *clinical situation* many individuals who use such atomistic approach in research insist upon a global view. Others would use this latter approach both in research and in clinical practice.

THE DIFFICULTIES IN THE PROJECTIVE APPROACH

The projective approach is a bold attempt to deal with very complex, unconsciously motivated, intricately intertwined facets of personality functioning. Instead of dealing with more easily accessible, overt, and conscious material already brought within the fold of scientific respectability, workers with projective material have struck out into uncharted territory with admittedly imperfect instruments and fragmentary theoretical navigation for their course.

It is hardly surprising that projective techniques have not lacked critics. Many criticisms when aimed at specific studies and particular interpretations would appear to be well justified, e.g., Cattell (4), Cronbach (5), Macfarlane (23). However, it must be noted that it is not in this field alone that poorly controlled studies and doctrinaire interpretations have been offered. In the growth of a young field certain excesses are perhaps inevitable. Many crudities will soon be forgotten and with the growth of psychology as a science, and of clinical psychology both as an aspect of this science and as a clinical art, there will be both a greater richness of findings and a closer rapprochement with the findings from other branches of psychological science. Moreover, it must be noted in fairness to clinical practice today that, barring some form of mass delusion almost universal among clinicians using projective devices, they hold a promise of much greater validity than it has been possible to demonstrate by the usual canons of scientific verification. The practicing clinician makes predictions and draws inferences which appear to enrich the clinical case study and to be accepted by his colleagues. But herein lies a paradox—what is enrichment in a clinical study becomes contamination of data in research. That is to say, in the clinical setting there is a healthy interchange of findings from psychological tests to other clinical data and back again. The psychiatrist's findings are often known to the psychologist when he interprets the test results; at the same time the psychiatrist often takes an inchoate idea from fragmentary psychological data and fortifies it with other clinical material. In such a way the findings of all the clinical team become so intermingled and amalgamated that there is a more or less unified picture of the patient, the exact contributions to which all clinicians have shared in varying and unknown ways. This, however, is an anathema in research, in which we are interested in unraveling the tangled skeins and precisely identifying the aspects making up the tapestry of the personality. The distinctive contributions of projective techniques to this picture are unfortunately obscured because they become lost by the very process of integration with other clinical findings.

Thurstone (20) points out that there are two reasons for appraising projective performance. On the one hand, a projective test may be used to elicit indirectly biographical material of clinical interest which may be emotionally blocked. In making a second, more important, point he goes on to say:

While this type of inquiry about a subject may be useful for some immediate purpose, we must remember that no amount of anecdotal or biographical detail will ever become science until someone organizes the individualistic material into some categories of fruitful classification so as to reveal the underlying parameters of the dynamical system that constitute a personality. This is the second purpose for which a projective test may be given. It should reveal, not only the biographical detail that is of interest in a particular case, but it should also reveal the subject as to the dynamical characteristics that describe his motivations and values. Even more fundamentally, it should reveal the style of his personality so that his behavior becomes at least in some sense predictable as to the style of response that he is likely to give to different types of life situations. But this cannot be accomplished as long as we stay within the narrow confines of responses to the ink blots. These must be interpreted in terms of larger classes and types of response that transcend the ink blots. If such interpretations can be made in a dependable way, then they should be described in every textbook in psychology. The student reader should be shown the experimental evidence and the psychological theorizing by which the color shock, the movement responses, the animal responses, the responses to the white spaces, become significant in the larger setting of psychological interpretation. (20, p. 473.)

In some measure the charge leveled at the Rorschach is true, since for a variety of reasons most Rorschach specialists have not been concerned with this larger issue. With other projective techniques this stricture is not as pertinent. Murray and his co-workers, and Rosenzweig and his associates have worked respectively with the TAT and the Picture-Frustration Study using the techniques merely as media through which they investigated personality functioning. Though some psychologists would not accept such attempts as scientifically valid, they are nevertheless prompted by the desire identical with that of Thurstone to reveal the "style of personality."

Following from the pioneering character of diagnostic efforts with projective devices are certain dangers. One of these is their great degree of dependence upon the insight, including self-insight, of the clinician. Goodenough puts this very well. She writes:

> One of the most curious features of much of the work in the field of projective methods is the extent to which the workers have been blind to the projection of their own personality characteristics and their own cherished wishes and beliefs upon their interpretations of the behavior of their subjects. *For projection is a tool that cuts both ways.* If it is true that the person under observation projects his own inner feelings and attitudes upon the situation to which he responds, it is equally true that the person who observes him does the same. Not only in his interpretations of the child's behavior, but in his arrangement of the situation and in the suggestions made in the course of the experiment can the examiner's bias be noted. When the only toy furniture provided in an experiment involving doll play consists of a bed, a toilet, and an armchair, it is not surprising to find that much of the play involves the use of the first two. When children are repeatedly told that they may break the toys if they wish, not much of importance can be assumed if they act upon the suggestion. (7, p. 128.)

The qualitative element in the interpretation of data from projective techniques has often been a source of criticism and justly so, since elimination of it is especially difficult in projective methods. What does not generally seem to be appreciated by critics of such approaches is that this reliance on qualitative features is not a matter of choice but is necessitated by the complexity of the process. Ordering the data to any sort of scale or scoring system is an enormously complicated procedure insidiously fraught with the very pitfalls the projective approach seeks to avoid—an oversimplified, segmented appraisal of the human personality.

The question of the relative absence of norms looms large as a difficulty in the projective approach, as was indicated earlier. Norms in the sense of some conception of what is common and what is unique in projective material are always held by the clinician. The question is not whether norms shall or shall not be used, but rather the extent to which these norms shall be objectified through being recorded in a fashion that makes public inspection possible. The position taken here is that anything making for greater precision should be utilized, and therefore recorded norms should be encouraged. This is not tantamount to rejection of subjective norms. In the present state of knowledge about the projective tests one must perforce use subjective norms to a considerable extent. It may be that there will always be a need for an intuitive element, in which an act of synthesis of the diagnostic material is aided by the use of subjective norms along with other personal elements of the personality and experience of the clinician. Nevertheless, to the extent that relevant standardized norms can be developed the position is taken that they should be used, thereby permitting a symbiotic relationship among clinicians whose data help to develop them.

The various criticisms of projective techniques reach sharpest focus when the question of validity is considered. A current controversy rages between the two more or less opposing points of view. There are those who would insist that projective devices be examined with and pass muster by the same techniques one would apply with any other test. Other psychologists would argue just as vehemently that rules of evaluation applicable to structured devices cannot be applied, and when applied merely demonstrate ignorance of the essential nature of projective findings, which demands intra-individual comparison. Indeed, it would appear that they take a perverse pride in the artistic element of such devices as rising above even the need for such evaluation.

It is the conviction of a more temperate group who are in the uncomfortable position of being in the middle that ultimately the truth will be found somewhere in between. With one side they would agree that there is a validity independent of statistical manipulation which has been demonstrated in clinical practice. With the other they would insist with equal vigor that projective devices meet the essential tenets of scientific verification. So far as statistical techniques are concerned they would argue that those now in use are inadequate and inappropriate in many instances.

As Rosenzweig puts it:

The challenge arises in connection with the far more intricate problem of intra-individual consistency from the standpoint of which the subject becomes to some extent his own standard of reference and the field of statistical operations is changed from a population of many individuals to a population of many responses within the same individual. The principle here involved is well exemplified in the card-by-card analysis demanded in any adequate Rorschach interpretation. It is maximally clear in the interpretive approach required in the Thematic Apperception Test. The assumption seems reasonable that methods will eventually be devised for solving the statistical problems here involved. It is, at the same time, not unlikely that even after such mathematical tools have been successfully applied, the skill of the individual examiner will always play an important part in clinical practice and make special demands upon his training and experience. (15, p. 459.)

With this quotation the writer is in hearty agreement. Eventually there will be a reconciliation of what essentially is a difference of degree, not a difference in kind. It must be emphasized that whereas projective techniques are at an early developmental stage, appropriate statistical devices are equally primitive for some standardization problems and as yet unborn for others. This, of course, is no excuse for not applying whatever appropriate techniques exist today.

In critically analyzing projective methodology, Macfarlane examines the various possible methods of validation, concluding that ordinary statistical devices used in other types of measurement are inadequate. She reviews the existing methods of validation, viewing each critically in terms of its applicability to the present problem. Her analysis is so cogent as to be worth quoting extensively:

1. *Correlation with outside criteria* is the most common method of validation. What can our outside criteria be, since it is the organizational processes of *individuals* which we are attempting to assess? Obviously, comparisons of the projective productions of many individuals via the same technique give us orienting and normative material and point to the frequencies of certain patterns from which some generality of statement is possible. Such normative material makes possible the comparison of an individual's picture with that of a similar age or sociological group, but it does not give us a picture of validity for individual dynamics. For example, a verbalized fantasy of a given individual may, on a manifest level, be similar to those of his group and yet have for him a highly special and idiosyncratic meaning.

Comparisons of the projective materials from the same individual via an array of "projective" techniques furnish a check for consistencies and disagreements. If consistencies seem absent, those with systematized concepts may be able validly with their conceptual tools to subsume under one embracing concept, material which on the surface looks incongruent. But, on the other hand, by interpretive classification they may produce a pseudo and non-valid congruence merely because they interpretively stick everything into a few categories. The congruencies they report may be due to the stability of their concepts and not to the congruencies of the material. Internal consistency alone docs not establish scientific validity, for what has more internal consistency than a paranoid's delusional system?

2. Another approach toward validation lies in the comparison of projective material with life history material. This is an essential check but it also offers difficulties, as life histories, too, must be organized according to concepts, and if the concepts used are the same, the congruencies again may be an artifact of simplicity and stability of concepts rather than consistency of the material. Or, the material from each source may, in point of fact, actually be highly congruent. How to sift pseudo congruencies from valid congruencies is the problem to be tackled. Let us look at a frequently encountered situation. A 10 year old boy on the overt level is reported by parents, teachers, clinic interviewers, and peers to be a very docile, well-mannered conformist, yet consistently discloses via all sort of projective tools, a fantasy full of brutal action. Can either the projective material or the overt material be ignored because they do not agree? Is the projective material to be considered invalid because it is in violent opposition to the child's persistent overt behavior? Obviously not! It is equally obvious, too, that overt behavior cannot be ignored because it is at variance with fantasy production. For it is by taking account of both aspects—overt behavior and fantasy—that we will understand these interlocking patterns we call dynamics. It is clear that a simple correlation between overt behavior and fantasy material is a tool completely inadequate to show the important organizational patterns involved in such combinations of explicit and implicit behavior. It may even mask dynamics discerned by other approaches. For a docile, well-mannered child may have fantasy (1) that shows a docile hero who receives kudos for docility; (2) fantasy that is neutral in this conformity aspect; (3) fantasy where the hero is belligerent and hostile and escapes unpunished; or (4) is caught and punished.

3. Another attack at validation is the search for through-time consistencies. Especially important is this in the study of pre-adult personality where personality patterns are less firmly entrenched. Longitudinal studies lend themselves to this approach to validation, since trends over time may be inspected without the distortion involved in retrospective reconstruction.

4. Collateral experimental approaches, too, should clarify the meanings of certain aspects of the protocols. Time precludes further discussion of this approach.

5. In the last analysis, the criterion *sine qua non* of validation is the degree of success in prediction. It is a criterion which in this complex

and difficult field of personality research the writer would hazard is the only one which will settle the arguments of the productivity of the various conceptual schools with their varying techniques of approach, and throw into relief, at least in studies where long through-time records are available, the significant tools of validation. This is the task for the future. The task for the present is to have many skilled but diversely conceptualizing clinicians and experimentally and statistically trained scientists attack jointly this complex and promising field.

The writer's opinion is that the utilization of the interpretive and predictive judgments of widely experienced clinicians later checked for predictive success, will offer at this stage the most productive leads. If an experienced clinician is able to predict with considerable success, then the data on which he bases his correct intuitive predictions can be inspected and validly weighted configurations can be established, quantified, and made available to less experienced people. Also, his wrong and partially right predictions in conjunction with the correct ones can serve for finer and more differentiating criteria. (23, pp. 283–285.)[3]

These as yet unsolved problems of validity are much in the forefront of thinking of at least some clinicians today. In a recent review of statistical techniques in present-day psychodiagnostics, Mensh (10) demonstrates both that such problems pervade all phases of clinical diagnostic work, projective and nonprojective alike, and that serious attention is being given to these issues by that relatively small but increasing body of professional personnel capable of both clinical acumen and statistical sophistication.

Closely enough related to the problem of validity to be considered briefly at this time is the question of the reliability of projective devices. Sargent summarizes in short compass some of the difficulties that face the psychologist in regard to this aspect of a projective technique. Her statement is as follows:

Reliability cannot satisfactorily be established on either the test-retest or split-half basis, due to the fact that some features of the tests are sensitive to actual personality changes which may take place from test to test, and because projective stimuli are not constant in the material evoked throughout a series. Reliability of both scoring and interpretation can, however, be checked by agreement between different judges. This is a precaution which ought to be taken against the tendency of interpreters to use the subject's protocol as a field for their own projections. At present some of these steps have been taken, but more systematic research on more subjects is essential to bring order in to a field

───────────
[3] Reprinted from "Problems of Validation Inherent in Projective Methods" by J. W. Macfarlane, by permission of the *American Journal of Orthopsychiatry.* Copyright 1942 by the American Orthopsychiatric Association.

in which the quality of experimental study as regards precision and control is decidedly uneven. (19, pp. 435–436.)

No one would disagree that for valid and reliable application of the techniques considerable skill and experience are needed. These, it must be emphasized, comprise not mere rote learning of scoring systems but a wealth of clinical experience. In addition, sound grounding in personality theory, the knowledge of that other language that is statistics, the ruthless application of the law of parsimony, dependence upon whatever scientific evidence has emerged, and some sort of personal analysis so that one is trained to recognize private projections are further safeguards.

THE NECESSITY OF MULTIPLE PROJECTIVE APPROACHES

The nature of individual projective technique is such that a multiplicity of approaches rather than a single technique seems advisable when making a diagnostic appraisal of a patient. In part this arises from the fact that certain techniques stress one aspect, while others emphasize another. Foremost among the distinctions is that between those which stress content and those which stress formal aspects. This distinction will be amply illustrated in later chapters. Suffice it to say here that it is not only the content of the responses but also the manner and form in which the material is organized that occupies the attention of the clinician.

These techniques complement one another because they appeal to the patient in diverse ways and carry in their very composition elements provocative of different aspects of the personality. Moreover, since intra-individual consistency is one of the bases of interpretation, it follows that choice of several instruments makes possible the collection of a larger array of data, in turn bringing greater certainty to the interpretation.

From among the representative projective techniques two have been chosen for presentation in subsequent chapters: the Thematic Apperception Test and the Picture-Frustration Study. As in preceding chapters, the primary criterion of selection is their relevance to the work of the clinician. Each in its own way supplies unique material of diagnostic value. Thus they may be said to complement each other and in conjunction with each other and with the Rorschach supply the clinician with a repertory capable of bearing the burden of many clinical tasks.

BIBLIOGRAPHY

1. Bell, J. E., *Projective techniques; a dynamic approach to the study of the personality*, Longmans, Green and Company, 1948.
2. Bellak, L., The concept of projection: an experimental investigation and study of the concept, *Psychiatry*, 1944, 7:353–369.
3. Caldwell, B. M., and Watson, R. I., unpublished manuscript.
4. Cattell, R. B., Projection and the design of projective tests of personality, *Character & Pers.*, 1944, 12:177–194.
5. Cronbach, L. J., Statistical methods applied to Rorschach scores: a review, *Psychol. Bull.*, 1949, 46:393–429.
6. Frank, L. K., *Projective methods*, Charles C. Thomas, 1948.
7. Goodenough, F. L., The appraisal of child personality, *Psychol. Rev.*, 1949, 56:123–131.
8. Hutt, M. L., The use of projective methods of personality measurement in Army medical installations, *J. clin. Psychol.*, 1945, 1:134–140.
9. Levinson, D. J., A note on the similarities and differences between projective tests and ability tests, *Psychol. Rev.*, 1946, 53:189–194.
10. Mensh, I. N., Statistical techniques in present-day psychodiagnostics, *Psychol. Bull.*, 1950, 47:475–492.
11. Munroe, R. L., The use of projective methods in group testing, *J. consult. Psychol.*, 1948, 13:8–15.
12. Rapaport, D., Principles underlying projective techniques, *Character & Pers.*, 1942, 10:213–219.
13. Rapaport, D., Principles underlying non-projective tests of personality, *Ann. N.Y. Acad. Sci.*, 1946, 46:643–652.
14. Rapaport, D., Gill, M., and Schafer, R., *Diagnostic psychological testing*, Vol. II, Year Book Publishers, 1945.
15. Rosenzweig, S., Projective techniques: their progress in the application of psychodynamics, in Lowrey, L. G. (ed.), *Orthopsychiatry, 1923–1948: retrospect and prospect*, American Orthopsychiatric Association, 1948, pp. 456–469.
16. Rosenzweig, S., Apperceptive norms for the Thematic Apperception Test. I. The problem of norms in projective methods, *J. Personality*, 1949, 17:475–482.
17. Rosenzweig, S., Levels of behavior in psychodiagnosis with special reference to the Picture-Frustration Study, *Amer. J. Orthopsychiat.*, 1950, 20:63–72.
18. Sargent, H., Projective methods: their origins, theory, and application in personality research, *Psychol. Bull.*, 1945, 42:257–293.
19. Sargent, H., Projective methods, in Pennington, L. A., and Berg,

I. A., (eds.), *An introduction to clinical psychology*, The Ronald Press Company, 1948, pp. 416–439.

20. Thurstone, L. L., The Rorschach in psychological science, *J. abnorm. soc. Psychol.*, 1948, 43:471–475.
21. White, R. W., Interpretation of imaginative productions, in Hunt, J. McV. (ed.), *Personality and the behavior disorders*, The Ronald Press Company, 1944, pp. 214–251.

Supplementary articles in Watson, R. I. (ed.), *Readings in the clinical method in psychology*, Harper & Brothers, 1949:

22. Frank, L. K., Projective methods for the study of personality. Pp. 259–278. (Also in *J. Psychol.*, 1939, 8:389–413.)
23. Macfarlane, J. W., Problems of validation inherent in projective methods. Pp. 279–286. (Also in *Amer. J. Orthopsychiat.*, 1942, 12:405–410.)
24. Rosenzweig, S., Fantasy in personality and its study by test procedures. Pp. 287–313. (Also in *J. abnorm. soc. Psychol.*, 1942, 37:40–51.)

CHAPTER 15

The Rosenzweig Picture-Frustration Study

The Picture-Frustration (P-F) Study is a technique designed to assess reactions to stress situations. It is especially appropriate as the first projective technique to be examined both because of its purposefully limited scope, reaction to frustration, and also because of its objective scoring system, similar in some respects to that of a psychometric device. Since it gives scores on a variety of rationally, empirically, and clinically interrelated factors—item scores, profiles, patterns, and trends—it does not suffer from the limitations of a single summary score approach. It is clearly a projective device in the sense described in the previous chapter.

DESCRIPTION OF THE P-F MATERIAL

The form for adults (fourteen years and older) consists of an eight-page booklet of twenty-four cartoon-like drawings, each depicting a situation which might occur in any ordinary day. Both adult male and female figures are involved in the action, although facial expressions are deliberately omitted and only enough details supplied in figure and background to suggest the general situation. In each scene some type of frustration is assumed to have occurred, with one or more persons being the perpetrator and one unmistakably the victim. The frustration may assume the form either of physical loss or injury or else of an accusation or incrimination by the frustrating agent. The subject is asked to respond by writing the reply that he thinks the thwarted individual would probably give. Illustrative of the situations is No. 17, a man searching for his car keys while the woman with him comments disparagingly about his misplacing them; or No. 13, one man telling another that he cannot keep his appointment with him despite an agreement made the day before.

ADMINISTRATION[1]

The P-F may be taken either individually or in groups, with instructions for both types of administration the same although the procedure must vary slightly. The subject is told to work as quickly as possible and was instructed in an earlier version to avoid being humorous. This admonition has now been deleted from the general instructions, since its omission was found to have no influence on the results (18) and because humorous responses themselves may be fitted into the same conceptual scheme. After the general instructions have been read the clinician requests the subject (or subjects) to open the booklet while he reads aloud the caption for No. I above the character at the left. The subject is then requested to write in the blank caption box above the picture representing the frustrated individual the first reply that comes to him and to go through the twenty-three other situations in order in the same way. Total time is recorded by the clinician.

In group administration the test is terminated at this point, but with individuals a further crucial step is taken, namely, an inquiry. This consists of having the subject read aloud the responses he has written, while the clinician notes for future reference any qualitative clues, such as inflections or tone of voice which may help in scoring. Ambiguous responses are clarified by questioning. Misunderstandings of direction, themselves qualitatively significant, are noted and corrections permitted (the original response is not erased but crossed out).

Following Rosenzweig (15), it is possible to demonstrate rather clearly the subjective (I), objective (II), and projective (III) levels of response in the P-F Study. Depending on the level at which a subject is responding, the modes of prediction are, respectively, extrapolation to other deliberately adopted and self-critical attitudes,

---

[1] The description in this section is not inclusive. Reference to the three articles which serve as the manual (14) (17) (19) is essential.

extrapolation to similar behavior in situations, and interpretation from manifest to latent content. Although designed to tap primarily the third or projective level, the P-F Study items are such that the patient may identify at any one of these levels. Rosenzweig feels that the way the patient construes the instructions is very cogent and suggests that the usual inquiry be extended to include questions concerned directly with this. He writes:

> One may thus ask, "What was the basis on which you gave your responses as you went through the Study?" If this indefinite prod fails to elicit the desired information as to level, it may be appropriate to ask more directly, "Have you ever been in any of the situations shown in the pictures?" One might sometimes proceed even more pointedly to ask whether the subject was thinking of himself or not as he gave his responses to the various items. A frank admission that the Study was taken at Level I—"I thought you wanted me to put down what I would say"— leaves little room for interpretation at Level III though both I and II are still possible. Naïve surprise that the replies were supposed to have any self-reference would reflect an adherence to the instructions favoring interpretation at Levels II or III. Statements to the effect that the responses were framed to exemplify what a person *should* say in the pictured situations would rather definitely imply Level I. The subject's replies to the interrogation itself would, of course, also have to be interpreted since rationalization might figure prominently in the usual case; but it would seem wiser to ask one or two questions for what they may be worth than to forego altogether the limited advantages of an inquiry. (15, p. 70.)

RATIONALE

Before turning to the scoring of the P-F Study it is appropriate to examine the rationale on which the study is based. It was developed by Rosenzweig primarily out of a desire to explore certain aspects of frustration theory and secondarily out of his interest in projective methodology. It is a logical outgrowth of his earlier studies (9) (10) (11) (12) (13) (22) concerned with other instruments. His point of view concerning the rationale of the P-F Study has found acceptance by many clinical psychologists and is therefore appropriate to discuss as an aspect of clinical methodology.

As a consequence of earlier studies in experimental psychoanalysis, Rosenzweig became interested in the sequelae of frustration—the types of reaction to it and the direction which any engendered aggression might take. Theorizing from these basic axes he developed a rationale which takes into account various forms of response, describing them as follows: "Under *direction* are included extra-punitiveness—in which aggression is *turned out* upon the environment; intropunitiveness—in which it is *turned in* upon the subject himself; and impunitiveness—in which aggression is *turned off*, i.e., evaded in an attempt to gloss over the situation. Under *type of reaction* fall obstacle-dominance—in which the presence or the nature of the barrier occasioning the frustration is emphasized in the response; ego-defense—in which the protection of the ego predominates; and need-persistence—in which the solution of the frustrating problem stands out." (28, p. 168.) A more detailed statement is given in Table 26 (including the scoring symbols considered in the next section). Examination shows that the type of reaction and the direction of aggression are considered to be related within a given behavior incident, so that both are revealed simultaneously. Thus, the type of reaction may be ego-defensive and extrapunitive, or need-persistive and impunitive, and so on.

The situations depicted in the P-F Study are divided by Rosenzweig (14) into two kinds, ego-blocking and superego-blocking. The former include those in which some personal or impersonal obstacle thwarts the depicted major character in some fashion, whereas in the latter there is some charge or accusation against the depicted character by another person. An example of the former, or ego-blocking, is seen in the situation where a man is awakened at 2 A.M. by a wrong number on the telephone (No. 11), and a direct charge of being a liar (No. 10) is typical of the superego-blocking experience.

SCORING

In scoring, the manifest content is always considered, and "deep" interpretative scoring (such as indicating compensatory mechanisms) is not recommended, although qualitative notes may be made. At the present time some theoretical work is in progress (cf. 16) which bears on this issue.

It will now be worth while to give closer scrutiny to Table 26, which identifies the symbols corresponding to the scoring categories proposed by Rosenzweig. A single or combined score which incorporates both *type* and *direction* components of the response is given for each of the twenty-four items. For example, a response in which the subject directs the aggression against himself (intropuni-

TABLE 26. Scoring Components of the Picture-Frustration Study[2]

Type of Reaction	Direction of Aggression		
	Extrapunitive	*Intropunitive*	*Impunitive*
Need-Persistive	E: A solution for the frustrating situation is emphatically expected of someone else.	i: Amends are offered by the subject, usually from a sense of guilt, to solve the problem.	m: Expression is given to the hope that time or normally expected circumstances will bring about a solution of the problem; patience and conformity are characteristic.
Ego-Defensive	E: Blame, hostility, etc., are turned against some person or thing in the environment. E: In this variant of E the subject aggressively denies that he is responsible for some offense with which he is charged.	I: Blame, censure, etc., are directed by the subject upon himself. I: A variant of I in which the subject admits his guilt but denies any essential fault by referring to unavoidable circumstances.	M: Blame for the frustration is evaded altogether, the situation being regarded as unavoidable; in particular, the "frustrating," individual is absolved.
Obstacle-Dominant	E': The presence of the frustrating obstacle is insistently pointed out.	I': The frustrating obstacle is construed as not being frustrating or even as in some way beneficial; or, in some instances, the subject emphasizes the extent of his embarrassment at being involved in instigating another's frustration.	M': The obstacle in the frustrating situation is minimized almost to the point of denying its existence.

[2] Reprinted from *Psychodiagnosis* by S. Rosenzweig with K. L. Kogan (28), by permission of Grune & Stratton. Copyright 1949 by Grune & Stratton.

tive direction) and at the same time attempts to effect a solution of the difficulty (need-persistive type) is scored i. Some responses, however, will resist analysis into a single element and may instead require inclusion of two scoring categories, e.g., ego-defensive type with both extrapunitive and impunitive components. The frequencies for all categories are then calculated.

A "Revised Scoring Manual" (19) has been published, providing ample illustrations of responses falling in the various categories. The scored response samples were drawn verbatim from approximately 500 records obtained from heterogeneous groups of subjects. For example, twenty-eight responses are supplied for No. 1 (driver apologizing to a pedestrian for splashing mud on his clothing). The response, "That's all right, I'll get it cleaned easily enough," although lacking a word-for-word counterpart, will be seen to be so close to response 7 (b) that there is no doubt that it is scored M′ (impunitive, obstacle-dominant). Likewise the response, "I'll bet you are (sorry)!" is similar enough to response 2 (c) to be scored E (extrapunitive, ego-defensive). The samples also provide assistance on such a response as "I'm sure you are sorry," identifying it as unscorable because of inadequate inquiry. The reply is ambiguous, carrying as it does the germ of sarcasm (in which case it would be E) or sincere humility (M).

Valuable though the scoring samples may be, it is important that the clinician be competent to judge the response on the basis of his familiarity with the rationale. The availability of scoring samples does not imply that all responses are to be scored by consulting them. In fact, Rosenzweig and his collaborators (19) estimate that about 50 percent of the responses of normal adults will not be found in the samples. It is obvious that the responses may be scored quite independently of the samples on the basis of meanings attributed to them. The scoring samples provide a means of increasing scorer reliability, not a substitute for clinical understanding.

The reliability of the scoring of the Picture-Frustration Study has been investigated (2). A series of three successive projects was carried out, not only to assess consistency of scoring but also to disclose the situations causing difficulties in scoring in order to eliminate them. The first two of these studies formed the backlog upon which the "Revised Scoring Manual" was based. The third and last of these investigations used the manual and, therefore, would be most representative for present practice. With two independent scorers, 86 percent agreement emerged. No item had less than 75 percent agreement. These figures probably would have been higher if individual administration with inquiry instead of group administration had been followed.

As the responses are scored they are entered on a specially prepared record blank, from which it is possible to calculate the Group Conformity Rating, profiles, patterns, and trends. These will be taken up in turn.

The Group Conformity Rating (GCR) indicates the subject's agreement with the modal response for a given item. The scoring factor or factors for a particular situation which warrant inclusion as a criterion score were computed on the basis of the significance of the difference between the factor of highest frequency and the next highest in the normative group. A q value of .01 or better was used. A scoring factor thus selected was considered characteristic enough of the item to serve along with the others similarly differentiated for determining group conformity of a new subject.

To facilitate calculation of the GCR the criterion scores are printed on the blank. On the adult form the number of responses agreeing with criterion scores has a maximum of twelve (the number for which a clear-cut modal score has emerged) and is calculated as a percentage, i.e., nine responses agreeing with criterion scores would yield a GCR of 75 percent.

The sums of scores and percentages for the three directions of aggression and the three types of reaction are presented on the record sheet in a nine-part table. From these tabulations four patterns are obtained, the first three of which are based on the profile of factors and concern the relative frequency of directional responses regardless of type, the relative frequency of type responses regardless of direction, and the size of factors most frequently found regardless of either type or direction. The fourth pattern is concerned with the frequency of superego ($\underline{E}$ and $\underline{I}$) variants expressed as percentages.

Trends concern change in the relative balance of factors from the first to the second half of the test both in direction of aggression and in type of reaction. Computation of these trends is important in order to determine the effect on the subject of cumulative frustrations and also of his response to his own pattern of reactions.

NORMATIVE GROUPS

The most recent norms presented by Rosenzweig (17) were based on 460 normal adults almost equally divided between males and females ranging in age from twenty through twenty-nine. Although he would have preferred to use twenty through thirty-nine as the adult standard, there were not enough thirty to thirty-nine subjects available to make it possible. However, since the differences between the data for the decades twenty to twenty-nine and thirty to thirty-nine were statistically nonsignificant, the present norms may be applied in these older years. The norms are presented in three tables in terms of the means and standard deviations of (1) the six scoring categories (E, O-D, etc.) and GCR by percentage, (2) the nine major scoring factors (E', i, etc.) by frequency, and (3) the superego factors by percentage.

Norms in terms of medians and interquartile variability for 175 young adult men and women, mostly college students or graduates, were prepared by Bernard (1). Comparison of these by the writer with Rosenzweig's revised norms for scoring categories shows very small percentage differences, never more than four percentage points, despite the fact that one author used means and the other medians. Bernard also reports norms for the first and second halves of the test separately, facilitating the study of trends. Analysis shows the two halves to be rather well balanced so far as total E, I, and M elements are concerned. Lists of GCR items were also derived for total, male, and female subjects with some deviation from Rosenzweig's list. Other norms for college students and for prison inmates are provided by Fry (6).

RELIABILITY

Although Rosenzweig (14) states that partially complete data concerning reliability are at hand, such studies have not yet been reported. Bernard (1) fortunately does present some evidence using as subjects about 100 of the norm group previously mentioned. Matrix reliability coefficients based on elapsed time of from three to nine months, with most at four months, were obtained. The correlations among types of reaction and direction of aggression range from .30 to .77 with six above .50. As Bernard points out, the results compare favorably with the reliabilities of scoring categories of other projective tests but also they are low enough to suggest caution in attempting prediction based on the P-F matrix alone. Since this is precisely what Rosenzweig (14) also warns against, urging that all data be used, they appear to be in agreement.

Item reliability was also investigated by Bernard through determination of the percentage of cases in which the test-retest scoring of a particular item was identical, plus one-half times the percentage of cases in which retest showed addition or subtraction of a single element, e.g., M;E on the original with E on retest. The consistency values obtained in this fashion ranged from 79 to 51 with a modal value around 55. Since shifts in type only, such as E to E′, or direction only, e.g., E to M, were given no weight in determining consistency, the values he found may be regarded as minimum.

VALIDITY

Like certain other projective measures the Rosenzweig Picture-Frustration Study has proved itself useful diagnostically in the clinical market place, as the case reports given in the bibliography will attest. Nevertheless, as Rosenzweig (14) stated in 1945, much remains to be done concerning validity. In fact, very little directly related to this topic has yet appeared.[3] To be sure there is some evidence, such as Rosenzweig's comment (given without embellishment) that a correlation of .74 was found between independent ratings for extrapunitiveness derived from the TAT and from the P-F Study, and several studies to be mentioned in a moment.

In view of the avowed purpose of measuring reaction to frustration it is not surprising that attention has been paid to the relation of the P-F Study to experimentally induced frustration. It is in connection with this that Rosenzweig (16) sounds the warning that the definition of the induced frustration must be carefully examined for purity, relevance, and unequivocalness of the independent criterion and that the experience of the subjects when faced with a presumably frustrating situation must be carefully defined. Here it should be remembered that the total scores of the twenty-four situations are fixed in a sense and that introduction of a frustrating situation may increase the intensity of all responses but not neces-

---

[3] Several studies which have not yet appeared in print are to be reported in a monograph now in preparation by Rosenzweig.

sarily strengthen the tendency for one sort of response to occur as compared with another (5). A change of score in any one category necessarily means a change in some other category.

A study by Franklin and Brozek (4) is pertinent in connection with some of these cautions. As an aspect of a larger study of semi-starvation and rehabilitation, the P-F Study was administered at the end of twenty-four weeks of semistarvation and again after twelve weeks of rehabilitation. It was the authors' contention that severe frustration was induced by the hunger, the physical weakness, and the overall suffering. The day-to-day behavior of the subjects in the semistarvation group, as compared with controls, showed generalized emotional states such as anger and anxiety and more specific states such as hostility and feelings of inferiority. Nevertheless, no test category of the P-F Study was significantly different after twenty-four weeks of semistarvation as compared with the testing after twelve weeks of rehabilitation. The authors consider that the findings bring into question the validity of the measure. In this instance, however, Rosenzweig (16) questions the study on the basis of two of the points made earlier; namely, without examining what significance the subjects attached to the experience in terms of frustration, variation with the P-F scores could not be expected, and just what the nature of the frustration might be is questionable. Furthermore, it should also be noted that they did not administer the P-F Study before starvation; nor did they have a matched control group of subjects as far as concerns the P-F.

In the study of French (5) some attention was paid to this matter. He used false reports of examination grades as a means of inducing varying degrees of frustration, raising by two letter grades the earned grade of some students, lowering some by the same amount, and keeping still others unchanged. Four subgroups of twenty subjects each, matched for sex and impunitive score on the initial administration, formed the experimental populations. Group 1 and 2 were matched for grades as were groups 3 and 4, but group 2 had grades raised and group 3 had grades lowered. Immediately after returning the graded papers the P-F was readministered. Quoting from French's summary:

Application of analysis of covariance to the results in each of the 15 Rosenzweig scoring categories revealed that: (1) good students given low grades did not differ significantly in any response category from good students given correct grades; (2) as compared with poor students given high grades, the poor students given their correct grades showed significantly fewer Intropunitive Ego-Defensive responses; (3) good students differed from poor students as a group in showing more Intropunitive Need-Persistent and fewer Extrapunitive responses. The results are interpreted as lending support to the validity of the test, although the small size of the changes produced is stressed as possibly qualifying this interpretation. (5, pp. 114–115.)

Incidental to a study of minority-group prejudice (the results of which so far as the P-F were concerned were negative and need not be considered) the P-F Study was submitted to an experimental test by Lindzey (7). The P-F and four selected TAT cards were administered to twenty experimental subjects who later were subjected to severe social frustration in a social situation, apparently not at all connected with the earlier portion of the study (different experimenter, etc.). Immediately thereafter they took the measures again. The frustrating experience included going from ten to twelve hours without food, drinking water and being prevented from urinating, having a blood sample taken and being wounded in the process. These experiences were but preludes to the primary frustrating experience, which consisted of having each subject individually perform, along with a group of the experimenter's confederates, in a competitive situation in which it was manipulated for him to perform personally very poorly and also to be the cause for the entire group to miss a sizable monetary award. Lindzey says that this produced relatively strong feelings of frustration—which the present writer is not prepared to doubt. The P-F Study was scored in the usual fashion, and the TAT protocols were scored for extrapunitiveness and intropunitiveness by counting respectively the number of incidents in which the self-figure carried out aggressive acts against non-self-figures and the number of incidents of aggressive acts the self-figure carried out against himself. Shifts in P-F Study scores following the frustration experience showed that the extrapunitive score increased after frustration at the .05 level of confidence, and intropunitiveness decreased at the .20 level of confidence. Impunitiveness remained the same. Among the types of reaction, need persistence decreased at the .10 level of confidence, while ego defensiveness, obstacle dominance, and the Group Conformity Rating showed no change. These are changes that appear plausible on the surface and lend weight to the belief that the P-F possesses validity reflected in a frustrating experience. However, the P-F Study data failed to correlate with the TAT either in an absolute sense or when shifts only were considered.

An interesting attempt to use the P-F to measure ethnic and cultural differences was performed by McCary (8). Using over 600 northern and southern high school boys and girls both Negro and white, he studied the differences among the groups. The northern groups were much more overtly aggressive and far less passive in their reactions to frustration than was the southern group. All females as compared to all males was significantly more conforming. The whites were more passive than the Negroes. These and other subgroups comparisons suggest that in interpreting P-F results the ethnic and cultural group from which the person comes is of some significance.

RELATION TO OTHER MEASURES

The question of the relation of the various components of the Rosenzweig P-F Study to indices arising from other measures has as yet been hardly touched upon. One study so far carried out is that of Falls and Blake (3), who used as subjects twenty-five college undergraduate and graduate students in psychology of high IQ, scholastic aptitude, and achievement. They proceeded to correlate a variety of measures, such as scales of the Minnesota Multiphasic Personality Inventory and the Bernreuter Personality Inventory, with extrapunitiveness, intropunitiveness, impunitiveness, and GCR. Of the eighty-eight correlations it so happened that three are (barely) significant at the one percent level of confidence, and five more are significant at the 5 percent level of confidence. They then proceed to analyze these and other "almost significant" correlations for trends, concluding that the relationships are consistent in general with theoretical expectancy. Although this appears to be the case, the study can hardly be said to offer very much support for it. It is made suspect by the few subjects and their testwise sophistication, failure to investigate level of response with consequent variability of attitude from subject to subject, dependence on eight "significant" correlations out of eighty-eight (where four might be expected to achieve the same level of significance by chance if the variables were uncorrelated), and, above all, the possible irrelevance of the whole investigation. It must be reiterated that this is not meant to imply that the P-F Study does not bear significant relation to other measures, merely that the Falls and Blake study does not demonstrate it.

INTERPRETATION AND DIAGNOSTIC USAGE

Basic to the interpretation of the P-F Study is the assumption that the patient either consciously or unconsciously identifies with the frustrated individual and projects his own point of view in his replies. The various percentages calculated as described in the earlier section represent the probability of his employing these various ways of reacting. Since norms are provided, both intra-individual and inter-individual comparison is possible. The Group Conformity Rating offers an apt illustration of the latter, since it provides a comparison of the degree to which the patient's responses agree with expectancy and thus affords a basis for appraising social adjustment in the form of capacity for conformity with conventional behavior.

The significance of total E, I, and M percentages and patterns should be clear from the earlier discussion of their meaning. This is likewise true of O-D, E-D, and N-P categories, although it might be mentioned in passing that Rosenzweig (14) advances the hypothesis that the total E-D score represents strength or weakness of the ego (with elevated scores pointing to weakness), whereas N-P, if not too high, indicates adaptive capacity.

Analysis of trends is predicated on the assumption that a patient may change with recognizable consistency in the course of the procedure from any type or direction of response to another and even back again. Thus, as Rosenzweig (14) points out, a record begun with considerable extrapunitiveness may shift to intropunitive emphasis, presumably reflecting sufficient feelings of guilt to bring about this shift.

Considering the question of interpretation of superego- and ego-blocking Rosenzweig writes:

As regards the types of frustrating situations included in the test, it may be noted that obstacle-dominant responses are rarely encountered in superego-blocking situations. These situations are thus usually scorable only for ego-defensive and need-persistive factors. In this connection the scoring of I′ deserves attention. In ego-blocking situations I′ ordinarily has the meaning of a martyr-like acceptance of the frustration—a transformation of the frustration into some sort of benefit—or occasionally as, for example, in situation No. 22, that of protecting the subject from outside help so that he may instead nurse his own wounds. In the superego-blocking situations, however, the I' response in the rare instances when it occurs represents the complement to E' in ego-blocking situations; i.e., the subject remarks his state of embarrassment at being involved in the frustration of others.

The distinction between the two types of frustrating situations is further of significance from the standpoint of scoring extrapunitiveness and intropunitiveness. In ego-blocking situations the aggression of the subject is usually directed against the frustrating person, whereas in superego-blocking situations, the aggression is expressed more often as a protest of innocence, as a denial of an accusation or charge, or, in general, as an emphatic self-justification. As has already been mentioned, the ego-blocking type of extrapunitiveness is distinguished from the superego-blocking type in the scoring by writing the latter as E. As regards intropunitiveness, responses in ego-blocking situations ordinarily take the form of avowed guilt or inferiority (I); but in the superego-blocking situations, where the subject is accused of having done something wrong, an admission of guilt in the response is often followed by an explanation intended to minimize this guilt in its essential import. In the latter case the I score is distinguished by being written as **I**. It should be observed that **I** in superego-blocking situations is closely allied in psychological significance to the **M** score in ego-blocking situations. (*14*, pp. 11–12.)

It is in keeping with its importance that Rosenzweig's conception of levels of behavior in personality appraisal, presented in general terms in the previous chapter, be examined against the background of the Picture-Frustration Study. This examination arises not only from the special fitness of this technique for discussion in such terms but also because of its important implications for the other projective techniques which are described later.

Rosenzweig considers that until experimental investigation of the levels of response in the P-F Study have been completed (an example of a research design for which he gives, *15*), the most plausible assumption to make, qualified by the findings of the inquiry, is that the patient is functioning at the objective, not the projective, level. Of course, evidence from the inquiry or from other tests and clinical data may make it possible to infer that functioning at the subjective or projective level is also present either in part or, though unlikely, entirely.

In examining further the matter of interpretation, he writes:

An example from item 13 in the P-F Study (which depicts one person approaching another to keep an appointment only to learn that the previously made arrangement has been abruptly terminated) may be useful. Some subjects respond with "That's quite all right" and in so doing reflect what they believe would be the polite or otherwise correct behavior in the situation. While such a response could actually represent what the subject would say or do in the circumstances, it may signify only an opinion of what should be said or done. In the former case Level II would be indicated; in the latter, Level I. The very same words can thus have two quite different interpretive meanings. Again, the item may elicit the response "Why didn't you let me know?" or, similarly, "You mean and inconsiderate person." Retorts of this kind may, of course, be made by some individuals in the scene depicted but it would seem more reasonable to suppose that such unrestrained expressions of aggression would be reserved for special and perhaps intimate occasions, remaining inhibited, if experienced at all, in the usual social situation. If the former circumstances apply, Level II would be indicated; if the latter, Level III. Different predictions would obviously be entailed in the two cases. (15, p. 68.)

An illustrative protocol may be found in Figure 3, following which the section of the diagnostic report devoted to the P-F is reproduced. The patient was a twenty-two-year-old single applicant for admission to a nurse's training program with two years of college. She had been referred for evaluation of her fitness for such training. On the basis of the protocol the following report was drawn up:[4]

The patient's pattern of reaction to frustrating situations reveals a highly individualized manner of responding. Although the amount of aggression engendered in such situations is no greater than is ordinarily expected, it is unusually intense for such minor frustrations. Her most typical response is an extrapunitive one offered in defense of the ego, which appears disproportionately threatened by any deprivation. However, her individuality is not expressed so much in terms of the direction of aggression as in terms of the choice of situations in which such aggression is expressed. Here she is extremely deviant from the cultural norm (GCR of only 33 per cent), displaying hostility in situations where cultural sanctions would tend to inhibit such behavior.

Although there are no overall trends in her response pattern, there are discernible short cycles in which one or another type of reaction will predominate. This is particularly true of extrapunitiveness, which is vehemently expressed through two or three situations, following which impunitiveness or intropunitiveness will prevail for a period. However, during this time frustration tolerance will gradually lessen and another extrapunitive release soon appear. For one who will be expected to be in a subordinate position for some time and be in constant association with authoritative figures (patient is entering nurse's training), such periodic outbursts do not appear salutary.

Judging from the patient's responses during the inquiry, she was for

---

[4] For the protocol and report I am indebted to Dr. Bettye M. Caldwell.

Fig. 3. Protocol for a Sample Rosenzweig P-F Study

	O-D	E-D	N-P	
1.		E		You could have at least watched where you were going.
2.		E		Accidents happen in the best of families. (Read in very aggressive tones.)
3.		E		Well, open your eyes.
4.			m	We can travel together then.
5.			i	I would appreciate your fixing it. (We will fix it as soon as possible, madam.)
6.		M		All right, thank you.
7.		I		You'll have to overlook my irritability.
8.	E'			What's this all about?
9.			m	All right, thank you.
10.		I		Silence.
11.		E		Silence.
12.			e;i	If he brings this back would you please notify me and I will return his.
13.			m	When may I see you?
14.	E'			In weather like this, too.
15.		M		Well, we all make mistakes.
16.		I	i	You're quite right how can I compensate?
17.		E		Hell, shut up! (*I* wouldn't say that because I don't curse but I imagine *he* would.)
18.			m	Silence.
19.		I		Sorry, Officer.
20.	M'			It makes little difference.
21.		I		Moral—never say anything if you can't say something good.
22.		E		No, I'm just lying here for the fun of it.
23.		E		I didn't marry you for *Auntie's Blessing*.
24.		M		That's quite alright.

Notes on Scoring

No. 3. Subject aggressively misinterprets situation.

Nos. 10, 11, and 18. Silence on the part of the subject is scored differently in the three situations, depending on the nature of the behavior sequence and the implicit meaning of such a response. In the Inquiry, the subject refused to elaborate on the responses simply insisting, "You wouldn't say anything."

No. 21. Although scored I, the tone of the response borders on sarcasm and thus has some E quality.

Summary

E %:	40	O-D %:	13	E > I > m	
I %:	27	E-D %:	60	Trends:	None
M %:	33	N-P %:	27	GCR:	33%

the most part responding at the objective level and thereby forecasting behavior which might be expected of her under similar external conditions. When questioned about this, her immediate reply was that she assumed this to be the proper and expected reaction, hastily adding, however, that this was difficult for her when the depicted characters were men. Assuming that difficulty in objective identification would facilitate a projective set, examination of her responses in these situations should permit deeper inferences. Such scrutiny actually reveals a significantly greater amount of extrapunitiveness (seven as opposed to three extrapunitive responses in scenes depicting women), suggesting that under the cloak of anonymity her low tolerance can find freer expression. Although this may merely represent the patient's stereotype of the way she expects men to react, the former hypothesis seems more feasible in the present instance, judging from the delay on several of these items (Nos. 8, 17, 22, and 23) and comments made by the patient while attempting them.

This vacillation between the objective and projective levels of response (in addition to a few instances of subjective responses, *viz.*, No. 21) may account for some of the atypicality of her response pattern and the cyclic behavior already described. Nevertheless, the amount of nonconformity which exists despite an avowed effort at self-censorship makes the total picture seem more ominous than would be apparent on casual inspection of the record.

THE ROSENZWEIG PICTURE-FRUSTRATION STUDY, CHILDREN'S FORM

Although the Adult Form has been the basis for this presentation, in all essential respects the Children's Form is identical (20). A short summary concerning it is, however, in order. The situations pictured are similarly twenty-four in number. A parallel between the pictures in the two forms may be observed in sixteen instances (20). (Strict parallelism would be impossible because of the difference between the worlds of the adult and of the child.) It is intended for use with children from ages four through thirteen and may be administered in approximately twenty minutes either by individual or group procedure. The instructions stress the gamelike aspect and attempt to turn away the subject from a self-critical attitude. Boys and girls and male (father) and female (mother) figures are introduced as frustrating agents, and a child is always the one who is frustrated. The inquiry concludes with questions concerning the level at which the responses are being given. The scoring and scoring guide (20) are organized similarly to those for the Adult Form. The scoring samples are based on 500 records from private and public school children, in nursery through ninth grade, aged four through thirteen years. The scoring norms are presented for two-year intervals for the ages covered. Preliminary investigations of reliability show it to resemble that of the Adult Form, stability coefficients of from .60 to .80 being found.

Validity is still under investigation, with clinical indications considered promising. Systematic studies are also under way. One completed investigation by Rosenzweig and Mirmow (21) is concerned with the validation of trends. Their evidence lends support to the belief that the sheer appearance of trends as such, irrespective of number or quality, is in itself an index of low frustration tolerance. For example, it was found that with a group of fifty private school children aged four through seven, for whom an independent criterion of adjustment was available, the presence of trends was greater (at the .07 percent level) in the socially inadequate group. Other lines of evidence tended to support this conclusion. In a larger group of 272 children four through thirteen the mean number of trends was found to be about two with a significant rise in the percentage of cases showing trends at age six though remaining relatively constant thereafter. This was interpreted as being related to the socializing process in childhood in that with increasing age there is a growing conflict created by the individual's reactions to frustration and hence the appearance of trends.

BIBLIOGRAPHY

1. Bernard, J., The Rosenzweig Picture-Frustration Study: I. Norms, reliability, and statistical evaluation, *J. Psychol.*, 1949, 28:325–332.
2. Clarke, H. J., Rosenzweig, S., and Fleming, E. E., The reliability of the scoring of the Rosenzweig Picture-Frustration Study, *J. clin. Psychol.*, 1947, 3:364–370.
3. Falls, R. P., and Blake, R. R., A quantitative analysis of the Picture-Frustration Study, *J. Personality*, 1948, 16:320–325.
4. Franklin, J. C., and Brozek, J., The Rosenzweig P-F Test as a measure of frustration response in semistarvation, *J. consult. Psychol.*, 1949, 13:293–301.
5. French, R. L., Changes in performance on the Rosenzweig Picture-Frustration Study following experimentally induced frustration, *J. consult. Psychol.*, 1950, 14:111–115.
6. Fry, F. D., A study of reactions to frustration in 236 college students and in 207 inmates of state prisons, *J. Psychol.*, 1949, 28:427–438.

7. Lindzey, G., An experimental test of the validity of the Rosenzweig Picture-Frustration Study, *J. Personality*, 1950, 18:315–320.
8. McCary, J. L., Ethnic and cultural reactions to frustration, *J. Personality*, 1950, 18:321–326.
9. Rosenzweig, S., Types of reaction to frustration, *J. abnorm. soc. Psychol.*, 1934, 29:298–300.
10. Rosenzweig, S., A test for types of reaction to frustration, *Amer. J. Orthopsychiat.*, 1935, 5:395–403.
11. Rosenzweig, S., Frustration as an experimental problem. I. The significance of frustration as a problem of research, *Character & Pers.*, 1938, 7:126–128.
12. Rosenzweig, S., Frustration as an experimental problem. VI. General outline of frustration, *Character & Pers.*, 1938, 7:151–160.
13. Rosenzweig, S., An outline of frustration theory, in Hunt, J. McV. (ed.), *Personality and the behavior disorders*, The Ronald Press Company, 1944, pp. 379–388.
14. Rosenzweig, S., The picture-association method and its application in a study of reactions to frustration, *J. Personality*, 1945, 14:3–23.
15. Rosenzweig, S., Levels of behavior in psychodiagnosis with special reference to the Picture-Frustration Study, *Amer. J. Orthopsychiat.*, 1950, 20:63–72.
16. Rosenzweig, S., Some problems relating to research on the Rosenzweig Picture-Frustration Study, *J. Personality*, 1950, 18:303–305.
17. Rosenzweig, S., Revised norms for the adult form of the Rosenzweig Picture-Frustration Study, *J. Personality*, 1950, 18:344–346.
18. Rosenzweig, S., The treatment of humorous responses in the Rosenzweig Picture-Frustration Study: a note on the revised (1950) instructions, *J. Psychol.*, 1950, 30:139–143.
19. Rosenzweig, S., Fleming, E. E., and Clarke, H. J., Revised scoring manual for the Rosenzweig Picture-Frustration Study, *J. Psychol.*, 1947, 24:165–208.
20. Rosenzweig, S., Fleming, E. E., and Rosenzweig, L., The children's form of the Rosenzweig Picture-Frustration Study, *J. Psychol.*, 1948, 26:141–191.
21. Rosenzweig, S., and Mirmow, E. L., The validation of trends in the children's form of the Rosenzweig Picture-Frustration Study, *J. Personality*, 1950, 18:306–314.
22. Rosenzweig, S., and Sarason, S., An experimental study of the triadic hypothesis: reactions to frustration, ego-defense and hypnotizability: I. Correlational approach, *Character & Pers.*, 1942, 11:1–19.

DIAGNOSTIC TESTING REPORTS INVOLVING THE PICTURE-FRUSTRATION STUDY

23. Bell, J. E., The case of Gregor: psychological test data, *Rorschach Res. Exch.*, 1949, 13:155–205.

24. Bernard, J., The Rosenzweig Picture-Frustration Study: II. Interpretation, *J. Psychol.*, 1949, 28:333–343.
25. Clarke, H. J., The diagnosis of a patient with limited capacity, *J. Personality*, 1946, 15:105–112.
26. Kogan, K. L., The diagnosis of a patient with organic defect, *J. Personality*, 1946, 15:113–120.
27. Rosenzweig, S., and Clark, R. A., The personality of a psychotic ex-soldier, in Watson, R. I. (ed.), *Readings in the clinical method in psychology*, Harper & Brothers, 1949, pp. 299–313. (Also in *J. abnorm. soc. Psychol.*, 1945, 40:195–204.)
28. Rosenzweig, S., with Kogan, K. L., *Psychodiagnosis: an introduction to tests in the clinical practice of psychodynamics*, Grune & Stratton, 1949, pp. 167–180, 190–207, 237–268, 271–286.

CHAPTER 16

The Thematic Apperception Test

The Thematic Apperception Test (TAT), developed by Murray and Morgan, presents itself as a technique for the study of the fantasies of the individual. Consisting of a series of pictures about which the subject is asked to tell stories, it provides a means whereby the interrelated traits, attitudes, needs, and conflicts underlying his behavior may be revealed. In short, it reveals a picture of his projected private world.

Like other instruments designed to elicit fantasy productions, it possesses certain advantages for the clinician. Reliance need not be placed upon the incidental comment, the evanescent dream, the occasional daydream related only after a stable therapeutic relationship has been built. Protected by the cloak of anonymity provided by the third person, the subject may not feel so strongly the need to detour and conceal when giving his responses to the TAT pictures. In this way fantasies may be brought forth at will rather than by dependence upon relatively unpredictable events. Furthermore, the material is standard in terms of the objective stimulus, thus permitting objectification of scoring of certain aspects of the individual's responses. However, as Murray (36) himself indicates, the TAT brings out a limited number of samples of the patient's thought. It is too much to expect that a complete portrayal of the personality will emerge. Also, sometimes TAT productions are almost entirely unfruitful because of their superficiality or impersonality just as there are therapeutic hours similarly sterile of results.

According to Murray (36), the projective hypothesis is manifested in this instrument through a tendency for individuals to interpret an ambiguous situation in terms of their past experiences and present needs and to draw upon these experiences and needs in expressing what they derive from the situations. The stories told in response to the TAT cards will reflect this interpretative tendency in the way the subjects meaningfully perceive (apperceive) the cards.

In clinical practice the Rorschach and the TAT are frequently used in conjunction with one another, since they supply complementary information. The former instrument is considered to supply essentially a formal or structural description of the patient, while failing to give as much psychodynamic *content* in the sense of conflicts and complexes as would be desired. The TAT is often the instrument of choice in seeking information on such matters. (For an illustration the case study of Harrison, 78, is excellent.) Of course, it is true that other tests also give information concerning thought content and attitudes, such as sex responses on the Rorschach or personal reference on the Wechsler-Bellevue, but such sources are often incidental and sporadic. By its very nature the pictured material supplies information on the patient's relationship to males, females, parents or other authority figures, and peers. In so doing it may not tell as much about the intensity of the needs thus expressed as does the Rorschach, but it does show a pattern of needs, providing the method of analysis used permits it to.

Another value of the TAT would appear to be its function as an "anxiety instigator." That is, the manner in which the patient meets the demands put upon him by the pictures reveals something about his defense against the anxiety stirred by the themes the particular picture suggests to him. How he expresses, disguises, or repulses his feelings of anxiety in the face of the instigating elements provides clues to his modes of defense against this anxiety. Here the term "anxiety" is used in its broader sense. Actually, in detection of anxiety reaction, as such, the TAT is not particularly fruitful (see, e.g., Schafer, 85).

Specifically included in the presentation to follow are discussions of the test material; the method of administration; the selection of shorter sets from among the cards; the interpretation of TAT material including the distinction beween form and content, norms, systems of interpretation, techniques of analysis, modes and principles of interpretation; validity; reliability; and application with various diagnostic groups. Closely related techniques, such as the Children's Apperception Test developed by the Bellaks, the Blacky Test of Blum, the Make-A-Picture-Story Test of Shneidman, the Picture-Story Test of Symonds, and the Four-Picture Test of van Lennep, are not discussed. On the other hand, the Thompson modification is included since he adapted the regular TAT pictures for use with Negroes.

TEST MATERIAL

The test material for any subject, regardless of age or sex, consists of twenty cards—nineteen containing black and white pictures and one blank card—presented one at a time. In the procedure Murray recommends the cards be divided into two series of ten each. To allow for selection of especially pertinent cards for boys, girls, men, and women, there are actually thirty-one cards in the set, eleven of which are suitable for either sex. This arrangement was chosen because of the experience of Murray and his associates (37) that validity of interpretation is increased if most of the pictures include a person of the same sex as the subject. In more general terms, Morgan and Murray (34) indicated that in most pictures there should be at least one person with whom the subject could easily identify.

The set of cards at present commercially available is the third revision of the original set—Set D, in the terminology of the *TAT Newsletter*.[1] Revisions were made in order to permit commercial distribution (some of the earlier cards were bound by copyright restrictions, and permission could not be secured to reproduce). Furthermore, as experience accumulated concerning the amount of information evoked by each picture, certain changes were seen to be advisable. In addition, the set under consideration was increased to twice the size of the original one. The major emphasis in the discussion to follow will be on this most commonly used set.

The description of these pictures as given by Murray follows:

---

[1] The "TAT Newsletter," edited by R. R. Holt, is now included as a special section of the *Journal of Projective Techniques* and is especially valuable as a means of keeping abreast of latest developments concerning the test.

Pictures of the First Series

1. A young boy is contemplating a violin which rests on a table in front of him.

2. Country scene: in the foreground is a young woman with books in her hand; in the background a man is working in the fields and an older woman is looking on.

3 BM. On the floor against a couch is the huddled form of a boy with his head bowed on his right arm. Beside him on the floor is a revolver.

3 GF. A young woman is standing with downcast head, her face covered with her right hand. Her left arm is stretched forward against a wooden door.

4. A woman is clutching the shoulders of a man whose face and body are averted as if he were trying to pull away from her.

5. A middle-aged woman is standing on the threshold of a half-opened door looking into a room.

6 BM. A short elderly woman stands with her back turned to a tall young man. The latter is looking downward with a perplexed expression.

6 GF. A young woman sitting on the edge of a sofa looks back over her shoulder at an older man with a pipe in his mouth who seems to be addressing her.

7 BM. A gray-haired man is looking at a younger man who is sullenly staring into space.

7 GF. An older woman is sitting on a sofa close beside a girl, speaking or reading to her. The girl, who holds a doll in her lap, is looking away.

8 BM. An adolescent boy looks straight out of the picture. The barrel of a rifle is visible at one side, and in the background is the dim scene of a surgical operation, like a reverie-image.

8 GF. A young woman sits with her chin in her hand looking off into space.

9 BM. Four men in overalls are lying on the grass taking it easy.

9 GF. A young woman with a magazine and a purse in her hand looks from behind a tree at another young woman in a party dress running along a beach.

10. A young woman's head against a man's shoulder.

Pictures of Second Series

11. A road skirting a deep chasm between high cliffs. On the road in the distance are obscure figures. Protruding from the rocky wall on one side is the long head and neck of a dragon.

12 M. A young man is lying on a couch with his eyes closed. Leaning over him is the gaunt form of an elderly man, his hand stretched out above the face of the reclining figure.

12 F. The portrait of a young woman. A weird old woman with a shawl over her head is grimacing in the background.

12 BG. A rowboat is drawn up on the bank of a woodland stream. There are no human figures in the picture.

13 MF. A young man is standing with downcast head buried in his arm. Behind him is the figure of a woman lying in bed.

13 B. A little boy is sitting on the doorstep of a log cabin.

13 G. A little girl is climbing a winding flight of stairs.

14. The silhouette of a man (or woman) against a bright window. The rest of the picture is totally black.

15. A gaunt man with clenched hands is standing among gravestones.

16. Blank card.

17 BM. A naked man is clinging to a rope. He is in the act of climbing up or down.

17 GF. A bridge over water. A female figure leans over the railing. In the background are tall buildings and small figures of men.

18 BM. A man is clutched from behind by three hands. The figures of his antagonists are invisible.

18 GF. A woman has her hands squeezed around the throat of another woman whom she appears to be pushing backwards across the banister of a stairway.

19. A weird picture of cloud formations overhanging a snow-covered cabin in the country.

20. The dimly illumined figure of a man (or woman) in the dead of night leaning against a lamp post. (36, pp. 18–20.)[2]

METHOD OF ADMINISTRATION

If the twenty cards are used,[3] the test is generally administered in two sessions of approximately one hour each, with at least one day intervening between sessions. Pictures 1–10 are administered during the first session and pictures 11–20 during the second. The patient is not informed of the two sets of cards lest he appear at the second session with a stock of previously prepared plots and destroy all vestiges of spontaneity. Two reasons are generally offered for presenting the pictures at two sittings: first, fatigue effects are obviated, and second, pictures 11–20 are generally more unstructured and "weird" than the first ten and can be responded to with less inhibition after "the ice has been broken" by the more structured first ten.

---

[2] Reprinted by permission of the publishers from Henry A. Murray, *Manual for the Thematic Apperception Test*, Cambridge, Mass.: Harvard University Press, 1943.

[3] The usual clinical practice is to administer fewer than twenty cards, generally ten or twelve as described in the next section of the chapter. Although the actual sequence in practice would be the selection of cards followed by administration, the reverse order of presentation of topics is followed here for the sake of clarity of exposition.

With respect to the arrangement of examiner and subject, it has been variously recommended that the patient be seated or lie on a couch, and either face the clinician or have his back to him. For example, Murray (36) and Rotter (52) prefer that the patient be turned away; Rapaport chooses the face-to-face position (39). It is the writer's impression that the face-to-face relation is more common in clinical practice. Since a couch is hardly standard equipment in the office of most clinical psychologists, the use of the reclining position could not by any stretch of the imagination be called common.

In essence, all methods of administering the TAT consist of asking the patient to tell a story about each picture with due regard for what is going on at the present, what events preceded the ongoing activity, what the outcome will be and what the characters are thinking and feeling. With this brief statement in mind the method of administration will be examined. Although particular attention to one generalized method will be given, variations will be noted. Other accounts of administration are given by Murray (36), Rapaport (40) (41), Rotter (52), Stein (61), and Tomkins (64). The account of the nature and technique of the inquiry by Rapaport (40) (41) is especially recommended.

There is some variation among clinicians in the wording used for introducing the first card, since no precise statement is prescribed. A variation of Murray's suggestion in the *Manual* (36) is used by the writer: "I am going to show you some pictures, one at a time. It is your task to tell me the story back of this picture—what is happening at the moment, what are the people feeling and doing, what led up to this, and how will it come out. In short, you make up a dramatic story about each picture, speaking your thoughts as they come. Since you will have about an hour for the pictures you can spend about five minutes or less with each one. Here is the first picture."

With subjects of limited education or intelligence and with children one may modify the instructions. Modifications according to circumstance are incomparably more important than adherence to set instructions. In any case, questions asked by the patient should be answered, although not to the point of supplying illustrative stories. As Rotter (52) indicates, any instructions may be used that convey to the patient the idea that an imaginative production, not a description, is wanted, and that do not suggest a particular story or kind of story.

When the entire twenty cards are to be administered, Murray (36) advises changing the instructions for the second session in order to stress giving freer rein to the imagination and disregarding commonplace realities. Whether card 16 (the blank card) is given during the second session or, as is more common, in the single clinical session devoted to the TAT, special instructions are necessary. The writer uses substantially the following instructions with this card: "With this blank card make up your own picture, describe it to me, and then go on to tell a story about it."

The recording includes the reaction time or the time elapsing before the story is begun after presentation of the card, and the total time for the story. The clinician tries to report as exactly as he can the words of the subject in addition to any questions or comments that he may make. If the patient talks too rapidly there is no recourse but to ask him to speak more slowly. Mispronunciations and verbal or syntactical peculiarities are underlined (so as to distinguish them from recording errors), and pauses in the voicing of the stories are identified by long and short dashes. Although mechanical recording is sometimes used, along with the practice of asking the patient to write out his own stories, it is generally discouraged. (See Stein, 61, for a discussion of these points.) All comments and remarks of the clinician are recorded at the point of occurrence and for ease of identification are placed in parentheses. Additional behavioral observations, such as changes of inflection, restlessness, signs of blocking or anxiety, or laughter are noted similarly. These are also enclosed in parentheses, thus making all such digressions from the story as such easily identifiable.

It is important to consider for a moment the role of the clinician during the time the patient is telling his stories. He is definitely more than a recorder. He must indicate to the patient an interest in what is being said without giving clues to his feelings. For example, a very morbid or aggressive story should produce in the language or the nonverbal behavior of the clinician no clues as to his feelings. Nor does he help the patient determine what various objects or persons (the "gun" in card 3, or the sex of the figure on the left in card 18 GF) might be. Instead, such questions are parried with something like "It can be anything you want it to be."

The question of the timing of various aspects of the inquiry arises. Rapaport (40) (41) urges that inquiry be given each card in order to lessen the likelihood of stereotypy and to avoid having the patient become forgetful and confused. On the other hand, Tomkins (64), feeling that inquiry after each story arouses suspicion, resistance, and a feeling that the stories do not satisfy the clinician, suggests that it be placed at the end. To the writer this contradiction may be resolved if practice is varied according to the nature of the patient and the skill of the examiner. If the clinician is unskilled or the patient judged especially prone to develop the difficulties mentioned by Tomkins, then inquiry should occur at the end. Otherwise Rapaport's procedure may be followed. Under all circumstances, however, the inquiry to complete the story should come immediately afterward or even during its recital. Certainly slips of the tongue or minor verbal obscurities must also be seized at the moment or they will be lost.

Despite the necessity for interjecting some comments on occasion, the clinician must whenever possible refrain therefrom until the patient signifies he has completed his account. Only questioning that is non-leading is permissible during the narrative. Nondirective procedures urged by Rogers and his followers are especially useful here (see Chapter 20).

The non-suggestive character of the inquiry is vividly described by Rapaport, who writes:

> For instance, a subject may describe the first picture as a boy with a broken violin, the inquiry, "How did it break?" or "How did he break it?" is suggestive to some extent. They suggest that it could have been broken by accident or by the boy. In many cases much suggestive inquiry may appear of no consequence, because the subject chooses the opposite possibility; yet without the suggestion, he might not have thought of the opposite possibility. "What led up to it?" or "How come, broken?" is a much safer inquiry. The more noncommittal the inquiry, the more significant the answer. "He didn't break it in anger" is much more revealing if the question was, "How come, broken?" than if it was, "How did he break it?" (40, pp. 411–412.)

When the subject has completed the story it is customary to note the length of time taken and to remind him, if necessary, of any aspect, such as outcome, omitted from the narrative. Questions may take various forms: "What led up to all this?" "How did this [the story told] come about?" "How does it end?" Sometimes the "story" may be primarily a description of the picture, in which case the clinician might state, "You did a good job describing the picture, but now I want you to make up a story about the picture." At this point a reiteration of instructions might be given. Refusal to tell a story at all, expressed in such statements as "It's a boy and a violin, that's all," are met with urging and restatement centering on "making it up" and a reminder that all of it is not in the picture itself. A detailed account of handling refusals is given by Rapaport (40).

A word of caution is well worth mentioning. Rapaport (40) warns against assuming that relatively stereotyped productions necessarily indicate ideational poverty. It may be that test anxiety, so common in the psychiatric patient, temporarily dries up the imaginative repertoire, and it is the task of the clinician by adroit inquiry to open up the sluice gates.

Somewhat greater delicacy must be used in framing questions about more specific issues. Of necessity, they vary from patient to patient. If some particular area of personality functioning is considered worth investigating, responses which deviate from "clinical" or derived norms (cf. the later section concerned with this topic) are especially important. If the gun in card 8 B is not noted (Rosenzweig and Fleming, 50, found that 62 percent of males note it) and aggressive or suicidal impulses have been reported in a particular patient, he might be asked to identify the object and to describe its function in the story. Or if on 13 MF no account is taken of the partial nudity of the female figure, it might be considered advisable to ask, "Is there anything unusual about the woman?" to see if the nudity is accepted. The danger, of course, is that the more suggestive the question, the more chance that the patient will become aware of the problem the clinician is attempting to explore and will become more cautious and suspicious about the general intent of the test.

The questioning heretofore described is to be distinguished from another inquiry which may take place either on the completion of the entire series or at the same time as the above. Instead of dealing with special points of interest suggested by either obscurities, unusualness, spontaneous comments in the stories themselves, or some particular purpose (such as investigation of "feminine identification"), one function of this inquiry is to determine something of the patient's conscious conceptions of and attitudes toward the characters in his stories. One more or less constant element in the inquiry is to ask the patient about the sources of the various stories. From the results of their intensive investigations, Murray and his associates (37) stated that there were four primary sources from which the plots were drawn, namely, books and motion pictures, actual events taking place in the lives of friends or relatives, personal experiences, and conscious or unconscious personal fantasies. This is not meant to imply that one is forthwith to reject as fortuitous the material from the first two sources, for there is selectivity even there. However, it does mean that more importance may be attached to those that spring from more personal and private experiences—incidents which the patient would not necessarily identify as personal or related to his own feelings in any way. To clarify this last point it should be added that the patient is only dimly or not at all cognizant of a relation between the plot and his own fantasy, and it is up to the clinician to tease out its origin. Often a patient will claim that it "just came to him," but further inquiry will supply the clinician with enough indirect information to be able to localize the source. An investigation by Combs (12) regarding the influence of personal experiences on TAT stories, described in the section of the chapter concerned with validity, is pertinent.

It is sometimes worth while to ask the patient to select those pictures he likes best and those he likes least and then to give his reasons for his choices. Still another fruitful procedure is to inquire into his feelings toward the hero of each story, obtaining value judgments such as whether the central character behaved as he should and did the sensible thing.

In the estimation of the writer, another important element in the general inquiry is to consider with the patient the level of interpretation at which he is functioning. It may be done in the conceptual framework of Rosenzweig presented in the previous chapter, and, although not necessarily common practice, it is believed to be a fruitful line of attack. Further attention will be paid this issue in discussing principles of interpretation.

For the psychologist in training many of these aspects of the inquiry just described may, with considerable justification, be omitted. They are refinements that may serve only to confuse the inexperienced examiner and the patient and introduce complicating elements into the interpretation. Therefore it is preferable at first to limit inquiry to securing the compliance of the patient with the in-

structions, i.c., to tell stories which include the four major components—what is happening, the feelings and acts of the people concerned, the antecedents, and the outcome.

In part, the nature of the inquiry will be influenced by the particular interpretative system or interpretative principles used by the clinician. The nature of these variations in inquiry will be implied in the
later discussion of interpretation.

THE SELECTION OF PICTURES

As was mentioned before, in clinical practice it is not customary
to give the entire twenty cards, but rather to select ten to twelve that
can conveniently be given during one session. The question arises as
to how the cards to be used are to be selected. Obviously the nature
of the patient and his difficulties decide this in some measure. On
the other hand, opinion would have it that certain cards, in and of
themselves, are more provocative and more revealing than others
and are more frequently employed in various short forms. It is considered advisable to marshal some opinions on the matter.

Among five staff clinical psychologists at the Washington University School of Medicine, including the writer, a discussion concerning the selection of the most generally useful TAT cards for men
and for women led to considerable agreement. This in turn stimulated a search for the thinking of other groups or individuals. What
are considered to be representative selections are reported in Tables
27 and 28. A brief description of the origin of these selections, other
than the one with which the writer was concerned, is in order.

Holt (23) reports that the Winter VA hospital group tried out a
variety of short forms and finally arrived at two sets of twelve pictures given in the tables. They do not administer them in the num-
bered sequence but for men use 1, 5, 3 BM, 4, 15, 10, 12 M, 6 BM,
7 BM, 13 MF, 18 BM, 8 BM, in that order. For women they usually
substitute 7 GF, 9 GF, 17 GF, and 18 GF in place of 6 BM, 7 BM,
12 M, and 18 BM. Twelve cards for men and a similar number for
women were selected for development of norms by Rosenzweig
(48) (50). A not inconsiderable advantage of using the shorter form
selected by him is the fact that it was made preliminary to the development of these now reported norms. In 1947 Levinson and a
group of psychologists in the Cleveland area (24) agreed upon the
eleven cards most fruitful for men and women separately. Subse-

TABLE 27.   TAT Cards Selected by Various Clinical Groups for Use
with Males

	Eiduson and Klopfer	Gar-field and Eron	Holt	Levin-son	Rosen-zweig	Watson	Total
1	x		x		x	x	4
2	x	x		x	x		4
3 BM	x	x	x	x	x	x	6
4	x	x	x	x	x	x	6
5		x	x				2
6 BM		x	x	x	x	x	5
7 BM		x	x	x	x	x	5
8 BM			x		x	x	3
9 BM	x						1
10		x	x		x		3
11	x						1
12 M	x	x	x	x		x	5
13 MF	x	x	x	x	x	x	6
14		x		x	x		3
15	x		x	x			3
16	x			x	x	x	4
17 BM							0
18 BM	x	x	x	x	x	x	6
18 GF	x						1
19							0
20		x		x		x	3
Total	12	12	12	12	12	11	

quently another card, No. 4 was added (29). A psychologist with the
Hacker Clinic in Los Angeles, Eiduson, with the assistance of Klopfer, worked out still another list suitable in their estimation for both
men and women (24). For comparative purposes it has been reported in both tables. Prior to a study of mood of theme, outcome
of story, and activity of the central character in the stories of veterans, Garfield and Eron (17) selected twelve cards on the basis of
estimated value for personality evaluation. Their selection is also
given in the table.

Disregarding the cards intended exclusively for boys or girls, the
cards for women alone in the case of men, and vice versa (unless
selected), it is disconcerting to note how few cards have not been
selected by one group or another. Only cards 17 BM and 19 were

TABLE 28. TAT Cards Selected by Various Clinical Groups for Use with Females

	Eiduson and Klopfer	Holt	Levinson	Rosen- zweig	Watson	Total
1	x	x		x	x	4
2	x		x	x	x	4
3 BM	x	x	x			3
3 GF				x	x	2
4	x	x	x	x	x	5
5		x				1
6 GF			x			1
7 GF		x		x	x	3
8 BM		x				1
8 GF						0
9 BM	x					1
9 GF		x		x		2
10		x		x		2
11	x					1
12 F			x	x	x	3
12 M	x		x			2
13 MF	x	x	x	x	x	5
14			x	x		2
15	x	x	x			3
16	x		x	x	x	4
17 GF		x				1
18 BM	x		x			2
18 GF	x	x		x	x	4
19						0
20			x			1
Total	12	12	12	12	9	

not selected for the males and only cards 8 GF and 19 for the females. Unanimous agreement was reached concerning 3 BM, 4, 13 MF, and 18 BM for men, and concerning only 4 and 13 MF for women. If the criterion be set up as agreement among all but one, cards 6 BM, 7 BM, and 12 M for men and 1, 2, 16, and 18 GF for women may be added.

Helpful as these selections may be, it must be remembered that they were made on a combined a priori and empirical basis; what is sorely needed is research evidence on the subject. Indeed, Levinson in 1948 (24) proposed such a research on a collaborative basis, but nothing has yet appeared. A study throwing indirect light upon this matter is that of Weisskopf (66). She was concerned with developing a measure of the extent to which individuals went beyond description when faced with TAT cards. Her hypothesis was that pictures in which the subject went beyond description when asked only to describe them were pictures with which he had difficulty in being factual and impersonal. Pictures in which the subjects transcended description would then be those in which it was easier to project. Accordingly, using college students as subjects she asked them to describe the TAT pictures in which human figures appeared. Her method of scoring was to count the number of comments which were not descriptions, such as ascribing emotions to the figures, including events temporally prior to or after the event depicted, stating relationships between the figures, and so on. For each picture a "transcendence index" consisting of the mean number of such comments per subject was calculated. Weisskopf does not report the transcendence indices for all cards used, but does state that the five highest were for cards 6 BM, 4, 7 BM, 7 GF, and 2. The five lowest were 12 M, 13 G, 17 GF, 20, and 9 BM.

It should be interesting to compare these results with the cards selected for clinical usage as reported in the earlier discussion. Using the criterion of selection by "all or all but one," cards 2, 4, 6 BM or 7 BM were included for either male or female or both. Although one card, 7 GF, with a high transcendence index did not meet this criterion, it was selected three out of five times for females. Of those with low transcendence indices, only 12 M met the criterion. This is an interesting discrepancy illustrative of one of the difficulties to which "objective" research such as this sometimes leads. Card 12 M pictures one man lying on a couch with another bending over him. It has been the experience of many clinicians that this card often supplies information pertaining to the status of the relationship between patient and clinician and consequently is extremely valuable. Granting that this card has a low transcendence potential, it is suspected that the special pertinence of the material which it supplies will far outweigh the relative paucity of projective material it might stimulate.

Another pertinent corollary of Weisskopf's study was the finding that M and BM cards did not have higher transcendence indices than F and GF pictures for male subjects, and vice versa. This throws some doubt on Murray's original hypothesis that male and female subjects are more prone to project upon cards in their particular sex series. Disregard of this assumption is also implicit in certain selections of cards reported in Tables 27 and 28, where sharp division into male and female cards was not made. In fact, Eiduson and Klopfer went so far as to select a set common for male and female subjects. However, no GF cards meet the selection criterion of all or all but one for males, and vice versa for females.

Another method of selection is to choose those cards particularly relevant to a given patient as judged from the information available about him and the diagnostic-therapeutic aims to be served by administration and interpretation of the TAT. If this procedure is followed one selection of ten or twelve cards may be used for one patient and a quite different set for another. Here a variety of sources of information become pertinent as aids in the selection. Variously described as accounts of "theme pull," "common stories," and "norms," data derived either from clinical experience or from quantitative studies are extremely helpful in the relevant selection of cards. The various sources are described in the subsequent section of the chapter devoted to norms.

Often, use is made of buffer or neutral cards to give the patient opportunity to recover from the anxiety engendered by a crucial one. According to Rapaport (40) (41), it is inadvisable to select only the cards on which the clinician expects to obtain decisive content. This is because unusual material given to a card which typically elicits an entirely different theme is relatively more conclusive than the same theme when given in response to a card on which its appearance is more or less expected. Furthermore, the stories on indifferent or buffer cards supply a base line for evaluating the stories to other cards. Or it may be, as Masserman and Balken (30) indicate, that a story particularly revealing of repressed strivings will be followed by a story which is particularly sterile, evasive, and noncommittal as a sort of unconscious defense against the earlier revelations. The adroit placement of buffer cards can help in this regard.

According to Rotter (52), the selection of cards for children reintroduces the hypothesis that the pictures used should involve individuals with whom the child might easily identify. He describes an unpublished study of Gerver involving 50 five- to ten-year-old children. The highest percentage of interpretation (as differentiated from description, enumeration, or refusal) was found on cards 7 GF, 18 GF, 3 GF, and 8 GF. The pictures failing to produce interpretations were 19, 18 BM, 11, and 12 BG. These findings uphold the hypothesis in that the former contain real people with whom it is relatively easy to empathize whereas the latter lack human figures. So far as the writer is aware, no definitive discussion of the selection of pictures for use with children has appeared, and this bit of evidence is the only help that can be offered concerning selection of pictures from the main TAT series for use with children.

A problem sometimes facing the clinician is the use of the TAT with Negroes. Consequently the discussion of the Thompson TAT, as it is generally called, becomes pertinent as an aspect of appropriate selection of cards. For a variety of reasons Thompson became concerned with the suitability of the TAT for Negro subjects. Was a projective test depicting white figures and standardized on a white population as valid for Negroes as for whites? This is especially pertinent when considering the assumption that identification is greatest where there is similarity of attributes of the figures on the cards and those of the subject. A case in point would be the special series of cards for women. The task to which Thompson (62) (63) addressed himself was that of determining if identification for Negro subjects would be increased if Negro figures were substituted for white figures without changing other significant aspects of the pictures. His modification consisted of introducing Negro figures on twenty-three of the original cards, the remainder being such as to make change unnecessary. Evidence that identification did increase with Negroes is advanced in a study in which various word counts showed that twenty-six student subjects in a Louisiana Negro college were more productive on the Thompson TAT than on the Murray TAT. The mean story lengths were 100 and 72 words, respectively. Statistically significant differences were found not only for an overall comparison such as this but also for each of the modified cards used. Qualitative findings were also evident—the matter-of-fact quality of the stories to the original cards, the tendency to place the white people in distant states and even foreign countries as contrasted with more warmth and closeness on the modified cards. Even more striking distinctions could be observed, such as pronounced violence and destructiveness shown on the Thompson TAT. It was, therefore, concluded that identification was likely to be greater for Negroes on the Thompson TAT than on the original because the pictorial material reflects the culture of the individual.

Although it is not unusual to use Thompson TAT cards with Negroes, the practice is not universal since there has been some informal criticism of the cards with exaggerated Negroid features. At least one psychiatric section of a Negro hospital staffed by Negro psychologists does not use it for this reason.

THE INTERPRETATION OF TAT MATERIAL

After administering the TAT the clinician has before him a series of stories, behavioral notes, the questions he has asked the subject, the reaction time, and the total time per card. There is also fairly general agreement that certain basic data concerning the patient need to be known for the sake of interpretative clarity and assurance. Specifically, knowledge of the age; sex; occupation; marital status; number, age, and sex of siblings and children; and presence or absence of the parents in the environmental constellation are considered essential by most clinicians.

Up to this point the procedure is more or less uniform; beyond this point there is relatively little agreement as to what is to be done. To be sure, there is considerable unanimity of opinion that for each card one will be interested in certain identifications (the hero or focal figure) and the way various figures are depicted, the frustrating or facilitating situations or persons (press), the interrelationships of the hero with other figures, the theme of the story, the nature of the outcome, and certain formal characteristics. However, the manner in which all this is done—in other words, the method of analysis and interpretation—is far from uniform among clinicians.

All analyses in one way or another involve the process of inspection and assimilation of the stories. This in one sense is the most fundamental technique of all, yet the one which is most dependent upon the skill and empathy of the clinician. As the stories are read through, repetitive and unique patterns are assayed until some sort of meaningful whole emerges. This process resembles in many ways the act of integration of clinical materials in therapeutic sessions, the diagnostic integration common to all clinical medicine. It is avowedly an artistic process—an act of creation with the creator guided by his past experience in a way not open to precise statement on the printed page. Murray (36) believes the only solution is immersion in many cases to give one the "feel" for the material and thus develop skill in creating valid and clinically meaningful interpretations of TAT stories. There are, however, other means of sharpening precision, namely, norms, techniques of analysis, interpretative systems, and interpretative modes and principles. Although it is possible for the sake of clarity of exposition to separate these four aspects of interpretation, they are apt to merge. In other words, a technique of analysis, including in this connection normative material based upon certain interpretative principles, is placed in the broader setting of an interpretative system. These aspects have in common the aim of making for valid, clinically appropriate interpretations.

These means of increasing precision, serving to widen and stabilize the vision of the observer, range from something as simple as underlining phrases and clauses of the written record, through sentence summarization of each story, to the application of elaborate manifold-step systems of pyramiding from categorization of every word unit of the record to a final summary.

Two topics must be considered—the question of the distinction between form and content, and the nature of the norms available for use with TAT stories—in order to set the stage for a discussion of interpretation. The interpretative significance of these two issues will be considered in the presentation subsequent to an examination of their nature.

THE DISTINCTION BETWEEN FORM AND CONTENT IN THE TAT

There is a certain amount of confusion or at least disagreement concerning the nature of and distinction between form and content in the analysis and interpretation of the TAT. Presumably form is concerned more with *how* the story is told and content with *what* is told. This may, on the surface, seem a relatively simple distinction but in practice it has worked out differently.

Rotter (51), in one of the earlier articles on the TAT, considers analysis of the structure (as differentiated from content) of the stories to include the predominant emotional tone (happy, humorous, unhappy, neutral), the nature of the endings (realistic or unrealistic), the logicalness and coherence of the stories, and the number of improbable interpretations. Rapaport, on the other hand,

considers "the prevailing tone" to be an aspect of the formal characteristics of the story content whereas compliance with instructions
and consistency within the production are "formal characteristics of
the story structure." Rosenzweig (83) specifies as formal features the
narrative level (whether enumeration, description, or interpretation), breadth of vocabulary, and other similar indications of creative capacity. Bellak defines as form analysis an aspect of his method
of analysis labeled "plot." Probably Mayman (31) in his review of
the literature goes farthest in what he considers to be subsumed under formal characteristics, using such headings as the adequacy of
the production, its coherence, its degree of significance, prevailing
mood, characteristic verbalizations, and so on through practically
everything associated with the TAT except depth interpretations,
need-press analysis, and other thematic methods, strivings, attitudes,
and personality traits.

In all this reference to form and content there is little or no discussion of the *criteria* of classification used. Fortunately, in the actual practice of interpreting a protocol this is of little moment and
would not be mentioned here at all if the literature were not rife
with such contradictions. Wyatt (72) suggests that the confusion
comes about because what at first appears to be content becomes
form when once it has been generalized. If this be the case it would
follow that discrepancies such as those mentioned earlier might be
resolved by gaining common agreement as to the level at which the
distinction is to be drawn, and maintaining it consistently. The
simplest for present classificatory and heuristic purposes is the concrete level—what the story says in the most literal sense—despite the
fact that under other circumstances it would be imperative to draw
the distinction at a higher level of generality. For a discussion of this
problem in all its subtlety at other levels the account of Wyatt (72)
is recommended.

The study of Hartman (22) is pertinent. He found in his study of
the TAT that the distinction between form and content elements
(including, in the former, fluency, speed of responses, interjections,
emphasis on past, present, or future, vocabulary level, and so on)
was of little aid in terms of distinguishing unique areas of personality
and in finding particular covert or overt levels of behavior with
which form or content was associated. Either, he found, may be
equally predictive in any of the personality areas studied.

One pragmatic distinction at this level between form and content, perhaps held more commonly than may be realized, is that "form" refers to those aspects of TAT material from which nothing about content can be inferred directly, i.e., reaction time, story length, total time, and the various measures such as those used by Balken and Masserman (3). This would mean, for example, that compliance with instructions and consistency as used by Rapaport would be contentual in nature since we need to know the content against a background of compliance or consistency. The distinction (given earlier at the concrete level) with a consequent narrowing of the scope of form is followed in subsequent discussion.

NORMS

The stand was taken in Chapter 14 that norms developed for a given projective instrument should be utilized whenever appropriate. Although the lack of commonly accepted and widely used norms for the TAT is deplorable, the deficit is easy to understand. The TAT is more or less standardized as to administration with considerable agreement on what the patient is to be informed about the task. But anything resembling standardization by administration to a normative population is almost completely absent. The reason is not far to seek. Since there is relative lack of agreement about what is to be "scored," there is a consequent lack of agreement about scoring summaries expressed in the form of norms. Moreover, clinicians are sometimes rather sensitive about the development of norms for projective devices, fearing that their presence will lead to mechanical application and that a sterile summarization of scores and ratios will emerge as the final product of the TAT. The question is not one permitting categorical answer except that, in the writer's opinion, it is not a two-pronged dilemma of having and using norms versus not having or using norms, but rather a question of *appropriately* using norms.

Murray (36) advises the development of subjective standards for evaluating individual variability by intensive study of numerous TAT protocols. This sort of knowledge is irreplaceable by any sort of appeal to objective norms. However, the usual weaknesses ascribed to them are inherent in such subjective approaches. If possible, normative data in the sense of explicit "norms" should also be available. Although one of the functions of normative material is to help the clinician select cards relevant to a particular patient, an even more important function is to serve as a base line for interpretation.

Difficulties of interpretation in the diagnostic area in the absence of norms are nicely demonstrated by the dual-purpose study of Cox and Sargent (14). First they set up a series of scoring categories based on a modification of Murray's system, scoring feeling, hero, need, threat, action, and outcome. These categories were then applied to fifteen emotionally stable and fifteen emotionally disturbed seventh-grade children. On the basis of these categories it was possible to determine a series of objectively measurable differences. On the basis of both independent case history material and the TAT scoring the two groups were demonstrably different. In the second phase of the study the TAT stories were sent to eight experienced clinical psychologists with the request that they be classified as emotionally disturbed or well adjusted. Each clinician had at his disposal all information that the experimenters had except the classification in which the subjects had been placed and the norms. In other words, they knew the pictures used, the criteria on which they were classified as stable or disturbed, and age and sex. They were also told that each pair of protocols submitted to them might include any combination of disturbed and stable (two disturbed, two stable, or one of each). Of the fifteen who had been classified as stable by the case history and the TAT, eleven were judged by the clinicians as disturbed.

In the opinion of the writer this study indicates with considerable cogency that two interrelated factors in the clinician's frame of reference help to account for these errors. First, the absence of normative data is very evident in these results. Second, since the clinician's knowledge of the pathological is so overwhelmingly greater than his knowledge of the normal, he appears sometimes to reason that the "normal" protocol should at least in certain respects be the opposite of the type recognized as disturbed—an inference which is presumptuous if not utterly fallacious.

APPERCEPTIVE NORMS. Rosenzweig (48) has observed that there are certain TAT norms relatively independent of any particular method of interpretation, which are related to the objective structure of the stimulus material. These are the statements made by the subject about the stimulus materials before him—in other words, the descriptive elements in his stories. Once it is known how much this structure has affected the response, the clinician is in a better position to infer the extent to which the personal or idiosyncratic mode of response of the individual is operative. This is made possible by apperceptive norms—those based on descriptions of the stimulus materials. Such norms as these make it possible to compare the responses of a particular patient with those popularly or commonly given to the same stimulus. The responses, of course, are not right or wrong as in many (but not all) psychometric devices; rather they show the degree of participation of the patient in popular ways of responding. Either agreement or lack of agreement with these common ways of behaving reveals certain discriminating characteristics of the patient. However, as Rosenzweig indicates, when agreement occurs it should not be interpreted as meaning psychodynamic neutrality. It may reflect the sharing with others of certain conflicts or inhibitions, not their absence. Thus, certain sexual stimulus situations on the TAT tend to be associated with elevated reaction times. An individual possessing this reaction time and thus agreeing with the group merely reflects his own inhibition or conflict, not a neutral way of responding. Of course, assessment among groups (inter-individual comparison) does not exhaust the value of apperceptive norms. It is equally important, if not more so, to consider them from a configurational point of view in intra-individual comparison.

Rosenzweig and Fleming (50) have developed apperceptive norms for twelve TAT cards for both men and women. These were the same cards presented earlier in Tables 27 and 28. The subjects were fifty men and fifty women selected by brief case history so as to assure the use of more or less normal individuals, although a fairly broad cross section of the groups deviated in the direction of being above average in intelligence and education. Mean age for both sexes was 27.5. The male and female subjects were matched by pairs with some exactitude in respect to age, education, religion, number of siblings, and marital status.

The verbatim responses of these subjects were classified under the headings of the presence of human figures, the objects noted, and the story content in terms of problem and outcome. The responses of the male subjects to card 3 BM might be illustrative. In terms of "figures," 44 percent saw the sole figure on the card as male, and 50 percent saw it as female. Twenty percent referred to the age of the figure, identifying is as a child. Likewise 20 percent identified it as a criminal or prisoner. Other characterizations included 44 percent as crying and 22 percent as asleep or resting. So far as "objects" were concerned, the blurred object on the floor was seen as a gun or other weapon by 28 percent. With reference to "problems and outcomes," childhood unhappiness was mentioned by 34 percent, and time as a remedy for the situation was proposed by 28 percent. Instead of childhood unhappiness 24 percent saw marital or romantic tragedy.

These norms are useful not only for interindividual comparison in order to cast light on uniqueness and commonality (with the cautions mentioned earlier) but also for intra-individual comparison. For example, by reading the table configurationally one may develop the paradigmatic story. Illustrating by using the larger percentages for card No. 1 (boy with violin), one could give a story such as the following (for female subjects): the boy (male = 100 percent; child = 100 percent) is looking at (violin = 42 percent; his violin = 36 percent) a violin (violin noted = 94 percent) because he is interested in music (54 percent) and is the son of parents who wish him to study music (36 percent). He is thinking of the future success (36 percent) which he will achieve (26 percent). This gives a skeleton on which the flesh of the individual nuances develops. As Rosenzweig points out, it is interesting to note that these norms seldom contradict the account of common stories given by Stein (61) on the basis of his clinical experience.

Viewing norms in this fashion, however, has introduced a shift of perspective from apperceptive (descriptive) norms to thematic content norms, which will be considered next.

THEMATIC (CONTENT) NORMS. Stein (61) presents the stories found in his experience to be common for the twenty cards used with males. They are presented both as summarizations and as illustrative stories. The account of Rapaport and his associates (40) (41) is unfortunately less useful than otherwise would be the case because the TAT edition used was the first Harvard Psychological Clinic revision of the original Morgan-Murray series. Therefore less than half the cards are identical with those appearing in the third revision (Set D), used by most clinicians today. However, the principles of interpretation based on the item analysis are still applicable and will be considered later.

A variety of sporadic pioneer studies, relatively limited as to scope, size of sample, and number of cards for which information was obtained, have appeared. Since each phrased the problems under investigation somewhat differently and used different kinds of subjects, it is not possible to bring them into any comparative perspective. Therefore they will be reported one by one.

The "theme pull," i.e., the appearance of certain themes in relation to a specific TAT card, is reported by Eron (16) for 1000 TAT stories of twenty-five hospitalized schizophrenics and twenty-five non-hospitalized college students. Both groups were comparable in age (twenty to thirty-four), IQ (at least 100), education, and marital status, and all were male veterans. All themes related by at least ten subjects are reported, with frequently more than one theme per subject per card. For card No. 1, pressure from parents and aspiration both showed a frequency of twenty-six out of fifty. The themes for other cards are reported in a similar manner. The data by card are reported for the normals and schizophrenics separately as well, and thus some preliminary norms are available from this source.

The roles ascribed the figures in ten TAT cards form the basis for norms supplied by Wittenborn (67) for 100 college men. For example, the boy in 7 BM is seen as impetuous by eighteen, compliant by twenty-eight, in conflict by eighteen, independent and indifferent by twelve, with twenty-five responses unclassified. The roles ascribed are presumed to throw light on the needs and attitudes of the subjects.

Although Garfield and Eron (17), whose reliability data are given later, supply normative data concerning mood and outcome for the selected TAT cards reported in Table 27, the findings are not necessarily of too great general significance as norms. The difficulty is that rating scales were used and only average ratings reported. They do bring out, however, that the predominating emotional tone or mood is very closely a function of the stimulus properties of the card and does not necessarily reflect the mood of the subject. Stories showing hope, satisfaction, pleasure, resolution of conflict, and so on were given "positive" ratings for emotional tone and outcome. On the other hand, stories with conflict situations, uncertainty, suffering, and unhappiness were considered "negative." A neutral rating fell in between. Characteristic values, card by card, are negative or neutral in mood or outcome with none predominantly posi-tive, i.e., none with means which would place them as character-istically bringing forth euphoric mood or optimistic outcome. This fact suggests caution in attributing a dysphoric mood to the patient when it is found on the particular cards making up the selection. More variability is found in outcome, suggesting this to be more a matter of the individual's projections.

Klebanoff's data (25) on the diagnostic appraisal of alcoholics, and Harrison's (19) (20) and Rotter's (51) studies of validity dis-cussed later supply incidental normative material. The need for a carefully planned comprehensive attack upon the problem of content norms in terms of theme pull, roles ascribed, or some synthesis of perspective is great indeed if the goal of explicit norms is to be reached.

NORMS FOR FORMAL CHARACTERISTICS. Reaction time, total time, and total wordage were investigated by Rosenzweig and Fleming (50) for the same sample as that for which apperceptive norms were developed. The general mean for reaction time was twenty seconds, with a range from fourteen (3 GF for women) to twenty-nine sec-onds (13 MF for men). This last reaction time, significantly larger, illustrates the use of these norms, since it shows that in evaluating the significance of reaction times more leeway must be allowed for 13 MF than for other cards. The general mean for total time was 3.7 minutes, with a range from 2.8 for one card to 4.7 for another, which finding corroborates the rule of five minutes or less per card including time for inquiry. The mean for total wordage was 143, with a range from 114 to 181. This is considerably shorter than the findings reported by Murray (36), who considers 300 words the standard length for adults. Clinical impression would support the shorter length found by Rosenzweig. For example, Rapaport (40) gives as his impression that in the clinical situation an average story is 100 words long and is given in three minutes after about twenty seconds' delay.

It is necessary, perhaps, to point out that the summary of Rosen-zweig's data is given in terms of an overall evaluation, whereas the usefulness of these results as norms resides in the report of the individual figures for men and women on specific cards given in the article itself. Sex differences, incidentally, are not in most in-stances of particular moment.

A variety of formal criteria were systematically applied to the stories of three neurotic patient groups by Balken and Masserman (3). From among a group of fifty patients on whom they had TAT protocols they selected five each from three subgroups of conversion hysteria, anxiety state, and obsessive-compulsive neurosis. To these fifteen subjects, eighty-five formal criteria of the language of the TAT productions were applied. Among these were the average number of words; the number of predicative participial and attributive adjectives; the relative number of active, passive, and intransitive verbs; the relative frequency of pro and con statements; and combinations of these indices which yielded quotients. An illustrative finding concerns the average number of words per production, with the least number of words used by cases showing anxiety states, next by cases of conversion hysteria, and the most by cases of obsessive-compulsive neurosis. In regard to the number of questions asked of the examiner, cases of conversion hysteria headed the list, with anxiety states next and the obsessive-compulsive cases by far the least. A further discussion of this study will be given in connection with diagnostic appraisal.

Although such studies are useful and revealing, they have not been carried on with very many groups. Furthermore, they do not extend to either a scope or a level which would make it relatively easy for the novitiate clinician to learn to apply them in the course of his diagnostic appraisal and are consequently overlooked all too readily.

INTERPRETATIVE SYSTEMS

Three broad systematic points of view concerning TAT interpretation may be discerned upon the present psychological scene. Although innumerable nuances are found, to the degree that almost every clinician has his own idiomatic way of deriving his interpretation, it would apparently be correct to designate the three main points of view as the interpretative need-press system of Murray and his associates and related systems, a more narrowly psychoanalytically oriented approach, and what may be called an eclectic approach. These, it is apparent, blend imperceptibly; Murray was influenced by psychoanalysis and is himself a practicing psychoanalyst. The psychoanalytically oriented TAT interpreters drew from Murray, as did Wyatt and Bellak, and both these points of view have had an influence upon the eclectic practitioner.

THE INTERPRETATIVE SYSTEM OF MURRAY AND ASSOCIATES, AND RE-
LATED SYSTEMS. The Thematic Apperception Test had its inception
not in psychopathology, as did the Rorschach, but in a comprehensive collaborative research project on the nature of the normal personality which culminated in the publication of *Explorations in
Personality* (37) under the guiding hand of H. A. Murray. It was a
complex theory of personality that Murray, MacKinnon, Morgan,
Rosenzweig, Sanford, White, and others brought forth. In this and
subsequent publications there was emphasis upon a collaborative
effort of a variety of specialists drawn from many fields. Early in this
effort it was discovered that a common meeting ground concerning
a tentative theory of personality was requisite. Following a series of
successive approximations there emerged what today may be considered an early stage of development of that theory as expressed in
this volume (37).

In the interpretative scheme of Murray (35) (36) (37), and in
its variants and extensions by Sanford (54) and Aron (1), the intertwined concepts of need-press are central. As Murray's manual (36)
illustrates, the method for analysis of each story is essentially that of
analyzing each event into the needs of the central character and the
forces emanating from the environment (press). Disregarding subdivisions, these needs and press are categorized by the authors into
twenty-eight needs and more than thirty press. Outcomes, e.g.,
happy or unhappy, are also studied. The interaction of the hero's
need and an environmental press, along with outcome, constitute
a thema (hence the term "thematic"). Strength (intensity, duration,
frequency, and importance in the plot) is scored for both need and
press by a rating on a five-point scale. After rating the twenty stories
for needs and press for each variable, a total score is found and
compared to normative material whenever available. Variables considerably above or considerably below the standard are examined in
relation to each other. A variety of leads to interpretation are then
offered, some of which will be taken up in a later section of the
chapter.

As can be profusely illustrated, this method of analysis produces
profound appraisals of the human personality both normal and abnormal (1) (37) (87). Nevertheless, it will not be elaborated in the
account to follow. Despite the brilliance of its conceptions and the

thorough work done with it, it is not appropriate for inclusion here. Murray and his associates were primarily interested in research in the psychodynamics of personality. Although their formulation contained some of the finest concerted thinking demonstrated upon the current psychological scene they arrived at a theory of personality which, while not uninfluential, is by no means commonly accepted among clinicians for reasons to be described.

Rotter (51), for example, stated that he failed to use the method of analysis under discussion because of its too close dependence upon an insufficiently validated theory of personality, the possibility that it covered up some individual differences, and a tendency to neglect content material with respect to attitudes, complexes, and the like. It has also been argued that since the theory reduces much of personality to conceptually separate needs and press, it does not capture much of the more elusive molar configuration which is considered by many the very essence of personality appraisal. Although Aron's attempt (1) at a method of analysis is explicitly designed to overcome this difficulty, it is quite possible, even probable, that the same charge will be leveled at her approach.

One reason for the failure of the need-press system to have received wide acceptance among practicing clinical psychologists is sometimes overlooked. By the nature of clinical practice the psychologist is not functioning alone or with the collaboration of other psychologists only; he is working intimately with psychiatrists, social workers, and others. Until his nonpsychologically trained colleagues are more impressed with this particular approach, it will continue to be somewhat neglected because of the necessity for a commonality of communication. This in no small measure contributed to the relative neglect of this particular theory in clinical practice. Reluctance to accept any interpretative system that conflicts with his own conception of the nature of personality arises in part from the fact that the content yielded from the TAT is similar in essence to the material found by the psychiatrist in diagnostic and therapeutic interviews. The psychiatrist may sometimes complain that Rorschach terminology is to some degree esoteric, but he is more receptive to it than he is to similar semantic secrets when contentual materials akin to his interview data are the matter of concern. In keeping with the aim here professed of avoiding theoretical constructs of limited acceptance whenever possible, it would not be appropriate to take the necessarily lengthy by-path into the nature of personality that the method demands.

Even if this were not the case, an additional reason is sufficient to bar inclusion of the Murray approach: the enormous amount of time necessary for working up each administration. In the foreword to the work of Aron (1), which is historically the latest manual resting essentially on Murray's need-press analysis, Sanford indicates that he does not use the TAT in his clinical practice because of its time-consuming nature. He contends that if there are but a few hours available for diagnostic study, other techniques, notably the interview, are more fruitful. He considers the TAT justified as a research instrument but not necessarily as a clinical tool. The same opinion is implicit in the work of Aron herself, who subtitles her book, "A Method and Technique for Personality Research." Although this position of uncertainty concerning the TAT as a clinical tool is an extreme one not shared by most clinicians, including the writer, it does illustrate the dilemma created by elaborate systems.

There have appeared manuals by Tomkins (64) and Stein (61) which bear in lesser measure the imprint of this need-press approach. They also share in even greater measure the characteristic of being considerably too complicated for daily clinical use. Although it may be argued that time should be taken if the analysis is worth while, the brutal fact is that it is not in most instances crucial to do so.

Nevertheless, not to use some system undoubtedly serves to weaken the yield to be secured from the TAT. One may stand in something akin to awe upon reading the forty-page analysis and interpretation of one protocol given by Stein in his manual (61) or the enormously detailed excerpts in Tomkins' book (64). They should be required reading for all clinical psychologists in order to keep alive that spark of dissatisfaction with their own efforts, and to serve as an incentive to more detailed and brilliant analyses by them. Although such publications as these can hardly serve as models to be imitated they may serve as sources of inspiration.

However, it is possible to make a general thematic analysis in the Murray tradition, or to follow Stein or Tomkins without scoring the variables. Indeed, Murray in the manual (36) suggests this practice. It is reasonable to conjecture that clinicians who do accept Murray's need-press conceptual system and use it in their clinical work do so without scoring in the sense just described. Indeed, an "intuitive" approach to TAT analysis was used in the original paper by Morgan and Murray (34) and in the account given in *Explorations in Personality* (37). The actual interpretative reports of Stein (61), and especially of Tomkins (64), although faithful to their own interpretative systems, certainly do not stress scoring as such.

THE PSYCHOANALYTIC INTERPRETATION OF THE TAT. Historically, the first interpretations of the TAT were rooted in psychoanalytic theory and technique.[4] The first communication of Morgan and Murray (34) concerning the TAT discussed depth interpretations with a patient under analysis, comparing the interpretations with other psychoanalytic phenomena including dream material.

Leaving aside the psychoanalytic influences on need-press theory, several writers on the TAT, notably Masserman and Balken (30), Bellak (5) (6) (7) (8), Rapaport and his associates (39) (40) (41), and Wyatt (70) (71), have shown most deeply the impress of this psychodynamic point of view. The techniques of analysis of Bellak and Wyatt, to be later described, bear the impress of a psychoanalytic orientation.

Masserman and Balken (30) were among the first to discuss the psychoanalytic significance of fantasy. Accepting conscious and unconscious psychic determinism, they considered that the stories might be interpreted as ways in which their patients would like to solve their intrapsychic conflicts. They related fantasy material to the mental dynamisms in what they considered to be typical cases. Fantasies such as those showing strong libidinal fixation on the mother and other oedipal situations, regressive urges, castration anxiety, and reflections of emotional conflict in childhood are typical centers of focus for their interpretations.

Although the fantasy production is determined by prior factors, the relationship of story to storyteller is not simple. The principle of overdetermination must be considered. It would appear that each aspect of the projected material may have more than one meaning, related to more than one level of personality organization. A portion of a story may consciously be attributed to a book read, yet be reported because of an important preconscious conflict and also have deep symbolic significance at an unconscious level.

The matter of the resemblance of dreams to TAT productions

---

[4] For a discussion of psychoanalysis see Chapter 20.

has been a matter of concern to psychoanalytically oriented psychologists. It seems deceptively plausible to attempt to draw analogies between dream productions and thematic apperceptions since they both involve fantasy material reflecting dynamic trends in the patient. In fact, the use of "forced fantasies" enjoyed something of a vogue in psychoanalytic practice about twenty-five years ago. As Wyatt (71) writes, one can even carry the analogy between dreams and TAT productions to the point of indicating the elements common to the manifest content of the dream and the actual story, while the latent content of the dream resembles the dynamic interpretation of the meaning of the story. Tendencies, strivings, drives, needs, or what you will, can be regarded as bearing some relation to the wish-fulfilling aspect of the dream. And yet, after mentioning the factors which have encouraged this analogizing, Wyatt goes on to point out that this kind of reasoning is superficial and premature since no clarification of the differences of induced fantasies from dream fantasies has been made so that one cannot treat TAT stories as if they were dreams. A TAT story, he indicates, is intentionally, even though artificially, produced in the setting of a relationship with another person; it is guided by instructions producing a conscious and to some degree reasoned creation. It thus differs in all these particulars from a dream. Moreover, "the basic condition of the dream, the reduction of mental activity to archaic forms as a consequence of the will to sleep and of concomitant physiological changes, does not obtain in the TAT at all." (71, p. 23.)

In psychoanalytic perspective there seems to be fairly general agreement that the TAT projections are often products of the mechanisms which defend the ego against unacceptable forces. Needs and drives do not necessarily show themselves clearly—their presence and strength sometimes can be inferred only from accentuation of the defenses against them, as in reaction formation or denial of a trend such as hostility. This is not to say that deep-lying desires and aspirations are not permitted expression in the TAT, but rather that one must make a distinction between these needs and the defenses against them. Strictly speaking, defense needs appear to be at three levels—accepted needs at the conscious level, rejected needs partly at the unconscious level, and unconscious defenses against repressed needs. Rapaport and his associates (40) indicate some of the forms that defense takes. The most obvious are constrictions of ideation, which may be likened to restriction of the ego. These constrictions may take several forms—stories with just enough life and movement to comply with instructions to the letter, if not the spirit; descriptions as such, without an account of preceding events or outcome; or overelaborate insistence that every detail in the picture be accounted for in the story. It would appear, then, that the very content is shaped, and perforce limited, by personality forces—drives and needs and defenses against them. Thus content is limited by defenses as well as stimulated by needs.

It is because of the recognition of both needs and defenses against needs that psychoanalytically oriented interpretation emphasizes more than the single "hero" figure per card. Wyatt, for example, writes of the self-evident but sometimes unappreciated fact that the opponent is just as much a creation of the patient as is the hero. He goes on to state:

Thus the interpreting psychologist should not argue that the subject identifies himself with the hero of the story and places himself in a setting as he remembers it from his own past experiences. Figures which counteract or complement his hero (that is, himself) are neither props nor just bits of past reality retrieved, although a good deal of either may be in them. . . . Schematically, one would suggest that the "central" figure will be more likely to show some of what the subject thinks he is, or wants to be; that means, features acceptable to his ego. This leaves room not only for the expression of ideals and moral standards but, of course, also for many unfavorable traits and for failure which may be fearfully anticipated or even secretly desired. Tendencies in other figures more likely will be dissociated and ego-alien, hence probably the castaways of earlier attempts at integration. (71, pp. 24–25.)

Repression of seeing the gun in 3 BM, displacement of the story to the Middle Ages, negations such as the hero's not being angry suggesting that at first thought he was angry, breakthroughs and slips of the tongue such as tendencies toward aggression followed by denial are all indicative of failures of defense which allow denied impulses to appear for a fleeting instant (6).

The psychoanalytic interpretation of TAT material has been neither systematically explored nor verified by research with TAT as the medium. Knowledge is scattered and incidental, and much remains to be done before any systematic method emerges. The foregoing account is in no sense complete, being merely suggestive of certain commonly stressed elements when TAT productions are seen in psychoanalytic perspective.

It might be well to point out that this description of the psychoanalytic interpretation of TAT material is not offered as a technique suitable for most psychologists. Training in psychoanalytic theory and practice is necessary before other than the most modest application should be attempted. To be sure, a certain skepticism that things are not always what they seem may come from adherence to the aforementioned principles of interpretation. Generally speaking it is psychoanalytic experience, not the findings on the TAT material, that makes such principles of interpretative value. Likewise, as Wyatt puts it, ". . . the interpretation of 'deep' complexes from a TAT, such as the Oedipus complex is, as a rule, a precarious enterprise, characteristic of the novice, but unbecoming to the experienced clinician." (71, p. 24.)

ECLECTIC INTERPRETATIVE SYSTEMS. The clinicians who use the TAT in an eclectic tradition are so diverse in points of view that it is impossible to do much more than illustrate. If they have any common ground, it probably is reflected negatively in the rejection of need-press theory and some of the defense mechanisms described by the psychoanalytically oriented clinician, and positively by the development of some categorization or list of drives, needs, and themes in keeping with their own theoretical predilections. In the account of techniques of analysis to follow, Rotter et al. are more representative of an eclectic tradition than are Bellak and Wyatt, who represent a fusion of need-press and psychoanalytic points of view.

Techniques of Analysis of the TAT

The techniques of analysis are essentially attempts to objectify interpretation by separation of analysis from the integrative interpretation ultimately made. Only to a limited degree are they successful, since the techniques themselves are based upon implicit or explicit interpretations which select certain aspects for analysis and relate them one to another.

The variety of more or less formalized techniques of analysis is quite great. Some are more adapted for research than for the clinical setting; others are not yet fully worked out. Still others with rather gross categories have been applied with some success in a clinical setting. Certain of these approaches are primarily eclectic with reference to the dynamics of personality, and others are more psycho-analytically oriented.

Rosenzweig has suggested a technique of TAT analysis (83) which he has called the Composite Portrait Method since the basic assumption is that the clinician can secure a composite portrait by superimposing and condensing the patient's productions. A detailed presentation is in process of formulation. Enough has been written to suggest that this technique of analysis should prove to be clinically useful. Combs' technique of analysis (10) may also be used. His approach, in an eclectic tradition, stresses desires and the outcomes of the actions told about in the stories. The situational analysis (as opposed to a need or desire approach) used by Arnold (73) may occasionally prove helpful in a clinical setting. She is particularly interested in isolating the situations in which traits are exhibited in the content material. Her technique of analysis is based upon the assumption that the sample situation in the picture will be reacted to in the same way as will the real situation. Habitual attitudes, whether clear-cut or ambiguous, to members of the same or of the other sex, parents, and other figures are sampled. Specifically considered in this section are the techniques of analysis developed by Bellak; Wyatt; and Rotter, Rodnick, Klebanoff, Plenk, and Mensh.

Although it might be possible to offer an integration of these various techniques of analysis, such is not attempted, owing to the conviction that any integration is tantamount to offering nothing more than still another system. Since the psychologist using the TAT clinically will probably develop his own system, modifying to a certain extent those systems now in use, material is presented which may aid him to do so. Pursuant of this aim, whenever possible, the descriptions of the methods of analysis are given in the form of direct quotations.

THE TECHNIQUE OF ANALYSIS OF BELLAK. Bellak (7) stresses the basic assumption that in responding to the TAT cards the patient is under relatively little constraint from the demands of convention or reality and depicts his inner feelings. The steps of recording, analysis, and summary are facilitated by the availability of a record blank (6). A copy of the analysis sheet needed for each TAT card used is given in Figure 4. The check system referred to in the following material is based upon the method of using one check for the mere presence of a given attitude or attribute, and double and triple checks to indicate increasing levels of importance to be assigned to the item. Using this blank as a starting point for elaboration of his system of analysis, Bellak writes as follows:

1. *The Main Theme.* The main theme is best understood as an attempt to restate the gist of the story. . . .

2. *The Main Hero.* . . . . The main hero of the story is the one who is most spoken of, whose feelings and subjective notions are most discussed, and, in general, the figure with whom the narrator seems to identify himself. . . .

By the adequacy of the hero we mean his ability to carry through tasks under external and internal difficulties in a socially, morally, intellectually, and emotionally acceptable manner. The adequacy of the hero frequently conforms to a pattern throughout the stories and is often in a direct relationship to the Ego-strength of the patient. . . .

3. *Attitudes to Superior (Parental) Figures, or to Society.* These attitudes are usually quite clearly brought out in TAT stories. They appear particularly in response to the pictures of people with obvious age differences, but also frequently in response to the boy with the violin. The sub-categories suggested are self-explanatory, and a pattern of behavior from story to story will usually become clear.

4. *Figures Introduced.* If a figure is not present in the picture, and the subject introduces it in his story, we can be doubly sure that it must be a figure of great significance for him and that it constitutes an exponent of an outstanding need or fear. One might note the role which that figure plays dynamically (e.g., punisher, supporter), and at the same time note whether it appears in the form of a male or female, parent or contemporary, etc.

5. *Objects Introduced.* Again, because these objects are supplied strictly by the subject's mind and not at all by the picture, they deserve special notice. Frequently one class of objects, such as books, objects of art, weapons, or money, etc., appear consistently in the stories of a subject.

6. *Objects Omitted.* This category is concerned with meaningful failure to include in the stories objects which are quite apparent in the pictures. Sometimes the rifle in 8 BM is omitted, and at other times the pistol in 3 BM, or the background of a half-dressed woman in Picture 4, etc. Under such circumstances one must look for other indications as to what problems the subject might have concerning aggression or sexual matters that cause him to exclude these objects from apperception.

7. *Attribution of Blame.* The qualities or forces which the subject blames as causing misfortune or tragedy in his story frequently constitute important clues to his conception of the outside world in relation to himself. The variables listed . . . [in Figure 4] . . . are the ones most frequently met with; others may have to be written in.

8. *Significant Conflicts.* The Super-Ego-Id variable is really more in-

FIG. 4.   Bellak Analysis Sheet[5]

TAT

Name...................... Story No......... (TAT Picture No.........)

1. Main theme:

2. Main hero (heroine): age........ sex......... vocation..................
   interests ....
   traits ....
   abilities...
   adequacy (√, √ √, √ √ √)...

3. Attitudes to superior (parental) figures, or to society: (√, √ √, √ √ √)
   autonomous ..... compliant........ respectful....... devoted........
   grateful......... dependent........ remorseful...... competitive....
   resistant......... aggressive........ abasive......... fearful........

4. Figures introduced: (√)
   punisher........ pursuer........... benefactor...... teacher.........
   friend........... reformer.......... lover........... supporter.......
   enemy...........

5. Objects introduced (symbols?):

6. Objects omitted:

7. Attribution of blame: (√, √ √, √ √ √)
   injustice......... indifference......... deception..................
   severity......... deprivation......... unfortunate influence.........

8. Significant conflicts: (√, √ √, √ √ √)
   Super Ego-Id ....   passivity-counteraction.............
   compliance-autonomy ....   achievement-pleasure.............

9. Punishment—for crime: (√, √ √, √ √ √)
   just ....   too severe............   lenient ....
   immediate ....   delayed ....   none ....

10. Attitude to hero: (√, √ √, √ √ √)
    detached and objective ....
    critical and abusive ....
    involved and emphatic ....

11. Signs of inhibition at aggression, sex, etc.: (√, √ √, √ √ √)
    pauses .... change of trend .... stammer ....

12. Outcome: (√, √ √, √ √ √)
    happy......... unhappy .... realistic......... unrealistic.......

13. Pattern of need gratification: (√)
    need-conflict.................
    need-fusion ....
    need-subsidiation ....

14. Plot: (√, √ √, √ √ √)
    structured ....   unstructured ....
    realistic ....   bizarre ....
    complete.............   incomplete ....

[5] Reprinted by permission of the Psychological Corporation and L. Bellak. Copyright 1947 by L. Bellak.

clusive than the other items under this heading; it indicates a general class of conflicts, while the other three items give a more specific indication of the main divergent tendencies. Nevertheless, all these items deal with the more molar level of major conflictual themes while need-conflicts, under Category 13, are concerned with the more molecular patterns of any number of needs occurring in the story.

9. *Punishment for Crime.* The relationship of the nature of the punishment to the severity of the offense gives us an excellent insight into the severity of the Super-Ego; a psychopath's hero may consistently get away in stories of murder with not more than a notion that he has learned a lesson for later life, while a neurotic may have stories in which the hero is accidentally or intentionally killed or mangled or dies of illness following the slightest infractions or expression of aggression.

10. *Attitude to Hero.* A subject will frequently depict his own conflicts by having the hero say or do things in the story and then stepping outside the narrative to severely criticize these actions. At times cynical remarks concerning his own story are simple defensive processes against real emotional involvement. Obsessive-compulsive intellectuals will frequently maintain a detached attitude, offering several possible themes with doubt pertaining to all of them. Hysterics and manics or hypomanics will frequents get dramatically involved in stories full of affectivity.

11. *Signs of Inhibition at Aggression, Sex, etc.* Pauses are sometimes so significant that it may even pay to time them occasionally to get a notion of the severity of the inhibition in the subject. Changes of trends of the story, or turning to an entirely new story are excellent indications that conflictual material was becoming too difficult to handle. Stammering, crossing out, omitting parts of the picture, rejection of all or part of a picture, or severe criticism of it are similarly points worth noticing in this context.

12. *Outcome.* The outcome will often make manifest the basic mood or adjustment of the patient and indicate his Ego-strength. It is interesting to note whether the subject (hero) arrives at a satisfactory solution after a continuous realistic struggle or uses a *deux ex machina* device to arrive at a simple gratification which is obviously on the level of a fantasy wish-fulfillment and has little relation to an overt, manifest achievement drive. If there is a failure to arrive at an acceptable outcome altogether, it probably results from very significant, nearly unsurmountable problems of the patient, and should be scored under the variables of the plot structure, Category 14.

13. *Pattern of Need Gratification.* The concept of conflict between various needs does not require any explanation. One story may actually show whole clusters of conflicts between various drives of varying importance. Murray's concepts of *need-fusion* and *need-subsidiation* are very helpful for the understanding of motivational systems in a given personality. For example, if a hero wants to buy a restaurant with the notion of giving people better and healthier food and at the same time enrich-

ing himself by means of this public service, we would speak of a *fusion* of the hero's need for nurturance and his need for acquisition. On the other hand, the hero may want to buy the restaurant because he expects it to be a good source of income which he needs to take care of his family. In this case we would say that his need for acquisition (of money) is *subsidiary* to his need for nurturance; namely, he wants to acquire money *in order to* be able to take care of his family. By means of these two concepts, whole hierarchies of motivation can be recognized in the TAT.

14. *Plot.* The form analysis of the TAT stories may be helpful to a certain extent. . . . It is this author's belief that there is a quickly diminishing return in this approach and that this is more strictly the province of the Rorschach Test. However, the categories of structure, bizarreness, and completeness probably permit a fairly good appraisal of the intactness of the thought processes and the Ego's ability to master the emotional material produced. . . .

The Summary and the Final Report. After having analyzed each of the picture-stories, one goes back over them and writes a thumbnail summary of each on page 4 of the *TAT Blank.* Following this one makes a Final Report on the cover, using the original analyses and the summaries as guides. On putting down the main data from each story in the Summary, the repetitive pattern ordinarily becomes clear. (7, pp. 5–8.)[6]

THE TECHNIQUE OF ANALYSIS OF WYATT. The technique of analysis of the TAT developed by Wyatt is one that he and his associates have used in their clinical work for some years. Its nature may be gathered most vividly and with the least chance of misinterpretation through his own statement. Figure 5 presents his work sheet, and in the following quotation in summary outline form is given a description of his system in his own words. He writes:

1. *Story—Description. Story* is everything which in either plot or description of the stimulus, goes beyond what is immediately given in the picture-stimulus. *Description* is everything short of *Story.* As there are transitions more often than clear-cut conditions, *Story-descriptions* or *Description-story* should be used to indicate how far *Description* tends to develop into *Story,* or if the response expands in any way upon the given scene of the stimulus. As in all other variables, standard abbreviations, such as *St.* or *Desc.* will be useful.

2. *Stimulus Perception.* This variable aims to define how the picture stimulus has been perceived and to what extent. The performance of a large normal group will be the norm against which any individual performance should be evaluated. . . . The stimulus may be perceived by the testee in the way in which it is commonly and most frequently done,

---

[6] Reprinted from *A Guide to the Interpretation of the Thematic Apperception Test* by L. Bellak, by permission of The Psychological Corporation and L. Bellak. Copyright 1947 by L. Bellak.

in which case nothing is to be recorded. Deviation from common performance can go in three major directions: *Omission, Distortion,* and *Detail,* e.g.: *Omission* of a person in Picture II, or of the object on the floor in III. *Distortion* of the girl in II into apparition. *Detail* description of the scence in II or of the furnishings in V.

FIG. 5. Wyatt Analysis Sheet[7]

TAT

Name..........................Education................Age........

Story Description			
Stimulus Perception			
Deviation from Typical Response			
Deviation from Self			
Time Trend			
Level of Interpretation			
Tone of Story			
Quality of Telling			
Focal Figure: Sex; Traits			
Other Figures: Sex; Traits			
Personal Relationships: Formal; Emotional			
Strivings Avoidances			
Presses			
Outcome			
Thema			

[7] Reprinted with permission of F. Wyatt.

3. *Deviations from Typical Response.* This variable denotes any major deviation from the several *plots* commonly used in response to a particular picture, or from the *perception* of the latter. It duplicates to some extent the previous variable but serves also to indicate unusual responses in the sense of an "original" response in the Rorschach Test. For quick scoring *deviation* may be marked with a check.

4. *Deviation from Self.* This variable should only be checked *after* all other stories have been analyzed. A concise statement of the nature of deviations will be indicated.

5. *Time Trend.* This serves to indicate the trend of the response as far as time is concerned: whether it gravitates toward the *past*; rests mainly in the *present* or projects into the *future*.

6. *Level of Interpretation.* This variable, together with (7) and (8) is among the most important, and most equivocal ones for analysis. The following qualities were selected as the ones most common in occurrence, and most significant for interpretation: (a) *concrete-factual* (on the level of realistic experience as distinguished from the following ones); (b) *endopsychic* (everything on the level of waking inner experience, thought or feeling); (c) *symbolic* (the scene means something beyond its immediate appearance, e.g. II. may mean the Good Earth or the Blessings of the Simple Life); (d) *dreamlike* (everything on the level of imagined subjective reality, as in a dream, in trance, in hallucination); (e) *past* and *mythical* (response, dealing with the more remote, "historical" past, no less than a generation ago, or any realm of Gods, ghosts, etc.); (f) *make-believe* (people in the story pretend to do, or feel, something which they do not really feel, or do, like play-acting); (g) *conditional* (the progress of events is made dependent on a certain interpretation in the beginning; e.g. if this is a gun then it means suicide; but if this is a toy then this may just mean that the boy is sulking after a disappointment. For the time being I would suggest that alternative responses to the same picture should be marked here, too).

7. *Tone of Story.* This refers to the feeling tone which pervades the entire response and is hence the complex effect of language and imagery, of story, and even of the perception of the stimulus. To become sensitive to it is one of the major tasks in learning to interpret the *TAT*. Twelve qualities were selected which seem to be the most frequent and psychologically the more important ones. If their use should seem too cumbersome or their meaning equivocal, it is recommended to describe *Tone* concisely, and as closely to the words of the testee as possible. The 12 qualities are: (a) *indifferent* (no particular feeling tone, flat); (b) *detached* (noticeable intention to be aloof); (c) *contemplative* (philosophically meditative, didactic); (d) *cheerful-expansive* (buoyant, vigorous drive); (e) *serene* (content but quiet, without much display of drive); (f) *melodramatic-pompous* (phrases, stereotypes of language or plot, soap opera); *unhappy-tragic* (any unhappy feeling tone other than the ones specified subsequently; frustration, suffering, thwarting, etc.); (g) *tense* (unresolved tension throughout the response, constrained; the

reason for it, as a rule, is not overt); (h) *anxious* (expression of anxiety, worry, concern; tension more definite than in (g) is important here); (i) *morbid* (this variable comprises, for the time being, any feeling tone of extreme moroseness; ideas of decay; disintegration, abandonment of self, gore, loss of orientation and control); (j) *aggressive* (with the connotation of pent-up hatred, vindictive lashing-out, critical asides, etc.).

8. *Quality of Telling.* This variable refers to choice of language, or diction, and to the style of telling, ranging from the structure of sentences to composition. The following qualifying terms seem most appropriate: (a) *simple* (average, every-day "spoken language"); (b) *primitive* (limited "words of one syllable" vocabulary, typical mistakes in grammar and syntax; (c) *verbose* (profuse on a simple or primitive level); (d) *stilted* (extravagant formality, stiffness, high-fallutin' words and phrases); (e) *cliché* (stereotype phrases of cheap literature); (f) *colorful* (variety, poignancy, originality of expression on a simple, not particularly literate level); (g) *literate* (diction and style showing influence of literacy and esthetic training). Two additional variables though of a somewhat different logical quality, may be used in combination with the preceding ones: (h) *critical* (if a good deal of emphasis is on a critical discussion of either the stimulus or the presumed conduct of the people in it); (i) *evasive* (if the purpose of the response is obviously to disguise the testee's true attitudes, to be noncommittal, to get by without saying anything).

9. *Focal Figure.* This figure, the former "hero," should not be selected according to his virtues but with regard to the extent to which the response centers around him. Space devoted to his description is a good but not an absolute indicator. In those frequent cases when the choice is doubtful, alternatives should be stated, too. Describe sex and the most important traits or activities which characterize this figure for a particular story, in the testee's own words. Avoid precocious interpretation which comes in by describing the focal figure in terms of its presumed psychological meaning.

10. *Other Figures.* Figures other than the focal one should be described in exactly the same way. If there should be too many—which is extremely rare in clinical testing—the more important ones should be selected.

11. *Personal Relationships.* Two classes of relationship should be distinguished: *formal* and *emotional* ones. *Formal* refers to institutional relationships (father, mother, husband, wife, etc.); *emotional* refers to love, hatred, dependence, etc.

12. *Strivings, Avoidances.* These should be abstracted from the response again as literally as possible. *Striving* refers to the manifest tendencies prior to any designation of unconscious significance, as does *avoidance*, the tendency away from something. If there is any question, refer first to the focal figure, then to his counterpart. Statement of *striving* or *avoidance* should include its object (e.g. boy—become famous).

13. *Presses.* This variable is defined in Murray's sense. It implies any influence from outside exercised upon the focal figure, his counterpart,

or upon any next-to-focal figure. *Friendly* (benign) presses should be distinguished from *unfriendly* (inimical, harm-intending) ones as well as from *impersonal* ones (e.g., forces of nature).

14. *Outcome. Success* or *defeat* in the end refer again to the *focal figure*. Both should be understood in a very wide sense, like gratification and frustration. *Unresolved tension* denotes the absence of an outcome, as when the situation is left dangling. A situation which by its very premises cannot have any outcome (e.g., description) is "no outcome" and is scored by a zero.

15. *Thema.* The main trend and main events of the story should be abstracted here in the most concise form. To learn how to shell out the core, or the thema of the story, how to epitomize from the response what is essential in it, is another skill which will only be acquired from experience with many responses of widely varied type. The thema-abstracts should be concrete and as close to the testee's words as possible. A descriptive newspaper headline will give a good example of what is intended.

A few general remarks should be added to the description of categories used for analysis. The rule has been mentioned several times that manifestly observable phenomena only should be described in the analysis form. So much for the principle; there are numerous incidents in the practical application of the test which fall in the middle between inference and manifest appearance so that they can neither be checked nor dismissed. They should be noted and characterized, perhaps best by being put in parenthesis. This is also suggested for slight or marginal tendencies which as psychological cues, are probably of a similar nature.

Scoring and Interpretation. After all 10 stories have been analyzed, a certain amount of numerical scoring is possible as indicated before. Variables are added up algebraically, like *story, description, description-story,* etc., and trends gleaned from the sum total. This is obviously possible only in some of the 14 categories. Qualitative (non-scorable) variables should be summarized with a view to regularity of trends and to the specific conditions of deviation. Following the suggestion of Rapaport and others, interpretation may well take its start from the deviations of the testee from the norm, and from his own trends. Naturally, this implies first a definition of pervasive characteristic trends in the testee's stories. If a printed form is employed similar to the one which I am using now, interpretation might start from the summary at the extreme right of the analysis sheet then work its way back vertically through the structural quality of the 10 stories while searching in horizontal direction for similar trends in different stories. Schematically speaking, the essence of analysis seems to consist in an appraisal of the change of variables connected with (and, possibly, dependent upon) the change of other variables, including the picture stimulus. (70, pp. 325–329.)[8]

---

[8] Reprinted from "The Scoring and Analysis of the Thematic Apperception Test" by F. Wyatt, by permission of the *Journal of Psychology.* Copyright 1947 by the Journal Press.

FIG. 6   Klebanoff, Plenk, and Mensh TAT Analysis Sheet

Name...   Date.................................

Group...   Session.............................

Analysis of Thematic Apperception Test

Thema										Picture											Summary
I	1	2	3	4	5	6	7	8	9	10	11	12	13	14	15	16	17	18	19	20	
Murder																					
Death																					
Suicide																					
II																					
Phys. viol.																					
Injury-acc.																					
Illness																					
Crime																					
Punish.																					
Arrest-capt.																					
Escape																					
Thr.-rep.-bul.																					
III																					
Quarrel																					
Domina.																					
Antag.																					
Dishon.-cheat.																					
Disloyalty																					
Ext.-confl.																					
Hate-revenge																					
Anger-rage																					
IV																					
Deprivation																					
Int. confl.																					
Emot. stress																					
Misfortune																					
Disappoint.																					
Separ.-reject.																					
Despondency																					
Jealousy																					
Fear																					
Anxiety																					
Rejection																					
V																					
Reassurance																					
Sex																					
Pity-forgive.																					
Grat.-friend.																					
Love																					
Happiness																					
Obligation																					
Affection																					
Repentance																					
Goal																					

Summary		Number		Percent
Category I.	Loss of life		Category IV.	Internalized emotional stress
Category II.	Physical aggression		Category V.	Positive
Category III.	Nonphysical aggression			

Length of Stories

1	2	3	4	5	6	7	8	9	10	11	12	13	14
				15	16	17	18	19	20				

Introduced Content

1. _____
2. _____
3. _____
4. _____
5. _____
6. _____
7. _____
8. _____
9. _____
10. _____

Hero Figure

1	2	3	4	5	6	7	8	9	10

Solutions

		Picture																			Summary
		1	2	3	4	5	6	7	8	9	10	11	12	13	14	15	16	17	18	19	20	
Failure Central	E																					
	S																					
	P																					
	L																					
Failure Minor	E																					
	S																					
	P																					
	L																					
Success Central	E																					
	S																					
	P																					
	L																					
Success Minor	E																					
	S																					
	P																					
	L																					
None																						

Symbols Used

M: man	C: child	P: power
W: woman	A: animal	L: love
B: boy	I: inanimate object	S: social
G: girl		E: economic

THE TECHNIQUE OF ANALYSIS OF ROTTER ET AL. A technique of TAT analysis which deserves more attention than it has received, even from its authors (since of four articles concerned with it only one has been published in other than abstract form), is that with which Rotter, Rodnick, Klebanoff, Plenk, and Mensh successively concerned themselves.

In 1940 Rotter and Rodnick (53), in a study of the reactions to experimentally induced frustration, introduced an objective scoring technique for the Thematic Apperception Test in order to present a standard method for handling TAT data. Their concern was with the development of a technique for research purposes and not necessarily to be used in clinical practice. In fact, Rotter, today, recommends for clinical usage a more subjective technique which is integrated with the individual's systematic approach to personality. The technique they developed was applied further and elaborated by Rodnick and Klebanoff (43) in a study of projective reactions to induced frustrations as a measure of social adjustment. More recently, Klebanoff (25) used the standardized scoring system to treat data obtained in a study of alcoholism. Shortly after this study, Klebanoff, Plenk, and Mensh modified the scoring system to its present form (26). Figure 6 supplies in the form of a work sheet the skeleton of the method of analysis.

The analysis of TAT data proceeds by thema content according to major category (loss of life, physical aggression, nonphysical aggression, internalized emotional stress, positive), length of stories, introduced content, hero figure identifications, and solutions (success or failure of central or minor character). The solutions also are identified by area (power, love, social, economic) and by character (man, woman, boy, girl, child, animal, inaminate object). The five categories of content include forty themas ranging from the three of murder, death, and suicide under Loss of Life to eleven under Internalized Emotional Stress. These are checked under the appropriate headings on the work sheet.

Each of these categories will be examined in more detail. The forty themas selected have been found to appear with sufficient frequency in TAT content to warrant their inclusion. Frequency of occurrence is entered in the summary column at the right of the blank. The themas are classified as subcategories of five major categories and are summarized by percent. Length of stories is reported by word counts. Introduced content concerns itself with additional significant material which elaborates the classification of thema. Such material may vary in quantity from one or two ideas to nearly a dozen. In the present form of the report, space is provided for ten instances of significant material not already accounted for under thema. Hero figure identification is handled by writing in the different forms which the hero figure assumes. Experience has shown that there are seldom more than eight to ten different hero figures produced.

It was also believed important to consider the characters to whom success or failure was attributed. Analysis of the solutions in terms of success or failure of the central figure and minor figures proceeded on the assumption of a tendency toward greater self-identification with the central character. The type (area) of solution was included, as it was believed that one could deduce from it some idea of the personal feelings of inferiority or superiority as related to specific kinds of insecurities. As shown in Figure 6 the examiner need only check the appropriate cell, insert the relevant symbol and offer short summarizations, then summarize these data to get range and frequency of thema, and direction of identification and solution.

The advantages (although some might consider them disadvantages) of this system are its relative simplicity with consequent ease of learning, its apparently fairly objective character, and its statement in commonly used clinical terms. Content evaluation, to be sure, proceeds at a rather superficial level, and depth interpretation does not necessarily follow. It must be added, however, that going beyond this system while continuing to use it is quite possible. For the comparatively inexperienced clinician it is perhaps all that can be expected; for the experienced it may serve as a base line or, when time is limited, the means of succinctly summarizing the material.

PRINCIPLES AND MODES OF INTERPRETATION

All techniques of analyzing TAT stories require a preliminary interpretative process on the part of the clinician in order to decide the appropriate categorization of the material under the rubrics of the system. Further, a post-analysis interpretative process is essential for clinical use. To be sure, for research interests one may stop with summarization of the results of the individual analyses, treating each of the items of the analysis as one element to be summed with other similar ones. Even in such studies, some sort of interpretative step beyond this is taken, although supported by appeal to the more objectified results presented in the summary of the analyses. In research this step, although desirable, is not necessarily essential, as when one is content to report measures of central tendency, variability, and correlation of the various single scoring categories. But in clinical practice the interpretative step, no matter how short or long, is mandatory. Imagine a clinical report on a TAT analysis reported to one's colleagues in the form of a neat copy of the work sheets! Subjective interpretation is present in *all* clinical work with the TAT.

The principles of interpretation offered as guides have been numerous and varied. Several psychologists, particularly Murray (36) (37), Rapaport (39) (40) (41), Rotter (52), Bellak (7), Wyatt (71), Rosenzweig (83), Stein (61), and Tomkins (64) (65), have actively considered the problems arising from this issue. It is manifestly impossible to give their contributions in full detail, so nothing more than a restricted sampling of the more important principles of interpretation may be given here. The reader is urged to consult the publications of these clinicians for more complete discussions.

Before dealing with these principles it is advisable to reconsider for a moment the situation created by the TAT. In building a story around a TAT picture, the patient gives *his* view of the picture, the antecedent events, what the figures are thinking and feeling, and the outcome. These are *his* thoughts (projections). It follows, then, that the characters into which he breathes life are his creations, and that in varying degrees he identifies with some figures while others are characters from his own private world (past and present) to whom he also attributes ways of thinking, feeling, and doing.

What principles may be applied in such a situation as this? It is at once apparent that the breadth of possibilities is just about as wide as the range of facets of the personality of the human individual. The principles of interpretation then are, as Harrison pointed out some years ago, "similar to principles that are used by everyone in everyday life with varying degrees of skill when opinions, comments, mannerisms, and various expressive movements are examined for the light they may throw on the attitudes and hidden motives of others." (78, p. 54.) If this conception of the task be accepted along with the previous emphasis on the personal and idiomatic, it may be seen that unusualness of theme, greater than usual frequency

of motif, interpretations of the patient foreign to the perceptual content of the picture, shift of emphasis, and so on are the clues to
which attention must be directed. Cutting across such indicators of
the personal and private are the characteristics of the stories with
which the clinician deals, such as hero, theme, mood, outcome, or
the nature of the material. It will be most convenient, since it reflects
current practice, to consider both the principles of identification of
the idiosyncratic and the characteristics of the stories in discussion
of interpretative principles. Generally speaking, the principles and
modes of interpretation which follow are not mutually contradictory
and presumably are such that all might be applied with a single case.
It would be too much to expect, however, that the busy clinician
would do this in every case. They are presented to give the gist of the
thinking of various experts—not to be adopted *in toto*, but as a
sampling of the way clinicians proceed in their task of interpretation.
In no sense are they given as a system to end all systems.

THE ATTITUDE OF THE CLINICIAN. The warning has been sounded
several times before, but it is worth repeating that projective devices
are two-edged swords, sometimes mirroring projections of the interpreter instead of the patient. To guard against this factor, partial
safeguards may be applied: the rule of parsimony, search for other
confirmatory evidence, and the use of the most objective method of
analysis commensurate with the nature of the material and the intent of the examination. Stein (61) suggests the specific safeguard
of making judgments only when substantiation may be found in two
or more stories.

It is also Stein who warns against too literal interpretation of the
stories. In this connection he writes:

Such interpretations will frequently be inaccurate because the objects
in the picture upon which an individual chooses to project his feelings,
attitudes, etc., are rarely as valid as the feelings and attitudes themselves.
For example, we cannot assume that a story to Picture #1 involving a
discussion of the boy's desire to play the violin reflects the patient's musi-
cal interests or aspirations. The patient may have projected his aspirations, which really lie in an entirely different area, upon the violin because it was the only object available in the picture. This fallacy may be
overcome by concentrating primarily upon the dynamics involved in the
stories, by knowing the common stories to each picture, by reserving
judgments about specific factors until they are corroborated by two or
more stories, and by then giving preference to those stories in which the
objects, people, etc., referred to are not suggested by the pictures them-

selves. (For example, if the patient says to Picture #1 "the boy wants to play the violin," to Picture #6 "the son is leaving his mother to play in a symphony orchestra," and to Picture #20 "the man is going to a concert," then we may postulate an interest in music.) (61, p. 23.)

Sarason (58) warns the clinician against adopting the mental set that one adopts when reading a book or newspaper story in which the words are accepted in their dictionary or literal meaning. Since the patient is expressing unconscious drives in a disguised fashion one wants to listen for their *other* meaning. Just as a therapist uses a sort of even-hovering, free-floating attention, so too must the TAT administrator listen not for the literal meaning but for what is behind it in the way of unconscious motivation. In this connection he suggests that the clinician read the story as if *he* were telling it— a procedure which may make the relation between what was said and what was felt somewhat clearer.

DERIVATION OF THE THEME. Most interpretations of a TAT story involve in some fashion the derivation of the theme of that story. It may be stated in terms of the relation of needs and press or, as is common in other approaches, simply as the summarized meaning or gist of the story. The particular kinds of episodes, characters, or moods constantly appearing as recurring motifs (see the later discussion of the principle of frequency) are identified. These themes may appear in many constellations and it is the task of the clinician to select the similarities from the different settings in which they are couched.

Bellak suggests considering the main theme in terms of five levels. The descriptive level is that in which there is a plain summary of the story's meaning. The four other levels are the interpretative, diagnostic, symbolic, and elaborative levels which he illustrates from a story to card 6 BM as follows:

This is a young successful engineer. . . . He is the only son in his family, his father is dead and his mother is very close to him. He is in the oil business and he has been offered a contract to go overseas to the East Indies. He has signed the contract and is about to leave. He obtains her farewell and they part heart-broken. After a while she feels very lonesome and decides to follow her son to the East Indies. It is wartime and somehow she obtains passage on a ship to the island on which her son is. An enemy submarine sinks her ship and she perishes. . . . Her son had not heard about her intentions but had independently planned to visit her as a surprise. He decides to return home for a surprise. . . .

The ship on which he had obtained passage is taking the same route which his mother had taken. . . . At the exact spot where his mother perishes, another enemy submarine attacks and he perishes also.

The theme on a *descriptive level* could be briefly restated as: a son lives alone with his beloved mother and leaves her—when they both try to rejoin each other they die on the same spot. On an *interpretive level*, one may go a step farther and put the meaning in a generalized form, assuming a meaning beyond this story: the patient believes that if one . . . permits oneself (incestual) fantasies, such as living with the mother, then both parties die. On a *diagnostic level*, one transforms these impressions into a definitive statement: this man has incestuous problems and oedipal conflicts which cause him severe guilt feelings. On a *symbolic level*, one may choose to interpret symbols according to psychoanalytic hypotheses; extreme parsimony and caution must be strongly recommended since this takes one relatively farthest away from hard facts. In our example one might, for instance, possibly want to interpret the torpedoes as paternal phallic symbols which endanger and destroy both mother and son for their illicit attempted get-together.

On an *elaborative level*, one must get the subject's elaborations and free associations to such specific data as: "East Indies," "engineer," to any proper names or dates, and any other associations he can give. (7, p. 5.)

In terms of the analysis sheet of Bellak introduced in an earlier section, the descriptive level is considered a crutch for which there is no need to give a written statement whereas the interpretative theme is given on the analysis sheet for the particular story with the diagnostic or higher level theme used in the summary statement only.

Other aspects of theme derivation have been discussed in the techniques of analysis previously described. Categorization of theme content is the crux of the analytic technique of Rotter and the others concerned with that particular approach. They take the additional step of not only using specific themes but further identifying the broader categories in which they fall.

DETERMINATION OF IDENTIFICATIONS. In analyzing a TAT story it is necessary to determine the figure with whom the patient has identified himself. Most often it is safe to assume that the patient has identified with the hero. In this connection Murray suggests commonly used aids to this identification. The character with whom he has identified may be:

(1) the character in whom the story-teller was apparently most interested, whose point of view was adopted, whose feelings and motives have been most intimately portrayed. He (or she) is usually (2) the one who

most resembles the subject, an individual of the same sex, of about the same age, status or role, who shares some of the subject's sentiments and aims. This character, called *hero* (whether it be male or female) is usually (3) the person (or one of the persons) depicted in the picture, and (4) the person who plays the leading role in the drama (hero in the literary sense), who appears at the beginning and is most vitally involved in the outcome.

Although most stories have but one hero (readily distinguishable by these criteria), the interpreter should be prepared to deal with certain common complications: (1) the identification of subject with character sometimes shifts during the course of the story; there is a *sequence of heroes* (first, second, third, etc.). (2) Two forces of the subject's personality may be represented by two different characters, for example, an antisocial drive by a criminal and conscience by a law-enforcing agent. Here we would speak of an *endopsychic thema* (internal dramatic situation) with two *component heroes*. (3) The subject may tell a story that contains a story, such as one in which the hero observes or hears about events in which another character (for whom he feels some sympathy) is leadingly involved. Here we would speak of a *primary* and a *secondary* hero. Then (4), the subject may identify with a character of the opposite sex and express a part of his personality just as well in this fashion. (In a man this is commonly a sign of a high feminine component and in a woman of a high masculine component.) Finally, there may be no discernible single hero; either (5) heroship is divided among a number of equally significant, equally differentiated *partial heroes* (e.g. a group of people); or (6) a chief character (hero in the literary sense) obviously belongs to the object side of the subject-object situation; he is not a component of the story-teller's personality but an element of his environment. The subject, in other words, has not identified with the principal character to the slightest extent, but has observed him as he would a stranger or disliked person with whom he had to deal. The subject himself is not represented, or is represented by a minor character (hero in our sense). (36, p. 7.)

Other related or similar principles useful in determining identifications have been suggested by Rotter (52). Among others he speaks of the repeatedly demonstrated clinical finding that the patient does not identify with a character whose behavior he personally finds reprehensible. It is unusual to find identification with a figure who is mean, cruel, or unjust. True, he may be punished for a crime, but either its nature is not stated or it is not of one of those just mentioned above. "Murder will out" on a TAT card, but not such a characteristic as miserliness. Signs of emotional involvement such as change of posture or tone of voice sometimes are a relatively simple clue to the identification figure.

Occasionally the hero's identity is not obvious because the patient may speak in the terms of those identifying characteristics more or less equally for two or more figures. If this be the case, it is frequently helpful to compare the data in the particular story with those of other stories, giving special attention to the figures' principal characteristics. Then, if the hero is aggressive in most of the stories, the figure who is aggressive may be presumed to be the hero in the story in question.

Earlier the thesis was advanced that most often the patient identified with the hero. Although this is correct so far as it goes, there are exceptions. As Murray indicated in the quotation just given, there may be a sequence of heroes or two component heroes. There may also be the phenomenon commented on in connection with the psychoanalytically oriented interpretation—identification with the hero's opponent, who is characterized by more unfavorable, denied, and ego-alien traits.

The determination of the roles attributed to characters other than the hero should not be neglected. Parental figures, marital partners, and siblings are important. By determination of the interaction between the hero and these other figures, insight into the nature and form of their interpersonal relations may be judged. Thus information may be obtained concerning the way the patient regards his world.

DETERMINATION OF MOTIVATIONS AND FEELINGS. In many, but not all, techniques of analysis there is emphasis upon the feeling and motivation of the hero and other characters. In the process of analysis a number of sets of concepts may be used. For example, Murray and his associates advanced a comprehensive list of needs for this purpose. Or the clinician may depend upon his own conception of the drives to action as postulated either by some systematic point of view or by an eclectic one evolving from his experience. Although determination of motivation and feeling is an important step in TAT interpretation by the very nature of the test, further consideration here is not indicated. (A full review would require examination of all aspects of personality psychodynamics.)

The strivings of the hero, it is assumed, are related to the strivings of the patient; the strivings of others are either ego-alien strivings or those of other individuals who serve to obstruct or further the aims of the patient.

INVESTIGATION OF ENVIRONMENTAL STIMULI AND OUTCOME. The influence of the needs of the figure or figures other than the one with whom the patient has identified shades imperceptibly into the investigation of environmental stimuli and the outcome of the focal figure's interaction with them. The concern is with the environment in which the patient behaves and the way in which it influences him. The description of the situation in which the focal figure is participating tells how the patient regards his environment. This, it is obvious, is partly secured from the theme as such but also deserves consideration in its own right. From the point of view of Murray and his associates this is the problem of press—the nature of which has been previously discussed. It is also an aspect of "outcome" as Murray formulates it. He writes very succinctly concerning outcome as follows:

. . . [Another] . . . matter to which the interpreter should attend is the comparative strength of the forces emanating from the hero and the forces emanating from the environment. How much force (energy, determination, enduring effort, competence) does the hero manifest? What is the strength of the facilitating or beneficial forces of the environment as compared to the opposing or harmful forces? Is the hero's path of achievement difficult or easy? In the face of opposition does he strive with renewed vigor (counteraction) or does he collapse? Does the hero make things happen or do things happen to him? To what extent does he manipulate or overcome the opposing forces and to what extent is he manipulated or overcome by them? Is he coercing or coerced? mostly active or mostly passive? Under what conditions does he succeed, when others help him or when he strives alone? Under what conditions does he fail? After committing an offense or crime does the hero get properly punished? does he feel guilty, confess, atone and reform? or is the misdemeanor treated as a matter of no moral significance and the hero allowed to "get away with it" without punishment or fateful consequence? How much energy does the hero direct against himself? (36, p. 12.)

Up to this point in the description of principles and modes of interpretation the emphasis has been upon various aspects of the stories as such—the theme, the focal figure or figures, environmental stimuli, and the like. Emphasis now shifts to the principles which aid in the isolation of the clinically important from the unimportant aspects of the stories, no matter what the phase of the story under consideration. In effect, not all themes, outcomes, and so on are important in themselves. Principles used to make this separation are next considered.

INTERPRETATION IN TERMS OF FREQUENCY. Recurrence of motif is one clue to the importance of material derived from the TAT. Just as in psychotherapy the patient keeps returning to that which is important to him, so does he in his TAT stories. Interpretation in terms of frequency has nowhere been more clearly and cogently stated than by Rotter. He writes:

Information or material obtained from the stories is considered significant when it occurs more frequently than might be expected, that is, when one attempts to determine what themes or plots are more significant in determining the patient's basic personality trends, complexes, and attitudes, a principle may be applied which states that a theme or plot which occurs repetitively is likely to be of greater significance than one which does not. The application of this principle requires that the examiner have formal or informal norms so that he has some idea of how frequently the ideas he is concerned with will occur in subjects who do not present serious problems. For example, if he wishes to conclude that the patient is overconcerned about death because death occurred as a theme in eight out of twenty pictures, he must first know how frequently it is likely to occur in a group of subjects who are not overconcerned about death. . . .

In a consideration of specific themes such as suicide, death, aggression, parental love, etc., the expected frequency may be determined only after considerable experience. However, when one is considering the frequency with which certain stories recur, it may be generally felt that if some specific plot in its important details occurs as frequently as twice to relatively different stimulus cards, it presents a greater than average frequency. For example, the occurrence in two or more cards, where the two pictures are objectively dissimilar, of a story involving a wife who was "talked into" getting married to a husband who later turns out to be a drunk and no good, usually presents a greater than average frequency of occurrence. In some instances themes will be repeated so often that even the relatively inexperienced examiner will be able to realize that he is dealing with a greater than normal average frequency. For example, a depressed patient may note that the expression on the face of the character is sad in as many as 18 out of 20 pictures. Relatively short experience is required to know that the occurrence of a suicide in 6 out of 20 pictures presents an unusually high frequency. Until the examiner feels relatively sure of normal expectancy, he must be cautious in attributing individual significance to specific themes that have occurred with some frequency. (52, pp. 78–79.)

Caution must be sounded, however, against blind application of the principle of frequency—psychological understanding of the belonging together or symbolic relationship of superficially disparate strivings is also needed. Rapaport (39) is particularly persuasive concerning this issue, showing that main strivings in various stories need not be identical to complement one another.

INTERPRETATION IN TERMS OF UNUSUALNESS. Several times reference has been made to the identification of the unusual, idiosyncratic, or personal aspects of a patient's TAT stories. For example, the explicit norms so far developed are useful in their detection.

Some of the various facets of interpretation are given by Rotter through consideration of the unusuality of the stories. He writes as follows:

The second general principle in determining the aspects of the subject's production of stories that are significant is the criterion of unusualness. A plot, theme, idea, or a choice of words may be unusual if it is rare, peculiar, or if the subject's emotionality, emphasis, or vividness makes it stand out.

Unusual responses may be discussed under three headings:

(a) *Choice and development of plot.* An entire story may be unusual in that it possesses any of the characteristics given above. So, for example, in Card 14 a story to the effect that the man in the picture believes that he can fly and is about to step through the window in an attempt to fly to the next building would be an unusual plot because it is rare. In considering plots and their development, knowledge of norms is again very necessary. Although the basic plot may be a very common one, a peculiar twist in the development of the story may make the story as a whole an unusual one. For example, in Card 6BM the story is given of a man whose mother is broken-hearted because he is leaving home to marry. When the man does leave home, the mother immediately dies of grief. The outcome of the story provides an unusual ending, which shows that one is dealing with more than the normal separation from mother and home, and it is likely that the subject is either expressing a pathologically strong mother attachment or a strong resentment to a maternal overdominance.

In considering the unusualness of plots, the stimulus nature of a card is important. For example, a story about suicide in Card 14 or in Card 3BM cannot be considered unusual. However, in Card I should the story told there end in suicide it could be considered unusual. *Should a plot from one of the pictures be one of a few frequently given plots and the basic idea or relationship does not occur elsewhere in the stories, one should be extremely cautious in attributing any significance to it.* For example, if in Card I a story of maternal dominance is given (the boy doesn't want to practice but his mother says he must), one should be extremely cautious in concluding that the subject has been overdominated or has dependent wishes without additional evidence from other stories.

(b) *Misrecognitions.* Misrecognitions are common, particularly with pathological cases. Some deviations occur so frequently in normal groups that it is difficult to attribute any significance to them. For example, the boy in M15 is frequently considered a girl, a young man, or a young woman. Most misrecognitions are significant of important personality problems and represent either an inability of the patient to accept what he sees or a pressing need to change the picture so that he may be given an opportunity to express his own emotional conflicts. Examples of the first kind of misrecognition are the ones where the subject sees an angry face as a pleasant one, or a nude of one sex as a member of the opposite sex. He may leave out obvious details in order not to deal with a situation which is catastrophic. . . . Where the patient is unable to accept physical violence or aggression because of a need to suppress his own aggression, misinterpretation of both objects in the picture and the facial expressions of the characters are common in order to avoid aggressive stories. Examples of the second type of misrecognition are those of seeing the violin in Card I as broken, seeing the expressions of the characters as portraying the same emotion as the patient feels, and changing the age and even sex of the characters in the pictures in order to make easier an expression of their own problems.

Misrecognitions also take the form of adding objects and even people to the pictured objects. Sometimes stories refer to objects which are behind other things which are in the picture and occasionally a specific object is claimed to be present in the solid black or gray background. . . .

(c) *Choice of words.* Not only may the stories and the development of individual themes be unusual, but occasionally the choice of words may indicate significant material. For example, one patient who was suspected of sexual desire for a half-sister referred in one story to the heroine (whom the hero later marries) with the awkward phrasing of "this girl is the daughter of a woman." In another story the hero marries "a girl he has known all his life and grew up with." One patient with two children, a girl who was conceived out of wedlock and a boy born five years after marriage, expressed an attitude toward the little girl by such unusual phrasing, an attitude which she would not admit in a direct interview. In card 9GF (a woman is running along what appears to be a beach), she stated that someone is drowning and then, "If it was a little boy the mother would be very anxious to get there."

Sometimes a word will occur repeatedly and in such unusual context that it may have some symbolic meaning to a patient. Usually, however, word symbolism is rare except with psychotic patients.

When it is discovered that some theme, plot, or idea occurs more frequently than may be expected or is unusual enough to warrant special consideration, there is still the problem of discovering the meaning of the repetition or unusualness. . . . The final interpretation regarding the personality of the subject is made from the discovery of the meaning and significance of the aspects of the stories which have been selected as frequent or unusual. (52, pp. 79–82.)[9]

INTERPRETATION IN TERMS OF DISTINGUISHING BETWEEN ESSENTIAL IDEATIONAL CONTENT AND CLICHÉS. From a different perspective— differentiation of clichés from essential ideational content—there is still another approach to the separation of the individual from the social, the idiosyncratic from the stereotyped. However, it is conducive to clarity to consider it separately from discussion of interpretation in terms of unusualness. The distinction between clichés and essential ideational content is clearly stated by Rapaport, who writes:

There are two factors which do not allow all T.A.T. stories to be "essential ideational contents." On the one hand, emotional experiences in the course of time lose their original quality, and when brought into the stories in the form of ideational contents may appear as stereotypes lacking the brand of individuality. On the other hand, much of what we remember has never been essential ideational content or emotional experience. Social stereotypes and clichés, or stories once heard or read, belong also in this category. The T.A.T. stories of clinical subjects are loaded with these stereotypes. These usually display not the subject's essential strivings, but rather his manner of avoiding their expression. Unlike stories which carry essential ideational content, a stereotyped story is not in itself revealing, but several of them together show the types of "defense," of relationships, and of figures, which the subject is prone to use. These types are integral parts of the subject's "private world" . . . and are evidence as to the subject's *principle of selection* in using clichés. Beyond this, the clichés have another significance: they serve as the baseline for appraisal of departures from the subject's narrative and story formation, and stories so departing will be found to contain essential ideational content. (41, p. 80.)

Other indications of the cliché, according to Rotter (52), are the patient's lack of emotional involvement in the rapid, effortless telling of the story, and the differences in tone of these stories from those in which essential ideational content appears.

Relatively superficial stories can frequently be recognized by appeal to the available norms. The paradigmatic story, detectable from the use of the norms previously described, helps the clinician to sep-

_____
    [9] Reprinted from "Thematic Apperception Tests: Suggestions for Administration and Interpretation" by J. Rotter, by permission of the *Journal of Personality*. Copyright 1946 by Duke University Press.

arate clichés from essential ideational content. If a story appears to be a cliché, the task of the psychologist is to examine the story for indications as to whether or not any really vital nuances "seeped through," as it were. As is the case with the "popular" response of the Rorschach it is well, however, not to dismiss too readily a story which at first glance appears to be merely a cliché.

INTERPRETATION IN TERMS OF COMPLIANCE AND CONSISTENCY. Rapaport considers compliance with the instructions and the test cards, consistency within productions (intra-individual consistency), and consistency with the trends exhibited in the general population (inter-individual consistency) very important aspects of TAT interpretation. These interrelated aspects of interpretation both supply a means of general appraisal of the patient and, equally important, are an aid in locating stories of special significance. Both compliance and consistency can be related to and compared with the norms which have been developed, especially the apperceptive norms of Rosenzweig. It is suggested by the writer that in drawing inferences about these characteristics comparison be made with explicit norms.

In connection with compliance and consistency Rapaport[10] writes:

Has he been really able to make up a story, or has he given merely a description of the picture? Has he given his story in the form of a plot, in which antecedents, situation, outcome, as well as the feelings and thoughts of the characters are indicated, or has he had to elaborate it into a circumstantial story? These are . . . questions which the examiner will want to ask himself.

Nearly as helpful as the consideration of the compliance with the instructions is the consideration of the degree of adherence which the subject shows to the implications of the pictures presented. The first question here is whether or not the subject has perceived and apperceived the picture adequately in all its parts. These two formal aspects of the stories lead us to a third most helpful basis for interpretation, which we shall refer to as *inter-* and *intra*-individual consistency. If a subject who usually describes the events antecedent to the situation shown in the picture suddenly avoids doing so in one picture, the examiner will have to pay special attention to that specific story. He may find that the content of this story gives a clue to explain the omission if it is assumed that the idea omitted is one which the subject is unable or reluctant to bring into his consciousness, or at least to verbalize. Such deviations in compliance occurring in a subject who otherwise adheres to the instructions, introduce into his stories an inconsistency which can

---

[10] A more detailed statement concerning this issue has also been given by Rapaport and his associates (40) (41).

easily be discovered by comparison of his stories, one with another. These deviations are labeled *intra-individual consistency*. An example of such a deviation is the following: a subject who had given the antecedent events in nearly all of his stories, avoided doing so in his story given to the picture in which a man in a dark room is silhouetted against a light window. His story was that the man was standing in the window pondering about his loneliness on a moonlit night; he was sleepless; he had been standing there all night and did not know what to do. The inference made by the examiner was that this omission of antecedents was significant and that, inasmuch as stories suggested by this picture are frequently suicidal stories, it was assumed that the omitted antecedents were suicidal ideas. This conclusion was supported by the clinical history.

The evaluation of the degree of adherence to the picture context is not as simple as the evaluation of compliance with the instructions. It can be done only by comparing the story of the subject with the stories given by other persons, i.e., by evaluation of *inter-individual consistency*. If, for instance, a prostrate figure whose face is not shown in the picture is seen by men usually as a man, and a certain male subject sees the figure as a woman, his perception of the picture deviates from the perceptions of others, and thus must be considered as significant. In such cases, especially if such misrecognitions occur repeatedly, there is sufficient basis for assuming that the subject has a female identification. Our comparison of such inferences with clinical material has demonstrated the validity of these inferences. The attention paid to *inter-individual consistency* of the stories given for each picture resulted in the recognition of the (for the most part) very obvious fact that certain pictures are prone to elicit the attitude of the subject toward certain types of problems. The picture of the elderly woman with the younger man, and that of the elderly woman with a young woman, usually bring out attitudes toward the mother figure. The picture of the woman on the bridge and the picture of the prostrate figure, on the floor, leaning against a couch are prone to elicit attitudes toward failure with suicidal implications. Space prevents us from going into the description of all these points here. Nevertheless, in evaluating the stories, the examiner will have to keep in mind the *specific significance of each picture*, in other words, the problem posed by each picture, to which the story of the subject is a response.

The formal characteristics here discussed thus help us to find the degree of *inter-* and *intra-individual consistency*, and the points at which this breaks down. The consideration of the specific significance of each picture, and the evaluation of the content of the story given to that picture by the subject, lead us to those thought contents of the subject which play a paramount role in his life. (39, pp. 107–111.)[11]

---

[11] Reprinted from "The Clinical Application of the Thematic Apperception Test" by D. Rapaport, by permission of the *Bulletin of the Menninger Clinic*. Copyright 1943 by Menninger Clinic.

IDENTIFICATION OF LEVELS OF BEHAVIOR. The patient is most often relatively unaware of the purpose that motivates the clinician to utilize this projective technique. The instructions are such that a frame of reference is created in which the patient conceives of it as a test of imagination. But as Gough (*18*) indicates, this is neither invariable nor absolute. The clinician must be prepared for the patient who does not adopt this frame of reference, and will need to adjust his interpretations accordingly. He must be on the alert to note just how the patient accepts the situation, and cannot expect the frame of reference to be always the same. This, in general terms, is the question of levels as formulated by Rosenzweig (*49*). He illustrates his concept as follows:

Let it be assumed that a subject tells a story in which he has identified with a hero who is involved in some relationship to a mother figure and in which the mother is depicted as a very kind and generous person. In such a production the subject may be functioning at Level I and reporting what he thinks is the socially approved conception of mothers—they are supposed to be kind and generous. In actuality he may be feeling and concealing considerable hostility toward his own mother. Again, he may be functioning at Level II and stating what he experiences consciously and demonstrates observably in relation to his own mother. Finally, if valid at Level III, the story would be revealing tender feelings of attachment, possibly even incestuous, toward a mother whom in real life the subject might reject with considerable conscious hostility. Needless to say, the interpretation that would follow from the mentioned production would vary greatly according to the level which was actually operative. (*49*, p. 67.)

In the course of interpretation of TAT protocols, examination of the levels of functioning tells us something about the relation of the story to the storyteller. It therefore is a relevant and valuable procedure in the same way as it is with the Picture-Frustration Study referred to in the previous chapter. This earlier discussion gives a perspective on placement of levels of behavior in an interpretative framework.

In connection with the levels of behavior at which the patient is functioning, another aspect attracted the attention of Tomkins (*65*). Convinced as he was of the selectivity and sensitivity of the TAT in revealing personality structure, he was struck by certain instances in which curious discrepancies arose. For example, in one instance a gifted scientist had indulged in a complicated fantasy concerning a hidden, faraway island populated only with males in which he, the daydreamer, was the ruler and seducer of new males brought to the colony. Since twelve years of age he had spent an hour or more each day in variations of this daydream. Yet there was no hint of this fantasy in his TAT protocols. Tomkins also noticed that instances of stealing do not appear in the TAT stories of noncriminals although other evidence points to their presence, whereas incarcerated criminals are apt to make reference to criminal activities. It would appear, then, according to Tomkins, that if two conditions—if the matter that is concealed is clearly in the awareness of the patient, and if he is motivated to conceal it—are present, significant material will not appear in the TAT. If one or the other of these conditions is not present the material may appear, e.g., the incarcerated criminal does not conceal his crimes and therefore they appear in his stories, and the patient who is not fully aware of certain of his own diffuse personality trends may project them into the TAT protocols.

THE INTEGRATION OF INTERPRETATIVE FINDINGS.   An assumption basic to the interpretation of a thematic story is that, in some ways at least, the story bears indications of characteristics of the individual telling the story. No two stories told to the same picture are alike because the experiences upon which they are based are not alike. That the same "theme," "outcome," and so on are given to the same picture by two individuals may result in identical categorizations. However, identity of categorizations, although more than a function of semantics if the system has any validity, does not necessarily correspond to all the operations that go to make up this relation between picture, story, and storyteller. Even in a single picture and a single story, no two persons use the same inflections, language, side incidents, stresses, asides, length, reaction time, total time, and handling of the inquiry, to name but a few variables. Let us even imagine some clinician's Wonderland in reverse, where things are what they seem, and the two stories are identical in letter and spirit. Even there the two stories would not have the same significance. For one thing, this "identity" does not extend to the next level of generalization, e.g., consideration of the relation of two or more stories and making inferences therefrom concerning intra-individual personality functioning. A Gestalt must be assumed even here. The relating of story meanings to one another is the acme of TAT interpretation.

The investigation of the interrelation of the stories, the integration into a composite portrait, to use Rosenzweig's term, is the cloudiest realm of TAT interpretation. It is here that clinical experience of an almost entirely unverbalized sort is most prominent. This integration requires grasping and holding simultaneously many of the elements of the story (and adroit ignoring of other aspects), a process of checking and rechecking, rejection and acceptance of hypotheses, and a search for confirmatory and contradictory evidence. This, then, is the epitome of TAT interpretation but one dependent upon all the clinical skills of the psychologist.

It is at the level of integration of the findings that TAT interpretation again becomes an artistic, incompletely verbalized task of the clinician. The integration of clinical materials is a function resting squarely upon his shoulders. He uses all his clinical skills in the manner suggested before, drawing upon his past experience, his theoretical predilections, his understanding of the purpose of the examination, the dictates of the particular clinical setting, and a myriad of other factors. A systematic point of view, psychoanalytic, eclectic, or what you will, is essential. Here theory and practice meet, and in keeping with the avowed intention in this volume of dealing with *method*, the question of interpretation is left to the clinician himself.

VALIDITY[12]

One omnipresent fact must be in focus when considering the validity (as is also true of reliability) of the TAT—the material being considered concerns a particular analytical and interpretative system applied by a particular clinician. Generalizing beyond a very limited distance is hazardous. A clinician is thrown upon his own resources when using the TAT, so that even a validity coefficient of .90 as determined by independent analysis of TAT material and criterion data has but remote implications for his own work unless he is using the same scoring or interpretative system with a similar population and on the basis of a similar experiential background to that of the clinician performing the study.

---

[12] The review of Tomkins (64) should be consulted for a penetrating account of some of the earlier studies. Here it was considered advisable to describe fewer studies but to present them in more detail. A special point is made to include studies appearing after his review.

To present some of the lines of evidence concerning the interpretative validity of the TAT, it was considered advisable to organize the material along certain methodological lines which seemed to reflect current interest and effort. Historically, the first evidence of validity came from studies involving the correlation of other clinical findings (interview data, etc.) to TAT findings, and vice versa. In the review to follow, they will be referred to as "Studies of Clinical Enrichment." Second, there are those more rigidly controlled studies in which the TAT data were treated as dependent variables to be used to predict variation on an independent variable or variables. Some of these studies will be summarized as "Independent Analyses of TAT material." Third, there are those investigations concerned with the reflection in TAT findings of some changes which take place in the subjects under investigation. These studies will be referred to as "Prediction of Experimentally Produced Change." Each of these sources of evidence will be examined in turn. Discussion of evidence of validity as found by differentiating between diagnostic groups and control groups will be reserved for a later section concerned with application of the TAT to diagnostic groups.

VALIDITY AS SHOWN IN STUDIES OF CLINICAL ENRICHMENT

One source of information concerning validity is the enrichment or congruency that the TAT supplies in the course of clinical appraisal. In generalized form it consists of the interpretation of the TAT as related to other sources of clinical data, for example, autobiographical material and dreams. Both are simultaneously examined, and points of similarity and dissimilarity explored in a process akin to TAT interpretation as such, but now in the larger context of TAT and other material. Eventually a more or less coherent appraisal emerges. The issue of whether or not this approach is really a test of validity will be considered after brief presentation of several pertinent TAT studies.

In the first publication on the TAT, Morgan and Murray reported for a single patient that the analysis of the stories "adumbrated all the chief trends which five months of analysis were able to reveal." (34, p. 305.) Their procedure was to isolate in the stories similarities to the course of events in the psychoanalytic sessions. With copious illustrative material, Sarason (55) showed that twenty-five institutionalized mentally defective girls produced the same major themes in TAT stories and in dreams when both were interpreted from the same basis—in this case, that of the TAT stories. Both kinds of thematic material were related to the life history of the girls with at least surface plausibility.

Combs (12) used, among other approaches to validity, the comparison of TAT content and autobiographical material. This was done on the plausible assumption that the latter mirrored, to some degree at least, the experience of the subject. Using forty-six college students, he secured autobiographies and TAT stories from each one. He then reduced each TAT story and autobiographical incident to a "thema"—a condensation of the story to its shortest possible compass—in terms of his own method of analysis, which will be described later. He then examined the two sets of data simultaneously, the autobiographical material and TAT themas, and isolated those instances in which a TAT thema could be substantiated from biographical material. The accuracy was checked for a portion of the data by another judge. He found perfect agreement with the previous analysis. Defined in the fashion above (autobiography representing life experience), about 30 percent of the TAT stories contained materials drawn from personal experience. In 3 percent, the entire thema could be substantiated in the autobiography. However, the majority of story plots (almost 70 percent) are not even partially taken from personal experiences as judged from the autobiography. Individual variations were rather wide, ranging from almost negligible (5 percent) to over half (58 percent) of the productions showing evidence of transfer. The pictures varied widely in their effectiveness in bringing out personal material, with cards 2, (the farm scene), 3 GF (woman in doorway with downcast head), and 16 (the blank card) being particularly effective. The last was especially effective in producing entire themas that could be substantiated. Card 11 (road on cliff with dragon) was the least productive.

It must be emphasized that these results are not capable of extension to other age and cultural groups. For example, the fact that the subjects were *students* made card 2 (girl in foreground holding books) easily capable of eliciting a "school" story.

It is also noteworthy that this is only indirect evidence of validity, since under the circumstances the TAT could be valid and yet not show appreciable resemblance between autobiographical materials

consciously given and TAT interpretation. The TAT may show unconscious fantasies and desires as well as conscious material. If the
results had been substantially negative it would merely have demonstrated that the contention of Murray (36) (that the subjects draw
upon past experience) was not substantiated. Since some agreement
was found, and it is plausible to think that other congruent material may have escaped Combs' attention owing to the subjects' various mechanisms of defensive behavior, the agreement is really quite
high and Murray's contention is substantiated.

Illustrative of the same approach to validity (detailed case study,
TAT and Rorschach interpretation) is the case report of Harrison
(78). According to Harrison, where there was overlap of TAT and
Rorschach material with case history data, there was agreement between the two sources of material on all except one or two minor
points.

The nature of these studies is such that most of whatever conviction the studies carry is lost in the process of summarization such as
that being carried out here. It is from appraisal of the details of the
evidence as presented by the clinician—the coherencies, interrelationships, and new perspectives—that the conviction of validity may
be brought out.

It would be harsh to call such studies "validity by plausibility," but
something approaching this is involved. Certain lines of relationship,
certain similarities of evidence in the two streams are seen. It is,
however, impossible to judge how much interplay takes place before
the consequences are seen. More important, clinically, than mere
verification of known facts (although this is the classical conception
of validity in operation) is the light which attempts at verification
may produce in the form of clarification of doubtful, unclear, or
previously unappreciated results, thus serving a valuable diagnostic
function. This, too, in the opinion of the writer, can be evidence of
validity although subject to the enrichment-contamination dilemma.
That is to say, once bringing together the case history material (the
independent variable) and the TAT and Rorschach data (the dependent variable), one can charge that any shift in perspective, any
realignment of thinking occurring from it is *post hoc, ergo propter
hoc* thinking in which the contamination prevents unequivocal evidence of validity. To be sure, rigorous separation of the dependent
and independent variables is lost; nevertheless every clinician has

had this happen as a closure experience. It is required that these findings, in turn, be validated through independent verification with new facts unearthed later.

Some psychologists protest that these are not studies of validity because of the cross-fertilization process going on between the two streams of data. The clinician's projections, not the patient's, they would say, are being studied. Others would as vehemently insist that validity is shown forthwith and nothing more need be done. There is, to the writer, a curiously pointless air about this discussion engendered by reification of the concept of validity. If these are not studies of "validity" in a strict sense, they at least point toward this chimera, validity. The source of difficulty is this—that there is still the possibility of the clinician's having organized the material to render his findings in line with his desires. Studies not suffering from this clinically advantageous but methodologically weak source of difficulty will now be examined.

VALIDITY AS DEMONSTRATED IN INDEPENDENT ANALYSES OF TAT MATERIAL

Broadly speaking, the studies of the validity of the TAT which are now to be discussed involve an analysis of TAT material in the form of ratings or interpretative summaries. Content of any nature is included, and then compared with already or simultaneously gathered but independently derived comparable material from other sources. These, then, are postdictive studies of validity, in the sense that there is independent verification of historically past or present material, *instead* of prediction of future behavior.

At the simplest level of postdiction the presence or absence of some major personality differentiation is judged on the basis of means other than the TAT, and an independent TAT evaluation is made. Illustrative is the study of psychotic, and non-psychotic but maladjusted children by Leitch and Schafer (28) (described in more detail later). Independent judgment of the psychiatrist and analysis of certain characteristics of the TAT resulted in disagreement as to the presence or absence of psychosis in but one case out of thirty. In still another such study, that of Murray and Stein (38), five cards were presented, by projection on a screen, to groups of ROTC men, who wrote five-minute stories to each of the pictures. Leadership qualification, judged on the basis of eight variables derived from the TAT and expressed in rank order, correlated .65 with the rank order given independently by their superior officers.

Two related validity studies were performed by Harrison (19) (20). The only essential difference between them is that in one he administered the TAT himself, and in the other he did not. In neither case did he have information in addition to the TAT stories although he was supplied with the sex of the subject in the blind diagnosis study. From reading the TAT stories he derived descriptive characteristics (mean of seventeen per patient) concerning biographical data and personality characteristics. (Many TAT deductions varying in nature from case to case had to be eliminated because of the lack of precisely comparable information in the case history.) In the study in which he administered the TAT, to forty state hospital psychiatric patients, his TAT evaluations were in 83 percent agreement with biographical data, and the inferred diagnosis was correct in 77 percent of the cases. In the blind diagnosis study, with fifteen psychiatric cases he found 75 and 73 percent, respectively. This study, then, demonstrated rather high correspondence between the two variables, i.e., the TAT characteristics and the independent clinical judgments, although the nature of much of the material utilized was on a relatively shallow, overt level. By definition, this information was already known about the person and contained little regarding his individual psychodynamics. It must be added, however, that there was little or no difference between ability to judge correctly biographical data (presumably more expeditiously gathered in actual practice by other means) and ability to judge personality characteristics.

Combs (11), using the TAT stories of forty-six college students, analyzed the motivating desires of the figure with whom the subject identified. The forty "desires" were derived, in part, from the terms expressive of desire used by Murray (37), and were in part based on Combs' clinical experience. Desires to continue the *status quo*, to control, to know, to care for, to avoid restriction, and to be accepted are illustrative. Experienced judges were used. Their independent judgments gave about 86 percent agreement with Combs' original categorizations. Combs then reviewed the classifications with them and presented evidence for his choices. This resulted in an increase in agreement to 91 percent.

The study of Hartman (22) involved a detailed analysis of the relation of fifty-six TAT category ratings to forty-two behavior variables. The subjects were thirty-five white boys of average or superior intelligence, ages thirteen to seventeen, who were undergoing examination in the psychiatric department of a juvenile court. Three clinicians were involved: (1) the psychologist with access to the case record, who tested the subjects using instruments other than the TAT, interviewed them, rated them on the rating scale, and subsequently administered the TAT; (2) the psychiatrist with access to the case records, who interviewed and independently rated them, again without seeing the TAT material; (3) another psychologist, who analyzed the TAT stories without information on the boys other than age and rated them a third time on the behavior rating scale. The behavior rating scale involved bipolar behavior and personality variables, the nature of which will become clear from the later account of relationships found. The TAT responses were categorized under the general headings of modes of response (degree of fluency, number of interjections, etc.), formal characteristics (relative emphasis on past, present, future, time, vocabulary level, number of rare details observed, etc.), thematic emphases (achievement, frustration, anxiety, conflict, etc.), feeling qualities (pleasant, paranoid, guilt, sadistic), and topics emphasized (age, neatness, sex activity). Biserial correlations were calculated and a variety of significant relationships found between TAT categories and the behavior ratings. There were also many significant correlations found among the three clinicians' ratings case by case (as well as variable by variable) when the ratings of the three observers on all of the personality variables (including, of course, the ones made by an observer on the basis of the TAT data alone) were compared. As the results are very detailed, only a representative sample or two can be given. In general, it may be said that the TAT data and the independently derived indices often seem consistent with clinical expectancy and tend to be consistent among themselves. Thus, emphasis on future time in the TAT stories correlates highly with certain personality variables —"feels superior," "extroverted," "popular," "realistic," and "prefers group recreation." A direct relation may also be indicated by the correlation of .44 between theme emphasis-frustration and the variable, emotionally deprived. Results of the blind analysis of the TAT were significantly above chance with many correlations significant at the 5 percent level or better.

Another study with implications for validity, although also concerned with diagnostic formulations, is that of Saxe (59). He compared independently derived TAT formulations with the opinions of the psychiatrists in regard to twenty children seen in therapy at a child guidance bureau of a city department of education. The full set of TAT cards was administered. Four hundred themas, in the form of statements about a subject, were derived from the twenty protocols. Duplicates were eliminated and similarities synthesized. Eventually an eighty-three-item questionnaire emerged. Such items as the following were included: S has been involved in active struggle for parental understanding; S reacts to anxiety with overt aggressions; S identifies with intellectual social deviates. This questionnaire was independently completed by the experimenter for all cases on the basis of the TAT data. The three psychiatrists, who had seen the patients therapeutically for four months, also completed the questionnaire. They possessed the usual clinical material regarding the subjects, including a psychological examination, but not the TAT. The results are stated in terms of agreement or disagreement on the items of the questionnaire (omitting those items considered nonsignificant or for which they had "no information"). For example, on case No. 17 there were thirty-seven agreements and nineteen disagreements. Significant agreement (below .05 level) was obtained in half the cases, positive but nonsignificant results in six cases, and disagreement exceeding agreement in the remaining four cases. Considering the "blind diagnosis" and the semantic difficulties so obvious in a study like this, the agreement is such as to lend confidence that in comparable clinical situations satisfactory validity is associated with this use of the TAT.

VALIDITY AS REFLECTED BY PREDICTION OF EXPERIMENTALLY PRODUCED CHANGE

Although studies of the effect of experimentally induced changes on TAT material may be treated as an aspect of repeat reliability, as Tomkins (64) treats them, it is possible to consider them as studies of validity. If the induced change causes corresponding changes in the TAT, we have concomitant variation presumably reflecting validity, and thus studies in prediction. It is true that such studies also tell us something about stability of results under different conditions. Changes which can be experimentally induced will indicate the extent to which the TAT is affected by the stability of the individual's environment.

That the TAT cards permit reflection of induced change has been neatly demonstrated by Bellak (5). The procedure was to administer five cards according to the usual approach. After the instructions no further comments were made until after the fifth picture, at which time violent criticism was made of the stories told. The criticism was repeated in modified form following each of the four stories thereafter. The hypothesis was that the subjects would project their aggression (i.e., ascribe aggression to subjects or objects of the external world) by introducing more aggression into these later stories than appeared in the ones told before the experimenter's criticism. Accordingly, the stories were analyzed as to the number of verbs and nouns connoting aggression. Analysis of variance, when applied to the results, and the overall difference in aggression between stories before and after criticism were highly significant at the 2 percent level of confidence. In addition to verifying the hypothesis, Bellak found that certain cards, irrespective of the presence or absence of criticism, produced more aggressive content. In other words, projection was, in part, a function of the stimulus.

That a milder and less ego-involving stimulus does not produce changes which will be reflected in TAT production was demonstrated by Coleman (9). Two sets of TAT cards, one set before and one after a fifteen-minute movie short, were administered to a group of children. No appreciable differences in the stories could be attributed to the movie.

The studies of McClelland, Atkinson, and their associates (2) (32) (33) are of interest since they too were concerned with experimentally produced changes. Two of their studies were, for present purposes, preliminary. They involved the relationship of the intensity of the hunger drive to perception of various stimuli and apperception on the TAT. They demonstrated that the contentual aspects of the TAT contain indications of the strength of the hunger drive. But, as they go on to indicate, no one is particularly interested in diagnosing hunger with the TAT. The remaining study (33) is concerned with more relevant materials. The area of investigation was "need achievement," to use Murray's term. Four pictures were selected to suggest achievement, two of which were from Set D, 7 BM and 8 BM. Stories were written by groups of thirty-nine college students under four conditions: *relaxed* (tests interpreted to them as being merely experimental), *neutral* (although tests were said to be experimental, students were urged to do their best), *failure* (tests were interpreted as standardized measures for which norms were available, after they had already been made to appear to fail on a series of paper and pencil tests), *success-failure* (same as failure except students succeeded on the first but not on subsequent paper and pencil tests). The scoring method, a carefully worked out adaptation of that used in the previous studies, showed agreement of ninety-one percent on independent scoring. Its nature will be apparent in a brief statement of the results. Analysis of the results tested the hypothesis that the relaxed and failure conditions represented low and high degrees, respectively, of induced need for achievement. Differences significant at the .05 level of significance or better were found on many categories of scoring such as on increase in achievement imagery, achievement-related deprivation themas, successful instrumental acts (*doing* something about a goal, not merely having it happen), and anticipatory goal responses (thinking about a future goal). Not only did this study define and measure an experimental change detectable in TAT material; it also opened up an area of rapprochement between the clinical usage of TAT and certain aspects of learning theory (for example, anticipatory goal responses).

Considering these studies in general, it would appear that ego-involved tasks or conditions influence TAT results much more profoundly than do such incidents as seeing a movie or working under relaxed, non-ego-involving tasks. This, so far as clinical practice is concerned, is as it should be for successful use. If any and every experience of change left its mark on the TAT protocol, little significance could be inferred from it. These studies demonstrate that predictable changes occur under defined conditions.

SUMMARY OF VALIDITY STUDIES

With all the diversity of methods of interpretation, populations studied, and methods of treating the data, there is one outstanding fact: in varying degrees, consistently positive results were obtained, pointing toward validities of the TAT. In fact, in the entire literature touching directly or indirectly upon validity, only one study can be said to be essentially negative. This is the one in which Richardson

(42) failed to distinguish stutterers from non-stutterers. In this study, described in somewhat more detail later when application with diagnostic groups is considered, no way is found by his methods of analysis to distinguish these groups. It may be, of course, that stutterers do not differ from non-stutterers in ways which the TAT can distinguish, or that his methods of analysis were inappropriate. Further attacks on the problem are indicated. With this exception, then, the TAT would seem under the conditions in which it has been studied to have surprisingly good evidence of validity. This does not mean that the point of diminishing returns in validity studies has been reached. Far from it, in fact, but there are encouraging signs for confidence in its continued clinical use.

Although, on the whole, carefully planned and efficiently and adroitly executed, the studies of validity suffer from the difficulties mentioned by Macfarlane as given in Chapter 14. A brief reminder is pertinent. Since, as she says, we are concerned with the organizational processes of individuals (intra-individual comparison), correlational studies with outside criteria do not give us much information about the TAT's validity for individual dynamics. The comparison of life history material with projective data suffers from the possibility that we are dealing with an artifact applied to both sets of data, rather than consistency of material. How, too, is it known whether or not inconsistencies and consequently lowered validity indices are not due to the difference of level of behavior, comparing, for example, overt docility with a fantasy life full of aggressiveness? Is the one correct and the other incorrect? It is owing to these difficulties that the material on validity has been organized in terms of "clinical enrichment" and "predictive efficiency." Although studies in both rubrics (the first category more than the second) are open to objection on some of the aforementioned grounds, it is considered that this method of organization throws the validity studies in clearest relief.

It is impossible under the circumstances to say that the TAT is "valid" or "invalid" since either would be a meaningless term. The evidence is suggestive of validity under many circumstances with but one study showing negative results. This does *not* mean that in the hands of an inexperienced person it will retain this relative level of validity. Rather, in the hands of a competent clinician, knowing the TAT and having a sound background of knowledge in personality and psychopathology, the interpretation of TAT protocols can be meaningful and valid.

RELIABILITY

Two aspects of the reliability of the TAT have been investigated —interpreter reliability and repeat reliability. (The pictures do not fall into equated halves, nor is there an equivalent set; thus the approaches to reliability which they imply are inappropriate.) Interpreter reliability is the degree of consistency with which the same or similar conclusions can be derived from the material by independent judges, whereas repeat reliability is measured by administering the same test on two occasions and judging the degree of similarity of the two sets of protocols. However, repeat reliability is affected by interpreter reliability since there is no objective scoring system.

INTERPRETER RELIABILITY

In a masterly summary of these studies, Tomkins (64) indicates that the reliability coefficients vary from .30 to .96. Detailed accounts are given by Tomkins, but for reasons that will shortly become apparent only two or three studies will be presented here.

The study of Harrison and Rotter (21) is perhaps typical and is also sufficiently clear-cut to be relatively easy to present in some detail. They were concerned with the selection of OCS candidates during World War II, and the TAT was being used as part of a trial battery in the task of judging the candidates' emotional maturity and stability. With only the protocols to five group-administered TAT cards on which to base their judgments, they independently rated seventy unselected candidates on both a three-point and a five-point scale without knowing them or anything about them. The findings are sufficiently similar on the two scales to justify presenting only the results for the three-point scale. They were in complete agreement on 64 percent of the cases, varied one scale step in 30 percent of the cases, and were in complete disagreement (varied two scale steps) in but 6 percent of the cases. The contingency coefficient was .73. It was concluded that good interpreter reliability had been achieved. This is interpreter reliability at its most general level, i.e., concerned with an overall evaluation along only a continuum of emotional stability-instability.

A somewhat more specific study, involving variables more closely allied with interpretative categories fairly characteristically derived from TAT protocols, is the study of Garfield and Eron (17) (referred to earlier in connection with the normative material they derived). Their three raters achieved 85 to 92 percent identical agreement in terms of tone and outcome, and 76 to 78 percent agreement concerning activity-passivity. Using tetrachoric correlation coefficients of the three aspects rated and the three raters, the authors reported a median correlation of .89.

The investigations of Combs (11) (one phase of which was described briefly in connection with the discussion of validity) also contain a reliability check in which the percentage of agreement between two judges was calculated to be 60 percent.

The relatively high interpreter reliability found in several of these research investigations is in considerable measure a function of interpreters' common prior acquaintance. (Harrison and Rotter, for example, had known each other and worked together for years; this is probably not the case with Combs and his unnamed collaborator, and in his study the percentage of agreement was lower.) The research tells us relatively little about what would happen to reliability in day-to-day clinical work. It is hazarded, however, that two clinicians trained at the same place and time, using the same interpretative framework and working in the same outpatient clinic, would probably exhibit higher coefficients of reliability between their interpretations than would be the case if training, experience, and focus of work were varied. Two or more clinicians varying in all of these areas of background would presumably show the lowest consistency of all. This is assuming that they could find a common universe of discourse in the form of agreement about what is to be rated. Studies systematically varying these characteristics would presumably be enlightening but have not been carried out. In addition, none of the specific techniques of TAT analysis described earlier in the chapter have been investigated as to reliability.

REPEAT RELIABILITY

The question of repeat reliability involves the difficulty that, on repetition of a projective device, it is not expected that the subject will give the same stories. Legitimate changes are taking place which serve to lower any correlation coefficient. Story replication, or reproduction of the same story, is hardly a source of interest. Again the most systematic analysis of this question is that given by Tomkins (64). Concerning the intertwined variables affecting repeat reliability—time and personality stability—he advances the contention that there will be changes after short periods of time if the personality is changing rapidly, but that longer periods will bring some change even in a more stable individual. Since his summary in a large measure concerns two of his own studies—one unpublished and the other published only in abstract form—a quotation is offered:

a) *As a Function of Time Between Successive Administrations*

In a study by . . . [Tomkins] . . . , 45 young women ranging in age from 18 to 20 years were given the TAT by group administration. Three groups of 15 members each were then chosen at random from the group of 45. The first group of 15 was given the test two months later; the second group, six months later; and the third group, ten months later. These stories were then rated according to Murray's quantitative need-press scheme. The ratings between the first administration and successive administrations were then intercorrelated. The reliability coefficients for the group given the test two months later was +0.80; for the second group, in which there had been a six month interval between repeated administration, the reliability coefficient fell to +0.60, and for the third group, after a ten month interval, to +0.50. The difference between repetition at two months and at ten months is clearly significant. Between two and six months and between six and ten months the differences are less reliable. It is clear, however, that as we increase the time between successive administrations the repeat reliability of the TAT declines. This however, is a genral group trend and need not be true of any particular individual. If the personality of the individual is extremely stable, the temporal interval between repeated administrations may make little or no difference. Let us examine the influence of this factor on repeat reliability.

b) *As a Function of the Stability of the Personality*

We shall compare the repeat reliability of three sets of data from individuals whose personalities differed in their stability. First, a group of rapidly developing adolescents, second a neurotic whose personality underwent spontaneous reconstruction, and third a neurotic of a particularly stable personality structure.

1. *Personality of low rigidity.* Childhood and adolescence represent the period of maximal plasticity of the individual—the organism is never again so malleable. We should therefore expect successive administrations of the TAT during this period to yield the lowest repeat reliability. This is in fact the case. Sanford . . . reported an average repeat reliability of +0.46 of the needs expressed by children and adolescents who had been given the TAT at yearly intervals over a three year period.

2. *Personality of moderate rigidity.* In the study of Joseph Kidd reported by White [87], the TAT was administered when Kidd was 19

and again when he was 22. This period was witness to a spontaneous process of reconstruction of his disorganized personality. Although psychoneurotic, his personality was not particularly rigid. Consequently we might have anticipated marked changes when the TAT was repeated three years later. This was the case. In the earlier test there were three main themes: the longing for lost love, the transformation of cruelty and greed by the sympathetic interest of an older man, and a theme of sadism and masochism. In the second set of stories the first two themes had virtually disappeared. This probably reflected Kidd's working through the grief occasioned by an unhappy love affair and the improvement in his relation with his father, with less need for regeneration and a greater tolerance of himself. There was also more open expression of the aggressive and acquisitive wishes from which he had previously been rescued by the older man. This represents a modification of the remaining theme. White does not report the coefficient of reliability between these two administrations. Although there are continuities between these two sets of stories, it is evident that the repeat reliability is not high, though perhaps higher than the correlation of +0.46 reported for adolescents. It is clear that the changes in the personality after a three year period had been reflected in the second TAT and thereby reduce its repeat reliability. Let us consider now a personality of marked rigidity.

3. *Personality of marked rigidity.* In a study by . . . [Tomkins] . . . a psychoneurotic subject, "Z," 18 years old, was presented five days a week with a different picture and asked to write a story about it. This was continued for a period of ten months. These were pictures other than those included in the TAT set and were used in order to assess the influence of the nature of the picture on the repeat reliability of the TAT. In addition the complete set (30) of TAT pictures was administered three times, at intervals of three months. The third administration was immediately followed by a fourth administration when the subject was under the influence of alcohol. Moreover, the subject's dreams were recorded over the ten month period and the results of approximately seventy-five hours of additional testing and experimentation were available. In general, the main themes that appeared in the first 30 stories given at the beginning of the investigation were repeated in the second, third, and fourth administrations of the TAT, as well as in the stories written daily. During a two week period of euphoria the subject was presented with very pleasantly toned pictures in an attempt to modify his typically unhappy stories, but despite this change of both pictures and mood the stories remained the same. The writer submitted half of all the stories to one rater and the other half to another rater. This procedure yielded a correlation coefficient of +0.91 between approximately 200 stories rated by one interpreter and 200 stories rated by another interpreter. It was clear that the constancy of these stories, despite differences in pictures, time of administration, mode of administration (spoken and written), condition of the subject (normal, euphoric, intoxicated, fatigued, etc.) was a function of the unusual rigidity

of this particular person. This rigidity was the consequence of Z's neurosis. . . .

Thus we have seen that for rapidly developing adolescents the repeat reliability of the TAT is approximately +0.46. In the case of a psychoneurotic who underwent a spontaneous process of reconstruction during a three year period there was a relatively low repeat reliability, but when the personality is extremely stable the TAT will reflect such stability in a repeat reliability as high as a coefficient of correlation of +0.91, in the case of stories told over a period of ten months. (64, pp. 6–8.)[13]

APPLICATION WITH DIAGNOSTIC GROUPS

The Thematic Apperception Test has found its greatest usefulness in helping to unravel the psychodynamics of the individual personality. Since stress has been laid on individuality, relatively less attention has been paid to the commonalities to be achieved through group studies. Diagnosis, in the sense of differentiating among psychiatric syndromes, such as conversion hysteria and anxiety, or between psychotic and non-psychotic states, is not the particular forte of the TAT. These factors, coupled with the difficulty in developing a generally satisfactory method of analysis and interpretation accepted by most clinicians, help to account for the fact that relatively few studies concerning diagnostic usage have appeared. Perhaps the relatively high standard set by those that have appeared may also be attributed to these same factors.

Generally speaking, the TAT has found its greatest usefulness in diagnostic appraisal as part of a battery of tests rather than as the sole testing instrument. A study which might be used to illustrate the point is that of Schafer and Leitch (60), who compared the effectiveness of the Stanford-Binet, the Rorschach, and the TAT in detecting maladjustment tendencies in nursery school children. The independent criterion of maladjustment was the rating of adjustment by the psychiatrist on the basis of case history, interview, and observation. The cases were classed by the psychiatrist as adequately adjusted, moderately maladjusted, and severely maladjusted. The Rorschach proved to be the most fruitful differential adjustment-maladjustment indicator; the TAT and Stanford-Binet were less effective. However, the TAT distinguished between moderately and

---

[13] Reprinted from *The Thematic Apperception Test* by S. S. Tomkins, by permission of Grune & Stratton. Copyright 1947 by Grune & Stratton.

severely maladjusted more effectively than the Rorschach, whereas the latter discriminated most effectively of all between the adequately adjusted on the one hand and the maladjusted both moderate and severe on the other. The major indicators of severe maladjustment on the TAT were an accumulation of unusually violent aggressive themes, blocking, and absurd perceptual distortions. It might be added that Schafer and Leitch's principal conclusion was that a battery of tests is more efficient than any one test alone in differentiating adjustment groups.

Despite the paucity of studies involving group evaluation, several are outstanding. Concern in these was not with labeling as such, but rather with the isolation of indices for diagnostic personality appraisal which would give a perspective on the dynamics of the individuals in the group.

The extent to which the nature of the dynamics can be isolated by an experienced clinician using the TAT with a patient group is vividly illustrated by the study of Klebanoff (25). He studied the personality factors in symptomatic chronic alcoholism, i.e., addiction being the dominant symptom in a basic maladjustment of neurotic quality. Seventeen male state hospital patients formed the experimental group, and "well-adjusted" males used in a previous study by Rodnick and Klebanoff (43) formed the control group. Klebanoff used an earlier version of the scoring system of Rotter et al., presented on pages 480–481. The major relevant variations from the system described are that instead of a "positive" thema category, a miscellaneous (more neutral and pleasant) one was used, and a thema subcategory, "intoxication" was included. Mean percentages were calculated for thema categories, successes and failures, and areas of failure.

Relatively little expression of aggressive tendencies, either physical or nonphysical, was found (21 and 17 percent versus 33 and 20 percent for the normal), whereas internal emotional stress was relatively very prominent (48 percent versus 25 percent in the normals). There was also a relative absence of pleasant miscellaneous themas. In terms of success and failure, failure of the central character predominated in 59 percent (35 percent in normals). Failure in the power and social area together made up 79 percent of the solutions. In terms of content, the themas most frequently involved intoxication, rejection or separation from a loved one, emotional stress, crime,

The Clinical Method in Psychology

and domination (of the central character by a minor one). Individual profiles agreed markedly well with the composite profile.

The study of Kutash (27) is of considerable interest because he was dealing with criminal psychopaths who were also mental defectives. On both counts one would expect to encounter difficulty in securing personality appraisal. Psychopaths are notoriously loath to reveal their personality, and mental defectives are frequently considered incapable of doing so. Kutash found in a study of sixty institutionalized, defective delinquents of Stanford-Binet IQ 70 or below that the TAT was valuable in enabling the psychologist to secure material which aided him in evaluating personality structure with particular reference to material of dynamic and etiological significance. He used fifteen cards of an earlier set of the TAT. The TAT was scored by breaking down each story into responses which represented a total whole and a statement of dynamic significance. Then each response was classified in terms of intrapsychic conflicts, inner motivation for the response, and the goal or drive which the response represented, or the complex or trauma to which the particular response was a clue. He found that the subjects often displayed a marked number of intrapsychic conflicts, although their emotionally impoverished level had led others to presume that they did not exist. Separation anxiety, conflicts about ambitions and family relationships, guilt feelings, and unconscious desire for punishment were very prominent. It is also interesting that card description, the mode of response Kutash might have expected on a priori grounds to be very prominent among criminal defective psychopaths, made up less than 10 percent of all responses.

The TAT has been applied to mental defectives by Sarason (55) (56). He modified the directions so as to make them appropriate for these subjects, who were studied in a fashion which should be useful with other mental defectives. The subjects were directed to stress an account of what was happening, how they felt, and what they were saying and thinking. Sometimes they would have to be shown the first picture as an illustration. Sarason found that plausible and coherent stories emerged in spite of much card description. Aggression, rejection, and ambivalence toward the parents, guilt, and fear of loneliness are the prevalent themes. After a presentation of the stories told by various boys and girls of mean IQ about 60 with other supporting clinical evidence, he concludes that this technique is useful with a mentally deficient population in gaining understanding of their behavior and adjustment, and especially as an aid in proper community placement.

It is impossible to summarize in short compass the findings of Rapaport, Gill, and Schafer (40) (41), and Schafer (85) about diagnostic indicators. They were concerned with both characteristic form and content for a large number of nosological groups, and were searching for prominent symptoms such as affective lability and depression. Bell (4) gives an outline summarization of the characteristic kinds of TAT response of various diagnostic groups drawn from various sources, including Rapaport, Gill, and Schafer (40) (41).

The TAT was consistently unsuccessful in discriminating a diagnostic group of stutterers from a matched normal control group in a careful study of Richardson (42). On the surface, the negative results seem somewhat difficult to reconcile with the positive findings heretofore reported. The meaning may simply be, however, that since stutterers are a heterogeneous group, the characteristics about which the TAT yields information are not particularly pertinent to discrimination of this group from normals. A modification of the Murray need-press method of analysis was used, and it may be that in these contentual aspects of personality functioning there are no differences between stutterers and normals.

The previously described studies were concerned with patient groups. The versatility of the TAT as a psychodiagnostic instrument is further exemplified in the investigations by Roe (44) (45) (46) (47) of eminent men in various fields. In her work with noted artists the TAT was of some value, but so many of her subjects became involved in aesthetic criticism of the drawings as to limit the amount of information obtained. The twenty very distinguished biologists whom she studied with Rorschach, TAT, and a verbal mathematical spatial test formed a group that aptly serve as an illustration of her work. Since she used Wyatt's system of scoring the TAT protocols (which has been previously described), it is unnecessary to consider the method of analysis further.

She writes in connection with her results that description was resorted to chiefly with card 11, probably owing to the objection of these men to anything amorphous and nonfactual. After briefly discussing material concerning stimulus perception and deviation from the typical response, she goes on to state that the time trend is extremely curtailed and that level is dominantly concrete-factual, and that tone is dominantly unhappy and tense, personal relations are somewhat more often formal than emotional, and outcomes, when given, are more often successful than not. Her summary of the qualitative features is worth quoting. She writes:

Qualitatively, outstanding aspects of the protocols are the generally nonaggressive attitudes, the mildness of heterosexual interests and feelings, and at the same time the importance of and security in marriage. Paternal attitudes are sympathetic. Some of the protocols have a strong feeling of determination and resulting success; but not all show this. There is, however, an almost total lack of any expectation of or reliance on luck, or fate, or any other nonpersonal intervention as an aid. The nonaggressive attitudes are firmly entrenched, but there is a hint of underlying resentment or rebelliousness, which, however, is generally attached to characters in early maturity, and which is usually not expressed in action and if it is, results unfortunately for the one expressing it. On the whole, there is a strong conventionality in most of the protocols, the only common break in this being in connection with religion, conventional forms of which most of them have discarded. (47, p. 239.)

Analysis of the formal characteristics have proved to be of as much value as analysis of content for the purpose of diagnosis, or proper placement in a nosological group. The TAT has been found clinically useful by Leitch and Schafer (28) in differentiating between psychotic and nonpsychotic but emotionally disturbed children of mean age eleven. Some of the intellectual and perceptual characteristics of the stories were analyzed. Intellectual factors which were found among the psychotic children and aided in differentiation were incoherence, contradictions, queer ideas, manneristic speaking, repetition of a phrase, and so on. Perceptual disturbances characteristic of the psychotic children were omission of important details, distortion of details, and perceptual uncertainties such as calling a particular figure both a man and a woman without later resolving the contradiction. By counting occurrences of these characteristics in each TAT record and arriving at a sum total, the authors were able to differentiate a small group of psychotic children from nonpsychotic children with practically no overlap.

The study of Balken and Masserman (3), previously referred to, includes an analysis of those formal TAT characteristics which differentiate conversion hysteria, anxiety state, and obsessive-compulsive neurosis. A quotation will bring out not only the nature of their findings (based on quantitative characteristics) but also rationale. They write:

> In *conversion hysteria* the characteristics of the phantasies are: productions of medium length, a plethora of leisurely descriptive material with little forceful action (low verb-adjective quotient), little vagueness, ambivalence or qualification of statement (high pro-con quotient as contrasted with low certainty-uncertainty and qualification-certainty quotients and with low alternative and "special expressions" ratings), and a minimum use of the first person or of identifications with the narrator. It is of great theoretical interest that these formal characteristics of the phantasies are consistent with the most striking psychodynamic mechanisms of the conversion hysteric; namely, the diminution of overt anxiety by the device of "converting" the repressed erotic or aggressive urge into organic dysfunctions which afford vicarious libidinal gratification and yet are sufficiently self-punitive to resolve in some degree the accompanying neurotic guilt. With his intrapsychic tensions thus autoplastically relieved, the conversion hysteric apparently can then indulge in rich, slow-moving, leisurely phantasies which need exhibit but little action or indecision and which are so lightly charged with projected anxiety that there are almost no direct references to the patient's own difficulties in the stories. Significant also is the fact that there is a corresponding minimum of interpersonal tension in the test situation, as shown by the freedom the patient feels in asking relatively casual questions of the examiner. (3, pp. 76-80.)

Lacking control groups as they do, several of these studies, notably Kutash (27) Sarason (55) (56), Rapaport, Gill, and Schafer (40) (41), Roe (47), and Balken and Masserman (3) are only indirectly studies of validity. Some others, i.e., Schafer and Leitch (60), Klebanoff (25), and Leitch and Schafer (28), since they establish differences between their respective patient groups and another group, either normals or patients, may be considered validity studies. They all found positive results. On the other hand, Richardson (42), who found no significant differences between stutterers and non-stutterers, offers essentially negative evidence.

SUMMARY

The Thematic Apperception Test often has been referred to in one fashion or another as the runner-up to the Rorschach in popularity among projective techniques. Introduced in 1935 by Morgan and Murray, it has gradually assumed a position of prominence. It takes no careful counting of usage in school and clinic or count of journal articles to be able to say that it is surpassed only by the Rorschach in practice and publication. And yet, probably owing in large measure to the fact that no generally accepted way of scoring or of interpreting the results has appeared, it is by no means a close second. As a result there is a curiously elusive quality about it. When one speaks of reliability or validity in a given study, it is likely to be quite amorphous.

Very few clinicians have concerned themselves with the necessarily exacting attempts needed to demonstrate conclusively the validity of their interpretations of the TAT. Most are content to accept their interpretations at face value as being self-evidently valid.

Some of the difficulty encountered in learning to interpret the TAT comes from the fact that the publications concerning it so often display a very high level of clinical competence. This seemingly paradoxical situation may be explained by pointing out that the novice cannot start at the level on which many of these accounts are couched. Therefore, several relatively "practical" methods of analysis and a series of interpretative principles have been presented. Both the methods of analysis and the interpretative principles have the characteristics of being simple enough to be learned by the novice who lacks extensive indoctrination. These "practical" guides do not demand adherence to any one theory of personality, although they do parallel, in some measure, certain theories. Two characteristic interpretative systems have also been presented: that of Murray and his associates and that followed when a psychoanalytically oriented framework is adopted.

As a rule, users of the TAT have not had the courage or temerity to make explicit the procedural principles on which they structure and integrate their findings. Illustrative cases abound, as attested by the selective bibliography on case studies at the end of the chapter. One can see what the clinicians did and their reasons for it, but the rules by which they did it are significantly lacking. That rules can be worked out may be too much to expect at present. In that case further research and clinical practice are urgently needed. The TAT is a promising procedure, useful and penetrating in research and clinical practice. Its scope, almost as wide as the whole field of personality, is both the source of its great clinical significance and the origin of the amorphousness which rises to plague the clinician who uses it.

BIBLIOGRAPHY
1. Aron, B., A manual for analysis of the Thematic Apperception Test: a method and technique for personality research, Willis E. Berg, 1949.
2. Atkinson, J. W., and McClelland, D. C., The projective expression of needs: II. The effect of different intensities of the hunger drive on Thematic Apperception, *J. exper. Psychol.*, 1948, 38:643–658.
3. Balken, E. R., and Masserman, J. H., The language of phantasy: III. The language of the phantasies of patients with conversion hysteria, anxiety state, and obsessive-compulsive neuroses, *J. Psychol.*, 1940, 10:75–86.
4. Bell, J. E., *Projective techniques; a dynamic approach to the study of the personality*, Longmans, Green and Company, 1948.
5. Bellak, L., The concept of projection: an experimental investigation and study of the concept, *Psychiatry*, 1944, 7:353–370.
6. Bellak, L., *Bellak TAT blank: for recording and analyzing Thematic Apperception Test stories*, Psychological Corporation, 1947.
7. Bellak, L., *A guide to the interpretation of the Thematic Apperception Test*, Psychological Corporation, 1947.
8. Bellak, L., Thematic Apperception: failures and the defenses, *N.Y. Acad. Sci.*, 1950, 12:122–126.
9. Coleman, W., The Thematic Apperception Test: I. Effect of recent experience. II. Some quantitative observations, *J. clin. Psychol.*, 1947, 3:257–264.
10. Combs, A. W., A method of analysis for the Thematic Apperception Test and autobiography, *J. clin. Psychol.*, 1946, 2:167–174.
11. Combs, A. W., The validity and reliability of interpretation from autobiography and Thematic Apperception Test, *J. clin. Psychol.*, 1946, 2:240–247.
12. Combs, A. W., The use of personal experience in Thematic Apperception Test story plots, *J. clin. Psychol.*, 1946, 2:357–363.
13. Combs, A. W., A comparative study of motivations as revealed in Thematic Apperception stories and autobiography, *J. clin. Psychol.*, 1947, 3:65–75.
14. Cox, B., and Sargent, H., TAT responses of emotionally disturbed and emotionally stable children: clinical judgment versus normative data, *J. project. Techniques*, 1950, 14:61–74.
15. Dymond, R. F., A preliminary investigation of the relation of insight and empathy, *J. consult. Psychol.*, 1948, 12:228–233.
16. Eron, L. D., Frequencies of themes and identifications in the stories of schizophrenic patients and non-hospitalized college students, *J. consult. Psychol.*, 1948, 12:387–395.
17. Garfield, S. L., and Eron, L. D., Interpreting mood and activity in TAT stories, *J. abnorm. soc. Psychol.*, 1948, 43:338–345.
18. Gough, H. G., The frame of reference of the Thematic Apperception Test, *J. clin. Psychol.*, 1948, 4:90–92.

19. Harrison, R., Studies in the use and validity of the Thematic Apperception Test with mentally disordered patients: II. A quantitative validity study, *Character & Pers.*, 1940, 9:122–133.
20. Harrison, R., Studies in the use and validity of the Thematic Apperception Test with mentally disordered patients: III. Validation by the method of "blind analysis," *Character & Pers.*, 1940, 9:134–138.
21. Harrison, R., and Rotter, J. B., A note on the reliability of the Thematic Apperception Test, *J. abnorm. soc. Psychol.*, 1945, 40:97–99.
22. Hartman, A. A., An experimental examination of the Thematic Apperception Technique in clinical diagnosis, *Psychol. Monogr.*, 1949, 63, No. 303.
23. Holt, R. R. (ed.), The TAT Newsletter, 1947, 1, No. 2 (mimeographed).
24. Holt, R. R. (ed.), The TAT Newsletter, 1948, 2, No. 2 (mimeographed).
25. Klebanoff, S. G., Personality factors in symptomatic chronic alcoholism as indicated by the Thematic Apperception Test, *J. consult. Psychol.*, 1947, 11:111–119.
26. Klebanoff, S. G., Plenk, A. M., and Mensh, I. N., personal communication, 1950.
27. Kutash, S. B., Performance of psychopathic defective criminals on the Thematic Apperception Test, *J. crim. Psychopath.*, 1943, 5:319–340.
28. Leitch, M., and Schafer, S., A study of the Thematic Apperception Tests of psychotic children, *Amer. J. Orthopsychiat.*, 1947, 17:337–342.
29. Levinson, D. J., personal communication, 1950.
30. Masserman, J. H., and Balken, E. R., The psychoanalytic and psychiatric significance of phantasy, *Psychoanal. Rev.*, 1939, 26:343–379, 535–549.
31. Mayman, M., Review of the literature on the Thematic Apperception Test, in Rapaport, D., Gill, M., and Schafer, R., *Diagnostic psychological testing: the theory, statistical evaluation and diagnostic application of a battery of tests*, Vol. II, Year Book Publishers, 1946, pp. 496–506.
32. McClelland, D. C., and Atkinson, J. W., The projective expression of needs: I. The effect of different intensities of the hunger drive on perception, *J. Psychol.*, 1948, 25:205–222.
33. McClelland, D. C., Clark, R. A., Roby, T. B., and Atkinson, J. W., The projective expression of needs: IV. The effect of the need for achievement on thematic apperception, *J. exper. Psychol.*, 1949, 39:242–255.
34. Morgan, C. D., and Murray, H. A., A method for investigating phantasies: the Thematic Apperception Test, *Arch. Neurol. & Psychiat.*, 1935, 34:289–306.

35. Murray, H. A., Facts which support the concept of need or drive, *J. Psychol.*, 1936, 3:27–42.
36. Murray, H. A., *Thematic Apperception Test: manual*, Harvard University Press, 1943.
37. Murray, H. A. et al., *Explorations in personality*, Oxford University Press, 1938.
38. Murray, H. A., and Stein, M., Note on the selection of combat officers, *Psychosom. Med.*, 1943, 5:386–391.
39. Rapaport, D., The clinical application of the Thematic Apperception Test, *Bull. Menninger Clin.*, 1943, 7:106–113.
40. Rapaport, D., Gill, M., and Schafer, R., *Diagnostic psychological testing: the theory, statistical evaluation, and diagnostic application of a battery of tests*, Vol. II, Year Book Publishers, 1946.
41. Rapaport, D., Schafer, R., and Gill, M., *Manual of diagnostic testing*. II. Diagnostic testing of personality and ideational content, Josiah Macy, Jr. Foundation Review Series, 1946, 3, No. 1.
42. Richardson, L. H., The personality of stutterers, *Psychol. Monogr.*, 1944, 56, No. 260.
43. Rodnick, E. H., and Klebanoff, S. G., Projective reactions to induced frustrations as a measure of social adjustment, *Psychol. Bull.*, 1942, 39:489 (abstract).
44. Roe, A., Artists and their work, *J. Personality*, 1946, 15:1–40.
45. Roe, A., Painting and personality, *Rorschach Res. Exch.*, 1946, 10:86–100.
46. Roe, A., The personality of artists, *Educ. Psychol. Measmt.*, 1946, 6:401–408.
47. Roe, A., Psychological examinations of eminent biologists, *J. consult. Psychol.*, 1949, 13:225–246.
48. Rosenzweig, S., Apperceptive norms for the Thematic Apperception Test: I. The problem of norms in projective methods, *J. Personality*, 1949, 17:475–482.
49. Rosenzweig, S., Levels of behavior in psychodiagnosis with special reference to the Picture-Frustration Study, *Amer. J. Orthopsychiat.*, 1950, 20:63–72.
50. Rosenzweig, S., and Fleming, E. E., Apperceptive norms for the Thematic Apperception Test: II. An empirical investigation, *J. Personality*, 1949, 17:483–503.
51. Rotter, J. B., Studies in the use and validity of the Thematic Apperception Test with mentally disordered patients: I. Method of analysis and clinical problems, *Character & Pers.*, 1940, 9:18–34.
52. Rotter, J. B., Thematic Apperception Tests: suggestions for administration and interpretation, *J. Personality*, 1946, 15:70–92.
53. Rotter, J. B., and Rodnick, E. H., A study of the reactions to experimentally induced frustration, *Psychol. Bull.*, 1940, 34:577 (abstract).
54. Sanford, R. N., *Procedure for scoring the Thematic Apperception Test*, Harvard Psychological Clinic, 1939 (privately printed).

55. Sarason, S. B., The use of the Thematic Apperception Test with mentally deficient children: I. A study of high grade girls, Amer. J. ment. Def., 1943, 47:414–421.

56. Sarason, S. B., The use of the Thematic Apperception Test with mentally deficient children: II. A study of high grade boys, Amer. J. ment. Def., 1943, 48:169–173.

57. Sarason, S. B., Dreams and Thematic Apperception Test stories, J. abnorm. soc. Psychol., 1944, 39:486–492.

58. Sarason, S. B., The TAT and subjective interpretation, J. consult. Psychol., 1948, 12:285–299.

59. Saxe, C. H., A quantitative comparison of psychodiagnostic formulations from the TAT and therapeutic contacts, J. consult. Psychol., 1950, 14:116–127.

60. Schafer, S., and Leitch, M., An exploratory study of the usefulness of a battery of psychological tests with nursery school children, Amer. J. Psychiat., 1948, 104:647–652.

61. Stein, M. I., The Thematic Apperception Test: an introductory manual for its clinical use with adult males, Addison-Wesley Press, 1948.

62. Thompson, C. E., Manual for Thematic Apperception Test: Thompson modification, Harvard University Press, 1949.

63. Thompson, C. E., The Thompson modification of the Thematic Apperception Test, Rorschach Res. Exch., 1949, 13:469–478.

64. Tomkins, S. S., The Thematic Apperception Test: the theory and technique of interpretation, Grune & Stratton, 1947.

65. Tomkins, S. S., The present status of the Thematic Apperception Test, Amer. J. Orthopsychiat., 1949, 19:358–362.

66. Weisskopf, E. A., A transcendence index as a proposed measure in the TAT, J. Psychol., 1950, 29:379–390.

67. Wittenborn, J. R., Some TAT norms and a note on the use of the test cards in the guidance of college students, J. clin. Psychol., 1949, 5:157–161.

68. Wittenborn, J. R., The implications of certain assumptions involved in the use of the Thematic Apperception Test, J. consult. Psychol., 1950, 14:216–225.

69. Wyatt, F., Formal aspects of the Thematic Apperception Test, Psychol. Bull., 1942, 39:491 (abstract).

70. Wyatt, F., The scoring and analysis of the Thematic Apperception Test, J. Psychol., 1947, 24:319–330.

71. Wyatt, F., The interpretation of the Thematic Apperception Test, Rorschach Res. Exch., 1947, 11:21–25.

72. Wyatt, F., The problems of quantification and objectification in personality measurement: a symposium: V. Measurement and the Thematic Apperception Test, J. Personality, 1948, 17:169–176.

Diagnostic Testing Reports Involving the TAT

73. Arnold, M. B., A demonstration analysis of the TAT in a clinical setting, *J. abnorm. soc. Psychol.*, 1949, 44:97–111.
74. Bell, J. E., The case of Gregor: psychological test data, *Rorschach Res. Exch.*, 1949, 13:155–205.
75. Bell, J.E., The case of Gregor: interpretation of test data, *Rorschach Res. Exch.*, 1949, 13:433–468.
76. Escalona, S. K., The use of a battery of psychological tests for diagnosis of maladjustment in young children—a case report, *Trans. Kans. Acad. Sci.*, 1945, 48:218–223.
77. Harris, R. E., Ulcerative colitis, in Burton, A., and Harris, R. E. (eds.), *Case histories in clinical and abnormal psychology*, Harper & Brothers, 1947, pp. 257–272.
78. Harrison, R., The Thematic Apperception and Rorschach methods of personality investigation in clinical practice, *J. Psychol.*, 1943, 15:49–74.
79. Meyer, M. M., Integration of test results with clinical observations: a diagnostic case study, *Rorschach Res. Exch.*, 1949, 13:325–340.
80. Munroe, R. L., A maladjusted college student, in Burton, A., and Harris, R. E. (eds.), *Case histories in clinical and abnormal psychology*, Harper & Brothers, 1947, pp. 628–649.
81. Rosenzweig, S., The dynamics of an amnesic personality, *J. Personality*, 1946, 15:121–142.
82. Rosenzweig, S., and Clark, R. A., The personality of a psychotic ex-soldier, in Watson, R. I. (ed.), *Readings in the clinical method in psychology*, Harper & Brothers, 1949, pp. 299–313. (Also in *J. abnorm. soc. Psychol.*, 1945, 40:195–204.)
83. Rosenzweig, S., with Kogan, K. L., *Psychodiagnosis: an introduction to tests in the clinical practice of psychodynamics*, Grune & Stratton, 1949, pp. 139–159, 208–236, 237–268, 271–286.
84. Sarason, E. K., and Sarason, S. B., A problem in diagnosing feeble-mindedness, in Watson, R. I. (ed.), *Readings in the clinical method in psychology*, Harper & Brothers, 1949, pp. 314–324. (Also in *J. abnorm. soc. Psychol.*, 1945, 40:323–329.)
85. Schafer, R., *The clinical application of psychological tests: diagnostic summaries and case studies*, International Universities Press, 1948.
86. Shakow, D., Rodnick, E. H., and Lebeaux, T., A psychological study of a schizophrenic; exemplification of a method, *J. abnorm. soc. Psychol.*, 1945, 40:154–174.
87. White, R. W., The personality of Joseph Kidd, I, II, III, *Character & Pers.*, 1943, 11:183–208, 318–338, 339–360.

LITERATURE, TESTING REPORTS INVOLVING THE TAT

72. Arnold, M. B., A demonstration analysis of the TAT in a clinical setting, J. abnorm. soc. Psychol., 1949, 44, 97-111.

73. Bell, J., The case of Gregor: psychological test data, Rorschach Res. Exch., 1949, 13, 155-205.

74. Bell, J., The case of Gregor: interpretation of test data, Rorschach Res. Exch., 1949, 13, 433-466.

75. Bellak, L., The use of a battery of psychodiagnostic tests for diagnosis of maladjustment in young children—a case report, Trans. Amer. Acad. Science, 1948, 10, 217.

76. Harris, R. E., Literature review, in Hutton, A., and Harris, R. E., Case histories in clinical and abnormal psychology, Harper & Brothers, 1947, pp. 93-102.

77. Harrison, R., The Thematic Apperception and Rorschach methods of personality investigation in clinical practice, J. Psychol., 1943, 15, 49-74.

78. Magnussen, M. The prediction of test results with clinical phenomena: a diagnostic case study, Rorschach Res. Exch., 1949, 14, 145-157.

79. Murray, H. A., Abridged manual college student, by Hutton, A., and Harris, R. E. (eds.), Case histories in clinical and abnormal psychology, Harper & Brothers, 1947, pp. 128-139.

80. Rosenzweig, S., The thematic test of imaginal personality, J. Psychol., 1949, 15, 121-142.

81. Rotter, J. B., and Clark, R. A., The personality of a psychotic veteran, in Watson, R. I. (ed.), Readings in the clinical method in psychology, Harper & Brothers, 1949, pp. 291-312. (Also in J. abnorm. soc. Psychol., 1945, 40, 105-124.)

82. Rosenzweig, S., with Kogan, K. L., Psychodiagnosis: an introduction to tests in the clinical practice of psychology, Grune & Stratton, 1949, pp. 220-250, 253-262, 371-380.

83. Sargent, H. R., and Sargent, S. R., A problem in diagnosing feeble-mindedness, in Watson, R. I. (ed.), Readings in the clinical method in psychology, Harper & Brothers, 1949, pp. 314-324. (Also in J. abnorm. soc. Psychol., 1944, 40, 41-47.)

84. Shakow, D., The clinical application of psychological tests, diagnostic summaries and case studies, International Universities Press, 1948.

85. Shakow, D., Rodnick, E. H., and Lebeaux, T., A psychological study of a schizophrenic: exemplification of a method, J. abnorm. soc. Psychol., 1945, 40, 154-177.

86. White, R. W., The personality of Joseph Kidd, J. H. III, Character & Pers., 1943, 11, 183-208, 318-360, 360-360.

III

Psychotherapy

CHAPTER 17

The Psychotherapeutic Values to Be Found in Diagnostic Materials

In discussing the clinical method in Chapter 2 it was demonstrated that the diagnostic phase shaded imperceptibly into therapy, and, likewise, that even the more narrowly diagnostic aspects have therapeutic effects either for good or for ill. From the first meeting with the patient, no matter how casual and incidental, therapeutic influences are at work. Moreover, the effect of diagnostic methodology in the test interview and case study need not be entirely casual, as test materials may be more consciously directed to therapeutic ends. Awareness of these therapeutic factors during ostensible diagnostic sessions is important lest they do become therapeutically damaging owing to the neglect of their effects. Although the psychologist may not be the therapist, knowledge of these processes will undoubtedly help him to understand the patient better and facilitate more efficacious therapeutic results.[1]

A psychologist must be familiar not only with these incidental therapeutic effects but also with some of the more active therapeutic efforts possible in diagnostic settings when the diagnostician is in charge of the case therapeutically as well. At all times the effective

---

[1] This alone is sufficient answer to those clinicians both from within psychology and from other disciplines who would deny to the psychologist therapeutic training. No matter what the aim, the psychologist cannot help but be therapeutically important.

clinician must be aware of the degree of anxiety created by the test situation and stimuli. Stirring up material close to the surface may be harmful unless the clinician is prepared to deal with the anxiety and guilt feelings that will accompany this disclosure of material. The patient may not have been ready to talk about the intimate personal experiences thus ruthlessly exposed. If the patient's anxiety becomes too severe or if his ego is obviously too weak to stand stress the clinician would do well to turn to other more neutral activities, unless as therapist he intends to follow through and use this upset state for therapeutic ends.

Almost all clinical psychologists who engage in therapeutic work as such have had previous experience in which their tasks were primarily of diagnostic nature. They are familiar with diagnostic interviewing, the importance of the attitudes of clinician and patient, and the necessity of rapport[2] when approaching these sessions. The inescapable therapeutic influence of such activities served to sensitize them to the nature of some aspects of therapy. They found in the course of the diagnostic session, whether structured for purposes of interview or test, that, no matter what its diagnostic intent, it was also an agent of therapy. In connection with interviewing, Font (12) indicates how the needs of the patient structure the session willy-nilly. If this need is for therapeutic help, even if the interview is set primarily for diagnosis, therapeutic effects are forthcoming. For example, the patient's need to release tension must be recognized and somehow met. If release is permitted by allowing him to pour out his troubles the psychologist must be skillful enough to forestall the ensuing guilt feelings. In most diagnostic situations, to be sure, it is preferable to attempt to stem the flow so as not to disturb the relationship between the patient and some other clinician who was assuming therapeutic responsibility; there is still the problem of doing this in such a fashion as not to have an adverse effect on the patient.

It is no exaggeration to say that all aspects of the diagnostic case study contribute to therapy. Roland (13), in discussing the entire psychological examination as a beginning in therapy with children, illustrates vividly the manner in which it may be so utilized. In the clinic she describes the child is seen by the psychologist before the therapist. The psychologist who accepts the child, who understands

---

[2] See Chapter 5 for a discussion of these factors.

what the child is facing in this new and often terrifying situation, is helping him so that he may enter the therapeutic sessions better prepared than otherwise would be the case.

Thorne (10), in discussing the therapeutic implications of the diagnostic case history, systematically reviews and illustrates many facets of therapeutic endeavor which are possible through this medium. The manner in which it is elicited is related to the ease with which *rapport* is established. Securing the diagnostic material concerning the patient under the guidance of the therapist sometimes allows the patient to see the matters which are troubling him in better perspective than before. These and other procedures allow a process of *desensitization* to be instituted. Closely related are the opportunities for *catharsis and abreaction* which a detailed case history allows. Still another major value of systematically eliciting a case study is the opportunity it gives the patient for perceiving the causal relationships of his difficulty. Thus *insight* to some degree may come into being.

Not all of these factors are necessarily operative in any one patient simply because a diagnostic study is made. Indeed, with many patients such therapeutic gains are nil. Nevertheless, with some patients these indirect returns from diagnostic endeavors are operative.

These factors of therapy—*rapport, desensitization, catharsis and abreaction,* and *insight*—are for present purposes important in another connection: They may be conceived as one way of stating some of the factors common to all forms of psychotherapy. Variously stated and differentially weighted in one or another of the therapeutic systems, these factors all play a part in therapy. It would appear, then, that in the diagnostic case study, the everyday activity of the diagnostician, there is the beginning of therapy. Like Molière's M. Jourdain, psychologists are discovering that they too speak (therapeutic) prose.

It is in the sphere of diagnostic testing that the psychologist is likely to be especially skilled. It is fitting, therefore, that a more detailed discussion of therapy use this already familiar medium as an introduction to psychotherapy in general and more specifically to the common factors in various psychotherapeutic approaches.

It is again pertinent to distinguish in this task between projective and nonprojective tests. For a variety of reasons so obvious as not to need discussion, projective materials such as the Rorschach and the

TAT are most useful. Although projective materials offer by far the greatest amount of activity of the patient of direct therapeutic value, the activity is not confined to such materials. Nonprojective material can also be of therapeutic worth. Doll and Brooks (7) report that the Vineland Social Maturity Scale when used with prison inmates allows catharsis and self-analysis against a standard.

Among projective tests the TAT is the most useful as a therapeutic device; consequently therapeutic procedures with this instrument will be examined, although this is not meant to imply that the TAT is universally or even usually used as a therapeutic tool. Rather, it provides a logically and pedagogically satisfactory means of introducing a discussion of psychotherapeutic procedures.

PSYCHOTHERAPEUTIC PROCEDURES USED WITH THE TAT

The therapist and patient derive knowledge of the patient's personality from many sources, including test material. This derivation is, properly speaking, an aspect of the diagnostic phase of the clinical method. It becomes therapeutic in intent when interpreted to the patient or when the patient interprets it himself through some sort of associational technique. Hereafter the term "interpretation" will be reserved for the therapist's offerings and those hit upon by the patient will be referred to as "self-interpretation." Interpretations may be offered by the therapist without direct reference to the sources of his inferences, or they may be supported by direct quotation of evidence from the interview or test materials.

In discussing when and how the TAT can be used in psychotherapy Bellak, Pasquarelli, and Braverman (4), after indicating as their first point that it may be used to become acquainted with the dynamics of the patient's thought, go on to what are more strictly psychotherapeutic uses. They write:

Second, the TAT can be used in cases or in particular episodes of cases in which the patient has difficulty in free associating or shows a dearth of associations. Instead of spending a great deal of time and effort in waiting for the patient to overcome the block, or in trying to prod him into further associations, the TAT, in whole or in part, will produce stories to which he can associate or which can, in themselves, reveal as much to the patient and to the therapist as the associations which may be evoked through the more lengthy process.

Third, the TAT can be used *in cases where the patient shows marked resistance,* either to expressing his thoughts or to the interpretations given by the therapist. In the former case, the TAT provides a situation which seems totally objective to the patient at the time he is asked to tell the stories. In the latter case, the patient will often be able to understand and accept the interpretation of his TAT story as it relates to himself since it is so undeniably a product of his own projected thoughts and yet can be seen more objectively, while he may have found it impossible to accept the interpretations of his associations, the patterns of which may well remain hidden to him. In his free associations, the interpretation is given on the basis of thoughts and behavior made known to the analyst during many sessions, associations which the patient may not be able or willing to relate to each other for any number of reasons. When presented with his TAT story, however, he usually accepts it immediately as his own production and can be made to see the thoughts and underlying behavior processes that were projected into the story.

Fourth, the TAT can be used *in cases where the patient feels the need for protectiveness* and produces associations which are completely superficial and innocuous. In such cases, since the TAT is considered an objective situation, the patient is not immediately aware of the fact that his stories are the products of his own thoughts and, therefore, as personal as his associations. Once the stories have been told, however, he can easily be made to see the stories as projections. Often in such cases the TAT will serve to break down the patient's protective shell and he will be able to continue psychotherapy on the basis of free association, if that is desirable. Should protectiveness appear again in the course of therapy, another TAT story can be taken up.

Fifth, the TAT can be used *in cases where the subject is depressed* and speaks little or not at all. In such cases, the TAT provides one of the few methods for getting in contact with the patient for psychotherapy. In connection with depressed cases, a TAT administered during sodium amytal interview often proves of particular value, particularly if the patient has been unable to respond to either the TAT or sodium amytal administered separately. (4, pp. 53–54.)[3]

Although the authors speak of using the stories therapeutically at the same session as they are given, they prefer the method of having them typed and later having each story read by the patient, followed by elaboration, discussion, and free association. "After all associations have been made, the therapist steps in and discusses all

---

[3] Reprinted from "The Use of the Thematic Apperception Test in Psychotherapy" by L. Bellak, B. A. Pasquarelli, and S. Braverman, by permission of the *Journal of Nervous and Mental Disease.* Copyright 1949 by the Smith Ely Jellife Trust.

the material again, with analysis and interpretation as indicated."
(4, p. 56.) That is, of course, only such interpretations are made as
the patient is ready for (3).

Arango and Lasaga (1) follow a very authoritarian use of the TAT
material. They consider that the TAT cards, as described in Chapter
16, give a clear picture of the conflict or conflicts which are acting to
disturb the patient. They therefore use the technique of administering the TAT, analyzing the stories for conflicts that are apparent in
them, verifying them from other clinical findings, and then employing them for more strictly therapeutic purposes. This includes discussion of the TAT by the patient, sometimes resulting in acceptance of the conflicts appearing in the stories as his own. If it does not
result in acceptance the task of the therapist at this point is to indicate to the patient his awareness that such conflicts exist and of what
they consist, but not of the details. This contention is strengthened
by mentioning some aspects revealed in the test and verified in the
history, but not in such a fashion that denial on the part of the patient will result. Since the conflict, according to the authors' view,
is primarily unconscious, it is realized that this may be a difficult
procedure; nevertheless, they report success in following it. After
acceptance of the personal nature of the material, the next step is
the presentation by the therapist of the solution he would suggest.
Solutions are classified as (1) modifications of objective reality, e.g.,
conflicts arising from a struggle between a patient's desire to please
her parents and an antipathy toward her present professional training resolved by abandoning her studies; (2) modification of subjective reality, e.g., convincing a boy who was upset by his sexual
practices that they were not "horrible" and arose from mere ignorance; and (3) modification of the patient's attitude toward an un-
modifiable reality, e.g., showing a girl whose conflict arose from
being in love with a man already married that he was unworthy of
her love. Arango and Lasaga realize that both intellectual and affective acceptance of the solution are necessary and devote considerable
attention to means of facilitating these. Although most clinicians
would find this approach objectionable on grounds of an almost
coercive character, it does serve to illustrate one therapeutic usage of
the TAT.

Deabler (6), who accepts a nondirective approach in psychotherapy, follows the procedure of allowing the patient ample time after

completing the test to express himself about the stories and the test as a whole. Interpretation is left largely to the patient, with the therapist serving primarily to mirror back to him his attitudes and feelings. Frequently elicited from the patients are comments about the general trends of the stories, such as their sexual elements, their aggressive elements, and so on. If the spontaneous evaluation the patient offers is rather meager, the stories are typewritten and at the next session given to him with the request that he verbalize his associations and interpretations.

Assessment of attitudes toward therapy is sometimes possible through the TAT stories, according to Tomkins (11). This is verified by the clinical experience of others. Card 12 M (young man reclining with older man standing over him with outstretched hand) is of special value in eliciting such material. Uncertainty about outcome, rejection of the therapist, pessimism or optimism, realistic expectation, etc., may be elicited.

Basically, then, the method in general use for utilizing the TAT therapeutically consists of confronting the patient with the products of his fantasies and allowing him to deal with them. This may be a direct by-product of telling the stories, of self-interpretation, or of interpretation by the therapist. The question now arises as to which factors that make for therapeutic change may be operating. This issue will next be considered.

COMMON FACTORS IN THERAPY AS EXEMPLIFIED THROUGH THE TAT

In considering the various therapeutic approaches it is apparent that many clinicians have a tendency to exaggerate the differences among them. It is possible, and in this setting desirable, to emphasize the factors which appear to be common to the various psychotherapeutic systems. Accordingly, through the medium of the TAT, the commonality of certain factors which in varying degree appear to be operative in seemingly diverse ways of handling therapeutic endeavors may be visualized. These common factors include the clinician-patient relationship, the circumvention of resistances in working through the difficulties of the patient, the effect of the personality of the therapist, the release of emotional tension in the therapeutic sessions, and the attainment of self-understanding or insight. Without attempting to deal with them exhaustively or systematically, a first approximation toward stating something about the nature of these phenomena will be given in relation to the TAT.

THE CLINICIAN-PATIENT RELATIONSHIP

Psychotherapy, it would appear, builds upon a substructure of relation between patient and therapist. The nature of this frequently described but nebulously defined term "relationship" will subsequently be explored from many angles and evidence introduced to justify its position of eminence, but for the moment description will suffice.

In any therapeutic contact a certain amount of time is spent in establishing this relationship between patient and therapist. This factor, known as "rapport," or "transference," needs to be developed lest the patient's defensiveness or cautiousness prevent a complete formulation and working through of his problems. Diagnostic instruments, particularly the projective variety, are considered by some clinicians capable of diminishing time spent in preliminaries. Therefore, when the TAT is used in an early session the hesitant patient is able to talk about himself without necessarily admitting he is doing so, and all the while increasing the number of experiences and thoughts shared with the therapist even if at a preconscious level.

RESISTANCE

As the relationship between patient and therapist strengthens there is not as much need for such devices. Nonetheless, it does not follow necessarily that all is smooth sailing once the relationship is established. Thus the TAT may be used (just as sometimes an entire diagnostic testing examination is used) to work through resistances to and defenses against therapeutic progress. When such "plateaus" in which no advancement is being made are reached, projective techniques may serve to loosen the situation and allow movement to occur. Their introduction at these points may break a vicious circle in which no change (movement) is taking place. The nature of the resistance by itself may be a valuable problem to analyze, particularly in a psychoanalysis proper. In brief psychotherapy, however, it is frequently a phenomenon to be avoided or overcome (3). The case to follow drawn from Bellak et al. (4) is introduced here because it illustrates the operation of such a resistance. They write:

Case I.-K., a 22-year-old white male military prisoner, diagnosed psychoneurosis, obsessional. On primary psychiatric interview it was recognized that the subject was theoretically amenable to psychotherapy. A full battery of psychological tests, including the TAT, was administered, and he co-operated to the best of his considerable ability. Throughout the first week of psychotherapy there was no progress whatever. The subject would clear his throat nervously and respond tersely to questions, and was extremely guarded and defensive. Owing to his superior intelligence he was successful in confining the conversation to completely neutral grounds. Because repeated efforts produced only barren verbalizations, the TAT was used as a "stirring rod." We have selected only one of his stories for presentation here. This particular story was chosen because we consider it a good example of the projection of wholly unconscious material into TAT stories.

(#14) "Well, I'd say that this takes place in Paris, just for the heck of it . . . That the papers have announced that there will be a . . . I would say that there will be . . . there will be meteors shooting across the sky on this date. This here person is a man . . . is watching . . . shall we say astral displays. . . . The room he is in is his bedroom and he has put the light out to make it easier for him to see what is going on. . . . He watches for about 15 minutes, closes the window, puts the light on, and gets undressed and goes to bed . . . And that's the end of that! . . . (Resistance) . . . The way the window opened up I always imagined that windows like that were to be seen in Paris. . . . I would say that before he went to the windows he was laying on the bed, reading a book, until the time came around at which time the newspapers said that meteors would be seen shooting across the sky. . . . I would say that he is more or less of an amateur astronomer and that he has a great interest in the universe . . . and . . . let's say . . . maybe we can make something out of this after all . . . that he is working on some small job which has no future . . . that he has always been interested in astronomy, but due to the fact that his parents did not have the resources with which to send him to school that he could not further his education in that field . . . (Resistance) . . . He has some knowledge of the stars, and this display fascinates him and only makes him yearn for that education he might have had . . . that's all!"

This is one of those TAT stories which is best interpreted by means of psychoanalytic symbols and treated like a dream or a fantasy. We are dealing here apparently with a primal scene: This person is watching "astral displays" in the bedroom, meaning, apparently, the watching of the parents. The "meteors shooting across the sky" are phallic symbols. The whole scene is placed in Paris as if to indicate the indecency of the event. "Windows" might actually be seen as symbols for the female genital, and it might convey the child's dismay at finding that his mother engages in such conduct. He himself feels only as an "amateur" who "works on a small job without a future"—that is, has only a small penis and masturbates. We understand, then, that the last sentence, the "yearning for an education" basically means to be as big a man as the father.

From the time that his unconscious projections in the TAT were in part[4] raised to the conscious level, K. began to work through his problems, established considerable empathy with the examiner and was able to produce much relevant material. The TAT served as an efficient neutral agent and intermediary wherewith the subject was brought into some real association with the therapist. (4, pp. 57–59.)[5]

The nature of this interpretation, psychoanalytically stated as it is, is not the point at issue. Whether or not one accepts this approach it does serve to illustrate the psychotherapeutic usage of the interpretation of TAT material when resistance is encountered.

The Personality of the Therapist

The relationship between therapist and patient is affected by the personality of the therapist. What he does and says and feels has its influence upon the relationship and thus upon the course of therapy. The TAT has been demonstrated sometimes to reflect the attitude the patient takes toward the therapist. The use of card 12 M, previously referred to, is a case in point.

The effect of the personality of the therapist also extends more generally throughout the TAT stories. The study of Bellak (2) described in Chapter 16 is an illustration of the influence of the personality of the clinician. It will be recalled that some TAT cards were administered in the normal fashion and then a second group was administered with the examiner adopting a punitive critical attitude. An increase in aggressiveness was shown in the stories of the second group of cards. Here, although the personality was an assumed one, there was a definite change which it is reasonable to assume had therapeutic implications. The fact that aggression was permitted to emerge, at least as projection (the stories), as a defense mechanism (preventing anxiety from arising), can be seen as an automatic self-therapeutic device (3).

---

[4] Choosing the most innocuous aspects first and only slowly increasing the more conflict-laden aspects (3).

[5] Reprinted from "The Use of the Thematic Apperception Test in Psychotherapy by L. Bellak, B. A. Pasquarelli, and S. Braverman, by permission of the *Journal of Nervous and Mental Disease.* Copyright 1949 by the Smith Ely Jellife Trust.

RELEASE OF EMOTIONAL TENSION

Expression of fears and other emotional experiences through projective material, particularly the TAT, forms in some instances a cathartic experience. This use as an instrument for catharsis may occur in the telling of the stories themselves or in the giving of interpretations either by patient or by therapist. The sheer presentation of the material by the patient may have some therapeutic value, as, for example, the relief obtained by giving vent to strong pent-up emotions. It may be blended with an insight by the patient into the nature of his difficulties through both self-interpretation and interpretation by the therapist. It is generally agreed that catharsis, by itself, is not very effective because tensions are likely to recur despite temporary relief. Therefore catharsis, to be therapeutically effective, must be integrated through interpretation by either the patient or the therapist.

The cathartic effect may sometimes be not so obvious during the TAT proper as it is immediately afterward. After going through the pictures the patient is likely to feel more freedom in expressing himself and subsequently go into significant aspects of his problems.

SELF-UNDERSTANDING

In discussing the emotional relief experienced during and after the TAT, indirect reference was made to the self-understanding of the patient as mediated through this technique. This self-understanding or insight is often hypothecated to be the most important of the factors involved in psychotherapeutic change. The self-interpretations offered in response to TAT stories shed light upon the patient's insight into his own personality make-up. A study of Bettelheim (5) is pertinent in this connection.

Bettelheim asked college students in his class to interpret their own performances on the TAT, which had been administered by him as an integral part of a course in personality dynamics. Three features were at work which are directly relevant to and modify the results obtained. During the administration the students were aware that they were talking about themselves in contradistinction to the usually assumed ignorance of the subject as to what is happening. They also were already in some degree in a transference situation with their instructor. Furthermore, the psychological sophistication of the subject group was considerably greater than it is in the general run of patients. In many clinical situations none of these features would obtain, and indeed these factors facilitated more self-interpretation than otherwise would be the case. The procedure that was followed involved administration by Bettelheim of the TAT, the lapse of several weeks, and the return of the stories to the students with a request that they analyze the psychological meaning of each story and also present an analysis of the validity of the findings of the test as a whole. He presents excerpts from these stories, their subsequent interpretations, and some general comments. No quantification is attempted but the following quotations will exemplify the obtained results.

A girl of twenty-one who clinically (including autobiographically) demonstrated an ambivalent attitude toward her mother and extreme religious convictions submitted the following story and interpretation to picture 7 GF (older woman on sofa, reading or speaking to a child beside her who, holding a doll, is looking away):

The little girl has just done something bad. Her mother, who is a very kind and wonderful woman, is telling her what she has done is wrong. She is reading verses from the Bible. The little girl is quite sad about it. She did not realize that she was doing the wrong thing. She is about to go to the party of her friend. All the time the little girl is listening to her mother, she is wishing she could be on her way.

Interpretation. Here again is a misbehaving, unadjusted daughter, and a kind understanding mother acting as a comforter; again I identified with the girl and express my wish for mother love and my feelings of guilt for something I have done. That the book is the Bible seems to show my need for religious influence. I make excuses by stating that I was ignorant of doing wrong. The mother is holding the girl back from a party and does not allow her the happiness which the other girls are having. She therefore resents her mother. (5, p. 89.)

Bettelheim then goes on to his own interpretation.

The interpretation reveals greater psychological insight than the story. In the story the girl wishes to go to the party. The interpretation adds that she resents her mother's preventing her doing so. It seems to indicate that Dorothy's religious feelings originate in her guilt-feeling, since the statement referring to it is followed by the assertion of the need for religious influence. It also indicates that Dorothy does not realize that the religious episode in her life is connected with her relationship to her mother. (5, p. 89.)

This small excerpt serves to illustrate that the method of presentation of results carries clinical conviction through the congruence of the two findings, but also the difficulties of teasing out the sequence of events which apparently took place. The findings appear to suggest that the girl knew something about herself and expressed this in her interpretation, and further, that this in turn seemed to be related to certain factors in her personal history. But there is no clear demonstration that these self-interpretations occurred *because* this story (and other stories) were told to the TAT cards despite the student's claim that she became aware of certain facets of her personality previously not recognized.

The results reported in Bettelheim's other illustrations parallel these findings and present the same difficulties. He cannot be said to have proved his thesis, since, for example, the transference situation of which he speaks might have contributed heavily, if not entirely, to the well-nigh unanimous agreement on the part of his subjects that they had learned significant facts about their personality make-up. The findings do, nevertheless, lend some support to the thesis that administration of the TAT can have psychotherapeutic effects.

Attainment of insight sometimes finds expression through the recovery of repressed memories. This the use of the TAT cards seems to expedite. Presentation of stories as reported by Tomkins (11) on occasion produces repressed memories of considerable import.

It would be entirely too superficial a view of therapy to believe that mere presentation of stories to a patient will forthwith make him capable of assimilating them insightfully and accepting their implications. Tomkins (11) distinguishes two phases of the denial or denials which may occur. There may be acceptance of the source from which the story comes but denial of the derivative interpretation offered by the therapist. Or there may be acceptance of the interpretation with repudiation, vehement or otherwise, of the source from which it comes. Be that as it may, the important point to realize is that, as with any kind of therapy, the readiness of the patient to assess the material must be taken into account. There must be a receptivity on the part of the patient; otherwise forcing (temporarily) inacceptable interpretations will only endanger the patient-therapist relationship and actually delay therapeutic progress. A patient proceeds, not at the pace of the therapist's insights, but at his own speed. The insight of the two eventually merge, but only in the patient's good time.

Illustrative of conditions which prevent assimilation of material revealed by projective instruments is the presence of a crippling anxiety. The material may, if dwelt upon, result in the intensification of anxiety—perhaps it submits too much for assimilation at any one time. Anxiety may be so pervasive as to prevent adequate emergence of material and the projective protocols (or interpretations) so barren of real dynamic content as to show nothing more than the presence of the all-pervasive dysphoric mood. In the Rorschach of the depressed, it will be recalled, there is a restricting, crippling effect upon the personality picture revealed. Similarly, in the TAT there may be a poverty-stricken record produced when acute anxiety is present.

THE NONDIRECTIVE AND DIRECTIVE APPROACHES

Terms currently in vogue in certain therapeutic camps are applicable in the present discussion as they reflect contrasting ways of handling the TAT material. On one hand we have interpretation by the therapist, illustrated best for this context in the work of Arango and Lasaga (1), and on the other hand self-interpretation, illustrated by the approach of Deabler (6).

Tomkins (11) points out very explicitly the use of the TAT as a guide in directive therapy. His remarks may be extended to include by implication other projective materials as well. An individual for whom other forms may appear inadvisable (e.g., too old, too rigid, etc.) may be offered reassurance or advice based on insights the clinician has achieved from the projective material. With an individual under various forms of treatment for twenty-five years Tomkins tells of using TAT material to demonstrate that sexual activity was equated with aggression and that his painful symptoms were an atonement for this. In describing the case Tomkins does not hold that the reassurance he gave him about sexual practices will effect a permanent change. He is properly pessimistic about its efficacy.

Although Deabler follows in the main a nondirective (client-centered) approach, his use of tests is not necessarily accepted by all who hold to this approach to therapy. Rogers (8) himself views with considerable reserve the use of tests if their introduction was initiated by the clinician and not by the patient. (He does *not*, as is sometimes mistakenly said, condemn the use of all tests with patients in therapy.) He maintains that the introduction of psychological tests and the usual array of diagnostic approaches (such as described in the earlier chapters) at the beginning of the sessions with the patient is likely to be a therapeutic mistake. With him there is, strictly speaking, no diagnostic phase of the clinical approach in the sense described in this volume. His argument for or against the use of psychological tests as diagnostic (and presumably therapeutic) devices hinges upon the way the situation is structured for the patient. The introduction of tests relatively early in the clinical situation, he believes, creates in the patient an expectancy that a tacit bargain is being struck in which in return for taking the tests the clinician will tell him what is wrong. Thus a preconception already strong in the patient to be dependent upon the clinician to tell him what to do is actually strengthened. Since his approach to therapy (to be discussed in detail later) rests upon the creating or reinstating in the patient of a desire to help himself and to assume responsibility for his own behavior, it may be seen that these tests may be used in a fashion which tends to defeat the goal. This is not necessarily the case, however. It is true that tests are sometimes given to a patient who is inadequately prepared for such sessions and that a false expectancy is created. If it does happen that an attitude of dependency and waiting to be told the answers develops, it may in part be due to inadequate therapeutic handling or preparation for the sessions. (This is not always the case—there are patients with such strong dependency needs that nothing can prevent the development of such an attitude.)

In short, the fault is not with tests as such, but in the way the tests are introduced.[6] If the patient is prepared for the examination so that he understands and accepts it as a means of gaining both for himself and for the therapist a better insight into his problem, then his objection becomes pointless. If the patient is provided with this understanding, tests actually can aid in the growth toward self-responsibility, as in such a framework participation in the examination implies a willingness to face his problems.

---

[6] See Chapter 7 for a discussion of preparation of the patient for diagnostic testing.

BIBLIOGRAPHY

1. Arango, C. M., and Lasaga y Travieso, J. I., Psychotherapy based on the Thematic Apperception Test, *Quart. Rev. Psychiat. Neurol.*, 1947, 2:271–287.
2. Bellak, L., The concept of projection: an experimental investigation and study of the concept, *Psychiatry*, 1944, 7:353–370.
3. Bellak, L., personal communication, 1950.
4. Bellak, L., Pasquarelli, B. A., and Braverman, S., The use of the Thematic Apperception Test in psychotherapy, *J. nerv. ment. Dis.*, 1949, 110:51–65.
5. Bettelheim, B., Self-interpretation of fantasy: the Thematic Apperception Test as an educational and therapeutic device, *Amer. J. Orthopsychiat.*, 1947, 17:80–100.
6. Deabler, H. L., The psychotherapeutic use of the Thematic Apperception Test, *J. clin. Psychol.*, 1947, 3:246–252.
7. Doll, E. A., and Brooks, J. J., The therapeutic uses of the Vineland Social Maturity Scale in its application to adult prisoners, *J. crim. Psychopath.*, 1942, 3:347–358.
8. Rogers, C. R., Psychometric tests and client-centered counseling, *Educ. Psychol. Measmt.*, 1946, 6:139–144.
9. Rosenzweig, S., The Thematic Apperception technique in diagnosis and therapy, *J. Personality*, 1948, 16:437–444.
10. Thorne, F. C., Directive psychotherapy: IV. The therapeutic implications of the case history, *J. clin. Psychol.*, 1945, 1:318–330.
11. Tomkins, S. S., *The Thematic Apperception Test: the theory and techniques of interpretation*, Grune & Stratton, 1947.

Supplementary articles in Watson, R. I. (ed.), *Readings in the clinical method in psychology*, Harper & Brothers, 1949:

12. Font, M. M., Therapeutic aspects of the psychological interview. Pp. 447–450. (Also in *J. clin. Psychol.*, 1946, 2:84–87.)
13. Roland, M. C., The psychological examination as a beginning in therapy. Pp. 451–460. (Also in *J. consult. Psychol.*, 1945, 9:171–177.)

CHAPTER 18

The Common Factors in Psychotherapy

┌─┐

In the previous chapter the TAT was used to illustrate certain phenomena which appear to be fairly common in psychotherapeutic practice, though no more than passing reference to the nature of the phenomena themselves was made. It is now necessary to examine these and other factors in psychotherapy both more systematically and more thoroughly. Accordingly, the nature of psychotherapy itself will be first examined in a general and necessarily introductory fashion. Following this the common factors in psychotherapy as expressed by psychotherapists of different orientations will be presented, after which an attempt will be made to present the common factors in what will be referred to as a dynamic (but not necessarily psychoanalytic) psychotherapy.

THE NATURE OF PSYCHOTHERAPY

In its most general aspect, the aim of psychotherapy is both to understand the behavior of the patient as an individual and to facilitate modifications to the extent that existing difficulties are relieved or minimized. In other words, the clinician attempts to make a diagnostic appraisal of the individual emphasizing the patient's unique configuration of personality attributes. The task of the therapist, either in conjunction with this activity or subsequent to it, is to aid the patient to become free of his anxieties and other feelings which stand in the way of his personal optimal adjustment, which affect his behavior and that of others in any or all major areas of life such as interpersonal relations, work, sex, or acceptance of oneself. These disturbances (neuroses and psychoses) are specific and not merely the pervasive problems of adjustment to which we all are heir.

Psychotherapy is best conceived in terms of its operations. In this process the application of the clinical method in deliberate, planned, and systematic and is guided by one or another theoretical point of view concerning the nature of human nature. Following from the premise that psychotherapy is systematic is the conclusion that training is necessary—training in psychotherapy and training in psychological theory. It is not unreasonable to affirm that psychotherapy, to be worthy of the name, must not only be consciously planned and executed but also require training for its proper execution. In short, in terms of its operation psychotherapy is an aspect of the clinical method. What follows is an attempt to state its operations.

The aim, but not this method, is shared with others. Since therapy is defined in terms of its operations it would appear that in the absence of certain definitive procedures there is no psychotherapy as such. This would rule out, in effect, therapeutic acts on the part of individuals who are by their very personality structure therapeutically helpful. Some individuals are able to help others to understand themselves more thoroughly and to act on these insights without themselves being psychotherapists. The minister, the family physician, the old and valued friend may under differing circumstances aid those with whom they come in contact to make more adequate and healthful adjustment by their very way of reacting to the difficulties of these individuals. They are intuitive and warmly sympathetic by nature but are not guided by a systematic clinical point of view or in any strict sense by a theory of the nature of personality organization.

A dynamic psychotherapy to be worthy of the name demands understanding of the behavior of the individual in terms of himself, and thus the goals should be patient-centered. In dynamic psychotherapy we are interested in an individual's reactions to his problems and the methods whereby he attempts to solve them, in the meaning for him of his symptoms and ways whereby he may be helped to overcome those difficulties which have brought him to the therapist. There is no single standard of normality; rather, there are many kinds of normality, many kinds of adjustments. The path to that adjustment which is desirable for a given patient may not lead to the solution for another. This view emphasizes the potentialities for growth possessed to a certain extent by everyone but often requiring rearrangement of conditions in order to unfold. The patient, to some degree at least, is responsible for his own goals in so far as he is able to formulate them, whether or not these correspond to the desires and aims of the therapist. Therapists and schools of therapy vary in the degree to which the responsibility is placed upon the patient, to be sure, but some freedom is allowed by all. The unique capacities and limitations of the patient also necessitate adherence to individual rather than group standards; hypothetical normality could not always be achieved even if this were the goal of the therapist. It is not some external, hypothetically ideal level of adjustment that is sought, but the most comfortable and efficient level for a given individual. The mentally defective child cannot be made normal in intelligence; the adult severely crippled by his psychoneurotic trends may never be able to give them up completely but can learn to live with them.

There is a deeper reason for rejecting the primacy of a statistical or conforming concept of normality as a guide in therapy. It is not the act itself but the motivating force which must be considered more fundamental. Washing one's hands is normal; a handwashing compulsion is not. The dividing line between persistence and perseveration is more in the motivation in relation to the situation than in the acts themselves. The need to produce flawless work may either reflect an entirely "normal" trend of behavior or be neurotically determined. Behavior is not abnormal or normal primarily because of what is done but because of the nature of the psychological individual-centered forces which produce it. It is this organization of the personality which gives rise to the differences in intensity and quality of normal tendency and abnormal impulse or normal caution and abnormal inhibition.

Despite this necessity for individual standards of behavior, man, to be in the fullest sense an individual, must learn to live with his fellow men and the world as it is. Therefore, the therapist must take the patient's reality situations into consideration not with the aim of "making him normal" in the sense of being similar to other people but in order to aid in increasing his ability to love and live with others without extinguishing the individualized expression of his needs. The concern is with his unique way of accomplishing this, not with a hypothetical norm. The desired goal is not what the individual should do to become like his fellow men but the manner in which the therapeutic relationship can provide an opportunity for the individual to handle his personal problems in a more realistic and less neurotically or psychotically determined fashion, and so to learn to live within a group structure.

"Norms" are not criteria of normality for the dynamic psychotherapist. They are points of departure from which to understand better the individual both intra-individually and in his relationship to the group. Group norms are thus necessary to delimit the behavior of the individual as being specific to him.

COMMON FACTORS IN PSYCHOTHERAPY AS EXPRESSED BY THERAPISTS OF DIFFERENT ORIENTATIONS

In any volume devoted to psychotherapy one could find somewhere references to insight, catharsis, growth, and other factors operative in the field. To lift them from their context and then to allege that they represent the common factors of psychotherapy might justifiably lay one open to the charge of bias. Therefore, relatively short explicit statements of the important variables were sought in the writings of leading psychotherapists. Care was taken to select concise statements which necessitated very little editing of passages to avoid the charge of selecting out of context only that which served the argument.

It is fortunate that such discussions are available. We have the succinct discussion of Thorne (25) who speaks of his point of view as directive. There is also available a relevant paper by Rogers (13),[1] who for some years has expressed a point of view referred to originally as nondirective and now as client-centered. Although the authors did not label their statements *common factors*—Thorne speaking of *objectives* of therapy in the general setting of the clinical method and Rogers of the *fundamental aspects* of the therapeutic process—it is felt that any difference is largely semantic and that

---

[1] Rogers (24) has also published another account of common factors in psychotherapy in a setting of child guidance practice.

they, as well as the author, are enumerating factors which are common to diverse psychotherapeutic systems.[2]

The points of view which they hold and the thinking they express have roots in psychiatric practice and theory. To place historically their approaches it will suffice at this point to say that Rogers was influenced by what will later be referred to as relationship therapy and by child guidance practice and somewhat less directly by Rankian psychoanalytic thinking. Thorne in an eclectic tradition was more influenced by general medical practice and psychobiology than any other points of view. The thinking of these two is of general significance both because of its representativeness in psychological thinking and because the differences between their positions are sufficiently great to warrant assembling of followers into separate camps.

The representativeness of the account of common factors of psychotherapy to follow would, however, be seriously circumscribed if it were not possible to include the contributions of psychoanalytic thinking. Most statements concerning the factors operative in psychotherapy as visualized by the psychoanalyst either are expressed in very lengthy fashion or else are so technically written as to be unsuitable at this point. However, Ackerman (1), a psychiatrist, in analyzing the dynamics of group psychotherapy found it necessary to preface his discussion with a short account of individual therapy, and in so doing presented the processes which this interpersonal situation provides.

Ackerman (1), Rogers (13), and Thorne (25), then, have offered a point-by-point specification of the fundamentals of therapy. It is possible to enumerate them here and thus to observe their inherent commonality.[3] This is done through Table 29.

---

[2] At this point, as well as at many others, a warning against provincialism might be sounded. Much of what various psychologists—Rogers, Thorne, and so on—have said about psychotherapy has also been said by therapists trained in other disciplines. Since this volume is written primarily for psychologists there is justification for cloaking the discussion in terms of the contributions of psychologists whenever pertinent. However, there is no justification for thinking that psychologists have a priority on thinking and writing and carrying out psychotherapy.

[3] It may be that Rogers would today not consider this 1940 formulation a fair statement of his position concerning psychotherapy. It was used because it is the latest known statement by him on this issue. Since that date he has been

TABLE 29. Common Factors in Psychotherapy According to Ackerman (1), Rogers (13), and Thorne (25)

Ackerman	Rogers	Thorne
"The patient develops an attachment to the therapist and may identify him with other persons with whom he has had previous relationships, thus re-living these past interpersonal patterns. From this attachment the patient may derive some feeling of security, variously experienced as a feeling of being accepted, respected, protected, loved, etc. Fundamentally, this sense of security arises from a feeling of trust and sympathy, and from the awareness of being deeply understood."[a] "Then there is the phenomenon of emotional release, the so-called catharsis, which takes place in psychotherapy. With some assurance of safety, the patient freely and spontaneously expresses his emotions, impulses, phantasies, etc."	"Rapport is established. There must be a warmth of relationship between counsellor and counselee if any progress is to be made." "There is free expression of feeling on the part of the client." "Recognition and acceptance, by the client, of his spontaneous self. . . ."[b] As material is given by the client, it is the therapist's function to help him recognize and clarify the emotions he feels. In the rapport situation, where he is accepted rather than criticized, the individual is free to see himself without defensiveness, and gradually	"Expressing and clarifying emotional attitudes. From the cathartic method of psychoanalysis to current nondirective methods of counseling, major emphasis has been placed on methods of securing emotional release and expression in a permissive, accepting environment."

a The order of these quotations is not necessarily that of the authors.

b Free expression of feeling, and recognition and acceptance by the client of his spontaneous self are treated by Rogers in the account from which these quotations are drawn as separate processes. As he points out, they are so closely related as to make it possible to class them together. This the writer has done.

"Finally, we have the phenomenon of insight which caps the foregoing processes. Insight emerges from the continuous clash of the patient's distorted conceptions with the true definitions of interpersonal reality, as embodied in the person of the therapist. In consequence of this, the patient's perceptions of his relation to himself and to others are modified in the direction of greater accuracy, greater discrimination, and this in turn encourages a higher degree of integration of the functions of the personality."

"In this individual therapeutic process an ever widening opportunity is afforded for a gradual correction of distorted perceptions, a higher degree of acceptance of reality, a finer discrimination in the process of interpersonal adaptation and a freer and fuller expression of emotion. This is essentially a process of personality growth. It is made possible by the special environment

to recognize and admit his real self with its childish patterns, its aggressive feelings, and its ambivalences, as well as its mature impulses, and rationalized exterior."

"The gaining of insight through assimilated interpretation. The foundation of insight seems to be the emotional acceptance of self mentioned under . . . [the second point above]. In addition, however, insight is often enriched by the therapist's interpretation of emotional patterns in the life of the individual which have not been recognized. Such interpretations, largely explanations of motives for behavior, serve no useful purpose, and may retard progress, if they are not accepted by the client. Hence, the use of the term 'assimilated interpretation.'"

"Growing into independence—with support. The final period of any therapeutic experience is the process of education or re-education which makes possible the effective continuance of the fundamental gains which have been made. In choosing new goals, the client may need new information which the therapist may supply or help him to obtain. In taking inde-

"*Self-understanding.* All psychotherapy has the objective of stimulating the client to understand and accept himself, to develop genuine insight into feelings, attitudes, and motivations."

"*Reeducation.* Since human behavior is regarded as being largely learned or acquired through experience, therapy seeks to reeducate and teach new modes of adjustment."

"*Catalysing maturation.* Recognizing that many morbid processes involve immaturity and regressive reactions, therapy seeks to catalyse maturation to the most complete state of development of which the therapist creates, in which the patient makes the therapist into anything he needs him to be. In this special environment, the therapist minimizes his own personality in order to permit an optimal expansion of the patient's individuality."

"There is also the process of gradual integration of unconscious tendencies into the conscious mental life, where these tendencies are reorganized and brought under conscious control."

"In addition, we have the process of reality testing through which there is an impact between subjective perceptions and objective realities, in consequence of which the patient learns the true nature of objective reality and acquires some mastery over it."

pendent steps to cope with his adjustment problems, there will be discouragements and defeats, which the rapport situation helps to neutralize. In these new experiences there are fresh opportunities for the client to see himself even more clearly and to make use of the insight he has previously gained."

"The making of responsible choices. Perhaps the sharpest difference between present day psychotherapy and earlier practice, is the degree to which the responsibility for the client's life is left in his own hands. The therapist at his best does not suggest, advise, or persuade."

which the individual organism is capable."

"*Resolving conflict and inconsistencies* Since conflicts and inconsistent attitudes threaten personality integration, therapy seeks to remove repression and ambivalencies in the mental economy."

On examining in Table 29 the statements concerning factors operative in psychotherapy by these three ostensibly different psychotherapists we see certain important agreements emerge. Although rapport, transference, or some other way of stating the relationship of patient and therapist is not mentioned by Thorne in the present formulation, the omission is not indicative of a rejection of the importance of this relationship. He offered the particular account quoted as a statement of the *objectives* of therapy. To him this relationship would be present, as other writings of his attest (17) (18), but not as an objective of therapy. With this amendment it is now possible to state categorically that all three therapists accept the following common factors in psychotherapy: the relationship established, expression of feeling, insight, and growth. Little comment is necessary, as the quotations speak for themselves. To be sure, there are obvious differences of emphasis, but this is much less striking than the considerable degree of agreement. Nevertheless, certain differences in formulation should be mentioned. Although all three accept the patient-clinician relationship as a factor, they differ in the weight attributed to it. Rogers and Thorne are concerned with rapport, and Ackerman, although he does not use the word, is concerned with transference. Insight or self-understanding and emotional release are more uniformly treated even though in the very formulation one can see incipient differences. Growth as a factor in psychotherapy is characteristically stated by each. Although Rogers would consider the choice of the term "teach" used by Thorne somewhat inappropriate, since it implies too directive a role on the part of the therapist, he nevertheless agrees on the importance of learning new means of adjustment. In regard to the other factors, Rogers states that current practice minimizes suggestion, advice, and persuasion. Thorne, who says nothing about this point in his account, would agree that there has been such a diminution but would not agree that "at his best" the therapist does not sometimes use these techniques, holding, it would appear, that sometimes they are essential. Presumably this difference is created by divergent attitudes toward the commonly accepted factor of growth. Rogers emphasizes the dynamic therapeutic value of

---

increasingly concerned with the client-centered approach. An exception in his review of psychotherapy in a volume connected with current trends in psychology (14), although he does not deal with the present issue systematically.

growth to a degree that Thorne could not accept. Rogers stresses growth toward independence more than does Thorne and consequently does not believe suggestion, advice, and persuasion are necessary.

The resolution of conflicts and inconsistencies mentioned by Thorne and not given directly by Rogers would appear to be implied in the quotation from Rogers at the point at which he speaks of recognizing and admitting "his real self with its childish patterns, its aggressive feelings, and its ambivalences, as well as its mature impulses, and rationalized exterior."

Ackerman alone speaks of unconscious tendencies and reality testing, as such. Rogers, to be sure, is not far from something approaching the concept of reality testing in speaking of growth and opportunities for fresh experience and making use of his insight. To "remove repression" that Thorne speaks of would certainly imply unconscious factors at work even if he prefers not to stress them.

The fundamental substratum of agreement shown by these individuals of different orientations is all the more striking when it is realized that the series of statements were drawn from articles prepared at different times, published in different journals, and, so far as references that they cite are concerned, without any direct attention to the work of the others except a passing reference by Thorne to Rogers' position concerning diagnosis.

Such views of the essential nature of psychotherapy as these are not held by these three psychotherapists alone. Although it is manifestly impossible to examine here all attempts to elucidate the basic factors in psychotherapy, it is believed that other accounts by writers of ostensibly quite different theoretical and procedural orientations would show as much agreement on fundamentals. For example, careful reading of Alexander and French (2) and Allen (3) reveals many points of similarity to the account just given. Speaking as a psychoanalytically oriented social worker, Gordon Hamilton offered as fundamental principles ". . . knowledge of and respect for human personality, and the right of a person to manage his own affairs . . . skilled use of relationship . . . improved interpersonal relationships and reality adaptations . . ." and the necessity of the patient ". . . to become aware of the pattern of his behavior if he is to change himself in any degree." (10, p. 213.) In addition, a symposium (19) on common factors in psychotherapy involving the participation of psychiatrists, psychoanalysts, social workers, and psychologists does not seem to be in contradiction so far as the general pattern which emerged is concerned.[4]

THE COMMON FACTORS IN A DYNAMIC PSYCHOTHERAPY[5]

To this point the intent of the discussion was to demonstrate the fundamental substratum of psychotherapeutic agreement by emphasizing the common factors which appear to be operative. Nevertheless, to go beyond to a more detailed discussion of each of these matters it is necessary to offer a synthesis of the common factors in a setting in keeping with that sketched previously in discussing the nature of dynamic psychotherapy. In other words, there is need for a working outline.

In view of the agreement described in the previous section, it is plausible to formulate more completely the nature of these common factors. In doing so certain limitations must be recognized. In keeping with the definition of psychotherapy in dynamic terms the intra-individual orientation will be maintained and, therefore, a systematic bias upheld. Despite this, the presentation to follow stresses methodology in general and not a personality theory in particular in so far as this is possible. This is both a weakness and a strength. Without a point of view concerning personality, actual therapy would be sterile, and even meaningless, yet this is not the place to consider this controversial and complex problem of the structure of personality. On the other hand, it is the conviction of the writer that these common factors are capable of assimilation into, or rather are integral aspects of, many psychotherapeutic systems. The classification will incorporate many of the ideas of Ackerman, Rogers, Thorne, and others but will not adhere strictly to their categories.

Any description of the process of therapy predicated upon categorization does violence to the stream of events. Instead of operating in isolation as the account to follow might imply, all factors are in fact interdependent. Nor is any sequence to be inferred from the

---

[4] In formulating the discussion of common factors in psychotherapy to follow I have been influenced by this symposium, which took place at a meeting of the American Orthopsychiatric Association.

[5] Many, if not all, of these common factors may, in another light, be viewed as examples of learning. To enter the realm of the relation of learning theory and these factors would, however, be inappropriate to this volume.

order of presentation, notwithstanding an attempt to present them in a psychologically realistic order.

THE PATIENT-CLINICIAN RELATIONSHIP

It is appropriate at this point to refer to the attitudes of the patient as discussed in Chapter 5 in connection with the diagnostic interview. Aside from instances in which coercion is used, the patient, unless in need of help, would not seek it. In seeking help the patient is especially prone to become dependent upon the therapist. He has certain expectations based upon previous experience in seeking help, especially the help that physicians have rendered in the past: after giving his complaints he anticipates the outlining of some program by the clinician whereby he will become better able to handle the complaints. In short, he expects a prescription. To be sure, the prescription may take the form of advice, exhortation, reassurance, or interpretation rather than medication but some capsule form of treatment is expected. This the clinician, except at one level of therapy to be referred to as supportive, cannot give. He has, in the words of Allen, "nothing to offer except himself." (19, p. 698.) It is the patient-clinician relationship which he offers—a series of experiences taking place in a particular setting at a particular time involving the interrelationship of patient and therapist.

All forms of psychotherapy demand a personal interrelationship of therapist and patient. In a sense this is a truism so obvious that it may be regarded as hardly worth mentioning. It might be said that you can hardly have psychotherapy without both there, any more than you can dispense with some means of communication between them. It is not in this sense of being required merely to permit such sessions—a necessary but not a sufficient cause—that the clinician-patient relationship is given a position of prominence here. The relationship is regarded by many therapists as effective in psychotherapy of and for itself. It is in this sense that Witmer (20) spoke of the distinguishing mark of a dynamic psychiatry as conscious use of a relationship. This relationship, if properly established, assures the emotional participation of the patient, an essential to the assimilation of the material that emerges. The patient must feel secure in this relationship and must feel that he is accepted whether he is expressing positive, ambivalent, or negative feelings.

That the patient-clinician relationship is a common factor in psychotherapy receives striking confirmation in three studies of Fiedler (7) (8) (9). The first proposition investigated was that good clinicians, irrespective of the particular approach followed, strive to create essentially the same relationship with their patients. Seventy-five statements concerning various possible characteristics of therapeutic relationships were prepared. Such matters as understanding the patient's feelings, hostility to the patient, and treating the patient like a child were included. The task of the therapist was to sort the statements as to the degree to which they were characteristic of an ideal therapeutic relationship from most to least characteristic. A group of therapists—psychoanalytic, non-directive, Adlerian, and eclectic—took part in this classification. The answers of each were intercorrelated and one general factor (in the statistical sense) was found. If there were real differences characteristic of each school, a factor representing each one should have emerged. Apparently, then, one type of relationship is actually considered maximally effective. Regardless of their systematic orientation they all can be said to have expressed a common goal in terms of the relationship they wanted to create. Some of those participating were experts, others novices. It was found that experts of *different* schools agreed more highly than experts and novices of the *same* school.

The second proposition was that better therapists were able to approximate this ideal of therapeutic relationship more closely than less skilled therapists. Wire recordings of interviews between the fifth and twentieth sessions from expert and from novice psychoanalytic, nondirective, and Adlerian therapists were made. Four judges listened to the recordings and assessed each of the sessions on the basis of the same seventy-five statements used previously. One judge was drawn from the psychoanalytic school, one from the nondirective approach, one had training in both, and a fourth was untrained in therapeutic theory or technique. Despite differences in training, the assessment agreed between judges with rank order correlations of .7 to .9; i.e., rank-ordering therapists by how closely they approached an ideal gave agreement despite bias and halo. Apparently it is the therapist's skill, not his school, which decides the quality of the therapeutic relationship within the limits of this admittedly incomplete study.

These ratings were used in a factor analysis, which yielded three factors for the nondirectively trained judge and four for the other judges. One factor related to the security of the therapist, another to the therapist's status in relation to the patient. A less prominent factor which emerged is related to the proper emotional distance between patient and therapist. Those factors which differentiated experts from nonexperts are related to the therapist's security, his ability to understand, to communicate with, and to maintain rapport with the patient. Differences between schools are most clearly apparent in terms of the status which the therapists assume toward their patients. The Adlerian and some, but not all, of the psychoanalytically oriented therapists tend to place themselves in a more tutorial, authoritarian role, whereas the nondirective therapists tend toward the opposite extreme.

So far as the results of these studies can be generalized, they seem to lend support to the contention that the therapeutic relationship is a common factor used in an astonishingly similar way in diverse therapeutic approaches. Nevertheless, there would appear to be at least one difference in the way the therapeutic relationship is handled which is best discussed in terms of the question of rapport as distinguished from transference.

The clinician may (and probably does if there has been adequate diagnostic study) recognize relatively early the conflicts giving rise to at least some of the patient's difficulties; nevertheless, he would be ill advised to rush into discussing them with the patient. Restraint is desirable, if not essential, because first there must be rapport with the clinician, and sometimes something more, commonly called transference. Although clinicians sometimes fail to distinguish between the two, it is considered essential to do so. Wyatt differentiates them as follows:

Individual psychotherapy is a peculiar relationship of two people. The specific quality of this relationship is referred to, often glibly, as a transference. I think it will be more helpful here to distinguish *rapport* from *transference proper*. The therapeutic situation is an unusual one in that the patient comes for help and talks about matters otherwise not disclosed. He is met by an attitude of unconditional acceptance, a point common to all systems of psychotherapy. The feeling of confidence fostered under these circumstances, a composite of trust, respect and liking of the therapist, is *rapport*. It makes it possible for the patient to communicate his problem and to accept the initial guidance of the therapist. Under certain conditions, as a rule those of intensive psychotherapy (psychoanalysis), when specific technical means are applied, this attitude may develop into one in which the therapist becomes the object of intense emotions on the part of the patient, who inevitably commits himself to an attitude of dependence upon the former. In his feelings the patient will regularly repeat patterns of early attachment to parental figures. This, then, is *transference*. (23, p. 83.)

Rapport is essentially a reality relationship in which the patient is consciously aware of the clinician as he really is. Transference, on the other hand, is an unconscious projection of the patient's attitudes toward figures from his past onto the clinician. Although rapport and transference have much in common, since both are ways in which the patient-therapist relationship is structured and are matters of degree and not dichotomies, they should for the sake of clarity be distinguished. The patient-clinician relationship is one of mutual trust and confidence (rapport) or the patient comes to identify the clinician with those persons in his environment of emotional significance and thus to relive past experiences (transference). Both exist in the therapeutic relationship; either one or the other may be in the ascendancy at a given moment.

In transference there is said to be a projection of unconscious contents upon the therapist. The person of the clinician may serve as a figure upon which emotion may be released directly. The clinician at one time or another may be the stern father, the despised and rejected, the loved, the source of security, the hunter, and the hunted—all these and myriads more of the figures from the past of the patient. There may be a fear of the clinician as a potentially destructive or malevolent being who threatens to annihilate the patient which arises from a hostile image of the parent and has been displaced to other authoritative figures. This may appear in a form in which the fear is evident, or it may be disguised by defiance, criticism, skepticism, or even aloofness and indifference. Preservation of one's integrity and intactness as a person is fundamental to everyone whether neurotic or normal, and this may be threatened in the therapeutic situation. Instead of a menacing figure the clinician may be seen as the very fountainhead of security, as a benevolent father or as a lover. Positive and negative feelings intermingle, as they do toward anyone for whom there is depth of feeling, with now one and now the other pole of feeling uppermost.

Transference phenomena are by no means confined to later stages of the therapeutic relationship. Indeed, the patient comes to the therapist and from the beginning demonstrates spontaneously what Bartemeier (4) and others aptly call the "preformed" transference. This is shaped by experiences with other authoritarian figures, physicians and so on, and by earlier life experiences. Thus, transference need not be shaped by therapeutic stratagems, psychoanalytic or otherwise, since its roots are already present.

The emphasis in the psychoanalytic approach upon transference implies not that transference does not exist in patients with whom other methods are used—or, for that matter, in other human relationships—but that it is viewed differently. Psychoanalysis deliberately arranges conditions so that the transference relationship is strengthened and, at the same time, not distorted by the patient's knowing too much about the therapist as he is in objective reality. Most important of all psychoanalysts use it more consciously and adroitly for therapeutic ends than do practitioners of other approaches. In fact, with some non-psychoanalytic practitioners transference is treated as an obstacle to therapeutic progress to be circumvented if at all possible, or at least rendered sterile in the event it appears. This is not the place to argue the relative merits of these opposed procedures, but it is worth while to realize that transference exists in other than psychoanalytic settings. For this reason it is discussed as a common factor rather than as an aspect of psychoanalysis.

The presence of transference demands of the therapist a heavy responsibility. He must be able to handle these emotional assaults upon him—for that is what they are—without losing objectivity or becoming involved, and yet without becoming wooden in his approach or impervious to the feelings expressed. This leads directly to, or rather is, the question of the personality of the therapist. He must be responsible and, in the fullest sense of the word, mature. In other words, he must be able to understand himself to the degree that he can accept and understand the projections of the patient without becoming that which is projected. He must have the kind of personality that shows the patient he is neither approved nor disapproved, but understood, that demonstrates he accepts the patient for what he is, and that implies respect for the dignity of the patient.

This is by no means an easy task in view of the fact that the therapist's own insecurities and countertransferences may be aroused. As a consequence, a psychological analysis of the would-be therapist is frequently insisted upon by psychotherapeutic training centers, whether this be a didactic psychoanalysis, so called, or some other form of personal experience with a psychotherapist. In his desire to understand the motivations of the patient, the inexperienced therapist sometimes feels he is outside the situation looking in on, but not influenced by, what is going on. Nothing could be further from the truth. His own anxieties, frustrations, and aggressions are a part of the therapeutic reality. The therapist and *his* problems are as much a part of therapy as the patient. He is, to use Harry Stack Sullivan's term, a "participant-observer." As in any social situation there is emotional interaction, and the personalities of both patient and therapist are involved in the process.

Korner (11) has recently discussed what he has called the process of "disengagement." After recognition of involvement the therapist "must attempt to draw back from the interactive process and determine the nature of his own functioning." (11, p. 207.) He then gives instances of undue involvement including such matters (paradoxically) as thoughts wandering, inability to grasp the material contrary to previous experience with the patient, a lack of sensitivity, boredom, and a feeling of not being up to par. These Korner believes are more often indications of resistance on the part of the therapist than instances of actual confusion on the part of the patient. He cites the curious phenomenon of having several patients on the same day exhibit similar patterns of adjustment difficulties and suggests that this is brought about by a special sensitivity on the part of the therapist, at the moment, for this sort of problem rather than a coincidental similarity on the part of the patients. He suggests that disengagement may take place during the actual therapeutic sessions without damaging the relationship to the patient at times when materials seem at low ebb, in terms of both the quality and the quantity of material. Although he does not speak of it directly, it would also appear that the therapist should be able to consider this matter retrospectively after the session, although with loss as to what may be done about it in that now past session. What the therapist might do in his period of "disengagement" he states as follows:

At such times the counselor can take stock of himself and his feelings. He can review the material and determine the adequacy of the reflections and interpretations given to the client. It is possible for him to examine his own conduct and watch for signs of involvement. The counselor removes himself from the place of an active participant, but he must remain alert to the client's reactions and sensitive to any sudden change in the situation.

If the results of the self-inventory are negative, it may be possible for the counselor to resume his activities with more awareness of the dynamics of the interview and with increased confidence.

In cases where the counselor discovers signs of involvement, he may not be able to discover the deeper lying sources of his disturbance. Without special and prolonged training, this is frequently extremely difficult. He can, however, take adequate precautions which will prevent damaging projections of these disturbances into the counseling process. The counselor, for example, may decide immediately to take a more reserved and cautious attitude toward the client. He may limit the quality and quantity of interpretations to an absolute and well-controlled minimum. He may desist from any step which would increase the speed and intensity of the interview. Last, but not least, the counselor may be alerted to the necessity to consult with associates in order to determine more clearly the nature, significance and the gravity of the disturbances. (11, pp. 208–209.)

Whether these specific suggestions are commonly followed or not is, for the moment, not the question. They do serve to bring out the nature of the therapist's involvement in the therapeutic process.

RELEASE OF EMOTIONAL TENSION

Release of emotional tension, although an objective of most therapeutic endeavors, can never be more than a limited or partial goal. In itself emotional tension represents the inroads made on the personality of the patient by one or more traumatic episodes. In the security of the therapeutic environment the patient reëxperiences the conflict situation and releases the tension created by the anxiety attendant upon this experience. Prior to this point he has been reluctant or unable to express some strong emotion—hate, fear, or sexual craving—but now it is either released gradually or expelled with considerable force. This release may take many forms, such as weeping, outbursts of temper, relating embittering experiences, or admission of previously denied impulses.

There appear to be certain prerequisites for therapeutically successful emotional release. Foremost is the fact that the setting in which the release is expressed must be a secure one where the patient can, without fear of condemnation or reproach, discharge any forbidden impulse. He must find it possible in the therapeutic setting to refer to or to experience emotionally practically any facet of human nature, providing it remains within certain limits set by ethical and professional standards. The patient is permitted to say anything he chooses, no matter how it might be judged in another social context, but he is not permitted to follow through these impulses in other forms of behavior. Realization of this freedom demands a non-judging therapist who accepts without either condemning or condoning (cf. Chapter 5). If release and release alone occurs there is apt to be an accentuation of guilt feelings, in which case it is necessary that the therapist be alert to support the patient. Therapists differ in the way they handle this problem. Some offer interpretations, whereas others merely clarify the emotional pattern being expressed. However, detailed discussion will be foregone for the present to be reopened when considering differences in therapeutic approaches.

The importance of emotional release in therapy with children has frequently been emphasized. Starting from the premise that therapy with children should use the method already adopted by the child for dealing with his emotional difficulties—that of imaginative play —Levy (12) developed a systematic approach to play therapy which he called "release therapy." In a sense the cases he treated through this technique exemplify the closest approximation to pure emotional release used in acceptable therapeutic practice. Naturally the cases for which it was considered appropriate are severely limited. The criteria he applied for selection were that the presenting symptom picture be one precipitated by some traumatic event, that the family and other interpersonal relationships of the child not be seriously disturbed, that the problem be of relatively short duration, that the patient be about ten years old or younger, and that the problem stem from incidents in the past and not be one existing at the time of treatment. An illustrative case follows:

An only child, a girl, aged 2 years, 5 months, was referred because of night terrors, onset 2 days before referral. She awoke frightened and screamed that there was a fish in her bed and refused to go back. The next night she started shrieking and screaming when put back to bed, shouting, "There's a fish in my bed." By advice of the pediatrist this was ignored. She continued screaming off and on for 2½ hours. The night terror was related to a visit to a fish market on that very day. The fish merchant, who was fond of the child, lifted her up to see the fish.

A second complaint was stammering, which had its onset 5 months before referral, although speech had developed normally up to that time. The stammering consisted of a repetition chiefly of consonants, e.g., to quote the mother: "It was almost like agony in getting the letter out in 'hello.' " This would occur probably once every minute of conversation.

There were 10 play sessions in all. A fish made of clay was introduced in the second session. To the question, why was the doll afraid of the fish, the answer was that the fish would bite, and the fish would go "in here," pointing to her eye, her ears and, finally, to her vagina. A few days before the night terror the patient had inquired about sex differences after seeing the father naked. Other than the introduction of the fish in various parts of the play sessions, the method was chiefly to facilitate her own type of play, whenever a difficulty in the play occurred. For example, she saw finger paint and wanted to play with it. I showed her how, but she wouldn't touch it with her finger, nor let me put a dot of paint on her hand. She said, "No, no, I don't like that—dirty, dirty." By playing with it myself and getting her to handle it gradually, she got to prefer it, and started each session with "I want to do paint." She played with it very freely, messed it on the floor, and on her legs. Similarly with water play, she got to drag a chair to the sink, playing with balloons, squirting water, breaking a baby doll, the latter becoming a frequent activity in the last two sessions.

Following her first appointment there was no change in behavior that could be related to it. Fear of the fish left after the third or fourth session and the stammering showed improvement after the sixth, disappearing two weeks before the last session. A follow-up was made 7 months later. Improvement was maintained; patient was developing normally and making good contacts with other children. She remained an orderly child, though no longer so fussy. (*12*, pp. 720–721.)

In instances exemplified by this case, release of emotional tension as such appears to be therapeutically efficacious. Even here, however, it is not pure release. The release of these forbidden impulses has taken place in an accepting environment, so that the impulses no longer seem so reprehensible to the child and may be acknowledged with less guilt, and hence brought more under conscious control. It is therefore seen to be merely an extreme of the more usual role of emotional discharge which relieves the accumulated tension and prepares the way for insightful assimilation of the interpretation either arrived at by the patient nondirectively or offered by the therapist. The patient after such discharge is generally less tense and more capable of viewing his problems objectively.

INSIGHT

No matter what school of psychotherapy one may favor and what the type of presenting symptoms the patient may demonstrate, no factor of psychotherapy is more fundamental than that of aiding the patient to gain insight. In psychotherapy there should be an enlargement of the patient's understanding of himself, of the relation of his symptoms to his personality pattern, and of his relation to other persons. This understanding is by no means intellectual; in fact, if intellectual understanding alone is achieved results will be limited and sterile. For insight in the fullest sense the patient must experience, not merely understand, what has been taking place. In other words, there is a large but inseparable component of feeling intertwined with the intellectual process. Man lives not by cortical processes alone; affect is a part of the functioning, ongoing organism. As a goal of therapy he must not only see interrelationships but also experience the appropriate affect—relief, guilt, anxiety, hatred—or, in short, there must be what Rogers called in the earlier quotation "assimilated interpretation." Fundamentally insight is self-acceptance and self-understanding. As a result of the therapeutic process, newly experienced factors or attitudes are assimilated, and a changed attitude toward life predicated upon the changed concept of the self emerges. This permits more satisfactory means of obtaining gratification of needs.

Insight may result in a changed attitude toward life, a realization that the world and the people in it are not menacing or hostile. As Wolberg states:

> The attainment of insight reflects itself in a changed attitude toward people wherein the patient feels neither threatened nor challenged to excel, wherein his expectations are neither so high that he is inevitably frustrated nor so low that he fails to permit himself to express his needs and strivings, wherein he is not excessively dependent on others nor compulsively determined to play the lone wolf, wherein his self-esteem is not forever in jeopardy, swelling and ebbing with the opinion of others, wherein he can express his instinctive longings without fear of condemnation and feel justifiably hostile without fear of injury. (21, p. 1222.)

The insight achieved is directly relevant to the treatment goals. It may be an essentially modest one—the realization of one's limitations and abilities in relation to some particular problem—or it may be wider in scope, such as a veritable reconstruction of the personality of the patient.[6] This will be discussed further in the next chapter.

In the various systematic approaches to psychotherapy the definition of insight is likely to vary. Insight in the sense of the recovery of infantile memories and the relation of these to existing systems as predicated by classic psychoanalysis is by no means certain to occur even when beneficial therapeutic changes have occurred (Wolberg, *21*). Minimal insight consists first in sensing to some extent the inadequacy of the present form and level of adjustment. Psychotics frequently do not have even this modicum of insight; it is a sign of improvement when they acknowledge that they "have been ill." In this sense, however, the great majority of patients seen in therapy have retained this level of awareness. They are cognizant that there have been symptomatic changes and that they are different from other people. They may or may not want to change these differences, since they gain something from the maladjustive processes at work, and do not entirely and whole-heartedly work toward a change. They recognize the symptoms, perhaps, but consider them alien to themselves and prefer not to hazard any modification. In such instances where insight remains minimal it is unlikely that any type of psychotherapy can have achieved more than the most modest goal.

Resistance and Working Through[7]

Both the insights capable of achievement and the emotional tension released pertain to experiences which the patient by himself is either reluctant or incapable of facing in a therapeutically beneficial fashion. It is not surprising that insightful emotionally tinged dis-

---

[6] This alone is sufficient answer to the various adherents of therapeutic schools who harbor the comforting delusion that theirs is the *best* therapeutic approach. "Best" depends on many things including the goal set. It was a realization of this that set many of the less doctrinaire psychoanalysts upon the long and fascinating journey into the broader area of therapeutic application. Cf., for example, Alexander and French (*2*).

[7] For the first time a new factor is introduced, not mentioned as a common factor in the preceding discussion. It is pertinent to offer a justification. To the writer the phenomenon of resistance and the concomitant procedure of working through are so self-evident in actual therapy, whatever the approach, that they cannot be neglected. In descriptive terms, something seems to happen to patients when asked to face their new insights. They parry the alien ideas and thrust forward extenuating material. They refuse to face them, and then they do, only to flee again. As the sessions continue they mull over the matters with the help

closures meet with resistance on the part of the patient. One "interpretation" does not remove the ego defenses of a lifetime.

Common sense suggests that the solution for people in the throes of emotional difficulties would be to tell them what should be done to correct the condition. A trained clinician often discovers the sources (or at least some of the sources) of the patient's difficulties rather quickly so why should he not impart this information? Such didactic instruction does not clear up the situation. Indeed, it may have the paradoxical result of producing what appears to be mild or even vehement opposition or resistance, which may assume protean forms. For example, resistance may express itself as follows: (1) exacerbation of symptoms; (2) diminution of symptoms so that the patient tries to convince himself and the therapist that he is well and in no further need of assistance; (3) withdrawal into uncommunicativeness or inconsequential talk; (4) evasiveness; (5) hollow verbalizations deceptively claiming understanding of his difficulties.

In every patient, this resistance which blocks therapeutic progress is just as much an aspect of the ongoing functioning personality as are his symptoms. In an effort to maintain psychic equilibrium the symptoms are an effort to solve the problems plaguing the patient; likewise as the sanctity of the symptom complexes is threatened the resistances are organized lest the organism be stripped of its last vestige of defense.

Wolberg states the matter in terms of opposing dynamic forces. He writes:

There are two opposing dynamic forces at work in the psyche of the neurotic person. One group constitutes basic biologic and social strivings, such as those for security, companionship, love, assertiveness, and creative self-fulfillment. There are more subversive strivings, too, in the form of irrational wishes, fears, and resentments. These strivings because of unfortunate conditions are so terror-inspiring and so repulsive that they can scarcely be acknowledged, let alone expressed, and it is the function of the second group of forces to oppose and to prevent their fulfillment. In most neurotic conditions an equilibrium is maintained between the

of the therapist, permitting partial assimilation to take place, and then the procedure repeats itself. Negative or hostile attitudes, as Rogers would probably prefer to call them, do occur and would seem to be just as much a factor in therapy as the more positive ones. In this we have a clue to the neglect of this factor in the short accounts of Ackerman, Rogers, and Thorne presented earlier. They were concerned primarily with the positive aspects. To the writer this negative aspect is just as important and irrefutable.

repressed and the repressing forces. The equilibrium is a shaky one, shifting constantly between the two opposing camps. When the integrity of the individual is threatened by forbidden impulses and demands, the defensive forces of the ego organize measures of counterattack in the form of drives and symptoms that constitute the various neurotic syndromes. As a result, the neurotic machine, complicated as it is with balances and counterbalances, never functions efficiently, and the slightest deviation may serve to throw it out of gear.

Psychotherapy, by providing insight into one's motives and behavior, constantly jeopardizes the delicate balance between the defenses and the repressed strivings and is unconsciously interpreted by the patient as a threat to his security. Destructive as they are, neurotic symptoms protect the individual from catastrophic helplessness and anxiety. To yield to them promises exposure to dangers far greater than the inconveniences that the patient already suffers. Furthermore, the ego gains through neurotic illness certain advantages of a positive nature, and resistance to cure is often based upon the fear of abandoning these secondary gains. A neurosis forces on the individual a distortion in his sense of values, and his neurotic drives become invested with subjective pleasures that make the ordinary pursuits of life mediocre and meaningless. Instead of seeking those goals accepted as normal by average people, the neurotic will engage himself in a frenzied search for vicarious satisfactions, such as for power, compulsive dependency, perfectionism, and detachment. These inevitably involve him in difficulties with people, for they make exorbitant demands on himself and others. The penalties he pays in the form of suffering are usually dissociated from his neurosis, and rarely does he consider his anxiety, tension, and hostility in any way related to his attitudes and objectives. Indeed, what he seems to seek in treatment is a formula whereby he can retain his neurotic trends without paying the price of suffering. During treatment, consequently, the patient will feel that his secret hopes and expectations are under attack. He will sense danger and almost intuitively he will retreat or rebel. In spite of his better judgment he will throw up smoke screens and camouflages to confuse the physician and to block his own progress. These reactions constitute resistances to change, and their exact form will depend to a large degree on the kind of defenses he customarily uses to avert danger. (22, pp. 1751–1752.)[8]

Resistance may be conceived as exhibiting two temporal phases— the first superficial and conscious, the second fundamental and primarily unconscious. The patient may come to the treatment situation with considerable resistance owing to the fact that the matters to be worked through are so personal and intimate. Frequently he

[8] Reprinted from "Resistance to Cure in Psychotherapy" by L. R. Wolberg, by permission of the *New York State Journal of Medicine.* Copyright 1943 by the Medical Society of the State of New York.

will mark off one or another area of life experience as sacrosanct, saying in effect, "This I will talk about, but not that, not even to let it be known that it exists."

The dissipation of this or other forms of initial resistance, superficial as it often is, probably comes about through the establishment of the patient-clinician relationship. If rapport is established reluctances are overcome and a certain amount of therapeutic progress may then be made. Initial resistance is sometimes dissipated by expressing appreciation of how difficult it is to accept help from another and by a frank searching discussion of this problem.

The second type of resistance encountered during the course of intensive psychotherapy is probably deeper, with roots of which the patient is unaware. It arises, in large measure, from the frequently observed clinical fact that the patient in the course of this resistance does not seem to be aware of the reasons he rejects or struggles against the course that psychotherapy appears to be taking. He does not understand, or he does not want to understand and tries to prove that the therapist is wrong.

In the course of therapy insight at first is but tentative and partial and grudging. The patient is not entirely convinced and if left at this stage would soon find reasons for losing any gain that had been made. There is, no matter what the form in which it is put, a period of "working through," as it has been aptly expressed in psychoanalytic literature, during which resistance is dissipated and insight assimilated. Bellak has given a statement of its nature in general dynamic terms. He writes:

Working Through.—The next step in therapy consists of the working through of the new insight:

(a) Intellectually: The patient now applies what he has learned to pertain to a few situations, as pointed out by the therapist, to a number of other situations to which the same general denominator applies. If a pattern was pointed out to exist for his present employer, his teacher, his analyst and his father, he may now remember situations involving an uncle, a superior officer in the Army, an elder brother, etc., as having been reacted to similarly.

(b) Therapeutically (Emotionally): In the therapeutic situation, psychoanalytically known as the transference situation, the patient originally "transfers" the emotional patterns of behavior which he has learned previously to the therapist as much as he had reacted with them to anyone else. Indeed, owing to the fact that earlier layers of behavior are discussed and the therapist becomes a much more important person than most other people and plays a parental role, these earlier learned behavior patterns are particularly brought out. As these patterns come up they are interpreted and then the patient works his problems through by relearning—by conditioning—his reaction pattern to the therapist first, and later by transference of training also changes his behavior in the real life situation. This is not the only way—other forms of relearning in the reality situation are discussed below. The transference situation and its therapeutic role, however, might be restated as follows: by transfer of training, the patient reacts to the therapist the way he reacted to the parents. Relearning takes place in the therapeutic situation by insight and reconditioning, and there is then a transfer of training from the therapeutic situation to the real life situation.

(c) Behaviorally: Outside the therapeutic session, the patient goes on meeting situations discussed and new ones similar to the ones scrutinized. While in the actual situations, he is aware of the insight he recently gained. Under the influence of that new "mental set" he reacts differently, in a progressive extent, to these situations in the corrective direction suggested by the analysis of the situation. New problems arising are re-analyzed, and the problem is worked out by persistent adjustment and readjustment between mental set and reality. (5, pp. 139–140.)

The phenomena of resistance and working through have been stated in psychodynamic terms, but an attempt has been made to remove them from the narrow interstices of the psychoanalytic path. Resistance, it would appear, is a fundamental factor (although exhibited in varying degrees), and a period of working through is essential to the conversion of the patient's insight from a grudging, partial, and intellectual awareness into emotional acceptance and understanding.

INTERPRETATION

Throughtout the previous discussion one significant aspect has been minimized—that of the interpretation made by or to the patient. It is sometimes implied or openly stated that in a therapeutic situation interpretation is minimal or even nonexistent. This occasionally is misunderstood, for what generally is meant is that no verbal interpretation is offered *by* the therapist *to* the patient. *There is always interpretation by the patient.* It does not matter whether it is on the basis of verbal explanations given by the therapist or of one or another of the less directive methods of communication with the patient. The patient perceives, i.e., interprets, the therapist's behavior—not so much what he says as his smile, tone of voice, or some indication of alertness or approval. The play therapist may say he offered no interpretation of the child's dismembering the dolls, but by his very permission to do so he has given the child a basis for interpretation in some fashion or another. Interpretation of a sort is implicit in the fact that, for example, an interviewer may guide the conversation from the patient's symptoms to the particular situations in which they arise. This implies an endeavor to find a connection between events and symptoms based on a point of view concerning the nature of that relation.

The position that Rogers takes is not incompatible with interpretation as such. (Indeed, if there were no interpretation there could be no therapy.) Estes writes cogently on this issue:

> Rogers advocates the avoidance in treatment of one clearly defined type of interpretation, namely, statements by the therapist in the form, "You do this or feel this because . . ." These avoided interpretations are mostly of the genetic variety, now much less stressed by the more liberal analysts. Interpretations of certain other sorts are not and cannot be avoided. The meaning of any act or statement by the client inevitably is determined in part by the response of the therapist to it. If no response or an ambiguous response is made, then the field is open for the client to supply meaning in accordance with his wishes or fears derived from his experience with significant others (sic). Here we face again the fact that ambiguity in the social stimulus situation is a critical determinant of invalid transferences or parataxic distortions. Another type of interpretation, common to Sullivan and Rogers, consists in a redirection of attention which raises that which is in the background of the momentary organization to explicit awareness. When this is done, whether by naming or otherwise, not merely is the nonconscious made conscious, but the existing phenomenal organization is often radically changed by the introduction of the new item, just as the introduction of an additional letter into a word can change the meaning of the word. Summary statements, bringing together items separated too widely in time in the report of the client for him to relate them, is another mode of interpretation used by Rogers and others. Closely related to summary statements are reformulative interpretations based simultaneously upon data given by the client and upon general social-psychological theory. (6, p. 80.)

Bellak presents a very able summary of the interpretation offered verbally by the therapist. He writes:

> *Interpretation.*—When the psychotherapist has become acquainted with a number of life situations of the patient, he may perceive a certain *common denominator* in the behavioral patterns and point them out to the patient in such doses as seem to him to be suitable at any time.
>
> (a) Horizontal Study: Principally, the therapist may find a common denominator of behavior patterns and of interpersonal relations of the

contemporary life situation, and we might speak of this endeavor as a horizontal study of patterns.

(b) Vertical Study: Sooner or later, it will be possible to trace by free association or otherwise the historical development of these patterns in the life history of the patient, leading to a more or less definite early set. We may speak of this part of the therapeutic investigation as the vertical study of relations of life patterns. Frequently, it will be necessary to point out both the vertical and the horizontal common denominator of the patient's current behavior to lead to a solution of his problems.

(c) Relationship to the Therapist: As a special case of current life situations of the horizontal pattern in its relation to the earlier historical ones, the relationship to the therapist may be discussed specifically, as what is known in psychoanalysis as *analysis of the transference situation*.

Interpretation, then, means the pointing out by the therapist to the patient of common denominators in his behavioral patterns—horizontally, vertically and in the special relation to the therapist.

A brief example might be of help here: the patient may have appeared with the presenting problem of vague anxiety attacks. It may appear sooner or later that these apparently puzzling attacks occur typically when the patient is in contact with a strict authority who produces hostility in him. After this horizontal pattern has appeared, at one time or another a vertical one may be found—the patient had a more or less specific relationship to his father who originally produced these feelings of hostility in him and the resulting anxiety. Further study will reveal a whole history of relationships to similar authorities prior to the current situation, and a similar attitude to the therapist. (5, pp. 137–138.)

A theory of psychotherapy, upon which interpretations are anchored, is essentially a theory of personality which focuses attention on the dynamic factors responsible for the present difficulties of the patient.

Implicit in Bellak's account just quoted is a psychoanalytic-genetic emphasis. The sources of the patient's difficulty are considered to have roots in the past and to bear upon the present therapeutic relationship. This is, to be sure, good psychodynamic doctrine and may be utilized quite apart from the narrowly psychoanalytic therapeutic procedures. But it is only one among other possible points of view. For example, in the next chapter a point of view will be advanced that activities, feelings, and experiences of the therapeutic session itself are the proper interpretative concern, with little or no attention given to genetic antecedents. Both this point of view and the historic-genetic are entirely tenable concerning the function of interpretation, and either one could have been selected for illustrative purposes.

Interpretation, whatever the theoretical framework in which it is set, has the function of uncovering and releasing feelings and securing acceptance of them by the patient. It also provides the basis whereby insight is achieved. For example, in discussing insight it was stated that it involved understanding on the part of the patient —understanding of himself. Interpretation, whether originating first with the patient or with the therapist, is essentially an explanation of the basis for past or present behavior. Such an explanation is often the immediate precursor of understanding.

The timing of interpretations is one of the most important problems to be considered in psychotherapy. In fact, one of the temptations to which a novice all too frequently succumbs is to disclose to the patient interpretations when he arrives at them, forgetting it is not his pace but that of his patient which is important. Or in his enthusiasm for his discovery he may insist upon the validity of his "offering" to the patient. The astuteness and truth of the interpretation are naught if the patient is not ready to consider acceptance of it. Too early or too pressing an interpretation means increased resistance—perhaps having the patient drop out of therapy or at least lengthening the treatment period. Sometimes an attempt to give the patient insight before he can tolerate it destroys his neurotic defenses without providing adequate substitutes for him. Appropriately timed interpretations result in increased movement, intellectual expression, and output of feeling and may prove to be a means of moving on to further insights.

It may be that one interpretative approach to therapy is destined to have a greater degree of validity than another. But it would be rash, short-sighted, and doctrinaire to prophesy the ultimate victor. Just as "schools of psychology" are disappearing, so warring points of view concerning psychotherapy may disappear in some sort of synthesis. No doubt there will be differences, even if the millennium does arrive—differences in patients created by differences in their problems, differences in therapists created by their personalities. Yet the therapist of today must "interpret" (if only to himself). In so doing he seems to help his patient in spite of his disagreements with his fellow practitioners, who may be equally successful with their patients despite different interpretations arising from different theories of personality.

A resolution of at least a part of this dilemma has been offered by

Rosenzweig (15) (16). He was concerned with what he called "implicit common factors in psychotherapy." Although he referred to such factors as catharsis and the personality of the therapist, his most distinctive contribution was a discussion of the present topic—the function of interpretation. In summary he writes:

5. Another common factor, which is somewhat more complex, may be summarized under the heading of the *function of interpretations*. If it is true that mental disorder represents a conflict of disintegrated personality constituents, then the unification of these constituents by any systematic ideology, regardless of its specific nature, would seem to be a prerequisite for successful treatment. Whether the therapist talks in terms of psychoanalysis or of Christian Science is, from this standpoint, relatively unimportant so long as what he says has a certain *inherent formal consistency* which gives the patient a schema for achieving that personality organization which he lacks. Since most forms of psychotherapy are based upon a systematic set of beliefs or theories about human personality, they all have this common possibility of providing a basis for reintegration.

6. There is a further aspect to the function of interpretations. Psychological events are so complex and many-sided in nature that they may well be *alternatively formulated* with considerable justification for each alternative. Thus any interpretation is apt to have a certain amount of truth in it, applying at least from one standpoint or to one aspect of the complex phenomenon being described. Moreover, it is generally recognized that personality represents an *interdependent organization* of dynamically related constituents. With this kind of organization it is impossible to change any constituent without affecting the whole, for the modification of any part entails reverberations throughout the rest. The conclusion would then be warranted that in attempting to modify the structure of a personality it would matter relatively little if the approach were to be made from the right or the left, the top or the bottom, so to speak, as long as some significant point were attacked; in the end the initial effect would alter the total organization anyway. Thus is added another implicit common factor overlooked when diversity of interpretations is stressed. (16, p. 522.)

These functions of interpretation, it would appear, do much to reconcile the discrepancies between apparently diametrically opposed systems of interpretation offered as theoretical structures of therapeutic efforts. This does not mean that we should not strive to enlarge and validate our understanding of human nature (indeed, Rosenzweig in writing the paper just quoted was doing so as a basis for future research with just this aim in view); it means rather that we should realize it is possible to proceed therapeutically without either a sense of insecurity about what is being done or a cynical despair that verbal magic alone is operating.

EMANCIPATION OR MATURATION

Just as injured tissues possess within their structure something which makes for a spontaneous search for restitution, so too in emotional illness the patient seems to possess a capacity for growth once the obstructions to this growth are weakened. The inherent impetus or drive to growth is obviously not enough for cure, for although there may be a desire, conscious or not, on the part of the patient to change, there is also anxiety about change. Each person wants to maintain his identity and fears the unknown. "I know what I am like now—I don't know what I would be like if I changed" is a recurrent theme appearing in basically insecure patients who are threatened by the therapeutic situation itself. Nevertheless, this capacity for growth is developed in the therapeutic situation by arranging conditions so that it may appear in spite of opposing trends such as fear of losing the crutch afforded by the symptoms.

As a consequence of the relationship with the clinician, whatever its nature and intensity, there comes a time when this relationship must be severed. There is an emphasis, although in varying degrees, in all psychotherapeutic systems upon giving responsibility for decisions as much as possible to the patient. He steadily learns to appreciate more and more that he is not "cured" by the clinician but that progress depends upon his own efforts. His gains through operation of the factors previously described make him better able to deal with the therapeutic hour and presumably with the problems outside that situation. Sometimes, although not always, he knows "when it is time to go." At first, he perhaps is not clearly conscious of this, but by various acts he demonstrates it—breaking appointments, wondering how many more sessions there are to be, and so on.[9] He has grown in confidence, in ability to take the initiative, to see and understand his behavior in a new light. Strivings for independence of the situation now begin to appear.

---

[9] It may be noted that these illustrations of behavior indicative of growth are the same as those given as examples of expression of resistance. However, in actual clinical situations little trouble is found in differentiating them, for by the time they are expressions of growth the entire climate of the therapeutic sessions has changed. Likewise the content of the material will differ, enabling the therapist to make a judgment about the amount of progress.

Sound psychotherapeutic procedure takes all this into account and strives to foster it. And yet, parting is sometimes a rude shock. It is not unusual for a patient to exhibit a resurgence of difficulties after a decision to close therapy has been reached. This increase in dependence or attachment in itself can be and is used therapeutically. It is another reality situation which by interpretation to the patient or by more nondirective methods such as reflection of feelings may be used to make the parting itself a growth experience.

SUMMARY

A summary may now be offered of some of the common factors, implicit and explicit, which appear in many psychotherapeutic approaches. A relationship is established between therapist and patient either at the level of rapport or at the level of transference which, while in itself therapeutic, permits other factors to operate. Interpretation of the personality of the patient takes place either as offered by the therapist, as self-interpretation on the part of the patient, or both. Many factors may impede the process of therapy, no matter what its theoretical orientation or the skill of the therapist. Common factors such as insight and release of emotional tension appear to be operative as therapeutic agents. Eventually maturation to a degree permitting separation of patient and therapist leads to the emancipation of the former. Although adherents of various therapeutic approaches may stress one or more and minimize or even deny therapeutic importance to some, it would appear that all of these factors are operative in varying degrees. With a specific patient a therapist may stress one and not even attempt to achieve others. In a sense, then, there may be an incomplete approach, but all seem to operate in any attempt at dynamic psychotherapy. So far as the dynamic point of view just sketched is concerned, it is eclectic in that it allows selection according to the needs of the patient and the proficiency and bias of the therapist. One may use, for example, a "nondirective" technique with one patient and a "directive" with another according to indications and contraindications in each specific case. It is necessary to emphasize, however, that many if not all of these factors are compatible with any system or school. In other words, they are conceived of as factors common to all psychotherapeutic systems. It is now appropriate not only to examine the nature of the different approaches but also to indicate the reasons for their presence. These issues the next chapters attempt to formulate.

BIBLIOGRAPHY

1. Ackerman, N. W., Group therapy from the viewpoint of a psychiatrist, *Amer. J. Orthopsychiat.*, 1943, 13:678–687.
2. Alexander, F., and French, T. M. (eds.), *Psychoanalytic therapy: principles and application*, The Ronald Press Company, 1946.
3. Allen, F. H., *Psychotherapy with children*, W. W. Norton & Company, 1942.
4. Bartemeier, L. H., Introduction to psychotherapy, *Psychoanal. Rev.*, 1943, 30:386–398.
5. Bellak, L., A note on some basic concepts of psychotherapy, *J. nerv. ment. Dis.*, 1948, 108:137–141.
6. Estes, S. G., Concerning the therapeutic relationship in the dynamics of cure, *J. consult. Psychol.*, 1948, 12:76–81.
7. Fiedler, F. E., "A comparative investigation of early therapeutic relationships created by experts and non-experts of the psychoanalytic, non-directive, and Adlerian schools," unpublished Ph.D. dissertation, University of Chicago, 1949.
8. Fiedler, F. E., The concept of an ideal therapeutic relationship, *J. consult. Psychol.*, 1950, 14:239–245.
9. Fiedler, F. E., The therapeutic relationship as a measure of therapeutic skill, *J. consult. Psychol.* (to appear).
10. Hamilton, G., Psychoanalytically oriented casework and its relation to psychotherapy, *Amer. J. Orthopsychiat.*, 1949, 19:209–223.
11. Korner, I. N., Ego involvement and the process of disengagement, *J. consult. Psychol.*, 1950, 14:206–209.
12. Levy, D. M., Trends in therapy: III. Release therapy, *Amer. J. Orthopsychiat.*, 1939, 9:713–736.
13. Rogers, C. R., The processes of therapy, *J. consult. Psychol.*, 1940, 4:161–164.
14. Rogers, C. R., Psychotherapy, in Dennis, W. (ed.), *Current trends in psychology*, University of Pittsburgh Press, 1948, pp. 109–137.
15. Rosenzweig, S., Some implicit common factors in diverse methods of psychotherapy, *Amer. J. Orthopsychiat.*, 1936, 6:412–415.
16. Rosenzweig, S., A dynamic interpretation of psychotherapy oriented towards research, *Psychiatry*, 1938, 1:521–526.
17. Thorne, F. C., Directive psychotherapy: IV. The therapeutic implications of the case history, *J. clin. Psychol.*, 1945, 1:318–330.
18. Thorne, F. C., Theoretical foundations of directive psychotherapy, *Ann. N.Y. Acad. Sci.*, 1948, 49:869–877.
19. Watson, G. (chm.), Areas of agreement in psychotherapy, *Amer. J. Orthopsychiat.*, 1940, 10:698–709.

20. Witmer, H. L., (ed.), *Psychiatric interviews with children*, Commonwealth Fund, 1946.
21. Wolberg, L. R., Recent trends in psychotherapy, *N.Y. St. J. Med.*, 1943, 43:1220–1223.
22. Wolberg, L. R., Resistance to cure in psychotherapy, *N.Y. St. J. Med.*, 1943, 43:1751–1754.
23. Wyatt, F., The self-experience of the psychotherapist, *J. consult. Psychol.*, 1948, 12:82–87.

Supplementary articles in Watson, R. I. (ed.), *Readings in the clinical method in psychology*, Harper & Brothers, 1949:

24. Rogers, C. R., Therapy in guidance clinics. Pp. 519–527. (Also in *J. abnorm. soc. Psychol.*, 1943, 38:284–289.)
25. Thorne, F. C., The clinical method in science. Pp. 49–63. (Also in *Amer. Psychologist*, 1947, 2:159–166.)

CHAPTER 19

Variations in Psychotherapy

In order to place with any degree of precision the current variations in psychotherapy it would be necessary to review in some detail the history of present-day psychiatry and psychology and related fields. However, all that can be done at this juncture is to present a short account of some of the more prominent variations. Accordingly, certain sources and consequences of variation will be presented, namely, psychotherapy as an artistic and as a scientific procedure, the personality of the therapist as a factor making for variation, variation created by differences in training and professional background, variation created by differences in the nature of the problem, variation created by external limitations, reconstructive psychotherapy as contrasted with supportive, curative psychotherapy as contrasted with symptomatic, and variation among schools of psychotherapy.

PSYCHOTHERAPY AS AN ARTISTIC AND SCIENTIFIC PROCEDURE

Psychotherapy as practiced today is a child of the times and bears their imprint. At present it is not entirely a scientific procedure; the variables are so complex and intertwined that it is an individualized experience essentially as much artistic in nature as it is scientific. This is not to deny that one of the goals of the psychologist is to assist in the scientific encroachment upon this artistic domain; rather it is merely a frank admission that psychotherapy is in a comparatively early stage of development as a scientific procedure.

Psychotherapy, then, is neither a well-integrated body of knowledge nor a single systematic point of view adapting itself within broad limits to varying kinds and conditions of patients. There is no standard concept of the nature of psychotherapy accepted by a majority of practicing psychotherapists. To be sure, there are common factors operative, as presented in the previous chapter, but in an all too human fashion psychotherapists are likely to stress the differences and find in the other man's approach not the beam of common agreement but the mote of disagreement. Considerable time in print and at professional meetings is spent in controversial debate. Though this may be interesting to all and professionally profitable to the more vocal of the representatives of the various schools, it is doubted that the returns in increased efficiency in the care of patients or in knowledge of the functioning of the human personality have been at all proportionate to the effort expended. Be that as it may, the large artistic element present today probably accounts for more of the variations to be found in psychotherapeutic practice and theory than any one other factor in spite of a gradually increasing core of scientifically verified material.

THE PERSONALITY OF THE THERAPIST AS A FACTOR MAKING FOR VARIATION IN PSYCHOTHERAPY

To the extent that artistic elements enter into any human endeavor the personality of the individual leaves its mark upon the product involved, whether it be a book, a painting, or the human experience that is psychotherapy. In an interesting study of the personalities of three early American psychotherapists—Austin Riggs, Thomas Salmon, and Weir Mitchell—Gildea and Gildea (6) point out certain resemblances in their personality backgrounds. The oldest was Weir Mitchell (1829–1914), whose professional career spanned the time from about 1850 to just before the First World War. Austin Riggs and Thomas Salmon became active in psychotherapy at about the turn of the century and were prominent in the history of psychiatry from that period on for the next twenty or twenty-five years. Relatively uninfluenced by Freud and his then small group of followers, all three lived and worked during the time psychotherapy was in its infancy. Nevertheless, so far as can be judged, they were about as successful psychotherapists as may be found in the present generation. In the account of the Gildeas are documented the many similarities in the development and personality of these men. In summarizing they write:

All were striking in appearance and unusually able through force and charm of personality to make immediate favorable contacts with people. All started life with roots in medical tradition, since all came from medical families. All were burdened by an extreme degree of responsibility beginning early and all through life. All were very sensitive and reactive. In fact the decision to work with medical, neurological and mental patients arose in part in each man as a reaction against blood and suffering, intense enough to cause each of them to veer away from the surgical approach. Each had a period of forced inactivity due to illness when he was in the very impressionable period between adolescence and young manhood. That this illness was in each case tuberculosis may have been accidental, but it is probably not accidental that this period of forced introversion brought with it the change in point of view that resulted in an intense interest in healing the mentally ill. This trend in their professional development probably sprung from a cognizance forced on them in their inactivity of mental problems in themselves.

They were vigorous men capable of very hard work. But they also suffered long spells of illness and fatigue or depletion. . . . All three were endowed with a high degree of controlled and directed extroversion. All had extraordinary vitality, intensity and conviction and all had great ability to focus their attention on the problem at hand, whether it was playing the traps, worrying over the problem of snake venom, struggling with a road in France or reconstructing a patient.

All were strongly emphatic, were particularly able to feel into and through the problems of their patients. This talent was made effective by the ability to verbalize and by an understanding of forceful emphatic communication which enable them to express their understanding in an arresting and dramatic manner. (6, p. 466.)

The work of these men bore the imprint of their personality characteristics. In view of their personalities it is not surprising to find that they had such success with their patients, living and working as they did in an era in which reassurance, suggestion, and supportive techniques in general were very important therapeutic tools. These very same tools of therapy in the hands of others often resulted in lamentable failure. They were the right men at the right time in the history of psychotherapy, and their personalities seemed to be the critical factor in their professional success.

The personality of the therapist is undoubtedly important in deciding the outcome of that uniquely interpersonal relationship which is psychotherapy. Whether favorable or unfavorable results are achieved rests in large measure with the personality of the therapist. It has even been said that the "right" psychotherapist will often achieve good results with the wrong method whereas the wrong person will fail despite using a more valid one. Undoubtedly this is a partial and even distorted view, but some modicum of truth is present in it.

Even variations within a systematic point of view, such as differences of opinion among psychoanalysts, may be due to personality differences. Oberndorf (10) indicates that variations in emphasis on certain aspects of psychoanalytic theory and practice are made by each psychoanalyst to meet his own clinical talents. Even the most cursory acquaintance with the history and vicissitudes of the psychoanalytic movement, including the defections of Adler, Jung, Rank, and so on, will bear this out. By a dynamic process, not unknown in their patients, certain therapists may ascribe to their own personal strengths a universality and primacy which other therapists would eschew.

Despite the permissiveness and self-determination accorded the patient, as described in the previous chapter, the personality of the therapist undoubtedly influences the goal he sets for the outcome of treatment. The desires of the therapist enter, in that he has to a greater or lesser degree a concept of what he feels the patient can become as a result of the therapeutic process. If he is temperamentally inclined to predict as an end result a completely changed personality, he will work toward that end. If his expectations are at a different and more modest level, he will set his sights accordingly. For example, one therapist would consider therapy highly successful if a homosexual was reconciled to his homosexuality; another might insist that anything short of a permanent transition to heterosexuality would be failure. Perhaps mere avoidance of hospitalization for certain patients would be and often is the realistic goal of many practicing therapists. Although such anticipations may violate the integrity of the patient and vitiate the therapeutic process in an academic sense, they can scarcely be eliminated and must continue to influence the course of therapy.

VARIATION CREATED BY DIFFERENCES IN TRAINING AND PROFESSIONAL BACKGROUND

Related to this source of variation are the differences in training with consequent deviations in both the practices and the settings in which therapy is conducted. A psychiatric practitioner of psychotherapy often, although not invariably, deals with relatively severely disturbed patients many of whom have been treated earlier by other medical specialists for the same symptomatology now presented. The psychiatrist is also a physician and carries out his practice accordingly. The psychologist as a consequence of his background, the nature of which is too familiar to need sketching here, is quite likely, although again this is not invariably so, to deal with less severely disturbed patients. These and similar differences in background on the part of other psychotherapeutic practitioners create variations in psychotherapy.

That one has had training as a clinical psychologist by no means sets the pattern of one's responsibility concerning psychotherapy. The degree of responsibility varies tremendously. In some clinical settings the only responsibility for therapeutic procedure the psychologist bears is related to his efforts as a diagnostician. At the other extreme are psychologists who, either as representatives of one or another of the systematic approaches or as eclectic practitioners, carry out intensive psychotherapy in a fashion which cannot be distinguished from the practice of their psychiatrically trained colleagues. There are also psychotherapists who practice within the framework of traditions more or less distinctively identified as psychological, e.g., the nondirective approach and school counseling. These last groups function more or less independently of psychiatric practitioners and other professional colleagues.

In settings in which the tripartite team of psychologist, psychiatrist, and social worker functions, the extent to which the psychologist participates in intensive and extensive psychotherapy is largely independent of the fact that he is a psychologist. His therapeutic duties depend on his personality and training, on his being the sort of person that others accept as a therapist, on the training and experience of the psychiatrist, or lack of it,[1] and the administrative

---

[1] Lack of training on the part of the psychiatrist may mean more psychotherapy being done by the psychologist, or his doing none at all.

policy of the clinic rather than the nature of the patients or their problems. Proper selection and adequate training will in increasing measure in the future make this less and less the case, but at the present time it seems a fair summary of the situation.

Of course, training as a psychologist does give him freer access to certain forms of treatment—for example, counseling as mentioned above. Remedial training in such cases as exhibit reading disabilities and speech correction is traditionally the concern of the psychologist. Nevertheless, the thesis may be defended that practice of therapy by a psychologist today is not so much decided by the fact that he is a psychologist but is more a matter of the setting in which it is done. In some clinics he will have little therapeutic responsibility despite training and interest in therapy; in another he may have more therapeutic responsibility thrust upon him than he cares to accept. Of course, in cases of inadequate training (and there are still a considerable number of psychologists who fall in this category), there is naturally every reason to deny therapeutic responsibility unless adequate supervision can be arranged and whole-heartedly accepted.

VARIATION CREATED BY DIFFERENCES IN THE NATURE OF THE PROBLEM

The procedures followed with a given patient, although partially the result of the personality of the therapist, are in large measure a reflection of the needs of the patient, and are also set by the conditions under which treatment is conducted, the severity of the difficulty, and many other similar factors. Psychotherapeutic efforts with a college student showing need of help in solving a specific problem which does not incapacitate him and in part is created by his ignorance of certain facts are quite different from those which would be used with an aged psychotic or a seriously disturbed neurotic. The student may be carried supportively for a few sessions through a relationship based upon rapport, and much of the help given may consist of supplying information. True, many of the elements present here—support, relatively few sessions, failure to investigate all facets of personality organization, and the supplying of information —may be such that some of the common factors described earlier either would appear not to be present at all or would operate only in a most emasculated form. Yet it is not a perversion of psychotherapeutic practice for such procedures to be conducted. It should be evident, without drawing upon the many illustrations available, that the nature of the problem of the patient is a fertile source for variations in psychotherapy.

VARIATION CREATED BY EXTERNAL LIMITATIONS

All psychotherapeutic systems, whatever the nature of their therapeutic goals, have in common certain limitations upon their efficacy. Incidental reference was made to this issue in discussing the nature of psychotherapy in the previous chapter, but the problem now deserves more detailed consideration. The more modest the goal, the less chance there is that these limitations will be operative. A summary of some of the limiting factors when the aim is reconstruction is offered by Knight. Although described in a setting specific to psychoanalysis, it is appropriate here.

Certain limitations, however, are imposed on the attainment of these aims in spite of the best application of the method of psychoanalytic therapy. (1) The intelligence level of the patient is a limiting factor. It may apparently be raised in some cases by lifting conflicts which interfere with intelligence functioning, but the native intelligence endowment cannot be increased. (2) Likewise there are definite limitations in respect to native ability. Talents cannot be instilled. Occasionally some new abilities may blossom forth in a patient when his instinctual energy is freed from the shackles of anxiety and inhibition, but it cannot be a regular expectation that psychoanalyzed patients will come to possess talents which they did not have before. (3) There are also limitations imposed by physical factors of size, muscular and skeletal development, personal attractiveness and specific handicaps of physical anomalies, sequelae of previous disease or injury, etc., which will affect in many ways the patient's full attainment of success in life. (4) Many emotional disorders are so deep-rooted, so early in their onset, that any improvement, even by the most thoroughgoing and successful psychoanalysis, can be only relative. The ego, or functioning, executive part of the psyche may be said to be crippled, just as the skeletal structure may be crippled by rickets or injury, the muscular structure by anterior poliomyelitis, or the organ integrity by rheumatic fever or malignant growth. (5) And finally, life and reality impose frustrations, stresses, privations and all sorts of difficulties against which the patient must do battle in spite of all he learns in psychoanalysis. The best analyzed patient might still relapse under a special stress, just as might any apparently quite normal person who had never had a neurosis nor been analyzed. (6) It probably goes without saying that the economic status of the patient imposes definite limitations on what he may accomplish—whether there be too little or too much money. (9, 436–437.)

With these limitations in mind it is desirable to illustrate the kinds of patients less amenable to psychotherapeutic efforts. Individuals with pronounced mental defect constitute one such group. With low average or even moron intellectual level the picture is likely to be somewhat brighter than is usually held to be the case, although controlled research evidence is sparse and confusing. Presumably lack of capacity to achieve more than very restricted insight is important when there are intellectual limitations. The inability to form a therapeutic relationship, although present in instances of severe mental limitations, is especially important in psychopaths and certain psychotics, primarily the schizophrenic. Although it is no longer considered impossible to form such a relationship (and it may well be more the problem of the therapist than of the patient), it is admittedly much more difficult to do so and often seems impossible.

RECONSTRUCTIVE AS CONTRASTED WITH SUPPORTIVE THERAPY

The term "reconstructive therapy" is used to indicate procedures which aim to modify an individual's personality structure. The contrasting term, "supportive therapy," implies no such changes; the aim here is to help the individual through some crisis by the use of reassurance and related measures. Some therapeutic procedures purport to correct underlying psychopathological difficulties; others aim only secondarily at the roots of the matter while supporting the individual through a period of stress. The distinction between reconstructive and supportive psychotherapy is by no means absolute but rather a matter of degree. It would appear that reconstructive therapy contains supportive elements. It is also true that supportive therapy may supply incidental reconstructive gains. Indeed, with any psychotherapeutic system there may be procedures which systematically stress support for one case and reconstruction for another. Instead of being an exception as it might first be conjectured, modified psychoanalytic practice is an excellent illustration, as Alexander and French (1) demonstrate. Even classical psychoanalysis has supportive elements.

Reconstructive psychotherapy goes beyond supportive therapy in that the therapist, guided by some concept of psychopathology and its genesis, follows a procedure in which the psychodynamics become evident not only to the therapist but also to the patient. It is on this basis that reconstructive therapy is referred to as "uncovering" or "insight" therapy. Since these latter terms refer to but way stations toward reorganization of the personality, the term "reconstructive therapy" is preferred. Supportive therapy may likewise be referred to as "covering-up" therapy in that various techniques such as reassurance, suggestion, the giving of information, and even hypnosis may be used to help the patient cover up, repress, or ignore troublesome difficulties.

Supportive elements, whether incidental or central, are present in any therapy. In some techniques support is nothing more than an inevitable by-product of the patient-clinician relationship, as, for example, in classical psychoanalysis. The clinician supportively waits out periods during which the patient is experiencing an increase in anxiety. This in no way vitiates attempts at reconstruction but actually increases the possibility that it may eventually succeed. In view of the stress in later chapters upon reconstructive psychotherapy, in the remainder of this present section supportive therapy will be stressed.

It is more common, however, to speak of supportive therapy not in reference to an incidental technique used only on occasions (as is the case with psychoanalysis) but as the major procedure employed. Advice or reassurance may be given and a protective role assumed in which the relationship with the therapist is the sustaining element. The therapist is needed, just as he is in reconstructive therapy, but his primary function may be to impart advice or guidance or to offer sympathy, encouragement, or other emotional rewards.

Much so-called counseling is essentially supportive psychotherapy. Counseling generally involves a shorter rather than a longer series of sessions, deals with reactive problems rather than intrapsychic conflicts, may stress intellectual factors rather than emotional ones, is likely to deal with non-incapacitating rather than severely disturbing and involved maladjustments, often places the symptom or symptoms in the center of focus, is likely to deal with relatively normal people rather than neurotics or psychotics, and is based upon a rapport rather than a transference relationship. These characteristics are precisely those typical of much supportive psychotherapy, whether labeled counseling or not. Reconstructive psychotherapy is also practiced under the name of counseling but less commonly.

The steady interest and sympathy of the therapist form the basis for this supportive relationship. It sometimes resembles what Axelrode (3) refers to as "old-fashioned case work"—an abundance of activity on the behalf of the patient. In the more narrowly therapeutic relationship this consists of interest and sympathy, advice and information, reassurance, favors arranged, etc. Axelrode would emphasize that the therapist plays a paternal role in which the affect hunger of the patient is at least partially met.

All therapy is a temporary relationship eventually severed at some point. If mere support is given there is likely not to be any essential change in the patient; he is carried over a rough spot or a series of rough spots and then must continue on his own. It may be that normal growth processes will be sufficient to allow the individual to go ahead thereafter without further assistance. Supportive therapy provides a means for helping the patient learn how to live in some measure of comfort with his uncured difficulties, or for guiding him through a stressful period until the time comes when these difficulties are no longer prepotent.

According to Alexander and French (1), supportive therapy is indicated in two opposite types of cases—the one in which no permanent personality change is needed because efficiency is only temporarily disturbed by difficult external conditions, and the other in which warping of the personality is so great that little hope of a reconstructive change can be held.

Supportive therapy may be illustrated by a discussion in turn of reassurance and imparting information. The first is characteristically a tool more often used with cases in which little or no change may be expected and the second where reconstructive effort is not necessary. It must again be stated, however, that these are also to some degree characteristics of reconstructive therapy, although in a much more incidental way.

REASSURANCE AS A SUPPORTIVE TECHNIQUE

Reassurance is a term which has several meanings. The crudest usage involves mere expressions of a general nature, such as "Don't be afraid to talk," "I'll not jump on you," "I'm interested, go ahead" and other such vague remarks better left unsaid. By his very manner the expert therapist *implies* this sort of reassurance without needing to verbalize it. What is essentially superficial and perhaps inane when spoken is, nevertheless, an important form of reassurance when otherwise conveyed. This comes from the therapist's attitude of permissiveness and understanding even in the face of the most "shocking" of revelations. Reassurance of this kind is closely related to certain aspects of what Snyder (12), writing as a nondirective therapist, refers to as "warmth." Among other techniques he speaks of friendly conversation, approval and encouragement, and permissiveness. The therapist lives this sort of reassurance—he does not need to speak it.

As bad as the crude reassurance mentioned at the beginning of the preceding paragraph are those instances in which the therapist permits himself to make guarantees beyond his patient's capacity of achievement. It is the mark of the quack to promise more than he can deliver, but sometimes the overanxious therapist traps himself by holding out that more profound changes will take place than are likely under the circumstances. This reassurance may produce temporary success at the time but ultimately will precipitate therapeutic disaster.

To be sure, the patient should be allowed to see that he is entitled to be hopeful, and the therapist is performing a legitimate function when he offers reassurance on this score. But reassurance should not be oriented only in the direction of the future. It is the patient's feelings here and now which are much more a matter of concern. Subtle indications that show he is accepted and worth while and entitled to self-respect are much more important aspects of reassurance, enhancing as they do his security and self-esteem. In this connection verbal statements of reassurance have some usefulness.

Reassurance of a verbal nature is also helpful and needed in other circumstances. For example, a patient's sense of being alone and unique in his suffering may be relieved by assurances that others like him have suffered and recovered. To know that he is not alone and that he is not the only one who has had these difficulties may lighten his feelings of guilt or anxiety. For a medical student to realize, in seeking therapeutic help during the traumatic years that are his lot in medical school, that he is not alone in seeking such help but merely one of a sizable proportion of his fellows in the same position often aids him to see his problems in better perspective.

As Thorne (13) points out, any method is valuable which helps a patient tolerate a period of acute stress until other treatment methods can be instituted. This, perhaps, is the most important usage of reassurance. It may often take the form of attempting to make the patient feel that his problem is soluble, or, if this cannot legitimately be indicated, that an improvement of some generally defined sort can be expected. Alexander and French (1) describe a case in which this sort of reassurance was used with a woman in an acute depression over her pregnancy.

Andrews (15), writing in a directive tradition, describes and exemplifies the use of reassurance with a variety of patient groups and states that it is especially indicated with the mentally defective, in combating simple reactive anxiety, in patients with feelings of inferiority and anxiety which appear to have no actual basis, and with children seen in child guidance clinics. Of course she did not mean to imply that all patients falling in one or another of the categories can be helped by reassurance but that these are patients with whom it is more often indicated.

Easy and irresponsible reassurance given to the patient may have exactly the opposite effect of that intended. If a patient is in an upset state, devaluating himself, his ability, and his relationships with others, and these feelings are met with a cheerful "Don't worry" or "I am sure you can get along with others," his anxiety rather than his confidence will be increased. The patient feels in mortal danger, and the reassurance merely proves to him that the therapist does not understand him or is belittling his problem. For example, to assure a patient that a symptom really amounts to nothing may plunge him into a further depression, since what is being dismissed as unimportant may be to him his only defense against a seemingly insoluble difficulty. This is sometimes avoided by the therapist who prefaces his encouragement with assurances that he understands the patient's suffering but still envisions a way out.

Sometimes reassurance succeeds too well, especially when reconstructive therapy is attempted. It is perhaps very human and natural to attempt to soothe an upset person. The experienced therapist will often resist this impulse because he wishes to see if something constructive may not come from such a glimmer of understanding as may accompany the upset state, or he may try to utilize this feeling as a wedge to open the door leading toward a solution of the patient's problems. If reassurance is given hastily, it may block any exploration and dry up at the source the spring from which therapeutic progress may be forthcoming. An incident described by Allen is pertinent:

> As he went into the therapist's office, Solomon smiled in a forced way. In appearance, he was pale, somewhat undernourished, and obviously fearful. There were a few facial tics. The therapist was friendly in a casual way as names were exchanged. Solomon made a feeble effort to cover the initial fear engendered by this new experience that separated him from his mother. For the moment he was cut adrift. He weakly said that the room looked cheerful enough but quickly got to his own anxiety and broke out into tears saying, "I'm just scared and I don't know what it is."
>
> The natural, human reaction at this point would have been to reassure this frightened child by saying there was nothing to be afraid of, or that he would not be hurt. A responsible therapist, however, recognizes the importance of helping Solomon express his fear and come to terms with it. The therapist, on the other hand, who feels the necessity to relieve the child of his fear keeps the source of the relief in himself and so postpones the child's discovery of his own capacity to live through and to overcome his fear. In this instance, the therapist supported Solomon in his fear by saying that he knew how frightened he was of coming to this strange place, of going off with a strange man and leaving his mother outside. He was encouraged to talk about how he felt. (2, p. 169.)

In this instance reconstructive therapy, not mere support, was being attempted. Yet Allen did offer support, but a kind which did not serve to gloss over the difficulties. Rather he brought out recognition and acceptance, not denial, of the fear. Reassurance used in this adroit fashion is also a means of building the patient-therapist relationship and on this count too is more than an aspect of supportive therapy.

IMPARTING INFORMATION AS A SUPPORTIVE TECHNIQUE

Many individuals who are seen by clinical psychologists lack the information necessary to reach some decision or to carry out some activity. They fall into that diagnostic category which Bordin (17) called "lack of information." He conceives of the category as reflecting both the reason they could not help themselves and also a way in which they could be helped. Some psychological disturbances are based on sheer ignorance or misinformation, and correcting this lack or distortion helps to alleviate the disturbance or perhaps remove it completely.

It has been contended by some therapists that imparting information has no place in the therapeutic situation since doing so is to commit the fallacy of ignoring deeper problems. Individuals who take this position contend that, for example, a person who comes for vocational advice may have such a problem but that it merely serves to cover a deeper one. Often it may do so, but in the opinion of the writer this is by no means always the case. At any rate, imparting information under certain circumstances is considered, by some clinicians at least, a therapeutically sensible procedure.

College students living in an environment in which there is known to be a counseling service turn quite naturally to the clinicians for information which will aid in making an adjustment. This information may be in the educational, vocational, or emotional sphere. In effect, then, their needs are often reactive in nature, arising not from intrapsychic conflict but from a situation with which they cannot adequately cope. Much college counseling is of this nature, and consequently the presentation of information is a very important function in such a situation. Many accounts of college counseling, e.g., Berdie (16), Sarbin (18), and Stogdill (19), stress the giving of information as a therapeutic service.

A cardinal principle in the correct use of information is to supply it only when the patient is psychologically ready to receive it. This implies in turn that the information thus shared is given not because it happens to be available but because the strategy of therapy calls for it at this particular time. In this connection the sharing of test information with the patient is pertinent. All too often, the psychologist spreads his wares in the form of test results before the hapless patient more or less as if he were a street vendor, inviting the patient to pick out a selection of gimcracks of dubious or unknown value. Scores, percentiles, and verbal classifications are thrust at the patient in a confusing mixture. In one easy lesson the patient is given courses in psychometrics and statistics, a personality evaluation, and a plan of action based on the test results. Such a puerile procedure, strange as it may seem, is sometimes confused with psychotherapy even by experienced psychologists.

Information should be given a patient with a full realization that it has emotional implications and that often the very fact that it was lacking is because of emotional reasons. For example, information concerning masturbation, intercourse, conception, and so on, frequently must be supplied by the therapist because proper knowledge allays curiosity and the anxiety and guilt which accompany it. Yet misinformation in the same sphere may not be eliminated by supplying correct information only. The frigid woman to whom all men are sensual brutes is not going to be helped by being informed that her belief is incorrect.

It may be hypothecated that the appropriate use of information as a therapeutic device has a direct relation both to the degree of maladjustment and to the emotional involvement the patient has with the area in which the information falls. The more healthy or integrated the personality the more useful is the giving of information likely to be. Retaining a fairly intact personality structure, the relatively well-adjusted individual is more likely to be in a position to profit from information, since his emotional resistance is probably less. However, if the information concerns an area about which there is some emotional disturbance, even the relatively well-adjusted individual is less likely to assimilate it and use it therapeutically. In short, if the information is not in itself disturbing, there is more chance that it will be assimilated and become part of the behavior repertoire of the individual.

Information and interpretation are often confused. In a sense, interpretation is a form of information centering upon self-understanding on the part of the patient. If he now recognizes that one of the origins of his present attitude toward authority is his earlier relationship with his father, he has certain *information* at his command. Customarily, however, this is referred to as the product of interpretation rather than imparted information. A distinction useful operationally, although by no means clear-cut, is to restrict the term "interpretation" to information involving the ego-identifications of the patient, whereas other information less individual-centered may be categorized by the term "information" itself. Thus, helping the patient understand about his night terrors is different from giving him information about the length of time and the complexity of the process involved in becoming a specialist in pediatrics.

It should not be inferred from the foregoing emphasis on college counseling and psychological test information that imparting information takes place solely in such settings. Often the more usual psychotherapeutic techniques go hand in hand with supplying of information. Alexander and French (1), for example, describe a case of a refugee physician who needed not only insight into the sources of his irritation with his young son but also practical advice on working out his beginning practice in a new country.

CURATIVE AS CONTRASTED WITH
SYMPTOMATIC THERAPY

Closely related to the previous discussion concerning reconstructive and supportive therapy is the issue of curative as contrasted with symptomatic treatment. Since the former is considered in great detail in the chapters to follow, attention here is focused upon symptomatic therapy.

Symptoms represent spontaneous and often unconscious attempts to adjust to the difficult aspects of life. They are indicators of underlying personality mechanisms at work but are not dynamic, being the resultant of forces operative, rather than the forces themselves. The clinician often regards them not as therapeutically significant in themselves but as indicators of deeper-lying aspects of inadequate adjustment. They are evaluated as a means of understanding the deformation of the patient's personality structure. With the correction of this deformity, the symptoms disappear. Although symptoms are not the focus of more intensive psychotherapeutic efforts, this is not to say that treatment is never directed toward alleviation of symptoms. In this type of therapy the clinician intends to reach a limited goal, either as a temporary milestone on the road to reconstructive treatment or as a final goal in itself. For example, certain environmental conditions, such as lack of time or money, to mention but two, may be present which prevent intensive treatment. Moreover, the patient's psychological resources may be so limited as to contraindicate any deeper probing, or he may be negatively inclined toward more intensive treatment. Again, the exigencies of the situation may be such that symptomatic treatment must without delay be instituted, as is the case when an acute panic occurs.

In any case, symptomatic treatment is sometimes justifiably practiced. In the course of mastering symptoms the individual may gain some freedom from distress, which is actually what he asks for and expects from the therapist. In other instances he may make an adequate adjustment. Therapeutic successes do occur, especially when the therapeutic efforts are supported by particularly fortunate circumstances in the post-treatment phase either through a continued process of self-mastery set into motion during therapy or by environmental circumstances of such a nature as not to precipitate repetition of the difficulties in the same or similar form. On the other hand, one should not minimize the superficiality of the symptomatic approach since the underlying sources of frustration, anxiety, and guilt remain unmolested. There is also the danger that symptom removal may leave the patient without an adequate substitute, since although the symptom may have been a poor attempt to reach healthful adjustment its removal leaves him without even this between him and a perhaps more serious psychological disturbance. Moreover, removal of a symptom, or symptoms, is sometimes a handicap to future therapy because the patient, now that what to him are his main difficulties are gone, may be unable to see any reason for continuing in therapy.

Although placed in a military setting and emphasizing somatic conditions, the account by Frank (5) of the psychotherapeutic effects of symptomatic treatment is of general interest and applicability. He considers the beneficial effects of symptomatic treatment under four related headings as follows: "(1) direct attack on the basic psychopathological process, (2) facilitation of approach to the underlying disturbance through alleviation of symptoms which tend to impede this, (3) diminution of emotional disturbances resulting secondarily from the symptoms, and (4) favorable modification of the patient's attitudes towards the physician." (5, p. 22.) Each of these will be discussed in turn.

Concerning symptoms which are at the same time etiological agents (symptomatic treatment thus being a curative measure) he illustrates with combat reactions in which exhaustion and anxiety arising from combat experiences are both manifestations and causes of the symptomatology. These and other reactive conditions may receive symptomatic treatment, but it is necessary to add that they hardly form the bulk of therapeutic practice. Accordingly the earlier advanced conception of symptoms as indicators, not as dynamic forces, still holds in the main.

If ventilation of the material that needs to be brought into the open in the therapeutic sessions is accompanied by exacerbation of symptoms, such as anxiety or fatigue, then treatment of symptoms may facilitate reaching these more fundamental issues. This second effect of symptomatic treatment is closely related to the third mentioned by Frank—diminution of the emotional disturbance created by the symptoms themselves. If cardiac palpitation due to anxiety leads in turn to a fear of heart disease, a patient is likely to be further upset by his symptoms and in a less favorable position to profit from psychotherapy than otherwise would be the case.

Modification of the attitude of the patient toward the therapist may come about with the use of symptomatic treatment since it demonstrates that the clinician has the patient's interest at heart and tends to increase the patient's confidence. Because the therapist has done something for the patient he is likely to be viewed more favorably.

In connection with symptomatic treatment Frank stresses, as do most physicians, somatic methods—treating reactive depression with benzedrine, battle reactions with sedation or ergotamine, back pain through physiotherapy, and weight loss by subcoma insulin treatment. Nonetheless, purely psychological means of symptomatic treatment are often indicated, including suggestion, persuasion, explanation, and reassurance.

VARIATIONS AMONG SCHOOLS OF PSYCHOTHERAPY

There is a tendency for adherents to a given school of psychotherapy to imply, if they do not assert, that their theories are correct and those of every other school are to some degree invalid—the degree of validity being decided by the degree of agreement between the two points of view. To be sure, bald statements as sweeping as this are seldom made, at least in public, but sometimes it would appear that this is the basis on which the more enthusiastic protagonists proceed. There are signs, however, that the period characterized by adherence to the "one true faith" and the persecution of unbelievers is disappearing. For example, it is recognized by some psychotherapists that the development of schools of psychotherapy (like the development of schools of psychology) is a sign not of considerable knowledge but rather of deficiency of knowledge. The greater security of the psychological professions in the family of clinical arts has also contributed to this more desirable tolerant state of affairs.

Although it is no longer true, to modify somewhat a well-known saying, that "psychotherapy is the art of applying a science which does not exist," it is nevertheless true that the scientific basis for the relationship between theory and practice in psychotherapy has not been established to the entire satisfaction of any but a few of the most doctrinaire adherents to one or another of the particular schools. This is not to say that one cannot point to successful therapeutic efforts demonstrating an apparently close correspondence between theory and practice. The issue is complicated by the fact that adherents of points of view in considerable measure opposed to the one under consideration can do essentially the same thing. Even practices entirely contrary to scientific thinking may claim cures. To be sure, many of these patients later appear in other clinical settings as disabled as before, but so do nondirectively treated persons, psychoanalytically treated patients, and so on through the entire gamut of psychotherapeutic approaches.

That there is a common core to psychotherapeutic systems, as sketched in Chapter 18, may account for a certain amount of therapeutic success. There are, however, sources of variation which make relative this question of "success." Success is always relative to the nature of the patient, his desires, the personality of the therapist, the training of the therapist, environmental limitations, and a great variety of other circumstances.

Since this chapter and the chapters to follow are either exclusively or in large measure concerned with schools of psychotherapy, it is inadvisable to deal exhaustively with the forms in which variation is expressed among the different schools. One form of variation, the approach to the therapeutic relationship at the level of rapport or at the level of transference, was considered in a previous chapter. A factor closely related to this, variation in the use of the therapeutic relationship, is also crucial. Another issue concerning which there is variation among schools of psychotherapy is the question of diagnostic appraisal in relation to psychotherapy. These two issues will be discussed here since they are crucial to an understanding of differences among therapeutic approaches.

VARIATION IN THE USE OF THE THERAPEUTIC RELATIONSHIP

The therapeutic relationship between clinician and patient, although having a common core of meaning, may be used differently according to the systematic orientation of the psychotherapist. Allen differentiates three types as follows:

The therapeutic relationship can be used authoritatively. This use is evident in the more direct efforts to tell a patient what to do, to lay out plans for his recovery and to fit him to a regime designed to ameliorate his difficulties. In less direct forms we see it in the subtle use of suggestion, in hypnosis or in the application of formulas and beliefs, such as "a military school will help" or in slogans such as "don't worry" or "be calm." The authoritative use of a relationship is characterized by the frank and purposeful utilization of an opportunity to bring about change. In this sense therapy has more in common with those methods which depend upon the employment of an external force, like a drug, to induce changes in behavior.

The second use of the relationship, which might be termed the "genetic" or "causal," strives to utilize the therapeutic experience as a means of getting at the historical background of the difficulties, of making conscious the unconscious trends and drives and re-creating the past in the therapeutic situation in order to release anxiety bound up with these earlier experiences. The emphasis is on the establishment of the "transference," from which insight proceeds. The focus is directed toward what the patient *was* in order to help him clear up conflicts in his present self. . . .

The third use will, . . . receive the major emphasis [in Allen's work]. . . . Here the therapeutic relationship is conceived as an immediate experience. The therapist begins where the patient is and seeks to help him to draw on his own capacities toward a more creative acceptance and use of the self he has. While maintaining an interest in understanding what has been wrong, the therapeutic focus is on what the individual can begin to do about what was, and, more important, still is wrong. (2, pp. 48–49.)

The first use of the therapeutic relationship is characteristic of many but not all eclectic practitioners. A directive approach such as that of Thorne would often use it in this fashion. Supportive treatment also may find expression through this form of handling the relationship. The genetic approach is characteristic of the psychoanalyst, and both relationship and nondirective therapy emphasize the immediate experience of the patient-therapist relationship. The genetic and present experience approaches often merge in actual practice. Reconstruction of the past often occurs as the patient experiences the feelings involved in the present situation.

VARIATION IN THE USE OF DIAGNOSIS IN PSYCHOTHERAPY

It must be evident from the discussion in the earlier chapters that a position is taken that diagnostic appraisal is necessary in application of the clinical method both for reasons specific to diagnosis and for the purpose of planning for psychotherapy. The entire process of scientific observation and classification demands it (8). Even if there were no other cogent reasons, the necessity of a valid diagnosis in order to detect or eliminate the presence of pathological processes which if undetected might result in harm to the patient would lead to the position. Our systems of classification are imperfect, and "labeling" is but a minor part of this endeavor. True, diagnostic appraisal may be and is with some therapeutic approaches such as psychoanalysis a continuing process not formally established at any one temporal point. Diagnosis and therapy may begin together and go along as one process of insightful development. Final diagnosis may come at the end of therapy, successful or unsuccessful. But diagnostic formulations are made even if subject to continuing change as further relevant material is obtained.

The importance of diagnosis and its acceptance as a necessary step is established with most psychiatric practitioners and many but not all psychologists and therapists. An exception is found in the non-directive point of view expressed by Rogers and his followers. With a commendable zeal to rid his approach of what he considered to be authoritarian trappings (and who today wants to be authoritarian?) Rogers rejects diagnosis as being too directive. In a well-known quotation he states baldly, "Diagnostic knowledge and skill is not necessary for good therapy. . . ." (11, p. 421.) This is not the appropriate place to explore the nondirective approach in detail, as this is done in Chapter 20. At the moment only the question of whether or not a diagnosis is necessary in clinical practice will be considered.

Hunt (8) has examined certain implications of this statement concerning the lack of necessity of diagnosis. Although he presents and dismisses as impracticable the possibility of referral by the non-directivist of all cases for prior psychiatric and neurological consultations, it would appear that what remains is for the psychologist to handle any and all cases with the nondirective technique presumed to be universally efficacious. Although this position is hardly verbalized in this fashion even by its most enthusiastic adherents, it appears to Hunt that such inference must be drawn from Rogers' statement concerning the superfluousness of diagnosis. Psychotics, organic cases masked as neurotics, psychopaths, suicidal risks, and so on, would seem, since preliminary diagnosis or screening is not necessary, to be accepted for nondirective treatment.

It may well be that with the great majority of college students (who still make up the bulk of nondirectively treated clientele) there is relatively less chance of serious difficulty emerging. But our concern must also be with that small minority to whom such dangers might come. It must be admitted that evidence, other than circumstantial and anecdotal, that this actually occurs is lacking. It can only be on the basis of general clinical experience (which is sometimes wrong) that one can at the present time criticize this lack of diagnostic appraisal. It would appear, on the other hand, as if the clinical experience of Rogers and his associates must be in direct contradiction. Had they found many difficulties, it is not at all unreasonable to suggest that they would have said so and changed their procedures accordingly. Thus at the moment there can be a choice between competing references to clinical experience, a hardly satisfying state of affairs either to Rogers or to his critics. When one considers the neurotic and psychotic patients in what for convenience may be called "psychiatric settings," the decision can be made on firmer ground. Although it is impossible to state precisely how far the method is applicable with such patients, since only further research and experience will tell, in the opinion of most present practitioners, a firm stand is warranted in favor of a diagnostic appraisal. To the best of the knowledge of the writer, no staff of a medical-psychiatric clinic or institution has taken the position that Rogers advocates and practices.[2]

BIBLIOGRAPHY

1. Alexander, F., and French, T. M. (eds.), *Psychoanalytic therapy: principles and application*, The Ronald Press Company, 1946.
2. Allen, F. H., *Psychotherapy with children*, W. W. Norton and Company, 1942.
3. Axelrode, J., Some indications for supportive therapy, *Amer. J. Orthopsychiat.*, 1940, 10:264–271.

---

[2] The question may perhaps be raised why the dichotomy, directive to nondirective, is not discussed as one of the results of variation in psychotherapy. Quite frankly it is seen as a pseudo problem. Some therapists are more active than others, directive if you will, but the great majority are so essentially "nondirective" in the sense of being permissive as to render discussion pointless. The same psychotherapeutic climate in which Rogers developed his point of view was simultaneously influencing other psychotherapists independently struggling with the passive-active dilemma. It might be argued that Rogers and his followers use different procedures from those of other psychotherapists. They do differ in carrying to logical extremes certain common psychotherapeutic procedures and thus advance one independent approach to psychotherapy. This position is taken up in the next chapter.

4. Bixler, R. H., Counseling: eclectic or systematic? *Educ. Psychol. Measmt*, 1948, 8:211–214.
5. Frank, J. D., Psychotherapeutic aspects of symptomatic treatment, *Amer. J. Psychiat.*, 1946, 103:21–25.
6. Gildea, M. C. L., and Gildea, E. F., Personalities of American psychotherapists: Mitchell, Salmon, Riggs, *Amer. J. Psychiat.*, 1945, 101:460–467.
7. Hoch, P. H., Summary of symposium findings, in Hoch, P. H. (ed.), *Failures in psychiatric treatment*, Grune & Stratton, 1948, pp. 224–238.
8. Hunt. W. A., Diagnosis and non-directive therapy, *J. clin. Psychol.*, 1948, 4:232–236.
9. Knight, R. P., Evaluation of the results of psychoanalytic therapy, *Amer. J. Psychiat.*, 1941, 98:434–446.
10. Oberndorf, C. P., Constant elements in psychotherapy, *Psychoanal. Quart.*, 1946, 15:435–449.
11. Rogers, C. R., Significant aspects of client-centered therapy, *Amer. Psychologist*, 1946, 1:415–422.
12. Snyder, W. U., "Warmth" in nondirective counseling, *J. abnorm. soc. Psychol.*, 1946, 41:491–495.
13. Thorne, F. C., Directive psychotherapy: VI. The technique of psychological palliation, *J. clin. Psychol.*, 1946, 2:68–79.
14. Thorne, F. C., Directive psychotherapy: VII. Imparting psychological information, *J. clin. Psychol.*, 1946, 2:179–190.

Supplementary articles in Watson, R. I. (ed.), *Readings in the clinical method in psychology*, Harper & Brothers, 1949:

15. Andrews, J. S., Directive psychotherapy: I. Reassurance. Pp. 654–673. (Also in *J. clin. Psychol.*, 1945, 1:52–66.)
16. Berdie, R. F., Judgments in counseling. Pp. 604–624. (Also in *Educ. Psychol. Measmt.*, 1944, 4:35–55.)
17. Bordin, E. S., Diagnosis in counseling and psychotherapy. Pp. 229–243. (Also in *Educ. Psychol. Measmt.*, 1946, 6:169–184.)
18. Sarbin. T. R., The case record in psychological counseling. Pp. 217–228. (Also in *J. appl. Psychol.*, 1940, 24:184–197.)
19. Stogdill, E. L., Techniques of student counseling. Pp. 598–603. (Also in *J. consult. Psychol.*, 1940, 4:176–180.)

CHAPTER 20

Some Systematic Approaches
to Psychotherapy

·On stopping to consider the psychotherapeutic approaches that are followed at the present time, one is struck immediately not only by their variety and scope but by the way in which they intermingle so far as the practice of specific individual clinicians is concerned. The stamp of individuality which each therapist places upon his work must be forgone for the sake of an examination of some of the various systematic approaches discernible in this field. In the present chapter there is a consideration of Freudian psychoanalysis, some variations from this the classic approach, nondirective psychotherapy, and eclectic psychotherapy. In the chapters to follow, devoted to psychotherapy with children and group psychotherapy, these points of view are again taken up in a fashion appropriate to the topics. In addition, relationship therapy is discussed in connection with child psychotherapy, as are activity group psychotherapy and psychodrama in connection with group psychotherapy.

PSYCHOANALYSIS

Modern psychiatry and clinical psychology have been greatly influenced by psychoanalytic theory and practice, often to the extent that the lay person confuses terminology and regards the term "psychoanalysis" as encompassing the entire field of the behavior sciences. That term, however, is in the most strict sense reserved for practitioners in a tradition stemming directly from Sigmund Freud and his followers operationally expressed in membership in the various psychoanalytic institutes and associations or in training under these auspices. This operational conception, some clinicians would argue, is to narrow. Although all psychoanalysis goes back ultimately to Freud there have been a number of variations such as those arising from the work of Jung, Adler, Horney, Rank, and Sullivan, for example, the followers of some of which insist they are "psychoanalysts." This has resulted in referring to those in "direct descent" as *Freudian psychoanalysts*. Without attempting to judge the merits of the varying claims, when the term "psychoanalysis" is used here without qualifying modification reference is intended to classic "Freudian" psychoanalysis, and the remarks may or may not apply to the aforementioned variations.

Psychoanalysis is, at one and the same time, a theory of the dynamics of human nature, a method of research, and an approach to psychotherapy. It cannot be properly understood without knowledge of its theoretical substructure. Understanding of dynamics must precede understanding of procedure, and the account which follows presupposes to a certain extent this understanding. Nevertheless, several salient points will be recalled in order to make the discussion of method more meaningful.

THEORETICAL PRINCIPLES BASIC TO PSYCHOANALYTIC THERAPY

The distinction between unconscious motivations and those of which the individual is consciously aware is central to psychoanalytic theory. The psychologist is familiar with experiments in posthypnotic suggestion and related studies demonstrating the influence of commands of which the subject is unaware. He is also familiar with the concept of unverbalized influences upon behavior and of involuntary conditioning (cf., for example, Maslow and Mittelmann, 33). By and large, however, his study and research have been concerned with conscious functioning, and among psychologists there is a relative lack of interest in unconscious processes. If practicing in the clinical field, however, he can hardly deny the influence of motivations of which the patient is unaware. Whether or not he subscribes to the analytic way of interpreting such phenomena, he cannot deny their validity or fail to ascribe at least some causation to them. The investigations of the psychoanalysts gave emphasis to the clinical

importance of unconscious forces in the development and maintenance of psychological disorders and, indeed, of all personality
functioning.

According to psychoanalytic theory, at every moment of life unconscious forces are contributing to an individual's behavior. In their
expression they are modified by being brought into relation with
conscious experience. Classic psychoanalysis as a therapeutic technique is a means of doing just this—bringing into consciousness the
emotions, motivations, and experiences of which the patient is unaware and, once they are revealed, extending his conscious control
over them or freeing their psychic energy with a consequent lack of
any necessity of control. It must be emphasized that "unconscious"
does not necessarily imply the disappearance of the emotions or ideas
from consciousness; it often means that there is an isolation or dis-
sociation of elements which belong together. Affects and ideas may
be separated and constituent parts of experiences isolated without
having these elements themselves unconscious.

Conscious control is brought about, or at least is believed to be
most efficiently and thoroughly achieved, by psychoanalysis. Mental
health to the psychoanalyst, in part at least, is indicated by the degree to which mental life is determined by conscious forces and
awareness of the effect of unconscious forces. This may also be stated
from a slightly different perspective as strengthening the ego by increasing its scope and power. It is also possible to reduce the influence of unconscious strivings and thus increase mental stability by
a strengthening of the ego; therefore the dynamics are changed and
behavior is altered, i.e., brought under the mastery of the ego. The
patient's personality is such that with the help of psychoanalysis he
is more able to handle his conflicts in a direct and mature fashion
and to meet life's vicissitudes without the complications of previously established, less mature patterns of integrated behavior. The
fantasy experience of the individual is more closely related to the
realities of the world about him as a result of psychoanalysis than it
was before.

The structure of personality is conceived in psychoanalytic theory
as involving Ego, Id, and Superego forces. The Ego serves as the
means of perception of internal and external events, an integrative
function, and an executive function. The Id refers to those unconscious, persistent, pleasure-seeking and hostile strivings which the

Ego must modify according to the dictates of reality. The Superego, on the other hand, is that compound of ideals, conscience, and self-critical factors which serves to spur the Ego to its task of combating Id forces.

The concept of the Ego is important for understanding psychoanalytic therapy. The conscious Ego is that portion of the personality which is in touch with the environment and is capable of independent judgment. In the adult psychoneurotic the Ego is usually of sufficient strength to deal with these unconscious tendencies of the Id by modification and sublimation if they are recognized. Through repression, however, they are not directly accessible to the conscious Ego, and, furthermore, the Ego militates against their being brought into consciousness by various mechanisms of defense (12). So, not only do the patient and analyst have the task of dealing with unconscious tendencies, but they must also take into consideration the Ego and its mechanisms of defense. They actually become aware of unconscious forces through the defense mechanisms.

Another major concept of psychoanalysis is that childhood experiences play a major role in the formation of the adult personality. This genetic formulation, for example, finds expression in the way the patient-clinician relationship is handled in therapy, as described in Chapter 19.

Closely related, although not so generally accepted, is the concept that conflict about sexuality, interpreted to include not only genital behavior but also varieties of pleasurable experiences occurring in childhood, is crucial and leaves an indelible imprint upon many aspects of the adult personality. For example, such psychological problems as the Oedipus and castration complexes, which are normal developmental phenomena, may not be satisfactorily integrated, thus predisposing the adult to certain behavior difficulties.

Finally, it might be mentioned that Freud was a thoroughgoing determinist in regard to psychological causation. He emphasized the importance of such matters as slips of the tongue, free association, and analysis of dream content in his unswerving determination to find in human activity and thought, no matter how ostensibly trivial or nonsensical, the sense that it contained.

These, of course, are but bald, short, and therefore to some degree inaccurate statements which can only serve to remind the reader already familiar with psychoanalytic theory of some of its salient aspects. It is hoped that they will serve as a means whereby the present concern with standard psychoanalytic therapeutic practice may be brought into some sort of perspective.

PRELIMINARY PROCEDURES

The following account of some of the preliminary procedures necessary before beginning analysis proper is based heavily, but not exclusively, on Freud's own work (17). Briefly, these preliminary procedures are concerned with provisional acceptance and diagnostic appraisal, matters of finance and schedule, the expectations of the patient, the warning against drastic changes during analysis, the principle of deprivation, and the use of the couch.

Before accepting a patient for psychoanalysis it is customary to allow a provisional period of two or three weeks in order to decide whether or not the problems presented are amenable to this approach. This provisional phase is in one sense not preliminary at all, since some analysts consider it the beginning of the analysis in no wise different from later phases. During this period, whether regarded as provisional or merely introductory, a decision can be reached regarding the suitability of the case for analytic treatment. Those disorders orthodoxly and conservatively considered amenable to psychoanalytic therapy include anxiety states, anxiety hysteria, conversion hysteria, compulsion neuroses, phobias, character neuroses, and the perversions. Within these categories psychoanalysis has been found most suitable for severe chronic cases.

Many analysts today use the preliminary interview or interviews to permit a diagnostic appraisal, perhaps also using the services of a psychologist to supplement this procedure, placing particular emphasis on the Rorschach findings. Lengthy preliminary discussions are objected to by Freud because of their adverse effect on the transference relationship, which is being structured to some degree in this preliminary period. For the same reason Freud pointed out that treating friends or acquaintances is fraught with special difficulties— the transference is already partially established in a form which otherwise it might not take.

During this period questions of schedule and finance are settled before proceeding. A definite daily hour (fifty minutes) is set aside, often, although not always, five (or six) days of the week, sometimes with the understanding that whether or not the patient appears he is financially responsible. It is considered by those following this practice that otherwise "involuntary" absences would be financially embarrassing in addition to providing the patient with a weapon whereby he can attempt to avoid unpleasant but therapeutically necessary phases of the treatment. Frequency per week is dictated (whether it be once, twice, or six times a week) by the finding that otherwise either the material becomes too diluted or, especially during unusually significant and productive periods, the pressure is too great to leave the patient without the safety the therapeutic hour provides. A fairly rigorous schedule is also necessary lest some aspects of the patient's behavior escape the attention of the analyst. The connection between the events of the previous day and the responses (associations) in the analytic hour is still fresh, enabling the patient to recount them with less difficulty than would be the case if longer periods of time elapsed. In cases already advanced in treatment a lesser number of hours per week will suffice.

As to the question of the duration of treatment, the analyst can at first only suggest to the patient he try it through the exploratory period before an answer will be ventured—which can then be only tentative. Certainly the length of time will not be inconsiderable, ranging from one year to several years, with perhaps two years being the modal duration.

The expectations that the patient may have about being treated— enthusiastic acceptance or extreme skepticism, not to mention open hostility—are actually of little moment. They are themselves attitudes not based upon considered judgment, and acceptance or distrust are but symptoms.

It is customary for the psychoanalyst to advise the patient to make no drastic changes in his way of life (home, school, job, marital status, and so on) during at least the earlier phases of the analysis until the unconscious motivations molding these changes have been explored in the analytic sessions. This is not only to protect the patient from impulsive desires to solve a problem in a way at least partially neurotically determined, but also to deprive the patient of this way of escaping his problems outside the psychoanalytic sessions.

Psychoanalysis, as has been said before, is a form of treatment in which neurotic conflicts must be raised to the level of consciousness. Since the patient was formerly not directly aware of these conflicts and has consumed quantities of psychic energy in keeping them at the unconscious level, it follows that he suffers in this uncovering process. He must, in order to avoid greater suffering later, suffer during the process itself. Since gratification of a desire and ability to analyze that desire are incompatible, it is the practice of psychoanalysts in many instances to arrange with the patient that the gratification of the desire represented in a symptom be frustrated; otherwise the symptom might merely be nourished and reinforced during treatment.

During the sessions the patient usually lies on a couch with the analyst sitting behind him at the head of the couch (although often in a position where he can see the patient's face). Freud (17) advances as reasons for this procedure the fact that it removes the analyst from the patient's gaze (eight hours' scrutiny per day by patients can become wearing) and also that it prevents the patient from being influenced by changes of the analyst's expression. Freud himself apparently rather insisted on this; others are more elastic about it, not requiring it, for example, when there are phobic reactions about lying down, or in instances in which the patient is apparently eager to lie down.

THE METHOD OF FREE ASSOCIATION

According to Freud (17), the subject matter with which the patient begins is left to his own discretion, since the particular choice on the whole is immaterial. No coherent consecutive account is either expected or encouraged. It is often necessary to sketch for him the nature of this fundamental rule of psychoanalytic technique, free association, as he is accustomed to suppressing all discursive ramblings. Freud's own words give this rule with clarity:

> Your talk with me must differ in one respect from an ordinary conversation. Whereas usually you rightly try to keep the threads of your story together and to exclude all intruding associations and side-issues, so as not to wander too far from the point, here you must proceed differently. You will notice that as you relate things various ideas will occur to you which you feel inclined to put aside with certain criticisms and objections. You will be tempted to say to yourself: "This or that has no connection here, or it is quite unimportant, or it is nonsensical, so it cannot be necessary to mention it." Never give in to these objections, but mention it even if you feel a disinclination against it, or indeed just because of this. Later on you will perceive and learn to understand the reason for this injunction, which is really the only one that you have to

follow. So say whatever goes through your mind. Act as if you were sitting at the window of a railway train and describing to some one behind you the changing views you see outside. Finally, never forget that you have promised absolute honesty, and never leave anything unsaid because for any reason it is unpleasant to say it. (17, pp. 355–356.)

This "letting one's mind go" is quite a different procedure from the more or less orderly thinking that takes up much of our time—something unique to the psychoanalytic sessions. That which comes unbidden appears to be a confused jumble of memories, fancies, daydreams, accusations, feelings, and reproaches. Many of these would not under ordinary circumstances be expressed. But in the analytic situation convention, shame, maintenance of a good impression are all to be disregarded by the patient.

Free association is generally found by the patient to be unexpectedly baffling. Although perhaps easy enough in the privacy of one's daydreaming, the associations often dry up at the source when the attitude is deliberately maintained. Or there is a struggle to hold back, to rearrange in acceptable form, to deny to oneself that one had thought that which just flashed. The sources of these tendencies which block free association (resistances) will be forgone for the moment.

The rationale of this procedure is extremely important. As mentioned before, it is based upon a thoroughgoing determinism. Psychological processes do not move from one to another experience without a connection, and a jumble is precisely what it is not— rather, free association is a means of exposing the associative links. Since many of these processes are unconscious in origin, the method was introduced as a means of reaching them when hypnosis, the method previously used by Freud, proved unsatisfactory to him. (Other competent therapists, most often of nonanalytic persuasion, would question this point.) The analyst knows that by this method the unconscious will betray its repressed content. Thus by making conscious the repressed tendencies and freeing the individual from their effects, the goal of analysis is achieved.

This technique might be likened to the working of a picture puzzle; the pieces are picked up as they appear and eventually fitted into a coherent pattern, although there may always be some pieces missing. The fragments accumulate and a pattern emerges; a formerly obscure corner takes shape while other areas are still unformed. It is a search unimpeded for a while perhaps but eventually hitting certain snags which retard the process, only to continue again by fits and starts.

It is sometimes believed that the analyst in his faithfulness to the method of free association never uses direct questions. This is erroneous, for he may use them as stimuli to further associations by saying, "And what did that make you think of?" or in getting more precise information, such as "How old were you when this happened?" Generally speaking, however, direct questioning is used sparingly, with reliance placed on a spontaneous shaping of the material.

Since the patient is with the analyst and expects help from him, he repeats in his relation to the analyst earlier attitudes toward other persons from whom he received help. Certain of his associations will center upon the analyst, and these too are to be expressed and eventually understood for what they are. These spontaneous reactions (known as transference phenomena) concerning the analyst, vague, deliberately "unseen" figure, develop precisely because of this relative incognito. The patient attaches to him his own particular projections, expectations, and distortions, unhampered by what the analyst may be like in reality. It is characteristic that in so doing emotional upheavals concerning his feelings toward the analyst are taking place, which will be shown in the nature and quality of his associations.

A guiding principle in the use of free association (17) is that so long as the patient associates freely the theme of the transference to the analyst is left untouched. Only when the transference is used as resistance is the time ripe to turn to this issue. However, before dealing with this extremely important problem in this exposition, it is advisable to consider dream material and actions as sources of psychoanalytic material.

DREAMS

The resemblance between what appears to occur in free association and what goes on in dreams has perhaps already occurred to many on reading the foregoing account. The jumble, the disorder, the apparently alogical nature of free association are also characteristic of dreams. And again, as in free association, it is possible to view them deterministically as a reaction of the dreamer to his experiences.

In fact, patients spontaneously refer to dreams in free association, as Freud (20) discovered. It is no wonder, then, that dreams too are used in the psychoanalytic technique. Freud, in fact, spoke of the dream as the royal road to the unconscious. From his studies (20) and those of others certain salient facts have emerged. As to the content it is recognized that things are not what they seem—that which is recounted by the dreamer, the manifest content, is but a kaleidoscopic screen hiding the latent content, or true meaning.[1] These latent meanings represent the many buried feelings and wishes concerning which the patient is so deeply involved that he cannot be aware of them by conscious effort. Each dream, as it were, is a struggle to solve unconscious conflicts, touched off, perhaps, by events of the previous day but having roots in earlier struggles. Unable to face them in their full glare of meaning, the human personality struggles with them and, by many of the familiar dynamic mechanisms such as condensation and displacement, dispatches elsewhere the central points of the dream and substitutes instead the disguised manifest content.

The method of dream analysis used psychoanalytically involves having the patient free-associate, not to the dream as a whole, but to details singled out either by the patient or by the analyst. As he does so, specific themes and trends will emerge and thus lead to the latent meaning in the unconscious content. In a sense, then, the patient is sharing in the experience of interpreting. Although the anlayst uses his own associations based upon his own experience, he must also have extensive knowledge of the patient. It must be emphasized that there is no universal dream symbolism to apply.

Speaking of the way in which the analyst should employ dream interpretation Freud (14) offers certain suggestions which help to illustrate its usage. Since the analyst must be aware at all times of what is occupying the experience of the patient at the moment, it is urged that only the amount of interpretation obtainable in a given hour is sufficient. Even though the dream may not be fully revealed, the topic which is uppermost with the patient should be taken up the following hour. If this is the earlier dream, no harm is done and

---

[1] In certain instances, e.g., the dreams of children, and in the dreams of adults concerning drives not taboo in our culture, such as the dreams of soldiers on short ration dreaming of steak dinners, the latent and manifest contents are quite similar.

interpretation may be continued, but if a new dream or association appears attention should be transferred and the old dream neglected. To do otherwise would violate the rule of taking whatever came first to the patient's mind at the beginning of the session. Not only are elaborate dream productions perhaps incapable of full elucidation, but also subsequent dreams will repeat the themes if they are essential. Indeed, Freud points out that the best way to complete the interpretation of a dream is to dismiss it, since the material will again be contained in future dreams. It is characteristic that initial dreams are relatively easily understood and more revealing because of the patient's lack of sophistication. As the analysis progresses, however, more obscurity enters. Freud warns against displaying too great an interest in dream material lest resistance be directed by the patient against dream production itself and he fails to dream any more.

Individual variations occur both in the manner of dream analysis and in the degree to which it is used. According to Lorand (32), some analysts start by investigating the influence of current happenings as instigators of the dream and follow this up with free association. Others use only the free associations. The depth to which a dream is investigated varies from time to time in the same patient and from analyst to analyst. Lorand also cautions against the interpretation of dreams early in analysis and suggests waiting until a good deal is known about the patient's difficulties and the conflicts which have precipitated them. He also urges that an explanation be given the patient of the origin and meaning of dreams. His illustrative account of actual analyses of dreams is especially instructive (32).

ACTIONS

Another source of analytic material is supplied in the actions of the patient. These nonverbal (and unintentional verbal) activities include some that are important, some that are trivial. They may occur both within the analytic hour and in outside activities (22). Within the hour they may include the care with which the male patient pulls up his trousers so as not to spoil the crease when first reclining on the couch; the anxious glance that he gives over his shoulder; his flirtatious manner; the mispronunciation of a word; the change in demeanor and expression which comes over him when the analytic hour is over. It must be remembered that these small segments of behavior are occurring in a situation which the analyst is attempting to keep as neutral as possible, so that they are in one sense projections upon a relatively unstructured environment. On the other hand, the activity may have taken place at home or work and be related by the patient. It may be a change from customary behavior in the sexual sphere; the disappearance or appearance of a symptom; reacting with less or more anxiety to a given situation; a change in ability to tolerate friends and relatives. Activities both within the analytic hour and outside of it, then, are another source of analytic material. "Acting out" to some degree replaces free associations within the analytic hour.

TRANSFERENCE AND RESISTANCE

The intertwined concepts of transference and resistance are central to psychoanalytic psychotherapy. Freud makes transference and resistance *the* nucleus of psychoanalysis and indicates that they are the means whereby psychoanalysis may be distinguished from non-psychoanalytic approaches. In view of their importance a quotation from Freud is offered:

It may thus be said that the theory of psycho-analysis is an attempt to account for two observed facts that strike one conspicuously and unexpectedly whenever an attempt is made to trace the symptoms of a neurotic back to their sources in his past life: the facts of transference and of resistance. Any line of investigation, no matter what its direction, which recognizes these two facts and takes them as the starting-point of its work may call itself psycho-analysis, though it arrives at results other than my own. But anyone who takes up other sides of the problem while avoiding these two premises will hardly escape the charge of misappropriating by attempted impersonation, if he persists in calling himself a psycho-analyst. (13, p. 298.)

In view of its universality certain characteristics of the transference were discussed in Chapter 18 in the account of the patient-clinician relationship as a common factor in psychotherapy. To summarize this previous discussion: Its distinction from rapport was presented, its irrational, projective, and ambivalent nature was indicated, and the presence of the "preformed" transference was mentioned. It was also stated that what is distinctive to psychoanalysis is the use to which it is put—its demonstration to the patient and the tracing of it to its origins. Nonanalytic usage places heavy reliance upon the dependence which is a by-product of the transference to influence by suggestion the behavior of the patient.

The irrational element of the transference stressed in the earlier chapter is used for therapeutic purposes. Since the analyst maintains neutrality and the analytic incognito, many of the emotional reactions of the patient are not a result of the actual situation but clearly stem from the patient's own tendencies. The analysis of these transference reactions may lead to uncovering childhood experiences important in creating the tendencies.

As Thompson (39) puts it, the patient is led by transference phenomena to puzzle about the origins of his behavior which heretofore had been, partially at least, outside of his awareness. With increased insight the irrational trends tend to fall away and thus a permanent personality change occurs. Thomspon illustrates this by speaking of the fact that a patient may persistently try to please the analyst. For him the patient has nothing but praise and admiration and shows no anger or annoyance even in the face of disagreeable facts that are brought to his attention. When this is pointed out to him he is surprised that anyone considers this unusual. Presently, however, he begins to relate similar instances of behavior in relation to other people. He can then become gradually aware of the sources of such behavior, recognizing that his fear of disapproval is overwhelming. On beginning to wonder why such situations frighten him, he is lead back by his memories into his childhood and eventually to incidents which gave rise to the fear. To a considerable degree psychoanalytic therapy consists of a series of such discoveries with a consequent favorable modification of the personality of the patient subsequent to these insights.

The transference is in itself a repetition (18) of the forgotten past transferred onto the analyst. The patient expresses this not by recollection of past events but by repetition of feelings that were so important to him in the past. He does not say how critical he was of his parents; he becomes critical of the analyst. He does not remember his searching for the truth of sexual matters; he describes his lack of getting anything done now. He does not remember his shame concerning sex practices; he is ashamed and secretive concerning his being analyzed. Because of resistance he does not remember; instead he acts out. This is handled by analyzing with him what he is doing in the transference situation.

In the transference relationship existing during the early stages of psychoanalysis the patient's symptoms may disappear and an illusion of health appear. This is due primarily to the relief of anxiety occurring because of confidence in the analyst. Since this confidence is an aspect of the transference, the phenomenon is referred to as a "transference cure." Theoretically this state is transient because the unconscious processes have not been worked through. Nevertheless the changes sometimes appear to endure surprisingly well (cf., for example, Oberndorf, 34).

The repetition of neurotic patterns in relation to the therapist is called the transference neurosis. A short description as presented by Rado (36) gives an admirable summary. Even when there are realistic (rapport) elements in the relation of the patient to the analyst, the analytic setting prevents retaining of these, and the relation develops into one which is irrational, emotional, and regressive. At least in some aspects the analyst is seen as an omnipotent deity. The patient desires to be loved by the analyst and to have his every craving, including genital cravings, satisfied. In this he is disappointed, and his feelings of frustration give rise to either anxiety or anger. If anxiety predominates, an ingratiating, submissive attitude occurs with the patient courting the favor of the analyst. If rage prevails, he becomes pugnacious, assertive, and resentful. As mentioned before, this stems from childhood behavior toward parents in which there is an illusion that the parents are but the tools of his omnipotence. The task of therapy is to correct this attitude, for the patient cannot be realistic toward the rest of the world until he is realistic toward the analyst. The analyst must be on the alert to prevent the patient from substituting his withdrawal into a therapeutic relationship for real life experiences.

Alexander offers a succinct summary concerning the transference neuroses:

> The transference neurosis as a dynamic reenactment of the pathogenetic past now became the basis of modern psychoanalytic therapy. Freud recognized the immense therapeutic possibilities that this revival of past emotional difficulties offered for therapy. In the transference neurosis the original conflicts appeared in much smaller quantities. Moreover, not only was the intensity of the transference emotions smaller than that of the original ones, but now the stronger Ego of the adult was exposed to the same type of conflict which had overpowered the weak, infantile Ego in the past. In the transference situation the patient has a

splendid opportunity to grapple once more with the same emotional difficulties which he had not been able to master in the past—with his envy mixed with admiration and gratitude felt toward his father, older brother or other rivals; with the guilt feelings and anxieties which followed his envy and hostility; with his dependent, help-seeking attitude he felt toward his mother together with all his embitterment and resentment when his demands for love were not fulfilled and with his rebellion against maternal over-protection. After Freud recognized that all the deeply-ingrained emotional patterns of the patient, the whole infantile nucleus of his personality, gradually became freely expressed during the treatment as the patient's later acquired defenses against them are analyzed, the transference became the center of the whole therapeutic procedure. (3, p. 111.)

From time to time in this discussion resistance has been referred to; it is now appropriate to examine the concept more directly. Operationally speaking, anything that interferes with the course of analysis is resistance. Interpretations are offered the patient and meet with his disagreement; he struggles against them, tries to prove the analyst wrong, and so resists the progress of the analysis. Basically resistance exhibits itself by breaking the fundamental analytic rule—not confiding all thoughts to the analyst.

A great variety of concrete forms which resistance may take quite apart from direct repudiation of the analyst's interpretations can be cited: superficially fluent associations, dearth of associations, pauses in free associations, sudden or prolonged silence, tardiness, breaking appointments, new symptoms, falling asleep, and inaudible speech, to mention but a few. Resistance may demonstrate itself as early as the first hour in the avowal of having nothing whatsoever to talk about in spite of the fact that the patient has his whole life history to date upon which free associations may take form. Or he may prepare his communications in note form, ostensibly to hasten the analysis but really as a means of guarding against the appearance of anything he does not wish to talk or think about (17). Blockings in the ordinary psychological sense are often indicative of active resistance.

It is not difficult in general to understand why resistance develops. The patient has made some sort of adjustment, has found some way of handling life's problems. He struggles against associating freely because a sensitive area has been touched. However psychoneurotically determined his present defenses may be, they are a buttress against the world, the sanctity of which is now threatened. Not only that, but certain of the patient's desires and drives emerging into consciousness are such that he cannot at first accept them. They are too terrifying, too reprehensible for him to accept. He is afraid of his own drives and therefore does not admit them.

It is precisely because there is resistance that mere explanation, or reading a book, or attending a lecture is not enough for successful therapy. It is not ignorance but resistance that prevents the patient from understanding his difficulties. The task of therapy, then, is to analyze resistances in order to demonstrate how they prevent appraisal of what is causing the present discomfort. Lest the patient take flight—the ultimate in resistance, as it were—a firm transference is necessary before the resistance can be dissipated.

Summarizing the phases of treatment from the point of transference and resistance, Lorand writes:

The central problem of technique is the management of the transference, since the corrective process is accomplished through that relationship. Therefore the emotional implications, including the resistances in connection with the transference relationship, are of cardinal importance in analysis. As one proceeds with treatment, it becomes obvious that the therapy automatically divides into different phases (to which Ferenczi drew attention early in the development of technique). The first phase is taken up with concentrating on the patient's life history given with free associations, getting a picture of his behavior patterns and the history of their development, especially through observation of the nature of the patient's transference manifestations. In this phase the analyst's job is to observe and to encourage the patient to express his thoughts and feelings. With the realization that he is not being criticized, the patient loses some of his fear and guilt, hence the spontaneous improvement in the first phase. It is necessary to give some superficial interpretation at times, but as nearly as possible the transference should be left out of the discussion.

The second phase is marked by slow development of resistance in the patient as he becomes aware of his problems and realizes that he himself must do something about them. The transference relationship becomes prominent and its continual interpretation is of the greatest importance. The analyst becomes the center of the patient's desires for love, guidance, help, and the solution of all his problems. The desires not being realized, he then becomes the focal point of the patient's aggression. When that happens, resistance moves into the foreground. Reviewing the patient's behavior, connecting his current attitudes with his attitudes to people in the past, especially to those persons whom the analyst replaces in the patient's thoughts and fantasies, must be done over and over again.

This phase leads gradually to a weakening of the transference (the third phase) and the patient slowly learns to do things by himself, to be self-reliant. From time to time there will be a revival of the old desires for dependence on the analyst, which will result in repeated feelings of frustration, leading the patient to again try to stand on his own feet. The ego of the patient becomes gradually stronger until he is actually able to give up his dependence upon the analyst. (32, pp. 15–16.)

Transference and resistance are the crux of psychoanalytic technique, and in their vicissitudes it is possible to trace the essentials of the procedure.

COUNTERTRANSFERENCE

Psychoanalysis is very much of an emotional experience to the patient expressed through the transference; it is also an emotional experience to the psychoanalyst. This may express itself as countertransference, in which the psychoanalyst responds emotionally to the patient's emotional trends. The training analysis required for all would-be analysts, it might be argued, should make this impossible. An analysis, however, is not an absolute in the sense that there are no blind spots remaining in the personality structure of the analyst. Control of feelings toward a patient, without in the process becoming wooden and unresponsive, is a problem for all therapists. When the transference relationship is utilized and not avoided, as it is in some therapeutic approaches, the emotional contagion is likely to become greater. The patient's positive transference is in one sense unreal, since it is displaced, but one may slip and treat it as a reality. The analyst not only must understand the patient and respond to him, but must also observe and control his own attitude. For an extended discussion of this aspect of the transference problem the reader is referred to Lorand (32).

EGO ANALYSIS AND INTEGRATION

In the preceding section the emphasis that Freud placed upon transference and resistance was mentioned. An emphasis upon analysis of the effects of repressed Id impulses was also maintained. Over the years there was a gradual appreciation that ego functions were also a part of the process of psychoanalytic therapy and by no means an insignificant part. To be sure, Freud (21) himself touched upon this as an aspect of technique (as well as creating the metapsychology upon which it is based), but it is to later analysts, particularly Anna Freud (12), that the present-day emphasis is due.

As has been implied, the investigation of the Id is a means to an end—the correction of a malfunctioning ego. Although it was felt that the ego could not be altered without some Id-interpretations (the person becoming aware of his impulses, or rather his wishes), these interpretations were often rejected by the patient. In order to circumvent rejection, the patient's conscious attitudes must be analyzed before the repressed mental contents, perhaps obvious to the analyst, can be brought to consciousness in the patient. As French (11) states, it is now standard practice to forgo Id-interpretation until analysis of the strength and particular nature of the patient's conscious attitudes and behavior that will influence the resistance to such interpretation has been made. This is referred to as ego analysis.

The analysis of the patient's defenses leads to an understanding of his habitual modes of defense and prepares the way for providing him with better methods of handling his problems through more healthful organization of the ego. This means, in effect, that the analyst attempts to understand not only the roots in the past but what aspects of the patient's current life are dynamic at the moment —he primarily works with the present; he cannot analyze the past, but can only reconstruct it.

In stressing the aim of psychoanalysis to strengthen the integrative function of the ego, French (11) makes the point that the analyst must focus not only upon repressed impulses and ego defenses but also upon the problem for which the ego at that time is attempting to find a solution. As to how this may be done he writes:

Obviously, in order to understand the ego's integrative task at a particular moment we must first discover both the nature of the repressed wishes that are struggling to emerge into consciousness and also the nature of the defenses of the ego against these repressed wishes. But we must also attempt to reconstruct something more. We need to know not only the motives that have been repressed but also the motives that have given rise to the defensive reaction. It is important to determine, for example, whether a disturbing sexual impulse has been repressed on account of fear of punishment, of fear of loss of the mother's love, of guilt, or of pride. Then when we have determined the motive of the

defense we are ready to reconstruct the integrative problem with which
the ego is faced at this particular moment.

In each of the four cases above mentioned, for example, the ego's
problems will be different. In one case the patient's problem will be
either to find some outlet for his sexual impulses without incurring
punishment, or to find some way of reconciling himself to the punishment. In another the problem will be either to find some way of making
the disturbing impulse acceptable to the mother or to find some substitute that will make the patient less dependent upon the mother. In still
another case the problem may be either to find some way of compensat-
ing for the patient's injured pride or to modify the disturbing sexual
impulse so as to make it consistent with the patient's pride.

In order to reconstruct the ego's problem, however, it is necessary not
only to determine the nature of the conflicting motives but also to take
into account the patient's real situation in relationship to them. A patient whose central problem is to reconcile sexual impulses with his need
for the mother's love, for example, will find his problem much simplified
if some mother figure has just indicated to him what he might do to
please her.

Formulated from a somewhat different point of view, the ego's integrative problem at any particular moment is the problem in adaptation
presented to the ego by the actual situation at that time. For the sake of
clarity, however, it is important to emphasize that it is not only the real
external situation that constitutes the ego's problem but rather the conflicting needs with which the patient is reacting to this situation. It
will be noted that such an approach to therapy focuses our attention
systematically upon the patient's actual conflict at the moment rather
than upon infantile memories. (11, pp. 337–338.)

INTERPRETATION

As the sessions roll on, meanings and connections related to the
main problems facing the patient begin to appear. Naturally it is
the analyst who first begins to grasp the meaning of an apparently
disordered jumble. One of the problems demanding considerable
clinical acumen is the decision as to when to interpret the material
to the patient. This decision is based on estimation of the patient's
ability to stand the interpretation. This in turn depends upon the
presence of a dependable transference (17) and an understanding
of the ego's defenses. Certainly in no instance should interpretations
be hurled at the patient as amateur analysts sometimes do. Such
obtuseness, as in informing a person at the beginning that his difficulty has its roots in an incestuous attachment to his mother, can
only act to discredit psychoanalysis forevermore in the eyes of that

particular patient. A pre-psychotic may be pushed over the brink or an anxiety neurotic sent into a panic state by too early interpretations. Psychoanalysis cannot be shortened by pushing the patient too hard and sometimes it results in actual harm. Fundamentally this is because mere intellectual understanding is not enough. Violent resistance is likely to occur unless the patient is in a position to accept emotionally the revelations. Of course, when resistance does occur, whether because of prior interpretations or not, the resistance itself is then interpreted.

Interpretation emphatically is not advice, persuasion, or exhortation. The analyst's opinions and interests, from which the patient may get a clue as to what he thinks the analyst wants him to think, are avoided, as is all suggestion in the conventional sense (16).

It is appropriate to reintroduce at this point the question of the attitude of the analyst. At first glance this might appear irrelevant to the question of interpretation, but this is by no means the case. It will be remembered from Chapter 18 that there is always interpretation by the patient, no matter how little the therapist indicates his opinions in words. Expressive movements—a gesture, a raised eyebrow—mean something to the patient and probably not what the therapist intends. The analyst's private life, opinions, and interests are exhibited as little as possible and social contacts avoided. He will not join with the patient in his attempts to establish a more "comfortable," casygoing relationship. For example, if a patient jokes about his illness in an attempt to make light of it, he will find the analyst unresponsive. Efforts to establish such contacts are not accepted and are met by silence or an analysis of what the patient is attempting to do. This is a partial explanation of why accepting friends and acquaintances as patients is discouraged and why the couch is arranged so as to prevent visual observation of the analyst.

All of these maneuvers help to prevent distortion of the interpretation. They serve to attenuate those irrelevant factors that enter into the interpretations made by the patient. To be sure, "analytic incognito," as it is sometimes called, is even more fundamentally an aspect of the deliberate use of the transference for therapeutic ends, but it also serves to partially free the interpretations from these perverting factors.

It has been said somewhat flippantly that the psychoanalyst "cannot lose" concerning his interpretations and constructions. If there is acceptance by the patient it is obviously correct; if it is contradicted, resistance is operative and the interpretation is still correct. Freud (22) answers this directly and to the point. He states that occasionally a mistake is made, but that what appears to happen is that the patient is untouched by what has been said. The test of passage of time in the analytic hours is applied. New material will arise, virtually nullifying the incorrect interpretation. Incompleteness, not incorrectness, Freud felt to give rise to rejection of the interpretation communicated to the patient. Interpretations, then, are not irrefutable; their validity depends upon verification by the patient in later sessions through free associations (including memories) and dream material.

Freud (22) makes the apt suggestion that often one should speak of construction, not of interpretation. The latter term, although applicable to a single element of the material, does not convey the precise nuance of meaning as well as the former. Construction involves building up from material supplied by the patient and mediation through the analyst's therapeutic skill. From fragments of a dream, a chance slip, and a bit of overt nonverbal behavior he constructs that which leads him to understand a particular aspect of the patient's personality—a process somewhat akin to synthesis. It is through construction that he arrives at the formulation which he uses for later interpretation to the patient.

The art of interpretation is, according to Freud (18), essentially for the purpose of identifying the resistances as they come up and then making the patient aware of their existence. When the resistances are removed, the patient can proceed through free associations to the material heretofore repressed and thus facilitate the process of making unconscious material conscious.

WORKING THROUGH

Working through may be described as continuing the analytic work in the form of further special interpretations in spite of the patient's failure to accept or assimilate emotionally the interpretation or construction that has been offered concerning certain "warded-off" components of the personality. Since it is affective and not merely intellectual acceptance which produces therapeutic results, this becomes a critical issue. It is also a very time-consuming one, since many analytic hours are spent in this "daily routine," to use Bergler's (5) term.

Of what does working through consist? Bergler describes it as follows: "Experience simply teaches us that we have to apply the interpretations of resistances to acceptance and renunciation of unconscious wishes, feeling of guilt, unconscious repetitiveness, and defense mechanisms often and chronically in the transference neurosis on varying or repetitious material until those interpretations finally work—and that is enough." (5, p. 449.) The patient clings tenaciously to his infantile behavior. The analyst responds either by waiting, pointing out the resistance, giving the patient time, and patiently going over the material again and again from different angles, as Freud (18) suggested, or by becoming more active, as Ferenczi (10) recommended. It is the period of working through that must be learned from actual case experience since it is at this level that each case differs markedly.

TERMINATION

The question of when the analysis should be terminated is not one which permits a categorical answer. Indeed, Freud (21) indicated that some analyses theoretically may be interminable. On the other hand, all *do* terminate, and most with the concurrence of the psychoanalyst. Barring incomplete analyses due to extraneous circumstances, there are some cues for judging whether the analysis should be terminated (or perhaps merely interrupted).

The discussion in Chapter 18 of common factors operative in psychotherapy supplies a partial answer, but a statement in terms of psychoanalysis is now desirable. Since psychoanalysis primarily is a reconstructive or curative psychotherapy, indications of changes in personality organization must be present. The questionnaire study of Oberndorf (34) in which experienced analysts were queried on results of psychoanalytic therapy is pertinent. There was considerable agreement on the criteria for terminating analysis: achievement by the patient of the capacity to accept sexuality; better social adjustment; and understanding of the mechanisms responsible for the presenting difficulties. Other criteria mentioned by Lorand (32) are the reduction in tendency to become anxious, to regress, and to escape reality, and changes to a positive attitude toward and tolerance of other people.

The removal of infantile amnesia was originally postulated as an important indicator. If there remained an amnesia concerning the second to fifth year of childhood, then analysis was not complete.

On this criterion there is some disagreement today, and perhaps more characteristic indices are mentioned earlier. Further discussion is reserved for the next section of this chapter.

One intent of psychoanalytic procedure is to dissolve the transference relationship which has been operative between patient and therapist. So long as the infantile emotional tie exists—whether it be to the parent or parental representative in the person of the therapist—the analysand remains emotionally infantile. Working through the transference relation helps to start the patient toward independence. With the first transference interpretation, and with each correct interpretation thereafter, the transference is weakened because the patient is to that extent less dependent and more mature.

Thompson (39) stresses, as did Freud, the effect of the attitude of the therapist throughout all psychoanalytic sessions upon the transference as making for its dissolution. By pointing out that he is not angry or condemnatory or the source of all virtues, he eventually dissolves his unique position in the eyes of the patient and thus the transference is dissipated. By showing the patient that his feelings did not originate in the present situation but are a repetition of earlier experiences, the analyst helps to dissolve the transference. Repetition is transformed to recollection and thus the patient is free not only of the transference to the analyst but also of the effect of these feelings upon other day-to-day experiences. In becoming free of the transference, he becomes free of his neurosis.

A valuable discussion of termination has been provided by French (11). He suggests considering psychoanalysis as a learning process, in which case the problem of termination becomes one of whether or not the patient will learn more inside analysis or outside analysis. If this is done it would appear that the last phase of an analysis consists of learning to dispense with the support of the analyst. He cautions against doing this authoritatively or dogmatically and against setting an arbitrary date. A mere suggestion that the analysis must, of necessity, be terminated at some time is often sufficient to mobilize the patient's conflict about getting along without the therapist. Then a probing of the reasons for clinging to analysis may be carried on. French also mentions various indicators by means of which the analyst may note when the topic of termination can be plausibly broached, e.g., material alluding to the length of the analysis, its unnecessary character, excuses for continuing the analysis (as if answering an unspoken question), or material centering upon birth and weaning. Gradual decrease in number of visits, "temporary" interruptions, and other technical devices aid the analyst in the process of termination.

The Relation of the Common Factors in Psychotherapy to Psychoanalysis

In psychoanalysis three aspects of a curative process generally are said to be taking place: emotional abreaction or discharge, intellectual insight or understanding, and the appearance of conscious awareness of formerly repressed memories, particularly infantile.[2] In view of the earlier discussion it is unnecessary to discuss insight and abreaction again at this point, except to say that free association, once repression is removed, leads eventually to the emergence of repressed material. Not only is there insight but also considerable excitement and relief accompanying it. Thus we have all these acting together in concert to produce therapeutic change.

The appearance of repressed infantile memories does need discussion. In standard psychoanalytic tchnique this recollection on the part of the patient is considered to be curative as such (18). Stimulation of these memories, Freud insisted, led to insight and thus to cure. Recovery of lost memories is essentially a descriptive way of stating the issue; dynamically conceived, the resistances caused by repression are being removed. The recovery of infantile memories is used by some psychoanalysts in an operational fashion as one of the indicators that the task of psychoanalysis is reaching its closing phases. Baldly stated, if infantile memories are recovered, it is a sign that the psychoanalysis is relatively complete; if not recovered there is still work to be done. Such a position achieves its validity from the position taken concerning the genetic origin in infancy and childhood of the conflicts which now give rise to the present difficulties. This position concerning the primacy and curative value of recall of infantile memories is challenged by some analysts, by whom the recovery of memories is thought more a sign of improvement than its cause. To the extent that it is curative it may be subsumed under

[2] It will be noted that this agrees in the main with Ackerman, whose psychoanalytic formulation was used in the account of common factors in psychotherapy in Chapter 18.

insight, since remembering and understanding the origin of neurotic patterns aid in the reintegration of repressed psychological content in the personality structure.

Even if the previous exposition of standard psychoanalysis were found to be technically accurate in all particulars, in one sense it would still be false: no psychoanalyst follows precisely such an exact course. Variations are inevitably introduced, and it is these with which the next section of this chapter is concerned.

VARIATIONS IN PSYCHOANALYSIS

Variations in psychoanalysis take two forms: modifications within the orthodox framework hit upon more or less individually and reflecting the personal predilections of the analyst; and variations advanced as avowed changes in theory and principle, empowered with a systematic rationale. That these two kinds of variation tend to merge is inevitable, with a systematic change crystallizing at some point in an individualized exploratory process. Nevertheless, many variations are never more than expressions of the personality of the particular psychoanalyst.

Individual minor variations of the more obvious sort are no better exemplified than in the questionnaire study of Oberndorf (34), published in 1943, concerned with the results of psychoanalytic therapy. Eighteen analysts out of twenty-four to whom the questionnaire was sent replied. All had over twenty years' experience and were located in various parts of the United States. There was variation in the kind of patients treated, with some working only with the classical compulsions, phobias, anxiety states, etc., and others working with borderline cases such as schizoid personalities, mild paranoid trends, mild depressions, and "constitutional inferiors." Concerning the type of cases with which the most satisfactory results were achieved, no two replies were very similar. Oberndorf summarizes the responses to this question by saying that all forms of mental deviation short of full-fledged psychoses were mentioned as best suited for psychotherapeutic success with psychoanalysis. Some of the analysts tapered off treatment by gradually decreasing the number of hours; about an equal number did not, terminating abruptly and decisively after two or three hundred hours. Criteria for termination varied, but not as greatly as for the other items, with general agreement concerning the patient's acceptance of sexuality, better social adjustment, and understanding of the mechanisms responsible for the development of the original presenting situation.

It appears that even the most doctrinaire adherent to one systematic point of view and therapeutic technique does not follow it in precisely the same fashion with all patients. This would patently be absurd. A psychoanalyst who adhered to a classical standard approach might refuse to accept modification in such factors as number of visits per week or in accepting patients falling outside the traditional scope of psychoanalysis. Nevertheless he would still be willing to help train psychiatric residents by offering a psychoanalytically oriented interpretation of their short-term eclectic efforts or to consult with a social worker concerning her case work treatment of a child. He is no less a psychoanalyst when he does this than when working with his own private patients, even if he adopts the illusion that he carries out these "extra-psychoanalytic" endeavors in his role as a "psychiatrist" rather than a "psychoanalyst."

It is only with the increasing maturity of a point of view that its adherents can afford to be tolerant. In the past psychoanalysts were quite rigid and inclusive about what did or did not come under their banner, and there are still residuals of this within the psychoanalytic ranks. Deviation was punished formerly by expulsion, often vituperative in nature. Today it is recognized that deviations may or may not have been serious or fundamental.

For a long time psychoanalysis as a method of investigation and as a therapeutic procedure remained practically identical (Alexander, 1). The reason is not obscure—the patient's therapeutic needs coincided with the analyst's investigative aim. Alexander, at least, feels it is now time for considering the advisability of therapeutic innovations. He writes:

No etiologically oriented therapy can be developed without a thorough knowledge of the causes and nature of the disease. Freud attacked a practically unknown territory. In order to develop a sound therapeutic procedure which is not based on mere empiricism he had to explore the nature of neurotic disturbances and that required a knowledge of the dynamic structure of the total personality. The fact that he could utilize for therapeutic purposes a method which at the same time was a method of investigation accounts for the fact that psychoanalytic therapy and theory have developed hand in hand and that an originally modest therapeutic aim has led to the foundations of a new discipline, a dynamic theory of personality. The price for this great initial advantage we had to pay much later. Freud's main interest was, of necessity, investigative. We inherited his highly developed and standardized technique in the shaping of which his investigative interest played such an important role and continued to utilize it in the same manner for almost 40 years. We must admit that our field has lacked flexibility in therapeutic orientation. As long as one knew so little about the pathogenesis and pathology of neurotic disturbances it was justifiable, desirable, and unavoidable to study each case in extenso: each patient was at the same time a subject of research. With the advancement of our knowledge the time has now come when we can utilize sound generalizations and well established principles for a more direct and economic therapeutic procedure. (1, p. 321.)

A brief exploration of some of the numerous systematic variations will be made.[3] This account of psychoanalysis, it must be confessed, is incomplete in the sense that many of the variations, healthy and fruitful though they may be, will be neglected. The influence of Horney and her associates upon understanding of environmental forces; the eclectic spirit displayed by the Washington School and the William A. White Institute of Psychiatry, at least so far as fruitful interaction of individuals from many disciplines is concerned, are but two examples of approaches that have been neglected in favor of the more thorough prior coverage of the basic Freudian principles. To be considered are the briefer and more flexible techniques developed primarily by Alexander and his associates at the Chicago Institute for Psychoanalysis, hypnoanalysis, the treatment of psychotics, and psychological counseling as practiced by Peter Blos.

TECHNIQUES OF THE CHICAGO INSTITUTE FOR PSYCHOANALYSIS

Although a tool of fine precision, "standard" psychoanalysis as just described has about it a certain unwieldiness. Its requirement of many closely spaced interviews, for example, is entirely impracticable for most patients with psychological disturbances. Then too, only patients of certain diagnostic categories were considered appropriate. Such a rigidly fixed method, which must select patients to fit it, invites experimentation to find "practical and flexible psychoanalytic techniques," to use a phrase of Alexander's (2). Accord-

---

[3] For reviews of other psychoanalytic variants, see Fromm-Reichmann (23), Thompson (40), Waelder (41), and Watson (42). From these accounts some appreciation of the considerable sweep and scope of variations in psychoanalysis may be obtained, with the necessary next step to take being the reading of the sources to which they refer.

ingly, a series of innovations was introduced at the Institute for Psychoanalysis in Chicago, under the leadership of Franz Alexander (4). It was a continuation of a process, although differing as to particulars, that had been going on during the entire history of the psychoanalytic movement. More often than not the innovators, such as Adler, Jung, and Rank, found continued association with psychoanalysis as a movement and point of view impossible to maintain. Others, such as Abraham, Klein, and Ferenczi, were able to work for the most part within this framework. Alexander and his associates not only found this possible but today are considered by many of their colleagues to be among the leading psychoanalysts.

Certain of these innovations consist of modification of frequency of interviews both from patient to patient and from time to time in the same patient; the use of periods of interruption; the use of face-to-face interviews instead of the couch; a radical reduction in the total number of sessions; manipulation of extra-therapeutic experiences; varying the use of the transference such as by choice of a therapist according to age, sex, and personality considerations in relation to the nature of the interpersonal problems of the patient, or actively working to prevent the development of a transference neurosis; and the planning of a preliminary dynamic outline of strategy to be followed.

As stated so far, these innovations are given merely at a level of the trappings or externals of the process. The rationale is, of course, much more important. Take, for example, the question of daily interviews as contrasted with more widely spaced sessions. In part a decision in favor of the former would be indicated when it was judged that emotional discharge and insight should take place gradually in small doses, as it were, whereas a patient with greater ego-integrative capacity might receive "highly-charged" but infrequent interviews (Alexander, 1). This depends not only on the patient but also on the stage in which therapy may be at the time. Active intervention in the daily affairs of the life of the patient, although not unknown before, as the work of Ferenczi (10) indicates, received impetus from the work of Alexander and his associates because of the systematic way in which they studied the problem.

Although acknowledging the curative value of insight, emotional discharge, and assimilation of recovered unconscious material, Alexander (4) attributes the highest therapeutic significance to what he calls the corrective emotional experience. Exposure of the patient to planned emotional experiences is the means whereby this principle is implemented. This is not necessarily an experience within the analytic hour, and hence one of the reasons for the active intervention in the daily living of the patient that is occasionally used. Nevertheless, since the analytic hour is more controllable, it is there that the more significant and certainly more frequent corrective emotional experiences take place. The objective attitude of the analyst constitutes the most common means of providing this experience. Instead of encountering repressive and punitive measures, the patient meets an attitude of helpful, active, warm understanding on the part of the analyst. He can express his aggressiveness without being punished, and thus he realizes he is no longer a child facing an all-powerful father.

In one case, for example, the patient had lived in his father's shadow all his life. Instead of maintaining an understanding but more or less impersonal attitude characteristic of standard psychoanalytic practice, the analyst reacted quite differently. In meeting the patient's attempt to reinstate the old father-son attitude of rebellion and passive admonition in the analytic hour with rules of conduct to be supplied by the analyst, Alexander met it with unusual effort to praise the patient for his qualities and to take an interest in his business and social activities. The patient thus experienced a new father-son relationship and, having lived through it, could surrender his old attitudes. As a consequence the presenting symptomatology and faulty interpersonal difficulties cleared up.

Another illustration may be found in narcosynthesis in which the patient relives in fantasy the dangers of combat. His anxiety is reduced by the narcotic and the presence of a trusted physician, so that he is enabled to reëxperience the situation with less anxiety.

Alexander offers an excellent statement of his general approach in the following:

> Reexperiencing the old, unsettled conflict *but with a new ending* is the secret of every penetrating therapeutic result. Only the actual experience of a new solution in the transference situation or in his everyday life gives the patient the conviction that a new solution *is possible* and induces him to give up the old neurotic patterns. By repetition, these corrected reactions gradually become automatic; the ego accepts the new attitudes and integrates them into the total personality. It is thus that therapeutic results become consolidated.

In the patient-physician relationship, the therapist has an unique opportunity to provide the patient with precisely that type of corrective experience which he needs for recovery. It is a secondary question what technique is employed to bring it about. The *standard* psychoanalytic technique is only one—and not in every case the most suitable one—of the many possible applications of fundamental psychodynamic principles that can be utilized for this kind of emotional training. Moreover, every therapy which increases the integrative functions of the ego (through reexposing the patient under more favorable conditions to those conflicts which have before been met with neurotic defense mechanisms) should be called psychoanalytic, no matter whether this duration is for one or two interviews, for several weeks or months, or for several years. (4, pp. 338–339.)

It is the contention of Eissler (9)[4] that Alexander and his associates systematically minimize the therapeutic significance of insight. This may be the case, although careful study of their work shows that they consider other experiences to precede and pave the way for insight. It is true that in supportive techniques insight is regarded as less important than in uncovering techniques, but this is hardly a heretical doctrine. Certainly in 1944 Alexander (1) called the appropriate combination of insight and emotional experience the very essence of psychoanalytic therapy, and Eissler's criticism scarcely seems justifiable.

HYPNOANALYSIS

For some years early in his professional career Freud used hypnosis as a primary therapeutic technique. The emotion discharged on reactivating under hypnosis a significant (especially a traumatic) memory was considered to have therapeutic value. Although he later rejected hypnosis as a technique, stating specifically that psychoanalysis came into being only after hypnosis was abandoned, this historical footnote is of some importance. For many years then psychoanalysts including Freud paid little attention to hypnosis. According to Brenman and Gill (8), the first simultaneous application of psychoanalysis and hypnosis was that of Simmel immediately preceding and during World War I. It is, however, only in comparatively recent years that more than sporadic attention has been paid to this problem. It is to the work of Brenman and Gill (8) (26), Lindner (30) (31), and Wolberg (43) (44) (45) (46) that much of the recent interest in this problem is due.

The manner of integrating hypnotic technique with psychoanaly-

---

[4] Eissler (9) offers an extensive critique of Alexander's position.

sis varies. For example, transference manipulation may or may not be used (8). A common element is the use of hypnosis to circumvent resistances (8). Lindner (30), for example, uses free association until he encounters serious resistance and then places the patient in deep hypnosis to obtain the withheld material. Another closely related function is the use of hypnosis as a device whereby material is uncovered, in contrast to other uses of hypnosis as a form of suggestion for covering up traumatic material. The therapist using hypnoanalysis consider the hypnosis a means to an end, and the common factors of insight, release, and so on presented in Chapter 18 are regarded as fundamental for any lasting modification.

TREATMENT OF PSYCHOTICS

The more difficult it is to form a therapeutic relationship, the more fragile and elusive are therapeutic results. Accordingly, if the individual is in some degree incapable of transferring emotional reactions, analysis becomes very difficult or impossible. This includes extreme narcissists and psychotics. Freud himself was exceedingly pessimistic of therapeutic success with these "narcissistic neuropsychoses," although holding that psychoanalysis could be used as an investigative technique. With the treatment of children in about the early 1920's by psychoanalytic principles (discussed in Chapter 21) many of the classical orthodox techniques had to be abandoned; the use of the couch, free association as a method, the passivity, the manner of interpretation, the number of sessions per week—all of this and more had to be modified in working with children. With these changes came the recognition that other changes, similar in spirit if not in form, might result in adaptation of psychoanalysis to the treatment of the psychotic.

The application of psychoanalytic principles and technique to the narcissistic disorders including schizophrenia is a fascinating modification of classic psychoanalysis. Originally deterred by Freud's stand concerning the essential untreatability of schizophrenia by psychoanalysis, it was characteristic that innovations and applications were attempted upon the American scene. Interesting as these variant and to some degree successful attempts may be, to explore them would go far beyond the present scope of the psychologist's practice. The interested reader might find in the representative references that follow some acquaintance with a variety of psychoanalytic approaches: Fromm-Reichmann (24) (25), Knight (28) (29), and Rosen (37) (38).

PSYCHOLOGICAL COUNSELING BASED UPON PSYCHOANALYTIC PRINCIPLES

Insights from psychoanalytic theory and practice are undoubtedly applied in many situations in which psychological counseling is called for. At the level of ego functioning many psychologists (including, of course, psychologists who are also lay analysts) are equipped to use successfully these findings. Even here extensive and directed prior training is necessary.

Blos has presented two papers (6) (7) on psychological counseling of college students which illustrate a psychoanalytically oriented approach to the matter. It is his experience in a college guidance clinic that when major mental disturbances and definitely neurotic cases are eliminated by referral to appropriate psychiatric sources a large proportion of emotionally disturbed individuals still remains. They have in common a dysfunction in a limited sphere of activity but no definite symptom complex or rigid, repetitive, neurotic patterns. He considers this kind of disturbance particularly prevalent among college students, where adolescence with all its usual turmoils is exacerbated by the artificially prolonged maturational period. If unchecked, these disturbances might well become full-blown neurotic patterns. Such a patient rarely comes to the attention of regular psychiatric services, since he is still seeking solutions on his own or is in the process of isolating conflicts by symptom formation. It is this sort of patient that Blos considers to be the legitimate field of psychological counseling.

In the description of his procedure he emphasizes the continuing character of the counseling process. At the level of ego defenses an attempt is made to resolve the presenting conflict—inability to study, ambiequal vocational preferences, desire to make friends but inability to do so, habitual evasion of responsibility, to name several. Resolution of conflict stimulates insight and growth, which gain after a lapse of time may in turn stimulate realization of other problems with the result that counseling is resumed. This, of course, in the college setting is quite possible and even appropriate.

It was mentioned that it was at the level of the ego that this approach functions. An ego too weak to withstand the conflict situ-

632 The Clinical Method in Psychology

ation is present. According to Blos, two characteristic reactions to the maturational crisis are ego restriction and ego regression. Both serve as protective measures, the former warding off anxiety through inhibition of function (for example, failing in spite of high scholastic aptitude) and the latter through archaic ego expression (as in attributing "magical" powers to one's thinking).

Blos's approach may perhaps be elucidated by the following quotation:

> Psychological counseling does not attempt to resolve unconscious infantile conflicts; in fact, it carefully avoids entering this sphere which is the realm of psychoanalysis. Psychological counseling deals with the derivatives of these conflicts in terms of ego reactions. In its interpretative aspect it restricts itself to the realm of the ego. . . . [In a case Blos described] it brought to awareness the relatedness of isolated facts, some of which come only very slowly to the surface. While dissociated conscious material could be related, an insight into ego defenses was gained through the interpretation of omissions, contradictions, denials, forgetfulness, etc. All these efforts would have been fruitless without a purposeful use of the transference. Here the unconscious conflicts which were recognizable during the counseling process found a mode of expression and communication where the direct verbal expression would obviously have been inadequate. (6, p. 632.)

Although present, transference is maintained at a level in which the therapist seeks at all costs to prevent the development of a transference neurosis. This is done for two reasons: first, he is not equipped to handle it since it would mean interpretation of unconscious material; and second, treatment may be carried out successfully without it, providing the individual was selected according to the principles previously outlined. If the conflict is fully internalized psychological counseling is not indicated. With these restrictions it may be seen that psychological counseling has a limited objective, since unconscious conflicts are of course as here described playing their part even if avoided in the therapeutic procedure.

NONDIRECTIVE PSYCHOTHERAPY

The appearance of Carl Rogers' *Counseling and Psychotherapy* (55) in 1942 constituted a milestone in the history of psychotherapy in psychology. The signs were uniformly propitious for its arrival—psychologists were becoming more interested in the practice of psychotherapy; the demand for such services in the college counseling field had increased; the military setting opened up new vistas for therapeutic personnel. To all these movements the book added impetus and interest. This was as true for psychologists who opposed Rogers' principles as for those who enthusiastically accepted them. In fact the new "school" was soon to be paid the dubiously valuable compliment of the development of opposing camps.

Two features of Rogers' method help to account for his immediate influence. Before his work there were a few psychologists with established reputations as psychotherapists, but most of them were functioning as representatives of one or another of what may be called *psychiatric* approaches to psychotherapy. For better or for worse, the nondirective approach was considered by psychologists to be their very own. Just as the social worker looked for an approach of his own "in order to feel authentic" (see Chapter 23), so did the psychologist find in nondirective psychotherapy a means whereby he could make a contribution *as a psychologist*. That this particular point of view had many roots in psychiatric thinking and practice is beside the point. Armed, at least in some respects, with an ignorance of past psychiatric work and separated from it by lack of professional contact, the young enthusiast could feel at ease about his status.

The second aspect of the development of this point of view in which all psychologists may feel some pride is the emphasis placed by Rogers from the first on research, in particular suggesting the use of electrical recordings as its medium. In keeping with the scientific tradition of psychology, this struck a responsive chord and gave the new endeavor a certain air of respectability.

Nondirective psychotherapy as presented in the book just mentioned is both a method and a theory of psychotherapy drawn from Rogers' experience in child guidance and student counseling. Since the original account appeared in 1942 there have been various modifications or extensions and ramifications. It is therefore appropriate, before examining the present nature of nondirective psychotherapy, to investigate critically this important volume especially since critics of the approach are occasionally guilty of writing as though this volume represented the final word on Rogers' point of view.

ROGERS' "COUNSELING AND PSYCHOTHERAPY"[5]

The point of view set forth in *Counseling and Psychotherapy*

---

[5] The assumption of some familiarity with this book (55) is made throughout this discussion.

(55) is much more eclectic than is the more fully developed and systematic one now advanced. The sources mentioned as giving rise to "a newer psychotherapy" (55, p. 27) are those which many non-Rogerian therapists would accept as admirably summarizing their own intellectual predecessors. Again, when Rogers describes the nature of this new point of view and the charactcristic steps in the therapeutic process, little will be found that can be called distinctive to the nondirective approach.

Superficial scrutiny obscures the uniqueness of anything, however, and it is important to examine more fully this question of the characteristics of the "newer" approach. Four features are mentioned by Rogers as distinguishing the modern approach to psychotherapy, nondirective therapy being one such approach. First it aims at the greater independence of the individual with freedom for spontaneous growth on his part. Second, the newer approach lays more stress upon emotional or affective elements than upon intellectual factors in the therapeutic process. Third, there is greater stress on the immediate situation than upon past events. Fourth, the therapeutic relationship is seen as a growth experience itself.

With one exception these have been stressed in the discussion of common factors in psychotherapy in an earlier chapter. The exception is the stress on the immediate situation versus the historical past. Of course, all psychotherapy deals with the present situation to some degree, but Rogers was referring to the therapeutic efficacy of the present experience without appealing to the past at all. In Chapter 19 this was seen as a source of variation in present-day psychotherapy, with Rogers, Allen, and others stressing the immediate experience, while classical psychoanalysis exemplifies the other point of view. As was pointed out, certain variations of psychoanalysis stress the immediate experience, and even classical psychoanalysis considers present defenses. Because of this and the fact that other present-day approaches stress etiology, it is reasonable to conclude that the statement is not necessarily correct concerning *all* modern points of view. It is characteristic of Rogers' approach, as well as that of Allen, John Levy, and others, but it is not a distinctive characteristic of all such approaches. The other three points, it must be emphasized, are quite acceptable to many psychotherapists of different theoretical approaches.

In the early chapters of the book there is a foreshadowing of the development of a negative attitude toward diagnosis which later became firmly crystallized. Here also is found the demand that therapy have complete freedom from coercion (which Rogers apparently thinks is characteristic of many therapists). In general the early chapters present an admirable introduction to psychotherapy but are open to the charge that the material is selective and not always comprehensive.

The criticism of "some older methods" of psychotherapy, i.e., ordering, exhortation, suggestion, catharsis, advice, and intellectualized interpretation, is open to some dispute. Treating each of them in isolation, as Rogers does, it is relatively easy to demonstrate individual weaknesses. Indeed, many of his arguments have their counterparts in an earlier discussion in the present book. The fallacy would appear to be this: proceeding from the premise that they have been misused, he concludes that they should be discarded (with the one exception of catharsis). This is felt by some psychotherapists, including the writer, to be unwarranted. In the present volume the intent has been to show they *do* have a place, although not a tremendously important one. Nevertheless, the position taken by Rogers can be pursued to a logical victory, once the desirability of the *completely* "nondirective" and "client-centered" nature of psychotherapy be accepted.

The study of Porter (52), used by Rogers in another section of the book to illustrate the characteristics of both directive and nondirective psychotherapy to set the stage for his later development of the nondirective point of view, is perhaps accepted too readily as personifying the techniques of both nondirective and directive counselors. In this early attempt to study counseling interview procedures, Porter, using college counselors, found the characteristics of some "directive" counselors—talking much more than the client, delimiting development of a topic to confirming it, denying it, or supplying specific items of information, and so on. Though his findings are undoubtedly correct for some counselors, they are not typical for other "directive" counselors and even less when counseling in the narrow sense is left behind and one enters the realm of psychotherapy in general. Certainly many non-Rogerian therapists talk less than their patients and do not define for them how they are to reply to their questions.

The individual case study which occupies the last third of the volume illustrates many of the characteristics of the nondirective approach. It is now conceived by Rogers (56) to show many subtly directive elements and thus is not typical of present-day practice.

The 1942 formulation (55) of the basic hypothesis of nondirective psychotherapy was stated as follows: "*Effective counseling consists of a definitely structured, permissive relationship which allows the client to gain an understanding of himself to a degree which enables him to take positive steps in the light of his new orientation.* This hypothesis has a natural corrolary, that all the techniques used should aim toward developing this free and permissive relationship, this understanding of self in the counseling and other relationships, and this tendency toward positive, self-initiated action." (55, p. 18.) Although in certain particulars it might be expressed somewhat differently today, this is by no means an outmoded statement. It remained for later thinking to formulate the theoretical substructure more clearly and completely than did this earlier statement.

There has been a relatively recent attempt to substitute the term "client-centered" for "nondirective" psychotherapy. The reservation of this term for nondirective psychotherapy quickly aroused some antagonism in other psychologists, who were quick to point out the connotation that no other approach centered interest in the patient. Since this is obviously not true and other therapeutic approaches do seek to work with and for the patient, the term is unfortunate despite the fact that the meaning thus attributed to Rogers' point of view is not the one he intended, as will be demonstrated shortly. Nevertheless, because this incorrect meaning is so readily and so often given, it was considered advisable not to use the term in this volume and, instead, to use the earlier, and still generally acceptable term, "nondirective psychotherapy."

The major aspects of nondirective psychotherapy to be considered in turn are the role of the nondirective therapist, the role of the patient and his interaction with the therapist, the presence of the common factors of psychotherapy, distinctive characteristics of the technique, the self concept, the scope of application of the method, and a brief review of some case studies available.

The Role of the Nondirective Therapist

The role of the nondirective therapist is crucial to an understanding of the nature of nondirective psychotherapy. It is the activities chosen by the therapist that determine the nature of any psychotherapy. As will be demonstrated shortly, the stereotype of passivity gentrally attributed to the nondirective therapist is hardly that—he carries on many activities which through research efforts have been rather sharply isolated and defined.

One excellent source for an account of the role of the therapist is found in the work of Snyder (59), who, in his study of the nature of nondirective psychotherapy, described certain categories of behavior by the therapist. This conceptual classification, it must be pointed out, did not necessarily originate with him. Many of the categories were stated by Rogers in his earlier account, *Counseling and Psychotherapy* (55), e.g., "recognition of feeling." Since Snyder's publication they have found more or less general acceptance as adequate for conveying the role of the nondirective therapist. Forty-eight therapeutic sessions by four therapists in the treatment of six cases formed the data for this study. A majority of the sessions were electrically or stenographically recorded. A classification system of statements and responses of therapist and patient was worked out, the nature of which will be described shortly. Snyder broke down each statement into the essential ideas and classified them according to this system. A reliability check more than a month later yielded about 80 percent for exactly the same category and 85 percent for main groups. An untrained scorer did somewhat less efficiently.

Figure 7, which presents the categories of activity of the therapist,

FIG. 7. Definitions of Therapist Categories[6]

Lead-Taking Categories. (Those which seem to determine the direction of the interview; which indicate what the client should be talking about.)

Structuring. Remarks which define the counseling situation. Remarks indicating the purposes the interview may be expected to accomplish, or the responsibilities of both individuals; i.e., telling "What we can do here." Also includes remarks setting the time and limits of the interview, but not those relating to the end of the interview; would include "You can have just an hour," but wouldn't include "I see you've come to the end of the hour."

Forcing client to choose and develop topic. Includes all efforts of the counselor to reject responsibility for the direction of the interview. For example: "What shall we talk about today?" or "Well, how do *you* feel about it?"

---

[6] Adapted from "An investigation of the Nature of Non-Directive Psychotherapy" by W. U. Snyder (59), by permission of the *Journal of General Psychology*. Copyright 1945 by the Journal Press.

Directive questions; specific types of questions. Asking an outright question which requires the giving of a factual answer. It does not include interrogative statements which are merely intended to redefine, clarify, or redescribe a feeling. It would include "What do you think of that?" "How old are you?" "Do they resent the fact that you are not aggressively going out after jobs?" It would not include "And you aren't too happy about it?" or "It's rather unpleasant for you, is that right?," particularly when such questions follow somewhat similar statements.

Non-directive leads and questions. Statements which encourage the client to state the problem further. This excludes leads that would greatly limit the client in what he could bring out about the problem or his feelings about it. It would include "Tell me more about it," or "Would you like to tell me how you feel about it?" or "How are you today?" (asked in a general sense). In general this type of lead is one that encourages a statement without limiting the nature of the response except in a very general way, as in "Tell me more about it."

Non-Directive Response-To-Feeling Categories. (Those which seem to attempt to restate a feeling that the client has expressed, but not to interpret or to offer advice, criticism or suggestions.)

Simple acceptance. "Yes," "M-hm," "I see," "That's right" (if not answering question) or similar responses. Must not imply approval or criticism.

Restatement of content or problem. A simple repeating of what the client has said without any effort to organize, clarify, or interpret it, or any effort to show that the counselor is appreciating the feeling of the client's statement by understanding it. The wording need not be identical with that of the client.

Clarification or recognition of feeling. A statement by the counselor which puts the client's feeling or affective tone in somewhat clearer or more recognizable form. "It makes you feel very much annoyed," "You love your mother but you resent her telling you what to do," "I think sometimes you wish you'd never been born."

Semi-Directive Response-To-Feeling Category. (Those responses which are interpretive in character.)

Interpretation. Responses in which the counselor points out patterns and relationships in the material presented. This category is always used when causation is implied or indicated. "You do this because . . ." If the counselor attempts even vaguely to say "why" the client does or feels something it is considered interpretation. "Perhaps you are revealing feelings of inferiority." "When people feel frustrated they often act the way you do." "There's your problem."

Directive Counseling Categories. (Categories of responses which imply a relationship in which the counselor attempts to change the immediate ideas of the client or to influence his attitude toward them.)

Approval and encouragement. "That's fine." "You've covered a lot of ground today." "You bet!" Any statement which lends emotional support or approval to the client's insecurity.

Giving information or explanation. Answers to any questions about the nature of psychology or any other informational material; anything which is recognized as a generally established fact; any personal information about the counselor.

Proposing client activity. Any statements which imply that the client should take any sort of action.

Persuasion. Attempts to convince the client that he should accept the counselor's point of view. "Don't you think it would be better that way, now?"

Disapproval and criticism. "You need to get hold of yourself."

Minor Categories. (Those responses which do not seem to be related to the principal problem of the client.)

Ending of the contact. Any responses dealing with the bringing to a close of the contact, or with the setting of a time for a future contact.

Ending of the series. Responses relating to the bringing to a close of the series of interviews, or to the beginning of the client's feeling that he does not need further contact.

Friendly discussion. Material unrelated to the client's problem, and serving only the pu'pose of establishing good rapport between client and counselor.

Unclassifiable. Any response which cannot be classified in one of the above categories.

exemplifies the nature of what the therapist does during the course of his sessions with the patient and is well worth careful study. It will be noted that so-called semidirective (interpretative) and directive categories are also included. One might fairly say, on the basis of Snyder's analysis, that the more important categories, in the sense that they are the ones nondirective therapists strive to use, are structuring, nondirective leads, simple acceptance, restatement of content or problem, recognition of feeling, and, above all, clarification of feeling.

In the results found with these categories, clarification of feeling comprises almost half the statements of the four nondirective therapists, decreasing from 44 percent of all responses in the earlier stages of treatment to about 26 percent in the late stages. Simple acceptance accounts for 25 percent of the therapist's statements at the beginning and at the end of treatment, rising to about 33 percent in the middle of the sessions. The therapist's use of structuring, persuasion, disapproval or criticism, approval or encouragement, and nondirective leads comprises less than 10 percent each of his total responses. Structuring and nondirective leads tend to decrease, and disapproval, persuasion, and especially approval and encouragement tend to increase as the sessions progress. Since the cases all followed roughly the same pattern, there would appear to be indications of a definite progression in nondirective psychotherapy.

It will be noted that certain directive techniques were used by nondirective therapists. Approval and encouragement, which are directive in nature, fell within the second largest grouping of counselor responses. Other directive categories together made up only a few percentage points of all therapists' responses. Thus the therapist attempts to use recognition or clarification of feeling, simple acceptance, and other nondirective techniques, while attempting to avoid the giving of information or advice, the use of verbal reassurance, argument, persuasion, the asking of questions, or the offering of interpretations. Most of these tools of therapy have been discussed in the previous chapters, so that redefinition is unnecessary.

No doubt as skill has increased and more consistent application has been made of the nondirective principles, there has been a trend to use fewer of these directive and semidirective procedures. This presumption receives confirmation in the study of Seeman (58), who in 1949 replicated in all essential details the study of Snyder. Whereas nondirective responses made up 63 percent of the total in Snyder's group, they had increased to 85 percent by the time of Seeman's sampling. A striking shift occurred in the category of "approval and encouragement." In the former study rather numerous responses were so classified; five years later there was only a single such response. The disappearance of this technique reflects current thinking. For the client categories there was substantial agreement with Snyder. As Seeman indicates, the peripheral elements of a hypothesis tend to fall away as it becomes clearer, making for sharper focus on the central components.

The account so far may have given the impression that nondirective psychotherapy is rather a cold application of certain rules in an intellectual game with no real personal interest on the part of the therapist. Sometimes the nondirectivist is depicted merely as repeating "M-hm," or "You feel . . ." in a mechanical parrot fashion as the sessions drone on. This is not the case. There is warmth in nondirective therapy. This was discussed specifically by Snyder (60) in a paper in which he demonstrates the ways in which the therapist "produces a high degree of rapport through warmth." (60, p. 491.) Thus the therapeutic relationship, posited as one of the basic common factors in psychotherapy (see Chapter 18), is again found to be acknowledged. After noting that phonographically recorded interviews in print do seem cold and formal and that novices, as in any approach, often appear wooden and stiff in their slavish attempt to be nondirective, Snyder points out that structuring, friendly conversation, approval, and above all permissiveness and clarification of feeling act so as to produce the warmth.

It will be noted that nondirective psychotherapy as described above is presumed to function at the level of rapport, not that of transference. Sometimes the nondirective approach is criticized for manipulating the transference situation while denying that this is done, e.g., Lowrey (50). It would seem that a recognition that nondirective therapy sometimes does function at a level properly called transference has appeared among nondirective psychotherapists. Snyder (64), for example, advances the opinion that "transference in the sense of fixation of normal and legitimate attachments on the counselor" and negative transference do take place in nondirective practice. The exact lines of relationship, similarity, and dissimilarity remain to be worked out. Although the nondirectivist does not offer interpretations of the transference, it is handled in a non-threatening manner operating to reduce defensiveness and release spontaneous growth processes by means of the permissiveness and neutrality of the therapist.

Thus far, nondirective psychotherapy at the level of technique is seen to consist of the application of certain procedures and the avoidance of others. In later developments Rogers has formulated the role of the nondirective therapist somewhat differently in that the emphasis is shifted from *technique* to *attitude*. Discussing the role of the pychotherapist in producing a nondirective therapeutic relationship he states that the necessary conditions will be present if the following elements are present:

(1) If the counselor operates on the principle that the individual is basically responsible for himself, and is willing for the individual to keep that responsibility.

(2) If the counselor operates on the principle that the client has a strong drive to become mature, socially adjusted, independent, productive, and relies on this force, not on his own powers, for therapeutic change.

(3) If the counselor creates a warm and permissive atmosphere in which the individual is free to bring out any attitudes and feelings which he may have, no matter how unconventional, absurd, or contradic-

tory these attitudes may be. The client is as free to withhold expression as he is to give expression to his feelings.

(4) If the limits which are set are simple limits set on behavior, and not limits set on attitudes. (This applies mostly to children. The child may not be permitted to break a window or leave the room, but he is free to feel like breaking a window, and the feeling is fully accepted. The adult client may not be permitted more than an hour for an interview, but there is full acceptance of his desire to claim more time.)

(5) If the therapist uses only those procedures and techniques in the interview which convey his deep understanding of the emotionalized attitudes expressed and his acceptance of them. This understanding is perhaps best conveyed by a sensitive reflection and clarification of the client's attitudes. The counselor's acceptance involves neither approval nor disapproval.

(6) If the counselor refrains from any expression or action which is contrary to the preceding principles. This means refraining from questioning, probing, blame, interpretation, advice, suggestion, persuasion, reassurance. (56, p. 416.)

It will be noted that only the last two elements concern techniques as such; the first four points are primarily concerned with the attitudes of the therapist.

In the formulations of Snyder in terms of techniques and Rogers in terms of attitudes we have the epitome of the role of the nondirective therapist and therefore of the nature of nondirective psychotherapy.

In nondirective psychotherapy the role of the counselor is not passive; instead it calls for very severe self-discipline. The counselor must trust the patient to solve his own problems and make his own decisions. The counselor must concentrate on what the patient is feeling through what he is saying so that he can select and clarify these feelings. This, it will be recognized, requires self-vigilance that can hardly be called passive.

The nondirective therapist would contrast this orientation with the more directive role that he claims traditional psychotherapy demands. With this one can take issue to the extent that stringent dichotomy is implied. Long before the appearance of the nondirective approach, psychoanalytic practitioners had demonstrated the errors of too much activity on the part of the therapist, expressed in overinterpretation, encouragement, deliberate suggestion, and so on. Misuse of directive techniques seems to lead to a desire to dispense with them altogether. In one sense the nondirectivist is correct, in that he has carried the position to a logical extreme.

THE ROLE OF THE PATIENT AND HIS INTERACTION WITH THE THERAPIST

Perhaps one would assume the role of the patient to be the same —to act so as to find relief from his difficulties—no matter what system his therapist represents. Nevertheless, just as a patient anticipates behaving differently if consulting a surgeon rather than a dermatologist, so must patients seeking psychotherapy modify their own behavior in the therapeutic sessions in accordance with the procedures of their chosen therapist. For illustrative purposes it will be helpful to refer again to Snyder's study (59), which classified behavior in terms of subject matter or content and the accompanying feeling observed.

In terms of content there were several major categories. There was the "problem" category in which the patient's statements describing his difficulties were classified. There were several so-called "simple response" categories, such as those involving requests for advice, answers to a question, and simple acceptance or rejection. Understanding or insight formed another major category, described in this context as indications by the patient that he had been able to see patterns or interrelationships (excluding what appeared to be rationalizations). The last major content category was that of the discussion of plans or the possible outcomes of plans. With regard to feeling, nine categories were used. These included positive, negative, and ambivalent attitudes toward self, the therapist, or other persons or situations. The patients' responses were classified and analyzed in the same fashion as were therapists' statements.

It was found that about one-third of the patients' responses dealt with statements concerning their problems. At the beginning of therapy problem statements comprised about 50 percent, falling off toward the end of treatment to about 18 percent. Insight responses formed about 12 percent of the responses at the beginning, 28 percent in the middle, and 30 percent at the end of treatment. Discussion of plans was practically zero at first, increasing to about 12 percent of responses in the last interview. Thus the initially important statements of problems decreased as the interviews proceeded, while insight and understanding, originally relatively insignificant, rose to an appreciable amount of the patient's interview responses toward the middle and end of the therapeutic sessions.

Affective tone also changed throughout the therapeutic sessions, with a marked predominance of negative attitudes in the first few sessions and a significant shift toward positive attitudes as therapy continued. Ambivalent attitudes were prominent in the mid-period, where the patient was still vacillating between positive and negative attitudes, with some patients never quite reaching positive attitudes. A study by Raimy (54) confirms Snyder's finding by showing that the positive changes in attitude increased toward the end of therapy with successful cases but not with unsuccessful ones. In Snyder's study the attitude of the patient toward the therapist was usually slightly rejecting at first and indifferent thereafter until the last session, in which there was a marked appearance of positive feelings.

The remaining major issue to consider at this point is that of the interaction between patient and therapist. Snyder framed this matter in terms of the tendency for certain types of patient responses to follow and others to be absent when certain types of therapist statements are made. Snyder (64) now feels that this sequel relationship was too atomistic, i.e., the patient's responses result from more than the just-previously-made response of the therapist. In 1942–43 there were not available the methods for studying larger units of interview material that have since been developed. However, to summarize Snyder's findings: statements of the patients' problems most frequently followed nondirective leads, such as simple restatements of what was said, and, in some cases, followed approval and encouragement. Problem statements almost never followed interpretation, persuasion, or criticism, and seldom followed structuring, questioning, or clarification of feeling. Acceptance most often was produced by clarification of feeling. Insight most frequently followed acceptance or approval and encouragement. Although clarification of feeling (the major therapist activity) did not seem to produce understanding and insight, its function of effectiing simple acceptance was judged to be important in the gaining of rapport and in the free expression of attitudes on the part of the patient.

The patients strongly rejected interpretation, persuasion, and disapproval, and frequently rejected direct questions and attempts to structure the situation. Such relations in Snyder's estimation strengthened the value of nondirective techniques, since positive changes were predominantly associated with their presence.

THE PRESENCE OF THE COMMON FACTORS OF PSYCHOTHERAPY

Emotional release and insight are spoken of as basic to nondirective psychotherapy by Rogers (55). Release of feeling leads to insight, which in this instance is conceived as the perception of new relationships, a willingness to accept the self, and a new choice of goals. There follows self-initiated action toward achievement of these goals.

Curran's study (47) admirably illustrates certain aspects of the interrelationship of these three factors in his analysis of the therapeutic process of a single case for which all twenty interviews had been electrically recorded. Among the major categories isolated were negative emotional responses, insight responses, and choice responses. Included in the first category were patient responses judged to demonstrate hostility or defense, dependency, rejection of self, escape (daydreams, rationalization, self-vindication), social maladjustment (feeling of frustration, conflict, insecurity), and expressions of confusion, fear, and unhappiness. Included in the second, or insight, category were patient responses considered as mediating attempts at facing reality, indicating willingness to accept responsibility and make decisions, seeking relationships and patterns of conduct, and working out solutions. Included among responses in the third, or choice, category were patient responses concerned with making decisions about himself or others, changing his pattern of conduct, and taking steps toward social adjustment. Expression of negative emotional responses was found to be a means of release. Insight responses were a means whereby new choices were visualized. New choices led to more satisfying ways of solving conflict problems. Using three independent judges Curran found that progress toward adjustment was correlated with high content of negative emotional factors in the earlier interviews, leading to a gradual falling off and a concomitant rise of insight responses in later interviews.

Three of the common factors posited in Chapter 18 are thus utilized. Nor is the factor of the patient-clinician relationship (expressed at the level of rapport as much as possible) neglected, as can be gathered from the previous discussion of the roles of the therapist and patient and their interrelationship. Likewise the growth factor is carried to its logical extreme.

THE DISTINCTIVE CHARACTERISTICS OF NONDIRECTIVE PSYCHOTHERAPY

Rogers (56) advances three characteristics as differentiating most sharply the nondirective approach from other procedures. Briefly, these are the predictable nature of the process of nondirective psychotherapy, its discovery of the constructive forces residing in the patient, and the "client-centered" nature of the therapeutic relationship.

In connection with its predictable nature Rogers leans most heavily upon the study of Snyder (59) previously discussed in detail. In this study it will be remembered that Snyder found the cases he analyzed to follow a roughly parallel course—an initial phase of release, followed by one in which insight is prominent, and a last phase in which positive action predominates. Consequently it is unnecessary to review this so-called distinctive feature further. This distinction between the nondirective approach and other ways of viewing the therapeutic relationship (which by implication are unpredictable) is one which adherents of other points of view may well dispute. With some justice they may claim, as can be gathered from the description earlier in the chapter of standard psychoanalysis and of the briefer techniques of Alexander and French, that with their approaches also there seems to be a more or less predictable course.

Turning to the second point—the discovery of the capacity of the client—it would appear that the nondirective point of view has carried this perhaps further than any other therapeutic system. Rogers writes, "The individual is capable of discovery and perceiving, truly and *spontaneously* [italics the present writer's], the interrelationships between his own attitudes, and the relationship of himself to reality." (56, p. 418.) The emphasis is on the spontaneity of the process and upon the fact that this "self-actualization . . . may act as the sole motivation for therapy." (56, p. 418.)

According to Rogers, the element of discovery is not original with the nondirective point of view. Other therapists have spoken of growth forces but never did trust them to function alone, introducing instead directive elements to help the process along by intervention. Rogers claims that there is acceptance of the patient by the therapist, but acceptance of a limited and grudging nature. He writes:

> There has, of course, been lip service paid to the strength of the client, and the need of utilizing the urge toward independence which exists in the client. Psychiatrists, analysts, and especially social case workers have stressed this point. Yet it is clear from what is said, and even more clear from the case material cited, that this confidence is a very limited confidence. It is a confidence that the client can take over, if guided by the expert, a confidence that the client can assimilate insight if it is first given to him by the expert, can make choices providing guidance is given at crucial points. It is, in short, the same sort of attitude which the mother has toward the adolescent, that she believes in his capacity to make his own decisions and guide his own life, providing he takes the directions of which she approves. (56, p. 418.)

The unguided use of the potential personality resources of the patient functions best in those situations previously sketched, i.e., he must retain sufficient personality integration to be capable of utilizing them. Research on this measure to indicate the limits to which nondirective therapy may go is obviously indicated. That there is a growth principle operative to facilitate therapy has been acknowledged to the extent of considering it one of the basic common factors of psychotherapy, but Rogers feels that "unguided" the patient may still reach psychological adjustment. Although this may be true of some patients, it has yet to be proved for the majority of patients and is probably the greatest focal point for criticism of his point of view.

In the previous chapter the position was taken that the dismissal of the necessity for diagnostic appraisal (along with the incidental dismissal of diagnostic tests) was untenable in at least most psychotherapeutic settings. Such a dismissal, erroneous though it may be, is seen to stem from this same principle.

The third distinctive feature—the client-centered nature of the therapeutic relationship—is closely related to the previous one, but emphasis is shifted to the character of the *relationship* between therapist and patient which implements spontaneous self-actualization. It is Rogers' contention that the client-centered attitude is maintained only when the patient's frame of reference is utilized. To the extent that the frame of reference of the therapist enters, the therapy is not client-centered. This implies, for example, that a psychoanalyst, who has had training in theory and practice of a particular point of view and applies this in his therapeutic work, is not "client-centered" because his frame of reference enters in the picture. From his background and experience he offers an interpretation to the patient, utilizing his own frame of reference rather than that of the patient. In nondirective psychotherapy the emphasis is upon understanding the patient in the way he understands himself. To use more common terminology: the patient must be accepted fully and whole-heartedly. Thus the concept of acceptance, it would seem, has been elevated to a position of supreme deity capable by itself of producing changes. This ennobling is evident in a further quotation: "The therapist must lay aside his preoccupation with diagnosis and his diagnostic shrewdness, must discard his tendency to make professional evaluations, must cease his endeavors to formulate an accurate prognosis, must give up the temptation subtly to guide the individual, and must concentrate on one purpose only; that of providing deep understanding and acceptance of the attitudes consciously held at this moment by the client as he explores step by step into the dangerous areas which he has been denying to consciousness." (56, p. 421.)

This emphasis on the client-centered attitude and the appreciation of its influence has gradually absorbed the former preoccupation with *technique*. In nondirective psychotherapy techniques for producing a permissive, accepting relationship developed before the theoretical explanation of their nature or the reason for their necessity. It is because of this that both techniques and attitudes were discussed in connection with the earlier section of the role of the therapist.

It may be noted that if appeal to a specific permissive attitude or other attitudes be made as basic to nondirective therapy on the theoretical basis of "personal integrity and self-directedness" and the "capacity for adaptation" (61), or a positive drive for growth (56), this opens up the possibility that techniques not now included within the nondirective armamentarium are consistent with the system. Some therapists would consider that questioning, giving interpretations, approval and disapproval, and the dissemination of information are consistent with these principles. At the present stage of evolution of principles of psychotherapy it would be difficult if not impossible to settle the issue. Rogers would contend that they are not permissible, presumably on the ground that they destroy the positive growth drive's chances of operating.

THE SELF CONCEPT IN NONDIRECTIVE PSYCHOTHERAPY

In a very important study in the history of nondirective psychotherapy Raimy (54) was concerned with the changes in personality of the nondirectively treated patient. On the basis of his objectively formulated study he concluded that the patient's improvement was primarily a matter of the manner in which he perceived himself and the persons and objects surrounding him. In comparing the incidence of positive, negative, and ambivalent self-references in successful and unsuccessful cases, he found distinct differences between the two groups. In the successful cases the positive self-references increased toward the end of therapy, while negative and ambivalent self-references decreased almost to the point of complete disappearance in the final interview. This did not take place in the unsuccessfully treated cases. Thus change in the self concept is viewed as a significant factor in nondirective psychotherapy.

The implications of Raimy's study initiated a very interesting and fruitful period in the development of nondirective psychotherapy. Indeed, Rogers (57) based his 1947 presidential address before the American Psychological Association on the relation of the organized perceptual field to behavior and the relation of the perception of self to adjustment and the conditions of change in self-perception.[7] Although differing in some respects from Raimy's formulation he agreed on the importance of the individual's perception of self as the basis of understanding what is happening in nondirective psychotherapy. Nevertheless, Rogers' observations were made "quite aside from any question regarding nondirective therapy as therapy." (57, p. 358.) Although present interest is centered upon "therapy as therapy" the implications of this remark might be explored further.

The inference the writer draws is that the self concept is not an essential feature of the nondirective approach. Quite apart from Rogers' comment, this can be inferred from its development *after* the appearance of a more or less systematic statement of the position. A stress on other features may be noted. Porter (53), for example, emphasizes the value of nondirective techniques in enabling the patient to learn new emotionalized attitudes. The importance

---

[7] For a critique of this presentation see Ellis (48).

of "acceptance" and "rejection" in describing the dynamics of non-directive therapy has been demonstrated by Miller (51). This is not to say that either Porter or Miller does not now accept emphasis on the self concept. Quite possibly, even probably, they do. It is in a sense the orthodox nondirective position. However, it is possible to accept the technique of nondirective psychotherapy but reject the self concept as a theoretical basis.

THE SCOPE OF APPLICATION OF NONDIRECTIVE PSYCHOTHERAPY

There is some confusion and divergence of opinion as to the scope of application of nondirective psychotherapy. On the one hand, some enthusiasts consider it a panacea for all psychological difficulties, no matter what their nature. This position is given impetus by Rogers' repudiation of diagnosis as described in the previous chapter. At the other extreme, excluding those who would not use it at all, are those who find the approach useful either with some patients throughout all sessions, with a particular patient, or during some (generally earlier) sessions with subsequent change to other techniques and approaches. They may be characterized as the extreme nondirective approach and the eclectic approach, respectively. Somewhere in between are the great majority of nondirective psychotherapists who apply it consistently or not at all, but apparently use some diagnostically derived discretion in its application.

Since 1942 when Rogers (55) offered certain cautions on the breadth of applicability of the nondirective approach he has written very little on the subject. Present practice makes it obvious that the rule (55) that it is most effective with relatively normal individuals with some capacity for personality integration still holds, but it can be inferred from such statements as Rogers' comment reported in Snyder (68) that with the psychotic in a controlled environment nondirective psychotherapy is definitely feasible. Also he makes passing reference (56) to a patient near a schizophrenic break with whom the method was used, suggesting that the boundaries have since been extended.

What is the nondirectivist position on this matter today? Rogers is sometimes inveighed against as claiming that the nondirective approach is suitable for any and all cases of individuals showing psychological difficulties. Although some of his followers have strengthened this impression, it would perhaps be fairer to say that recently he has *not* said with what cases it is *not* suitable. This semantic difference apparently means that Rogers reserves the right, which is his due, to be silent on this matter until actual trial and research reveal the limitations that should be placed on its application. By implication it does not mean, however, that the approach is suitable for any and all instances in which psychotherapy would seem to be necessary. Undoubtedly misuse of nondirective therapy has occurred and will continue to occur until its limitations are better and more widely appreciated.

A positive statement of scope by Snyder (63) is worth summarizing. He considers the nondirective approach most applicable with college students, since their problems generally lie within themselves rather than in environmental sources. Marital adjustment problems, vocational counseling, parent-child relationships, and the problems of mildly psychoneurotic persons (especially anxiety states and some of the hysterical syndromes) would appear to be well suited for its application. It is used less frequently with psychotics, those of low intelligence, those over fifty years of age, those who find it difficult to verbalize (including those who are so emotionally disturbed as to be unable to do this), and the excessively dependent person.

Turning from the position of avowed nondirective therapists it is informative to examine what others have said about the matter of its scope. Thorne (65) (69), a very vocal and severe critic of the nondirective approach when used in extreme form to the exclusion of all other methods, has also written on this subject. Thorne, unlike Rogers, does not consider a lapse from complete nondirectiveness a grave therapeutic error. Rather he considers that from one case to another, from one session to another, and even within a single session there may be varying degrees of directiveness and nondirectiveness. This attitude represents the position taken by many therapists who use nondirective approaches not at all times but from time to time as need dictates. Thorne claims that there is a continuum involving degrees of directiveness. This is strongly supported by an analysis offered by Wrenn (66), suggesting that a great deal of therapeutic effort falls at points other than at the extremes of this continuum of emphasis. To Wrenn the essence of skillful therapy consists in knowing when to use the varying procedures along the continuum. Thorne (65) would state the nondirective-directive continuum in terms of indications for the use of nondirective and directive methods. Only extreme cases are amenable to pure directive or nondirective methods, with the modal case being most effectively handled by a judicious combination of both methods. Even if nondirective methods were originally emphasized, sooner or later there will be indications demanding active intervention. Thorne (65) further finds nondirective therapy generally valuable in creating rapport and transference and in eliciting from the patient an expression of his most urgent problems. In addition, if the patient shows reasonable progress with nondirective techniques because he is capable of maintaining a healthy independent state, then it is proper to continue unless and until an impasse is reached.

In private practice Thorne has used the nondirective approach consistently in initial contact with 200 cases, continuing to do so until in his clinical judgment other techniques became necessary. On the basis of his opinion, which he states may have suggestive value only, he summarizes:

The numerical distribution of case results has no significance because of the uncontrolled conditions. The small number of cases in each category, and the lack of rigidly controlled procedure make impossible any reliable or valid analysis of results. However, a number of tentative conclusions may be stated based on the totality of clinical impression. First, it will be noted that nondirective methods appear to have more valid application with the minor personality problems and transient reactions to acute stress. With the more severe syndromes of psychoneuroses, pathological personalities and psychoses, nondirective methods were rarely the method of choice and were used only for limited objectives to supplement more directive methods. Second, nondirective methods were most commonly used in initiating therapeutic contacts, to build up rapport, to elicit the case history in uninterrupted manner, and to facilitate emotional expression. Thirdly, consideration of all the various types of syndromes encountered emphasizes the importance of diagnostic studies in evaluating counseling and psychotherapy. It immediately becomes apparent that a wide variety of methods are indicated for a wide variety of different conditions. Finally, although it might be argued that nondirective methods had not been carried out intensively enough to give them a fair trial, and also that they were perhaps not executed with maximum proficiency, we believe it fair to state that they were applied as conscientiously as *possible* in the situation of private practice where it is necessary to compromise between many different pressures. The conclusion from this preliminary qualitative appraisal of nondirective methods is that they are of very definite value for certain specific indications but that they have no universal validity as a complete system of therapy.

With minor personality reactions, and in the presence of unimpaired resources, nondirective methods may be sufficient. But with the more severe psychoneurotic and psychotic syndromes, nondirective methods operate only on superficial levels and are of only limited value. (65, pp. 259–260.)

These findings, although interesting and informative, may be challenged by the nondirectivist on the grounds that Thorne gives no description of the actual procedures which he calls "nondirective." There is evidence from Snyder (68), speaking from the point of view of a nondirectivist, that Thorne can be said to misuse nondirective techniques. With this caution and the obvious fact that Thorne used nondirective techniques only to the point where he felt it advisable to give them up, it is significant that he found them of considerable value.

In the opinion of many clinicians, the needs of patients cannot be met with only one technique of treatment. The gamut of human suffering associated with psychological factors is wide; the nondirective approach is but one among many.

Case Studies

As mentioned before, Rogers now believes that the case given in his 1942 volume, *Counseling and Psychotherapy* (55), shows what appears to be directive elements. The case of Mr. M. presented by Snyder (67), although perhaps more characteristic, also is said by Rogers to show this deficiency. It is important, however, as the means whereby a penetrating criticism of the entire approach was made by Thorne (69), to be followed by a spirited rebuttal on the part of Snyder (68). Another and undoubtedly the best complete · source is the casebook edited by the same writer (61). Five cases, one each from the therapeutic practice of Snyder, Rogers, Muench, Combs, and Axline, exhibiting a variety of problems, are described. Large sections of the therapeutic sessions are quoted verbatim from the recorded materials. Footnotes commenting on the therapist and patient responses add enlightening information. For at least one interview of each case presentation Snyder has categorized all statements according to the classification system described earlier in this chapter. The cases bring out very lucidly the nature of nondirective therapy and also, as some critics including Ellis (48) point out, highlight certain possible limitations.

ECLECTIC APPROACHES TO PSYCHOTHERAPY

A psychotherapist can utilize one approach, use interchangeably a number of approaches, or, more commonly, develop his own approach from an intermingling of many sources. Eclecticism may follow the pattern of using a particular systematic point of view and its related procedures with one patient and a different point of view with another patient. This is likely to create a somewhat distressing if not faintly humorous situation, described very well by Bordin (70). To paraphrase him, a psychotherapist is well entitled to be appalled at the thought of being a psychoanalyst at nine o'clock, a nondirective therapist at ten, and a release therapist, à la Levy, at eleven, not to mention an afternoon spent with Anna Freud, Alexander and French, and Thorne. Fortunately most therapists do not face quite so grim a schedule. There is usually selection of patients at least as to age and severity of illness and a consequent reduction in the variety of approaches necessary.

The ludicrousness of the above situation makes apparent the fact that eclecticism seldom expresses itself as the assumption of one systematic role with a given patient and a different one with a new patient. Instead, what is generally seen is an intermingling of procedures with each patient, drawn from many sources, with modifications governed by the needs of the particular patient.

Eclecticism is most often manifested in the utilization of a variety of approaches selected not in terms of their consistency with a given system but in terms of their efficacy for particular disorders as supported by the experience of the therapist. To carry the discussion one step further, one might inquire why this is done and why it seems to make for therapeutic success. Although no definitive answer can be given, the reasons for their selection and success apparently reside in the sources of variation described in Chapter 19.

By the very nature of this type of eclecticism it is impossible to describe it generally. Presumably the common factors in psychotherapy are operative, but again this is an instance in which differential emphasis on some now, others later, is placed.[8]

---

[8] Among psychologically trained therapists, Thorne's writings in the eclectic tradition are well known. From time to time articles describing his approach have appeared (73) (74) (75) (76) (77) (78) (79) (80) (81) (82) (83) (84) (85) (86) (87) (88). In the main they are concerned with descriptions

Saslow and Buchmueller (72), working in an eclectic tradition, admirably capture some of the nuances of variations in procedures in a description of cases in which they have observed improvement in spite of the following:

1. Change of therapist's behavior (from "passive" to "active," from completely non-judgmental to skeptical or critical, etc.) within an interview, or from one interview to another.

2. Shift from one therapist to a second, or a third, of different sex, age, ability and experience—when, in the patient's view, there is acceptable reason for the shift.

3. Responsibility of one therapist for the patient *and* for one or more signficant persons in his environment (mother, spouse, child, etc.). The other person(s) may be seen in separate interviews over the same period of time as the patient is seen; or after the patient's visits are over, for the time being; or in joint interviews with the patient during all or some of the original patient's therapeutic work.

4. Deliberate use of as many avenues of access to the patient's behavior as possible, all with the patient's consent. This includes obtaining school, health and employment records; interviewing significant persons (spouse, children, employer, teacher, doctor); therapy for any of these who wish it; use of two therapists with one patient (one seeing him for particular purposes, such as to review his situation at the moment, or to intensify his concern with a particular problem, or to habituate him to forthright dealing with some one less close to him than the regular therapist); use of physical therapy; use of occupational therapy; use of vocational counseling; use of effective drugs, surgery or medical consultation.

5. Considerable variation in the therapist's interaction with the patient after the early interviews (in which he tries to adjust himself as perfectly as he can to the patient's behavior). Thus, interrupting, disapproving, doubting, rejecting, praising, forbidding, warning (as of too large steps in learning new behavior), suggesting, ordering, are all within the tolerance of many patients and actually speed-up their mastery of desired behavior.

6. Very variable intensity and therapeutic importance of the transference relation. Strong transference is rare, even in seriously disturbed

---

of procedures together with discussions of indications and contra-indications. An integrated presentation in book form is to appear shortly. Illustrations from the work of other men may be found in Watson (42). The account by Lewis (71) in the *Readings*, although related to a nondirective point of view, is considered to describe essentially eclectic psychotherapy at a relatively simple level. Her acceptance, permissiveness, sensitivity, nonmoralizing attitude, and lack of emphasis on "technique" combine to create an atmosphere conducive to psychotherapeutic gain.

patients. Direct use of the transference relation (as by the Chicago Psychoanalytic Institute) is rarely practiced. The patient-therapist relationship is treated explicitly as a transference one only to the degree made necessary in the individual situation—very rarely may this be to the maximum degree.

7. Very variable intensity, duration and importance of narrated and re-experienced infantile and early childhood experience. In general, only enough seems necessary for the patient to recognize that his present behavior has origins which seem relevant and convincing, and to come to terms with a specially disturbing early interpersonal relation. . . .

8. Failure to use Freud's conception of an invariant relation between the adult personality and the management of infantile physiological drives, and of his tripartite theory of personality structure. . . .

9. Infrequent and minimal "resistance" seems to us to be encountered when the process of therapy takes place as described above, as contrasted with frequent and severe difficulty in learning other types of problem-solving techniques. Repeatedly we find evidence (for example, in psychological testing) that inflexibility is manifest in less significant or non-traumatized areas of living, as well as in intensely involved ones. . . .

10. The expression of minimal affect in interviews. Face-to-face, pertinent, intellectual discussion with minimal associated affect seems often to be extremely effective in leading to successfully altered behavior. With moderate frequency, brief intense affect can be expressed.

11. The effect of interview discussions upon severe phobias. These may disappear without special repeated desensitizing procedures or unusually long therapy.

12. Failure to work through all the problems uncovered. Only a few need to be worked out, since the therapist attempts to raise the patient's self-awareness to a high level of generalization of his problems and problem-solving techniques. The starting point is the specific, easily observed dysfunctions, and the patient learns to define the larger context of such dysfunctions and to act more successfully in relation to such a context. Hence he learns a technique of general applicability to many problems not discussed with the therapist. . . .

13. Very variable number and length of interviews and the total duration of therapeutic relationship. Two interviews (one day apart) may terminate a problem of two years' standing, and no more may need to be done. Seven interviews may most effectively be spaced over seven months. Very rarely do the interviews exceed 50 in number, or extend for more than one year. The first few interviews may be very short. Increases and decreases in the length of, or interval between, interviews, and changes in the therapist's behavior can all be suited to fluctuating needs of the patient, with apparently little

risk of "dependency reactions," "acting out," psychotic episodes, etc. (72, pp. 9–10.)[9]

It is apparent that simultaneous application of these procedural variations runs counter to the tenets of at least two systematic approaches previously described. For example, they shift from a "directive" to a "nondirective" therapeutic role; the transference relation is found by them to be a factor of variable intensity and relative importance; the amount of affect compatible with improvement is also considered to be very variable including instances in which there is "minimal associated affect." Nevertheless, they demonstrate in their case presentations that therapeutic success has been achieved. From the writer's point of view the common factors in psychotherapy are felt to be operative, even though it would be difficult, if not impossible, to discern their operation from this necessarily short statement.

BIBLIOGRAPHY

PSYCHOANALYSIS

1. Alexander, F., The indications for psychoanalytic therapy, *Bull. N.Y. Acad. Med.*, 1944, 20:319–332.
2. Alexander, F., Practical and flexible psychoanalytic techniques, *Digest Neurol. & Psychiat.*, 1945, 13:283
3. Alexander, F., Individual psychotherapy, *Psychosom. Med.*, 1946, 8:110–115.
4. Alexander, F., and French, T. M. (eds.), *Psychoanalytic therapy: principles and application*, The Ronald Press Company, 1946.
5. Bergler, E., "Working through" in psychoanalysis, *Psychoanal. Rev.*, 1945, 32:449–480.
6. Blos, P., Psychological counseling of college students, in Watson, R. I. (ed.), *Readings in the clinical method in psychology*, Harper & Brothers, 1949, pp. 625–637. (Also in *Amer. J. Orthopsychiat.*, 1946, 16:571–580.)
7. Blos, P., Indications and contra-indications for psychological counseling, *Amer. J. Orthopsychiat.* (to appear).
8. Brenman, M., and Gill, M. M., *Hypnotherapy: a survey of the literature*, International Universities Press, 1947.
9. Eissler, K. R., The Chicago Institute of Psychoanalysis and the sixth period of the development of psychoanalytic technique, *J. gen. Psychol.*, 1950, 42:103–157.

---

[9] Reprinted from "Flexible Psychotherapy in Psychosomatic Disorders" by G. Saslow and A. D. Buchmueller, by permission of *Human Organization*. Copyright 1949 by the Society for Applied Anthropology.

10. Ferenczi, S., *Further contributions to the theory and technique of psycho-analysis*, Hogarth Press, 1926.
11. French, T. M., Ego analysis as a guide to therapy, *Psychoanal. Quart.*, 1945, 14:336–349.
12. Freud, A., *The ego and the mechanisms of defense*, Hogarth Press, 1937.
13. Freud, S., On the history of the psycho-analytic movement, in *Collected papers*, Vol. I, International Psychoanalytical Press, 1924, pp. 287–359.
14. Freud, S., The employment of dream-interpretation in psycho-analysis, in *Collected papers*, Vol. II, Hogarth Press, 1924, pp. 305–311.
15. Freud, S., The dynamics of the transference, in *Collected papers*, Vol. II, Hogarth Press, 1924, pp. 312–322.
16. Freud, S., Recommendations for physicians on the psycho-analytic method of treatment, in *Collected papers*, Vol. II, Hogarth Press, 1924, pp. 323–333.
17. Freud, S., Further recommendations in the technique of psycho-analysis: on beginning the treatment, the question of the first communications, the dynamics of the cure, in *Collected papers*, Vol. II, Hogarth Press, 1924, pp. 342–365.
18. Freud, S., Further recommendations in the technique of psycho-analysis: recollection, repetition and working through, in *Collected papers*, Vol. II, Hogarth Press, 1924, pp. 366–376.
19. Freud, S., *Collected papers*, Vol. III, Hogarth Press, 1925.
20. Freud, S., The interpretation of dreams, in Brill, A. A. (ed.), *The basic writings of Sigmund Freud*, Modern Library, 1938, pp. 179–549.
21. Freud, S., Analysis terminable and interminable, in *Collected papers*, Vol. V, Hogarth Press, 1950, pp. 316–357.
22. Freud, S., Construction in analysis, in *Collected papers*, Vol. V, Hogarth Press, 1950, pp. 358–371.
23. Fromm-Reichmann, F., Recent advances in psychoanalytic therapy, *Psychiatry*, 1941, 4:161–164.
24. Fromm-Reichmann, F., Problems of therapeutic management in a psychoanalytic hospital, *Psychoanal. Quart.*, 1947, 16:325–356.
25. Fromm-Reichmann, F., Notes on the development of treatment of schizophrenics by psychoanalytic therapy, *Psychiatry*, 1948, 11:263–273.
26. Gill, M. M., and Brenman, M., Treatment of a case of anxiety hysteria by an hypnotic technique employing psychoanalytic principles, *Bull. Menninger Clin.*, 1943, 7:163–171.
27. Gill, M., and Menninger, K., Techniques of hypnoanalysis illustrated in a case report, *Bull. Menninger Clin.*, 1946, 10:110–126.
28. Knight, R. P., The place of psychoanalytic therapy in the mental hospital, in Glueck, B. (ed.), *Current therapies of personality disorders*, Grune & Stratton, 1946, pp. 59–69.

29. Knight, R. P., Psychotherapy of an adolescent catatonic schizophrenic with mutism; a study in empathy and establishing contact, *Psychiatry*, 1946, 9:323–339.
30. Lindner, R. M., *Rebel without a cause: the hypnoanalysis of a criminal psychopath*, Grune & Stratton, 1944.
31. Lindner, R. M., Hypnoanalysis as psychotherapy, *Dis. nerv. Syst.*, 1945, 6:371–374.
32. Lorand, S., *Technique of psychoanalytic therapy*, International Universities Press, 1946.
33. Maslow, A. H., and Mittelmann, B., *Principles of abnormal psychology: the dynamics of psychic illness*, Harper & Brothers, 1941.
34. Oberndorf, C. P., Results of psycho-analytic therapy, *Int. J. Psycho-Anal.*, 1943, 23:107–114.
35. Oberndorf, C. P., Constant elements in psychotherapy, *Psychoanal. Quart.*, 1946, 15:435–449.
36. Rado, S., The relationship of patient to therapist, *Amer. J. Orthopsychiat.*, 1942, 12:542–543.
37. Rosen, J. N., A method of resolving acute catatonic excitement, *Psychiat. Quart.*, 1946, 20:184–198.
38. Rosen, J. N., The treatment of schizophrenic psychosis by direct analytic therapy, *Psychiat. Quart.*, 1947, 21:3–37, 117–119.
39. Thompson, C., Transference as a therapeutic instrument, in Glueck, B. (ed.), *Current therapies of personality disorders*, Grune & Stratton, 1946, pp. 194–205.
40. Thompson, C., *Psychoanalysis: evolution and development*, Hermitage Press, 1950.
41. Waelder, R., Present trends in psychoanalytic theory and practice, in Lorand, S. (ed.), *The yearbook of psychoanalysis*, Vol. I, International Universities Press, 1945, pp. 84–89.
42. Watson, R. I., Treatment as an aspect of the clinical method, in Watson, R. I. (ed.), *Readings in the clinical method in psychology*, Harper & Brothers, 1949, pp. 674–718.
43. Wolberg, L. R., *Hypnoanalysis*, Grune & Stratton, 1945.
44. Wolberg, L. R., Hypnosis and psychoanalytic therapy (hypnoanalysis), *Amer. J. Psychother.*, 1947, 1:412–435.
45. Wolberg, L. R., *Medical hypnosis: the principles of hypnotherapy*, Vol. I, Grune & Stratton, 1948.
46. Wolberg, L. R., *Medical hypnosis: the practice of hypnotherapy*, Vol. II, Grune & Stratton, 1948.

NONDIRECTIVE PSYCHOTHERAPY

47. Curran, C. A., *Personality factors in counseling*, Grune & Stratton, 1945.
48. Ellis, A., A critique of the theoretical contributions of nondirective therapy, *J. clin. Psychol.*, 1948, 4:248–255.
49. Ellis, A., review of Snyder, W. U. (ed.), *Case book of non-directive*

counseling, Houghton Mifflin Company, 1947, in *J. soc. Psychol.*, 1949, 29:125–129.

50. Lowrey, L. G., Counseling and therapy, *Amer. J. Orthopsychiat.*, 1946, 16:615–622.
51. Miller, H. E., "Acceptance" and related attributes as demonstrated in psychotherapeutic interviews, *J. clin. Psychol.*, 1949, 5:83–88.
52. Porter, E. H., Jr., The development and evaluation of a measure of counseling interview procedures. I. The development. II. The evaluation, *Educ. Psychol. Measmt.*, 1943, 3:105–126, 215–238.
53. Porter, E. H., Jr., The learning of emotionalized attitudes in the counseling situation, *Pers. Counselor*, 1947, 2:174–179.
54. Raimy, V. C., Self reference in counseling interviews, *J. consult. Psychol.*, 1948, 12:153–163.
55. Rogers, C. R., *Counseling and psychotherapy: newer concepts in practice*, Houghton Mifflin Company, 1942.
56. Rogers, C. R., Significant aspects of client-centered therapy, *Amer. Psychologist*, 1946, 1:415–422.
57. Rogers, C. R., Some observations on the organization of personality, *Amer. Psychologist*, 1947, 2:358–368.
58. Seeman, J., A study of the process of non-directive therapy, *J. consult. Psychol.*, 1949, 13:157–168.
59. Snyder, W. U., An investigation of the nature of non-directive psychotherapy, *J. gen. Psychol.*, 1945, 33:193–224.
60. Snyder, W. U., "Warmth" in nondirective counseling, *J. abnorm. soc. Psychol.*, 1946, 41:491–495.
61. Snyder, W. U. (ed.), *Casebook of non-directive counseling*, Houghton Mifflin Company, 1947.
62. Snyder, W. U., The present status of psychotherapeutic counseling, *Psychol. Bull.*, 1947, 44:297–386.
63. Snyder, W. U., Client-centered therapy, in Pennington, L. A., and Berg, I. A. (eds.), *An introduction to clinical psychology*, The Ronald Press Company, 1948, pp. 465–497.
64. Snyder, W. U., personal communication, 1950.
65. Thorne, F. C., Further critique of non-directive methods of psychotherapy, *J. clin. Psychol.*, 1948, 4:256–263.
66. Wrenn, C. G., Client-centered counseling, *Educ. Psychol. Measmt.*, 1946, 6:439–444.

Supplementary articles in Watson, R. I. (ed.), *Readings in the clinical method in psychology*, Harper & Brothers, 1949:

67. Snyder, W. U., A short-term nondirective treatment of an adult. Pp. 528–578. (Also in *J. abnorm. soc. Psychol.*, 1943, 38:87–137.)
68. Snyder, W. U., Dr. Thorne's critique of nondirective psychotherapy. Pp. 591–597. (Also in *J. abnorm. soc. Psychol.*, 1945, 40:336–339.)
69. Thorne, F. C., A critique of nondirective methods of psychotherapy. Pp. 579–590. (Also in *J. abnorm. soc. Psychol.*, 1944, 39:459–470.)

ECLECTIC PSYCHOTHERAPY

70. Bordin, E. S., Counseling points of view, non-directive and others, in Williamson, E. G. (ed.), *Trends in student personnel work*, University of Minnesota Press, 1949, pp. 120–129.
71. Lewis, V. W., Intensive treatment with adolescent girls, in Watson, R. I. (ed.), *Readings in the clinical method in psychology*, Harper & Brothers, 1949, pp. 513–518. (Also in *J. consult. Psychol.*, 1940, 4:181–184.)
72. Saslow, G., and Buchmueller, A. D., Flexible psychotherapy in psychosomatic disorders, *Human Organization*, 1949, 8:5–12.
73. Thorne, F. C., Directive psychotherapy: II. The theory of self-consistency, *J. clin. Psychol.*, 1945, 1:155–162.
74. Thorne, F. C., Directive psychotherapy: III. The psychology of simple maladjustment, *J. clin. Psychol.*, 1945, 1:228–240.
75. Thorne, F. C., Directive psychotherapy: IV. The therapeutic implications of the case history, *J. clin. Psychol.*, 1945, 1:318–330.
76. Thorne, F. C., Directive psychotherapy: VI. The technique of psychological palliation, *J. clin. Psychol.*, 1946, 2:68–79.
77. Thorne, F. C., Directive psychotherapy: VII. Imparting psychological information, *J. clin. Psychol.*, 1946, 2:179–190.
78. Thorne, F. C., Directive psychotherapy: VIII. The psychology of satiation, *J. clin. Psychol.*, 1946, 2:261–266.
79. Thorne, F. C., Directive psychotherapy: IX. Personality integration and self-regulation, *J. clin. Psychol.*, 1946, 2:371–383.
80. Thorne, F. C., Directive psychotherapy: X. Constitutional analysis, *J. clin. Psychol.*, 1947, 3:75–84.
81. Thorne, F. C., Directive psychotherapy: XI. Therapeutic use of conflict, *J. clin. Psychol.*, 1947, 3:168–179.
82. Thorne, F. C., Directive psychotherapy: XII. The client's Weltanschauung, *J. clin. Psychol.*, 1947, 3:277–286.
83. Thorne, F. C., Directive psychotherapy: XIII. Psychological antidotes and prophylactics, *J. clin. Psychol.*, 1947, 3:356–364.
84. Thorne, F. C., Directive psychotherapy: XIV. Suggestion, persuasion and advice, *J. clin. Psychol.*, 1948, 4:70–82.
85. Thorne, F. C., Directive psychotherapy: XV. Pressure and coercion, *J. clin. Psychol.*, 1948, 4:178–188.
86. Thorne, F. C., Directive psychotherapy: XVI. Situational analysis, *J. clin. Psychol.*, 1948, 4:290–298.
87. Thorne, F. C., Principles of directive counseling and psychotherapy, *Amer. Psychologist*, 1948, 3:160–165; 159.
88. Thorne, F. C., Theoretical foundations of directive psychotherapy, *Ann. N.Y. Acad. Sci.*, 1948, 49:869–877.

CHAPTER 21

Psychotherapy with Children

In psychotherapy with children the aims are essentially similar to those operative with adults. Modifications in technique, however, are introduced to the extent that the child differs from the adult. Since the child is more plastic and his resistances and defenses to problems are less "overlearned," simple disuse by change of environment may make for therapeutic gain. In older children procedural differences in direct psychotherapy are not so remarkable, but with the younger child extensive modification of the therapeutic situation must be expected because of the variety and strength of the intrinsic differences between children and adults. Play, for example, may be used as a means of communication rather than words because, as has often been said, it is the natural medium of expression for the child. As the difference just mentioned as well as certain others are fundamental to an understanding of psychotherapy with children, they will first be explored.

DIFFERENCES BETWEEN ADULT AND CHILD PSYCHOTHERAPY

An obvious difference between psychotherapy with children and that carried out with adults is predisposed by the verbal level of the child. Verbal conversation of any sort, let alone the conversation of a therapeutic session, is very difficult. To be sure, children talk, but often there is a minimum of verbal language. Facial expressions, mannerisms, gestures, and body movements are used purposively by children to a greater degree than is usual among adults. Children also react to facial and bodily movements of adults to a great extent. Since the therapist is an adult accustomed to communicating in accordance with adult standards, the child may feel threatened by the language barrier so introduced. Not talking the same language, literally and figuratively, creates a situation in which suspicion and hostility are almost inevitable. Dependent as he has been upon adults, often frustrated as he is in his contacts with them, the child expresses his hostility again with this new enemy until a basis of understanding and common ground may be established.

This difficulty is likely to be encountered with very young or intellectually dull children, or those on the defensive with adults such as young delinquents. Bright children coming to therapy because of neurotic symptoms or emotional conflicts usually are willing to engage in conversation. The difference here is not so much in the verbal level as that different situations are required for verbal communication. In other words, a formal conversational situation is suitable for adult therapy, whereas an informal situation in which the child can play or draw is suitable for children, and it is usually from some play activity or some picture the child draws that meaningful conversation originates.

In contrast with adults, children are less aware of the need for therapy. Children do not spontaneously seek psychotherapeutic help, and in some instances they do not desire it initially once they are made aware of its existence. True, some children, especially those showing strong anxiety, may be motivated for treatment prior to being seen by the therapist. The child who is afraid of his terrorizing dreams or that his mother may die may desire treatment if it is depicted as a means of lessening his fears and thus making him more comfortable. Or if another boy has attempted some activity, such as attending school, but has found it impossible to continue because of his symptoms, he may be willing or even eager for treatment for relief of these symptoms. The child starved for affection may develop what is almost a mania concerning therapy. But by and large a child neither seeks nor welcomes psychotherapy. Once in therapy, however, he is likely to swing back and forth during treatment from periods of wanting it and finding comfort in the therapeutic relationship to periods of wishing to repudiate it. Therapy cannot proceed unless he changes so that he continues willingly, even if he started unwillingly.

Another barrier to therapy is created by the fact that the therapist and child are not united by a common purpose as readily or as completely as is possible with adults. The adult is more aware of his own and the therapist's role and can appreciate at least to some degree the nature of the situation. The nearest approach by the child to an appreciation of the therapeutic process, which is hardly accurate, is a fear (shared with some adults) that the therapist will do something to "make him over." Fear of punishment is still another obstruction to therapy. These attitudes are dispelled by effective therapy, but their initial appearance does necessitate differences in the approach used with children.

There is even greater fluidity of progression in therapeutic sessions with children than with adults precisely because the patient is a child. Ego boundaries are not as well fixed in the child, with an intermingling of realistic and fantasy material taking place. This may express itself horizontally during a play session in the child who intermingles behavior arising from the present situation as observable objectively with a conglomeration of fantasy materials and full recollections of actual events. Longitudinally through several sessions there may be periods in which a deep crucial conflict is being worked through, only to be followed in the next session by a desire to play checkers or by some considerable excitement over a movie recently attended, a test taken, or a home incident. Although it may be argued that there is in this a rather strict progression from one theme to the next, with the difficulty lying in the obtuseness of the therapist who fails to see the connection, it is the conviction of the writer that there is actually greater unpredictability in work with children than in therapy with adults. Despert (5) expresses substantially the same conclusion. It is also in keeping with knowledge of the general developmental process of the child, in which, although continuity may be in the ascendance, discontinuity and unpredictability also appear. One facet of this fluidity of development was touched upon in Chapter 12 in which tests of intellectual development of infants were discussed. This, again, is a relative difference since discontinuity, and intermingling of reality and fantasy also appear in adult patients, but not to as great a degree or as often.

In psychotherapy with children as distinguished from treatment of adults one relative difference is that therapeutic planning is seldom restricted to just one patient but has instead to be carried on with the parents and other persons in the environment of the child. (This, of course, sometimes is done with an adult.) The child's difficulties are inextricably bound with those of the adults about him and frequently are exacerbated, if not created, by their problems, and often lasting therapeutic benefits cannot be obtained without their coöperation. The treatment of the child is often conducted either wholly or partly at the level of changing some aspects of his environment or outright removal to another environment. Since the child is the focus of interest in the present context, the treatment of adults to alleviate his difficulties, as well as environmental changes instituted for his sake, is regarded as an indirect method of treatment and will be discussed in Chapter 23, which is concerned with this problem.

As a consequence of the differences between adults and children in the therapeutic situation, the use of the mother as an informant is common practice. Before entering upon treatment it is necessary to have some sort of diagnostic evaluation of the symptoms and environmental etiological factors in order to derive a tentative therapeutic plan. An adequate history resembling in many respects that described in Chapter 5 may be secured.[1] This is not to imply that there is not room for variation in procedure—often much valuable diagnostic material is gathered in the course of later therapeutic situations. On the other hand, at least a preliminary history is generally obtained from the mother, a process permitting also an evaluation of her emotional difficulties, the role she plays in the child's present disturbance, and a tentative decision as to her position in the treatment plan and some idea of the family organization. In short, it gives an opportunity for the evaluation of the total emotional environment of the child. Such sessions also permit the foundation of a positive relationship with the parent without which, if the child remains in the home, very little therapeutic progress could be made and without which the child is seldom kept in therapy.

Probably the greatest difference between child and adult psychotherapy, as it is customarily practiced, is created by the child's de-

---

[1] A discussion of the parental interview is given in Frankl (21).

pendency needs. As a consequence of his status as a child he is more subject to change and stress than is an adult. The adult has immeasurably more control over his environment than does a child. The latter's personality is still in the formative stage and as a consequence the therapist gives direct help and assumes a greater amount of responsibility for the welfare of his patient. Consider a child who has no opportunity for learning healthful adjustments, has a poor sense of reality, and lives in a disturbed home environment with confused parents. He has little opportunity for learning from others, and the therapist or clinic team supplies this lack. The therapist "shares experiences" with the child, bringing him to see in some perspective the consequences of his behavior. To an impulsive child, for example, it is indicated that immediate satisfaction must sometimes be forgone for the sake of future goals. It is the task of the therapist to permit the formation of identifications which will give the child some emotional support. The therapist, in short, uses a more outgoing and winning approach with active intervention in the affairs of the child.

It is the task of the child therapist to provide a common ground for a therapeutic relationship. The approaches to child psychotherapy to be discussed—the use of play technique and the specific systematic approaches—essentially are means of doing this. They also illustrate other modifications introduced as a consequence of these differences between adult and child psychotherapy.

AN ILLUSTRATION OF THERAPY WITH CHILDREN

Therapy with children most often takes place in certain clinical settings such as child guidance clinics, in private practice, and in medically oriented institutions. It is, however, not confined to these settings, and may be effectively applied in situations quite apart from these. Application in "non-psychiatric" settings is especially important for the psychologist, since he may carry out such therapy in psychological clinics, through nursery schools, or through other educational settings. Since psychotherapy with children in psychiatric settings will be considered in discussion of the various systematic psychotherapeutic approaches, a detailed illustration of play therapy will be drawn from the work of a psychologist in an educational setting, albeit an unusual one.

An especially vivid account of therapeutic procedures as part of the educative process in a school of education is given by Baruch (20). The children, eighteen months to six years old, in the pre-school and kindergarten came from an upper-middle-class group. The home atmosphere, as is common in this stratum of society, served to introduce certain frustrating cultural impositions. Most of the children had been breast fed only for short periods of time, if at all, had not been fondled very much, had been given early toilet training with an overemphasis on cleanliness, had been required to conform to a relatively rigid feeding schedule, had been permitted to cry it out rather than being "spoiled," and had been severely restricted in expression of aggressive and angry behavior. Some of the children had in varying degrees developed rather serious personality difficulties, others much less serious problems, and apparently all, or almost all, were in need of some satisfactions to offset the frustrations so characteristic of their cultural background.

Basic to Baruch's presentation is the use of what she called "contacts" and "release." To make provision for contact a variety of approaches are used. Since the child's entrance into the school is a crucial cleavage, arrangement is made for one of the teachers to serve as his "school mother" and special teacher. This teacher is present when he arrives and takes over when the departure of the mother occurs. She attempts to make her procedures with the child similar to those of the mother by calling him by the same nickname, holding his cup for him when he drinks if this is what the mother has done, and so on. At the same time she seeks him out when he is hurt or in some way distressed. This contact is carried on in the group with one teacher assigned to from three to five children. If the child is more disturbed than others such contacts within the group do not seem enough. Therefore she makes special provisions for "time alone" with the particular child, in which fifteen or twenty minutes a day she leaves the group with the child and goes to a quiet place with him. The child is made to understand that this is his time and that he can have her all to himself. An illustration is given in a quotation:

One day as he is playing, his teacher goes up to him. She tells him that he is to have time with her all alone and asks what he would like to do. He wants to take the baby doll and go to see the ducks in the kindergarten. Holding hands, they walk slowly toward the duck pond. As they walk, the teacher chants, "Harry and his teacher are going all alone, going to see the ducks, going all alone." She interjects that she thinks he's a nice boy. He climbs on her lap when they reach their destination and from that vantage point, while she cuddles him, they watch the ducks together. (20, p. 504.)

Provisions for *release* are supplied in general through such outlets as finger paints, clay, earth, soapsuds, water, and so on. Many of these children who had been subject to early toilet training and never allowed messing of any sort took to the use of the materials just mentioned with special enthusiasm. There was also a release through the permissive atmosphere in regard to using "unmentionable" terms and execution of aggressive and hostile activities with these materials and others especially suitable such as dolls, hammer and nails, etc. All the materials in the playrooms are of such a nature that there is no need for the usual admonishment of "don't touch" so common in the middle-class homes from which these children came. As in the case of contact experience there was also provision for experiencing release within the group. For example, one 3½-year-old girl had been brought up with overemphasis on cleanliness. Her interest in messing was pronounced. She was therefore given the opportunity to experience satisfaction of this need in a variety of ways. For example, she was in charge of cleaning the rabbit cage, helping the teacher to mix finger paints and mash for the chickens, watering the plants, and so on. Within reasonable limits fighting was also permitted. For example, boxing matches were arranged, and opportunities provided to destroy various objects, such as tearing apart old towels.

All this was done in a permissive, non-evaluating setting in which the teacher maintained a consistent solicitous attitude toward the child. In evaluating the effect of this way of working with children, Baruch felt that in many ways these children had improved in their ability to get along with other children, that they got along better with their parents and were freer and happier within themselves. It is necessary, however, to sound a word of caution. Often indiscriminate contact and release are not enough. The teacher or supervisor must be therapeutically oriented with a keen awareness of the nuances of the therapeutic experiences for the children. This is true in spite of the fact that strictly speaking not one of these children was regarded by anyone as a "patient." To be sure, if deprived of this therapeutic experience as part of their educative program, some of them would have been referred to a child guidance clinic.

PLAY AS A THERAPEUTIC TECHNIQUE

Play is a means of establishing a therapeutic relationship. If this relationship is lacking, there may be play but not play *therapy* in any strict sense. Accordingly the term "technique" (despite its somewhat mechanical connotation) is considered more appropriate than "therapy" for this very reason. As Blanchard (9) remarks, to speak of play therapy risks being misunderstood in that it might be construed as intimating that the therapist is concerned primarily with the play rather than with the child. Moreover, she goes on to indicate, the term "might be taken to imply that the child's play life is, of and by itself, the therapeutic agent, that the therapist need only observe the child at play, or control or guide the play activities, in order to bring about therapeutic results." (9, p. 514.)

From the point of view expressed earlier in reference to the common factors in psychotherapy, the proper perspective is clear. Play is a *medium* of therapy. It is a means for allowing a therapeutic relationship to develop, for guided emotional release to take place, for insight to develop, as well as the other factors previously posited.

Psychotherapy with children requires that the child be given an opportunity to interact with an adult (the therapist) who takes a different attitude toward his problem from that he has previously experienced. This the therapeutic attitude supplies, no matter how it is expressed. Of course, merely making it available is not enough; the child must experience it. Although play may share in the development of this interaction, the attitude may be maintained in its absence. Play is merely one way of allowing the therapist to interact with a child patient.

Even when restricted to a means of releasing tension, play techniques may be therapeutically valuable. Illustrative is the release therapy of Levy (35). Even here there is no doubt that some form of therapeutic relationship exists, but it is minimized. Play technique with perhaps certain exceptions such as release therapy is not a means of treatment in itself. It is a means of facilitating interaction with the therapist through a medium readily available and natural to the child.

THE MATERIALS OF PLAY TECHNIQUE

Although leaving ample room for minor deviations, the materials and setting for play technique have considerable similarity. Privacy is essential (even if group play is being used). A room that can take it, with easily washed walls, smooth surfaces, and free space, is desirable. Access to a washbowl and toilet in an adjoining room is also of value, not only for conventional demands but also to provide outlets for primitive desires to mess. Clay, crayons, finger paints also should be available. Some toys to satisfy aggressive impulses, such as pegboards to be hammered, are frequently provided. Guns, trucks, soldiers and other instruments of destruction and violence are similarly indicated. Dolls are probably the most characteristic item used in play techniques. (In fact, if play therapists should ever feel in need of a coat of arms, a Betsy Wetsy doll standing on one leg in a pool of water flourishing in one hand a dismembered leg is apropos.) Often a variety of dolls are on hand, selected to permit identification as baby, father, mother, sister, brother, and so on.

The materials vary according to the interests of the therapist, the setting in which the therapy takes place, and the problems for which they are used. Sometimes one sort of play material will be used by a few clinicians with considerable skill and acumen in spite of the fact that the specific material and technique are not widely used elsewhere—as, for example, puppets.

Bender and Woltmann (3) (19) have had considerable success with hand puppets both in facilitating understanding and in working through emotional difficulties of behavior problem children. Puppet plays enacting themes are produced, often with the same central character who represents, in so far as one character may represent, the strong infantile desires which demand satisfaction. He, the puppet, is faced with reality situations after giving vent to his childish impulses. Thus after he snatches food, other characters grab from him. The play proceeds with his learning to live with others. Aggression is exhibited, followed by a solution of the problem depicted in which love and affection are expressed. Not only do the children participate in the on-the-spot development of the scenario, offering advice to the hero and shouting warning of danger, but they are also asked in later private discussions to retell the story. This provides an opportunity for projective self-reference as the story unfolds and yields significant material in terms of distortions, omissions, and palpable emotional reactions to specific parts of the plot.

The Uses of Play Technique

Regardless of the approach and the way in which materials are utilized, play technique would seem to have the potentiality for stimulating a child to verbalize and dramatize experiences and conflicts and to allow the opportunity for emotional discharge. These two basic patterns—expression and release—are inherent in the nature of play *per se* but achieve therapeutic stature only when a therapeutic relationship is established. Whatever else is accomplished is due primarily not to the play itself but to the skill and orientation of the therapist, for out of these two basic attributes more refined uses may be built.

This further refinement finds apt expression in what Amster (2) has called "differential uses of play." After describing the use of play for diagnostic understanding, which is outside of our present framework, she goes on to describe with particular vividness other uses as follows:

Play can be used to establish a working relationship. This use of play is helpful with the young child who lacks the adult's facility for verbal self-expression and with the older child who shows resistance or inability to articulate. . . .
Jeannette, 9, is referred for her hostile behavior toward her younger siblings and for refusal to permit her mother out of her sight. History material reveals she has suffered alternate over-indulgence and cruel punishment from her father, rejection by her mother, and many traumatic hospitalizations. At the first interview, with a fearful expression in her eyes and rigidity in her body, Jeannette eyes me apprehensively but slowly enters the room when she sees the play material. For several interviews she models animals in clay or draws stilted landscapes, keeps her head lowered, and speaks to herself in whispers. Gradually, she permits me to assist her and I confine my comments to the play activity and to her real abilities. When Jeannette achieves the first therapeutic objective of thawing out, she confides that now she is sure I will not send her away as her mother threatened.

In this situation, the therapist provides play material from which the child can select and through which she can safely express herself; remains passive until invited to share; confines comments to play activity and to the child's abilities; helps the child thaw out; and prepares the child for a relationship. Jeannette slowly releases some tension through her activity; slowly permits the activity to become a sharing one; feels encouraged to again extend herself as a person and to expect warmth from an adult; learns that all adults are not punitive like her mother; feels the therapist is her ally; and establishes a working relationship with the therapist. . . .

Play can be used to help a child verbalize certain conscious material and the associated feelings. This use is helpful when a child blocks in discussing certain material and an impasse in treatment is created.

Stanley, 10, doggedly refuses to discuss his encopresis and his mother's attitude toward him. As he is interested in building with blocks, I suggest he build a house. He builds one but omits the bathroom. We discuss what such omission might mean to the imaginary family who lives in the house. Stanley then builds an ornate bathroom but places it outside the house. We discuss this in terms of the inconvenience to the family. The boy comments that he dislikes the simple bathroom in his home. Later, he relates that he soils himself; and that his mother punishes him by whipping and by rubbing his faeces on his face; and that he gets even because she has to wash his trousers. We discuss the pleasurable aspects of his soiling and whether through his "getting even" he can achieve the escape he wants from his mother's domination.

In this situation, the therapist uses material in which the boy is interested at this point in treatment; initiates a general play situation and permits the boy to fill in the details, discusses his omission of a reality, makes interpretative remarks, geared to the content of the play and, later, when the boy makes his own associations, the therapist makes interpretations which point up the symptomatic nature of his soiling and which fits this into his general problem. The boy is helped to verbalize material which represents failure, punishment and retaliation; secures release of his feelings, surrenders some of his negativism, gradually accepts the reality of bathrooms, verbalizes his role in his relationship to his mother, and is helped to doubt the effectiveness of his method. Some of his discomfort is alleviated and an impasse in treatment is worked out. . . .

Play can be used to help a child act out unconscious material and to relieve the accompanying tension. This cathartic use of play deals with symbolic material which has dangerous significance to the child. The therapist must be aware of how much release in play the particular child can tolerate without panic and must be aware of the kind of participation and interpretation in which to engage.

Morton, 7, is referred for a sudden onset of sleeplessness. He anxiously relates that Max is the name of the neighborhood bully who beat him severely. He slowly writes out: "Max is a triple based (bastard)," and walks restlessly about the room as he shows me how well he can bounce a ball. He quickly accepts my suggestion that he make up a story about a little boy and a big boy. I draw the stick figures while Morton tells the story. He relates that the little boy meets the big boy who beats the little boy until the little boy loses his nose and legs. The little boy manages to escape by running home on his hands. The little boy is disappointed because his mother does not kiss him. A doctor makes the little boy well. The second scene shows the little boy challenging the big boy to fight. This time Morton and I decide the little boy has grown and has muscles. In the fight the little boy knocks off the bully's nose, legs and arms. The last scene shows the big boy, covered with bandages, confined to his bed and weeping. A doctor is preparing painful remedies and the little boy who is standing outside the bedroom window is laughing heartily.

In subsequent interviews, Morton acts out through stories and jokes, various dangers which overtake small boys and how these boys emerge victorious. After this play activity Morton spontaneously relates that he and Max are friends and share activities. His mother reports that Morton is now able to sleep.

In this situation, the therapist initiates a general play situation in which the boy can act out his fear and relieve his tension, permits the boy to fill in the details of the play activity, participates in a manner which helps the boy work out his feelings, and interprets only through activity geared to the content of the play. Morton acts out his fear of injury by stronger males, his feeling of weakness, and his desire for strength and retaliation. He becomes less anxious and develops strength through the repetitive play. In his daily life he forms a friendship on equal terms with a stronger male whom he formerly feared and avoided. He regains his ability to sleep.

The boy contributed through play activity additional diagnostic understanding. He revealed his feeling of weakness, desire for consolation from his mother, concern about injury, and his need to feel strong. (2, pp. 63–67.)[2]

These are three very important differential uses of play technique, but they do not exhaust its possibilities. For example, play technique may be used in order to reach a decision as to whether or not a given child will react favorably or unfavorably to therapy. It is obvious that the release function of play also serves as a differential usage. Since it has been discussed previously, mention is sufficient at this point.

It is evident that again we find the common factors in psychotherapy—relationship, insight, release, and so on—operative in these differential uses. Play is used to establish the relationship, aids in the development of insight through the verbalization of con-

[2] Reprinted from "Differential Uses of Play in Treatment of Young Children" by F. Amster, by permission of the *American Journal of Orthopsychiatry.* Copyright 1943 by the American Orthopsychiatric Association.

scious material with its accompanying feelings and through acting out of unconscious material and accompanying tension, and allows release as such.

THE KINDS OF PLAY TECHNIQUE

Over the last twenty years a vigorous controversy has developed between two positions concerning play technique variously described as "active" and "passive," "free" and "controlled," "spontaneous" and "standardized." These are now recognized as merely extremes of a continuum and it is not a question of either one or the other's being correct, but of the adroit use of a technique stressing now one end of the continuum, now the other. Activity and passivity, to single out these two for the moment, cannot be used to imply complete passivity or complete activity since it is impossible, as Lowrey (9) says, for the therapist ever to be completely passive or completely active and still have a therapeutic relationship with the patient.

The stress on activity and passivity as characterizing this difference of degree seems objectionable on other grounds. Blanchard (36), in discussing the active approach of Solomon to be described shortly, points out that since free play (the term considered by Solomon to be suitable for the contrasting method) is hardly "passive" the term "active" might be replaced by controlled play. In support of this a quotation from Blanchard is offered: "In Dr. Solomon's approach, it seems to me that the most strikingly different activity on his part, from the activity of the therapist using other methods, is that of *control* of the child's play activities—perhaps even, attempts to control the child's thoughts (since he speaks of directing the future thinking of the child by means of therapeutic suggestions). Therefore, if he would describe his method as 'controlled play therapy,' which seems to me its chief differentiating characteristic, I could agree that this is a valid distinction." (36, p. 498.)

Accordingly, the practice of referring to "free" and "controlled" will be followed in the ensuing discussion. A characteristically "free" approach was used by Amster and Baruch in illustrations given earlier in the chapter. Moreover, in the systematic approaches to be discussed later in this chapter, a free approach is used in which freedom of choice on the part of the child of the material he wants or needs to use and a minimum of activity on the part of the therapist are exhibited. It is therefore plausible to stress at this point the controlled approach.

In the setting of an eclectic approach, a kind of controlled play technique in therapy with children has been described by Conn. In a relatively recent statement of his position (30) he indicates that he emphasizes concrete difficulties which have arisen at a specific time in the child's life situation. Illustrations include car sickness, enuresis, sibling rivalry, parent-child relationships, fears, and sex attitudes. A controlled type of play session is used in which the child selects from a family of dolls supplied by the therapist those with which to play. Questions are interspersed by the therapist as to what the dolls are doing and thinking.

In this variety of controlled play technique the therapist takes a very active role in securing diagnostic information, offering at the same time therapeutic suggestions (36). Thus there is little chance for free play, as the child is confined for the most part to play situations created for him. In structuring these situations the therapist is guided by previous information from the case history and from what the child says or does. An illustration may be drawn from a case of Solomon (36) in which a five-year-old girl was brought to the clinic for head-banging. Part of the first interview follows:

The examiner secured a doll representing a little girl.
Q: Here is a little girl, what is she going to do?
A: She is going to play ball.
Q: All right, let's see, who is she going to play ball with?
A: Her sister.
Q: How many sisters does she have?
A: She has three sisters.
Examiner picked up some dolls representing sisters.
Q: Who else is in her family?
A: Her mother and father.
Examiner selected appropriate dolls suggesting one as mother and the other as father.
Q: Whom does the little girl like the best?
A: She likes all her sisters and she likes her mother too.
Q: Does she ever get mad at anyone?
A: She gets mad at her mother.
The examiner placed the little girl in bed.
Q: What is the little girl thinking about?
A: She is thinking about her mother.
Q: What else?

A: She is thinking about the Lord.
Q: How does she feel then?
A: She feels very sorry.
Q: Does she ever do anything when she feels sleepy?
A: She bumps her head.

Examiner asked patient to show how the little girl does it. She showed the doll bumping its head in bed.

Q: Why does the little girl bump her head?
A: Because she wants to be a lady.
Q: Do ladies bump their heads?
A: My mother does.

The examiner then placed the mother in bed.

Q: With whom does the mother sleep?
A: She sleeps with the father.
Q: What does the little girl think about when the father and mother sleep in bed together?
A: She is thinking about bumping her head.
Q: Why?
A: Because the mother and father are bumping their heads together.
Q: Why does the little girl want to bump her head?
A: She doesn't like to see her mother in bed with her father.

The patient took the mother out of the bed and placed the little girl next to the father.

Q: Does the little girl hear the father and mother bumping together?
A: They shake the bed and make noise and wake the children up.
Q: Then how does the little girl feel?
A: She feels very angry.
Q: What would she like to do?
A: She would like to hit the mother. (36, pp. 481–483.)

Commenting on his procedure ten years after the foregoing quotation was written Solomon (18) indicated that, although he has not abandoned the use of controlled play situations, he has become more cautious of dosages than he was at that time. The emphasis is now placed on the emotional response of the child rather than on the dramatic aspects of the constructions.

The sibling rivalry studies of Levy (13) illustrate a controlled approach. The method in essence consisted of exposing the child to doll play in which the sister (or brother) doll observed a baby doll at the breasts of the mother doll. Activity on the part of the child is encouraged by referring to the baby and instigating the child to enact what might happen next. Encouraging remarks, such as "Go ahead," "Don't be afraid," were used liberally. Although hostility was by no means the only form of behavior exhibited it was characteristic. Following release of hostile feelings on the infant or mother doll, the child carried out self-redeeming behavior, self-punishment, and restoration of the dolls as much as possible to the pre-attack state, or perhaps introduced various defensive measures such as lies and justifications. Since it was primarily an experimental study little systematic evidence of therapeutic effects was collected, but enough is presented to show at least a plausible efficacy.

In an excellent review of the literature on play technique to about 1940, Newell (14) summarized the advantages and disadvantages of the controlled and free approaches. Controlled play, aside from the ease and speed with which it provides diagnostic information, is asserted to have special usefulness in the treatment of specific symptoms, especially those of relatively short duration. For example, he considers it unsurpassed in desensitizing a child to some specific fear. It should be evident that he considers controlled play a tool to be used under certain circumstances rather than a general technique. Levy, one of the experts with controlled play, is mentioned as believing it to be contraindicated in neuroses of some duration or with problems arising from disturbances in family relationships. As Newell indicates, since it may be used before adequate rapport develops, the child may feel tricked when he realizes what has been revealed by his ostensibly benign activities. This may constitute a genuine setback to therapy.

Free or spontaneous play is considered to be less artificial than controlled play. It is a natural method and because of this encourages a closer relationship with the therapist. It allows the child to select his own problems and proceed at his own pace. However, this in itself may be a disadvantage since the child may proceed very slowly. Just as the adult may express his resistance by circumlocution or repeated discourses on one or another irrelevant topic, so may the child reveal his by keeping his play within the realm of safe, innocuous activity. Newell considers free play especially suitable for children showing neurotic traits and difficulties which stem from disturbed family relationships. It is especially useful with inhibited children who repress their hostility and also those excessively trained in cleanliness.

APPROACHES TO THERAPY WITH CHILDREN

Perhaps the book concerned with psychotherapy with children which best catches the modern scope and spirit of such endeavors is that edited by Witmer (38). Eight contributors of presumably quite diverse orientations present in detailed fashion their methods of work with children. Instead of following a stylized "textbook" approach, they preserve the breadth and vitality of the process and show living and breathing children (and therapists) following rules of the game, contributing a most realistic account of the hurly-burly of therapeutic activities. There are no presentations of the beliefs of several schools neatly categorized pro and con, but different children presenting unique problems with whom different therapists formed a variety of relationships. These relationships, forming what Witmer called "the dynamic of therapy," were the common thread uniting *not* approaches but competent therapists working with children.

If this is the case, the question may be raised as to why "approaches to therapy" are presented as a matter of concern at this juncture. The answer is simple. Concurrent with appreciation of similarity must go awareness of differences. This the following discussion of relationship therapy, nondirective therapy, and psychoanalytically oriented therapy with children supplies in some measure.

RELATIONSHIP THERAPY WITH CHILDREN

It is the conviction of Frederick H. Allen and his associates that the guiding principle for child psychotherapy lies in the concept that the child can be helped to help himself. Consequently, in his book *Psychotherapy with Children* (23) he is concerned with a description of the normal psychological growth processes. Growth occurs in a setting in which biological and social realities merge and in which a principle of individuation may be witnessed. This process, although biological, occurs in a framework of events and human relationships, particularly the family. These relationships and events give meaning and direction to the emerging self of the child, a self which has within it the qualities of creativity and spontaneity. Thus in therapy a child is accepted as an individual in his own right—a human being with a capacity for change. Therapy demands participation of the child since no change can be effected without this.

Psychotherapy is adapted to the differentiating functions of growth and is in itself a growth experience. In one sense Allen's approach might be called differentiation therapy since this element is so prominent. As people live and consequently learn they arrive at a sense of selfhood. The goal of therapy is to help the child to be and accept himself in a world of other and different human beings. This can be done only as he senses and respects his relatedness to others. "Being an individual carries a responsibility to the group as well as to the self." (23, p. 296.)

The relationship between therapist and child is considered the primary therapeutic element. The quotation from Allen (23) in Chapter 19 gives the essence of his position, showing how he differentiates it from the "authoritative" and "causal" uses of relationship. He uses the therapeutic relationship for the immediate experience that it is, not to explore the past of the child or to establish what he should do. The relationship should deal with what the child does and feels here and now, accepting the child as he is, not as what he has been in the past or what he should be in the future. This means that he is put into a position where he can use his current habitual methods of behaving and can meet the therapeutic experience on his own terms. As Allen writes:

The child is taken at the point he is at in his own development and he will react with his own feeling to meet this experience. It may bring out the overt fear that emerges around each new experience which requires leaving behind the supports he never has been able or willing to let go. He may enter this relation with a guarded, cautious attitude that allows little if any participation. He may attempt to assume complete control by an assertive, aggressive attitude which may be directed against the therapist or be a part of his activity which aggressively shuts him out. He may try to establish a side of himself that is completely adequate and then show he needs no help from anyone. He can do all his own changing, or even prove those changes have occurred before he came. But the important fact to be understood is that the child starts this experience with his own feeling, whatever form it may take, and, in putting his own feeling into it, the experience immediately takes on a significance that links it with his growth problem. The therapist then has the opportunity to give meaning and direction to this new growth experience because he is a part of it. He is in the position to give immediacy to the child's turmoil and help him to a more livable balance as this relation is established, as it moves and, finally, as it ends. He begins to discover certain unique features of this new experience. Here he may be afraid without having efforts made immediately to remove his fear. He has met with a person who understands and accepts both his need and his right to be afraid without melting before it. He finds that he can be aggressive and hostile, and, at the same time, finds a person who can both accept the feeling and give limits to its expression. He finds a person who is interested in what he says, in what he is, and is not trying to squeeze him into a preconceived mold. He can have his own power without having it overwhelmed by the greater power of another. He comes expecting to be changed and finds a person interested and related to what he is now. Truly, this is a unique experience which is started with himself in the center of it. (1, pp. 738–739.)

The therapist is there not to correct or to probe but to understand what is going on. In this connection Allen indicates that the therapist must maintain his integrity in spite of the variety of ways in which the child will use him. Although cast in manifold roles by the child, the therapist provides a constant background. The child "may use the therapist to symbolize the more unacceptable parts of himself, may see in him his 'bad' self, or the 'perfect' self he is vainly trying to become; or he may attempt to place the therapist in the role of the mother or the father with whom his relationship has miscarried." (23, p. 60.) The task of the therapist is to maintain himself as himself.

Because of the crucial effect on the growth-inducing experiences to follow, the period of entry into therapy may be examined in more detail. Allen writes:

Thus, the first seeking of help by the parent, and the subsequent coming together of parent and child, with the separation and reunion that takes place, has in it the essence of the entire therapeutic process. If no positive significance is attached to parent and child reactions to this structure of working, the direction and meaning of the whole experience will be altered. For example, if the fear that is set up in a child by coming to the therapist is seen principally as a barrier to therapy, to be removed by reassurance or by interpretation in order that therapeutic work can begin, the direction will be quite different than when the fear is seen as the first evidence that something is beginning to happen between the therapist and the patient. Real help can be given to the child by understanding his need to be afraid, and by supporting him as he finds what he can do with that feeling in this new experience. (23, p. 64.)

The problem of handling initial resistance is typical. Allen uses the term not in the psychoanalytic sense of the struggle by a patient against the emergence of unconscious material with feeling directed toward the analyst, but in the sense of the efforts made to handle negative feelings manifested by distrust, antagonism, and the like.

In the course of the therapeutic sessions play materials are used to organize the experiences of the child not as in controlled play sessions but in the broader sense previously described of relating to the child through play. The child is told the material is available for use as he chooses. The choice is the important fact, not whether he decides to play or not, or what particular materials are selected. How he reacts—attempting to shift the choice to the therapist, rushing over immediately to the toy shelf, or playing in a way that shuts out the therapist—is the most important material for observation.

Consistent with Allen's total theoretical framework is the pattern for instigating the close of therapy. This phase also is used as a therapeutic experience. Briefly, it provides a means whereby the child can demonstrate that he is now different and can go on alone. He has found himself in his relation to an adult.

NONDIRECTIVE THERAPY WITH CHILDREN

Historically speaking, relationship therapy developed before the nondirective approach, and the debt of Rogers to Allen is acknowledged (15). It is apparent that in certain ways the two approaches are very similar. Allen, however, does introduce interpretations and does not hesitate to use supportive techniques on occasion. Set rules do not apply so rigorously as they do in the nondirective approach in that no technique is always to be unvaryingly followed.

Therapy with children in the setting of the nondirective approach has been described by several workers (12) (24) (25) (26). In most of these accounts emphasis has been placed upon illustrative rather than systematic material. There has also been a tendency to advocate its use with children in a setting combining play techniques with group therapy. Axline (24) emphasizes case illustrations and makes no attempt to relate her work to that of other therapists. An excerpt from one of her cases, a boy aged seven, illustrates the application of this approach:

Dickie gets out the clay and comes over to the table and sits down across from the therapist.
Dickie: Let's make something.
Therapist: You want to make something out of clay.
Dickie: I said "Let's." You make something, too.
Therapist: What do you want me to make?
Dickie (frowning, scratching his head): I want you to make a cat. You hide it back of a big rock.

Therapist (*beginning to make a cat out of clay and also a rock to hide it behind*): You like to boss me around.

Dickie: You do as I say. (*Therapist and Dickie make the clay figures. Dickie makes a rabbit and a pile of rocks to hide his rabbit.*) Now come out and fight. (*Therapist edges her cat toward his rabbit. He immediately jumps his rabbit on top of therapist's cat and mashes it.*) There. That's the end of the old cat. Make another cat.

Therapist (*making another cat*): You ruined my first cat and now you want me to make another one.

Dickie: Yes. (*The therapist's cat again meets the same fate*). Make another, and this time you have your cat jump on my rabbit. (*Therapist does, but just at the right moment Dickie's rabbit knocks the cat's head off and he pinches the rest of it out of the therapist's fingers.*)

Therapist: You like to get the best of my cat.

Dickie: Sure I do. I like to fight.

Therapist: You like to fight, too.

Dickie: Sure I do. And I like to get the best in a fight, too. You make a snake now.

Therapist: You want me to make a snake. (*She does so. Dickie makes one also. He reaches over and takes therapist's snake and measures it alongside of his. Then, very deliberately, he makes his snake longer than the therapist's.*) You want your snake to be bigger than mine.

Dickie: Yes. And it is going to knock your snake's head plum off. Here. Hide yours behind this rock. Mine is hiding here. (*Dickie has his snake protected by a large pile of rocks.*)

Therapist: You want your snake well protected.

Dickie: Now this time I'm going to let your snake kill my snake. Come on. Hssss. Sssss. (*The snakes are edged toward each other, but just as the therapist's snake is about to strike Dickie's snake, he drops a big ball of clay down on top of it and then pushes his hand down on top of the clay and mashes the therapist's snake. He laughs gleefully.*) I tricked you. I fooled you.

Therapist: You like it when you can trick me and get the best of me.

Dickie: Sure. Now you see if you can trick me. You really try and see if you can.

Therapist: You want me to see if I can trick you.

Dickie: Yes. You just see if you can.

Therapist: You don't think I can.

Dickie: No. I don't think you can, but you try it. (*The therapist and Dickie maneuver the clay snakes. The therapist's snake knocks Dickie's snake's head off. He springs up from the table and shouts at the therapist.*) Look what you did! Look what you did to my snake!

Therapist: You told me to try and trick you, and then when I did you didn't like it.

Dickie: No. I don't like it. Now you fix my snake's head back on. Now you give it first aid.

Therapist: You want me to fix it again since I was the one that knocked its head off.

Dickie: I want you to do what I say.

Therapist: You like to boss me around.

Dickie (laughing suddenly): This is fun. I really don't care about the old clay snakes. I'm just playing. *(He waits until the therapist has fixed his snake, then he picks it up by the tail and mashes it all up in a ball. Then he goes over to the shelf and gets the soldiers and begins another battle, with his back to the therapist this time.)*

Therapist: You're having quite a battle.

Dickie: Why don't you keep still?

Therapist: You want me to stop talking when you tell me to.

Dickie: Yes. Why don't you? *(Therapist does. Dickie peers around at the therapist and looks very pleased with his success at silencing her.)* Can I come back again?

Therapist: Yes, if you want to.

Dickie: I'm really just playing with you. You said I could play any way I wanted to.

Therapist: Yes. That's what I said. I meant it.

Dickie: I can say anything I want to say to you, too?

Therapist: Yes.

Dickie: I could even swear in here if I wanted to?

Therapist: If you want to.

Dickie (laughing hilariously): When can I come again? Every day?

Therapist: You may come every Wednesday at this same time.

Dickie: You're a grown-up lady and I can say anything I want to say to you *(laughs)*.

Therapist: You think it's fun to say anything you feel like saying to a grown-up.

Dickie: Yeah. *(Grins.)* Shut up, Mrs. X [the house-mother's name]. Shut up Mrs. X.

Therapist: You would like to tell the house-mother to shut up sometimes.

Dickie: Shut up, Mr. M. [the superintendent of the Home]. Shut your damn big mouth!

Therapist: You sometimes feel like telling Mr. M. to shut his "damn big mouth."

Dickie: I'd like to, but I wouldn't dare!

Therapist: You would like to tell him that, but you wouldn't dare.

Dickie (sitting down across from the therapist): Know what?

Therapist: Hmm?

Dickie: I want to drink from the nursing bottle.

Therapist: There it is, over on the shelf. Drink from the nursing bottle if you want to.

Dickie: Know what?

Therapist: Hmm?

Dickie: I want to crawl on the floor and drink my bottle.

Therapist: You want to act just like a baby. Well, go ahead. (*As Dickie hesitates.*) You don't know whether you should or not.

(Dickie gets the nursing bottle, sits down across from the therapist and closes eyes and drinks from the bottle; then he gets down on the floor, lies down, sucks on the bottle with his eyes closed.)

Dickie: Me little baby.

Therapist: You like to be a little baby.

Dickie: Ummhumm. (*Lies on the floor, drinking from the bottle for the remainder of the hour. (24, pp. 173–176).* [3]

It is evident from this excerpt that in many ways the procedure resembles closely the use of nondirective therapy with adults. This is confirmed by Landisberg and Snyder (12), who performed a study in which they investigated a variety of factors casting light upon the nature of nondirective play therapy. Essentially they followed the method of investigation used by Snyder in his earlier study (16) of adult cases described in Chapter 20. Four cases were selected for study, and each statement and response was categorized for counselors by content and for clients by content and feeling. Considerable similarity to the previous study was found, with the counselors consistently nondirective in the sense previously described. Of all activity and verbalizations occurring in the therapeutic sessions, about 25 percent consisted of statements by the children supplying information; in another 25 percent they took positive sorts of play actions; and about 30 percent of all activity consisted of nondirective responses by the therapist (simple acceptance, restatement of content of action, reflection of feeling or action). In studying sequel relationships, nondirective statements precede 85 percent of all responses by the children. In fact, reflection of feeling, one type only, preceded 57 percent of the children's responses. Much feeling was released by the children, ranging from 50 percent of their actions or statements during the first two-fifths of treatment to about 70 percent during the last three-fifths. Differences from the adult cases studied by Snyder centered upon the presence of physical activity and, more important, absence of anything which might be classified as insight. In this connection the authors write:

[3] Reprinted from *Play Therapy* by V. M. Axline, by permission of Houghton Mifflin Company. Copyright 1947 by Houghton Mifflin Company.

Insight is, of course, a very significant aspect of the adult counseling experience, and the apparent lack of such responses in the children's situation has suggested to some that play therapy produces a cathartic effect but does not bring the child to additional insights. In other cases than the four analyzed in this study, we have observed statements which we believe might be classified as a type of insight. For example, a statement by the child such as, "I don't like to have people boss me." This would seem to indicate that the child is acquiring knowledge about himself. It is our belief that the degree of insight achieved in therapy is considerably affected by the age and intellectual maturity of the child. One should not expect the child to reach more advanced levels of insight in play therapy than are expected for other children of the same stage of mental development. An older child would be more likely to answer some of the questions about himself that start with "why." The children in this study ranged in age from five to six years. To reach an insight such as, "I act mean to my brother because I resent my mother's obvious preference for him" would require a high degree of maturity in any child. The most that may be expected is insight commensurate with the child's ability. (*12*, p. 213.)

Although verbalized insight is minimal it would appear from close scrutiny of case reports that more than mere release is operative, and the criticism sometimes offered that it is exclusively a release technique is open to question. The problem is not whether the child can verbalize his insight but whether it is exhibited in his behavior. Kohler's ape, Sultan, showed insight in his bamboo and banana experiment through changed behavior, not in talking about it.

PSYCHOANALYTICALLY ORIENTED PSYCHOTHERAPY WITH CHILDREN

In 1909 Freud (7) wrote a paper entitled "Analysis of a Phobia in a Five-Year-Old Boy," concerning a case whose treatment he had directed four years earlier and in which are to be found the beginnings of both play technique in psychoanalysis and child analysis proper. Treatment was actually carried out by the father, with the help of interpretations by Freud, and the uses of play, including drawing, were merely casual and indirect. About 1920 Hug-Hellmuth (10) made a more deliberate attempt to use play as a substitute for free association by arranging for play situations rather than depending on the emergence of spontaneous incidents. She supplemented this by seeing the child at home and trying to become fa-

miliar with his day-to-day life. It was not, however, until the work
of Melanie Klein and Anna Freud became known that child psychoanalysis was at all widely practiced. Melanie Klein, who settled
in England, attracted a considerable following and contributed a
great deal to what came to be known as the English school of psychoanalysis. Anna Freud, the daughter of Sigmund Freud, first
practiced in Vienna, which fact gave rise to the custom of referring
to her work and that of her associates as the "Vienna school." Since
the views of Klein and Freud[4] differ considerably and in many ways
oppose each other, their procedures will be examined separately.

THE APPROACH OF MELANIE KLEIN. The definitive step of systematically applying play technique as a substitute for free association
was taken by Melanie Klein (34) about the same date Hug-Hellmuth was working, but it was not until 1932 that she published a
systematic account of her work. Play technique is considered to be
a direct substitute for the adult association technique. The child is
conceived to be so close to certain traumatizing events and his unconscious in such close contact with his conscious life that psychoanalysis with children is considered to be more successful than with
adults. The child's symbols are not those of speech but of action
expressed in play.

The essence of Klein's approach is direct verbal interpretation to
the child concerning the symbolical nature of his acts, drawing
upon his use of play materials for this purpose (11) (34). She
makes available toys, pencils, paper, string, and, as she emphasizes,
water (11), for the child to use as he sees fit, with free rein in releasing destructive impulses. When he uses the play material the
meaning is interpreted directly to the child when it first appears in
symbolic form. This is done because she believes she must reach
the depths of anxiety in order to relieve it and bring the child into
and continue treatment. Interpretations are offered to the child
even in the first hour. From excerpts presented in her various publications (11) (34) it would appear that they are very direct and
uncompromising (bumping of toys together signifying intercourse
of the parents, questions about a sequence of alternating long and
short words in a poem indicating thoughts of sex differences between boys and girls, a girl playing an "office" game meaning a de-

---

[4] In order to avoid awkwardness when the name Freud is mentioned in this
chapter, hereafter it refers to Anna, not Sigmund, Freud.

sire to be a man, overturning a toy suggesting an aggressive impulse against the father, etc.). It is only fair to point out that these symbols are not presumed to have one invariable meaning. Klein explicitly points out that a single toy or a single bit of play may have many meanings which can be known only by an understanding of the total situation. Although such may be the case, the interpretations offered in her published accounts do not always show this judicious postponement for more evidence but instead suggest a direct plunging into interpretations based presumably upon her extensive prior experience which the new bit of play behavior now revives.

Her approach for a variety of reasons aroused considerable criticism (4) (9) (28) (31). It is unnecessary to dwell upon it in detail since the approach is little used in this country. Suffice it to say that many competent therapists feel that sweeping interpretations are offered prematurely, thus decreasing the child's anxiety rather than relating the feeling to the therapeutic experience; that she has made unwarranted and unverified statements about the behavior of the young child; that her point of view and terminology teach him a new vocabulary and otherwise make him feel "apart" from his contemporaries so that it is all the more difficult for him to adjust to reality; that her point of view demands acceptance of the belief that infants have "innate unconscious knowledge" (4, p. 88) and that all play behavior has a deep symbolic function as well as being a simultaneous expression of current happenings, never reflecting superficial experiences alone; that one cannot equate play with free association since the child cannot assume the same free attitude as does the adult; that immediate interpretation closes the door to learning more about traumatic events behind the play (9); and that the play of the child may become too eroticized (9).

Whether these criticisms are valid or not, her position has not had as much influence on therapy with children in the United States as has that of Anna Freud. Accordingly the approach of the latter will now be described in some detail.

THE APPROACH OF ANNA FREUD.[5] In distinct contrast to the relationship approach of Allen, Freud feels that therapeutic progress follows a clearly delineated therapeutic sequence, rather than un-

---

[5] The account which follows leans heavily on her definitive statement of technique, *The Psycho-analytical Treatment of Children* (31).

folding full-blown, as it were, from the moment of introduction of the child and the therapist. Accordingly, in descriptions of her technique she spoke of three phases of the treatment process, each possessing unique characteristics and warranting individual inspection and consideration. Modification introduced as experience grew will also be considered.

The Pre-Analytic Phase of Treatment. Freud (31) spoke of some of the differences between children and adults discussed in an earlier section of this chapter—immaturity, non-self-dependence, failure to reach decisions to come for treatment, failure to perceive the trouble as emanating from themselves—as contributing to the development of her method. These differences certainly have much to do with the development of the pre-analytic or introductory phase of the method. In this phase her intent is to make the patient analyzable, as the adult is—inducing the beginnings of insight into the source of difficulty, developing a confidence in the analyst, and helping the child make his own decision to proceed with analysis rather than accepting a course of action forced upon him by others. As yet there is no real analytical work—no analytical influence, and no question of making unconscious processes conscious.

A variety of expedients are used to produce this attitude, described by Freud in some detail. If the child is suffering in one way or another his distress can be turned to therapeutic advantage, as when she offered to help "take out" a "devil" which one child was convinced she possessed, or when another child accepted her as an ally against her parents when the child was in home difficulties. Perhaps more typical cases are those in which it is not so easy to begin because such factors are not present. This is in the case of a boy referred for a number of anxieties and difficulties within the home situation and various thefts. There was no conscious conflict about home conditions and, in the analytical situation, his reaction toward the psychoanalyst was that of thoroughgoing mistrust and a desire for concealment. There was no opportunity of dealing with a "split off" part of the personality, as with the child who had a devil, nor was there any opportunity of offering oneself as a partner against his surroundings, since he was not consciously aware of any difficulties. Other courses of action appeared to be indicated. At first Freud did nothing but follow his moods in the analytic hour, doing what he did, falling in with his caprices, and accepting his behavior no matter how odd. If, as he did, he showed her some knots and rope tricks, she tied even more remarkable ones; if he made faces, she pulled better ones. In talk he was allowed to take the lead with nothing barred. She also wrote letters and made things for him during these early sessions. Thus, she was not only interesting but also useful to him. She showed him that she could protect him against his misdeeds if they were first told to her and through her to those in whose charge he was placed. This last was especially hard for him to believe, and he tested her in it time and again until finally there were no more doubts. Interesting and useful before, and now powerful and trustworthy, she was, in summary, indispensable, and a state of dependence necessary for analysis was thus created.

The discussion thus far may be seen to reflect only minor innovations in practices followed by all analysts in dealing with their adult patients. Freud, for example, compares this procedure to the awakening in an adult melancholic patient of interest in the analytic work by a sympathetic attitude, and the immediate dream interpretation which one might, contrary to usual procedure, introduce at the outset of treatment of an educated, compulsive neurotic who is thus offered a demonstration of what the analyst is capable of doing. Actually this last is essentially similar to showing a youngster that the analyst can do much cleverer tricks with a piece of string than he can himself. Still another analogy may be found in the way the analyst allies himself on the side of the antisocial child just as an adult neurotic is supported by the analyst in conflicts with his family.

This period of "wooing," once considered indispensable, has been found (6) (28) (Preface, 31) not to be as necessary as originally thought. This was realized by applying direct psychoanalytic techniques through study of the ego's methods of defense in a way not foreign in spirit to that described in Chapter 20. Various members of the Vienna school found that through analysis of the ego the child can give up his defenses against anxiety. Analysis of the resistances, in this instance the first resistance to treatment, is described in another publication of Anna Freud (6). Thus it is now often used as the substitute, or partial substitute, for the introductory phase. Bornstein (28) gives numerous illustrations of the manner in which the analysis of the defenses which the ego erects against libidinal impulses or against environmental stresses may be used as a tool of analysis.

The Analytic Phase of Treatment. Once confidence is established, the second phase of analytic work with children begins, namely, the analytical work proper. Freud employs primarily four techniques.

First, a case history is taken both from the child and from his parents. Since the child often cannot contribute too much of the history or appreciate the nature of the abnormality manifested the expedient of using the parent is necessary.

Second, dream interpretation is used. In this instance the technique can be applied to children in the same manner that it is used in the analysis of adults. As with adults the transparency or obscurity of the dream content conforms to the strength of the resistance. Surprisingly enough, the child, according to Freud, finds it relatively easy to grasp the practice of dream interpretation. He is set upon the task of the individual dream illustrations and seems to show great satisfaction in tracking them down. In part, the readiness to coöperate in dream interpretation arises from the fact that he has never been faced with the view that dreams have no meaning. Even if dream interpretation fails, it is possible to infer from the child's reactions the significant circumstances which permit the analyst to apply from his background of experience the missing links necessary for such an interpretation to be congruent and valid. The following is given by Freud as an illustration:

In the fifth month of the analysis of a nine-year-old girl I eventually arrived at the discussion of her masturbation, which she could only admit even to herself with a strong feeling of guilt. She felt very hot sensations when masturbating, and her revulsion against her handling of her genitals extended to these feelings. She began to be afraid of fire and rebelled against wearing warm clothes. She could not see the flame burning in a gas water heater next her bedroom without fearing an explosion. One evening when the mother was away the nurse wanted to light the heater, but did not know how and called the elder brother to help. But he did not know how either. The little girl stood by and had the feeling that she ought to know how. The following night she dreamed of the same situation, but in the dream *she actually did help, but did it wrong and the heater exploded. As a punishment the nurse held her in the fire so that she would burn up.* She woke up in a great state of anxiety and awakened her mother at once to tell her the dream, adding (from her analytical knowledge) that it was certainly a punishment dream. She brought up no other ideas, but I could easily supply them in this case. Manipulating the heater stood for manipulating her own body, which she assumed her brother did too. "Doing it wrong" was the expression of her own condemnation, and the explosion probably represented her form of orgasm. The nurse, who was the natural person to admonish against masturbation, appropriately carried out the punishment.

Two months later she had another fire-dream with the following content: "*On the radiator there were two bricks of different colours. I knew that the house was going to catch fire and I was frightened. Then somebody came and took the bricks away.*" When she woke up she had her hand on her genitals.

This time she associated an idea to a part of the dream, the bricks; she had been told that if you put bricks on your head you do not grow. From that the interpretation could be completed without difficulty. Stopping growing was one of the punishments for masturbation which she feared, and we recognized the significance of fire as a symbol of her sexual excitation from the earlier dream. Thus she masturbated in her sleep, was warned by the remembrance of all the prohibitions, and was frightened. The unknown person who took away the bricks was probably myself, with my soothing reassurances. (31, pp. 19–20.)

Children tell their dreams freely and occasionally make use of free association in connection with the manifest dream content. The analyst, however, must often supply the missing links because the free associative attitude is neither consistent nor lasting.

As a third technique interpretation of daydreams plays an important role, and the relating of all fantasy seems to be of great assistance. The usefulness of this material arises from the fact that children are much less ashamed and self-condemnatory about daydreaming than are adults.

A fourth technique involves the analysis of drawings, in which symbolic interpretations akin to those used in dream interpretation are made to the drawings.

With these techniques available the question may be raised as to why psychoanalysis of children is considered by some to be so difficult. In this connection a further quotation from Freud is appropriate:

The solution is not far to seek. The child cancels all the foregoing advantages by reason of the fact that it refuses to associate. The analyst is thus plunged into perplexity, for the very method on which the analytical technique is founded becomes to all intents and purposes useless. It is obviously contrary to a child's nature to assume the easy recumbent position prescribed for the adult, to expunge by an effort of its own will all criticism of emerging ideas, to exclude nothing from its communications, and so to explore the surface of its consciousness. It is indeed true that when one has attached a child to oneself in the ways I have described, and made oneself indispensable to it, one can make it do anything. Thus for once in a way it will occasionally associate on being invited to do so, for a short time to please the analyst. Such an interpolation of associations may certainly be of the greatest use and bring sudden enlightenment in a difficult situation. But it will always be of the nature of temporary assistance and not the secure basis on which the whole analytical work can be founded. (31, p. 24.)

The role of transference as conceived by Anna Freud must be considered and evaluated. As is evident from her attempts to establish a strong attachment, described earlier, she regards the role of the relationship of therapist and patient as most significant. She equates this directly with positive transference, which may or may not be appropriate. In terms of the discussion in Chapter 18 it is also possible to consider this state of positive attachment what the writer has formulated as rapport as distinguished from transference. Be that as it may, she rejects the essential element of the transference relationship as broadly conceived, namely, the development of a transference neurosis. She takes the stand that no such neurosis develops. In this respect her arguments are quite cogent. First of all she points out that the child, unlike the adult, is not ready to reproduce in the analytical situation a parent or parental figure relationship precisely because the original relationship with parent or parent surrogate still exists. The relationship with the parents is not a fantasy one but actually occurs in reality at the very time the child is being seen by the therapist. In other words, the parents are actually in existence as love objects and a transference neurosis cannot, therefore, occur. Secondly, the "analytic incognito" is not maintained as it is in the analysis of adults. The analyst is very much more than a "shadow" since he is concerned with all sorts of day-to-day activities with the child, exemplified in the first phase of making himself useful, interesting, and attractive to the child. Sharing as the analyst does the child with the family and working with this family in the way to be described shortly also serves to prevent the development of a transference neurosis.

It is concerning her formulation of the transference relationship

that many competent psychoanalytically oriented psychotherapists diverge from the position taken by Anna Freud. Although conceding that the negative aspects of the transference relationship must be minimized and if possible avoided, there remains a feeling that the transference though partial is stronger than she implies. In this connection Blanchard writes:

. . . There are young patients who put themselves much more completely into the relationship with the therapist, make a much more complete transference, than this distinction [advanced in a case discussion by Gerard] between child patients and adult patients implies. Children who are not living with their own parents, some of the five and six year olds, children who feel greatly in need of help with their illness symptoms, certain very confused and disturbed children, are perhaps the most likely to enter intensely and rather fully into the transference relationship. In these cases, I doubt if there would be much therapeutic progress unless the child's varied and changing feelings toward the therapist and the transference phantasies were understood and interpreted. Moreover, the adequate handling of the transference relationship often offers the shortest way to the unconscious feelings and material. (33, pp. 419–420.)

This, it seems, does imply that a transference neurosis sometimes develops, especially in those instances in which the conditions sketched by Freud (working closely with the family, etc.) do not hold.

Freud in describing her approach to child analysis says very little about the use of play materials and play technique. To be sure, she falls in with the interests of the child in the pre-analytic phase and considers play technique useful for diagnostic observation and drawings in the analytic phase proper. By no means, however, does she employ the relatively elaborate paraphernalia now available in the child therapist's office. The word "available" is used advisedly. Child therapists working in the tradition of Anna Freud, using a "free" rather than a controlled play technique, see to it that materials are available to the child but not forced upon him. Play materials, today, however, assume greater prominence than they did in her early formulations. It would appear that she regards dreams, daydreams, and drawings as more useful for active interpretation than play technique as such, whereas her American followers have reversed this emphasis. There seems to be general agreement by these workers that not all activities carried out in the play setting

have emotional or symbolic value; some play activities are conscious repetitions of everyday experiences and are not symbolic at all.

Interpretations are delayed until there is a reduction of anxiety and defensiveness to the point where the child can handle the problem and work it through. For example, in a case of a seven-year-old girl worked with by Gerard (32) (33), there was much evidence of preoccupation with sexual differences. As Blanchard (33) indicates in discussing the case, when concern was shown about Pinnochio's endangered nose or a doll's broken arm, Gerard did not rush in with interpretations, but instead waited until it was exhibited much more openly and less disguised in peeping under a doll's dress. In other words, interpretations are made only when the child has so worked through the material as to be ready to appreciate its significance. There is no guessing what is back of the child's productions; if given time, the child will narrow the potential field of interpretations to the point where confirmatory evidence is available. What is important will appear again and again.

The Post-Analytic Phase of Treatment. Freud found necessary a third phase, after analysis proper. This is necessary simply because the child *is* a child who is still dependent upon the parents or other adults. The child is so open to the influence of the environment that regressive behavior in the absence of a parental figure is common. For example, habits of cleanliness may be lost when separation occurs from the person who has inculcated cleanliness. Now since the parents themselves are the very persons who have contributed something at least to the development of the difficulties of the child and since the child is without the strengths of the adult, it is necessary for the analyst to see to it that the parents are able to carry on an educational task after the analytical work is done. Therefore throughout analysis and in the post-analytic phase a sympathetic and understanding family circle is worked toward, with advice on handling the child in the home being considered quite apropos. There is often a period following the analysis in which the child is less inhibited. Not only must he be educated in self-control but also the parents must be counseled to prevent repetition of the same patterns of behavior which helped originally to lead to the development of the neurosis.

The post-analytic phase was formerly standard practice for the child therapist; in her 1946 Preface, however, Freud points out that

enlightened public opinion makes it unnecessary, since school-teachers and parents have had so much better training than they did formerly. Presumably in the child guidance clinic as it exists in the United States today members of the clinic team other than the child's therapist, especially the social worker, would make sure this somewhat optimistic note is a true one through sessions with the parents and teachers.

Summary. In summarizing this approach to child analysis three stages are discernible. The introductory stage is one in which the therapist attempts to understand the child and his problems and to develop a positive trusting relationship (whether through wooing or through analysis of the ego's mechanisms for defense). The second stage is the analysis proper in which the child works through his conflicts and the techniques typical of psychoanalysis are used, except that free association must be used sparingly, if at all. There is some question as to whether or not a transference neurosis develops. The third stage is one in which the child is aided in using his new methods of behavior to express himself outside the therapeutic situation. In some instances this last stage is unnecessary and in many instances is carried on by other clinic personnel.

BIBLIOGRAPHY

1. Allen, F. H., Trends in therapy. IV. Participation in therapy, *Amer. J. Orthopsychiat.*, 1939, 9:737–743.
2. Amster, F., Differential uses of play in treatment of young children, *Amer. J. Orthopsychiat.*, 1943, 13:62–68.
3. Bender, L., and Woltmann, A. G., The use of puppet shows as a psychotherapeutic method for behavior problems in children, *Amer. J. Orthopsychiat.*, 1936, 6:341–354.
4. Bibring, E., The so-called English school of psychoanalysis, *Psychoanal. Quart.*, 1947, 16:69–93.
5. Despert, J. L., Play therapy: remarks on some of its aspects, *Nerv. Child*, 1948, 7:287–295.
6. Freud, A., *The ego and the mechanisms of defense*, Hogarth Press, 1937.
7. Freud, S., Analysis of a phobia in a five-year-old boy, in *Collected papers*, Vol. III, Hogarth Press, 1925, pp. 149–289.
8. Gerard, M. W., Trends in orthopsychiatric therapy. V. Treatment of the young child, *Amer. J. Orthopsychiat.*, 1948, 18:414–421.
9. Gitelson, M. (chm.), Play therapy, *Amer. J. Orthopsychiat.*, 1938, 8:499–524.

10. Hug-Hellmuth, H. von, On the technique of child-analysis, *Int. J. Psychoanal.*, 1921, 2:287–305.
11. Klein, M., *Contributions to psycho-analysis, 1921–1945*, Hogarth Press, 1948.
12. Landisberg, S., and Snyder, W. U., Nondirective play therapy, *J. clin. Psychol.*, 1946, 2:203–214.
13. Levy, D. M., Studies in sibling rivalry, *Res. Monogr. Amer. Orthopsychiat. Assoc.*, 1937, No. 2.
14. Newell, H. W., Play therapy in child psychiatry, *Amer. J. Orthopsychiat.*, 1941, 11:245–251.
15. Rogers, C. R., *Counseling and psychotherapy*, Houghton Mifflin Company, 1942.
16. Snyder, W. U., An investigation of the nature of nondirective psychotherapy, *J. gen. Psychol.*, 1945, 33:193–224.
17. Solomon, J. C., Play technique as a differential therapeutic medium, *Nerv. Child*, 1948, 7:296–300.
18. Solomon, J. C., Trends in orthopsychiatric therapy. IV. Play technique, *Amer. J. Orthopsychiat.*, 1948, 18:402–413.
19. Woltmann, A. G., The use of puppets in understanding children, *Ment. Hyg.*, 1940, 24:445–458.

Supplementary articles in Watson, R. I. (ed.), *Readings in the clinical method in psychology*, Harper & Brothers, 1949:

20. Baruch, D. W., Therapeutic procedures as part of the educative process. Pp. 496–512. (Also in *J. consult. Psychol.*, 1940, 4:165–172.)
21. Frankl, A. W., Diagnostic methods in child guidance and psychological counseling. Pp. 366–384. (Also in *Ment. Hyg., N.Y.*, 1937, 21:579–598.)
22. Frankl, A. W., Play interviews with nursery school children. Pp. 385–394. (Also in *Amer. J. Orthopsychiat.*, 1941, 11:33–39.)

RECOMMENDED CASE STUDY READINGS

23. Allen, F. H., *Psychotherapy with children*, W. W. Norton & Company, 1942.
24. Axline, V. M., *Play therapy: the inner dynamics of childhood*, Houghton Mifflin Company, 1947.
25. Axline, V. M., and Rogers, C. R., A teacher-therapist deals with a handicapped child, *J. abnorm. soc. Psychol.*, 1945, 40:119–142.
26. Bixler, R. H., Treatment of a reading problem through nondirective play therapy, *J. consult. Psychol.*, 1945, 9:105–118.
27. Blanchard, P., 1937 case for symposium, and symposium, *Amer. J. Orthopsychiat.*, 1937, 7:383–422.
28. Bornstein, B., Clinical notes on child analysis, in Freud, A., et al. (eds.), *The psychoanalytic study of the child*, Vol. I, International Universities Press, 1945, pp. 151–166.
29. Bornstein, B., The analysis of a phobic child; some problems of

theory and technique in child analysis, in Freud, A., et al. (eds.), *The psychoanalytic study of the child*, Vol. III–IV, International Universities Press, 1949, pp. 181–226.

30. Conn, J. H., The play-interview as an investigative and therapeutic procedure, *Nerv. Child*, 1948, 7:257–286.
31. Freud, A., *The psycho-analytical treatment of children*, Imago, 1946.
32. Gerard, M. W., Case for discussion at the 1938 symposium, *Amer. J. Orthopsychiat.*, 1938, 8:1–18.
33. Gerard, M. W., The 1938 symposium, *Amer. J. Orthopsychiat.*, 1938, 8:409–435.
34. Klein, M., *The psycho-analysis of children*, Hogarth Press, 1932.
35. Levy, D. M., Trends in therapy. III. Release therapy, *Amer. J. Orthopsychiat.*, 1939, 9:713–736.
36. Solomon, J. C., Active play therapy, *Amer. J. Orthopsychiat.*, 1938, 8:479–498.
37. Solomon, J. C., Active play therapy, further experiences, *Amer. J. Orthopsychiat.*, 1940, 10:763–781.
38. Witmer, H. L. (ed.), *Psychiatric interviews with children*, Commonwealth Fund, 1946.

CHAPTER 22

Group Psychotherapy

In the history of group psychotherapy two major trends appear to have been operative—a desire to reach more patients therapeutically and an appreciation that the group itself offers opportunities for unique therapeutic influence.

Sometimes, however, group procedures are introduced for the sake of convenience or of necessity created by a dearth of therapists and an abundance of patients. Implicit in such an arrangement is the assumption that group psychotherapy is just a matter of applying with fifteen people what would be utilized with each person individually if time were available. In short, according to this view group psychotherapy is merely diluted individual therapy. This idea of dilution, and the accompanying principle that the effects of bungling by inexperienced therapists would be less noxious, manifested itself in a tacit agreement that workers other than psychiatrists could effectively carry out so-called group therapy long before there was similar acceptance of these therapists for individual patients. To be sure, there was a recognition that the educational background of the psychologist and the environmental emphasis of the social worker might stand them in good stead in dealing with groups of patients (and the lines between group psychotherapy, group "work," and pedagogy are not well drawn even today), but more important was this feeling that it was "diluted" therapy and, therefore, involved less danger in inexperienced hands. This point of view reached its climax in the armed services during World War II but fortunately today is somewhat less prevalent.

This discussion does not mean to imply there has been no recognition and appreciation of the importance of group dynamics, from which point of view stems the concept of group psychotherapy as more than a cluster of patients. Pioneers in group therapy—Burrow, Schilder, Wender, Slavson, and Moreno—recognized that interplay, intercommunication, and interdependence all played their part in the group therapeutic relationship. In short, they recognized that group psychotherapy was to some degree unique, possessing advantages and disadvantages, indications and contraindications. At the same time there was a realization that points of difference between individual therapy and group therapy might often be matters of degree or emphasis. In fact, it will become apparent that one of the theses of this presentation is that the common factors in psychotherapy described in Chapter 18 are operative in group as well as in individual psychotherapy. The similarities are conceived as far outweighing the differences despite the necessary emphasis on the latter in this chapter.

Group psychotherapy is not a substitute for individual treatment and is indicated for some cases no matter what else may be done. In others it may be as desirable as individual therapy, and in still other instances pressure of cases may render it administratively feasible despite the greater desirability of individual therapy. Also there are some patients for whom group association would be contraindicated, since their very disturbance may be such that an aim of treatment is to bring them to the point where they can associate with others.

The Distinction Between Group Work and Group Therapy

It is difficult to make a clear-cut distinction between group psychotherapy and many other attempts to modify the behavior of individuals through group participation. For example, typical YMCA or settlement house groups have many aims in common with those of group therapists. The therapeutic values of spas probably reside less in the drinking of the waters than in the opportunity of associating with other individuals with similar problems and a common conviction of the benefits to be derived. Alcoholics Anonymous, combining as it does individual and group advice and exhortation, partakes of many of the qualities, procedures, and purposes found in group psychotherapy. Indirect methods of treatment such as occupational therapy (described in Chapter 23) often involve groups of patients and yet are not considered group therapy. The distinctions between therapeutic helpfulness and psychotherapy presented in Chapter 18 as well as the emphasis on training would seem to hold in connection with group therapy as well. Even more fundamental is the quality of the therapist-patient relationship. In group psychotherapy there is one therapist and a group of patients each with a direct relationship with the therapist and consequent direct psychotherapy, whereas in occupational therapy the OT specialist works as an aid to the actual therapist. The therapeutic relationship is still on an individual basis in group psychotherapy; in group work it is ancillary and indirect.

INTERVIEW AS DIFFERENTIATED FROM ACTIVITY GROUP THERAPY

Slavson (14) and others have found it useful to draw a distinction between interview and activity group psychotherapy which will be found useful in this presentation as a heuristic device. In the interview approach verbal communication is paramount. The patients discuss problems that come up with as much freedom as their anxieties permit. According to Slavson, if verbal communication is blocked, acting out in an accepting environment may be the only road to therapeutic effectiveness.

The interview approach is much more commonly used. It embraces the work of many diverse therapists—nondirective, eclectic (including pedagogical), and psychoanalytically oriented. Activity group therapy, associated more directly with the work of Slavson and his associates, is so designated in the account to follow. In using this approach a favorable social environment is created in which children may work with arts and crafts, and in so doing interact with one another. The role of the therapist is that of an ally in using the material, not an interpreter of behavior. Moreno's psychodramatic technique with its stress on spontaneity is also an activity (acting-out) approach in many respects, but also partakes of interview group psychotherapy. In the actual practice of much

group psychotherapy the interview and activity aspects are intermingled.

Children who have not learned to work and play together with
one another and to be members of a group need the experience of
belonging together which pure activity group therapy affords. Adolescents and adults often have learned this lesson but not how to
solve their intrapsychic conflicts; therefore interview group therapy
is indicated. This is a brief outline of the essential difference. Obviously it is merely a sketch subject to correction and amplification
in the discussion to follow. It is appropriate to stress that hereafter
general statements are to be understood as applying to interview
group therapy but not necessarily to activity group therapy as such
unless so specified.

THE STRUCTURE OF GROUPS

In order to understand properly the nature of groups an examination of group structures is helpful. Luchins' (7) description of
the development of group psychotherapy programs in an army hospital serves as an excellent introduction. He found that four distinguishable group structures emerged: a mere assemblage of patients,
an audience of passive spectators with no apparent interaction, a
spectator audience, and an interacting group.

It is often the case that when a group of patients is brought together the only uniting influences are the words of the therapist
and the confines of the room—and, sometimes, the presence of
ward attendants. Even during the time the therapist is with them,
and certainly before his influence is felt, some patients read, walk
about, wander in and out of the group, "show off," and so on. Certainly there is no group feeling evident.

This motley assemblage often, although not always, becomes a
passive audience with attention centered on the therapist. However, most of the flow of activity is from the therapist to the patients with no apparent interaction between patients. Spontaneous
questions or comments are rare, and only when the therapist refers
them back to the group for answer is there any particular response.
Specific comments addressed to specific patients may or may not
produce a reply.

A spectator audience is formed when the relationship between the therapist and the patients changes sufficiently for some or most patients to become interested and respond overtly. The questions raised are more or less appropriate, and discussion is carried out with the leader. The element of interaction between patients is, for the most part, still lacking. In effect, a private conversation between therapist and patient in the presence of the others is being conducted. Nevertheless, some interest in others is now displayed by members of the group, and occasionally by redirecting and amplifying a patient's question or statement the therapist succeeds in getting members of the group to interact. However, it is only through the leader's mediation that interaction takes place.

Structure in terms of an interacting group is one in which the patients manifest interest, sympathy, or some other attitude concerning the other patients' behavior and verbalizations. Directing of remarks to one another or to the group as a whole may take place. Individuals who monopolize the time, or several people who talk at once may arouse criticism in other members of the group and attempts to control this situation. Debates concerning the worth of the group therapy sessions may be sponsored by some patients. In this structure there is a definite feeling of being a member of a group.

In his own experience Luchins found that no session was precisely one or the other, and the groups did not necessarily proceed consecutively through all the various types of structure. Some groups skipped or reverted or became fixed at one or another of these levels.

An analogy with the classroom setting might make clearer these group structures. Most classroom groups before classes begin correspond roughly to the assemblages. When the class is called to order something analogous to a passive audience is involved. The flow of activity is from teacher to group, with little observable response arising from those in the audience. Some class activities pass into the stage of a spectator audience in which there is a reciprocal flow from teacher to student and vice versa, but still little interaction among students except that brought about by the teacher serving as a mediating agent. The fourth structure, the interacting group, would be exemplified by the discussion group or seminar. It is relatively easy to see also how skipping, reversion, or fixation might also occur in classroom groups.

To anticipate the future discussion of approaches to group therapy, we shall find that certain forms of pedagogical group therapy, in which the therapist talks to the group about a chosen topic, is sometimes at the level of a spectator audience, although elements of a participating audience may also appear. The level of an interacting group is characteristic of other approaches to group psychotherapy described later in the chapter.

THE COMPOSITION OF GROUPS

It is generally held by therapists that adult and adolescent groups should be relatively homogeneous and represent approximately the same problems. This opinion, it must be admitted, is not backed by very impressive evidence, and other therapists would disagree and point to quite diverse groupings with which they have had success. Be that as it may, it is a fairly commonly held opinion that homogeneity in the composition of the groups makes for therapeutic progress. With children's groups, however, this is not considered essential. Slavson's remarks are typical:

It was to prevent overstimulation, with possible traumatization, of some of the patients in the group that we suggested the grouping of members with the same psychological syndromes. . . . It is also helpful for the members of groups to have more or less common problems and some degree of social, intellectual, and language parity. There needs to be some degree of similarity of life patterns among people before they can establish emotional and intellectual contact. Without some such homogeneity catalyzation does not take place, and the supportive value to each other is at a minimum.

Homogeneity, however, is not so essential in children's groups, except that extremes are to be avoided here as well. In activity and play groups heterogeneity is essential. Children with the same characterological syndromes reinforce one another and increase the density of pathology. What is rather necessary here is neutralization, which is supplied by a variety of psychological syndromes. . . . In adolescent and adult groups the members confine themselves to verbal formulation of their emotional difficulties, and therefore there must be a greater commonness among them. (13, p. 175.)

Other issues relating to the composition of groups are more appropriately regarded as aspects of the larger issue of indications and contraindications for group psychotherapy which are examined in the following sections.

THE ADVANTAGES OF AND INDICATIONS
FOR GROUP PSYCHOTHERAPY

Differences between individual and group psychotherapy may be further highlighted by centering attention upon the advantages of and indications for the use of group sessions. This also serves to illuminate further the factors operative. According to Slavson (27), the most important value of group experience "is the modification or elimination of egocentricity and psychological insularity. It increases the ability to feel with other people, that is, to establish positive identifications." (27, p. 1.) The child, beginning with family members and extending in an ever widening horizon, broadens his interest and positive feelings beyond his own person to family, school, neighborhood clubs, and other groups. Likewise within the therapy group the same process of social evolution may be witnessed—the originally self-centered attitudes are modified to permit responsiveness to others and a more allocentric orientation.

Group therapy is more realistic in the sense of a social and socializing experience than is individual therapy. The interpersonal relationships of the group approximate more closely experiences in ordinary social life than does the two-person relationship of individual therapy. Social relationships can be improved through actual trial-and-error experience in the group itself.

A tangible social reality is present in the group situations. Therapy may deal simultaneously and successively with the individual's inner experiences and this social reality (19), a process supplying something which many individual psychotherapeutic settings lack. Psychoanalysis, for example, lacks this social reality—a lack deliberately encouraged by the analytic incognito for other important therapeutic values, such as allowing freedom of expression of repressed urges by the patient. The analyst actually plays a role that minimizes the menacing aspects of reality. To use Ackerman's expression, psychoanalysis is a therapy " 'from inside outward.' " (19, p. 152.) He goes on to state:

Group psychotherapy functions somewhat differently: it seems to operate in both directions. In contrast to the analytic situation, a tangible social reality is always present in a group in the form of dominant aims, ideas, values, and interpersonal patterns. The patient's contact with this tangible social reality is immediate and inescapable, and the therapeutic process moves back and forth between this social reality and the emotional life of each individual patient.

From these considerations a significant speculation arises. It is common knowledge that even those patients who have had a successful analysis seem to experience some amount of confusion and often a considerable lag in effective social readjustment in the immediate post-analytic period. This is entirely logical, since the patient uses this period to re-orient his ego-patterns to his newly achieved insights. Often, however, such patients experience a real distress in their efforts to translate the analytic understanding into new and more constructive forms of social experience. One is tempted to wonder in this connection if group psychotherapy would not be a valuable supplement to psychoanalytic treatment as a bridge between the newly structured insights and the establishment of new forms of interpersonal relationships. (19, pp. 153–154.)

The patients in a group for the first time in their lives meet on common ground with others who have similar symptomatology. This may give the group a cohesion based on mutual interest and empathy. Group psychotherapy affords the opportunity of evaluating the problems of others and thus gaining insight into one's own. Since the attention of the individual is directed away from himself and toward interest and intent common to the group, the individual sees his problems in a new perspective. Realization that others have similar difficulties tends to lessen the feeling of being alone and to remove some of the stigma accompanying the disturbance. It makes easier the expression of these difficulties and relieves anxiety and guilt.

Baruch and Miller (2), in summarizing the relationship between group and individual psychotherapy with allergic patients, stress the coördinate value of individual and group therapy. They tend to supplement each other, with individual therapy "going deeper at a greater speed." The group sessions stimulate material which can then be explored further in individual sessions.

The therapy group provides each individual patient with a controlled, protective medium in which his tentative steps toward growth in social adjustment may first be tried. The group is a social situation in which he may feel adequate. An equally safe trial experience is somewhat difficult to provide outside the office of the therapist in individual psychotherapy. Group psychotherapy has it ready-made in the very situation itself. The patient is participating in social life when he participates in group psychotherapy. Working out his problems in the group theoretically should make him better able to move out from this group to the larger world about him, as group psychotherapy more nearly approximates natural, everyday living. In dynamic terms, the attributes described make group therapy especially valuable for reintegration of personality at the level of the ego. This would seem to be the opinion of Ackerman (1) (19) and Slavson (13) (14) (15) (27).

It is not always the presence of a certain syndrome which does or does not indicate the desirability of group therapy. In other words, it is impossible to say that all patients of a given type will be suitable for group therapy whereas those of others will not. It depends much more fundamentally upon individual needs than any nosological grouping. For example, incompletely repressed strong homosexual impulses in an individual with paranoid trends contraindicates group therapy. On the other hand, in another homosexual patient the group may be the only acceptable treatment medium, since passive homosexual wishes may be unbearably stimulated in individual therapy. However, more often than not, certain kinds of patients are not considered suitable for group psychotherapy. These include psychopathic personalities, paranoids, and anxiety neurotics in near-panic states.

It must again be indicated that the number of patients in relation to the number of available therapists is also taken into consideration. Group psychotherapy serves the need when individual therapy is impracticable. This consideration is misused only when other factors are ignored or minimized.

CONTRAINDICATIONS FOR GROUP PSYCHOTHERAPY

The fact that the disadvantages and contraindications can be sketched more briefly is not an indication that they are relatively unimportant or unimpressive. Rather, they are sometimes so important and far-reaching as to outweigh all advantages.

A not insignificant limitation on the usefulness of group therapy is the enormous complexity of the processes involved. Instead of being "easier," group therapy is for many purposes more intricate than individual therapeutic efforts. Just as playing twenty games of chess simultaneously is vastly more complicated than playing one game, so is group therapy more complicated. And unlike chess, the patient does not wait his turn quietly but makes extra moves when the therapist's back is turned. The superficiality of some group psychotherapeutic efforts reflects not the simplicity of what is being done but rather the inadequacy of the therapist. Actually group psychotherapy requires as much, if not more, skill than individual therapy which is roughly at a parallel level.

In most, but not all, instances group psychotherapy brings about more acceptable adjustments in some areas of life but does not produce profound changes in basic personality structure. It is often more than merely supportive therapy, to be sure, but individual psychotherapy would still appear to be necessary in instances of deep intrapsychic conflicts. According to Slavson (13), children constitute an exception to this principle, as changes of a reconstructive sort can be produced by group therapy in a considerable number of cases. With adults the factor of insight becomes more prominent than with children, thus restricting the value of group therapy. "Deep" interpretations are contraindicated and working through is difficult, if not impossible, to carry out successfully.

There are, of course, a large number of patients who should not be placed in the group therapeutic situation because of the harm which might come from the multiple relations and tensions. Some patients are ill precisely because they cannot tolerate such situations and are unready to join such a group. According to Ackerman (1), group therapy is either contraindicated or is at best a partial therapy with patients who show serious intrapsychic distortion and deep unconscious conflicts. When the patterns of emotional conflict are internalized, group therapy is less suitable. Since cases of this sort form an impressive number of those seen in psychotherapy, the use of group psychotherapy is subject to a very real restriction.

FACTORS OPERATIVE IN GROUP PSYCHOTHERAPY

The focus of treatment is always the individual; the group is a treatment tool, not the treatment focus. It is evident that group therapy, dynamically conceived, assumes that the group experience —the contacts and the relationships of the individual members of the group one with another—has in itself a therapeutic effect on the individual patient. This is felt to represent a special case of the therapist-patient relationship previously posited. It expresses itself in patient-patient relationships in which the therapist also plays a part. A patient, for example, may accept an interpretation from another patient more readily than he would from the therapist, just as a child will reject a statement from the parents only to accept it when proffered by a playmate. However, Luchins (7) reminds us that to attribute therapeutic efficacy to group influences when the structure is not that of an interacting group is to attribute more to group cohesion or activity than should be the case. In such instances therapeutic effects are presumably due to the relationship with the therapist or to the knowledge gained and not to group influences as such. Hereafter, it is understood that an interacting group is being discussed.

Although limited to a psychoanalytically oriented position, the discussion of the factors operative in group psychotherapy by Ackerman is sufficiently general to be worthy of note. His presentation follows:

> The therapeutic aims in employing the group methods with the neuroses are the following:
> (1) To provide emotional support through group relationships.
> (2) To activate emotional release in the area of specific anxiety-ridden conflicts; in particular, to encourage the release of pent-up aggression. This process entails the utilization of group psychological influences for the selective re-enforcement of some emotional trends and involves the suppression or dilution of others.
> (3) To reduce guilt and anxiety, especially through the universalization of common forms of conflict.
> (4) To provide opportunity for the testing of various forms of social reality as personified in individual members of the group or in the group as a whole.
> (5) To provide opportunity for the modification of the concept of the self in the direction of increased self-esteem and recognition of constructive capacities. This in turn tends to increase the acceptance of other persons and tolerance for frustrating experience.
> (6) To foster the development of insight arising from an actual living out of emotional drives in the context of the multiple relationships within the group. Interpretation is employed only when the expression of specific emotional trends has been sufficiently solidified.
> (19, pp. 136–137.)

Slavson states the dynamic view by similarly mentioning transference, release, insight and/or ego strengthening, and reality testing. It would appear that the factors described in Chapter 18 as operative in individual therapy are closely similar to, if not identical with, those operative in group therapy.

APPROACHES TO GROUP PSYCHOTHERAPY

There is no one approach to group psychotherapy suitable for all patients, since various kinds of procedures would appear to be indicated according to the therapeutic needs of the patient. No one method is universally applicable. Likewise therapists differ in psychodynamic orientation and attempt to transpose their procedures to be compatible with demands of the group situation and yet maintain the integrity of the dynamic system. Accordingly some of the approaches which have appeared have recognizable counterparts in individual therapeutic practice. In the eclectic (as expressed in a pedagogical variation), nondirective, and psychoanalytic orientations there is distinct similarity, whereas in activity group therapy and psychodrama there are no directly related counterparts in individual therapy. These aforementioned points of view, with the exception of the nondirective,[1] will be discussed in subsequent sections.

PEDAGOGICAL GROUP PSYCHOTHERAPY

It is the contention of Hadden (3), Klapman (24), and others that educational procedures are to be considered therapeutic in that they impart knowledge in order that man may live more happily. In essence the "class" method, as it also may be called, is one in which a group of people having at least roughly similar difficulties are brought together and the therapist explains the causes, nature, and solution of their particular kinds of difficulties. The material imparted may be oriented according to the bent of the particular therapist. For example, Hadden's approach stressed content perhaps best described as common-sense, non-dynamic, and eclectic, and Klapman's is somewhat more psychoanalytically oriented. This last, it must be emphasized, refers to the *content*, not the procedure. Notwithstanding the nature of the content, these and similar approaches are essentially eclectic. This is one of the oldest, if not

---

[1] Nondirective group therapy (aside from group play therapy) is a field about which relatively little has been reported. In a study by Peres (10) no particular differences in procedure from that found in individual nondirective therapy are isolated or even mentioned. The article by Baruch (20) suggested as a case reading demonstrates some similarities to Rogers' approach. The studies of nondirective group psychotherapy directed by Nicholas Hobbs are appearing in print too late for inclusion.

the oldest, medically oriented attempt at treatment of groups. As early as 1905 Pratt (17) had established a class method as a supplement to somatic methods of treating tuberculosis. Many of the later developments in group treatment of somatic conditions in outpatient clinics stem from this beginning.

Group therapy through a textbook or prepared script is used by Klapman (24). Lectures (and sometimes assignments) are given, systematically covering certain topics. In Klapman's own work, adapted to the composition of the groups (neurotic, psychotic, etc.), they concern emotional problems and mental hygiene, with emphasis on mental mechanisms and general personality descriptions. Using a specially prepared textbook, each class member reads a paragraph, summarizes, and then offers any comments he considers apropos. Questions may be asked at any time, and every effort is made to create an informal discussion group. The therapist himself is not primarily concerned with the amount of knowledge acquired but tries to be especially sensitive to the feelings and the personal implications that each patient might find for himself in the discussion. It is Klapman's contention that the material, when therapeutically effective, touches off the patients' identifications.

The work of Hadden (3) is very close in spirit to that of Klapman, although there is less emphasis upon a prepared script. He speaks of his work as training by a "class technic" and describes its application to groups varying in size from six to seventeen in the outpatient services of a neurological department of a large hospital. Patients were referred for whom no "organic basis" could be found for their complaints. A personal interview preceded their admission to the class. In the class it is again stressed that they are being referred because no evidence has been found for the presence of organic disease. Since new members are admitted weekly, if scheduling permits, it is necessary to review this matter of the nonorganic basis of their difficulties and other things that have taken place previously under the guise of helping the new members but actually for the purpose of reinforcing certain fundamentals for the entire group. Stress is placed on explaining to and demonstrating for them the appearance of symptomatology as a result of a psychosomatic disturbance, for example, calling their attention to experiences which they might have had as a result of a stage fright or other upsetting situations, and analogies are drawn with their present difficulties. Older members of the group are called upon to state in their own fashion how their emotions produced the symptomatology which they demonstrate. Thereafter in the session the effect of physical tension upon the nervous system is described, followed by instructions in methods of relaxation. These methods include assuming a comfortable position and focusing attention upon a simple object in the front of the room while the therapist in a monotonous tone of voice offers suggestions concerning relaxation. While in this "relaxed" state members are asked to visualize a scene which he describes, generally tranquil in nature. In this hypnotic-like state, suggestions, encouragement, and a description of the dynamics of some particularly common symptoms are presented. Later the particular symptom or syndrome that has been described is the focus of an informal discussion with particular attention on those who have had personal experience with it.

This approach to group therapy has a somewhat "academic" air and presumably suffers from the defects of a pedagogical approach to therapy. It would appear not only that it is educational in nature but also that a large suggestive element is present. It is open to the obvious criticisms of such an approach. Nevertheless, Hadden claims considerable effectiveness for the methods just described.

These and similar procedures stress the therapeutic role of explanation, but do not necessarily neglect other factors. Klapman speaks of a living-through process, and Hadden refers to the relaxing, the inspirational, and the cathartic effects. It is obvious from the description of the latter's procedure that suggestion is operative in an undisguised form. Certain "repressive-inspirational" elements, to use Merrill Moore's term, seem to be present, e.g., urging the patient to control and to suppress the symptomatology.

Although such approaches appear to involve both insightful and release factors in varying degrees, it is pertinent to note that emphasis upon one or the other may be varied according to the type of patients involved. To cite only one from many examples, Teicher (16) used a rather rigid lecture series with groups of naval servicemen in whom anxiety predominated, while arranging for opportunities for ventilation in groups composed of individuals in whom hostility and resentment were very prominent. The therapist served as a guide so as not to allow the sessions to become mere "gripe sessions."

PSYCHOANALYTICALLY ORIENTED GROUP PSYCHOTHERAPY

Generally speaking, no one specific group psychotherapy has emerged which has found common acceptance among psychoanalytically oriented psychotherapists. Many workers in the field—Schilder (12), Wender (18), Ackerman (1) (19), Foulkes and Lewis (21), Sarlin and Berezin (26) among others—have persuasively presented their points of view. They do have in common the conception of group psychotherapy as an extension and amplification of individual psychoanalysis, and the behavior of the individuals in the group is considered to be in many aspects similar to that observed in individual sessions. As in individual psychoanalytic treatment, emphasis on transference and resistance, insight and abreaction, and working through appear.

It is characteristic that individual interviews are combined with group therapy sessions (12, 18, 26), with the latter regarded essentially as a supplement to individual psychotherapy. Foulkes and Lewis (21), however, warn against combining full psychoanalytic treatment with group sessions if for no other reason than the fact that the transference is changed and blunted by the group sessions. It would appear that often the individual interviews used conjointly with group sessions are some form of "briefer" psychoanalysis rather than the classic variety. Early individual sessions make possible some formulation of the patient's difficulties, and then later individual sessions are used to follow up preceding group sessions in regard to matter that the latter stimulated but did not work through. The individual sessions are also used for whatever "deeper" interpretations the therapist sees fit to give, especially those which may prove to be extremely anxiety-provoking at first. Generally speaking, interpretations in the group are kept on a somewhat more superficial level, commensurate with the patient's level of insight.

Since psychoanalytic technique with the individual is carried over to the individuals in the group by most psychoanalytically oriented group therapists, some degree of difference needs to be stressed.[2] Dream interpretation and free association are used by

[2] This is not to say that completely new innovations are not introduced. Schilder (12), for example, used written reports and questionnaires, searched out "ideologies," and so on. Neither these nor other innovations have been widely adopted and, therefore, may be disregarded.

some therapists. Many therapists commented on the relief experienced by the patients when ordinarily tabooed subjects came out in group sessions. When group psychotherapists utilize psychoanalytic concepts and procedures it is fair to say that their approach is likely to be more active than is customary in the individual approach. There is more give-and-take between therapist and patient.

Since transference is basic to the psychoanalytic approach it is appropriate to stress this aspect. Schilder's remarks seem of general significance, so he is quoted:

The phenomena of positive and negative transference to the analyst are not less outspoken in the group than in the usual psychoanalytic treatment. They express themselves in generally known terms. The reaction of one patient to the transference situation of another patient is very often remarkable. The patient in a state of positive transference feels a need to defend the analyst against the negative transference of another patient. In the negative transference, the group particularly stress that the physician is not sufficiently interested in their fate, that as a public employee he must spend his hours with them regardless, and that he is less interested in the fate of the patients than in the scientific problems they offer. Very often discussions of problems of this type have a very important effect upon the fate of a group. They can be shown that nobody has the right to expect the complete emotional surrender of another person—that the other person has to live his own life even if he does happen to be one's father or one's relative or one's physician. (12, pp. 91–92.)

There is another aspect of the transference phenomenon in group psychotherapy worthy of comment. This is the patient-to-patient transference, to use Wender's term (18). It is found to take place and is used to facilitate the transference to the therapist through the identification of one patient with another when one of them is already in a transference relationship with the therapist.

Foulkes and Lewis (21) point out that in group psychotherapy the therapist cannot remain in the background but must emerge as an actual person, which, of course, affects the transference situation in that the patient faces (literally and figuratively) a real person. This serves to keep transference reactions somewhat blunted and prevents reaching the deepest unconscious levels.

Slavson, on the other hand, offers what at first glance appears to be contradictory to this point of view. He writes:

Transference is greatly facilitated because the group is a protection against the therapist and what he stands for: a symbol of parental and environmental authority. At the same time, however, transference at times becomes greatly intensified, particularly its negative phases. There is reinforcement of the hostile trends against the therapist, which makes his role rather difficult. But because of this very fact, and the opportunity for acting out, therapy is accelerated. Transference in groups is also intensified on its positive levels when there is sibling rivalry and the patients make a bid for the love of the therapist. (15, p. 26.)

It may be that this apparent contradiction can be resolved by a reminder that the advantages sketched by Slavson—ease of formation, freedom in expression—are not necessarily correlated with depth of transference or the subtlety of its manipulation.

Schilder (12) believed on the basis of his experiences with psychoanalytical oriented group psychotherapy that it was most successful with cases characterized as social neuroses. These are individuals who do not feel comfortable in the presence of others. Sweating, blushing, awkwardness, palpitation, a feeling of being conspicuous, a feeling of self-consciousness, etc., may help to identify them. Schilder used the group method with a wide variety of other patients but with less success. Wender (18) reports benefits from his approach with mild schizophrenics, mild but not retarded depressives, and hysterics.

Activity Group Psychotherapy

Developed in the setting of a case work agency whose clients included a large number of behavior problem children, activity group psychotherapy as described by Slavson (15) (27) stands in sharp contrast to the verbal give-and-take of interview group psychotherapy. Activity takes the place of words—the child does things with materials available for him and others to use. To be sure, there is conversation among the children and between the therapist and the children, but it is at the level of the activities in which they are engaged, such as comments from one child to another about the boat he is building, or instructions from the therapist on how to operate the jig saw.

The keynote of these club meetings, for it is as such that the groups are organized, is permissiveness. The time of the meeting, the clubroom, its furnishings and equipment, and even the food served at the end of each meeting are decided upon by the children themselves. At first there are no restrictions at all in most of the groups. Rules that are instituted arise naturally from the members of the group as they realize that infringement on the rights of others must somehow be handled if they are to get along together in the group.

A brief generalized sketch will serve to illustrate activity group therapy in operation. Leaving aside for the moment the basis of selection for the eight boys averaging in age ten years who form this hypothetical group, the first, second, and some of the subsequent meetings will be described. The group therapist, a specially trained social case worker, arrives at the meeting room early and sets out the material. Wood and metalworking tools, clay, electric toys and apparatus, leather work, crayons, paints, and water colors might be supplied, as well as games such as tenpins and indoor quoits. As the boys arrive at their "new club" they find him working with the material; he introduces himself by his first and last name. As others come in they are introduced to one another (for generally they do not know one another before). The therapist does not volunteer to get things started but instead permits them to wander around, watch him, or do what they please. Rather shortly there will be inquiries from some of the boys if they can help him or can use the other things. To this the therapist replies that they may do or make what they please—the materials are there to be used if they so desire. Some late arrivals will find what other children have settled on to their interest; one or two will cluster around or work near the therapist; others will stay off entirely by themselves. Naturally there is some constraint on the part of the boys and much uncertainty at this meeting. This the therapist does nothing more to relieve than to maintain a quiet, warm interest. Neither now nor later does he start conversations, make suggestions, or offer reproofs. The refreshments at the end of the session break the ice somewhat, since most of the boys sit around the same table to eat and drink.

At the time of the second meeting, there is not as much constraint. Some of the boys know one another a bit better; one or two have found some long-range activity such as building a boat; two or three flit from one activity to another; others just sit or wander around the outskirts. Activities at first undertaken hesitantly with frequent anxious glances at the therapist (who continues to have some activity of his own to turn to when not called upon by the children to do something else) are now tackled with more assurance and vigor. However, there is little interaction with one another, each boy going about his own business with little or no coöperative activity. Such comments as are made are generally directed to the therapist. The refreshments bring them together again, with perhaps a bit more relaxation on their part.

The next few sessions may show essentially the same trends, with greater accentuation of those making for security in the group. Or there may be variations. For example, the meal together, heretofore more or less orderly, may suddenly "go wild." There may be a concerted grab by two or three of the boys, which starts others throwing the food around the room or at others, while another may attempt to stuff the remains in his pockets. This outbreak is again met by steady acceptance on the part of the therapist. If asked about his inactivity by the boys he will only point out that it is their club. There may be a wave of destroying the materials, followed by neither condemnation nor replacement of the broken materials. There may be fist fights, "ganging up," cursing and vulgarities, and still the therapist refrains from intervention. Or there may be variation in the setting of the meeting. Using the club's allowance, the boys may decide to have a hike or go to a movie instead of having one of their usual meetings. Here again the boys decide. However, the budget is finite, and if used up too quickly or spent in a way later considered foolish, no more is forthcoming until the next budget period. This financial limitation and other restrictions such as a decision for therapeutic reasons to forbid attendance of a member or to bar "guests" is not a function of the therapist. The "front office" takes care of such matters, so that the therapist is allowed to maintain his neutral role.

It is perhaps appropriate to explain the therapist's neutral role more completely at this point. Steadily maintaining his permissiveness, he is what the children make him. Some seek him out; others do not communicate with him in any way. These and other roles he accepts as they come. Emphatically he does not play favorites, as all children receive his regard. He does not permit outside contact with the children nor see as patients any of them who might be receiving individual therapy. It is the therapist's intent that the child relate himself to the group in the same way in which he relates to them, i.e., showing attitudes toward one another of friendliness, appreciativeness, and acceptance. He gives praise to all chil-

dren for their constructions and accomplishments, unless it is judged that the child is not ready to accept it. He does not praise a child for doing something for the good of the group—coöperative effort is taken for granted. He himself acts in this manner. For example, toward the end of the session the room is likely to be in some disorder, but no one is requested to clean it up. Instead, the therapist points out the time and goes about doing it himself, often alone. When time for the meeting is up there is again no direction. He puts on his coat and hat and goes to the door, perhaps pretending to read. Sooner or later someone notices this, calls it to the attention of the others, who then proceed to pile out.

As has been emphasized, he is permissive, but not uncritically. Some groups have more limitations placed upon them from the very start, whereas others have restrictions gradually applied. For example, lack of restriction on fighting or destruction is characteristic of early sessions only, since participation in everyday activities demands restraint.

The changes in activity which show therapeutic progress are varied and numerous. With the same activities which were previously used to illustrate maladaptive aspects of group interaction, it is possible to illuminate some of the positive changes. The boys overcome their lack of self-confidence by finding out that they can build or create things from the materials supplied. They take over (generally unasked) the task of arranging the materials before the meeting proper. They learn to work together in creative activities and introduce games, formerly more or less absent, which require interpersonal contact and observance of rules. Their need for committing antisocial and destructive acts seems to disappear. The ganging up and fighting drop away, although normal roughhousing may remain. Conversation becomes easy, informal, and non-stressful after fears and tensions have disappeared. Planning the use of the club's money and rules about cleaning up may be instituted. Aspects of something approaching family living become evident. The meals become a high point of the activity, and pride in observing decorum (at least what would pass for decorum in ten-year-old boys) may appear. Plates are passed, and conversations are carried on about matters of mutual interest. Friendships develop which are sometimes carried over to life outside the group. Thus many salutary behavior patterns are established.

The impression may have been given that shy and withdrawn children have no place in activity group therapy. Such is not the case, since agressiveness is not a threat. In view of the very nature of the group, which clearly permits social mobility, they may withdraw from the danger spots and make themselves inconspicuous. Provided the child has some desire for acceptance by others (social hunger), he too will eventually find himself in the group.

With this background, it is now possible to examine the rationale on which the technique is based. It was developed originally to work with children with primary behavior disorders, meaning in effect those children who show hostility and aggression or withdrawal arising in large measure from early emotional deprivation. Neurotic traits are also often present. However, work with psychoneurotic children with internalized conflicts has recently proved successful (Slavson, 15). The unhampered, unrestrained acting out permitted in such groups would exacerbate the difficulties of the psychopathic child. Considerable precision, then, is necessary in selecting patients for whom activity group therapy is indicated. With respect to age, it is considered primarily suitable for children between the ages of about seven and fourteen.

The intent of activity group therapy is well summarized by Slavson himself:

> Generally, Activity Group Therapy provides spontaneous discharge of drives, diminution of tension and reduction of anxiety through physical and emotional activity in a group setting that permits unimpeded acting out within the boundaries of personal safety, and through free interaction with fellow-members that leads to a variety of relationships. Interpersonal and social situations constantly arise through which each discharges tensions, expresses emotions, discovers limitations, builds ego strength, finds some status for himself, develops relationships and a limited degree of derivative insight. The total situation is designed to supply substitute gratifications, give vent to aggression, reinforce the ego, particularly in regard to feelings of failure and inadequacy, counteract deflated self-evaluation, release blockings to expression in some, and build self-restraint in others. (15, pp. 33–34.)

Permissiveness within the broad limits set up is very important in that it is a means of breaking down resistances to the world as it is. Activity catharsis, or expression of feeling through actions, is considered to be crucial. Group therapy encourages security, ego development, leisure time interest, and acceptance by the group. The

group is presumed to be a substitute family with the therapist a parent surrogate. This is not entirely a hypothetical analogy; children often speak of it in such terms, referring to the group leader as a parent and to the other members of the group as a family. With this adult and other children the child establishes relations which make possible a transition toward a more realistic and balanced perception of the world and its demands upon him. Insight is gained by the child *in* the activities experienced in the situation, not through interpretation, as contrasted with the work of Redl to be mentioned later. Slavson (6) also considers the usual common factors of psychotherapy to be operative. Among those mentioned earlier he includes catharsis, insight, and relationship as having counterparts in activity group therapy. They are considered to come from different sources and to warrant different relative emphasis. Insight, for example, does not achieve much importance as a therapeutic factor, and instead ego strengthening is regarded as its counterpart (14).

The question may be asked as to why these goals are to be achieved through activity group therapy and not through individual psychotherapy? The answer at its most basic level is relatively simple: these children need to relate to other children rather than to an adult (15). They need to enjoy constructive personal relations with their contemporaries. It must be borne in mind that the child coming to such an agency as that in which Slavson and his associates function is one in whom the need for constructive group experience is very great. In varying degrees he has been rejected at home, school, settlement house, or street gang.

In the foregoing account many aspects of activity group therapy have not been explicitly formulated, especially the selection of the patients, the formation of groups so that they are therapeutically balanced, and modifications to suit particular problems and ages. Slavson's interpretation of dynamics in a psychoanalytic framework has also been relatively neglected. His *Introduction to Group Therapy* (27) is a basic source which considers these and other omissions.

In the setting of a smaller group within the population attending a day camp Hewitt and Gildea (22) described their experiences with several girls chosen for the group after the start of camp. Its therapeutic purpose was unknown to the children, although not to the parents. The unique feature of the group was a relatively well-adjusted youngster included to serve as a catalyst. For an account of the use of activity group therapy in a setting different from that of Slavson and his associates this study is especially useful and interesting.

Two characteristics appear to stand out in activity group therapy —the complete lack of interpretation and the permissive neutrality of the therapist. It is concerning these two points that the criticisms of Redl (11) are pertinent. The critique arose from his own experience in agency group work. On the basis of this experience he rejects the concept of unconditional acceptance. He also attempts to show that interpretation, when used properly, is a very potent tool for therapy. In this connection he gives three criticisms essentially as follows: First, in view of the fact that there are so many varieties of disturbing causal factors and kinds of children treated, he is suspicious of any single technique which promises to be useful for all these cases and feels that a variety of approaches would be needed. Second, the idea of unconditional acceptance reminds him of the mistakes made in its name in the early history of the psychoanalytic treatment of children. Third, he wonders why, if it has been found unsatisfactory within the confines of individual therapeutic sessions, it is reasonable to assume it would work better in a group setting, especially with the differing backgrounds of the children. Interference on the part of the leader is demanded either for the manipulation of the entire group or because the needs of one child make it obligatory. How and when to interfere is by no means easy to decide, but he unequivocally rejects the theory of unconditional acceptance. His experience has been that interpretation is a very valuable buffer in this occasionally necessary interference. Group interviews of an interpretative nature as well as periods of time with individual children are considered valuable.

It is exceedingly difficult to arrive at any definite conclusion concerning the justice of these criticisms. Quite possibly the environmental "climate" of Redl's groups is somewhat different from Slavson's and, in effect, they are two quite independent approaches to group therapy with children.

PSYCHODRAMA

Perhaps more than is the case with any other approach to group psychotherapy, psychodrama is largely the work of one man, J. L.

Moreno. In certain phases the development of this point of view resembles that of a cult in that he has surrounded himself with a group of assistants independent of the main stream of professional clinical thought and has established a training school, a private hospital, a publishing house, and a theater all dedicated to the advancement of psychodrama to the exclusion of other points of view. In fact, he would claim for psychodrama primacy in the entire field of group therapy both historically and in breadth of application. In his hands psychodrama takes different forms from its use in the day-to-day practice of other individuals in hospitals and institutions. It is, therefore, necessary to describe some aspects of his procedure and also to illustrate the more sober use of the technique when removed from his direct influence.

Moreno (8) (9) points out that psychodrama uses five instruments—the stage, the patient, the director (therapist), the staff and therapeutic aids (auxiliary egos), and the audience. These will be briefly described in turn.

The stage at Beacon House, one of the settings for psychodrama under Moreno's supervision, is circular in nature, is bare of properties except perhaps a chair or two, is arranged in three concentric circles one above the other with the largest at the bottom practically at the level of the floor, and has above it a balcony. The setting for the audience is of more conventional design. Moreno contends that the stage is an important but not essential element of psychodramatic productions, since it is also possible to have what he refers to as "psychodrama on the spot," meaning in effect psychodrama conducted anywhere. The arrangement of the stage is designed to encourage freedom of movement and to permit expression at one or another "level."

The second instrument is the patient himself, who is asked to play a part—to portray himself and his own private world. He may be expected to play the part of someone else who is therapeutically important to him, such as his father, his wife, etc., or even to improvise spontaneously a fictitious (imagined) role, such as the district attorney, sheriff, or the Devil (25). There may be enactment of a past event, a problem presently pressing, or a projection of oneself into the future. Since most patients have had no dramatic experience and it is necessary for them to become familiar with and attuned to the situation of playing a role, Moreno introduces into their activity a variety of preliminary procedures for warming-up purposes. Suppose, for example, that a patient when asked to portray his wife has been extremely stiff, wooden, and self-conscious in trying to do so. Someone else might be called upon by the director to play the part while the patient watched. Very shortly the patient would find the portrayal not true to life and would be in a position to criticize the performance. He would then be asked to portray the character with fidelity. It must be emphasized that at no time is there a prepared script for the patient to use. He is to act freely and spontaneously, creating life on the stage. Once warmed up to his role of the moment, it is Moreno's experience that the patient finds it relatively easy to proceed freely.

The third instrument of psychodrama is the director or therapist. It is his task to turn every possible clue which the subject offers through prior acquaintance with him into dramatic action and to guide the production in whatever direction would be therapeutically efficacious.

In addition there is a staff of supporting players called "auxiliary egos." They are used to play the role of absentee members involved in the patient's network of interpersonal relationships. In other words, they portray the roles required by the patient's world. Often they know relatively little about the patient and are dependent upon him for clues as to how to act during the psychodrama sessions and upon cues given by the director prior to the situation. They act only as suggested and try to adapt to the therapeutic situation as it arises. In a sense they are psychological *agents provocateurs*.

The fifth instrument is the audience, composed of other patients, professional personnel, and the like. Since their comments are solicited, they serve as a sounding board of public opinion.

A psychodramatic session, then, consists of the enactment of a spontaneous dramatic incident. This particular situation is either selected by the director because of its relevance to the person's difficulties based on a prior private interview or suggested by the patient himself as an area in which personal problems lie. Immediately before the session the incident is briefly outlined. Merely the background is given; e.g., the wife has told the patient she is leaving him. How the patient is to handle the situation is not described, it being essentially self-directed with the person reacting as he sees fit.

The fundamental premise of the method is that, by turning the personality free upon a stage in spontaneously enacting some incident, one brings about emotional release. The patient is given an opportunity for emotional liberation in a group situation. He externalizes and shares his troubles in a situation in which the other participants are nonhostile and accepting. He releases not only verbally but physically.

In this momentary situation on the stage, according to Moreno, the patient is presumed to show basic aspects of his personality, his strivings, and his conflicts. Thus diagnostic material is obtained, but an even more important process of catharsis is taking place by the acting out of conflicts and by analysis later in a post-dramatic interview with the director. Training in spontaneity is offered both in reëxamining past situations and in meeting some not heretofore faced. This factor of spontaneity is considered to be the core of psychodramatic therapy. It is presumed that a mobilization of personality characteristics on the spur of the moment on the psychodramatic stage creates a resourcefulness in meeting life's situations which, if sufficiently developed, increases the individual's adjustive capacity.

Turning to the use of the technique outside Moreno's coterie we find it in mental hospital practice to be somewhat more sober and pedestrian. Preparation for return to outside life of patients nearly ready for discharge is a typical situation where it may be utilized. The report of Kline (4) (5) is pertinent. A variety of scenes were prepared, including "quest for a job," "marriage and children," "inquisitive neighbors," and "the in-law problem." The search for employment may be used as an illustration. Having to seek employment is often very threatening for individuals who have been in mental institutions. In addition to the usual problems of employment seeking they are troubled by the question of the advisability of whether or not they should admit their mental illness and hospitalization. Therefore, within the less threatening protective setting of the hospital they are confronted with this potential perilous situation and are thus able to prepare for it when they face it in actuality. In the setting as Kline uses it are a desk and two chairs, with the cast including the interviewer and the job applicant, who, of course, is the patient. The meeting is supposedly taking place in the interviewer's office about one month after discharge from the hospital. The interviewer makes a general inquiry into the man's qualifications for the job for which he is applying. The patient responds as he sees fit. If he is reluctant to talk about any aspects of his background, including his mental illness, it is the task of the interviewer to probe into these areas. Before leaving the interview situation the patient is forced to face his period of hopsitalization and to account for it as best he can. The interview is terminated with the statement that the man will be notified if and when an opening occurs. After the interview, other patients, who have been present throughout, are called upon to comment or to criticize the performance and the way the patient handled the situation. The interviewer himself is asked whether or not he would have been inclined to hire the man and to give reasons for his opinion.

The major criticism which may be offered of the psychodramatic approach is that Moreno's theory of psychodynamics is not generally accepted. Dependent as it is upon the theory of spontaneity as the mainspring of human conduct, it appears to be open to the criticism that it is relatively one-sided, neglecting, if not denying, the other factors common to psychotherapy. Insight is minimized at the expense of emotional release, and the procedure is presumably beset with the same difficulties which appear when release is the only element operative. Since fantasy living is very much encouraged, as when Moreno encourages a psychotic patient in his delusional system through psychodrama on the spot, the already tenuous distinction between reality and fantasy is sometimes further weakened.

When psychodrama is not regarded as *the* therapeutic technique but as one among many psychotherapeutic approaches, these criticisms are not as tenable. In addition, the technique itself may be used while the spontaneity theory is rejected, the approach being viewed as one aspect of the main stream of psychiatric-psychological thinking.

BIBLIOGRAPHY

1. Ackerman, N. W., Some general principles in the use of group psychotherapy, in Glueck, B. (ed.), *Current therapies of personality disorders*, Grune & Stratton, 1946, pp. 275–280.
2. Baruch, D. W., and Miller, H., Group and individual psychotherapy in the treatment of allergy, *J. consult. Psychol.*, 1946, 10:281–284.
3. Hadden, S. B., Treatment of the neuroses by class technic, *Ann. intern. Med.*, 1942, 16:33–37.

4. Kline, N. S., Psychodrama for mental hospitals. I, *J. clin. Psychopath.*, 1947, 8:817–825.
5. Kline, N. S., Psychodrama for mental hospitals. II, *J. clin. Psychopath.*, 1948, 9:96–107.
6. Lowrey, L. G., (chm.), Group therapy: special section meeting, 1943, *Amer. J. Orthopsychiat.*, 1943, 13:648–691.
7. Luchins, A. S., Group structures in group psychotherapy, *J. clin. Psychol.*, 1947, 3:269–273.
8. Moreno, J. L., *Psychodrama: first volume*, Beacon Press, 1946.
9. Moreno, J. L., Psychodrama and group psychotherapy, *Sociometry*, 1946, 9:249–253.
10. Peres, H., An investigation of nondirective group therapy, *J. consult. Psychol.*, 1947, 11:159–172.
11. Putman, M. C., and others, *Proceedings of the second Brief Psychotherapy Council, January 1944*. Psychotherapy for children, and group Psychotherapy, Institute of Psychoanalysis, 1944.
12. Schilder, P., Results and problems of group psychotherapy in severe neuroses, *Ment. Hyg., N.Y.*, 1939, 23:87–98.
13. Slavson, S. R., The field and objectives of group therapy, in Glueck, B. (ed.), *Current therapies of personality disorders*, Grune & Stratton, 1946, pp. 166–193.
14. Slavson, S. R., Differential dynamics of activity and interview group therapy, *Amer. J. Orthopsychiat.*, 1947, 17:293–302.
15. Slavson, S. R., General principles and dynamics, in Slavson, S. R. (ed.), *The practice of group therapy*, International Universities Press, 1947, pp. 19–39.
16. Teicher, J. D., Experiences with group psychotherapy, *U.S. Nav. med. Bull.*, 1945, 44:753–756.
17. Thomas, G. W., Group psychotherapy: a review of the recent literature, *Psychosom. Med.*, 1943, 5:166–180.
18. Wender, L., Group psychotherapy: a study of its application, *Psychiat. Quart.*, 1940, 14:708–718.

RECOMMENDED CASE STUDY READINGS

19. Ackerman, N. W., Interview group psychotherapy with psychoneurotic adults, in Slavson, S. R. (ed.), *The practice of group therapy*, International Universities Press, 1947, pp. 135–155.
20. Baruch, D. W., Description of a project in group therapy, in Watson, R. I. (ed.), *Readings in the clinical method in psychology*, Harper & Brothers, 1949, pp. 638–653. (Also in *J. consult. Psychol.*, 1945, 9:271–280.)
21. Foulkes, S. H., and Lewis, E., Group analysis: a study in the treatment of groups on psychoanalytic lines, *Brit. J. Med. Psychol.*, 1944, 20:175–184.
22. Hewitt, H., and Gildea, M. C. L., An experiment in group psychotherapy, *Amer. J. Orthopsychiat.*, 1945, 15:112–127.

23. Holland, G., Lister, L. Slavson, S. R., and Ackerman, N. W., Treatment of a case of behavior disorder through activity group therapy, in Slavson, S. R., (ed.), *The practice of group therapy*, International Universities Press, 1947, pp. 107–132.
24. Klapman, J. W., Didactic group psychotherapy with psychotic patients, in Slavson, S. R., (ed.), *The practice of group therapy*, International Universities Press, 1947, pp. 242–259.
25. Moreno, J. L., Inter-personal therapy and the psychopathology of inter-personal relations, *Sociometry*, 1937, 1:9–76.
26. Sarlin, C. N., and Berezin, M. A., Group psychotherapy on a modified analytic basis, *J. nerv. ment. Dis.*, 1946, 104:611–667.
27. Slavson, S. R., *An introduction to group therapy*, Commonwealth Fund, 1943.

CHAPTER 23

Indirect Methods of Treatment[1]

In previous chapters concerned with treatment, emphasis was placed upon the therapeutic effects arising from the direct inter-personal relationship of patient and therapist. Although the environment in which the patient moved was not entirely neglected, his direct relationship with the therapist was conspicuously in the foreground. Events occurring outside the therapist's office were seen only in relation to therapeutic sessions. And yet, one of the goals of therapy is the preparation of the patient for the time when the outside world is the only reality and the therapist's office but a remote past aspect of that reality. Even during the therapeutic sessions the patient lived and moved and had his being in this world. The environment was the soil from which came the experiences and behavior with which both patient and therapist were working; it was also a present reality modifying the therapeutic sessions. Human activities, no matter what the particular area under consideration, are furthered or hindered by situational opportunities or ob-

---

[1] The use of indirect methods of treatment is especially well developed in social work agencies. The account in this chapter does not do justice to the complexity, adroitness, and clinical acumen displayed by social workers in using these approaches, since many of their applications are not directly related to the theme of our presentation. For example, children's protective societies, children's homes (orphanages), and foster home care agencies very commonly use indirect methods, but in a setting somewhat removed from the province of the psychologist.

stacles. A child buffeted by circumstances—a brutal father, a neglectful mother—is not in any opportune position to profit from individual psychotherapy. Psychotherapy is not alien to this reality. Ancillary procedures to psychotherapy proper are as a consequence implicit in the clinical method.

Indirect methods of treatment are dependent upon mediating adjuncts—books, recreation, work, or persons other than the therapist. Indeed, the use of testing material, through which the present discussion of psychotherapy was introduced, was such an indirect method (see Chapter 17). Emphasis now shifts to other devices employed or the manipulative procedures utilized.

THE INTRODUCTION OF INDIRECT PROCEDURES

The appropriate timing of introduction of these ancillary procedures is not as simple as it may seem. We hear of "total push" implying use of all available means of treatment simultaneously. It might at first glance appear plausible to decide that every method of treatment should immediately be instituted. This is done sometimes in the uncritical manner of a blanket prescription or shotgun technique in which therapeutic shots are sprayed over the patient in the hope that some will hit the target. Assuming psychotherapy is more often than not the primary method of treatment a caution must be offered. Psychotherapy is an activity demanding much from the patient. Other procedures to be effective are not introduced until the clinician has asked himself whether or not the patient can tolerate the additional treatment and whether or not it is therapeutically indicated and has been able to answer in the affirmative. Attendance at a summer camp might be used as an illustration. The experiences at such a camp may be challenging and often are helpful, but if the child is already overwhelmed by the changes in his life introduced from psychotherapy he may find it too much to tolerate. Only when the child is soundly established in the clinician-patient relationship are such supplementary procedures indicated. Positive reasons for the choice of camping as a supplementary therapeutic experience need to be identified as well. The child must be seen as one in whom the socializing experiences of the camp will be of some therapeutic value. The discussion in Chapter 22 of group therapy is pertinent.

As in any application of the clinical method, indirect procedures of treatment ideally require appropriate diagnostic appraisal. Unfortunately, environmental change is often the only treatment step taken, and a diagnostic phase worthy of the name may be omitted, e.g., most, but not all, commitments for delinquency. In other instances, as in institutionalization for mental deficiency, the diagnostic phase will be of varying degrees of depth and may well be accompanied by other treatment measures. Movement to another home, whether foster home, institution, camp, or other setting, does not in itself cause the behavior problem or emotional difficulty to disappear. The patient brings to the new environment his personality structure, his attitude toward authority, and his symptoms. If environmental change is to be utilized with full effectiveness it is ancillary, requires a prior diagnostic justification, and is specific to the needs of the individual.

Indirect methods may be variously classified. Emphasis may be placed (1) on the general field of endeavor as in occupational and recreational therapy; (2) on the nature of the adjunct introduced, as in bibliotherapy; (3) on the environmental changes introduced, such as environmental modification and manipulation. In the following account each of these ways of classifying indirect methods will be illustrated by the examples given above. However, bibliotherapy, an adjunct so named to emphasize the nature of the material used, will be regarded as an aspect of occupational-recreational therapy.

OCCUPATIONAL AND RECREATIONAL THERAPY

There is no fundamental difference between occupational and recreational therapy. The former, it is true, may be said to emphasize handicrafts and the like and the latter games and sports. Since both "work" and "play" in this context are used for therapeutic ends, the distinction is rather pointless. Both occupational and recreational therapy are to be distinguished from occupational training and recreational activity on this basis of intent. The therapeutic values are sought, not the work or the recreation.

Custom and the efforts of specialists in the field have emphasized the former term, "occupational therapy." It will be used hereafter when the general field is to be indicated. The occupational therapist is a professionally trained person whose basic credo is that the practice of his profession is an adjunct to the activities of the physician. Therapeutic efforts are carried out in a setting in which there is a prescription either general or specific by the physician of the activities to be implemented by the occupational therapist.

Occupational therapy is a means of treatment through participation in activities of the sort suggested by the term "occupation." It is necessarily broader than its application in the psychological-psychiatric field, including treatment for primarily somatic diseases such as orthopedic conditions or tuberculosis.

In relatively recent years there has been an increase both in the quality of training and in the number of occupational therapists. Certification of occupational therapists is designated by O.T.R., which implies graduation from an accredited school and passage of a national examination. Four- or five-year courses (including at least two prior years of general college work) are offered in twenty-one schools throughout the country (Willard and Spackman, 31).

OCCUPATIONAL THERAPY IN A PRIVATE HOSPITAL

Occupational therapy is practiced in a great variety of settings—general hospitals, mental hospitals (state and federal and private), workshops, and so on. The clientele of a private mental hospital, which caters to patients whose financial means permit such treatment, generally consists of neurotics and psychotics in relatively early stages of development. The number of patients is usually small, and they have a high level of cultural interests. The private hospital permits a greater variety, richness, and subtlety of treatment than does the overcrowded state hospital with its greater number of chronic or deteriorated patients. Consequently occupational therapy in such private sanitariums has greater scope and depth than it does in state hospitals. It is appropriate under these circumstances that the program for occupational therapy at a specific private institution, the Menninger Institute, be described.[2]

At the Menninger Institute (27) recreational therapy is prescribed individually and consequently varies from patient to patient, depending upon the psychiatrist's conception of the needs of the patient. This is predicated upon the assumption that "re-creation" means to create anew, or, more specifically in this instance, to build toward an adult level of functioning in society. With many deeply

---

[2] Since the series of articles appeared several years ago it must be pointed out that they may not reflect current practice.

disturbed patients this is a gradual process—first recreation with the therapist, then in small groups, and only later in large groups. Thus, resocialization is a fundamental aim of the therapeutic process.

Other values and goals are also operative, one of which is the task of making reality more pleasant. The patient whose delusional system involves many unpleasant aspects such as "rotting insides" may, when occupied recreationally, ignore in varying degrees these prominent symptoms. Moreover, recreation gives the patient an opportunity to vent his feelings upon objects in the environment in a socially acceptable manner. One such example is the patient who when driving golf balls named each after a hated relative. Another patient who destroyed objects in her environment derived considerable pleasure from knocking down bowling pins. Artistic pursuits, such as music, the graphic arts, dancing, and dramatics, also allow freedom of fantasy expression and serve an especially useful purpose with narcissistic patients.

This same hospital, according to Bellator (7), uses educational courses modified to suit the needs of the patients to accomplish similar objectives. Sometimes a patient has been forced by his illness to leave school before completion. After the acute stage of the difficulty has passed, the patient may resume his work toward a diploma or degree through correspondence, extension, or actual attendance in local classrooms. Hobby training in music, wood carving, horticulture, and so on are also used. In a later paper Menninger (26) gives further details concerning organization. He reports considerable success with educational procedures.

Social gatherings are also used with some success at this same hospital. Anderson states that the purposes are as follows:

The purpose of the occasion is to create a real situation in which there is an opportunity for the satisfying of social needs. Some of these needs are: (1) Many patients have found themselves inadequate to most social demands and shrink from all contacts. A means must be found to bring them out of the shell into which they have retreated and to help them to face reality by giving them an opportunity for some accomplishment with protection from failure. (2) Some patients seek all their social satisfactions in phantasies in which they are the leading character. They need an opportunity to live out in a real situation some of those dreams which have a tendency to absorb their entire interest. (3) Many patients are handicapped socially by strong hostilities toward other people which render them either unpopular or else completely inactive. They need an opportunity to express these hostilities in socially acceptable ways. Such a need is usually met more satisfactorily in sports and contests than at social affairs when politeness is emphasized, but occasionally a suitable outlet can be devised in the Social Hour. (4) Praise is necessary to all individuals, yet many have received little or none. This deprivation often contributes to the development of mental illness. Opportunities for earning praise can easily be provided in social situations. (4, p. 57.)

It is apparent that these various facets of occupational therapy as practiced in this private hospital have in common certain fundamental aims. Although the media through which the aims are accomplished vary (recreational activities, educational courses, social gatherings), they are integrated by the goals set, such as resocialization, ability to meet with and deal with other individuals, and the like. If in turn integrated with psychotherapy they are far from time fillers but actually comprise therapeutically beneficial experiences.

THE PRESCRIPTION OF OCCUPATIONAL THERAPY

Throughout the preceding description of various aspects of occupational therapy implicitly and explicitly the matter of prescription —the therapeutically correct occupation or recreation for a particular patient—has run as a theme. Occupational therapy properly used has a definite therapeutic objective. As Willard and Spackman (31) say in this connection, simple distraction and easing the rigors of the environment are not the whole intent. They summarize the purposes of occupational therapy as guiding mental attitudes into healthy channels, promoting a desire to get well, restoring self-confidence and a feeling of security, substituting encouragement for discouragement, establishing and maintaining good work habits, and affording an opportunity for socialization. Laudable as these general motives may be, they are not specific enough to meet the needs of the individual patient.

The prescription of occupational therapy when used with clinical acuteness is neither simple nor general. "Sending the patient to OT" is not enough. A valuable account specific to this problem is offered in a book by Dunton (14), written primarily with the physician in mind rather than the occupational therapist. It is valuable in demonstrating how the clinician prescribes occupational therapy. The advantages (and limitations) of occupational therapy may be illustrated by a quotation from this book.

In discussing occupational therapy with schizophrenic patients Dunton speaks of their asocial tendencies, their habits of daydreaming, and their lack of contact with reality. In connection with daydreaming he writes:

> The habit of day-dreaming may be best overcome by giving those occupations which require concentration of attention. An excellent example is using a scroll saw to make puzzle pictures or other objects. The small, delicate blade is easily broken unless close attention is given. This acts as an alarm, bringing the patient back to reality. Replacing the blade is troublesome and annoying so the patient learns to concentrate better in order to avoid this task. Attention must also be given to make the cut in its proper place, outlining pictured objects or lines of the pattern, and the pedals must be worked steadily to keep the saw moving. Basket weaving requires close attention, even though it is a stereotyped occupation, in order that the winder may be placed before and behind proper stakes. Errors must be corrected by undoing work done, a thing which no one enjoys. Loom weaving may be used for the same purpose, the patient necessarily concentrating on the use of pedals or levers and making a proper shed if work done is not to be taken out. (14, pp. 53–54.)

Such instances bring out clearly that although this sort of approach is valuable, the activities sketched can hardly be more than supplementary. Often the therapeutic change occurred not in the event taking place in the shop, the classroom, or the recreation hall but in the use the psychotherapist was able to put it to in the subsequent psychotherapeutic sessions.

This leads directly to an important, but sometimes neglected, aspect of the comprehensive use of occupational therapy. Just as it is not enough to prescribe occupational therapy in a general or cursory fashion it is not sufficient to have it carried out in isolation from the therapist. Once it is prescribed, the manner in which the patient responds should be observed or noted by the therapist—not only to evaluate progress more or less passively but also to accomplish the more clinically relevant objective of utilizing the experiences of the patient in subsequent psychotherapeutic sessions.

BIBLIOTHERAPY

The use of books as an adjunct for therapy is a firmly established indirect method of treatment. In one direct sense bibliotherapy is an aspect of occupational therapy along with handicrafts, games, classes, and social gatherings. It is different from other techniques, however, in that it is often used by the therapist directly rather than through an intermediary in the person of an occupational therapist.

Although there has been some attention to bibliotherapy in the literature, most accounts are unfortunately general and superficial. A distinguished exception is the discussion by Menninger (25). This is especially fortunate since it applies to the same setting, the Menninger Institute, as did the discussion of other aspects of occupational therapy.

Menninger considers the purpose of bibliotherapy to be three-fold—education (information, interest, contacts with reality, and evolution of insight), recreation, and identification with the social group (book club, library, newspaper columns). Serving these purposes necessitates a prescription which considers the patient's needs, background, and symptoms.

As Menninger sees it, there are four methods by which benefits may occur. He writes:

Perhaps the most common therapeutic benefit from bibliotherapy is derived by identification of the patient with some particular character or experience in the book with a subsequent abreaction of emotion regarding the material absorbed. In such identification the person obtained vicarious gratification from the hero's struggle and victory. He may obtain relief from the recognition that other people have problems similar to his own. This method of benefit has been especially noted from reading fiction, particularly in instances where the hero or heroine has a struggle and does achieve. Thus, one elderly patient who felt that her family had deserted her found great satisfaction in reading Pearl Buck's Exile. The struggle that the author's mother experienced stimulated the patient to write of her own mother, but it was apparent that she was writing a good deal about herself. Another patient whose home had been temporarily closed by her married children found a great deal of solace and satisfaction in reading Hale's A Man Without a Country. . . . This same mechanism of identification and abreaction has at times a deleterious or at least dubiously beneficial effect. Thus, a paranoid woman whose delusions centered about clothes that other women wore, but which she claimed as her designs, was always greatly disturbed by fashion magazines. A hypomanic woman, who proclaimed and exhibited her hypererotic desires, was always demanding sex stories and risqué books. . . .

A special form of identification in which benefits are apparently derived is through the mechanism of projection in which the patient uses the opportunity to attribute his or her own traits to some villain in the story, or to the "bad parents" or to the "unfaithful partner." By so doing, he vicariously expresses these traits with varying degrees or relief. Thus, one patient who consciously had a great deal of hostility for her husband felt that Rhett Butler, the character in Mitchell's *Gone With the Wind*, was by all odds the best character in the book. This ruthless individualist who in the story runs the blockade, speculates in food supplies, and finances a prostitute, she could identify with her husband and could project on to him her own character and wishes. . . .

Therapeutic benefit results when the patient is stimulated by his reading to make a comparison between the author's standards or ideas and his own. This is particularly true when the author's statements or principles have been such that the patient could accept and adopt them. Thus, one individual with an agitated depression had found some ideas in Jackson's *Outwitting Our Nerves* which were apparently of more help for her insomnia than any direct psychotherapy that the physician had been able to give her. Beneficial results have been obtained in various ways through affording the patient some narcissistic gratification. This we feel has been accomplished by several different methods. First, by the patient finding a means of fantasy expression in some reading material whereby he momentarily escapes his own conflict. Particularly is this true with books of fiction, as illustrated by the case of a paranoid schizophrenic young man who found satisfaction and benefit in Jim Tully's novels. Frequently we see such escapes in adventure fiction such as Zane Grey's books in which the identification mechanism of the patient with the hero is not so apparent as is the momentary escape from conflict. The choice of mystery stories by patients addicted to alcohol seems in part to be beneficial because of this form of gratification.

A second type of narcissistic gratification is seen in those individuals who make an effort to maintain their contact with reality through reading newspapers and magazines. This is well illustrated by an instance of an epileptic patient whose mental age was not more than 12 years, who insisted on receiving *Time*, *The Review of Reviews*, *The Nation's Business*, and the *Wall Street Journal* with unfailing regularity. It was apparent that he never gained very much information from his reading of any of these, and yet the narcissistic value to himself was of great importance in maintaining his self-respect. . . .

A third method of gaining narcissistic gratification is seen in the patients who want to increase their general fund of knowledge and perhaps thus strengthen and enhance the ego. This has been particularly noticeable in physician-patients who in many instances have asked for various medical journals from the hospital library. One patient voluntarily chose such books as Stockard's *The Physical Basis of Personality*, Carrel's *Man, The Unknown*, Zinsser's *Rats, Lice, and History*, and Merejkowski's *The Romance of Leonardo Da Vinci*.

A fourth method of obtaining narcissistic gratification has apparently been through the patient's desire to gain social approval, often through the therapist's or the physician's interest and affection. This has been shown by various patients who have accepted books and attempted to read them but, we felt, gained little by the reading, making the attempt chiefly because they felt it was the proper thing to do. In some instances this was because the group was doing it and in other instances because they thought the physician wanted them to do it. (25, pp. 269–273.)[3]

These reported benefits—identification with a character or experience with subsequent abreaction of emotion, maintaining contact with reality, enhancing the ego by increasing the general fund of knowledge, and gaining social approval—will immediately be recognized as worth-while therapeutic objectives and encourage wider usage of or experimentation with this method.

ENVIRONMENTAL MANIPULATION AND MODIFICATION

Environmental manipulation and modification will be considered here in reference to the child and adolescent because of the general conviction of clinicians that these methods are more fruitful with younger people than with adults. For example, although institutionalization, a form of environmental manipulation, is often indicated for adults, this is not always because per se it is considered to be of any more than incidental value but because methods such as direct psychotherapy are there more conveniently and expeditiously applied, or for custodial or protective reasons. The incidental values arising from freedom from distraction, the neutral environment, the regularity of the regimen, and on occasion the freedom from contact with relatives are very real and worth while for adults, but it is in work with children that these indirect methods are most fully developed and successful.

The reason for the greater success with children is not difficult to comprehend, since the child is in a formative period and not yet as rigidly established in his ways of behaving. With changes of certain aspects of the environment or removal to a less traumatic one, the child's capacity for growth exerts itself and the disturbing methods of handling his problems may disappear.

Since the child is dependent upon the family setting, he cannot be treated successfully if this setting is psychologically destructive. Growth released in the therapeutic setting will be stultified if the child cannot apply the results of his therapeutic experience to his

---

[3] Reprinted from "Bibliotherapy" by W. C. Menninger, by permission of the Bulletin of the Menninger Clinic. Copyright 1937 by the Menninger Clinic.

life in the home. For the child the home is the basic social environment. Influences operative here far outweigh all others combined. Nevertheless, other factors—the school, the church, play groups, gangs, neighborhood houses, radio, movies, and so on—are operative although in varying degrees of importance. These influences upon the child may be changed or modified in such ways as to introduce therapeutic growth.

It is in connection with this aspect of treatment that the social worker takes primary responsibility. Working with the family and other facets of the social structure is one of his special areas of competence.

ENVIRONMENTAL MODIFICATION AND MANIPULATION DISTINGUISHED

Indirect techniques of treatment aimed at the environmental milieu rather than at working with the patient directly involve two separable aspects. Environmental modification stresses changes of some aspects of the present milieu of the child without removing him from it. Attempts at modification of the ways in which the parents handle the child or in making arrangements that a disruptive influence such as a punitive grandmother is removed from the home are illustrative. Environmental manipulation refers to removal of the child, himself, from the present disturbing environment and placement elsewhere. These steps are taken when they would seem indicated for the best interests either of the patient, of society, or of both.

Both techniques, environmental modification and manipulation, have in common the intent of removing the present stimuli which may be contributing to the disturbances of the child. If this is successful the stimulus constellation is different, permitting now the extinguishing of old inadequate patterns of behavior and the formation of newer, more adaptive ones. If the environment is judged to be one in which the child could never learn to adjust or to attain personal stability, then removal from it is indicated either temporarily or permanently. If, on the other hand, it would appear that modifying certain factors through working with the disturbing influences (individuals) or adding new experiences will create a changed field, then environmental modification is indicated.

Interference with therapy arising from the home may come from many sources. The negative attitudes toward the therapist or therapy on the part of parents may prevent the formation or maintenance of a therapeutic relationship. The personality needs of an adult in the home may be such that he or she cannot tolerate any change in the behavior of the child, with a consequent blocking at every turn of any attempts at change. The child then finds that new techniques learned in therapy for dealing with his needs actually do not work as well at home as did his less mature ways of handling his problems.

HISTORICAL DEVELOPMENT OF ENVIRONMENTAL PROCEDURES

As originally utilized environmental techniques were likely to be somewhat crude and blunt. Instead of being adapted to the particular needs of the child, environmental manipulation was almost entirely a group approach in which institutional placement loomed large. Modification of parental attitudes and behavior patterns was rather pedagogical and intellectual. Principles of child care and management were patiently taught to parents with the hope that if they "knew better" they would be able to handle their child's problems more intelligently. In these earlier days emphasis in treatment was placed upon outer life forces—attempts at the development of understanding on the part of the parents, provisions for additional recreation, removal to an institution, and so on. It was hoped that these would provide an external impetus for growth (Dawley, 13).

Two developments played a major part in changing this conception of child treatment although they themselves are causally intertwined. Initially there developed the recognition that the child's personality is a composite of internal and external forces, followed closely by the appearance of clinical tools which permitted successful direct treatment of the child. Psychoanalytically oriented thinking, the relationship approach, and play therapy all played their part in both developments. There was a gradual acceptance of a more individual-centered dynamic approach and a recognition that emotional needs are fully as important as, if not more important than, intellectual needs.

At this stage of maturation there was a reaction against environmental manipulation as a tool. Sometimes there was even a disdain of the environmental forces operative with a tacit agreement among clinical personnel to ignore them in so far as possible. It became rather fashionable to consider institutions, hospitals, and foster homes as either last resorts or rather old-fashioned treatment media employed only by those incapable of using or reluctant to use the newer approaches. This adolescent revolt against environmental manipulation has now abated, so that there is room for a more mature evaluation of this technique as an indirect form of treatment.

It would appear that there is today an increasing respect for the potentialities of environmental manipulation. It is recognized that institutions, for example, given sufficiently trained personnel and a definite operating policy, can meet the needs of the individual child. Some outstanding clinicians have come to accept the fact that, entirely disregarding custodial considerations, economy, and convenience, sometimes the best treatment is institutional *because* it is institutional.

Environmental modification did not suffer this temporary minimization attendant to the development of a more dynamic point of view. Rather, it was gradually changed in character from being primarily pedagogical to being primarily therapeutic. It was recognized that it was not ignorance of principles of child management on the part of parents but rather their own personality difficulties which prevented application of these principles. It was also recognized that successful treatment of the parent often demanded as much, if not more, skill than work with the child.

ENVIRONMENTAL MANIPULATION

The choice of therapeutic tools—psychotherapy, environmental manipulation, or environmental modification—depends upon the diagnostic appraisal which is formulated. As a general rule, the less drastic form—personal therapy occurring simultaneously with attempts at environmental modification—is indicated first unless obviously contraindicated.

In part this arises from the long-prevalent dictum that a poor home is better than a foster home and that a foster home is better than an institution. As in all such generalities the modicum of truth obscures the many treatment errors that have been committed in its name. An economically poor home may well be the best for the child providing it supplies the security of a warm understanding and the steady emotional relationship that makes for growth. Unfortunately, this security-enhancing warmth is precisely that which is lacking in many of the parental homes of child patients seen in clinics and agencies.

That rejection is injurious to the child is another shibboleth of child treatment. On the other hand, removal from the home to a foster home or institution may in itself be interpreted as a threat. It may be that fear of being unloved is already present and the contemplated move merely intensifies such feelings. Or it may be that this is an additional traumatic injury. In any case, removal from the home is likely to cause a deep narcissistic injury. Interpreted as rejection and punishment, removal may exacerbate immediately the child's most socially disturbing tendencies. This is not invariable, since often the early period will be one of watchful and cautious waiting until the environment can be tested out to find the limits of permissiveness. Only later will aggressive feelings be released.

The social worker, as with all aspects of indirect treatment, is the specialist most concerned with carrying out environmental manipulation. Treatment of parents and helping the parents accept the foster home are characteristic duties. Investigation by the social worker of foster parents and institutions with a view to evaluating their adequacy is also an important aid in proper use of environmental manipulation.

CONDITIONS INDICATING THE DESIRABILITY OF THE USE OF ENVIRONMENTAL MANIPULATION

No hard and fast rules can be laid down which indicate infallibly when environmental manipulation is to be used. In spite of the oversimplification that is necessary it is appropriate to indicate briefly certain of the conditions which may make desirable removal of the child from his present environment: (1) The parent rejects the child in a fashion which indicates that he is apparently inaccessible to change in this attitude with the aid of the resources available; (2) the parent is so deeply personally involved in the child's problems because of his own neurotic needs as to prevent therapeutic progress and yet cannot accept treatment for himself; (3) the child is delinquent and lives in an unwholesome family group which contributes to such delinquency; (4) the mother is absent from the home and provides no adequate mother substitute; (5) the care of the child places a disproportionate drain upon the resources of the parental home, as in low-grade feeble-minded;

(6) the child has failed to be helped by other facilities; (7) diagnostic opinion is that environmental manipulation would have great positive value.

Other considerations enter the picture, whether directly relevant therapeutically or not, such as the convenience of the family or of society, the protection of society, accessibility to appropriate therapeutic resources, etc. In the past these considerations far outweighed more directly therapeutic aims and gave rise to the view, still prevalent, that changes were not for the good of the child but for the convenience of others. Under such circumstances a punitive element in open or disguised form also seemed prominent in many institutional placements, though this is certainly not true in all cases.

THE CHOICE BETWEEN FOSTER HOME AND INSTITUTION

In broadest and simplest terms, the choice between an institution and a foster home is to be decided on the basis of whether or not the needs of the child are likely to be met most adequately through an individual, personal, and intense relationship or through a group, impersonal, and diluted relationship. To be sure, some institutions, such as the Orthogenic School to be referred to shortly, do stress personal relationships, but the typical institution and typical foster home can be thus distinguished.

A major consideration of society in this choice, irrespective of the needs of the child, is the capacity of the environment to tolerate the child. With regard to the limits of tolerance the institution has the greater capacity for standing severe or antisocial forms of behavior. There are just not enough foster homes that can tolerate the behavior of some emotionally disturbed children. The acting-out behavior of some aggressive children, or the continuous rejection of some withdrawn children, is beyond the capacities of all except the most unusual foster home. The institution permits control of all aspects of the child's life with consequent direction, so far as possible, upon a therapeutically healthful course. It also has specialized medical and physical facilities impossible in the home.

It would appear on the basis of these considerations that the child would be better off in an institution if he is seriously crippled or suffering from acute physical conditions, is psychotic or a low-grade mental defective, is an advanced delinquent, or has symptoms

742 The Clinical Method in Psychology

difficult to tolerate in another setting. The great majority of children showing mild behavior difficulties, neurotic conditions, or symptoms arising from needs for interpersonal relationships would seem to be better suited for foster home placement.

A factor not yet mentioned which cuts across those previously indicated is that of age. Clinical opinion is apparently practically unanimous that the younger child, other things being equal, is better suited for foster home placement. In fact, institutionalization is indicated only under severe conditions for children younger than five years of age. Age is important in foster home placement because, generally speaking, the younger the child the greater the possibility of positive therapeutic change. In part this is due to the pliability of the child. The younger child finds it much easier to accept foster parents as parent figures than does the older child and therefore is in a position to profit more basically from foster home placement. The adolescent, who is in the process of learning to be emancipated from the home, often seems to prefer and need the group life found in institutions as compared to the more intense and yet limited interpersonal relationships of the foster home (24). Rogers (40) concludes, after careful study, that foster home placement after thirteen years of age is prognostically unfavorable.

Since the psychologist has more direct concern with and experience in institutions, the following account will be centered upon these rather than upon foster homes.

THE INSTITUTION AS A METHOD OF TREATMENT

KINDS OF INSTITUTIONS FOR CHILDREN

There are many kinds of treatment institutions both public and private for the care of maladjusted children. Jenkins (21), Clothier (11), and Davidoff (12) describe and classify them. For present purposes it is sufficient to say that they include children's wards of general hospitals, training schools for delinquents, training schools for the mentally defective, private psychiatric hospital-schools set up for intensive treatment, resident schools for emotionally disturbed children, children's wards for psychotic children in mental hospitals, institutions for epileptics, and a host of others. Some of these operate with the expectancy of long-term care, as in the case of training schools for mental defectives and wards for psychotic children; others are much more temporary in nature, such as resident schools for emotionally disturbed children.

Not all institutions meet the level of therapeutic adroitness that the earlier discussion would demand. Many of them are merely custodial despite claims to the contrary. Many are inadequately staffed as to both quality and quantity of personnel.[4]

THE INFLUENCE OF THE PERSONNEL

The attitude of the personnel of the institution probably has more to do with its therapeutic efficacy than any one other factor. This is as true of the nurses, house mothers, and attendants as it is of psychiatrists, social workers, and psychologists. The amount of time they spend with each child enormously exceeds that possible for the individual therapist. They should be capable of relating to children with warmth and affection but without sentimentality; they should be fair and just without being harsh or punitive or impersonal. They need to appreciate the rights of the child to be what he is. They must not build up in the children anything which will contribute to the development of a gang spirit. This is especially important because all too often the child will build loyalty and attachment not to the adults of the institution but to other children, united against a common enemy, the "keepers." If the staff is regarded as hostile or even distant, the pernicious effects commonly attributed to institutions as breeding grounds for further delinquency or abnormal behavior will be forthcoming. The social worker often serves as the liaison agent between the home, social service agency, institution, and clinic. Through his activity as such a cohesive element which helps to prevent working at cross-purposes is introduced. It is also his task to work toward eventual return of the patient to the home if this be indicated by the nature both of the case and of the home.

THE GOAL OF TREATMENT INSTITUTIONS

Aside from the goals expressed in this description of the personnel, what are these therapeutically oriented institutions attempting to do? Jenkins aptly expresses the spirit of the best of institutions for the disturbed child:

---

[4] Rogers (40) gives a detailed and well-tempered account both of institutions in which the personnel are motivated by therapeutic aims and of those geared to custodial or repressive care.

At its best the institution may be regarded as a community which has accepted as a profession the readjustment of children committed to its care. It bears much the relation to the larger community that a therapist does to the parents of a child under treatment. It does not take over the functions of the larger community to which the child must ultimately return. It does not seek to wean the child's affections from this lay community, but rather, uses its temporary relationship to help him adjust himself so that he can return to it. This professional community can afford to be more tolerant, more understanding, and less judgmental than can the lay community. It is able, if it chooses, to exercise a closer control than the lay community. It is able, under favorable conditions, to utilize this control therapeutically. (21, p. 515.)

The institution exerts its therapeutic influence not through the passive influence of a presumably beneficial environment but by creating in the patient a desire to reorient himself actively, both in the institution and later in the outside world.

ILLUSTRATIONS OF TREATMENT PROCEDURES IN INSTITUTIONS

Although space considerations permit only brief mention it is advisable to name certain procedures characteristic of the more therapeutically oriented institutions. Institutions for neurotic and behavior problem children, delinquents, and mental defectives will serve as illustrations.

EMOTIONALLY DISTURBED CHILDREN. Illustrative of a specific attempt to capitalize upon the institutional setting as a method of treatment of neurotic and behavior problem children are the procedures of the Orthogenic School of Chicago. In part they take as their point of departure the well-established fact (Goldfarb, 16, 17, Bettelheim and Sylvester, 8, 9) that the child raised in an institution, in spite of psychometric normality, may be astonishingly immature. One of the indicators of this immaturity, according to Bettelheim and Sylvester, is their inability to form meaningful personal ties with an adult. Living as they often do under a set of impersonal rules and changing and infrequently seen adult personnel they have not learned to relate to adults. They are out of contact with them, do not know how to respond to them, sometimes do not even remember the names of the adults in the institution.

One of the principles which the Orthogenic School, a school for emotionally disturbed children, emphasizes is that of the therapeutic milieu. Bettelheim and Sylvester describe this principle as follows:

In a therapeutic milieu . . . the child's development toward increasing mastery must be facilitated. Training in skills and achievements, specialized programs and activities, are of peripheral importance only. They are therapeutically justified solely if they originate from the central issue of the therapeutic milieu. A therapeutic milieu is characterized by its inner cohesiveness which alone permits the child to develop a consistent frame of reference. This cohesiveness is experienced by the child as he becomes part of a well defined hierarchy of meaningful interpersonal relationships. Emphasis on spontaneity and flexibility—not to be misconstrued as license or chaos—makes questions of schedule or routine subservient to the relevance of highly individualized and spontaneous interpersonal relationships. Such conditions permit the emergence and development of the psychological instances, the internalization of controls, and the eventual integration of the child's personality. (8, p. 192.)

In another article, Bettelheim and Sylvester (9) go on to say that this form of therapy is indicated when the child either is one whose ability to maintain an interpersonal relationship with a parent figure has been destroyed or is one who, because of prior deprivation, lacks the tools for building up this or any other personal relationship. Illustrative of the first group would be the boy whose presenting symptoms were truancy and an inhibition of learning. He had interpreted his mother's divorcing two husbands in rapid succession as being brought about by him. "His need for gratification and reassurance made him hunger for closeness to adults and made him approach them, while his fear of destroying them made him flee from them in panic. In this sense, his truancy was an attempt to escape from his own destructiveness, and he had further to avoid all learning because of his doubts about his own personal identity and that of his delusionally destroyed victims." (9, pp. 56–57.) The second group typically would include many children who had grown up in orphanages. In such an institution as the one described there is a positive advantage to institutional treatment in which the milieu, to use the term of Bettelheim and Sylvester, is oriented toward treatment.

DELINQUENTS. A description of a modern psychiatrically oriented institution for the treatment of delinquents is given by Grossmann (20). Emphasis is placed on the understanding of the individual child and an individual program is geared to his needs. Admission is selective in that those who are considered unable to profit from the program are not accepted. Parole is not an automatic matter but is based on criteria of adjustment in the institution and a prediction of adjustment in the community. If the child is to return home the social worker works with the family to modify their patterns of reaction to the child so that they will accept him with more understanding.

MENTAL DEFECTIVES. A vivid account of the experiences of institutionalized feeble-minded girls is given by Abel and Kinder (1). Psychotherapy, as such, is used relatively little; instead habit training is stressed. This is quite understandable since such training of mental defectives if successful makes them more self-sufficient. Within their own and the institution's limits emotional problems are also considered. These writers hold that if there is any chance the girl can hold a job, even an unimportant one, or her parents can support her without undue strain, institutionalization should not be used.

Some procedures used in aiding mentally deficient boys to make an adequate institutional adjustment are discussed by Stogdill (37). The psychotherapist's function was to be available at all times to the boys, who would come to him with their problems. He deliberately had no administrative authority, which lack served to minimize if not eliminate the authoritarian element. The problems that came to his attention were regarded as specific environmental situations, and once some solution was reached contact ceased for the time being. It must be remembered that these were feeble-minded boys for whom extended psychotherapy would not be indicated. Problems were seen in simple concrete terms and handled accordingly. For example, the boy who believed his cottage father was giving him "all the dirty work" was assured after a three-way conference of boy, cottage father, and therapist that once he had demonstrated he could handle more responsible work he would be given it. Shifting from one cottage to another is occasionally beneficial, but must necessarily be used sparingly lest such changes be engineered by the boys to avoid responsibility.

ENVIRONMENTAL MODIFICATION

In many instances the child's maladjustments may be treated satisfactorily in the home provided certain influences which appear to be operative can be modified. The modifications may take various forms. Some require elimination of pernicious influences in the home in the person of some peripheral member of the family group.

For example, arrangement may be made for a boarder or an aunt to live elsewhere, though such arbitrary maneuvers are used relatively infrequently. More common than elimination of a person is the variation of some aspect of the environment through change of attitude of one of the members of the family. Also useful is the introduction into the life of the child of some new environmental experiences. These three forms of environmental modification—elimination, change, and addition—are often used in conjunction with one another. Usually they are carried out by the social worker.

TREATMENT OF THE PARENT IN CHILD THERAPY

Most child guidance clinics and related agencies have some arrangements for regular visits of both parent and child. The child usually meets with the psychiatrist; the mother (or father) sees the psychiatric social worker. There may be variation of this pattern, such as having the child seen by the social worker or psychologist and the parent by the psychiatrist. Variations like these are often motivated by a conviction that the most severely disturbed individual should be seen by the psychiatrist. Other factors are also pertinent, such as whether a patient may be more readily worked with by a person of the same or opposite sex, administrative convenience, or other matters. Regardless of the therapeutic arrangement, the therapeutic experiences of the parent are generally oriented around her relationship with the child and the meaning of the child to her. In this sense the therapy is child-oriented, with the therapeutic effects for the mother secondary.

Certain more or less commonly accepted principles guide work in this aspect of environmental modification, in which the child is considered to be the basic unit. Arising from the primary focus on the child is a fundamental guiding principle—that the treatment of the parent is indicated only to the extent that his or her problems contribute to the child's problems. This restriction is necessary if for no other reason than that the organization of a clinic (or the private practice of one individual) is geared to the treatment of a limited variety of patients. It arises logically from the centering on the child as the primary patient and justifies the present discussion as an aspect of environmental modification.

Conception of the child as the patient, it must be remembered, is also the position the parent adopts. She comes to the clinic, not for treatment herself, but to do something or have something done about the child. In fact, this idea is so firmly entrenched in the practice of many clinics that, even if the referral is originally instigated by a school, another agency, or a physician, the parent is required to make the arrangement with the clinic and to accompany the child. This is in keeping with the usual requirement that one parent at least be an active participant in clinical treatment.

Both from the clinic's and from the parent's point of view, then, the child is the patient. The mother at first is likely to interpret her role as merely that of an adult who necessarily accompanies the child to and from the clinic as an informant about his difficulties. The first task the social worker has is to allow her to see and express some appreciation of her role in the child's difficulties. The mother comes essentially as a *parent* and will continue to do so unless and until there is some clarification that her role is other than this (Wickman and Langford, 30). In making clear the last point Green offers an apt illustration from one parent interview as follows:

The mother of an eight year old girl was in the clinic for her first interview. She talked a great deal of Linda's bed-wetting and thumb-sucking. The mother said she feared Linda had not had as much affection as she needed (many illnesses and hospitalizations); also, that she herself had had no affection and frankly expressed hostile feelings to her own mother. She resented her mother's influence with Linda, and against herself. She felt somehow that Linda's bed-wetting might be tied in with this conflict. Among other points of activity, the case worker helped this mother to describe and discuss the behavior that worried her. With much feeling for the mother, the worker's activity focused clearly on the mother's involvement in her relationship problems with her daughter. In all her inquiries and responses, the worker remembered that this mother had come to the clinic because of her *responsibility as a parent.* Toward the end of the interview, the mother was able to say she thought Linda's behavior was retaliative: "When I lose my temper, she sucks her thumb: and when she sucks her thumb a lot, she wets the bed." (19, p. 444.)

She goes on to intimate that focusing on the mother's role as a parent probably gave rise to the insight on the mother's part. Focusing on the mother's resentment toward her own mother would have been inappropriate because this acceptance of her in the role of a "daughter" would have disregarded the impetus which brought the mother to the clinic. If she, not the child, had been the "patient"

this other course might have been indicated. The mother's own relationship with the child continued to be stressed in subsequent sessions and served as an important means of strengthening her sense of responsibility to make effective the direct treatment of the child.

In many instances, however, the behavior of the parent in the current difficulties with her child is, to an important degree, the result of childhood experiences with her own parents. Sometimes the only way in which the child may be helped is to deal with the mother's relation to her parents. Because of this relationship or other exacerbating forces it becomes necessary on occasion to see the mother for intensive psychotherapy and to deal with the child on a much simpler or even superficial therapeutic level. This does not, however, vitiate the primary aim of helping the child.

Work with parents is often of crucial importance. Indeed, Ackerman and Neubauer (2) emphasize that failures in psychotherapy with children are often due to the inadequacy or impossibility of handling of the problems of the parents. The child is brought not because of his own needs but because of the parent's needs. This circumstance often defeats the treatment of the child, or prevents the child from entering a therapeutic relationship at all. The authors report the following illustrative case:

Isa is eight and a half years old. She was brought by her mother because she was unmanageable, did not want to go to school and was enuretic. She was born out of wedlock. The mother gave a history of a depressive reaction during which time she would cling excessively to the child. The child felt frightened without the mother, particularly in the dark or during a rainstorm. Her play fantasies revealed that she harbored strong death wishes against her mother. Early in treatment she established a strong transference to the therapist. The mother soon began to produce difficulties for the child's treatment. She became depressed and told the therapist that she was unable to bring the child for treatment. When a volunteer worker agreed to fetch Isa and bring her to the clinic the mother managed to leave the apartment with the child before the worker arrived. The mother finally confessed her fear that Isa did not love her any more, and subsequently discontinued treatment for the child. The therapist in charge of the case had been aware since the beginning of treatment that the mother herself was in need of therapy. She was therefore seen at a clinic where she had gone previously during her episodes of depression. In spite of this help she was unable to accept the improvement in Isa, and almost completely interrupted her own treatment. (2, p. 89.)

In an account of interpreting psychological data to parents, Blanchard (34) describes the present point of view quite well. She believes that the relationship between clinician and parent is at the level of a participating give-and-take with the parent recognized and accepted as the individual that he is. An excerpt from a case that she gives is so similar to many that occur every day in clinics that it is worth quoting:

Perhaps this participating kind of discussion may be illustrated from the case of a mother who brought her inhibited, fearful little boy to the clinic stating that she wished him to be cured of his fears. After a few interviews with the therapist, the little boy began to be somewhat less fearful, but also he became less docile and obedient. "He refused his spinach one day last week," said his mother. "He never did that before. I never even knew that he disliked spinach." She went on to question whether she could continue to bring the boy to the clinic, giving as a reason that the trip was too long and expensive. The social worker did not leave the question of the mother's continuing to bring the boy to the clinic on the basis of the trip, but inquired whether the mother might be worried over the changes in the boy and his being a little less obedient. The mother replied that he never had been disobedient before she brought him to the clinic, but then she was able to go on to talk of how she always had demanded docility and obedience of the boy. She ended this description with the query as to whether this way of bringing up the boy might have some connection with his having become such a fearful child. The social worker agreed that this was a real possibility and the mother decided that she would continue to bring the boy for treatment because she preferred him to be less fearful even at the expense of his being a little less submissive to authority. (34, pp. 475–476.)

A specific approach to the treatment of mothers has been referred to by several clinicians as "attitude" therapy. There is major emphasis on therapeutic sessions devoted to modification of the mother's attitude toward the child by facilitating insight into her influence on the child's behavior. Attitude therapy was first stated in terms which distinguished it rather sharply from psychiatric case work (23). Originally it was to be used with parents when case work methods failed (23). It also bore the imprint of that earlier more prevalent pedagogical influence (28). It now has been changed somewhat in all of these respects. Just as it arose in case work it re-fertilized and became a part of case work. Today the social worker, instead of needing her own therapeutic approach to feel "authentic," to use an expression of Levy's applied to attitude therapy, finds

herself comfortable as a therapist without having to have her work marked off as "social worker" therapy. She does not use therapy only when case work fails, with a consequent reformulation of her role, but instead is herself all along. This has in turn meant a minimization of the pedagogical, advisory methods used earlier. The social worker is concerned with understanding the needs of the patient, whether this be case work or therapy.

The patterns of treatment heretofore sketched as an aspect of environmental modification do not exhaust by any means the ramifications that dual treatment of parent and child may take. Not only may all kinds of therapeutic approaches be followed, such as relationship, Freudian, Rankian, and so on, but also there may be a reversal of the child-centered approach or possibly a balance between the emphases on child and parent. Illustrative is the psychoanalytically oriented report of an analysis of a seriously disturbed adolescent girl and the collaborative psychiatric treatment of her mother by Johnson and Fishback (22). In this case, details of which are unnecessary here, the girl and the mother derived such mutual gratification from their neurotically determined needs that without collaborative treatment little could have been done for the girl. The parent received so much satisfaction of her unconscious forbidden impulses from the girl that without treatment she would not have permitted continuation of the treatment of the girl.

INTERPRETATION AS ENVIRONMENTAL MODIFICATION WITH PARENTS OF MENTAL DEFECTIVES

One area of environmental modification which occupies the time of a certain number of psychologists is that of interpreting psychological diagnostic findings to parents of mentally defective children. Because the psychologist is an expert with diagnostic tests and because test results often loom large in decisions about mental deficiency he sometimes has the task of discussing the findings with the parent. The psychologist (or other clinician) in doing this is endeavoring to produce changes in the attitudes of the parents toward the child and his disability and to break ground for further solution. In many instances the parents are not in themselves emotionally disturbed beyond the confines of this particular problem and therefore are not so much in need of extensive therapy. This does not mean that they are not upset, ashamed, suspicious, defensive, or even belligerent when first seen in the clinic. Rather, their own problems do not so much obtrude upon the treatment of the primary patient, the child, as to make them patients as well.

Parents, although aware that their child is "different," characteristically have seized upon the well-meaning but misguided advice that the child "will outgrow it." When they come to the clinic, they generally have been brought up short by something that cannot permit refuge in this comforting illusion. The child's exclusion from regular school classes or some other event prevents their hiding from the problem any longer. Psychometric and other clinical findings are gathered, but it is not therapeutically sensible merely to impart this information and then advise a solution. Such a direct intellectual approach is almost certain to produce considerable resistance and defeat its own purpose.

As Rheingold (36) points out, the first step is to guide the parent toward an emotional acceptance of the fact of the child's retardation. She goes on to suggest means whereby this may be accomplished. Indeed, she finds an interview that successfully interprets mental retardation to the parent to follow a regular sequence (although varying in detail according to sex, age, degree of retardation, and so on).

Such interviews are opened with expressions indicating awareness that the parent has been concerned with the child. With this the parent almost invariably agrees. A recognition of the problem in this fashion often stimulates the next step, a description of the child's behavior. Spontaneously or with subtle guidance by the clinician this centers upon evaluation of the child's development as compared to the achievement of other children of comparable ages. When at this point the clinician introduces the question as to what age child the patient resembles, parents have revealed themselves to be astonishingly accurate in guessing the age given by the diagnostic tests. Such a discussion gives the parent a self-deduced measuring rod, not foisted upon her by others. At this juncture the parent will usually ask what the clinician thinks, in response to which the clinician reviews the results of the test, although in general terms rather than a precise mental age or IQ. The parent then is likely to turn to the future—schooling of the child, jobs that he might be able to hold, and so on—thus admitting the implications of mental retardation. In answering the questions the parent raises about the future, the clinician keeps pace with expressed needs and feelings, not forging beyond the questions posed. Questions about etiology and treatment are apt to occur next. The clinician encourages the parent to give her own formulation, which may take various forms —heredity, accidents of birth, or prenatal experiences. If the explanation seems reasonable or constructive the clinician may encourage it, but more often than not he can but refer to the lack of definite etiological knowledge. In so doing he emphasizes points which will help relieve feelings of guilt or responsibility. This leads directly to consideration of treatment. Often the parent seeks some cure, grasping at any surgical, medical, educational, or social straws that offer the slightest hope. Responsibility for retardation felt by the parent receives special attention in Rheingold's account at this point. She emphasizes the necessity of allowing, or rather encouraging, the parent to express these guilt feelings, without which he or she can scarcely view the situation with sufficient objectivity. After this is worked through the parent is usually ready to consider the last step —the solution of the problem.

The exact nature of such solutions is inextricably tied to individual circumstances to a degree that precludes blanket prescriptions. The previous discussion of institutions, however, is relevant. If it is advisable that the child be institutionalized or that some other drastic step be taken, it is the function of the clinician to work with the parent concerning the doubts, fears, and guilt feelings which will appear before the contemplated step becomes acceptable.

INTRODUCTION OF NEW ENVIRONMENTAL EXPERIENCES

Without removing the child from the home it is possible to introduce him to new environmental experiences which may have therapeutic value. One of his difficulties may be inability to relate to other individuals of his own age. Accordingly, the use of clubs and social groups and summer camps often is warranted for inducing a more healthful relation of the patient to other persons. Such groups also offer the opportunity for release of therapeutically valuable feeling if the leader is sympathetic and understanding. As Rogers (40) says, if gangs are potent in the development of delinquency, may they not also be used constructively? Direction to other groups such as clubs, settlement houses, Boy Scout troops, and so on may be indicated.

An individual prescription or recommendation is necessary; the clinician must be familiar not only with the needs of the child but with the dynamic matrices of the group in which he will be placed. It is also his responsibility to enlist the coöperation of the leader and to give him some insight into the child's difficulties. He must be in a position to secure subsequent information about the child's experiences in the group setting which will enable him to evaluate progress in dealing with the problems that formed the basis for the referral. Summer camps will serve as an illustration.

SUMMER CAMPS. The maintenance of summer camps for their clients has been part of the procedure of many social agencies. Perhaps with no more than a vague idea that it will "get them off the streets," give them a regular life for a time, and build them up physically, children have been sent to such camps for brief or prolonged periods. The need for specialized camps became apparent when it was found that camps designed for the ordinary child were not successful in helping problem children as often or as effectively as might be hoped. For example, a timid child might find the competitive spirit so rampant in some camps that an actual detriment to his development would occur, leaving him at the end of the camping experience with a greater sense of failure. The overly aggressive child would, in most camps, be found to be a nuisance if not something worse.

Hence there is a need for specially sponsored and staffed camps oriented toward therapeutic procedures and goals. Since inability to coöperate with one another and with adults is one of the major problems occurring in such camps, selection of appropriate counselors looms large as a problem. According to Young (32) maturity is one of the essential characteristics, even at the expense of previous camp experience. It is generally considered desirable so far as possible that counselors be trained to observe, accept, and interpret behavior but not judge it (cf., for example, Amsden, 3).

Such camps differ outwardly in no wise from hundreds of other camps scattered throughout the recreation areas of the United States (3, 15). Their setting and many of the activities are the same. Athletics, swimming, lifesaving, handicrafts, nature study, hikes, and campfires are as much a part of these as of any other camp. The difference is primarily in the attitude taken toward the campers by the camp personnel. There is generally a minimum of authority used, just enough to avoid actual danger. The necessary regulations, however, are promptly and impartially enforced. There is also a focus upon the individual personality needs of the campers instead of the view that all should have the same program. In describing the actual program of treatment in a boys' summer camp for child guidance clinic cases Galkin (15) indicates that some of the values to be achieved, although not for every single boy, include habit training, initiation of greater independence from the mother, the first opportunity to feel that the world outside the home is not punitive, the receiving of much-needed recognition and feeling of acceptance, the prevention of delinquent associations, contact with reality, clarification of needs, and progress toward socialization.

Obviously not all children who are being seen in treatment clinics and agencies are suitable for such camp experiences. Again the therapist in charge must feel that the camp is a logical step in treatment (32). For the patient to be selected for such treatment the clinician-patient relationship must be well established and the patient must have at least some glimmering of insight into the nature of his problems.

An illustrative case cited by Young of the use of a summer camp for therapeutic purposes follows:

One unhappy eleven-year-old boy, unable to get along with other children, was helped to work through his problem in the clinic to the point where he realized that, by teasing and playing mean tricks on his schoolmates, he was expressing the antagonism that he felt toward his unsympathetic foster parents. Spurred by this knowledge, he was eager to overcome the traits that caused him so much unhappiness. Camp was suggested as a place where he could put into practice the more wholesome attitudes gained through his new insight and where he might also experience satisfactory group living. He was not eager to go, as past experience made him realize how difficult it would be for him to adjust to group life. He reasoned that since he had never had any satisfying relationship with any boy, it would be unbearable to have to live several weeks with boys who he was sure would not accept him. The legitimacy of this objection was not minimized. However, reassured by the therapist that he was now able to take this forward step, and that he would be helped to meet whatever unpleasant situation arose, he consented to go. . . . The aggressive eleven-year-old boy, once in camp and faced with the social situations there, reacted by the same obnoxious behavior that had made him so unpopular with his classmates. He made himself heartily disliked by teasing and threatening to tell the counselors of misconduct on the part of other children. He had many emotional upsets which ended in crying and in demands that he be allowed to go home. These were usually the result of teasing on the part of the other children as retribution for something he had done to them. During these emotional storms, his insecurity and the realization that their dislike was brought about by his own behavior became more apparent to him. The therapist took advantage of these upheavals to sit down with him and discuss the situation calmly. At other times when he was showing behavior that was annoying to the other boys, he was quietly called from the group and his actions pointed out. He appreciated this help and it was evident that he was genuinely attempting to alter his behavior. During the last week in camp, a decided improvement was noticed; he became more sociable and self-reliant, less frequently seeking the attention of staff members. The other boys had begun to accept him to a certain extent, but unfortunately the bad impression he had made on them at the beginning of camp could not be completely forgotten. (32, pp. 245, 249–250.)

MODIFICATION OF SCHOOL EXPERIENCES

School activities, no matter what the individualization attempted, cannot be expected to gear themselves to the needs of an individual child, especially a rather severely disturbed child. Nevertheless, consultation and mutual planning with school authorities and teachers often yield important treatment gains.

The importance of the school is readily apparent. Many problems first become acute on entrance into school. Heretofore protected in the home, the child reacts to the greater demands put on him by school experiences by releasing tendencies previously held in check by the home. In other words, the school requires the first major social adjustment by the child outside of his own home.

The various school systems have in varying degrees been imbued with a mental hygiene point of view. Teachers and supervisors in many school systems have accepted a doctrine which recognizes the diversified emotional needs of children. On the other hand, certain teachers are probably even today as repressive and as punitive, with the exception of physical punishment, as in the most rigid intellectualized period of education. But the classrooms of even the most enlightened school systems are not equipped, nor should they be, to deal with all behavior problems and manifestations of neurotic behavior. Sometimes these emotional problems arise in or are exacerbated by the school; more often than not the classroom is merely one of several settings in which behavior having its roots elsewhere is expressed. It is too much to expect the school system to be equipped to deal with all individual problems of its pupils. Geared as it is to group instruction and group methods, it cannot supply sufficient individualized attention to handle the problems discussed here. Though there is specialization in many school systems, it is in terms of school *subjects*, not school *children*.

In many schools, however, specialized services are provided, including attempts to deal with adjustment problems (35). These include the visiting teacher and sometimes the services of a school counselor, psychologist, social worker or psychiatrist, or even a child guidance clinic. If such personnel or clinics are to be found in a given school system they carry out some, or all, of the clinical functions of diagnosis and treatment described in this volume. Sometimes the psychologist is limited by professional or administrative restrictions to giving psychometric tests; sometimes he carries out all aspects of the clinical method. It is, then, manifestly impossible to present a "typical" account of practices related to environmental modification in the school. In the following presentation the assumption will be made that skilled clinical personnel are available whether through the school system or through outside clinical facilities. In such instances much clinical work is conducted through advisement of others in the school system who come in direct contact with the child in question.

It is in this sense, working through others as intermediaries, that the present discussion becomes an aspect of environmental modification. Interpretation of the behavior of the child to the teacher, with suggestions for dealing with manifestations of the child's difficulties; arrangements for special remedial work such as tutoring; shifts of the particular classes attended; reclassification to a lower or higher grade; and interviews with parents in reference to school problems exemplify some of these varied activities.

The clinical functions also include explanation to the teacher of what is going on in direct therapy. Especially effective are case conferences to which teachers are invited. The whole concept of psychotherapy is likely to be somewhat mysterious and forbidding to the teacher. If it is explained in terms of the individual child and his problems, the teacher's whole-hearted, enthusiastic coöperation may very often be secured. However, the emotional relationship between the child and the teacher cannot be disregarded and the contacts with the teacher limited to didactic instruction as to what may be done. Expression and clarification of feelings are important in this setting just as in the more intimate family situation, though the feelings are presumably of lesser intensity and more readily interpreted and modified.

Problems of the interaction of clinician and teacher therefore loom large. Cason (10) describes many of the pitfalls which make this interaction ineffective. She speaks of the psychologist's failing to report back to the school at all, failing to make any helpful recommendation or making impossible ones, making recommendations outside his field of competence, expressing his recommendations in terms impossible for the teacher to understand, or implying blame of the teacher. These same pitfalls would also apply to clinicians other than psychologists.

So far the modification of school experiences has been couched in rather general terms. In order to make the treatment procedures useful in a school setting more tangible, one specific aspect—tutoring—will be examined in greater detail. Tutoring, as Arthur (6) describes it, is temporary individual teaching of children who, although they have the intellectual capacity to grasp at least some of the schoolwork, are not doing satisfactorily. This failure to do satisfactory work may arise from a variety of causes—previous inadequate teaching methods, special physical defects, prolonged illness, or emotional adjustment problems.

What can be done by the collaboration of a psychologist, supervisor, and tutors (generally teachers specifically employed for the given case) in educational remediation is graphically described by Arthur in a series of publications (5) (6) (33). In many instances the behavior difficulties of the children, such as withdrawn or antisocial behavior, bore only a very indirect relation to the educational difficulties as such. Since these also cleared up with special educational remedial work without other treatment procedures, she calls her work tutoring as therapy. Although she offers no explicit discussion, some of the common factors operative in psychotherapy are certainly present, including the clinician-patient relationship and consistency of interpretations. In other instances she recognizes that tutoring is a procedure supplementary to direct psychotherapy.

Schumacher (5), in discussing one of Arthur's papers, makes the important point that there are two groups in which tutoring seems indicated. On the one hand, there are cases in which the educational maladjustment is primary to the behavior difficulties; on the other, those cases in which the primary problem antedates and complicates the educational maladjustment. He goes on to say:

It is in this type of case, when the parents and the child cannot be brought readily to understand the issues involved that tutorial work is often of great value in making a contact with parents and child and establishing working relationships. Parents will talk more readily if it seems to them that it will be of assistance in understanding and treatment of the problem for which they have brought the child to the Clinic's attention. In such cases, however, the tutor should be an experienced therapist, for in the last analysis, success depends on the treatment of the underlying neurotic disturbance. The tutorial situation is, then, a treatment situation and interpretations are made of the material brought out as in any treatment relationship and is "curative" in the same sense as is any treatment relationship. Tutoring as a medium for therapy would in our opinion, be a more expressive title for such therapeutic effort. (5, pp. 184–185.)

SUMMARY

In this chapter, indirect methods of treatment have been described and evaluated. By their very nature they are most efficiently utilized when the focus of concern is with the individual patient, whether treatment merely consists in the clinician's prescribing particularly suitable forms for the patient to take, or arises as a supplement to individual psychotherapy. Bearing the imprint, as indirect methods do, of many of the factors common to individual psychotherapy—opportunities for release and the appearance of insight, and so on—yet it lacks in large measure that most subtle and amorphous feature of all, the strong, abiding, and dynamic patient-therapist relationship.

BIBLIOGRAPHY

1. Abel, T. M., and Kinder, E. F., *The subnormal adolescent girl*, Columbia University Press, 1942.
2. Ackerman, N. W., and Neubauer, P. B., Failures in the psychotherapy of children, in Hoch, P. H. (ed.), *Failures in psychiatric treatment*, Grune & Stratton, 1948, pp. 82–102.
3. Amsden, R. L., The summer camp as a behavior clinic, *Ment. Hyg.*, N.Y., 1936, 20:262–268.
4. Anderson, M., The role of prescribed social gatherings in the treatment of the mentally ill, *Bull. Menninger Clin.*, 1941, 5:56–60.

5. Arthur, G., Tutoring as therapy, Amer. J. Orthopsychiat., 1939, 9:179–185.
6. Arthur, G., Tutoring as therapy, Commonwealth Fund, 1946.
7. Bellator, N. S., An educational therapy program in a mental hospital, Occup. Ther., 1938, 17:147–152.
8. Bettelheim, B., and Sylvester, E., A therapeutic milieu, Amer. J. Orthopsychiat., 1948, 18:191–206.
9. Bettelheim, B., and Sylvester, E., Milieu therapy: indications and illustrations, Psychoanal. Rev., 1949, 36:54–68.
10. Cason, E. B., Some suggestions on the interaction between the school psychologist and the classroom teacher, J. consult. Psychol., 1945, 9:132–137.
11. Clothier, F., Institutional needs in the field of child welfare, Nerv. Child, 1948, 7:154–177.
12. Davidoff, E., Institutional treatment of children, Nerv. Child, 1948, 7:178–194.
13. Dawley, A., Inter-related movement of parent and child in therapy with children, Amer. J. Orthopsychiat., 1939, 9:748–754.
14. Dunton, W. R., Prescribing occupational therapy, Charles C. Thomas, 2nd ed., 1945.
15. Galkin, J., The treatment possibilities offered by the summer camp as a supplement to the child guidance clinic, Amer. J. Orthopsychiat., 1937, 7:474–482.
16. Goldfarb, W., The effects of early institutional care on adolescent personality, J. exper. Educ., 1943, 12:106–129.
17. Goldfarb, W., Infant rearing as a factor in foster home replacement, Amer. J. Orthopsychiat., 1944, 14:162–166.
18. Goldfarb, W., Effects of psychological deprivation in infancy and subsequent stimulation, Amer. J. Psychiat., 1945, 102:18–33.
19. Green, R., Trends in orthopsychiatric therapy. VIII. Treatment of parent-child relationships, Amer. J. Orthopsychiat., 1948, 18:442–446.
20. Grossmann, G., The role of the institution in the treatment of delinquency, Amer. J. Orthopsychiat., 1938, 8:148–157.
21. Jenkins, R. L., Institutional treatment of maladjusted children, in Harms, E. (ed.), Handbook of child guidance, Child Care Publications, 1947, pp. 514–527.
22. Johnson, A. M., and Fishback, D., Analysis of a disturbed adolescent girl and collaborative psychiatric treatment of the mother, Amer. J. Orthopsychiat., 1944, 14:195–203.
23. Levy, D. M., Attitude therapy, Amer. J. Orthopsychiat., 1937, 7:103–113.
24. Lippman, H. S., Newer trends in child placement, Family, 1941, 21:323–328.
25. Menninger, W. C., Bibliotherapy, Bull. Menninger Clin., 1937, 1:263–274.

26. Menninger, W. C., Experiments with educational therapy in a psychiatric institution, Bull. Menninger Clin., 1942, 6:38–45.
27. Menninger, W. C., and McColl, I., Recreational therapy as applied in a modern psychiatric hospital, Occup. Ther., 1937, 16:15–23.
28. Moore, M. U., The treatment of maternal attitudes in problems of guidance, Amer. J. Orthopsychiat., 1933, 3:113–127.
29. Moore, M. U., Attitude therapy, Amer. J. Orthopsychiat., 1940, 10:681–696.
30. Wickman, K. M., and Langford, W. S., The parent in the children's psychiatric clinic, Amer. J. Orthopsychiat., 1944, 14:219–225.
31. Willard, H. S., and Spackman, C. S. (eds.), Principles of occupational therapy, J. B. Lippincott Company, 1947.
32. Young, R. A., A summer camp as an integral part of a psychiatric clinic, Ment. Hyg., N.Y., 1939, 23:241–256.

Supplementary articles in Watson, R. I. (ed.), Readings in the clinical method in psychology, Harper & Brothers, 1949:

33. Arthur, G., Tutoring and remedial teaching as educational therapy. Pp. 461–465. (Also in J. consult. Psychol., 1940, 4:173–176.)
34. Blanchard, P., Interpreting psychological data to parents. Pp. 473–477. (Also in J. consult. Psychol., 1940, 4:120–123.)
35. Cornell, E. L., The psychologist in a school system. Pp. 131–146. (Also in J. consult. Psychol., 1942, 6:185–195.)
36. Rheingold, H. L., Interpreting mental retardation to parents. Pp. 478–487. (Also in J. consult. Psychol., 1945, 9:142–148.)
37. Stogdill, R. M., Some behavior adjustment techniques in use with mentally retarded children. Pp. 488–495. (Also in J. except. Children, 1938, 5:25–30, 45.)
38. Zehrer, F. A., The school psychologist as a mental hygiene specialist. Pp. 466–472. (Also in J. consult. Psychol., 1942, 6:218–222.)

ADDITIONAL READINGS

39. Louttit, C. M. Clinical psychology, Harper & Brothers, rev. ed., 1947, pp. 134–154.
40. Rogers, C. R., The clinical treatment of the problem child, Houghton Mifflin Company, 1939, pp. 63–278.
41. Towle, C., Social case records from psychiatric clinics, University of Chicago Press, 1941, pp. 10–27, 41–82, 83–105, 106–124, 157–196, 284–312, 313–353.

INDEXES

Name Index

Subject Index